The Twentieth Century
A Brief Global History

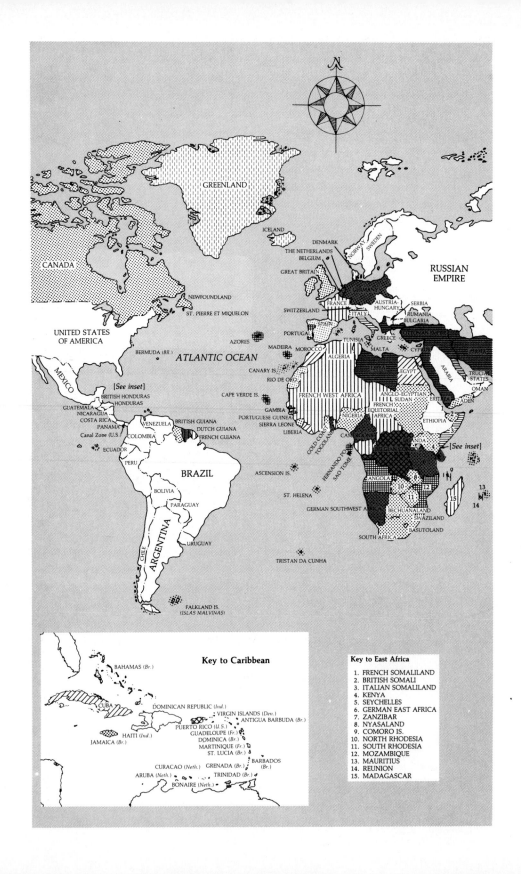

GREENLAND

ICELAND

CANADA

NEWFOUNDLAND

ST. PIERRE ET MIQUELON

UNITED STATES
OF AMERICA

BERMUDA (*Br.*)

ATLANTIC OCEAN

MEXICO

[See inset]

BRITISH HONDURAS
HONDURAS
GUATEMALA
NICARAGUA
COSTA RICA
PANAMA
Canal Zone (U.S.)
COLOMBIA

VENEZUELA

ECUADOR

PERU

BOLIVIA

PARAGUAY

BRAZIL

ARGENTINA

CHILE

URUGUAY

AZORES

MADEIRA

CANARY IS.

RIO DE ORO

CAPE VERDE IS.

ASCENSION IS.

ST. HELENA

TRISTAN DA CUNHA

FALKLAND IS.
(*ISLAS MALVINAS*)

PORTUGAL

SPAIN

MOROCCO

ALGERIA

TUNISIA

MALTA

GREECE

CYPRUS

DENMARK
THE NETHERLANDS
BELGIUM

GREAT BRITAIN

NORWAY

SWEDEN

GERMANY

FRANCE

SWITZERLAND

AUSTRIA-HUNGARY

ITALY

SERBIA
RUMANIA
BULGARIA

OTTOMAN EMPIRE

PERSIA

RUSSIAN
EMPIRE

LIBYA

EGYPT

ARABIA

TRUCIAL
STATES

OMAN

ADEN

FRENCH WEST AFRICA

ANGLO-EGYPTIAN
SUDAN

ERITREA

GAMBIA
PORTUGUESE GUINEA
SIERRA LEONE
LIBERIA

NIGERIA

FRENCH
EQUITORIAL
AFRICA

ETHIOPIA

GOLD COAST

TOGOLAND

CAM

FERNANDO PO
SAO TOME

ANGOLA

GERMAN SOUTHWEST AFRICA

BECHUANALAND

SOUTH AFRICA

SWAZILAND

BASUTOLAND

1

2

3

4

5

6

7

8

9

10

11

12

13

14

15

[See inset]

Key to Caribbean

BAHAMAS (*Br.*)

CUBA

JAMAICA (*Br.*)

HAITI (*Ind.*)

DOMINICAN REPUBLIC (*Ind.*)

PUERTO RICO (*U.S.*)

VIRGIN ISLANDS (*Den.*)

ANTIGUA BARBUDA (*Br.*)

GUADELOUPE (*Fr.*)
DOMINICA (*Br.*)
MARTINIQUE (*Fr.*)
ST. LUCIA (*Br.*)

CURACAO (*Neth.*)

ARUBA (*Neth.*)

GRENADA (*Br.*)

TRINIDAD (*Br.*)

BARBADOS
(*Br.*)

BONAIRE (*Neth.*)

Key to East Africa

1. FRENCH SOMALILAND
2. BRITISH SOMALI
3. ITALIAN SOMALILAND
4. KENYA
5. SEYCHELLES
6. GERMAN EAST AFRICA
7. ZANZIBAR
8. NYASALAND
9. COMORO IS.
10. NORTH RHODESIA
11. SOUTH RHODESIA
12. MOZAMBIQUE
13. MAURITIUS
14. REUNION
15. MADAGASCAR

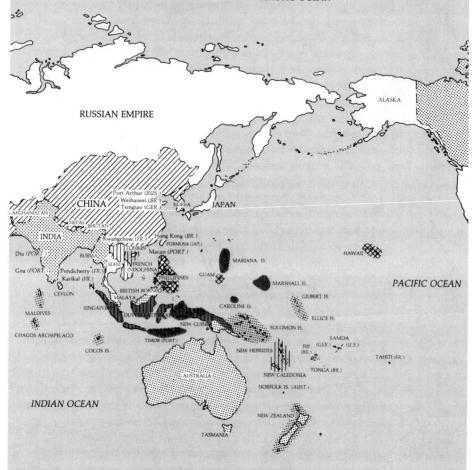

ARCTIC OCEAN

RUSSIAN EMPIRE

ALASKA

CHINA

Port Arthur (RUS.)
Weihaiwei (BR.)
Tsingtao (GER.)

KOREA JAPAN

AFGHANISTAN

NEPAL BHUTAN

INDIA

Kwangchow (FR.) Hong Kong (BR.)

Diu (PORT.)

BURMA TONKIN FORMOSA (JAP.)

Macao (PORT.)

HAWAII

PACIFIC OCEAN

Goa (PORT.)

SIAM FRENCH
INDOCHINA

MARIANA IS.

Pondicherry (FR.)

Karikal (FR.)

PHILIPPINES GUAM

CEYLON

BRITISH BORNEO

MALAYA

MARSHALL IS.

MALDIVES

SINGAPORE

DUTCH EAST INDIES

CAROLINE IS.

GILBERT IS.

CHAGOS ARCHIPELAGO

NEW GUINEA

ELLICE IS.

COCOS IS.

TIMOR (PORT.)

SOLOMON IS.

SAMOA

NEW HEBRIDES

FIJI (GER.) (U.S.)

(BR.)

TAHITI (FR.)

AUSTRALIA

NEW CALEDONIA

TONGA (BR.)

INDIAN OCEAN

NORFOLK IS. (AUST.)

NEW ZEALAND

TASMANIA

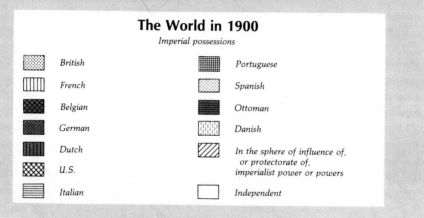

The World in 1900

Imperial possessions

British		Portuguese	
French		Spanish	
Belgian		Ottoman	
German		Danish	
Dutch		In the sphere of influence of, or protectorate of, imperialist power or powers	
U.S.		Independent	
Italian			

The Twentieth Century

A Brief Global History

FOURTH EDITION

Richard Goff

Walter Moss

Janice Terry

Jiu-Hwa Upshur
Eastern Michigan University

McGraw-Hill, Inc.

New York St. Louis San Francisco Auckland Bogotá Caracas
Lisbon London Madrid Mexico City Milan Montreal New Delhi
San Juan Singapore Sydney Tokyo Toronto

This book was set in Palatino by The Clarinda Company.
The editors were Niels Aaboe, Pamela Gordon, and Sheila H. Gillams;
the production supervisor was Leroy A. Young.
The cover was designed by Wanda Lubelska.
R. R. Donnelley & Sons Company was printer and binder.

Part opening photo credits:

Part 1: The Mansell Collection.
Part 2: (Mussolini) UPI/Bettmann Newsphotos; (Hitler) AP/Wide World Photos; (Hirohito) UPI/Bettmann Newsphotos; (Nuremberg) The Bettmann Archive.
Part 3: (Astronaut) NASA; (atomic explosion) Defense Nuclear Agency.

Acknowledgments:
Chapter 2, p. 25: *Reproduced with permission of Curtis Brown Group Ltd., London, on behalf of the Estate of Sir Winston S Churchill. Copyright the Estate of Sir Winston S Churchill.* Chapter 22, p. 321: *From* A Precocious Autobiography *by Yevgeny Yevtushenko, translated by Andrew R. MacAndrew. Translation copyright © 1963 by Yevgeny Yevtushenko, renewed 1991 by Yevgeny Yevtushenko. Translation copyright © 1963 by E.P. Dutton, renewed 1991 by Penguin USA. Used by permission of Dutton Signet, a division of Penguin Books USA Inc.* Chapter 30, p. 463: *From* Freedom from Fear and Other Writings *by Aung San Suu Kyi; foreword by Vaclav Havel; translated by Michael Aris. Translation copyright © 1991 by Aung San Suu Kyi and Michael Aris. Used by permission of Penguin, a division of Penguin Books USA Inc.* Chapter 32, p. 500: *Reprinted with the permission of Macmillan Publishing Company from* Kaffir Boy *by Mark Mathabane. Copyright © 1986 by Mark Mathabane.* Chapter 33, p. 521: *Copyright © 1989 by The New York Times Company. Reprinted by permission.*

THE TWENTIETH CENTURY
A Brief Global History

 This book is printed on recycled, acid-free paper containing a minimum of 50% total recycled fiber with 10% postconsumer de-inked fiber.

1 2 3 4 5 6 7 8 9 0 DOC   DOC 9 0 9 8 7 6 5 4 3

ISBN 0-07-023566-X

Library of Congress Cataloging-in-Publication Data

The Twentieth century: a brief global history / Richard Goff . . . [et al.].
   —4th ed.
     p.   cm.
   Includes index.
   ISBN 0-07-023566-X
   1. History, Modern—20th century.   I. Goff, Richard D.
II. Title: 20th century.
D421.T9   1994
909.82—dc20   93-37280

About the Authors

RICHARD GOFF is Professor of History at Eastern Michigan University. He received his A.B. from Duke University and was a Woodrow Wilson Fellow at Cornell and a James B. Duke Fellow at Duke, where he received his Ph.D. He has taught twentieth-century world history since 1975. He is the author of *Confederate Supply* and of articles in the *Encyclopedia of Southern History* and the *Encyclopedia of Southern Culture.* He is the editor and co-author of two other college textbooks, *A Survey of Western Civilization* and *World History.*

WALTER MOSS is Professor of History at Eastern Michigan University, where he has taught history since 1970. He attended Xavier University in Cincinnati and received his Ph.D. from Georgetown University. He is a co-author of *Growing Old* and the editor of *Humanistic Perspectives on Aging.* He has written numerous book reviews and several articles on Russian history, literature, and philosophy and has traveled on many occasions in the former Soviet Union. He has recently completed a manuscript entitled "Alexander's Time: A Portrait of Rulers, Writers, and Revolutionaries in the Era of Alexander II." He is currently working on *A History of Russia,* to be published by McGraw-Hill in 1996 or 1997.

JANICE TERRY is Professor of History at Eastern Michigan University. She received her Ph.D. in modern Middle East history from the School of Oriental and African Studies, University of London. She is the author of many publications in anthologies and journals and of *The Wafd, 1919–1952: Cornerstone of Egyptian Political Power* and *Mistaken Identity: Arab Stereotypes in Popular Writing.* Dr. Terry has lived and traveled extensively throughout the Middle East and Africa. She is a co-author of another college textbook, *World History.*

JIU-HWA UPSHUR is Professor of History at Eastern Michigan University. She received her B.A. from the University of Sydney and her Ph.D. in Chinese history from the University of Michigan, where she was a Rackham Prize Fellow. She is the author of articles and book reviews on Chinese history and two catalogs on Chinese art. She is co-author of a college textbook, *World History,* and co-editor of *Readings in World History,* scheduled for publication in 1994. She has been elected to the advisory board of World History of the Educational Testing Service.

Contents

Part One
THE ERA OF IMPERIALISM

Part Three
THE ERA OF THE COLD WAR AND
THE COLLAPSE OF EMPIRES

Appendixes

Special Features

Maps and Charts

Autobiographical Boxes

Preface

This book is designed to facilitate teaching and learning twentieth-century world history. As experienced instructors, we saw the need for a compact text that would provide a balanced perspective and that would be pedagogically effective for students in introductory college history courses.

The Twentieth Century: A Brief Global History combines thematic and chronological approaches, thus leading students from the late nineteenth century to the present with a firm sense of historical order. Chapter 1 introduces five themes that are covered throughout the text: science and technology, economics, political and social developments, international relationships, and cultural trends. Following Chapter 1 we have divided the century into three parts. Each part opens with a "general trends" chapter that explains how these themes pertain to that era of the twentieth century. The chapters that follow the "general trends" chapter apply these themes where appropriate. Although we present twentieth-century developments with sufficient historical information to make them clear, we have nonetheless kept the text brief, thus allowing instructors the flexibility to add supplemental material.

In the Fourth Edition our main challenge has been to provide perspective on the tumultuous events that have occurred since the Third Edition was published in 1990—the reunification of Germany, the collapse of communism in eastern Europe, the disintegration of the Soviet Union, and the withering of communism around the rest of the world. We have substantially reorganized Part Three, The Contemporary Era, and brought it to a conclusion with the collapse of the Soviet state in December 1991. Chapter 34 concludes the text by covering events since the end of 1991 and offering overviews of the development of the five themes throughout the century. In addition to keeping abreast of recent developments, we have included more social history, particularly the history of women. We have also added new maps and autobiographical excerpts.

Through all of our editions we have kept the student foremost in mind. This book is short enough not to be intimidating and includes many learning aids. It features a series of excerpts from autobiographies and diaries of significant twentieth-century figures as young adults. Short annotated lists of additional sources appear at the end of each chapter. These lists highlight well written historical sources, relevant fiction, and films and television programs that students may view outside the classroom. We have also prepared uncluttered time charts and useful maps. Because most college students lack knowledge of geography, we have provided an appendix that briefly surveys world demographic and economic patterns.

In the absence of a uniform practice on transliteration of proper names, we have applied the system we considered most appropriate for the historical situation. For Chinese names, we have used the pinyin convention when referring to the People's Republic since 1949; otherwise we have employed Wade-Giles and traditional usages. For Arabic, we have generally employed the commonly accepted Western usage.

ACKNOWLEDGMENTS

For the Fourth Edition we are grateful for the support provided by the staff of McGraw-Hill, Inc., and particularly by our editors, Niels Aaboe and Pamela Gordon. We would also like to thank the reviewers of the various editions for their helpful insights: Eric Dorn Brose, Drexel University; C. Stewart Doty, University of Maine-Orono; Louis Menashe, Polytechnic Institute of New York; William Morris, Shelby State Community College; Gersham Nelson, Frostburg State University; Robina Quale, Albion College; Barbara Reinfeld, New York Institute of Technology; Paul Scherer, Indiana University at South Bend; and John Snetsinger, California Polytechnic State University. We remain indebted to Sally Marks, professor emerita of Rhode Island College, for her encouragement.

Many of our colleagues, unfortunately too many to name here, have graciously assisted us with their comments. We are especially indebted to the following colleagues at Eastern Michigan University who were kind enough to read and comment on major portions of the original manuscript: Richard Abbott, Donald Briggs, Donald Disbrow, Della Flusche, James McDonald, and Lester Scherer. Michael Homel was particularly helpful in revising material pertaining to the United States, and Raymond B. Craib provided material on women in Latin America. Joseph Engwenyu has been particularly helpful on Africa, and Roger Long on the Indian subcontinent. George Cassar, Louis Gimelli, Theodore Hefley, Neil McLarty, and Reinhard Wittke gave professional advice; James Waltz and Ira Wheatley provided administrative support. We are especially indebted to Nancy Snyder, who has untiringly helped us prepare all four editions, including the instructor's manuals.

Richard Goff

Walter Moss

Janice Terry

Jiu-Hwa Upshur

The Twentieth Century

A Brief Global History

CHAPTER 1

1900: A Preview of the Twentieth Century

In 1900, on the sandy, breezy shores of Kitty Hawk, North Carolina, two bicycle mechanics from Dayton, Ohio, tested their first flying machine, a glider weighing fifty pounds. Within a few years, these brothers, Orville and Wilbur Wright, kept a powered airplane aloft for more than half an hour. Other aviation pioneers were right on their heels.

The Wrights' airplane symbolizes the emergence of a technology based on new scientific knowledge, a technology that became one of the central forces shaping twentieth-century life. In the following decades, scientists rapidly expanded their insights into the basic properties of chemistry, biology, and agronomy. Medical and sanitation practices based on these insights dramatically improved health and longevity. New concepts of mathematics, physics, space, and time revolutionized the thinking of many on the meaning of history and the nature of the universe.

This notable twentieth-century advance in scientific knowledge led to a spectacular technological explosion. Automobiles and airliners, motion pictures and television, atomic energy, plastics and synthetics, vaccines and antibiotics, satellites and space probes, missiles, lasers, and computers are only a few examples of the technological outpouring of the decades after 1900. The changes that resulted from twentieth-century science and technology came with increasing rapidity and ensured that each new generation lived in a world markedly different from that of preceding generations. Few living in 1900 imagined, for example, that by 1930 many would be spending evenings listening to voices coming out of a box or watching people moving and talking on a screen. Even fewer dreamt that in 1969 hundreds of millions of people around the world would sit in their homes and see men walking on the moon, or by 1993 would see simulcasts of disasters via cable television.

Unfortunately, scientific and technological breakthroughs frequently have had negative as well as positive consequences and have often strained humanity's capacity to adapt to them. By 1993, life expectancy for many people had doubled since 1900; yet enough nuclear weapons still existed to extinguish all human life in a few hours.

At the same time that the Wright brothers were pursuing their dream, famine was destroying hundreds of thousands of lives in India. Observers wrote of the sunken eyes, hollow stomachs, and emaciated arms and legs of multitudes of suffering Indians; by the end of 1900 over a million had died. According to one estimate, 15 million Indians died from famine in the years 1875–1900, ten times the number who had died from hunger in the first fifty years of the nineteenth century. The British government tried to provide relief, blaming the tragedy primarily on rapid population growth, aggravated by drought.

In actuality the 1899–1900 famine in India dramatically illustrated the role that another force, economics, played in the twentieth century. Although the famine in India was immediately precipitated by drought, its more fundamental cause lay far away from the stricken villages and urban slums of India, in the boardrooms of the cartels that operated in a global economic context. Even though food production had increased as a result of scientific and technological improvements, the companies or governments controlling the global supply of essential grains often created an unequal distribution of such foodstuffs.

In this context, Great Britain during the nineteenth century had encouraged the great landlords of India to produce export crops for Britain's global trading empire. The opening of the Suez Canal in 1869 and the rapid expansion of the Indian railroad network dramatically cut the time and costs of importing Indian products into Great Britain and other parts of the Empire. Landowners were encouraged to utilize their lands and peasant labor for the production of jute, cotton, tea, and wheat for sale abroad rather than to cultivate food crops for the growing population. In 1901, when some were still perishing from hunger, landowners in India exported two and one-half times more food grains than they had in 1858. In addition, British-imposed land taxes and other agricultural policies were driving more and more Indian peasants into poverty.

As illustrated by the situation in India in 1900, a major economic theme of the twentieth century was the continuing disparity between the impoverished and the affluent areas of the world. Particularly in Asia, Africa, and Latin America, malnourished people remained tied to meager local economic resources, while at the same time the great international businesses that controlled the world's resources helped to create prosperity for a few favored nations, particularly in Europe, North America, and parts of East Asia and the Middle East.

Climatic conditions, overpopulation, political rivalries, civil war, and domestic economic policies also contributed notably throughout the twentieth century to the recurrent tragedy of famine, a tragedy that occurred in nations of varying economic systems. In the 1930s, for example, millions starved in the Soviet Ukraine as a result of the policies of Joseph Stalin, even though Ukrainians produced enough food to feed themselves. Owing to a variety of governmental and international business policies and natural disasters, in the decades following 1960, millions died of hunger in such varied nations as China, Nigeria, Bangladesh, India, Cambodia, Ethiopia, Mozambique, and Somalia. In the same period, on the other hand, the international marketing of an array of industrial and consumer products brought a comfortable standard of living not only to many in the United States, Canada, and Western Europe but also to increasing numbers in Japan, South Korea, Taiwan, Hong Kong, Singapore, and the petroleum-rich states of the Middle East.

Economic inequality helped to stimulate another significant twentieth-century phenomenon: social and political conflict. No one personifies this better than Emma Goldman, a dynamic Russian Jewish emigré to the United States who was a major figure in the rise of anarchism. In the belief that the rich exploited the poor and that the state was merely a tool of wealthy interests, anarchists advocated doing away with all government. Leo Tolstoy, the famous Russian nobleman writer who was also an anarchist, urged the use of nonviolent means to bring about this goal, but most anarchists advocated violence.

In 1900 Goldman was a delegate to the Anarchist Conference in Paris. Sitting in a cafe one day, she read of the assassination of the Italian King Humbert by a fellow anarchist who had come from the United States to perform the deed. Her reaction was that such acts were inevitable as long as centralized governments continued to exist. King Humbert had been the fourth royal figure or chief of state to be assassinated within six years. In 1901 U.S. President William McKinley became a fifth victim at the hands of a young man named Leon Czolgosz. Earlier in the year, Czolgosz had attended a Goldman lecture, and he allegedly stated later that her fiery rhetoric had influenced his decision to commit his bloody act.

Goldman viewed herself as a spokesperson not only for the economically downtrodden but also for all oppressed people, including women. Although she criticized U.S. suffragettes for seeking what seemed to her meaningless voting power and for ignoring the problems of working women, her thoughts on the liberation of women echoed down through the decades. Goldman argued that a woman had the "right to support herself; to live for herself; to love whomever she pleases, or as many as she pleases."[1]

Anarchism and women's rights became just two of the many ideas and ideologies stirring political waters after 1900. Marxism, liberalism, conservatism, syndicalism, populism, and progressivism were some of the others. Later in the century, communism, fascism, and Nazism became particularly powerful examples of the quest of men and women for political solutions to their various problems. Much blood flowed in many parts of the world as a result of the conflicts among these ideologies and the men and women who espoused them.

---

[1]Quoted in Alice Wexler, *Emma Goldman: An Intimate Life* (1984), Pantheon Books, N.Y., p. 94.

The Boxer Rebellion in China was one of the most dramatic events of 1900. An antiforeign group known as the "Boxers" (the Society of Harmonious Fists) besieged the compound that housed the diplomatic community in Peking. Persistent Chinese hostility to predatory outsiders, coupled with a drought and other natural disasters in northern China, and patronage by a parochial dowager empress culminated in the Boxer fury. Almost two months after the beginning of the siege of the foreign legations, an eight-nation force rescued the survivors. Before his soldiers departed from Germany on this mission, the bombastic Kaiser Wilhelm II encouraged them to be as merciless as the barbarian followers of Atilla the Hun. Upon occupying Peking, many soldiers from the invading armies did their best to live up to the kaiser's militant exhortations.

The Boxer Rebellion and its quick suppression illustrated another dynamic force of the twentieth century: turbulent, often aggressive, international relations. For decades before the Boxer Rebellion foreign powers had used imperialist policies and superior military might to impose unfair treaties on the Chinese and to carve China into spheres of influence. Even the United States' "Open Door" policy was little more than a U.S. plan to gain a share of the wealth of helpless China. As the twentieth century proceeded, the international scene continued to be a key forum for the expression of nationalism, imperialism, and militarism.

Many great powers displayed the imperialism by which stronger countries imposed and maintained their rule over weaker nations. Early in the century, for example, France forced Morocco to accept its "protection," the United States took de facto control of a number of Caribbean nations, and Japan annexed Korea. After World War I, Great Britain and France took over part of the Middle East. In the 1930s and 1940s Japanese militarists sought to impose their will on China; Hitler saw it as a German right to conquer and dominate the nations of Europe; and Stalin annexed the Baltic republics. Following World War II, the Soviet Union imposed its control over the states of Eastern Europe.

As China's twentieth-century resurgence from the Boxer defeat of 1900 indicated, however, the force wielded by powerful nations to impose their will on weaker states often failed to snuff out the nationalistic aspirations of conquered peoples to be free from outside controls. Thus France failed to "assimilate" the Moroccans, and Latin Americans resisted "Yankee imperialism." A harsh Japanese colonial policy failed to make Koreans into docile subjects, and the Soviet Union failed to make the Baltic peoples into happy Soviet citizens or Hungarians into willing allies.

After World War II, one after another, colonial empires collapsed. Hundreds of millions of the peoples of Asia and Africa became citizens of new independent nations. Between 1989 and 1991 the "Soviet Empire" also collapsed, and the subjugated states of Eastern Europe regained their independence.

In 1900 the philosopher Friedrich Nietzsche died in Weimar, Germany, at the age of fifty-five. His ideas posed a major challenge to the traditional Western religious beliefs and morality of his day. At a time when Western imperialists thought of themselves (in the words of the poet Rudyard Kipling) as taking up "the white man's burden" to bring their civilization to "inferior" peoples in Africa and Asia, Nietzsche's writings undermined confidence in Western civilization itself. The son of a Lutheran minister, Nietzsche preached that "God is dead" and that Christianity—"the one great curse"—was a strategy of the weak, intended to enslave the strong. He advised individuals who dared to go "beyond good and evil" to become new "supermen." He had contempt not only for the spirit of Christianity and much of the Western culture that had evolved from it but also for democracy and the ideal of equality. He predicted a future of uncertainty, revolution, war, and turmoil.

Even after Nietzsche's death, his ideas lived on, testifying to the importance of culture—that is, philosophical ideas and cultural values—as another force that shaped the twentieth century. Many European poets, artists, playwrights, and composers fell under the sway of Nietzsche's ideas. During the twentieth century, a world increasingly interconnected by ever more effective systems of communication presented individuals with an unprecedented array of often conflicting ideas and values. Both new ideas from thinkers in technologically advanced nations and older ideas from traditional cultures were propagated around the world. Although Nietzsche's ideas represented, for many, a very powerful challenge to traditional Western values, even more of the world's people in the twentieth century felt liberated—or threatened—by the theories of Charles Darwin, Karl Marx, and Sigmund Freud. Some observers repudiated what they considered to be the cultural and religious anarchy of the modern era; others celebrated the multiplication of cultural and religious choices.

The discontent with traditional Western values that Nietzsche stimulated led some to seek enlightenment from other cultures. The French artist Paul Gauguin, disenchanted with Western materialism, sought what he considered a nobler existence in Tahiti, while Nietzsche's faithful friend Paul Deussen became one of Europe's leading experts on the religious philosophies of ancient India. Later, some in Europe and the United States adopted Zen Buddhism, or, like the boxer Muhammad Ali, converted to Islam.

To conclude, these five sketches from 1900—the Wright brothers at Kitty Hawk, the famine in India, Emma Goldman's activities in Paris, the Boxer Rebellion, and the death of Nietzsche—offer a preview of the years ahead. They illustrate the five major forces that this text will focus on throughout its discussions of the history of the twentieth century: rapid scientific and technological innovation; an increasingly global economy coupled with persistent economic inequality; continuing social and political conflict; aggression and reactions to it in international relations; and the broad dissemination of conflicting philosophical ideas and cultural values. These forces did not work in isolation but combined in unique patterns to create important results throughout the twentieth century. An example of how these factors intertwine is this Boxer leaflet that cites both technological change and the clash of cultural values in explaining the Boxers' hostility to outsiders:

The arrival of calamities is because of the foreign devils. They have come to China to propagate their teachings, to build telegraph lines and to construct railways. They do not believe in spirits and they desecrate the gods. It is the desire of the gods to cut up the telegraph lines, to rip up the railroads, and to cut off the heads of the foreign devils.[2]

This book will show how the forces underlying these five events combined in different ways to shape the history of the twentieth century.

[2]Quoted in William J. Duiker, *Cultures in Collision: The Boxer Rebellion* (1978), Presidio Press, San Rafael, Calif., p. 37.

The Era
of Imperialism

TIME CHART I
1900–1918

Year	South & East Asia	Middle East & Africa	Europe	Western Hemisphere	Trends in Culture, Science, Technology
	AGE OF IMPERIAL DOMINATION			UNITED STATES PREDOMINANT IN LATIN AMERICA	Industrial West
1900	Boxer Rebellion	Boer War, 1899–1902	Triple Alliance in effect (1882)		
1901	Philippine insurrection, 1898–1913				
1902					Growing influence of Darwinism, Marxism
1903					
1904	Russo–Japanese War, 1904–05				
1905	All-India Muslim League formed	First Moroccan crisis	Continuing British–German naval race	Roosevelt Corollary	Einstein's theory of relativity
1906					Decade of arms build-up Birth of modern art and music

1907	Triple Entente completed				
1908	South Africa self-governing	Austria annexes Bosnia and Herzegovina			
1909			Advent of motion pictures, airplanes, automobiles		
1910	Japan annexes Korea				
1911	Manchus overthrown in China		Beginning of Mexican Revolution		
1912	French protectorate in Morocco	Balkan Wars, 1912–13			
1913			Tagore first non-European to win Nobel Prize for Literature		
1914	Ottoman Empire joins Central Powers; German colonies taken by allies, 1914–18	**WORLD WAR I**	Panama Canal completed		
1915	Japan serves 21 demands on China		Submarines, trench warfare		
1916					
1917		Russian Revolution, 1917	United States enters war; Dadaism founded		
1918	United States–Japanese intervention in Siberia, 1918–25	Allied intervention and civil war in Russia, 1918–20			

CHAPTER 2

General Trends
before World War I

The twentieth century opened on a world dominated by the West. Major European nations and the United States led the world in scientific discoveries and technological innovations and controlled most of the globe with overwhelming economic and military power. Among non-Western nations, only the partially Westernized nation of Japan had joined a Western-dominated world.

Westerners believed that their preeminent position was a reflection of their superior culture. By the beginning of the twentieth century, most Western peoples enjoyed an unmatched standard of living as well as the opportunity for better education, health care, and social services. For the West the future offered the prospect of continued progress and power.

As it turned out, Western power was not as overwhelming as it seemed. Many Western nations were beset by ethnic and religious strife as well as by political conflicts among liberal, conservative, and socialist forces. In addition, most European nations nursed hostilities toward their neighbors. These tensions stemmed in part from long histories of national rivalries in Europe and from competition for control of territory around the world. When European nations embarked on military build-ups and alliances for additional security from their rivals, these policies added to the stresses of the era and eventually led to a general war. This war, World War I, weakened European power around the world.

SCIENCE AND TECHNOLOGY

The people of Europe and the United States took great pride in a wave of Western scientific discoveries and technological improvements in the nineteenth and early twentieth centuries. In biology, Charles Darwin's *On the Origin of Species by Means of Natural Selection* (1859) and *The Descent of Man* (1871) had revolutionized perceptions of humanity's history. Darwin had theorized that different animal species, including humans, originated through a process of natural selection whereby the "fittest" survived and flourished. His concept became widely accepted, although many could not reconcile it with the Biblical account of creation. Darwin's ideas, along with advances in the study of geology and paleontology (fossils), led to further discoveries that brought many to a greater understanding of early humans and their society.

Psychologists brought forth a new field of investigation that opened human mental functions to study and interpretation. At the beginning of the twentieth century, Sigmund Freud was in the vanguard of psychological prac-

An age of science: Marie Curie, twice a recipient of the Nobel Prize, in her laboratory. (*American Institute of Physics/Niels Bohr Library*)

titioners. His theories revolved around his belief that humans were driven by unconscious pleasure-seeking forces such as sexuality. The conflict of these unconscious desires with other psychological forces more attuned to social "reality" often led to inner psychological conflict. To deal with serious cases, Freud developed psychoanalysis, a method of probing the unconscious mind, frequently by analyzing dreams. Freud's theories and methods were both supported and attacked by later experts in the field.

In 1895 Wilhelm Roentgen discovered a form of radiation that could penetrate opaque materials. These "x-rays," as he called them, were gradually applied in many areas of physics and medicine. Meanwhile, Antoine Becquerel discovered the radioactivity of uranium. Starting from this discovery, Marie and Pierre Curie investigated other radioactive elements, discovering radium and polonium in 1898. Their work helped to provide a foundation for twentieth-century research in the composition of atoms.

As Darwin changed thinking about the nature of humans, Albert Einstein, in the first two decades of the twentieth century, changed thinking about the nature of the universe. He demonstrated that energy is mass multiplied by the square of the velocity of light. Joined with the conclusion of Ernest Rutherford and others that the atom is a combination of particles moving at enormous velocity, Einstein's theorem suggested that useful thermal energy would be released if the nuclei of atoms could be altered.

In addition to his studies of the atom, Einstein's theory of relativity and his other discoveries changed scientific understanding of the forces that make up the universe. During the two centuries before 1900, scientists believed that the universe was a three-dimensional spatial arrangement and that its properties could be measured from an absolute point of reference. Einstein proposed that time was a "fourth dimension" interrelated with the other three. According to him, the velocity of light is the same whether or not the observer is in motion, and thus there is no absolute point of reference. Measurement is in that sense "relative."

Westerners were particularly proud of the advances in health and longevity that had taken place. The work of Joseph Lister in the nineteenth century improved hygienic conditions in hospitals; puerperal fever, the main cause of death for women in childbirth, was eradicated. The introduction of anesthesia techniques enabled doctors to perform more complicated operations, which saved countless lives. Louis Pasteur and Robert Koch proved that bacteria were the cause of many previously incurable diseases and could be controlled through inoculations, medication, and hygienic measures. As a result, anthrax and rabies, which had destroyed many animals around the world, came under control, and four major causes of child mortality—smallpox, diphtheria, typhoid fever, and scarlet fever—appeared to be on the road to elimination in the Western world. Soon after 1900 chemists discovered vitamins and developed sulfa drugs, which helped humanity combat disease-causing bacteria.

Improvements in health care and in the control of disease contributed to a marked population increase late in the nineteenth century, not only in Europe and the United States but also throughout much of the world. The population of Europe more than doubled between 1800 and 1900, primarily because of a lowered death rate. On the other hand, population increases often created overcrowding in many Western cities. As better health care spread through the rest of the world to areas such as India and China, it, too, contributed to population increases that often outstripped the available food supply.

Scientific insights spawned a multitude of technological breakthroughs. Engineers who developed turbines and dynamos dramatically accelerated the production of electropower. New petroleum-refining techniques produced gasoline and diesel fuels to power the new internal combustion engines. The chemists and technicians who produced rayon and artificial dyes in the laboratory brought in a new era of synthetic material, while their discovery of new metal alloys promised greater diversity in manufactured products. Industrial innovators used interchangeable parts and created the assembly line to make production more efficient, thus making manufactured goods cheaper. The development of structural steel, reinforced concrete, and the electric elevator allowed cities to grow upward as well as outward.

By 1900 physicists studying electricity and its relationship to magnetic waves had already revolutionized concepts of communication. The telegraph had been well established in the nineteenth century, and underseas cables already linked the world's continents. The telephone also began to make its impact in urban centers at the beginning of the twentieth century. Perhaps the most exciting development in communication came in 1895, when Guglielmo Marconi sent messages through space with a "wireless" transmitter. The age of the radio soon followed. Advances in photography created a new wonder, the motion picture.

For those living early in the twentieth century, perhaps no single invention marked the breakthrough into a new era more than that of the electric light. Thomas Edison had rolled back the darkness and promised a revolution in the pattern of daily life. For many in the West, in particular, home illumination was now safer, cleaner, and more effective. Activities of every kind could now be carried on around the clock.

In transportation, the advent in the nineteenth century of steam-driven locomotives and steamships had already greatly accelerated travel on land and water. After 1903, through the efforts of Orville and Wilbur Wright and many others, the age-old dream of air travel was realized. The achievement in aviation soon meant that people could traverse the world in a matter of days or hours instead of months or weeks. More important to the average Westerner was the development of the internal combustion engine, which led to the automobile. While only in its infancy in 1900, the automobile already promised to transform work and leisure patterns throughout the West and eventually around much of the world.

Ironically, the same spirit of scientific and technological advance that was enhancing the life of human beings was also busily devising new means to destroy them. Scientists and metallurgists produced explosives and propellants such as cordite, TNT, and nitroglycerin. Their improvements in the

techniques of rifling and metal casting brought forth a new class of artillery—howitzers, mortars, and long-range naval guns—and new or improved fragmentation weapons, such as shrapnel shells, antipersonnel mines,
and hand grenades. These projectiles could now be delivered with great accuracy through new guidance systems, thus increasing the number of casualties per projectile expended. Technicians working on new fuel and hydraulic
technology produced the submarine; additional propellants and guidance
technology armed the submarine with a reliable torpedo. Applications of
chemistry and physics created poison gas, the flame thrower, and the machine gun.

The military establishment also adapted a number of techniques originally
developed for civilian use. Mass production of textiles and clothing, plus the
invention of canning and refrigeration, meant that nations could raise, equip,
and feed larger armies and navies. Utilizing new modes of transportation and
communication, military leaders could move about, supply, and coordinate
their forces over long distances.

Whether for good or ill, there was an explosion of scientific and technological advances in this period. Indeed, it was difficult for many to see how this
pace could be sustained. In 1899 the head of the U.S. Patent Office asked President William McKinley to abolish the bureau: "Everything that can be invented has been invented."

ECONOMIC TRENDS

The dawn of the twentieth century saw the West in economic control of the
world. Before the eighteenth century, economic systems had been primarily
local and regional, but by 1900 the rapid expansion of the Industrial Revolution, coupled with advances in transportation and communication, had created a worldwide economy. The heart of this new global economy lay in Western Europe, particularly in Great Britain and Germany, and in the United
States. These nations had created a complex of heavy industry in which iron
ore, petroleum, and electricity provided power for the production of iron and
steel, machinery, chemicals, and textiles. Great Britain had been the world's
greatest industrial nation early in the nineteenth century, but by 1900 it was
losing its lead to Germany and the United States.

The rise of industry in Western nations had a major impact on other areas
of the world. As their industries outgrew local resources and markets, industrialized Western nations began to pursue a policy of imperialism (see below),
seizing economic control over parts of Latin America, Africa, and Asia in
order to ensure a ready supply of raw materials for their factories and to gain
secure markets for their surplus goods. The growing power and aggressiveness of the established industrial powers spurred some of the less developed
nations such as Russia and Japan to protect themselves by commencing intensive industrialization programs of their own.

Although European investors had built a few textile factories around the globe, overall there was little heavy industry outside Europe, the United States, and Japan. Mineral, fiber, and hide processing was the most common form of manufacturing in the British dominions of Canada, New Zealand, Australia, and South Africa and in the Latin American nations of Mexico, Brazil, Argentina, Uruguay, and Chile. These nations depended on Western Europe and the United States for the bulk of their manufactured goods.

Paralleling their industrial expansion, Westerners over the centuries had been developing a global network for producing and distributing agricultural products. By 1900 they had organized many areas of the world into large plantations, "agricultural factories" that poured out enormous quantities of foodstuffs. As a result, citizens in Western Europe and the United States could sit at their dinner tables and enjoy Honduran bananas, Brazilian coffee, East Indian spices, Cuban sugar, Hawaiian pineapple, Ceylonese tea, and many other products from around the globe.

As the industrial and agricultural factory system spread around the world, people moved—or were forced to move—from continent to continent to provide the labor necessary for economic development. For centuries, Westerners had imported black Africans into the Western Hemisphere to work as slaves on plantations. By 1900 the slave trade had ended, but new human migrations were underway. Millions of Europeans were encouraged to settle in North and South America, Australia, and New Zealand. Chinese and Japanese—many of them contract laborers—went to work on the plantations of Hawaii and the railroads of North America. Indians worked in the mines of eastern and southern Africa and on Caribbean plantations. Many of them later rose in economic and social status in their new homes.

An effective worldwide economy would have been impossible without a concurrent revolution in the technology of commercial transportation. Ships of ever greater capacity and speed, paced by the British merchant marine, hauled raw materials and finished products into every nook and cranny of the globe. Where water traffic was impeded by land formations, engineers constructed the Suez and Panama canals, created canal networks in Western Europe and the United States, and built or enlarged harbors all over the world.

On land, the tremendous cargo-hauling capacity of steam-driven engines operating on rails gave an enormous boost to economic development by the early twentieth century. Railroads crisscrossed northwestern Europe, Japan, and much of North America. Elsewhere in the world, however, railroads were much rarer. The cargo-hauling potential of the internal combustion engine used in automobiles remained uncertain because no cheap permanent road surface had been developed.

The massive economic development underway around the world was fueled by investment money, and Great Britain was overwhelmingly dominant in this matter at the turn of the century. London was the center of world finance, setting the standards in investment, banking, and insurance. "Insured by Lloyds of London" was the ultimate guarantee of protection and security.

SOCIAL AND POLITICAL TRENDS

The rapid transformation of the world economy had brought many social changes by the opening decades of the twentieth century, particularly in the nations of Western Europe. These changes were also apparent in the United States and, to a lesser degree, in Latin America and Japan. As the century progressed, some of these social changes spread to other parts of the world.

Population Mobility and Social Classes

One social consequence of the industrialization process was that many people left the countryside to work where the factories were located. Old cities grew rapidly, and new ones appeared. The populations of new urban areas grew so rapidly that the authorities were technologically and psychologically unprepared to deal with the change. Industrialized nations soon faced a host of problems—poor sanitation and housing, crime, a shortage of schools and hospitals, and many others—in their urban centers.

The impact of industrialization and worldwide commercial activity was to create changes in the social classes in Western nations. The upper class was now comprised of an uneasy combination of the traditional titled, landed aristocracy (except in the United States) and a new group of wealthy industrial and commercial entrepreneurs. Whatever their background, the members of the upper class dominated their nations. In Great Britain, 5 percent of the population controlled 75 percent of the earnings from private property. The European hereditary aristocracy still occupied most of the high civil and military posts in their governments, but an increasing percentage of the important posts were now being filled by men with a "common," though often affluent, background. The new rich, although usually products of the "work ethic," matched the traditional aristocrats in lifestyles of "conspicuous consumption." They built and furnished mansions; consumed huge quantities of expensive food and clothing; bought technological marvels such as automobiles, phonographs, telephones, and radios; patronized the arts; and indulged in expensive travel and recreation.

The middle class, while sharply separated from the upper class in income and status, was growing in size, prosperity, and complexity. Traditionally, the middle class had consisted of shopkeepers, skilled artisans, and such "white-collar" professionals as academics, physicians, and clergymen. By the twentieth century it also included new professionals such as engineers, business managers, and architects. These newcomers were joined by a large mass of less affluent professionals, such as teachers, business clerks, and civil servants. Living in modest comfort, these groups saved money for a better home, for their children's education, and, if not protected by one of the new business or government pension plans, for retirement.

Perhaps the greatest social change brought about by the changing economy was the improvement in the condition of urban working classes. Mass production and improved agricultural techniques were providing cheaper clothing, shoes, and food at the same time that wage increases were outstripping inflation. In Western Europe just before World War I, two-thirds of the urban work force, now rapidly outnumbering the rural labor force, earned wages above the subsistence level. A small minority of skilled workers and foremen enjoyed an income greater than some in the lower middle class. Many workers could afford to add meat, dairy products, and vegetables to a diet that had previously consisted almost entirely of bread and potatoes. Better nutrition and improved health care increased average life expectancy in Western Europe from about forty years in the mid-nineteenth century to about fifty years just before World War I. Increased wages and new laws forbidding child labor (although not in the United States) allowed children to go to school.

Despite improvements for the upper ranks of the working class, however, many problems remained. Housing was cramped and uncomfortable; workplaces usually remained noisy, unhealthy, and dangerous. One-third of urban workers, especially those employed in textiles, mining, hauling, and other relatively unskilled occupations, still eked out a living at a bare subsistence level. In 1900 in the United States, the average work week was fifty-nine hours at $13 a week. Some were no better off, and some were worse off, than farmers or peasants working on agricultural estates. It was estimated that in 1900, one-third of the inhabitants of New York and London lived in poverty.

There were some modest shifts in the status of women. The advent of the typewriter and other office machines opened new opportunities for "respectable" women, especially single women, to work in business offices instead of remaining at home. Others became teachers or nurses. On the other hand, the rise in income for many working-class families allowed some wives to leave factory work and stay home to look after their children and households. The statement "My wife doesn't have to work" became a status symbol for many working-class husbands. Some upper- and middle-class women, particularly in the United States, obtained higher education and entered the professions. Many women wanted political power commensurate with their heightened economic and social status, and increasing numbers of them agitated for the right to vote.

In western and central Europe, two trends were underway in the countryside. First, farmers who already owned substantial land expanded their holdings and mechanized their operations. Along with the nobles on the great estates, many converted from producing grain to raising beef, dairy herds, and vegetables in order to meet the changing consumption patterns of the city dwellers. These peasants were able to maintain a comfortable lifestyle, but their incomes often barely kept pace with inflation. At the same time, small farmers often lost their land and joined the mass of farmhands who were struggling to subsist in the countryside. Millions went to work in factories, where they had to make the difficult transition from the work habits of the country to the continuous discipline demanded by the factory work routine. Millions more emigrated to the Western Hemisphere, where some secured farms of their own or worked as farm laborers. Most immigrants, however, stayed in the cities and worked in factories. At the turn of the century, especially in the United States, the flood of immigrants outpaced the growth of industry; and workers faced low wages and poor working conditions.

Outside the industrialized West, social changes came much more slowly. In Japan, and to a much lesser extent in China and India, partial industrialization had enlarged the traditional middle class and created a small class of factory workers. However, most of the people of Asia, Africa, Latin America, eastern and southern Europe, and the southern United States remained workers or tenants laboring on the lands of a few affluent landowners. Because of imperial domination, local landowners in parts of Africa and Asia had been displaced by European settlers and corporations. In any case, whether dominated by a local elite or by Westerners, the rural masses lived below or close to subsistence levels.

Competing Political Forces

The struggle between liberals and conservatives was a major source of dissension in the Western world. Conservatives usually came from the more privileged groups in society and supported existing class distinctions, autocratic government, and special economic privileges for the upper classes. They also generally defended institutions that embodied traditional practices and values—the established church, a divine right monarchy, and a powerful military. Conservatism was still a powerful force in such central and eastern European nations as Germany and Austria-Hungary, and particularly in Russia.

Liberals tended to come from the rising business and professional classes and wanted to change society so that they would have a secure and powerful place in it. They wanted freedom of speech, press, religion, and assembly; the right, for men with modest amounts of property, to vote and hold office; elected governments responsible to the voters; and commerce free from restrictions. Some who were very liberal wished to allow all adult males, even those without property, the right to vote and hold office. Americans had achieved this for white males by the middle of the nineteenth century. Generally speaking, liberalism had been gaining power in Europe since the French Revolution in 1789, and by 1900 was a strong force in Great Britain and France, among some groups in Italy, and in some of the small western European nations. By the turn of the century, some liberals, hoping to avoid socialist revolution, advocated such welfare state programs as unemployment compensation and pensions.

Liberal-conservative differences were often contests between people of property, and such battles did not seem particularly relevant to many factory workers. One response of Western workers to their exploitation was to organize into trade unions to force improvements from their employers through collective bargaining, picketing, strikes, and boycotts. Trade unionists were not necessarily interested in bringing an end to the capitalist system but instead concentrated on improving their wages and working conditions and on acquiring pensions and other forms of security. Trade unions met with great resistance from employers and their political allies, but they slowly gained strength, especially in Great Britain, after the turn of the century. Other people concerned with the plight of the workers turned to a more radical approach than trade unionism: the destruction of capitalism through socialism.

Karl Marx, who died in 1883, was one of the world's most important political theorists. The core of Marx's "scientific socialism," which he developed along with his fellow German Friedrich Engels, was the theory of historical or dialectical materialism. This theory proclaimed that such productive forces as technology, material resources, and labor determined economic relationships. According to Marx, these productive forces and economic relationships together made up the foundation of society and in turn determined the "superstructure" of government, laws, religions, and culture that the dominant class in any historical period used to strengthen its position.

Productive forces, Marx declared, had changed in the course of history. Therefore, economic relationships had changed, and as a result, new classes had emerged to replace the old dominant classes and create new superstructures. However, no ruling class ever surrendered its power peacefully. It had to be overthrown by the rising class associated with the new productive forces. Thus class conflict was inevitable and would continue until the golden era of communism was established. In his own time, Marx believed that he was witnessing in Western Europe the overthrow of the feudal landowning class by capitalist merchants and industrialists. Just as inevitably, said Marx,

Karl Marx, founder of one of the most influential modern ideologies. (*The Mansell Collection*)

the industrial working class, or "proletariat," would associate itself with still newer productive forces even then evolving out of capitalist society. This working class would clash with the capitalist class and would eventually overthrow it. The working class would then establish a "dictatorship of the proletariat" in order to set up a new socialist system and deal with any remaining class enemies. That dictatorship and all the machinery of government would then wither away, to be followed by an age of equitable social relations, humanized labor, and increased leisure.

By the turn of the century, both trade unionism and Marxism in its various interpretations had numerous followers in the industrial nations. It was clear that both liberals and conservatives faced formidable political opposition. Despite their differences, Marxists and trade unionists influenced each other. Marx had stated that the conditions of workers under capitalism would grow worse and that they would become increasingly radical. On the contrary, salaries and working and living conditions in capitalist countries such as Great Britain and Germany began to improve as capitalist politicians instituted reforms in order to ward off socialism. Many workers became more interested in continuing such improvements, and perhaps in gaining a share of political power, than in overthrowing capitalism through revolution.

Before World War I, responding to the moderate outlook of most workers, many socialists in Europe and in the United States had decided to replace capitalism through the political party system rather than pursue violent revolution. In nations that allowed a popular vote, Marxist parties such as the German Social Democratic party increased rapidly in size. In the United States, the presidential candidate of the Socialist party, Eugene Debs, twice received nearly a million votes.

As some socialist parties became less revolutionary, two other movements, anarchism and syndicalism, became more prominent. Anarchists believed that governments exploited people on behalf of the wealthier classes, and so they wished to destroy all governments and to reconstruct the social order without them. From 1894 to 1912 anarchists assassinated a president of France and one of the United States, two Spanish premiers, the king of Italy, and the empress of Austria. Syndicalists believed that a trade union-led general strike would paralyze society and destroy its government, after which the unions would be the basic organizing structures of society. The movement developed in France but influenced workers and radicals elsewhere. In the United States, the Industrial Workers of the World (the "Wobblies") was the largest group that reflected syndicalist ideas.

Liberalism, conservatism, socialism, and other political movements also had some impact outside the West. At the start of the twentieth century, liberalism was already strong among Western-educated Indians, some of whom founded the Indian National Congress in 1885. At about the same time, some Japanese, influenced by Western ideas, advocated adopting a constitution, which was finally granted in 1889. Although Marxism eventually proved to be a potent influence among non-Westerners, it was a negligible force before World War I. A major example of Western influence in Asia was

Sun Yat-sen, who overthrew the old regime in China in 1911 and attempted to replace it with one founded on democratic, liberal, and moderate socialist principles.

Although Western political ideas gained some ground in non-Western areas, most traditional leaders sought to perpetuate the old customs and cultures of their societies and often used religion as a powerful force to prevent or limit Westernization. Because these traditional leaders sought to maintain the status quo, they bore some resemblance to European conservatives.

Nationalism

Nationalism was another political force at work at the turn of the century. Concentrated in the West and in Japan in 1900, it spread around the world during the twentieth century. Nationalism is a learned emotional loyalty that individuals direct toward a group with which they perceive common bonds. It gives to individuals a sense of membership and belonging. Nationalism is nurtured by a number of common bonds—language, religion, social and institutional traditions, territory, and history. The most recurrent basis for nationalism in recent times has been loyalty to one's ethnic group. It is not necessary for a national group to share all the bonds mentioned. Switzerland, for example, has a long national history, but it comprises several major language groups.

A common history is an important ingredient in nationalism. National groups and states glorify their past and sometimes create or rediscover a past history if one is lacking. For example, Germans sought to overcome regional, political, and religious differences by emphasizing triumphs in their distant tribal past. Nationalistic Indians, chafing under British rule, rediscovered Asoka, an emperor of the third century B.C.E. under whom the subcontinent was unified and made powerful. His insignia, the wheel and the lion, became the symbols of the newly independent state of India in 1947. After the 1910 revolution, Mexicans of predominantly Amerindian extraction stressed their Aztec and Mayan past rather than their Spanish heritage.

In nationalism, the nation itself is often glorified. Nationalists evoked old, even primitive, feelings based on myths that nations are eternal. As the Italian writer Joseph Mazzini expressed it, "Our country is our Home, the house that God has given us. In laboring for our own country, on the right principle, we labor for humanity."

By 1900 nationalism as a unifying force was well established in western Europe and the United States. Leaders in these areas, where literacy was high, used the printed word and the educational system to indoctrinate individuals into supporting their government as the paramount symbol of their nation. Because of the heterogeneous population of the United States, nationalism in that country was a complex and contradictory phenomenon. There was the traditional doctrine of an ethnic and religious "melting pot" whose citizens gave primary allegiance to the concepts of economic opportunity and political democracy. This was counterbalanced, however, by a cultural tradition that reflected the values and prejudices of the politically and economically powerful persons descended from the ethnic groups of northern Europe.

In Europe the dramatic unifications of Germany and Italy in the 1860s and 1870s demonstrated the power of ethnic nationalism. Many Germans, however, considered their unification incomplete because millions of Germans still lived outside the boundaries of the new Germany. Demands by ultranationalistic Germans for *Anschluss* (union) of all Germans into a single state disrupted the history of Europe well into the twentieth century.

In many areas, nationalism was a divisive rather than a unifying force because it sometimes inspired a dominant group to persecute minorities within a nation. These actions were often based on ethnic antagonism, economic jealousy, and religious hatred. Pogroms (government-instigated mob attacks) in Russia against the Jews and Turkish suppression of the Armenians were examples of such persecutions at the beginning of the twentieth century.

Nationalistic sentiments were also divisive in another way. In some countries, certain populations that were under the dominance of other groups aspired to break away from that control, either to form their own independent nations or to join a neighboring nation governed by their kindred. Austria-Hungary and the Ottoman Empire, in particular, were torn by nationalistic dissension because these states governed a host of ethnic minority groups that were becoming increasingly nationalistic. The Austro-Hungarian Empire was largely held together by loyalty to the monarchy and the Catholic Church. When the dominant Germans and Magyars (Hungarians) began to stress that the empire was primarily a German one or a Magyar one, the Slavs and other minority ethnic groups within the empire responded by pushing for their own national states. The tensions and hatreds of nationalism made the Balkans the "Tinderbox of Europe." In the Ottoman Empire, which had been held together by a common belief in Islam, religious bonds were no longer sufficient; Arabs and Kurds, though Muslims, sought their own national independence from a state dominated by the Turks. Such local nationalisms and ethnic prejudices contributed powerfully to the collapse of both of these formerly great empires.

In the early part of the twentieth century, Western doctrines flourished that asserted the inherent superiority of the so-called Aryan group and of Aryan nations and stressed the inferiority of other groups—Jews, Slavs, Gypsies. This was the clearest example of the use of racial myths to foster nationalism.

By 1900 nationalism in its different forms was also taking hold in Asia. The Japanese justified their aggressiveness in Asia by asserting that they were a superior race. A small Indian elite, influenced by the West, worked to throw off British rule by attempting to instill the concept of a united India into a population divided by ethnicity, language, and religion. In China also, another Western-influenced elite worked to rally the Chinese on two nationalistic crusades simultaneously. They channeled Chinese resentment of the ruling Manchu minority into plots to overthrow the Manchu dynasty, while at the same time they tried to rally all ethnic groups in China to resist Western and Japanese imperialism.

INTERNATIONAL RELATIONS

At the beginning of the twentieth century, international relations around the world were poisoned by tensions emanating from a number of sources. New levels of nationalistic pride spilled over into international affairs, heightening existing fears and hostilities inherited from the past. Often, nationalism manifested itself in general feelings of national or racial superiority; the British referred to non-Westerners as "Wogs," to the French as "Frogs," and to the Germans as "Huns." Nations fought one another over territory and power while accusing their opponents of having a vicious character and a history of wrongdoing. "The policy of the German Empire . . . has always been one of undisguised blackmail," asserted a British official in 1899. Imperialist competition for the control of territories around the world added more fuel to the flames, driving nations to search for security in arms races, alliances, and plans for war.

Imperialism

Imperialism, the process by which a small number of industrial nations extended their economic and political control over much of the rest of the world, was the main driving force in international relations at the turn of the century. As one of Great Britain's leading imperialists put it, "The day of small nations has passed away; the day of empires has come." Actually, the process was not new; from the fifteenth through eighteenth centuries, searching for foods, fibers, and precious metals, Europeans had taken control of the entire Western Hemisphere, Australasia, large sections of Asia, and a few spots in Africa. Thereafter, although imperialist conquests never entirely ceased, they proceeded at a somewhat slower pace before imperialism intensified dramatically in the last third of the nineteenth century. The cast of imperialist nations had now changed. Spain, Portugal, and the Netherlands, three stalwarts of an earlier era, were no longer very active. However, three other traditional imperial powers, Great Britain, France, and Russia, were fully involved in the new era. They were now joined by Belgium, Germany, Italy, the United States, and Japan.

There were many reasons for the resurgence of imperialism, economic considerations being one of the most important. With new economic forces at work, Western and Japanese industrialists continually searched for new markets, cheap labor, industrial raw materials, agricultural products, and places for investment. Often, complex patterns of economic interdependence developed. For example, British textile manufacturers encouraged the planting of cotton in India and Egypt, both crucial parts of the vast British Empire. Cheap local labor grew and harvested the cotton, which was shipped to Great Britain to be manufactured into cloth. Cotton cloth was then made into shirts and other articles of clothing that were in turn sold back to the laborers in India and Egypt. In such a fashion, industrialists not only enjoyed cheap labor and raw materials but also profited from new markets for their manufactured goods.

Imperialism was also fueled by nationalism, which engendered in many countries a relentless urge to compete with other nations to become the most powerful in the world. Frequently, special-interest groups or such lobbyists as explorers and adventurers encouraged national governments to extend their influence.

Strategic imperialism, a concern for control of key waterways, ports, and military outposts, was another important factor leading nations to take over distant territories. The British government, for example, used a powerful navy operating out of strategically located bases to protect its international trade routes. The Suez Canal and the surrounding Middle Eastern territory, in particular, were viewed as crucial for controlling the lifeline to India and East Asia. The British took over Singapore, Aden, and other territories as bases to protect this vital trade route.

One complex aspect of imperialism, part motive, part rationalization, part result, has been termed "cultural imperialism." On the basis of the alleged natural superiority of the white race, Westerners argued that it was the "white man's burden" to bring the benefits of "superior" Western civilization—its technology, its religion, its institutions—to the "inferior" nonwhites of the world living in "darkness and ignorance." The virulently imperialistic Kaiser Wilhelm II of Germany proclaimed, "God has called us to civilize the world. We are missionaries of human progress." A U.S. senator put it in a more folksy way: "We will lift Shanghai up and up, ever up, until it is just like Kansas City." Some Westerners went even further, arguing that nonwhites had few cultural or historical achievements to their credit and could never reach the cultural, political, or technical heights that the predominantly white societies of the West had attained.

Social Darwinists such as Herbert Spencer argued that biological evolution, which involved competition, elimination of the weak, and "survival of the fittest," should be applied to competition among cultures, nations, and peoples. They argued that it was right or "natural" for "strong, superior cultures" to control or even to eliminate "weaker, inferior cultures." Thus, after France conquered Algeria, it attempted to eradicate local traditions, language, and religion. When the Algerians fought against the destruction of their society, the French responded that there was no such thing as an Algerian nation and that they were bringing the benefits of the "superior" French civilization to wandering, ignorant tribes.

Christian missionary zeal was another manifestation of cultural imperialism. It was often said that the flag followed the cross. Missionaries from Europe and the United States sought to spread Christianity in Africa and Asia, as they had earlier in Latin America. Often these missionaries and their converts became embroiled in misunderstandings and quarrels with adherents of the local culture. Imperial powers would then send military forces into the local area to protect the missionaries, both as compatriots and as symbols of Western culture. In China, when a French missionary was killed by Chinese in the 1850s, Napoleon III seized on this incident to wage war against China and, as a result of France's victories, gained concessions.

The Outlook of a Young Imperialist

It did seem a pity that . . . the age of civilized wars had come to an end forever. If it had only been 100 years earlier what splendid times we should have had! Fancy being nineteen in 1793 with more than twenty years of war against Napoleon in front of one! However, all that was finished. The British army had never fired on white troops since the Crimea, and now that the world was growing so sensible and pacific—and so democratic too—the great days were over. Luckily, however, there were . . . Zulus and Afghans, also the [Mahdi's followers] in the Sudan. Some of these might, if they were well-disposed "put up a show" someday. There might even be a revolt in India. . . . These thoughts were only partially consoling, for fighting the poor Indians, compared to taking part in a real European war, was only like riding in a paper-chase instead of in the Grand National.*

◆◆◆◆

Here Winston Churchill, a member of one of the great ruling families of Great Britain, recalls his outlook when he was a cavalry cadet in the 1890s. The confidence in Western superiority over non-Western peoples that young Winston displayed here reflects the attitude of cultural imperialism that typified the era before World War I. Churchill retained his imperialist attitudes throughout his career and resisted the dissolution of the British Empire after World War II.

*From *My Early Life: A Roving Commission* by Winston Churchill. Copyright 1930 Charles Scribner's Sons; copyright renewed © 1958 Winston Churchill. Reprinted by permission of Charles Scribner's Sons, an imprint of Macmillan Publishing Company.

For cultural, religious, and racial reasons, many imperialists believed that the West's domination over the globe would go on forever. Western nations attempted to recreate their empires in their own images. Entire societies in Africa, Asia, and Latin America were modified and, in some cases, totally destroyed. In virtually all instances of imperial domination, the conquered people were changed. In many instances, they tried, but failed, to overthrow outside control and to recapture control over their own destinies. On the other hand, Western encroachments and cultural claims gave impetus to Asians and others to reexamine their traditional values and to offer reforms.

Sometimes, imperialist competition led Western rivals to the brink of war. One dangerous situation in 1898 in Africa was a prime example. The British were interested in building a colonial empire, and perhaps a transcontinental railroad, that would extend from South Africa north to Egypt, from "Cape to Cairo." Equally enthusiastic French imperialists dreamed of a transcontinental empire extending from western Africa to the east coast. This rivalry brought about a confrontation in 1898 at the Sudanese village of Fashoda. The Fashoda crisis was an outstanding example of extreme nationalism, or jingoism, a term deriving from a British beer hall song of the day: "We don't want to fight,/But by Jingo! if we do/We've got the ships,/We've got the men/And got the money, too!" Goaded by articles in the new mass media of journals and news-papers, people in France and Great Britain rushed thoughtlessly to support their nations—"my country right or wrong." Neither the French nor the British gave a thought to the Sudanese in the conflict. Only the intercession of more moderate diplomats, and second thoughts by the French, averted open warfare between Great Britain and France in 1898.

On a few occasions, imperialists went to war with one another to further their interests, but in most cases nations settled their rivalries peacefully. For example, Japan and Russia fought over Korea and Manchuria, and the British battled Dutch settlers in South Africa. For the most part, however, the imperi-alists preferred to hammer out diplomatic agreements in which territories were parceled out as in some gigantic Monopoly game. For example, fourteen nations met at the Berlin Colonial Conference of 1885 to decide the fate of the Congo in Africa. No Congolese were included, and the European nations de-cided the fate of one of Africa's largest areas without ever asking the people of that region what they wanted.

Although major powers generally had not gone to war over imperialist claims, a number of them continued to nurse grievances. Japan, Germany, Russia, and Italy, in particular, believed they did not have their fair share of possessions and looked for ways to increase their global holdings. Some na-tions, such as Great Britain, France, and the United States, were essentially sat-isfied with the territories they had annexed and the areas of indirect economic control they had accumulated.

Arms Races, Militarism, and Alliances

In a period filled with nationalistic and imperialistic tensions, the major na-tions moved to strengthen their security. They stockpiled the new weapons of the era, built up the size of their military establishments, and made alliances. In the nineteenth century, Prussia had led the way in military build-up, creat-ing a mass army of short-term conscripts. Men were drafted, trained, and then sent home to their civilian occupations. This procedure created a large reserve of trained men that could be called up to form a formidable army at the out-break of war. Prussia also set up a general staff organization charged with planning and conducting future wars. Prussia's large army of conscripts and reservists, well trained, equipped, and led, defeated France's smaller army of long-term professional soldiers in 1870. Learning from its defeat, France switched to the Prussian system and built up its own mass army. Such a sys-tem required huge amounts of money and disrupted the civilian occupations of a large percentage of a nation's population.

To protect itself from Western imperialism, Japan built up a Western-style military machine and demonstrated its strength by winning wars against China in 1895 and Russia in 1905. It won more praise from the West for these victories than for any other aspect of its modernization and gained equality in international affairs. Japan saw that a strong military brought results and thereafter steered an increasingly militaristic and imperialistic course. On the

A symbol of the arms race: In 1906, the New British battleship *Dreadnought* made other battleships obsolete and spurred expensive naval building programs in several major nations.
(U.S. Navy Department)

other hand, Great Britain and the United States were protected by the sea and regarded large standing armies as possible threats to popular government; they maintained relatively small armies. By 1914, however, both nations were building up reserves and both had created general staffs.

The build-up in armies was matched by a naval arms race. Until the 1880s, the naval situation had been relatively stable. The British navy led in both size and quality. The French navy was a distant second, and France was not disposed to challenge Great Britain. Germany, however, began a naval building program in the 1890s, and the United States and Japan followed with more modest efforts. Both Germany and the United States were rapidly developing interests around the world and needed substantial navies to protect their supply lines. Japan also sought to protect its regional interests with a strong navy. Great Britain feared that the German naval building program was intended not only to protect German interests outside Europe but also to threaten Great Britain itself. As a consequence, the British launched a determined effort to keep their navy well ahead of Germany's. This naval race was enormously expensive and created a further strain on the economy of both nations.

The arms race, begun as a defensive measure, only created more tension and fear and led national leaders to the conclusion that if war should break out, the best protection would be to take the military offensive. Basing their calculations on the Austro-Prussian and Franco-Prussian wars of 1866 and 1870, European military planners believed that the next war would be a short one of open maneuver, although the Civil War in the United States and wars in the Balkans suggested that the next war might be a long one of trenches and attrition.

The build-up of armies and navies was accompanied by the rise of militarism, the concept that military aspects of a society are the most important. The German general Friedrich von Bernhardi, reflecting the influence of Charles Darwin, wrote that war was a biological necessity, a law of nature. Darwin's ideas led the Russian writer Leo Tolstoy to lament in 1906 that science "has decided that the struggle and enmity of all against all is a necessary, unavoidable, and beneficent condition of human life." Friedrich Nietzsche wrote, "You say it is the good cause that hallows even war? I say unto you; it is the war that hallows any cause. War and courage have accomplished more great things than love of the neighbor."

Advocates of militarism stressed that war was good because it developed the qualities of loyalty, cooperation, courage, and sacrifice that were important for the development of humanity. President Theodore Roosevelt and Kaiser Wilhelm II agreed on the bracing effect of war on a nation's population. Roosevelt said, "No triumph of peace is quite as great as the sublime triumphs of war." Japanese patriotic writings glorified both war and the warrior. This Japanese attitude owed much to the sense of solidarity and sacrifice among the *samurai* (the former hereditary warrior class). A code of conduct, called *Bushido* (Way of the Warrior), governed *samurai* behavior. It taught service, loyalty, and willingness to die for nation and cause. Japanese leaders relied on the traditional respect accorded to *samurai* superiors to inculcate the same values in the ordinary citizen.

In addition to building up their military forces, European countries sought to obtain security in alliances or in a balance of power between blocs of nations. Long before 1900, European nations had made it a leading principle of diplomacy to balance their economic, military, and strategic power against competing nations so that a rival nation would not have a clear-cut advantage and seize that advantage to attack. Often, a major power, unsure of having parity with a competitor, sought to create a balance by forming a partnership with a third nation. Great Britain, for example, traditionally maintained a balance of power by formulating understandings with other nations based on loans and other economic arrangements.

Other nations, such as the European rivals France and Germany, believed their security lay in constructing formal military alliances. Both nations built up an alliance system that was designed to deter their enemy from attacking. If war did break out, the alliance would add to their military power.

Occasionally, smaller nations used the concept of balance of power to protect themselves from more powerful ones. For many decades the Ottoman Empire, the so-called Sick Man of Europe, prevented Russia and others from taking its territory by playing off the competitors against each other. Thus, while Russia envisioned carting the "Sick Man" off to the undertaker, the British, fearing that a Russian defeat of the Ottoman Empire would upset the balance of power in the eastern Mediterranean region, wanted to keep the patient alive. The Ottomans were thereby able to retain vast amounts of territory that otherwise would have been lost to more powerful nations. Likewise, China resorted to a strategy of "using barbarians to control barbarians" in an attempt to play off the Western nations against one another and against Japan. Thailand remained independent because it served as a buffer state between British Burma and French Indochina. Similarly, Ethiopian emperors preserved their sovereignty by propagating the idea that if one European nation controlled Ethiopia, the balance of power in Africa would be destroyed.

The balance-of-power idea was also used in a global context. Great Britain, fearing growing German strength in East Asia, concluded a rare formal peacetime alliance with Japan in 1902. Leaving Japan to watch the Germans in East Asia, Great Britain concentrated its forces to meet opponents elsewhere in the world, for example, confronting Russia in Persia.

At times, the attempt to achieve a balance of power fomented war rather than sustained peace. Nations were not content to maintain the balance of power in all its various aspects—military, economic, and diplomatic; they also struggled to shift that balance in their own favor. Consequently, the balance-of-power concept became a source of ever-spiraling economic and military competition and, eventually, war.

Alliances, in theory constructed to deter war, in practice threatened to bring on wars that otherwise might not have occurred. Nations backed by allies sometimes acted more aggressively than they would have alone. In some situations, such as in the summer of 1914, European nations in both alliance systems urged their allies to refuse compromises, thus creating an explosive situation.

In reaction to the atmosphere of nationalistic tensions pointing toward war, many people became interested in fostering a spirit of international cooperation to preserve the peace. Delegates met at international peace conferences at The Hague in the Netherlands in 1899 and 1907, where they worked on disarmament propositions and international arbitration techniques and established the Hague Tribunal for the arbitration of disputes. The presence of the tribunal induced a number of nations to settle their disputes through arbitration. The peace movement also benefited from the participation of prominent individuals. Alfred Nobel, the inventor of dynamite, instituted the Nobel Prize for Peace, among others. The iron and steel magnate Andrew Carnegie set up the Carnegie Endowment for International Peace and also built the Peace Palace at The Hague. Compared to the onrush of nationalistic hostilities, however, the international peace movement proved to be feeble; the Hague Tribunal was given only insignificant cases such as technical boundary questions. Meanwhile, the major nations continued to put their energy into building up their war machines.

CULTURAL TRENDS

In the West, many significant new forms of expression developed in religion, literature, and the arts. Non-Western cultures were modified to varying extents by contacts with the West. Non-Western cultures also had some impact in the West, but not nearly to the same degree.

The West before World War I witnessed a continual conflict between secularism and traditional religions. In Europe and the United States, secularists (people who would greatly limit the role of churches and their teachings in society) strongly challenged the privileged position of the established churches. Scientific and technological changes and urbanization disrupted traditional living patterns, which in turn affected religious customs and beliefs. Despite their differences, the ideas of Darwin, Marx, Nietzsche, and Freud all challenged, in whole or in part, long-standing religious beliefs.

Within Judaism and Christianity, some individuals tried to reconcile their religious beliefs with some of the new influences and ideas. Reform Judaism and liberal Protestantism were two such responses, but Orthodox Jews and Protestant fundamentalists were much less ready for compromise. The Catholic and Orthodox Churches also were usually not enthusiastic about modern ideas.

Another conflict in Western culture concerned differences among Western thinkers and artists about how to view and depict the world around them and inside themselves. In the decades immediately before 1914, many began to question the dominance of an objective, scientific, and strictly rational approach to reality. Einstein's theory of relativity seemed to deny certainty in science. French philosopher Henri Bergson emphasized intuition rather than reason, and Freud, preceded by Nietzsche, stressed the role of unconscious, nonrational motivation. Writers and artists increasingly questioned the realistic modes of artistic expression that had been dominant since the mid-nineteenth century and that tended to be dependent on an objective, scientific approach.

Modern art, music, and literature came out of this questioning, and out of new ways of seeing and portraying the external world and the reality within oneself. Modern art embraced a range of expression, from the postimpressionist paintings of Paul Cézanne, Vincent van Gogh, Paul Gauguin, and Georges Seurat to the fauvism of Henri Matisse, the cubism of Pablo Picasso, and the abstractionism of Wassily Kandinsky. In music, Arnold Schoenberg was the most significant innovator. Between 1906 and 1909, he developed what came to be called atonal music, a step that led the artist Kandinsky to write that Schoenberg had "discovered mines of new beauty in his search for spiritual structure." In literature, the symbolist poets of France and Russia, such as Stephane Mallarmé and Alexander Blok, were among the most notable challengers of literary realism and naturalism and the world they continued to depict. By using words as symbols, they attempted to suggest a more meaningful, mysterious, and hidden reality.

In addition to changes inside Western culture, another noteworthy trend was that non-Westerners sometimes altered their values after contacts with the West. The major religions and philosophies of Africa and Asia, such as Islam, Confucianism, Buddhism, and Hinduism, were confronted by Christianity, secularism, and other aspects of Western culture. While some local religions were destroyed or transformed, in general the major world faiths were little

Picasso's *Young Ladies of Avignon* (1907) reflects the movement away from realistic representational art and also the influence on Picasso of primitive art.
(Pablo Picasso, Les Desmoiselles d'Avignon *[1907]. Oil on canvas, 8′×7′8″. Collection, The Museum of Modern Art, New York. Acquired through the Lillie P. Bliss Bequest.)*

affected before 1914. In India, Hindu reformers attempted to reconcile traditional teachings with modern science and with the concept of the equality of all human beings. Some Chinese scholars attempted a reinterpretation of Confucianism to accord with democratic ideals. In both instances, however, such attempts were rejected by the orthodox majority.

While the influence of Western culture on the non-Western world was certainly greater than the reverse, there were also some notable non-Western influences on Western artists, writers, and thinkers. As a result of imperialistic expansion, Westerners became increasingly interested in foreign cultures. The publication of the first two volumes of Sir James Frazer's *The Golden Bough* in 1890 opened the world of "primitive" societies to many, including Freud and others, who eventually made use of Frazer's material in formulating some of their psychological theories. Some modern Western artists who rejected traditional Western perspectives were influenced by Japanese, South Pacific, and African art. Paul Gauguin, for example, went to Tahiti in 1891 and was influenced by its art. Vincent van Gogh was much indebted to Japanese woodblock prints. Picasso was studying African art when, along with Georges Braque, he founded Cubism in 1907–1908. By the mid-nineteenth century, religious ideas of India had already begun to influence such Western thinkers as the German philosopher Arthur Schopenhauer and the American writer Ralph Waldo Emerson. In 1912, the famous Irish poet William Butler Yeats called attention to the poetic writings of the Indian religious thinker and writer Rabindranath Tagore, who the following year would become the first non-European writer to win the Nobel Prize for Literature. Commenting on Tagore's writings, Yeats noted, "They stirred my blood as nothing has for years."

SUGGESTED SOURCES

CHURCHILL, WINSTON S., *My Early Life: A Roving Commission* (1930). A recounting of Churchill's youthful experiences as a soldier and correspondent at home and abroad; gives insights into the British aristocracy and imperialism.* (Also a film, *Young Winston*.)

HOBSBAWN, ERIC, *The Age of Empire, 1975–1914* (1989). A panoramic history of European dominance.*

KNAPP, VINCENT J., *Europe in the Era of Social Transformation: 1700–Present* (1976). A penetrating study of the changes in the lives of Europeans, with emphasis on the nineteenth and twentieth centuries.

MASSIE, ROBERT K., *Dreadnought: Britain, Germany, and the Coming of the Great War* (1992). An engrossing study of a fatal rivalry.*

MOSSE, GEORGE L., *The Culture of Western Europe*, 3d ed. (1988). Standard cultural history, with analysis of links between romanticism and nationalism.*

PALMER, ALAN, *Dictionary of Twentieth Century History, 1900–1982*, 2d ed. (1983). Useful and readable resource.

RUIS (EDUARDO DEL RIO), *Marx for Beginners* (1979). A humorous but sophisticated explanation of Marx by means of cartoons.*

SHAFER, BOYD C., *Nationalism: Myth and Reality* (1955). A general treatment of the subject that deals with myths regarding both nationalism and its historic development.*

TAYLOR, EDMUND, *The Fall of the Dynasties: The Collapse of the Old Order, 1905–1922* (1963). A comprehensive survey of one of history's great upheavals.

TUCHMAN, BARBARA W., *The Proud Tower* (1972). A detailed and well-written look at politicians, anarchists, socialists, imperialists, nationalists, militarists, and leading figures in the arts in Europe and the United States from 1890 to 1914.*

WARD, BARBARA, *Five Ideas That Change the World* (1984). A survey of five important ideologies that have had and continue to have a significant impact.*

WARE, CAROLINE F., K. M. PANIKKAR, and J. M. ROMEIN, Eds., *History of Mankind: Cultural and Scientific Development*, Vol. VI, The Twentieth Century (1966). A comprehensive overview of twentieth-century trends.

*Paperback available.

CHAPTER 3

The Great Powers of Europe

The history of the period before World War I can be best understood by examining the characteristics of the powerful European nations that dominated much of the globe. Although each of these nations had its unique historical experiences, strengths, and weaknesses, each was also heavily influenced by the major trends of urbanization, nationalism, militarism, and secularism discussed in the previous chapters. These nations will be taken up beginning with the more democratic nations in Western Europe, then moving eastward to consider the more autocratic nations.

GREAT BRITAIN

In 1900 Great Britain was generally considered to be the most liberal and prosperous nation in Europe. The British people enjoyed the benefits of a highly industrialized economy fed by raw materials shipped in from a huge colonial empire. The empire also supplied many vital foodstuffs, for Great Britain's large urban population needed much more food than the farmers of the small island nation could provide. The widespread economic prosperity led both old landed aristocrats and new industrialists to agree that it was "the best of all possible worlds."

Political life in Great Britain, a constitutional monarchy, was characterized by growing tendencies toward social reform and liberalism. The Reform Bill of 1867 and the Franchise Bill of 1884 had created virtually universal adult male suffrage. The Parliament Bill of 1911 in effect gave the House of Commons, the elected chamber of the British Parliament, control over the government budget. It also somewhat diminished the "gentlemen's club" atmosphere that had previously pervaded the Parliament. Before World War I, Emmeline Pankhurst, her two daughters, and many other women organized a suffragette movement to demand voting rights for women. Pankhurst adopted effective but controversial militant tactics such as processions to the Houses of Parlia-

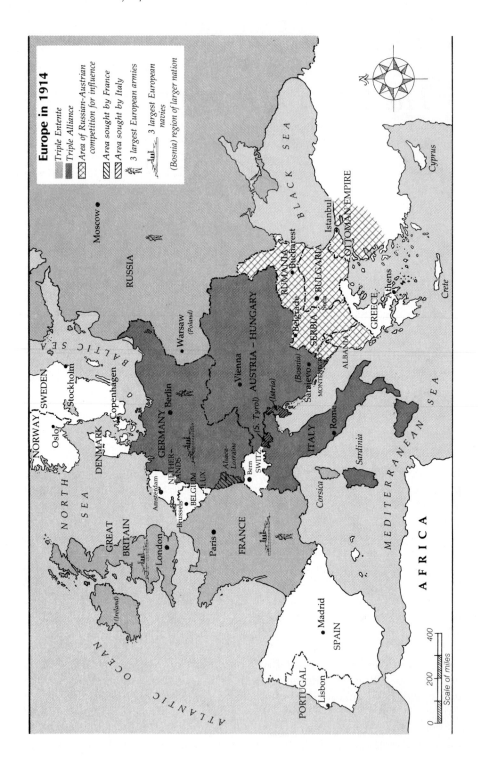

Europe in 1914

Triple Entente
Triple Alliance
Area of Russian-Austrian competition for influence
Area sought by France
Area sought by Italy
3 largest European armies
3 largest European navies
(Bosnia) region of larger nation

ment, window smashing, and bombs in letter boxes to draw attention to the issue of women's rights. When they were arrested and jailed, the suffragettes went on hunger strikes. The British government retaliated with a "cat and mouse" strategy whereby the suffragettes were released from prison when their health was threatened by the hunger strikes and then rearrested when they had recovered. The war delayed the full franchise for women, which was not secured in Great Britain until 1928.

British politics developed in a two-party context, in contrast to the multi-party system common in France and many other European nations. The two-party system eliminated the necessity of forming party coalitions in order to gain a governing majority and thereby contributed to a more stable political system. As a result, the British were able to modify many of their economic and political institutions without bloody and divisive revolutions. However, ethnic separatist movements in Wales and Scotland and the struggle for "Home Rule" in Ireland placed continued demands on the centralized political structures.

Although the general economy was prosperous, the industrialization of Great Britain during the eighteenth and nineteenth centuries had brought with it oppressive working conditions. Many remained so poor that the poet Alfred Lord Tennyson could write: "White chalk and alum and plaster are sold to the poor for bread." Workers demanded better pay, improved working conditions, and fringe benefits. In contrast, industrialists believed in a laissez-faire system in which the government kept a "hands-off" policy toward business, a system that permitted them to do precisely as they wished. Relatively unhampered by government controls, the industrialists tenaciously fought labor union demands for better working conditions. In spite of the owners' opposition, however, labor unions steadily gained power and influence. Workers rallied

Suffragettes, attempting to extend voting rights to women, are escorted away from Buckingham Palace by police in 1914.
(*BBC Hulton/The Bettmann Archive*)

around the new Labour party, whose rapid growth demonstrated the rising political power of workers and their supporters and threatened to displace the Liberals, one of the traditional gentry-dominated political parties. Labour politicians and their political friends in Parliament created legislation that limited monopolies, assisted the unemployed, and improved working conditions. They also made similar reforms in the fields of education and social welfare.

Beyond the British Isles, as a popular saying went, "The sun never sets on the British Empire." By 1900 Great Britain had amassed the largest collection of overseas possessions in the world. In northern Africa, Great Britain dominated Egypt and the vital Suez Canal; it held Nigeria and other territories in western Africa. In eastern and southern Africa, Great Britain had taken control of Kenya, Uganda, the Rhodesias, and South Africa. In Asia, it held Hong Kong, other concessions on the China coast, the Malay peninsula, Burma, Ceylon, key areas along the Persian Gulf, and above all India, "the Jewel in the Crown." Halfway around the world, Great Britain had created two new "Britains" in Australia and New Zealand, almost completely displacing the original populations and populating the areas with settlers from the British Isles. Through its control of Canada, extensive Caribbean possessions, and islands off South America, Great Britain still maintained a formidable presence in the Western Hemisphere. Self-governing dominions such as Canada, Australia, and New Zealand had their own armed services but relied on the British navy for overall protection and followed Great Britain's lead in foreign policy.

This vast imperial domain, so vital to the survival of Great Britain, required a large navy to protect the supply lines from the colonies and to secure the British Isles from invasion. "Rule Britannia! Britannia rules the waves," the British sang as they spent millions of pounds to support their navy, the largest in the world. Conservatives seeking to increase the number of dreadnoughts, battleships with heavy-caliber guns, adopted the slogan, "We want eight and we won't wait." Naval units were stationed around the world at strategic outposts such as Gibraltar, Suez, the Cape of Good Hope, Aden, and Singapore. The British also used numerous islands in the oceans of the world as coaling, watering, and supply stations for the navy.

In contrast to their enormous navy, the British maintained a small but efficient volunteer army. Great Britain did not aspire to make conquests on the Continent; protected primarily by the navy, the British thus had no need for a huge standing army of conscripts. Nor did the empire require large land forces. A surprisingly small number of British officers and men, supported by a substantial number of local troops commanded by British officers, kept the peace throughout the colonies. For example, only 4,000 Britons were stationed on the entire Indian subcontinent.

FRANCE

France was also an industrialized nation with a large empire; compared with Great Britain, it had a much more substantial agricultural base but a less developed industrial system. As in Great Britain, the French had been moving toward liberalization; French liberals advocating more democratic political forms clashed with conservatives who tended to support more authoritarian policies. The multiparty system of French politics before World War I reflected many gradations of conservatism, liberalism, and radicalism and often made French governments unstable. After France's disastrous defeat in the Franco-Prussian war in 1870–1871, an essentially moderate, middle-class group of politicians founded the Third Republic. They were opposed both by the political Right, which wanted a return to conservative monarchy, or what was jokingly called "the man on horseback," and by forces on the Left, which wanted a more revolutionary, socialist government.

The Dreyfus case, which dragged on from 1894 to 1906, reflected the deep divisions within French society. Alfred Dreyfus, a French Jew and a junior army officer, was wrongly convicted of selling military secrets to a foreign power. Many Frenchmen, including such noted intellectuals as Emile Zola, were convinced that Dreyfus was innocent and that he had been used as a scapegoat to protect important judicial and military officials. The case became a cause célèbre and brought into serious question the extent to which French society had eradicated age-old privileges and prejudices. Dreyfus was finally found innocent in 1906. His exoneration resulted in the downfall of the conservative forces and the victory of the republicans and the socialists.

Successive liberal coalition governments reformed the military and subordinated it to the civilian government, while limiting the political power of the Catholic Church. One politician stated unequivocally, "Clericalism, there is the enemy." Organized labor sought to institute sweeping economic reforms and gained widespread political support. With increased power within the Chamber of Deputies, French radicals from 1905 to 1910 pushed through measures formally separating church and state and creating old-age pensions and other legislation to improve the lot of working people. However, before World War I, British workers still had more basic rights than did unionists in France.

France also faced problems in international affairs. Its population was smaller than that of other major continental powers and was growing more slowly. In addition, French industry lagged behind that of Great Britain, Germany, and, later, the United States. These problems in turn led to military weakness. The French army was smaller and less efficient than that of its neighboring enemy Germany, and its navy had fallen to fourth place behind those of Great Britain, Germany, and the United States.

To compensate for these weaknesses, the French government sought to create an alliance system that would bolster French power. Concerned about further German expansion, France sought to limit German power on the Continent by finding allies to counterbalance Germany and its Triple Alliance. In 1894, France signed a secret convention with Russia whereby if France were attacked by Germany or Italy, Russia would attack Germany, and conversely, if Russia were attacked by Germany or Austria, France would move against Germany. France later enlarged this agreement by including Great Britain. Traditionally suspicious of European alliances, Great Britain hesitated before finally joining in an entente (informal understanding) with France in 1904 and Russia in 1907. With the resulting Triple Entente, which was in part no more than a "gentlemen's agreement," the French believed they had formed a powerful balance to Germany's growing strength in Central Europe.

France controlled the second-largest colonial empire. In North Africa, France held Algeria and Tunisia and, by 1912, Morocco. In sub-Saharan Africa, France dominated vast stretches of West and Equatorial Africa. In Asia, the French held Indochina, which was subdivided into Vietnam, Laos, and Cambodia. In the Western Hemisphere, France possessed a number of Caribbean islands and French Guiana in South America. France also controlled numerous small islands in the South Pacific and in the Indian Ocean.

GERMANY

The opening of the twentieth century also witnessed Germany's emergence as perhaps the most powerful nation in Europe. Although not unified until 1871, Germany moved forward rapidly. It had a sound agricultural base and had used its large resources of coal and iron ore to develop into one of the world's top industrial nations. By and large, Germany's industrial plant was newer and more efficient than that of its major economic rival, Great Britain.

Politically, the German government reflected autocratic tendencies characteristic of the Prussian monarchy, the dominant entity within the federal system of German states. The German constitution provided the chancellor with wide executive powers in relationship to those of the German parliament. The Reichstag, elected by males above the age of twenty-five, was never as powerful a voice for citizen representation as was the British House of Commons or the French Chamber of Deputies.

As in other industrialized nations, Germany's growing industrial strength caused a rapid movement toward unionization. Ironically, it was Otto von Bismarck, the conservative "Blood and Iron Chancellor" who had masterminded the unification of Germany, who brought about many of the changes the workers desired. Hoping to cripple the socialist movement in Germany, the conservative and paternalistic Bismarck inaugurated social welfare programs in the 1880s, several decades before the more liberal governments of France and Great Britain and half a century before the United States. Through his social welfare program, Bismarck instituted social insurance compensating workers for illness or accidents and providing the aged with pensions.

German successes in the Franco-Prussian war of 1870–1871 not only completed the unification of Germany but also shifted the center of European politics. Under the Treaty of Frankfurt, France was forced to surrender the provinces of Alsace-Lorraine to Germany, to pay an indemnity of about $1 billion, and to allow Germany to occupy key French fortresses until the amount owed was paid. Bismarck knew France would be set on revenge. Indeed, the unification of Germany was viewed with hostility and fear not only by the French but also by other European nations, particularly Russia and Great Britain.

Fearing French retaliation, Bismarck set out to form new political and military alliances; he compared this diplomatic maneuvering to a giant chess game. In order to isolate France and to avoid fighting a two-front war against

France and Russia, Bismarck sought alliances with Austria-Hungary and Russia. He failed to conclude a lasting agreement with Russia, but he did forge an alliance with the declining Austro-Hungarian Empire, which wanted support to protect itself from possible conflict with Russia. In 1879, Germany and Austria-Hungary signed a secret Dual Alliance whereby both would make war together if either were attacked by Russia, and if either were attacked by another power, the other would remain neutral.

Three years later, in 1882, Bismarck enlarged the Dual Alliance to include Italy. Under the secret terms of the Triple Alliance, all three nations would fight together if Italy or Germany were attacked by France; if any one of these nations were attacked by any two great powers, all three would give mutual assistance. The Italians, fearing British naval power, stipulated that the treaty did not apply if Great Britain was involved in any of the attacks. Italy was willing to align itself with Germany because it was angry over the 1881 French takeover of Tunisia and because Germany offered to assist in securing Libya for the Italian empire.

Bismarck also tried to prevent Austrian-Russian conflict in the Balkans, but such efforts were often threatened by Austria-Hungary's ambitions for territorial gains there. Indeed, Austria's aggressive foreign policy against both Italy and the Balkan nations directly conflicted with the surging nationalism in these areas and contributed to the destruction of Bismarck's carefully constructed alliance system. Initially, Great Britain, secure with its naval superiority, remained aloof from these maneuverings. However, after Germany announced that it intended to build a first-class navy and in general to become a major industrial and military power, Great Britain's policy of isolation rapidly changed.

In 1890, Bismarck resigned under pressure from Kaiser Wilhelm II, who wanted to be his own chief minister. Wilhelm II sought to reestablish a more autocratic government, a move that was opposed by the German socialists. Wilhelm also supported the growth of the German military and the stockpiling of armaments. With continued economic prosperity and successes in expanding the German empire, Wilhelm II had little difficulty in repelling socialist attempts to take control of the government.

Like Italy, Germany came late to the imperial scramble and had to pick up the leftover pieces. Germany acquired a block of islands in the western Pacific and a sphere of influence in China. The Germans also obtained several scattered territories in Africa: Togoland and Cameroon in western Africa, German East Africa (Tanzania), and German Southwest Africa (Namibia). Other imperial powers, hardly pacifists themselves, considered the Germans particularly aggressive in their prowling around the world looking for opportunities to expand their colonial power. The United States feared that the Germans were even trying to establish a base of power in the Western Hemisphere.

RUSSIA

To Western European eyes, tsarist Russia was a gigantic, backward nation. Territorially three times as large as the continental United States, it was overwhelmingly populated by peasants. Despite significant industrial growth in the preceding quarter century, by 1914 only about 3 million out of a population of approximately 170 million were industrial workers. Nor was it a homogeneous population. The Russians (or Great Russians) were not quite half of the population of the empire. Ukrainians, Byelorussians, Poles, Lithuanians, Latvians, Estonians, Finns, Jews, Armenians, Georgians, and various Muslim Turkish groups made up the bulk of the remaining population, along with numerous smaller ethnic groups. Most of the non-Russians had their own cultural and religious tradition and were held in the empire only by the greater strength of the Russians. The Russian school system had recently been expanded, but on the eve of World War I, less than half of the Russian population was literate.

Like his predecessors, Nicholas II, "Tsar of All the Russias" from 1894 to 1917, believed that he alone was chosen by God to rule the Russian Empire. Only a revolt in 1905 persuaded him of the necessity of allowing the creation of a Duma, or Parliament, which had very limited legislative powers. Once the turmoil quieted, Nicholas promptly began to retreat from reforms. When he found the composition of the first two Dumas not to his liking, he changed the electoral law in 1907 so as to obtain more conservative representatives. Disparaging the determination of the tsar to remain an autocratic ruler, his opponents grumbled, "The Duma is dead, long live the Duma." As a result of the tsar's interference, the next Duma was so cooperative that it was allowed to serve the maximum five-year term. The Fourth Duma had almost completed a full term when the first 1917 revolution occurred.

A symbol of the old order: Russian Tsar Nicholas II and his family around the turn of the century.
(*UPI/Bettmann Newsphotos*)

Finding it difficult because of geographic constraints to move overseas to acquire colonies, Russians expressed their imperialism by moving overland. By the nineteenth century, the Russian Empire had expanded eastward to the shores of the Pacific. Russia also moved southeastward into central Asia, or Turkestan, conquering and holding these territories until the collapse of the Soviet Union in the 1990s. Russian growth eastward was in some ways comparable to the westward expansion of the United States across North America. Both American and Russian settlers pushed aside scattered tribes. Like the United States in dealing with Mexico, Russia also made extensive gains at the expense of established nations on her border, including the Ottoman Empire, Persia, Afghanistan, and China. In 1891, the Russian government began building a transcontinental railroad, the Trans-Siberian Railway, to knit together the vast stretches of its domain. In 1903, Russian railroad workers completed their task, having built a 5,500-mile single track from Moscow to Vladivostok on the Pacific Ocean. Since Vladivostok was icebound for part of the year, Russia in 1896 forced China to allow a branch line of the railroad to pass through Chinese Manchuria to ice-free Port Arthur on the Yellow Sea. In Manchuria and Korea, Russian imperialism openly confronted Japanese imperialism, which sought to expand into the same territories.

SUMMARY

Before World War I, Europe was rich and powerful, but it was also plagued with internal problems. Domestically, all European governments struggled with the conflict among the forces of conservatism, liberalism, and socialism. In Great Britain, France, and even Germany, these internal political divisions resulted in reforms that improved the lives of middle-class and working-class people. In Russia, however, the conservative aristocrats continued to be the dominant political force. While both Britain and France were characterized by a trend toward liberalization, the more autocratic governments of Germany and Russia continued to maintain their ascendancy.

The mounting trend of nationalism also escalated old rivalries among the various European nations. These nationalist rivalries poisoned the atmosphere and led European nations to increase their armaments and to forge alliances in order to achieve security. Despite the known problems in creating and maintaining alliances, both Germany and France designed alliance systems that were as likely to cause war as to keep the peace. Increased arms stockpiles and the alliances added to tensions instead of providing a sense of calm or security.

Finally, Europeans felt superior to the Asians and Africans whom they were eagerly incorporating into vast empires. Great Britain and France had the largest empires. Having unified late in the nineteenth century, both Germany and Italy were relative newcomers and struggled to secure whatever territories remained independent in Africa and Asia. Russia was another major European imperialist power, whose interests clashed with those of Austria-Hungary in the Balkans. These imperialist rivalries added to the international tensions and further exacerbated hostilities among European nations.

SUGGESTED SOURCES

GILBERT, FELIX, *Europe Since 1890,* 2d ed. (1979). A brief, general survey for students, with illustrations.*

HALE, ORON J., *The Great Illusion, 1900–1914* (1971). A survey of technological, economic, cultural, and political developments in Europe before World War I.*

MASSIE, ROBERT K., *Nicholas and Alexandra* (1967). A popular, sympathetic biography of the last Russian tsar and tsarina. Gives a feeling for the world of royalty before World War I.* (Also a film.)

RICH, NORMAN. *Great Power Diplomacy 1814–1914* (1992). Survey of the often complex relationships among diverse European nations.*

STONE, NORMAN, *Europe Transformed, 1878–1919* (1984). A scholarly, readable, and comprehensive work that emphasizes the decline of liberalism.*

TANNENBAUM, EDWARD R., *1900* (1977). A depiction of Europe in 1900 with special emphasis on the European response to modernization.*

Upstairs-Downstairs, BBC television series. A look at life among the British upper class and their servants during the early part of the twentieth century.

*Paperback available.

CHAPTER 4

The European Conquest of Africa

In the late nineteenth and early twentieth centuries, the major European nations were in the full tide of imperialistic conquest across the globe, particularly in Africa. In 1869, at the opening of the Suez Canal, Europeans directly controlled only a scattering of outposts on the African coast and some settlements in Algeria and on the southern tip of Africa. By 1912 they had partitioned nearly all of the continent and incorporated vast areas into several colonial empires.

Only two states in Africa, Liberia and Ethiopia, remained independent after the partition. Liberia, partly settled by former slaves from the United States, remained heavily dependent economically on U.S. companies such as Firestone. The other independent state, Ethiopia, had the unique distinction of defeating a European nation when it repulsed an Italian attempt to conquer it in 1896.

AFRICAN SOCIETIES

The African continent in the late nineteenth century contained a vast mosaic of tribal peoples who lived in a varied landscape of desert, rain forest, savannah, mountain, and coastal lands. All these peoples had adapted their social and economic organizations to their environments; hence some were hunters, and others were agriculturalists, nomads, food gatherers, or herders. Their political systems varied from large empires to tribal groupings under chieftains. From the eleventh century onward, Africa south of the Sahara had experienced an influx of newcomers from Islamic Arabized North Africa and from western Asia. In the seventeenth century small numbers of Europeans began to arrive. As a result of the confrontations among these different groups, many traditional societies were disrupted or destroyed.

THE PARTITION OF AFRICA

European nations looked on Africa as a target for imperialism from a broad spectrum of motives—economic, strategic, cultural, and nationalistic. Leaders of several of these nations watched with particular interest the activities of a private commercial association organized by King Leopold II of Belgium in 1876 for the purpose of exploiting the resources of the Congo basin. As Leopold had commented, "I want my share of this wonderful African cake." The Congo Free State, as the area controlled by Leopold's company was called, was headed by the king in his private capacity, although his prestige as king of the Belgians was crucial to the success of the association. The company's oppressive policies in the Congo Free State and its exploitation of the people justified accusations that modern tropical colonization by Europeans was motivated only by economic greed. Joseph Conrad captured this greed in his novel *Heart of Darkness*. He said: "To tear treasure out of the bowels of the land was their desire, with no more moral purpose at the back of it than there is in burglars breaking into a safe." In 1908 the Belgian government replaced the king's regime in the Congo with a less exploitative one.

Leopold's early success played a key role in sharpening the mutual suspicions of European nations about each other's intentions in Africa, and they began to elbow one another in earnest after 1880 to get what they wanted on that continent. At the Berlin West African Conference in 1884–1885, European colonial powers agreed on "first come, first served" as the basic rule of dividing Africa. Any power that effectively occupied an African territory and notified others would be recognized as having established sole possession. After 1884, the scramble intensified as the older colonial powers—Portugal, Spain, and particularly Great Britain and France—expanded inland from their original outposts on the coast. The new nations of Italy and Germany gained footholds on the African coast, often in neglected areas, and pushed inland as well. By 1912 almost all Africa was under European control. Between 1871 and 1900, Britain added about 4.3 million square miles of territory and 66 million people to its African empire, and France about 3.5 million square miles and 26 million people. The possessions of the other imperial powers were smaller and less populous. Since Great Britain and France dominated the partition of Africa, their actions will be the focus of this chapter.

As Europeans sought to consolidate their holdings, Africans saw in the coming of the Europeans the disruption of their traditional ways of life. They resisted bitterly; there were at least twenty-five conflicts with Europeans before World War I. Besides the Ethiopians, other key resisters were the Ashante in present-day Ghana, the Hereros in present-day Tanzania, and numerous peoples in Islamic northern Africa. Two of the most determined groups fought for years: the followers of the Mahdi in the Sudan and the Zulus of southern Africa, both treated in the following discussion. In the end, except for the Ethiopians, all of these resisters lost.

The scramble to divide Africa created a number of intense hostilities among the imperialist nations, particularly among Great Britain, France, Ger-

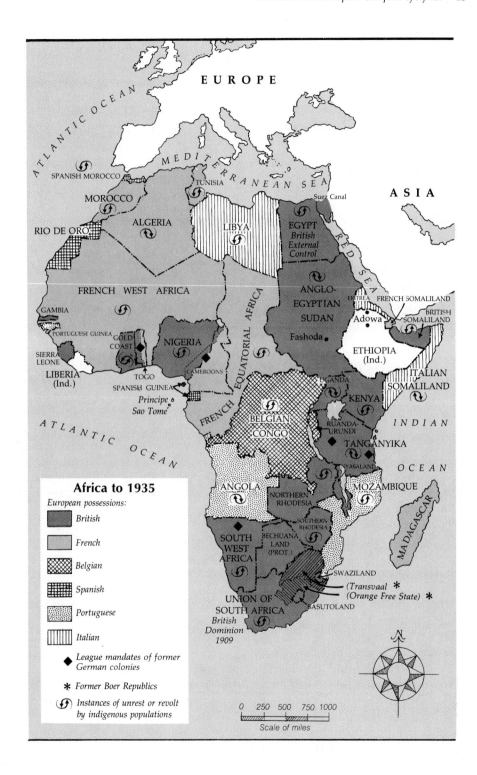

Africa to 1935

European possessions:

- British
- French
- Belgian
- Spanish
- Portuguese
- Italian

◆ League mandates of former German colonies

∗ Former Boer Republics

Ⓕ Instances of unrest or revolt by indigenous populations

0   250   500   750 1000

Scale of miles

many, and Italy. Nevertheless, these problems were settled peacefully at conference tables in European capitals. After partitioning Africa, Europeans found through surveying and exploration that few areas could produce immediate wealth without large capital investment. Therefore it is not surprising that once Africa had been divided up and there was no longer a reason to fear rivals, most European governments lost some of their interest in their newly acquired possessions. The following will detail the partition of Africa by regions by major European powers in the late nineteenth century.

NORTH AFRICA

North Africa between the Mediterranean Sea and the Sahara Desert was a land of ancient civilizations. Since the eighth century C.E., most peoples of this region had become Muslim. This land was called the *Mahgrib*, because it was the westernmost extension of Arab culture. Most of North Africa came under British or French control.

British Control of Egypt and the Sudan

Great Britain's interest in this region was primarily strategic, focused on the Suez Canal which shortened the distance between Europe and Asia. The Suez Canal, designed by a French engineer and built by an international company, was opened in 1869. The canal provided a shortcut between Europe and Asia. Because of their far-flung empire and global trading network, the British were the most interested in the canal. In 1875 Great Britain acquired control of it when the ruler of Egypt sold his shares in the company to the British government to avert bankruptcy. In order to protect the canal, Great Britain looked for an opportunity to gain control over Egypt. In 1882 Great Britain made Egypt into a de facto protectorate, although it nominally remained a province of the Ottoman Empire. British advisors supervised all important Egyptian government offices and became the real rulers of the country.

Egypt claimed authority over the Sudan, which controlled the water supply of the Nile River. The Sudanese, who resented Egyptian control, rose in revolt in 1883 under the Mahdi (Rightly Guided One), the leader of a nationalist Muslim movement. Since Great Britain controlled Egypt, it too became involved in putting down the Sudanese uprising. Between 1896 and 1898, General Sir Herbert Kitchener undertook the reconquest of the Sudan. After its pacification, Great Britain and Egypt established joint rule over the land, which in effect meant British control.

When the British reached Fashoda in southern Sudan in 1898, they found a French expedition, which had arrived overland from the west, occupying the village. France hoped to control the Sudan so that its African empire might extend from the Atlantic Ocean to the Indian Ocean, and at the same time put pressure on the British downriver in Egypt by controlling the source of the Nile. The ensuing standoff was called the "Fashoda Incident." France backed

In 1898, an Anglo-Egyptian force commanded by General Kitchener conquered the Sudan. Here the Twenty-first Lancers charge at the battle of Omdurman.
(Walker Art Gallery, Liverpool)

down in 1899 and renounced all claims to the Nile valley in return for British recognition of its claims in the Sahara. This crisis illustrates the intensity of rivalries among the colonial powers in Africa, although these rivalries never led directly to war.

The French Conquest and Settlement of Northwest Africa

Outside Egypt and the Sudan, France was the dominant colonial power north of the Sahara. Between 1830 and 1869, France had conquered Algeria, which it then used as a base for further advances. By the end of the century the French had made Tunisia to the east a protectorate, in the teeth of a strong claim by Italy. As in Egypt, a facade of native government was allowed to exist. The French also moved southward across the Sahara and finally westward into Morocco.

Unlike the British, who made no attempt to send settlers to Egypt, the French from the start encouraged the immigration of Europeans into Algeria. Algerians found themselves pushed off their best agricultural lands to make room for European colonists. By 1911, out of a total population of 5.6 million people in Algeria, 752,000 were Europeans. Tunisia had a European population of 130,000.

In both Algeria and Tunisia, there was friction between the privileged European minority and the Arab majority. The Muslims were treated in every respect as a conquered people. Under the circumstances, it is hardly surprising that a "racial problem" developed between the Europeans and Muslims. In no other part of the Islamic world were Muslims confronted with so large a number of foreigners settled in their midst.

In addition to economic advantages, the privileged European settlers enjoyed the right of political representation in the legislature of metropolitan France. Under the French constitution, the *colons* (French settlers) in Algeria sent six deputies and three senators to the French legislature in 1900. The Muslims had no representation. Established in a position of superiority, many *colons* regarded the Algerians with open contempt. "The Arab must accept the fate of the conquered," wrote one *colon*. "He must either become assimilated to our civilization or disappear. European civilization can have no sympathy for the life of the savage."

Gradually, the abuses of the colonial system became widely known in France, and a spirited debate on colonial policy ensued in the Chamber of Deputies (the lower house of the French legislature), which enacted reforms early in the twentieth century. Given the tenor of French thought, the ideal of most reformers was progressive assimilation. Upper-class Algerian Muslims were encouraged to attend French schools and adopt French ways, for which they would be rewarded with a share in the power structure of the French Empire.

The policy of assimilation never took off, however, for three basic reasons. One was the resistance of most Algerians, who were not prepared to renounce their culture and their religious law for those of their masters. Second, not all French opinion supported the assimilation plan, and it was therefore extremely limited in the scope of its execution. The *colons* were the third factor. Unwilling to give up their privileges, they opposed most measures designed to lessen or dilute their power.

Morocco was the last French acquisition in North Africa. At the beginning of the twentieth century, it was an independent kingdom beset by internal problems. For a time, the government of Morocco was able to delay French imperialistic advances by exploiting the Franco-German rivalry in international affairs and appealing to the German government for help. Germany was at first happy to play this game, but in the face of European opposition it eventually backed down and recognized Morocco as a French sphere of influence. In 1912, the Sultan of Morocco was forced to sign a treaty that handed his country over to French protection.

WEST AFRICA

This huge territory contained some of the harshest desert and some of the lushest rain forest in Africa, in addition to grasslands. Before European colonization, the peoples in this area lived in societies ranging in scope from large empires like that of the Muslim Hausa-Fulani peoples in today's northern Nigeria, through well-organized kingdoms like that of the Ashante in today's Ghana, to small groups who still lived by hunting and gathering in the equatorial rain forests. Except for those areas south of the Sahara that had become largely Islamic, traditional religions prevailed in West Africa.

Indirect Rule in Great Britain's Scattered Colonies

In West Africa Great Britain ruled four colonies strung out on the coast and mostly surrounded by French possessions. There the British opened mines and encouraged cash crops grown by African peasants. They made this development profitable by building railroads to connect the coast with the interior. The Gold Coast (Ghana) was the best example of a successful and prosperous colony. Here, the railroad system made it possible to exploit timber, open up cocoa farms, and develop gold mines in the hinterland. British-owned trading companies and their shareholders became rich from these operations. This economic process also provided jobs for some Africans, but it disrupted the previous economy.

In administering Africa, the British applied no preconceived notions of colonial government but devised practical, day-by-day solutions to the problems of governing. The policy Great Britain eventually applied in West Africa was called "indirect rule," a system developed by Lord Lugard, governor-general of Nigeria, Great Britain's largest and most populous West African colony, to administer a district easily and cheaply. Because the British administrative staff was small, the African chief and his advisors were delegated the task of running the day-to-day matters of government. They were supervised by a British official who also saw to it that British interests in the area were upheld.

Climatic conditions and an already large population made West Africa unsuitable and unattractive for British immigration. The absence of a British immigrant group eager to compete for local jobs meant more opportunities for Africans. Many were very anxious to acquire a Western education to qualify them for the new skilled positions opening up in a rapidly changing economy. British official opinion was responsive and sometimes enthusiastic about West African demands for more schools and job opportunities. Sir Frederick Guggisberg, governor of the Gold Coast during World War I, appointed a committee that drew up a new educational plan for the colony. This plan provided a foundation for the modernization of the Gold Coast, paving the way for the independent nation of Ghana.

France's Vast West African Empire

By the twentieth century, France had acquired a huge block of colonial territory south of the Sahara that stretched 3,000 miles from the extreme west coast of Africa to the Congo River deep in central Africa. In Senegal, the oldest French colony in West Africa, the colonial administration encouraged the population to grow groundnuts on their farms as a cash crop. The peasants sold the nuts for cash, part of which they used to pay the head tax that was for many years the chief source of revenue for the government of Senegal. The French worked hard to implant French culture in Senegal, with some success.

With its boulevards and shops filled with French-speaking Africans and Europeans, Dakar (the capital of Senegal) was often referred to as the "Paris of Africa." Senegalese units fought in the French army around the world. In France's other coastal colonies, Guinea, the Ivory Coast, and Dahomey, cash crops such as palm oil and cocoa were introduced and proved profitable.

The French colonies in the interior of West Africa were sparsely populated, limited in resources, and difficult to reach. Formidable rapids made the three major river systems in this area—the Congo, the Senegal, and the Niger—difficult to navigate. New cash crops, such as cotton in Niger, were introduced, but until railroads could be built to penetrate the interior, few products could be brought out. These colonies were therefore a financial drain.

Pending the completion of new railroads to move interior products to market, the quest for economic efficiency led the French government in 1904 to gather the West African territories into a single unit, called French West Africa, under a governor-general who ruled from Dakar. The economic benefits that emerged from the formation of French West Africa led the French government to follow the same policy in its territories in the Congo basin, joining them in 1910 into a single colonial unit called French Equatorial Africa, under a governor-general who ruled from Brazzaville. In both cases, the greater resources of a consolidated colonial government resulted in faster economic development.

BRITISH EAST AFRICA: THE ADVENT OF A MULTIRACIAL SOCIETY

Geographically, East Africa is dominated by mountains and high plateaus that extend southward from Kenya to the Cape of Good Hope. Although near the equator, the temperate climate of the uplands soon attracted British settlers. To a British Colonial Office in search of revenue, the prospect of settlement by British farmers seemed a good step toward economic development. Up to World War I, the number of British settlers in East Africa and Central Africa remained small—around 3,000 in what is now Kenya, and a few hundred in Uganda. While some English settlers congregated in what were previously sparsely populated lands, others took over lands already settled by Kikuyu tribes, displacing them or making them tenant farmers. Thus British colonists became a disruptive factor in the region, competing with Africans for land and exploiting labor. Many Africans became migrant laborers on European farms. This development caused political and social problems in the next generation.

The interracial tensions of East Africa were further inflamed when the British government allowed large numbers of Indians to immigrate, some as indentured laborers to build railroads and others to work as clerks in government offices and commercial companies. Indians settled in towns and villages, and many also became traders. In the early decades, it was the Europeans who resented the numerous and articulate Indians in their midst. In a later era, as a result of growing African nationalism, Indian British subjects became the victims of African majorities who did not think Indians belonged in Africa. Thus, in British East Africa, a pluralist society was formed in the early twentieth century that had disturbing consequences in later years.

SOUTHERN AFRICA

In this temperate part of the continent, European colonies dated back to the mid-seventeenth century and European settlement made by far its largest penetration. The early inhabitants of southern Africa were the San and Khoi; small in number, they lived by hunting and gathering and were easily subdued by white settlers. Meanwhile, Bantu-speaking peoples, who engaged in both herding and agriculture, had been immigrating in large numbers from the north over a long period. Clashes among the Bantu tribes and between the Bantus and Europeans brought about the emergence of the Zulus. Zulu leaders forged their people into a fighting nation that defeated and subjugated other tribes and fought white colonists in several Zulu wars. While the white settlers eventually defeated the Zulus, they were not able to prevent the movement of Bantu peoples into southern Africa. As a result of both Bantu and European immigration, South Africa became a land with a black majority and a white minority, the basis for race problems in the twentieth century.

The Rise and Fall of the Boer Republics

South Africa attracted large numbers of white colonists over the years because of its benign climate, good soil, and, in the late nineteenth century, the discovery of large gold and diamond deposits. When Great Britain acquired the Dutch colony located at the Cape of Good Hope in 1815, it also inherited the Dutch colonists of the land, who called themselves Boers (farmers). The Boers resented British rule, particularly a law passed in 1833 that forbade slavery and forced the Boers to emancipate their slaves. To escape British control, many Boers made a mass migration called the "Great Trek" into the interior of Africa between 1835 and 1841. There they founded two independent republics, the Orange Free State and the Transvaal. Meanwhile, British settlers poured into the Cape Province and into Natal, a new colony to the east. The relationship between the Boer republics and Great Britain became increasingly tense, especially after gold was discovered in the Transvaal. Non-Boer prospectors, including many British, swarmed into the Transvaal, where they encountered discrimination at the hands of the Boer government.

In 1899, war broke out between Great Britain and the two Boer republics. The Boers were ably led by Paul Kruger, the president of the Transvaal, and for three years Boer commandos (guerrillas), who perfected hit-and-run tactics, successfully resisted the might of the British Empire. British forces resorted to the same harsh but effective antiguerrilla measures used in that period by the Spanish in Cuba and Americans in the Philippines. In order to deprive the commandos of sanctuary and resources the British burned farms and herded women, children, and other noncombatants into concentration camps. The Boers finally surrendered in 1902.

Out of their dogged resistance emerged modern Boer, or Afrikaner, nationalism. In an attempt to conciliate the defeated Boers, Great Britain let them decide whether black and other nonwhite inhabitants should be given the vote; true to their white supremacist tradition, the Boers denied suffrage to all of them. When the two former Boer states federated with the two British colonies of Natal and the Cape in 1910 to form the Union of South Africa, a self-governing dominion in the British Empire, black people were denied political rights.

The Rhodesias: One-Man Imperialism

North of Transvaal and the Orange Free State was an area of high plains and good soil where in earlier centuries an African state had been centered at Great Zimbabwe. Here Cecil Rhodes, the "Empire Builder," an English adventurer who had made a fortune from diamond mining in South Africa, carved out two new colonies for Great Britain. At his request Britain annexed the territories and called them Northern and Southern Rhodesia, entrusting Rhodes' South African Company to govern them. An unabashed imperialist, he once exclaimed, "I would annex the planets if I could!"

During the 1890s, the company's army was responsible for winning Portuguese acquiescence in the British takeover of that area and for the defeat of the Matabele and Mashona tribes who bitterly resented the company's demands on their land and labor. Fighting did not stop until 1897, after which company-sponsored European immigrants began to arrive, eventually constituting 5 percent of the total population.

THE IMPACT OF COLONIAL RULE ON AFRICA

The positive and negative effects of colonial rule of Africans varied greatly and differed from society to society. As always under conditions of change, some groups benefited. They were either lucky or farsighted enough to cooperate with the new masters and to take advantage of new circumstances, thereby winning favors, prestige, and sometimes additional land. Such beneficiaries were the Baganda people of Uganda and the Ibos in Nigeria, who welcomed chances for a British education and cooperated with the British authorities. They were rewarded with positions in the colonial bureaucracy.

Conversely, large numbers suffered from colonial rule, especially in areas where Europeans sought to settle or to extract minerals. In some instances, tribes were split under different European jurisdictions, while in others several traditionally hostile tribes were grouped under a single administration. In parts of Kenya and the Rhodesias, for example, hundreds of thousands of Africans lost their land. Many were forced to live on inferior lands designated as "native reserves" or became tenants of and laborers for the new white landowners.

It would be an exaggeration, however, to imagine that all Africans were directly affected when European countries annexed their lands. Large areas, in fact, remained untouched by white rule. Until World War I, colonial officials frequently had little control over the local scene and had to work within the restraints of local kinship groups, village communities, and tribal ties. In Morocco and Tunisia, European diplomatic entanglements compelled the French to retain native rulers in power.

The indirect effects of imperialism were much more widespread. Europeans investing in Africa demanded laborers to work in mines and on plantations and to build roads and railroads. Whether laborers were paid or not, their service was compulsory. On the issue of forced labor, European reaction was contradictory and tinged with hypocrisy. Although Europeans abhorred slavery, they permitted the forced labor of Africans. Yet when facts about King Leopold's methods for exacting labor services in the Congo Free State were made public, adverse European public opinion forced the Belgian government to take over responsibility for its administration in 1908.

Despite the violence generated by the imposition of colonial rule, some forms of violence in Africa decreased after colonization. Colonial authorities largely suppressed the tribal wars, cattle rustling, and slave raids that had caused much bloodshed before the European takeover. Peace, better public health programs, development of cash crops, and agricultural improvements led to large increases in population. In some areas, rural peoples moved into the newly established cities for work, causing problems of social adjustment.

European control was invariably accompanied by Christian missionary activity, which had an important impact. In many inaccessible villages, the missionary teacher and preacher was much more likely than the colonial administrator to be the first white person that an African encountered. In the early days, the teachers in the missionary "bush schools" were Europeans, but soon the African pupils themselves became teachers and missionaries. By the early twentieth century, in many parts of Africa, Western education and Christian religion were expanding hand in hand. Christian missionaries and teachers brought with them not only a new religion and education but also medical care and a general acquaintance with the scientific, technological, and intellectual bases of Western civilization.

In much of northern Africa, Islam remained the rallying point of the people and Christianity had little impact. Thus, in Algeria, the majority of Algerians resisted conversion to Christianity, as did the peoples of Morocco, Tunisia, and Libya. At the same time, Muslim missionaries continued to be active in spreading their religion and culture south of the Sahara.

Early in the twentieth century, a new kind of leadership began to emerge in Africa. It consisted of Western-educated black Africans who rejected the authority of the traditional chiefs and willingly seized the new opportunities created by colonialism. Some of the new elite received further education in the ruling nations, where they gained a better perspective for judging the colonial administrations of their lands. They found that the colonial practices of the European imperialist states invariably fell short of their professed democratic

Western cultural impact on Africa: A drawing of missionary Robert Moffat preaching to the Tswanas.
(*African Museum, Johannesburg*)

ideals. Consequently, these European-educated Africans began to develop anticolonial movements. Even before World War I, these new leaders were demanding that African Christian churches be placed under black African leadership and that African independent states be established based on modern democratic concepts.

SUMMARY

In the late nineteenth and early twentieth centuries, European imperialism, based on a mixture of economic, strategic, cultural, and nationalistic motives, expressed itself in the partition of the African continent. The preeminence of European nations in industrial, technical, and military development made it relatively easy for them to defeat tribal societies and seize their territories. Although nationalism created intense rivalries between the imperialist states, diplomacy triumphed and these states were able to avoid war against each other as they carved up Africa.

During this period, Great Britain and France seized the largest amount of African territory, but Germany, Italy, and Belgium also made extensive acquisitions. Spanish and Portuguese holdings dating from an earlier century were enlarged. Africans often resisted European imperialism, but with the exception of the Ethiopians and Liberians, all Africans were eventually subjugated. Many African groups were dislocated or destroyed in the process.

Europeans in Africa extensively exploited the continent's mineral and agricultural products, often by means of forced labor and sometimes with labor imported from other parts of their empires. On the other hand, colonial authorities sometimes introduced programs for health, education, and social welfare and suppressed intertribal violence. While Europeans ruled some areas of Africa indirectly and allowed the local indigenous cultural patterns to continue, in many cases their colonial administrations eliminated the traditional political leadership and imposed Western systems of government, taxation, and justice. Both Christian and Muslim missionaries worked to win converts from adherents of local African religions.

SUGGESTED SOURCES

ACHEBE, CHINUA, *Things Fall Apart* (1978). A novel on the profound effects of British contact on Ibo society in Nigeria.*

DINESEN, ISAAK, *Out of Africa and Shadows on the Grass* (1989). Good stories based on first-hand experience, also a movie, *Out of Africa*.*

GANN, L. H., and PETER DUIGNAN, *Burden of Empire: An Appraisal of Western Colonialism in Africa South of the Sahara* (1967). A well-documented interpretive history.*

The Horizon History of Africa (1971). A thoughtful text, with lavish illustrations and maps.

HUXLEY, ELSPETH, comp., *Nine Faces of Kenya: Portrait of a Nation* (1991). A rich anthology with many contributors.

KENYATTA, JOMO, *Facing Mount Kenya* (1962). A collection of studies that favorably depict the customs of Kenya's Kikuyu tribe before they were altered by the impact of imperialism.*

MORSE, MAGALI, *North Africa 1800–1900: A Survey from the Nile Valley to the Atlantic* (1984). An analytic account of the peoples and societies of North Africa before and during the period of European imperial expansion.

OLIVER, ROLAND, and ANTHONY ATOMORE, *Africa Since 1800,* 3d ed. (1981). A standard survey of Africa and European imperialism.*

ROBINSON, ROLAND, and JOHN GALLAGHER, with Alice Denny, *Africa and the Victorians* (1961). A study of European expansion and the strategic reasons for imperialism.*

"Search for the Nile," BBC television series. A six-part account of British explorers in Africa. A good visual account with numerous personal vignettes of nineteenth-century imperialists.

*Paperback available.

CHAPTER 5

The United States and Latin America

By 1900 the United States had become the first world power to emerge from the Western Hemisphere. As its economy, military, and national pride grew, the United States, like major European nations, became increasingly imperialistic. Its main interest, the Caribbean, was predominantly Latin American in culture. It was essentially a two-class culture where a white-descended landowning elite dominated a mass of mixed-blood, Indian, and African-American workers. U.S. imperialism in Latin America tended to start with military action or coercion and end with a combination of direct and indirect military, economic, and political controls short of outright annexation. U.S. business and political officials became part of the ruling class of the Caribbean nations in particular, often putting these Americans and their government on the wrong side of movements aimed at bettering the lot of the masses.

THE UNITED STATES AT THE TURN OF THE CENTURY

General Characteristics

At the turn of the century, most citizens of the United States of America looked upon themselves as heaven-blessed. Far from the tumult of Europe, Americans had been left alone for almost a century to develop one of the richest areas of the globe. The United States was the largest nation in the Western Hemisphere in arable land. It contained five times the population of the next-largest nation in the hemisphere and ranked fourth in population worldwide. Whether measured by property ownership or by per capita income, the standard of living for most Americans far exceeded that of the other nations in the hemisphere and rivaled that of the powerful European nations. The overall affluence and high educational level of Americans made possible a stable political system.

The United States was fast becoming an economic powerhouse. The nation's farmers and ranchers produced an enormous quantity of food and fibers, enough to feed and clothe its citizens cheaply and to lead the world in the value of agricultural exports. The United States dwarfed the rest of the hemisphere in general manufacturing and led all nations in railroad mileage, in iron ore and coal output, and in iron and steel production. American business leaders were aggressively entering the world of international trade and finance and were gaining rapidly on European nations in the value of capital invested abroad and in the total value of all exports. To protect its rapidly growing international trade, especially with Europe, the United States had built up the third largest navy in the world.

Populist and Progressive Struggles

Despite its general affluence, economic power, and self-confidence, the United States at the turn of the century was beset by divisions. Most Americans were brought up on farms or in small towns and were struggling to adapt to a rapidly industrializing and urbanizing society. The rise of big business, such as Standard Oil, U.S. Steel, and the Morgan Bank, had brought with it a number of problems, as it had in western Europe. U.S. factory workers, like their European counterparts, labored long hours under unsafe conditions, received low wages, and lived in city slums and rundown housing in company towns.

Some workers organized for collective bargaining to improve their situation. The American Federation of Labor, an association of skilled artisans led by Samuel Gompers, was the most effective of the early labor organizations. Unskilled workers trying to improve working conditions in the steel industry participated in massive strikes, such as the one at Homestead, Pennsylvania, where they fought with police and with armed strikebreakers. After 1900 labor unrest spread to the mining towns and lumber camps in the West, where some workers were led by the radical syndicalist Industrial Workers of the World, or Wobblies. On the whole, however, unionization lagged behind that in industrialized Europe; only about 4 percent of all industrial workers were organized at the turn of the century.

Farmers, especially in the South and in the Plains states, comprised another major group that felt threatened by business consolidation. They found themselves facing monopolies in railroad shipping, commodity storage, and meat packing. They received low prices for the products they sold and paid high prices for the goods they purchased. To remedy their plight, farmers organized politically, capturing control of several states in the agricultural belt. These farmer-controlled state legislatures then passed legislation regulating the operation of railroads, grain elevators, cotton gins, and stockyards.

On the national level, farmers formed the Populist party and seized temporary control of the Democratic party. Populist politicians then allied with small business interests and other reformers to frame national legislation that curbed the growing trend toward monopoly. The Populists and their allies were basically responsible for creating the first independent regulatory commission, the Interstate Commerce Commission, which they empowered to regulate railroad freight rates. The reformist political coalition also secured the first antitrust legislation and a graduated income tax. Populists also tried but failed to manipulate the value of currency for the benefit of debtors.

However, farmers and workers weakened their causes by competing politically with each other. Supreme Court decisions also tended to favor big business interests. Thus, in 1900, big business essentially controlled politics at every level and despite attacks was stronger than ever.

By 1900 a growing middle class, consisting primarily of professionals, white-collar employees, and the owners of small business establishments, took the lead in working for reform. Located primarily in the towns and cities of the East and Midwest, these groups often had different goals, but when united constituted a formidable constituency in support of social and political change. Small business entrepreneurs found it difficult to survive in a corporate world and were afraid of political and social polarization between supporters of the big business interests and those of the farmers and workers. Some of them resented the corrupt subservience of politicians to big business and detested the political machines that manipulated the new immigrants. Still others demanded equality for women, the abolition of child labor, and the elimination of gambling, prostitution, and alcohol.

This restless middle class, at times in uneasy alliance with certain business interests, led the nation into an era of reform called Progressivism. The movement spread through both the Democratic and Republican parties, although in one election it fielded its own slate of candidates. Presidents Theodore Roosevelt, William Howard Taft, and Woodrow Wilson gave varying measures of support to the Progressive movement.

The Progressive era was one of extensive reforms in political structure and process, including the direct election of senators and the institution of party primaries. Progressives also reformed the structure of city government. New procedures, especially the initiative, the referendum, and the recall, gave citizens more leverage in creating legislation and in reducing corruption in office.

One of the most dramatic political reform movements was the drive to secure the vote (suffrage) for women in national elections. Carried on at the same time as the enfranchisement campaign in Great Britain, the women's suffrage movement in the United States, dating back to the mid-nineteenth century, flourished in the reform atmosphere of the Progressive era. The movement became steadily more effective and more militant as more women became willing to take such "unladylike" actions as picketing or chaining themselves to the White House fence to call attention to the cause. The final drive, first led by Susan B. Anthony and later by Alice Paul, centered on pushing an amendment to the U.S. Constitution through Congress and then through the ratification process in the states. In 1918 Congress approved an amendment giving women the vote in all elections; by August 1920 the requisite three-quarters of the states had ratified the amendment, in time for women to vote in the 1920 general election.

In addition, the Progressives expanded the power of both the state and the national governments to regulate the economy, to protect the public from big business, and to provide increased public services. Using this power, they se-

Confronted by Poverty

[We were] taken to the East End [the London slums] to witness the Saturday night sale of decaying vegetables and fruit. . . . [W]e saw two huge masses of ill-clad people clamoring around two hucksters' carts. They were bidding their farthings and ha'pennies for a vegetable held up by the auctioneer, which he at last scornfully flung, with a gibe for its cheapness, to the successful bidder. . . . [T]he final impression was not of ragged, tawdry clothing, nor of pinched and sallow faces, but of myriads of hands, empty, pathetic, nerveless and workworn, showing white in the uncertain light of the street, and clutching forward for food that was already unfit to eat.

I have never since been able to see a number of hands held upward, . . . without a certain revival of this memory, a clutching at the heart reminiscent of the despair and resentment which seized me then.*

This 1880s scene in London, which might have been witnessed in urban centers

all over the world at the turn of the century, was one of the experiences that propelled Jane Addams to take action to combat poverty. An upper-middle-class young woman from a small town in Illinois, Addams had come to believe that her college education and comfortable financial circumstances not only put her in an elite minority among women but also gave her a responsibility to help the less fortunate. In 1889, she founded Hull House, the famous urban complex in Chicago that addressed itself through a broad spectrum of programs to the needs of the poor. She became a powerful advocate, through her work and writing, of improved working conditions, women's rights, and peace. She received the Nobel Prize for Peace in 1931. The "settlement house" and the new profession of social work were major components of the reform spirit that marked the Progressive era.

*From *Twenty Years at Hull House* by Jane Addams. Copyright © 1910 by Macmillan Co. Reprinted by permission.

cured legislation that improved sanitation and education and upgraded working conditions, especially for women, children, and those in dangerous occupations. The states, often in conjunction with innovative individuals such as Jane Addams, now took a more active and creative role in dealing with poverty. One aspect of poverty led to the birth control movement, whose champion, Margaret Sanger, had been stirred to action by the ideas of Emma Goldman, among others.

At the national level, the Progressives reformed the monetary system and introduced the graduated income tax, the eight-hour day for railroad workers, pure food and drug regulations, laws mandating conservation of natural resources, and lower tariffs. They increased the network of laws and agencies regulating big business and through the Federal Reserve System improved the nation's financial structure. The wave of reform was in full tide by 1917, but the entry of the United States into World War I turned energies toward the war effort, and the reform spirit ebbed.

Mulberry Street, New York: A neighborhood of new immigrants, a sight that often aroused fears in many Americans at the turn of the century.
(Library of Congress)

Racial and Ethnic Problems

A divisive nationalism, taking the form of ethnic and racial prejudice and repression, constituted another major problem in the United States. White Americans of northern European descent, who controlled the economy and politics and set the social norms of the nation, subjected African Americans, Hispanics, and Asians to legal segregation in housing and education and prohibited Asians from owning land. In the South and elsewhere, the white majority, by such tactics as literacy tests, poll taxes, threats of job loss, and lynchings, was in the process of depriving African Americans of the political and legal gains made during Reconstruction. While some African Americans fought back through the press, the courts, and the National Association for the Advancement of Colored People (NAACP), most submitted to the dominance of the white majority.

Moreover, many Americans of northern European descent looked down upon whites of eastern and southern European descent. These "nativist" Americans attacked the traditional policy of open immigration because it allowed millions of new immigrants, mostly Slavs, Jews, Italians, and Greeks, to enter the United States annually. They sought to restrict immigration and succeeded after World War I.

The Turn Toward Imperialism

When Americans looked overseas at the turn of the century, imperialism was rampant in world affairs. Americans were ambivalent about imperialism, in part because of contradictions in their history. On the one hand, Americans were the prime example of a people who had won freedom from European colonialism. In the years after independence Americans had supported, at least in oratory, liberty for all peoples under foreign imperial control.

On the other hand, most Americans were strongly nationalistic and, in practice, imperialistic. They believed that they were a chosen people and that it was their "Manifest Destiny" to expand throughout North America and perhaps the whole hemisphere. Regarding the interior of the continent as open land, the United States had aggressively moved westward during the nineteenth century at the expense of the Indians, Spain, and Mexico. In this period the Russians similarly were moving southward through central Asia. Only the power of Great Britain had prevented Americans from marching northward as well.

By the 1890s most Americans considered their nation a great global power. Many still opposed imperialism in terms of crossing the seas to conquer and exploit the lands of alien peoples, as the Europeans were doing in Africa. However, an increasing number had concluded that as a great nation the United States should have its share of colonies, protectorates, and spheres of influence, as did the other great powers. U.S. capitalists were already in the process of exploiting the economy and influencing the government policy of some Latin American nations. Sharing fully in the cultural imperialism of the major European powers, many Americans believed that they were justified in joining the march to control, and hopefully "civilize," the "backward" parts of the world.

As it turned out, Americans practiced two forms of imperialism at the turn of the century. In Asia (see Chapter 7) the United States in effect joined Europe in seizing the territories of non-Western peoples overseas and turning them into colonies. However, Americans pursued their foremost area of interest, the Caribbean nations of Latin America, quite differently. Instead of acquiring colonies, they used force or threats of force to establish indirect economic and political control over neighbors that were a part of Western culture.

SOCIAL, ECONOMIC, AND POLITICAL PATTERNS IN LATIN AMERICA

Latin America was the only major area of the world where substantial numbers of persons from three races lived together. Much of the region was still dominated by the white minority, who had conquered it and controlled it for four centuries. A wave of immigration from Europe in the late nineteenth century substantially increased the proportion of white people in southern South America. Despite white conquest, exploitation, and epidemics, Indians were still in the majority in parts of Central America, the Amazon jungles, and the Andes Mountains. Centuries of cohabitation between Indians and white people had resulted in large numbers of mestizos (people of mixed white and Indian parentage), a rising group that would play a major role in twentieth-century developments. White people had also brought millions of slaves from Africa to the Caribbean and to sections of Brazil, where their descendants remained in the majority. Cohabitation between white people and African Americans had also created a significant number of mixed-blood mulattoes.

European conquerors also dominated Latin America culturally. Indian customs and languages survived to some extent in areas where Indians remained a majority, but in most places Indian culture had been supplanted by Iberian (Spanish and Portuguese) values and customs. The vast majority of people, whatever their race or origin, spoke Spanish (Portuguese in Brazil and various European languages in the Caribbean region) and were members of the Roman Catholic Church. Literature, art, and music, while distinctively Latin American, were based on the cultural forms of Latin Europe. The mestizos were caught between adherence to the dominant Iberian culture of the upper classes and respect for the culture of their Indian ancestors.

In the early twentieth century, most Latin American nations were characterized by two classes separated by a great gulf. At the top were a small group of European-descended white people, the *patrones* (landlords or patrons), who, along with foreign investors, owned the ranches, mines, and plantations of each nation. Like the established families of most societies elsewhere in the world, the *patrones* monopolized the wealth, social prestige, education, and cultural attainments of their nations. Many of them aspired to the ideal of nobility, with high standards of personal morality and a parental concern for those who worked for them. Some *patrones* lived up to these ideals, but most, consciously or unconsciously, exploited their workers. Allied with the *patrones* was another small group, the socially inferior middle-class professionals, some of them mestizos, who wanted to join the propertied class.

In general, Latin American landowners, content to follow the relaxed traditional lifestyle of landed aristocrats, had not efficiently exploited the extensive array of natural resources in their region. For the most part, they neglected the abundant industrial raw materials and clung to the production of traditional colonial agricultural products—sugar, tobacco, coffee, and meat—that faced stiff competition on the world market. Agricultural production was low because of poor land-use methods. The owners preferred to employ cheap hoe-wielding hand labor rather than use expensive plows and tractors. They did not fertilize the soil, and much of the land was left fallow after being depleted of its nutrients. As a result, a number of Latin American nations had to import food.

Late in the nineteenth century, investors from Great Britain, France, and the United States began to move into Latin America. They reorganized plantations for efficient sugar and fruit production, mined ores for industries abroad, created factories to process agricultural and ranching products, and built up transportation and communications networks. In the process, Latin America became an economic colony of the advanced Western nations.

Far below the "establishment," the huge mass of rural and urban workers—Indians, mestizos, African Americans, mulattoes, and some newly arrived white immigrants—comprised the great majority of the population. In the rural areas, the *campesinos* (country people) worked generation after generation on the estates of the elite, bound to the land by tradition, ignorance, and debt. A few *campesinos* owned tiny parcels of land that were often too small to support their families. In either case, they lived in shacks with dirt floors, lacked water and sanitation facilities, and had little medical attention or education. Malnutrition was common, and starvation also occurred. The high birth rate was paralleled by a high death rate, especially for infants. Life expectancy in some areas was in the thirties. Some of the rural people were Indians, most of whom spoke no Spanish or Portuguese and followed their traditional culture. Most *campesinos* were docile, respectful, and orderly; on the whole they complained little and rarely rioted or rebelled.

By 1900 several Latin American nations, such as Mexico, Argentina, Brazil, and Chile, were beginning to expand mining operations and to industrialize, and as a consequence an urban working class was swiftly developing. In the city neighborhoods and in the mines, factories, and workshops, workers experienced the same miserable conditions commonly found all over the world at the onset of industrialization: overcrowded housing, poor sanitation, inadequate health care, unsafe working conditions, low wages, and no provision for accident, sickness, or layoff.

When the Latin American nations became independent early in the nineteenth century, their leaders placed republican forms and procedures in their national constitutions. However, widespread poverty and illiteracy and the lack of a democratic tradition quickly produced a system in which political power was often seized and held by the *caudillo* (leader). The *caudillo*, a dictator, ruled with the support of the dominant elements—the Church, the armed forces, the landlords, and foreign investors—and by force of personality. The *caudillo* system, however, was unstable and was often marked by violent changes in leadership.

THE UNITED STATES TAKES OVER THE CARIBBEAN

U.S. interests in Latin America centered on the Caribbean and the nations adjacent to it. Economically, the United States wanted to control investment and trade in this area in order to import fruit, coffee, minerals, and petroleum and to monopolize the sale of foodstuffs and manufactured items. Strategically, U.S. leaders feared that the political instability and military weakness of the republics of Central America, coupled with the economic attractions of the region, would tempt European powers to interfere. As early as 1823, in what was later called the Monroe Doctrine, the United States had stated its opposition to European nations expanding their colonial holdings in the Western Hemisphere. Although it was initially too weak to enforce its position without the concurrence of Great Britain, by the end of the nineteenth century the United States was powerful enough to carry out this policy. Thus in 1895 it intervened in a boundary dispute between Venezuela and Great Britain with the ringing declaration that "the United States is practically sovereign on this continent."

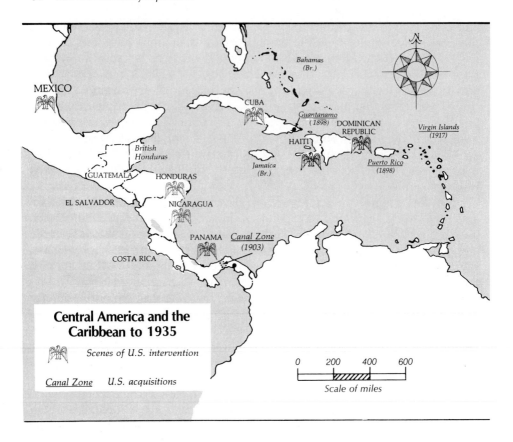

Central America and the Caribbean to 1935

Scenes of U.S. intervention

Canal Zone   U.S. acquisitions

0   200   400   600

Scale of miles

The Spanish-American War and Its Results

In 1898, an opportunity arose for U.S. expansion into the Caribbean. For many years Americans had been particularly interested in the Spanish colony of Cuba; some had wanted to annex it, some to free it, and some to exploit it economically whether it remained a Spanish colony or became independent. Since 1869, some Cubans had been fighting a predominantly guerrilla war for independence. The Spanish government had retaliated with an internment program that confined civilians to detention camps. On February 15, 1898, the battleship *Maine,* sent to Havana to demonstrate U.S. concern, was blown up and 260 men were killed. An influential segment of the U.S. public and press blamed Spain and clamored for revenge, and Congress declared war on Spain. The U.S. navy easily destroyed Spanish squadrons in Cuba and the Philippines, while a small U.S. volunteer army forced the Spanish garrisons in Cuba and Puerto Rico to sue for peace. Admiral George Dewey and Theodore Roosevelt's Rough Riders became the heroes of the day as the public hailed them for winning a "splendid little war" in four months.

In the peace treaty, Spain ceded Puerto Rico to the United States and gave Cuba its independence. U.S. imperialists and antiimperialists clashed vehemently over what to do with the Spanish possessions now under the military control of the United States. The imperialists favored annexation of Cuba, but the antiimperialists in Congress were able to push through the Teller Amendment, in which the United States disavowed any intention of exercising "sovereignty, jurisdiction, or control" over the island. However, situated only ninety miles from the Florida coast, Cuba was too important strategically for the United States to ignore, and in the long run imperialism won out. Cuba became a virtual U.S. protectorate, as its constitution permitted the United States to intervene in time of political or economic crisis. During the first decade of its so-called independence, Cuba was twice under U.S. military rule. It also agreed to lease military sites to the United States. The navy developed a base at Guantanamo Bay that, along with facilities in Puerto Rico, enabled the United States to dominate the Caribbean and the routes to the future Panama Canal. Puerto Rico became a possession but not an integral part of the United States. The Supreme Court ruled that "the Constitution does not follow the flag"; that is, Puerto Ricans did not have the full range of constitutional rights that citizens of the continental United States enjoyed. In 1917, the United States purchased the Danish section of the Virgin Islands, which solidified its strategic grip on the Caribbean. Great Britain gave tacit recognition to U.S. supremacy by withdrawing its naval forces from the region.

Acquiring the Panama Canal

President Theodore Roosevelt, a dedicated imperialist, next pressed for the completion of an old project of international interest—the construction of a canal through Central America that would link the Atlantic and the Pacific oceans. The government of Colombia had earlier granted a French company the right to build a canal through its Panamanian province. When this company failed, the United States pressed Colombia for a treaty granting rights to build the canal. The Colombian Senate, which was irritated by the pressure and also interested in holding out for more money, rejected a treaty that had been negotiated by Colombian representatives and ratified by the U.S. Senate. President Roosevelt was enraged by the action of those he termed "contemptible little creatures . . . the Bogotá lot of jackrabbits" and was determined to obtain a canal that could be controlled by the United States. In 1903 a motley group of Panamanians, Europeans, and Colombian soldiers revolted and declared Panama an independent country. The U.S. navy blocked Colombian attempts to recapture the province, and the U.S. government immediately recognized Panama as a sovereign state. In return, the new nation, in fact a new U.S. protectorate, granted the United States a permanent lease to a zone across the isthmus enclosing the partially built canal. The United States fortified the zone and completed the Panama Canal in 1914, conquering both yellow fever and rugged terrain in the process.

U.S. imperialism in Latin America: President "Teddy" Roosevelt helps dig the canal he "took."
(*Harvard College Library*)

Increased U.S. Intervention in Latin America

As it was building the Panama Canal, the United States also took action to defend its expanded interests against European intervention in the region. Several European nations had sent naval expeditions to the Caribbean either to force Latin American states to pay their debts or to protect European residents and their property from brigands and from political turmoil. In 1902 several European powers jointly blockaded and bombarded Venezuela in a typical example of imperialist "gunboat diplomacy" against a weak nation. Roosevelt feared that if European nations were allowed to continue this practice, they might take over the Caribbean nations and threaten U.S. interests there. The United States therefore made a statement expressing its concern over continued European armed interference in the region. To preempt future European intervention, President Roosevelt then declared that in the future the United States would assume the "international police power" against those Latin American nations that were guilty of "chronic wrongdoing." This was called the Roosevelt Corollary to the Monroe Doctrine. No European nation directly challenged this doctrine by attempting new interventions.

On the other hand, in applying its new doctrine, the United States repeatedly intervened in the Caribbean. Between 1900 and 1934 it sent armed forces at least once into Cuba, Mexico, Honduras, Haiti, the Dominican Republic, and Nicaragua. In the last three nations, the marines stayed for many years.

Whereas the United States restricted direct military intervention to the Caribbean, its economic penetration, called "dollar diplomacy" by critics, was applied throughout Latin America. Two-thirds of all U.S. foreign investment dollars were spent in Canada and Latin America. U.S. capitalists were attracted to Mexican petroleum, Chilean copper, Colombian coffee, Brazilian rubber, Central American bananas, and numerous other products. In addition to importing these raw materials and foodstuffs, U.S. entrepreneurs competed aggressively in selling their products, and by 1913 the value of U.S. exports to Latin America outstripped those sent by any other nation. With extensive economic and strategic interests at stake, the U.S. government was interested in stability in Latin America and backed dictators if democratic governments failed to maintain order.

The Impact of U.S. Imperialism

By 1914 the United States had emerged as a major world power. It was the dominant power in the Western Hemisphere, and one with a stake in the Pacific and Far East (see Chapter 7). It was a heady time for Americans and their leaders, for events of the preceding twenty years had confirmed their self-perception that they were a special people with a glorious future.

Problems attended the exercise of imperialist power, however. While some Latin Americans benefited from and supported U.S. economic, political, and military activities in their nations, many reacted with hostility. They resented the seemingly incessant interference by the "Colossus of the North" and called it "Yankee imperialism." The fact that the United States often supported dictators was interpreted as indifference or hostility to the masses of peasants exploited in such nations. Later in the twentieth century, many reform leaders in Latin America came to regard the United States as their chief enemy.

THE UNITED STATES AND CANADA

From the days of the War for Independence, Americans had been interested in absorbing the British possessions to the north, and as late as the middle of the nineteenth century many Americans still expected to incorporate that area. Between 1867 and 1871, however, Canadians frustrated U.S. hopes by uniting several colonies and the possessions of the Hudson's Bay Company into a federation called the Dominion of Canada. Initially, the new dominion was firmly attached to Great Britain through an arrangement in which the Canadians governed their internal affairs while Great Britain controlled trade, foreign policy, and military matters. By the twentieth century, Great Britain had granted Canada substantial control over its external affairs as well. This development was the first example of an imperial nation's peacefully granting political freedom to a former colony, a process called devolution.

By 1900 Americans sought to dominate Canada economically rather than annex it politically. By 1914 almost one-quarter of U.S. foreign investments were concentrated in Canada, although this was less than one-third of British investment there. Initially, U.S. investments were centered on Canadian mines and transportation; later they expanded into manufacturing as that sector developed during and after World War I.

SUMMARY

By the end of the nineteenth century, the United States had emerged as the greatest power in the Western Hemisphere and was ready to press its interests around the world. Despite internal social and economic tensions, Americans lived in a relatively affluent and stable nation. By 1914 the United States was an economic power on par with the most powerful European nations. It was ready to exercise that economic power, often in conjunction with its naval might, in other regions of the world, especially in Latin America, but also in Asia and the Pacific.

Between 1898 and 1917, mostly through war and intimidation, the United States turned the Caribbean into a U.S. lake. It acquired Puerto Rico, Guantanamo, the Canal Zone, and the Danish Virgin Islands and established economic and political control over Cuba, Panama, and other Caribbean nations. By assuming the responsibility of policing the Western Hemisphere, the United States made sure that European powers had no grounds for intervention in the region. U.S. military and economic domination of the Caribbean aroused hostility among other peoples of the Western Hemisphere and led to the charge of Yankee imperialism.

SUGGESTED SOURCES

BURNS, E. BRADFORD, *Latin America: A Concise Interpretative History,* 5th ed. (1990). A well-written text; opening chapters provide historical background for twentieth-century latin America.*

COOPER, JOHN MILTON, JR., *Pivotal Decades: The United States, 1900–1920* (1990). Easy-to-read survey of the Progressive period.*

FREIDEL, FRANK, *The Splendid Little War* (1962). A lively account of the Spanish-American War.

LINK, ARTHUR S., and RICHARD L. MCCORMICK, *Progressivism* (1983). A short, lively overview of the period.*

MORGAN, H. WAYNE, *America's Road to Empire* (1968). A description of the beginnings of U.S. imperialism.*

SINCLAIR, UPTON, *The Jungle* (1906). A searing novel depicting the plight of exploited immigrants in Chicago at the turn of the century. The book ends with a socialist appeal.*

*Paperback available.

CHAPTER 6

European Imperialism in Asia and the Pacific

Western domination of Asia was almost complete by the year 1900. In that year, a last futile attempt at resistance in China was crushed by a joint imperialist force. With a few exceptions, Europeans (and the United States and Japan, whose interests on the Asian continent will be taken up in Chapter 7) were primarily interested in raw materials and markets in Asia and not in settlement. Industrialized European nations prized Asia's mineral wealth and also needed such agricultural raw materials as rubber, hemp, and sugar. On plantations developed to grow these items, local or imported labor under European supervision produced goods for a world market.

In addition, Europeans coveted for their manufactured goods the markets that the peoples of Asia would supply. The large population of China especially excited the imagination of European merchants. As one wishful thinker said, "If every Chinese would buy a British-made shirt each year, Manchester shirt manufacturers would never suffer economic recession!" By 1900 only Japan, China, Siam (Thailand), Nepal, Afghanistan, Persia, and the Ottoman Empire still retained formal independence. However, with the exception of Japan, these nations were really no more than "semicolonies," which Europeans influenced or controlled indirectly.

Western states gained and maintained dominion over Asia for a number of reasons. They possessed overwhelming military power, which in turn was the product of an advanced technology and a modern industrial base. Nationalism was another important factor, as highly competitive Western nations vied constantly with one another for real and imagined advantages. Conversely, the people of Asian states, except for the Japanese, lacked a sense of modern nationalism. Because of these factors, as well as local circumstances and ineffective governments, Asian states were unsuccessful in resisting foreign intervention and domination—and sometimes even invited it.

Eventually, European rule introduced to Asians the ideas of modern nationalism, which in turn provided the impetus for the dominated peoples to revolt against European imperialism. It also exposed Asians to Western sci-

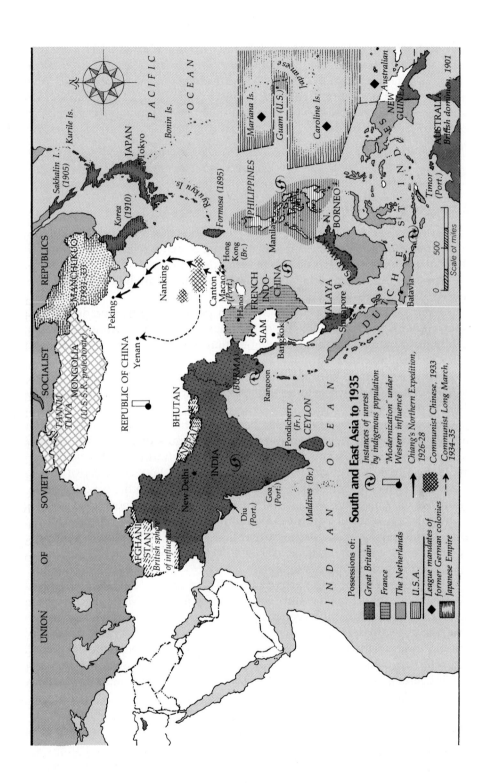

South and East Asia to 1935

UNION OF SOVIET SOCIALIST REPUBLICS

PACIFIC OCEAN

Kurile Is.

Sakhalin I. (1905)

JAPAN
Tokyo

Bonin Is.

MANCHUKUO (1931-33)

Korea (1910)

Ryūkyū Is.

Formosa (1895)

Mariana Is.

Guam (U.S.)

Caroline Is.

Japanese

PHILIPPINES

Manila

Peking

Nanking

Canton

Hong Kong (Br.)

Macao (Port.)

TANNU TUVA

MONGOLIA (U.S.S.R. protectorate)

REPUBLIC OF CHINA

Yenan

Hanoi

FRENCH INDO-CHINA

N. BORNEO

SARAWAK

DUTCH EAST INDIES

Batavia

Timor (Port.)

AUSTRALIA
British dominion, 1901

NEW GUINEA

Australian

BHUTAN

NEPAL

BURMA

SIAM

Bangkok

MALAYA

Singapore

Rangoon

AFGHANI-STAN
British sphere of influence

New Delhi

INDIA

Pondicherry (Fr.)

CEYLON

Goa (Port.)

Diu (Port.)

Maldives (Br.)

INDIAN OCEAN

0   500
Scale of miles

Possessions of:
- Great Britain
- France
- The Netherlands
- U.S.A.
- League mandates of former German colonies
- Japanese Empire

Instances of unrest by indigenous population

"Modernization" under Western influence

Chiang's Northern Expedition, 1926-28

Communist Chinese, 1933

Communist Long March, 1934-35

71

ence, technology, political philosophy, and cultural norms, much of which could also be turned against the conquerors. Thus, while Western imperialism was at its height, European empires had already sown the seeds of their own destruction. In the twentieth century, Asians would use what they had learned form the West to counter it. Nowhere was this process more apparent than on the subcontinent of India.

INDIA

A Fragmented Society

India boasted one of the world's oldest continuous major civilizations, dating from approximately 3000 B.C.E. It was the home of many religions and philosophies, one of which was Hinduism, the religion of the vast majority of Indians. Another was Buddhism, which was almost extinct in its homeland but was nevertheless a major world religion.

Hinduism taught its believers that each person's life was predetermined by his or her actions and behavior in previous lives. Only spiritual perfection, or nirvana, attainable through a combination of devotion, good works, and spiritual learning, released one from the wheel of births and rebirths. Hinduism divided people into hereditary castes, ranging from the exalted Brahman, or priest-scholar caste at the top of society, to the outcastes, or untouchables, at the bottom.

Throughout its history, India had been the victim of many invasions. After the eighth century C.E., most invaders were Muslims of Arab, Turkish, and Persian ethnic groups, some of whom had settled in India. In time, many Indians, especially those from lower castes, attracted by Islam's promise of equality among believers before Allah, or God, had converted to the conquerors' religion. Muslim majorities dominated the northwestern and northeastern parts of the subcontinent but constituted a minority community in the rest of the land. A multiplicity of languages further divided the Indian people. While the oldest cities in India dated back to over 4000 years, most Indians lived in villages ruled by village and caste elders.

Europeans seeking trade arrived in India by sea in 1498; soon afterward the Moghul Empire gained control over the subcontinent. Moghuls came from Central Asia, were Muslim in religion, Turkish in ethnicity, and Persian in culture. The first Moghul rulers were great builders who left behind many impressive monuments (one of the seven wonders of the world, the Taj Mahal, was the mausoleum of a famous Moghul empress). However, by the eighteenth century, the Moghul dynasty was in decline, challenged by both its Hindu and Muslim subjects.

British Rule in India

The disintegration of Moghul political power was accompanied by civil wars and foreign intervention. By the middle of the eighteenth century, Great

Britain and France were fighting for colonial supremacy throughout the world, and India became a prey of these imperialist rivals. Great Britain prevailed over France and by the 1760s was well established in India. In the nineteenth century the British won a series of wars against major princely states and consolidated their grip on the subcontinent. They put parts of India directly under their control and assigned other parts to be ruled by Indian princes under British supervision.

In order to protect its interests in India, Great Britain proceeded to take control over adjacent territories and make them into buffer zones. To the east, it defeated the Burmese in three wars and incorporated Burma into the Indian Empire. To the south, it secured the island of Ceylon from the Dutch by treaty, gaining a new colony. To the west and northwest, Great Britain sought to protect India from both raiding Afghans and expansionist Russians by creating a protectorate over Afghanistan and a sphere of influence in eastern Persia (see below). The Himalayas protected India from attack by China from the north, and in any case a weak China was in no position to threaten British interests. To secure trade routes between the Indian Ocean and East Asia, Great Britain purchased the tip of the Malay peninsula from the local ruler. Here it developed a free port and a major naval base called Singapore.

Since the main motive for their control of India was commercial, the British paid close attention to developing the Indian economy in order to expand trade. They undertook large irrigation projects to bring new land into cultivation and introduced new crops such as tea and coffee. They revitalized old crops such as cotton and jute to supply raw material to British mills. To bring the crops to the seaports and to distribute their manufactured goods to Indian consumers, the British built railroads that linked the coast to the interior. They introduced new processing industries to India and opened coal mines to provide fuel.

Reflecting the atmosphere of cultural imperialism prevalent in that era, the British administration introduced measures to correct Indian practices that were considered wrong by Western standards. They abolished *suttee* (or *sati*, burning upper-caste widows alive on their husbands' funeral pyres) and suppressed the *thuggees*, who robbed and murdered in the name of religion.

Many Indians accepted the reforms as beneficial and responded to the Western challenge to their traditional values by reexamining and reevaluating their religion and society. As a result, many Indians actively supported such reform measures as the Age of Consent Act of 1891, which raised the marriageable age of girls. These Indians advocated the introduction of further reforms. Hindu traditionalists, however, bitterly resented this act as an example of British interference in Indian society and organized riots in several cities to protest it.

Confident of the superiority of its educational system, Great Britain had since the early nineteenth century used public revenues in India to support British-style schools. Private Christian schools, both Catholic and Protestant, had also been established by missionaries from Britain in many cities. Although many upper-caste Hindu girls were educated at home, there were no girls' schools. English missionaries opened the first school for girls in 1849. Missionaries did not convert many Indians to Christianity, but their schools for Indian children were crucial in the spread of Western values and knowl- edge to many Indians.

Gradually, the lines of contact between British and Indians broadened, and new ideas about social reform, popular sovereignty, and modern nationalism took root among the Western-educated Indian elite. Without question, nation- alism was the most powerful force in India from 1900 onward. Western liberal ideas and modern nationalistic feelings, either introduced by contact with the British or generated in reaction to British rule, profoundly changed the nature of Indian upper-class society. Most Indian nationalists of the twentieth century wanted not only independence but also independence based on Western con- cepts of nationhood. They sought democracy and representative government, not a return to the authoritarian monarchies of ancient India. British-educated Indians insisted that democracy and self-government were universally applic- able ideals; therefore, they argued, Indians should govern themselves and the British should leave India.

In 1885 a group of British-educated Indians, mostly lawyers, and some of their British friends formed an organization called the Indian National Con- gress, whose goal was to gain for Indians the right of political representation that Britons enjoyed in their homeland. The Congress met in annual sessions to formulate goals and programs. Between sessions, its members lobbied for reforms. All Indians were welcome to join the Congress, which professed no

English ladies and gentlemen served afternoon tea by Indian servants. Even minor British officers and officials lived well in India.
(*"Afternoon Tea,"* © *1976, Aperture, Inc., as published in* The Last Empire, Photography in British India, 1855–1911, *Aperture, 1976.)*

religious biases. However, few Muslims joined, initially because Muslims lagged behind Hindus in political consciousness and later because they feared that majority rule would mean Hindu suppression of the Muslim minority. As a result, most Muslims regarded the Congress as a Hindu organization that did not represent them.

In the face of determined Indian pressure, the British government, with no clear vision of where it wanted to move, slowly and reluctantly made concessions to Indian demands for self-rule. Indian Muslims were ambivalent about self-government, since they feared that any representative government would be Hindu-dominated and thus override the interests of their community. To safeguard their interests against possible Hindu oppression, the All-India Muslim League was founded in 1906. The League demanded "separate electorates" for Muslims (Muslims electing their own representatives) in any elected Indian legislature. The Congress from the beginning vehemently opposed the idea of separate electorates, but its opposition merely made the Muslims more adamant. The identification of Indians primarily by their religion is called communalism.

In 1909 Great Britain took a first major step toward Indian self-rule. The British Parliament passed the Indian Councils Act (generally known as the Morley-Minto reforms), which provided for a limited male franchise and for limited powers to the elective councils and assemblies at both the provincial and central government levels. This was far from true self-government because British-appointed governors and officials still held the reins of power and made most of the important decisions. The reforms did, however, provide a constitutional platform where Indian representatives could voice their opinions, and they introduced Indians to the concept and practice of elections and representative government. They also set the pattern for future constitutional development. Muslims won the right to separate electorates and insisted on being guaranteed separate electorates in the future. Finally, they demanded a separate nation to ensure their identity. Conversely, Hindus and the Congress interpreted separate electorates and other concessions to Muslims as a ploy of "divide and rule" to prolong British dominance of the subcontinent.

Neither the Congress nor the League was satisfied with the concessions of the Morley-Minto reforms. Both saw self-government as the logical goal of Indian nationalism. They coined a new word, *swaraj*, or self-rule, to represent their goal. By 1914 *"swaraj"* was on the lips of every Indian political activist.

A faraway event added to Indian restlessness—news of Japanese victories on land and sea over Russia in the Russo-Japanese war of 1904–1905 (see Chapter 7), the first victory by an Asian nation in modern times over a major power of the West. As a foreign traveler observed at the time, "Even the remote villages talked over the victories of Japan as they sat in their circles and passed around the pipe at night."

AUSTRALASIA

The name "Australasia" applies to the island continent Australia and the North and South Islands of New Zealand. At the time of Western settlement

Australia was sparsely inhabited by people of the Australoid race who did not practice agriculture or herding and lived in scattered groups by hunting and gathering. New Zealand was populated by earlier immigrants of the Polynesian race called Maoris. They were more "advanced" than Australian aborigines, lived in tribal societies, and offered stiff resistance to English settlers.

Although discovered and first explored by Dutch people, Australasia was colonized by Great Britain; it therefore became British in population, culture, and institutions. The climate of parts of Australasia resembles that of Europe, and imperialism in this area stressed the settlement of Europeans, a pattern similar to colonizing North America in previous centuries. The first Britons (a load of convicts and their guards) arrived in Sydney, Australia, in 1788. It was intended as a dumping ground for convicts when the North American colonies refused to accept them after independence. Most of Australia, however, was not set up as penal colonies, and the entire continent was soon opened up to regular immigration from Europe. A total of six colonies were established "Down Under," and each received self-government as soon as local conditions warranted. In 1901, like Canada, the six self-governing colonies were federated to form the Commonwealth of Australia and became a dominion in the British Empire. Until World War II, Australia remained overwhelmingly British in culture and sentiment and enjoyed the protection of the British navy. With the exception of a small number of native aborigines, Australians maintained racial and cultural homogeneity by keeping out Asian immigrants through the White Australia Policy.

New Zealand was also discovered by Dutch explorers in the seventeenth century. British settlers came in the early nineteenth century and subjugated the Maoris in wars. New Zealand was never a penal colony, and Great Britain had no hesitation about granting the settlers self-government. In 1907, the North and South Islands joined to form a dominion within the British Empire. Like Australia, New Zealand passed laws to restrict Asian immigration, which ensured the British heritage of the white New Zealanders.

The small populations of Australia and New Zealand enjoyed a high standard of living based on an economy that emphasized export-oriented farming, animal husbandry, and mining. Both Australia and New Zealand exported wheat, wool, meat, and dairy products, mainly to Great Britain, and depended on Great Britain for manufactured goods. By the early twentieth century, there were only a few industries, most of them processing agricultural and livestock products or minerals.

The labor movement, expressed in unions and in labor parties, was strong in both Australia and New Zealand, with the result that both nations were in the vanguard of social legislation in such areas as old-age pensions, financed by heavy taxes on large properties. New Zealand granted women suffrage in 1893, and the Australian states did so beginning in 1894, leading the world. In 1910, as evidence of growing national maturity, Australia instituted compulsory military training for its young men and began to organize a regular military force. New Zealand followed suit in 1911.

FRENCH INDOCHINA

The Indochina peninsula was the meeting ground of Chinese and Indian cultures in ancient times, hence the name. Steady immigration by settlers from China ensured the predominance of peoples of the Mongolian race. Over 2,000 years ago Chinese conquest and control of northern Vietnam brought in advanced agriculture and irrigation, Chinese writing, social organization, Confucian ideology, and Chinese-style Buddhism. Since about 900 C.E. Vietnam had had its own government but acknowledged Chinese overlordship. The southward expansion of the Vietnamese people to the tip of the peninsula was completed in the eighteenth century. Indian culture, expressed in Hinduism and Buddhism, came to the region through Indian merchants and missionaries beginning in the early Christian era and prevailed in the western half of Indochina, in Laos and Cambodia.

Although French Catholic missionaries had been active in Indochina since the seventeenth century, French imperial ambitions in the region did not become a factor until the middle of the nineteenth century. Indochina was important for several reasons; it provided natural resources, a domain for Catholic missionary work, a back door for expansion into southern China, and a deterrent to British imperialism. The advance of French power in Vietnam during the nineteenth century was a good example of "the flag follows the cross," because French annexations during the nineteenth century were sometimes brought on by Indochinese attacks on French missionaries and native converts. In 1885 France defeated China in war; China was forced to give up its position as overlord of Vietnam, which was annexed by France. In 1887 France joined together Cochin-China, Tonkin, and Annam (the three components of Vietnam) and Laos and Cambodia to form the Indochina Union. Within the Union, France ruled Cochin-China directly and the others as protectorates. The governor-general, headquartered in Hanoi, controlled overall policy, while the native rulers in the protectorates were allowed to supervise routine administration. The goal of the French was to extend their control in that area gradually through the policy of association, whereby French resident officials closely supervised the administration of the native states.

French economic policy in Indochina aimed at exploiting Indochinese, especially Vietnamese, resources. The French greatly expanded rice and rubber production and developed the mining of coal and metals. To facilitate economic development, they built roads and railroads, expanded the irrigation system, and introduced modern public health and educational facilities. The average Vietnamese paid dearly for these improvements and benefited little from them. As late as 1939, only 15 percent of school-age children in Indochina were receiving any education.

As in Africa, France pursued a policy of cultural "assimilation," a concept aimed at creating a "New France" in Indochina by establishing French schools and promoting French language, culture, and customs. France hoped that eventually a new elite class sympathetic to French rule would emerge among the Indochinese. Physically, cities in Indochina acquired French-inspired architecture, but the small minority of French-educated Indochinese, like their British-educated Indian counterparts, used their new knowledge to oppose colonial rule and to advocate independence for their nations.

The Vietnamese elite who received a French education became the standard-bearers of modern Vietnamese nationalism. Japan's victory over Russia in 1904–1905 spurred Vietnamese nationalists to organize and publicize their aims and goals. Vietnamese students in Japan organized and openly agitated for throwing out the French. Chinese reform movements that culminated in the successful revolution of 1911 gave additional stimulus to the Vietnamese anti-French activities. They were so widespread that the years after 1905 were known as the "era of plots," all of which were suppressed by France. An example of the contradiction inherent in France's colonial policy was the closing down of the University of Hanoi because it was a center of revolutionary activities. The university was a creation of the French colonial government, opened to promote its policy of assimilation by imparting French culture and values to Vietnamese. Yet it was precisely these French-trained Vietnamese who led the nationalist movement to oust the French from Vietnam. Temporarily, the French repression succeeded. Some activists fled to China to continue their work; others, most notably Ho Chi Minh, went to Europe, where they kept up their anti-French activities.

THE DUTCH EAST INDIES (INDONESIA)

The Dutch had been involved in the East Indies since the seventeenth century, after they had ousted the Portuguese, but had not extended effective control outside Java to the rest of Indonesia until early in the nineteenth century. From the beginning, the Dutch showed little interest in exporting their culture or religion to their colonies; rather, they regarded them as valuable sources of raw materials and later as a market for the sale of manufactured goods. The plantations, financed by the Netherlands and other Western nations and worked by Javanese and Chinese laborers, produced tea, coffee, indigo, tobacco, spices, sugar, and palm oil. Petroleum and tin were other valuable raw materials.

At the turn of the century, the Dutch introduced reforms called the "ethical policy," to protect ordinary Indonesians from the more flagrant forms of economic exploitation. This paternalistic policy established state-supported elementary schools and stressed the moral obligation of the Netherlands to improve the welfare of the local people. Despite this policy, economic prosperity benefited the Dutch rather than the Indonesians.

Dutch rule in Indonesia before World War I was authoritarian. A Dutch-appointed governor-general ruled from Batavia (located on Java, renamed Jakarta after independence), assisted by an all-Dutch advisory council and a cabinet. No popular assemblies of any kind existed beyond the village level. Even though Dutch rulers did not attempt to bring Western ideas and methods to the natives, young Indonesians, like colonials elsewhere, became exposed to them. Indonesians were also impressed by the rising stature of Japan and the respect it received from European powers; for example, in 1899 the Japanese were granted equal status with Europeans in Indonesia.

An Indonesian nationalist movement emerged in reaction to Dutch colonial rule. Most notable among the nationalist groups was the Sarekat Islam, formed in 1910. As the title indicates, the movement was a Muslim organization and as such it represented the majority of Indonesians. In 1911 the Sarekat Islam organized anti-Chinese riots, a reflection of native resentment of the strong economic role of the Chinese community in Indonesian life and the fact that the Chinese were Buddhists and Confucians, not Muslims. By World War I the Sarekat Islam had become a mass movement aimed at reviving Islam, attaining independence, and eliminating the economic power of the Chinese.

CHINA

A Tradition-Bound Society

For millennia, China, geographically isolated from other major cultures, dominated East Asia. Like India, China boasted a continuous civilization spanning some 4,000 years. In the third century B.C.E., to protect itself from the nomadic peoples on its northern borders, China built the 1,500-mile-long Great Wall, the biggest man-made structure on earth. In its isolation, China developed a unique writing system (ideograms and pictograms), local religions (ancestor worship and Taoism), and a political and moral philosophy (Confucianism). Although caravans and sailing boats had carried goods between China and the eastern Mediterranean since ancient times, the only outside culture that had an important influence before the coming of modern Westerners was that of India. Indian Buddhism was accepted enthusiastically by the Chinese in the early centuries of the Christian era.

For more than 2,000 years China had been an empire headed by ruling dynasties that could be overthrown for incompetence. Bureaucrats were selected based on educational attainments demonstrated in examinations based on Confucian moral philosophy; they ruled a predominantly rural society. There were no hereditary social classes, but there was a class system that exalted scholars, honored farmers and artisans, but denigrated merchants as social parasites. Although most Chinese lived in nuclear families, multigenerational families headed by a senior male or patriarch were admired. Men enjoyed higher status than women, but age regardless of sex merited great respect.

Since China was the largest, most advanced, and strongest state in East Asia, its civilization, even more than its political power, dominated the area. Korea and Vietnam were under direct or indirect Chinese political control for 2,000 years and absorbed major aspects of Chinese culture. Even though Japan was never under China's political sway, it voluntarily adopted much of China's culture. China's traditional role as the giver but not the receiver of cultures contributed to its ethnocentrism and reluctance to learn from other peoples, an attitude that proved to be disastrous during the era of imperialism.

From its traditional cultural and political perspective, China thought of itself as the "Central Kingdom" and all foreign nations as tributary vassal states. When the monarchs of the Manchu (or Ch'ing) dynasty received modern seaborne Westerners in the late seventeenth and eighteenth century, they, like their predecessors from the Ming dynasty, regarded the foreigners as tribute-bearing vassals.

In fact, the Westerners had come to China to trade. Tea, silks, and porcelains from China were in great demand in Europe. Until the late eighteenth century, however, Europeans had little to trade in return. This balance of trade in China's favor further reinforced China's self-perception of superiority and indispensability. Westerners, however, rejected China's claim of superiority; they not only believed in legal equality between nations but in fact often looked down on the Chinese as inferiors.

The Twilight of the Manchu Dynasty

In the nineteenth century, Chinese traditional culture and Western imperialism met in headlong confrontation as China became the main target for imperialism in Asia. Differences on such issues as diplomatic equality, international relations, laws, and trade all made conflict inevitable, but opium precipitated the clash. The Chinese government had banned opium, but it was a lucrative trade item for Western merchants. Great Britain's insistence that its merchants had the right to sell opium to the Chinese triggered war between the two nations in 1839–1842 and again in 1858–1860.

In each case, China was defeated and forced to sign (in the eyes of the Chinese) humiliating, "unequal treaties." The Chinese not only had to accept opium and other trade but also to cede territory and pay an indemnity. A clear manifestation of contemptuous Western cultural imperialism was the extraterritoriality provisions of these treaties. By these provisions Westerners residing in China were exempted from Chinese laws, which by Western standards were considered too harsh and barbarous. In addition, China was forced to accept Christian missionaries.

While few Chinese converted to Christianity, the missionaries introduced modern medicine, the sciences, schools, and other ideas to the Chinese with revolutionary consequences. In the early twentieth century modern Western-style schools would replace traditional ones and Western medicine would gain acceptance. Above all, missionaries introduced new ideas about social relationships that would contribute to the republican revolt against the traditional imperial institutions and to a social revolt of the individual against the all-powerful family and of women against male dominance.

By 1900 China had been carved up into "spheres of influence" controlled by Russia, Germany, Great Britain, France, and Japan. In the German sphere of influence, for example, Chinese authority was limited; Germany alone could exploit the resources there and sell mainly German goods to the Chinese residents there. Similar conditions applied in the other spheres of influence. China appeared to be destined for full colonization.

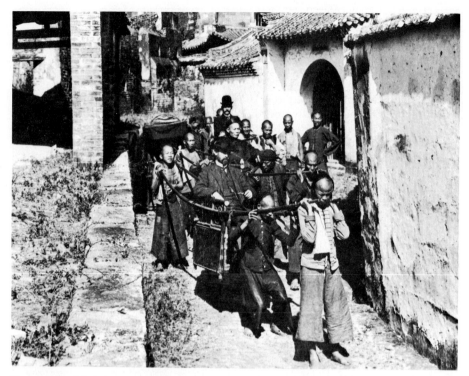

Extraterritorial rights and wealth gave Westerners special privileges in China. Two well-dressed gentlemen carried in litters as they sightsee.
(Museum of American China Trade, Milton, Mass.)

These humiliations weakened and discredited the ruling Manchu dynasty. During the last decades of the nineteenth century, China was plagued internally with rebellions, brigandage, and natural disasters, while externally it struggled unsuccessfully to maintain itself against increasing foreign encroachments. It was China's misfortune that in the most critical years of its contact with the West, its destiny was in the hands of an ignorant, corrupt, and unscrupulous woman, Yehonala, better known to the world as the Dowager Empress Tz'u-hsi. From 1862, when she became coregent for her young son, to her death in 1908 (with the exception of a few years), she ruled China as an autocrat. Hating all foreigners, she threw her support behind a militant and superstitious group who shared her xenophobia (fear of outsiders), popularly called the Boxers, who believed they could rid China of foreigners by their magic.

In the summer of 1900, the Boxers inflicted a reign of terror on the capital city Peking and its environs, especially against foreigners and Chinese Christian converts, and besieged the foreign diplomatic quarters in the city. Meanwhile, their ally Tz'u-hsi went so far as to declare war on all the Western nations and to order all foreigners in China killed. Fortunately for China, its diplomats abroad refused to obey her order, and many local authorities at

---

A Foe of the Manchus

From 1885, i.e., from the time of our defeat in the war with France, I set before myself the object of the overthrow of the Ch'ing [Manchu] dynasty and the establishment of a Chinese Republic on its ruins. At the very beginning I selected for my propaganda the college at which I was studying, regarding medical science as the kindly aunt who would bring me out onto the high road of politics.

Ten years passed like one day. In Canton Medical School, I made friends with Chen Shih-Liang, who had a very large circle of acquaintances amongst widely traveled people who knew China well. When I began talking of revolution, advocating its ideas, he gladly agreed with me, and declared that he would immediately enter a revolutionary party if I would agree to lead it. . . . attracted also by the thought that there I should have a wider field for my revolutionary propaganda, I went to Hong Kong to continue my education. For four years I gave up all my free time from studies to the cause of revolutionary propaganda, traveling backward and forward between Hong Kong and Amoy.*

Dr. Sun Yat-sen, 1866–1925, father of the Chinese Republic, wrote here about how he became a revolutionary. Born near Canton of poor parents, Sun was taken by an elder brother to Hawaii as a youth and was educated in a Christian missionary school. He converted to Christianity. While in medical school Sun was drawn to revolutionary politics by the incompetence of the Manchu government. He dedicated his life to overthrowing the Manchus and to modernizing China.

*From *Memoirs of a Chinese Revolutionary* (1918), quoted in *The China Reader*, vol. 2: *Republican China, 1911–1919*, Franz Schurmann and Orville Schell, Eds. Copyright 1967 by Random House, Inc. Reprinted by permission of Random House, Inc.

---

home also ignored her and succeeded in restricting Boxer activity to Peking and parts of northern China. Eight nations with nationals in China organized an international force to relieve the besieged foreigners and succeeded in doing so in August 1900. Just before the relief forces entered Peking, Tz'u-hsi fled the capital disguised as a peasant woman.

The Boxer fiasco ended in 1901 with China's acceptance of a protocol dictated by the victorious powers. The Boxer Protocol provided for punishment of Boxer leaders, a huge indemnity, and an armed and walled legation district to safeguard the foreign diplomatic community in Peking.

As a result of the Boxer Rebellion, China lay prostrate at the feet of the imperialist powers. This disaster had also stripped the Manchus of the last remaining claim to authority. U.S. and British-educated Sun Yat-sen became the foremost revolutionary dedicated to the overthrow of the dynasty. He proposed to replace it with a republic and formulated a program that combined nationalism, democracy, and social reforms. Sun lamented that China in the early twentieth century was a semicolony, the prey of all and the responsibility of none. The impotent Manchu dynasty remained in power until 1911, at least partly because the imperialist nations were for the moment satisfied with their gains and did not wish to risk war among one another by demanding additional concessions from China.

THE MIDDLE EAST

Middle Eastern Society: The Bond of Islam

Like China, the Middle East was held together by a common history. Peoples of that area could look back on the glorious Golden Age of Islam from about 800 to 1100, which occurred at the time when Europe was in the depths of economic and cultural depression, the so-called Dark Ages. During this period, Islamic culture, economy, and political power reached its zenith.

The Muslim religion was another important cohesive factor in the Middle East. Islam came out of the same traditions as Judaism and Christianity. Muslims (submitters to Islam) believe in one God (Allah) and in his prophets of the Old and New Testaments, including Jesus, who is considered a great prophet but not God. All people who accept the belief in one God and in Muhammad as his prophet are seen as equal before that God and as equals within the Muslim community. It was largely on the basis of this egalitarian philosophy that Islam spread rapidly to peoples of many diverse cultures.

The Koran, the Muslim holy book, contains instructions for every aspect of a Muslim's life. The leaders in Islam were viewed as both political and religious figures; in its early formation Islamic society did not separate the role of the government from that of religion. For millions of Muslims, Islam was perceived as a dynamic force for social change, particularly in the treatment of women. Although women were regarded as inferior to men, they nevertheless could inherit property, initiate divorces, and remarry in the event of widowhood or divorce. Largely as a result of its stable and complete nature, Islamic society remained resistant to outside forces. Thus, while the political apparatus of the Arab world fell to Western colonialism, the culture and religion remained relatively unchanged. As in Africa, Asian Muslims rarely, if ever, converted to Christianity, nor did they lose their traditional values of respect for the family and loyalty to one another. Hence Islam was to play a major role for many Muslims in their struggle against Western domination.

European Imperialist Inroads

By 1900 the states of the Middle East, which had long been in decline, were at a low ebb. The Persian and Ottoman empires, which had formerly produced able and vigorous leaders, were headed by incompetent and sometimes unstable men. These governments had lost much territory and in some cases had to submit to European control in areas that remained in their nominal jurisdiction. They had, however, managed to play off competing foreign forces to retain control in parts of their empires. Great Britain and Russia were rivals who had interests and ambitions in both the Persian and Ottoman empires, while Germany had extended its influence into the Ottoman Empire. The German government sent officers to train the Ottoman army and planned to build a Berlin-to-Baghdad railway; German banks loaned money to the Ottoman government and invested in financial enterprises in the Ottoman Empire.

Russia expanded its empire at the expense of the Ottoman Empire around the Black Sea in a series of wars that began in the eighteenth century. In the nineteenth century the Russian Empire also advanced southward at the expense of the Persian Empire and more importantly into Central Asia against loosely organized tribal states. Russian gains in Central Asia during the nineteenth century equaled half the size of the United States. Thus whereas 2,000 miles divided British- and Russian-controlled lands in Asia in 1800, only twenty miles separated British India from Russian Central Asia in 1900.

Competition between the British and the Russians came to a head in Persia. Sharing a long border with Persia, Russia was in an advantageous position to infiltrate and penetrate that nation. Russian officers had been sent to Persia to organize the Persian army, Russian banks loaned money to the Persian government, and Russian firms won concessions to build Persian railroads. In return, Russia controlled the Persian customs office and other departments of the Persian government.

Great Britain feared that Russia had ambitions in India and believed that the easiest way for Russia to attack India was via the Western frontier between Persia and Afghanistan. Based on this assumption, the key to British policy toward Persia was to thwart Russia's southward advance. For this reason, Great Britain was satisfied with the results of the Russo-Japanese War, which forced Russia to turn its attentions to rebuilding its army and navy and to retrench in Persia. It was in this context that Russia and Great Britain began to negotiate their outstanding differences in 1907, which resulted in the Anglo-Russian Convention and Entente. According to the terms of the Convention, Russia agreed not to encroach on Afghanistan and conceded it as an exclusive British sphere of influence. Both powers agreed to "respect" Persian "independence," but they then proceeded to divide it into their respective spheres of influence. Russia got the lion's share, or the entire northern half of Persia, including the capital city, Tehran. Great Britain's sphere in the southeast was smaller, but was strategically located on the border between Afghanistan and India. What remained of Persia was designated a neutral zone. As a result of this settlement, tension between Russia and Great Britain eased.

Meanwhile, Persians who had traveled and studied in Europe were convinced that Persia needed to reform its antiquated political system if it was to survive. They launched a dual program that involved agitation for Westernization and constitutional reforms on the one hand, and on the other the creation of a national consciousness based on deep-rooted traditions and Persia's long history. In the bloodless 1906 revolution, the shah (ruler of Persia) was forced to give up his absolute powers and to convene an elected parliament to draw up a constitution, which was promulgated in December of that year. A civil war broke out in 1908 between conservatives and reformers, complicated by a Russian invasion. In 1909 the Anglo-Persian Oil Company began production in southwestern Persia, and Persia soon became a leading producer of oil. It remained neutral during World War I, and Western pressures were much reduced for the duration of the war.

Among Europeans during the nineteenth century, the Ottoman Empire was often called the "Sick Man of Europe" and was viewed as a dangerous power vacuum that tempted major European powers to intervene. The Austro-Hungarian, Russian, and German governments had conflicting imperial ambitions in the Balkan provinces of the Ottoman Empire. They encouraged and sometimes helped the predominantly Christian subject peoples such as the Serbians, Bulgarians, Rumanians, Albanians, and Greeks to rise up against the failing Ottoman Empire. Six independent states were created as a result of successful uprisings. By 1914 the Ottoman Empire retained only a foothold in Europe. However, to prevent Russia from gaining access to the Mediterranean Sea, the British and French encouraged the Ottomans to hang on to this foothold and to retain their hold on the vital Dardanelles Straits.

In Asia, restlessness among the unassimilated Christian Armenian minority caused the Turkish-Ottoman government great alarm and resulted in harsh repression. A sizable Arab subject population in the Middle East (which indeed outnumbered the ruling Turkish population) had also awakened to the pulls of nationalism and was threatening secession from the empire. North Africa and Egypt, still technically Ottoman provinces, had long since come under French and British control, respectively. Italy annexed the Ottoman Empire's last African possession, Libya, in 1912.

In attempting to hold on to what remained of the crumbling empire, the Ottoman government enlisted German aid. Kaiser Wilhelm II was only too happy to comply, for he saw in such aid an opportunity to expand German influence into the Middle East. As previously noted, German instructors helped to modernize the Ottoman army and, in so doing, helped to awaken a spirit of nationalism among Turkish officers. These officers styled themselves as "Young Turks" and formed an organization dedicated to the modernization of the Ottoman Empire. In 1908, the Young Turks staged a successful revolution, and their leader, Enver Bey, became the de facto ruler of the empire. Between 1909 and 1914, the Young Turks attempted a program of "Turkification" of Armenians, Arabs, and other subject nationalities of the empire; this, however, only deepened local nationalistic feelings among these peoples. Then in World War I, led by German trained officers, the Ottoman Empire joined the Central Powers.

From the experience of the Arabs, Armenians, and others, it can be seen that Western nations were not the only practitioners of imperialism. The Ottoman Empire provided an ironic example of a state, itself the victim of European imperialism, which in turn sometimes imposed a harsh rule on its subject nationalities.

SUMMARY

Western imperialism was at its height in Asia at the beginning of the twentieth century. With the exception of Japan, all of Asia was under either the direct or the indirect control of Western imperial nations. Large areas and ancient civilizations—the Indian subcontinent, Indochina, the East Indies, and other smaller territories—had become colonies of the imperial powers. Other once-powerful empires were in decay and only nominally independent: Persia and the Ottoman Empire had been reduced in size by successful revolts of subject nationalities and by Western encroachments. China had been stripped of vassal states and was but a semicolony itself.

Even as Western imperialism stood at its most triumphant, however, movements had been set in motion that would eventually topple it. Victims of imperialism, Asian peoples were among the first non-Westerners to experience a new sense of nationalism. This desire to control their own destinies inspired a new generation of Asian nationalists not only to free their homelands of Western imperialism but also to get rid of their traditional governments and to reform their moribund societies and cultures along Western lines.

Traditional life in Asia was also changing, as a result of the technological and scientific innovations introduced by Western imperial powers. While traditionalists had resisted Western-inspired changes and reforms, modernizers in Persia, the Ottoman Empire, and other lands sought to adopt Western technology and institutions. In China, the ignominious defeat of the Boxer movement, which sought to counter Western science and technology with superstition and magic, opened the way for forward-looking leaders. These leaders set as their goal learning from advanced Western nations so that Chinese peoples could throw off the yoke of subjugation.

Australasia had a different historical experience. Australia and New Zealand had been colonized by people of predominantly British stock who enjoyed a prosperous economy. Great Britain did not repeat the mistake it had made with its North American colonies; by the early twentieth century, Australia and New Zealand, like Great Britain's other white-majority colonies, had gained self-government within the Empire.

SUGGESTED SOURCES

CLAVELL, JAMES, *Tai-Pan* (1966). An epic novel about British traders on the China coast in the mid-nineteenth century.* (Also a film.)

DEAN, VERA M., *The Nature of the Non-Western World* (1966). An easy-to-read introduction to general problems of modernization and culture clash.*

FLEMING, PETER, *The Siege of Peking* (1959). A good account of the Boxer siege of Peking in 1900.

FORSTER, E. M., *A Passage to India* (1924). A novel about English men and women in India and their interactions with Indians.* (Also a film.)

HOPKIRK, PETER, *The Great Game, The Struggle for Empire in Central Asia* (1990). This is the exciting story of Anglo-Russian competition for empire in Central Asia in the nineteenth century.

MACMILLAN, MARGARET, *Women of the Raj* (1988). Concentrates on the role of English women in India c. 1650–1947; richly illustrated.

MANSFIELD, PETER, *The Arab World* (1976). An introduction to the Arab world by a journalist.*

ROBINSON, DONALD H., *The Raj* (1981). An interesting view of British rule in India.* (Also a BBC television production.)

TAN, CHESTER C., *The Boxer Catastrophe* (1967). The best book on the uprising of the Boxers and their effort to drive Westerners out of China.*

WARNER, MARINA, *The Dowager Empress: The Life and Times of Tz'u-hsi, Empress Dowager of China, 1835–1908* (1972). A Colorful biography.

YAPP, M. E., *The Making of the Modern Near East, 1792–1923* (1988). A readable and extensively researched survey.*

*Paperback available.

CHAPTER 7

The United States and Japan in Asia and the Pacific

As European nations consolidated their hold over most of Asia, two rising powers—the United States and Japan—also began to assert their claims in that region. Many in the United States believed in its Manifest Destiny, and the Japanese felt great pride because Japan alone among non-Western nations had successfully modernized and escaped the fate of other Asians. Nationalistic pride turned into imperialism as both upstarts, the Americans and the Japanese, elbowed their way into Asia, defeating relatively weak European rivals in the process. Eventually the United States and Japan would become each other's major competitor for dominance of Asia.

THE UNITED STATES CROSSES THE PACIFIC

Acquiring Hawaii and the Philippines

Although the United States was primarily absorbed in Latin America, by the turn of the century it had also become interested in Asia. Throughout the nineteenth century, U.S. merchants had engaged in the famous "clipper ship" trade, for silk, tea, and porcelain from China and spices from the Dutch East Indies. To ensure its share of widening trade possibilities, the United States had sent naval squadrons to force the opening of commercial contacts with Japan and Korea. In 1867, the United States purchased Alaska from Russia and occupied Midway Island in the central Pacific for use as a coaling station for its commercial and naval vessels.

In the 1890s, a rush of events propelled the United States into the dominant position in the central Pacific. One of the main centers of activity was the Hawaiian Islands, the key to controlling the region. This Polynesian kingdom had already been conquered economically by U.S. sugar and pineapple planters, who imported Chinese and Japanese laborers to work the plantations. By 1887 the United States had concluded commercial treaties with

Hawaii and acquired Pearl Harbor for a future naval base, in effect making the islands a U.S. protectorate. In 1893, U.S. settlers toppled the Hawaiian monarchy, and in 1898, by mutual agreement, the United States annexed Hawaii. Unlike Puerto Rico, Hawaii was given territorial status, a stepping-stone to statehood. The United States rapidly developed Pearl Harbor into a major naval base. One year later, the United States annexed Wake Island, thereby filling a gap in its trans-Pacific supply line.

Also in 1898, as a result of the Spanish-American War, and after payment of $20 million to Spain, the United States acquired the Philippines and the strategically important Pacific island of Guam. As in the case of Cuba and Puerto Rico, the question of what to do with the populous Philippine Islands became the chief focus of debate between pro- and antiimperialist politicians. Antiimperialists argued that the Philippines possessed a hodgepodge of unassimilable peoples and cultures and that the islands were not necessary for the security or economic development of the United States; therefore, annexation of these islands would be a deplorable act of imperialism and a repudiation of U.S. ideals.

Those who supported annexation argued that the Philippines were valuable economically as a producer of such tropical items as sugar, coconut oil, and hemp, and as a consumer of U.S. products. They were also concerned that some powerful European nation or Japan might seize the islands if the United States did not. In Subic Bay, they saw an excellent base for a U.S. naval squadron that would protect U.S. trade and other interests in Asia. Imperialists further argued that the "backward" Filipinos needed a period of tutelage under the United States before they could operate successfully as an independent nation. In annexing the islands, therefore, the United States was only assuming its responsibility, as the British imperialist writer Rudyard Kipling had advocated when he urged Americans to "take up the white man's burden." Protestant ministers also favored annexation as an opportunity to save souls for Christ, even though the majority of Filipinos were already Catholics.

At a crucial point in the debate, President William McKinley told the public that prayerful contemplation had convinced him that the United States should keep possession of the Philippines. The annexationist point of view prevailed both in Congress and in the presidential election of 1900, when anti-expansionist William Jennings Bryan was defeated by McKinley for the second time. Thus, like Puerto Rico, the Philippines became a U.S. possession.

Politically active Filipinos, who had already been fighting the Spanish for independence, opposed annexation by the United States. In 1899 they proclaimed a Philippine republic. Emilio Aguinaldo, a hero of the fight against Spain, was named its first president. However, the United States refused to recognize this government and waged war to suppress it. In 1901 General Arthur MacArthur (father of General Douglas MacArthur) captured Aguinaldo. The independence movement eventually collapsed, but the Muslim Moros, a minority community that lived on several islands of the archipelago, continued their rebellion until 1913.

Imperialism in Asia: U.S. troops suppress insurrection in the Philippines.
(Culver Pictures)

During this struggle, the United States had sent many more troops to conquer the Philippines than it had sent to pacify Cuba. On occasion, U.S. soldiers committed the same atrocities and pursued the same policies of internment that Americans had condemned when they were used by the Spanish in Cuba and the British in South Africa. About 200,000 Filipinos died from various causes during the fighting, and U.S. dead numbered over 4,000.

Because of this unhappy experience, U.S. attitudes toward the Philippines were tinged with guilt. While suppressing movements for immediate Philippine independence, the U.S. government also played an active role in preparing for its eventual realization. In 1913 and again in 1919 President Woodrow Wilson formally pledged that it was U.S. policy to grant independence to the Philippines at an early date. To prepare Filipinos for the responsibility of independence, Governor-General William Howard Taft and his successors launched an ambitious program of public education that doubled the literacy rate in just over a generation and introduced English as the second language for a significant minority.

Qualified Filipinos found the doors to civil service jobs open to them. By 1912 half of all ranking judges were Filipinos. In 1907 local elections were held for an assembly, in which two major political parties competed for power. The assembly was the first popularly elected legislative body in Southeast Asia. An upper house in which Filipinos had a majority was added in 1913. However, political reforms were not matched by economic ones. Wealth in the Philippines remained in the hands of U.S. business firms and a few rich Filipinos and Chinese.

Expanding U.S. Interests in China

By the turn of the century the United States controlled a string of islands and bases across the Pacific to the threshold of the Asian mainland. Now that their trade routes were protected, U.S. businesses wished to increase their share of Asian commerce, and missionaries were anxious to spread the Gospel. Unfortunately for U.S. capitalists, most of the Asian trade had already been preempted by European nations through their colonial possessions and their spheres of influence in China. In 1899 and again in 1900 Secretary of State John Hay announced that he had secured an agreement from the European powers and Japan for an "Open Door" policy that would allow all nations equal opportunity to trade throughout China while respecting its political independence and territorial integrity. In fact, there had been no uniform agreement, but the Open Door principle became the cornerstone of United States policy toward China up to World War II. In contradiction of its own policy, however, the United States also attempted to carve out a sphere of influence in Fukien on the southern coast of China but was thwarted by Japanese opposition.

The pace of U.S. contacts with China accelerated during the early twentieth century. In 1900 U.S. marines joined the international relief force that rescued the besieged Westerners in Peking and suppressed the Boxer Rebellion. Although some U.S. merchants and missionaries moved into the interior, the majority remained clustered in the autonomous foreign settlements in coastal cities. Like other privileged foreigners protected by unequal treaty rights, Americans enjoyed immunity from Chinese justice wherever they were. To safeguard U.S. lives and property, gunboats patrolled the Chinese coast and the Yangtze River.

Although the United States had become a significant imperialist presence in East Asia and the Pacific, its position there was much weaker than in Latin America. U.S. interests in the Western Hemisphere were backed by overwhelming military might, but in Asia the United States faced strongly entrenched European interests and the rapidly rising economic and military might of Japan. Controversy among Americans over the U.S. presence in East Asia also weakened the United States. As a result, U.S. policy in Asia tended to be tentative and reactive.

THE RISE OF JAPAN AS A GREAT POWER

The swift transformation of Japan from an isolated, traditional nation to a respected modern industrial power has fascinated the world. Japan's remarkable feat has been studied closely by those anxious to unlock the secrets of its phenomenal success. In 1900 Japan was the only Asian nation that had made the transformation to modern nationhood. Having broken the shackles that the West had placed upon it half a century earlier, Japan was ready to challenge Western dominance of Asia.

The Opening of Japan and the Meiji Restoration

Whereas Great Britain had taken the lead in the opening of China, it was the United States that forced Japan to open its doors to the world. In 1853 a U.S. naval squadron commanded by Commodore Matthew Perry arrived in Japan with an ultimatum that Japan sign a treaty. Perry invited Japanese leaders aboard his ships and showed them his formidable cannons, as well as displays of U.S. science and technology, including model trains and tracks. The Japanese were suitably impressed. They knew what had happened to the Chinese who resisted British might, and they bowed to the inevitable. Japan signed the treaty as demanded. Great Britain, Russia, France, and the Netherlands followed in the wake of the United States. These treaties opened up Japanese ports for trade with the West, fixed the tariff that the government of Japan could charge on imported goods, and granted extraterritorial rights to the Western signatory states.

In 1868, revolutionaries overthrew the ineffective feudal government that had bowed to the humiliating Western demands and returned authority to the figurehead emperor and his advisors. The event was called the Meiji Restoration, named after the young emperor who gained power as a result of the revolution. During the early years of the Meiji Restoration, Japan reconciled itself to the limitations that the unequal treaties had placed on its sovereignty. With the same zeal that they had manifested in learning from China over a thousand years earlier, the emperor and his youthful advisors began a program of reforms based on what they perceived to be the best Western models. As the Meiji emperor officially proclaimed in 1868: "Knowledge shall be sought throughout the world so as to strengthen the foundation of imperial rule." For example, the Japanese decided to build an army on the French model because it was commonly believed then that the French army was the best in the world. When France was resoundingly defeated by Germany in the war of 1870–1871, the Japanese quickly switched mentors and patterned their army on that of victorious Germany. Following the same logic, they established a navy based on the British model.

The crowning political achievement of the Meiji Restoration was the promulgation of a constitution in 1889, which made Japan the first Asian nation to commit itself to the daring innovation of constitutional government. In the early 1880s, a constitutional commission had spent several years studying the forms of government of Western nations. They found the political system of Germany most congenial to Japan's needs and drafted a constitution that approximated it closely. The Meiji Constitution, promulgated as a gift of the emperor to the people, pronounced the imperial line as divinely descended, protected many imperial prerogatives, and made the emperor commander-in-chief of the military forces. However, in a dramatic departure from Japanese tradition, it created a bicameral legislature, known in English as the Diet, which consisted of a largely hereditary House of Peers and a popularly elected lower house. The Diet's consent was needed in all money matters and in making permanent laws. Adult men who paid a certain level of taxes (about

The Meiji emperor proclaiming the constitution in 1889.

5 percent of adult males) were eligible to vote in the 1890 election. In subsequent years the qualifications for male eligibility to vote went down progressively, but women were denied the vote until after World War II. Political parties were permitted to contest the elections. The Meiji Constitution also provided for government by a prime minister and his cabinet. In time it was accepted that the prime minister and cabinet must receive majority endorsement by the Diet. It also guaranteed a host of freedoms.

The goal of the early reforms was to strengthen Japan so that it would not have to suffer further losses to its sovereignty. A later goal was to help it recover lost sovereign rights by convincing Western powers that the Japanese were as good as Westerners. In the following pages we will look at the important areas of change and modernization.

A Modern Economy

Japan's successful transition from an agricultural to an industrial nation was the result of government planning and cooperation between the government and private enterprise. The government took the lead in developing a modern economy by providing a modern transportation and communication network and by denoting certain key industries and mines as national enterprises. Japan was leery of contracting foreign loans because of the onerous conditions such borrowing entailed, and so it financed modernization by squeezing tax revenues out of the farming sector. After defeating China in 1895, Japan exacted a monetary indemnity from China and used it to finance further industrial expansion.

To plan and ensure steady growth, the government created a ministry of industry that coordinated strategic nationalized industries with nonstrategic private enterprises such as the textile industry. After the key industries were firmly established, the government sold them at low prices to private capitalists. Thus a strong private sector developed, dominated by a few large firms called *zaibatsu*, conglomerates that worked hand in glove with the government. The two largest *zaibatsu* were Mitsui and Mitsubishi, each of which had many affiliates that straddled all segments of the economy.

Up to World War I Japan's heavy industries were mainly designed to meet its strategic and military needs. Since it lacked key raw materials such as iron ore and coal, Japanese military strategists were concerned about the security of the sea lanes and the reliability of the foreign sources of raw materials. In light industry, the early emphasis was on building silk and cotton mills, which required little capital, had a traditional base, and mostly employed low-paid, docile young women from the farms. The Japanese government desired not only a rapid industrialization but also a peaceful one. To forestall industrial unrest, it provided legislation that ensured factory safety and provided workers with some welfare programs. At the same time, the Peace Preservation Law of 1900 outlawed strikes.

Japan's transition from an agrarian to an industrial society was not without dislocations and problems, but since its industrialization came relatively late, these problems were not as acute as those experienced by earlier industrializing nations such as Great Britain. As "latecomers," Japanese planners, like those in Germany, benefited from knowing and avoiding many of the economic problems that had beset Great Britain and other pioneering nations in the industrial revolution.

The pattern of Japanese industrialization differed from those of European nations and the United States. This was partly a result of the uniquely Japanese employment system, which had three distinctive and interrelated characteristics that have persisted throughout the twentieth century. First was the low turnover rate in the labor force. Second was a strong mutual loyalty between employer and employee; both prefer a lifelong commitment to each other, and workers identify with their employer, who tries not to lay them off. Third was the prevalence of company-provided welfare and benefits programs for employees. These factors contributed significantly to Japan's successful and rapid industrialization.

Farmers, through payment of high taxes, financed Japan's industrialization and supplied its labor force. They also produced agricultural goods for export in exchange for foreign machinery and raw materials, and grew the food for the expanding urban population. Adoption of modern farming techniques and the introduction of chemical fertilizers increased the per acreage yield on the limited arable land available in Japan. Thus, up to about 1900,

Japanese farmers were able to feed a growing population and maintain a tolerable standard of living despite the high burden of taxes they endured.

Whereas the population had been relatively stable in the premodern era, the introduction of modern science and medicine resulted in a rapid increase. Between 1903 and 1919 the population grew from 46 to 56 million people, about 20 percent. Since all arable land was already under intense cultivation, the land could not support additional people. The surplus was siphoned off to the new commercial and industrial cities such as Tokyo, Yokohama, Nagoya, Osaka, and Kobe. By 1900 only about half of the population remained on the land; but even in a period of rapid industrial growth, the supply of labor increased faster than demand. Wages, therefore, remained low, and the standard of living for the average person did not improve significantly during the early twentieth century.

After 1900 Japanese farm production could no longer keep up with urban population growth, and food began to make up a significant part of Japanese imports. This growing dependence on imported food, a situation similar to that faced by Great Britain, worried planners, who feared what this might mean in wartime. Aware that Great Britain's situation was eased by the dominance of its navy and by food produced in its colonies and dominions, Japanese leaders also sought to acquire colonies that would supply a dependable food source. They created a strong military force that was ready to implement an expansionist foreign policy.

Modernizing Education, the Bureaucracy, and the Military

A fundamental reason for Japan's successful modernization was the system of universal education instituted in the early years of the Meiji Restoration. By 1907 universal compulsory education lasted for six years, and about 5 million boys and girls were attending 27,000 elementary schools. Secondary schools emphasized vocational and technical training and thus provided a firm base for Japan's industrial advance. The imperial universities trained the sons of the elite for the bureaucracy and the professions. Teachers' and women's colleges trained females for teaching, nursing, and other selected professions. A highly organized educational bureaucracy monitored the school system and, after 1903, compiled all textbooks. Illiteracy virtually disappeared.

Several themes were stressed in textbooks for the Japanese student: loyalty to the emperor and the state, selfless patriotism, and duty to family. An Imperial Rescript on Education that stated these values was issued in 1890. A copy of the rescript was hung beside the emperor's portrait in every classroom. It became the basis of the moral and ethical instruction of all Japanese children.

The bureaucracy and the military were the twin pillars of Meiji Japan, and Japan's modern education system became the foundation of its efficient bureaucracy. At the heart of the civil service were several thousand graduates of the elite Imperial (later Tokyo) University. Civil servants enjoyed high respect, both because of their rigorous academic training and as "officials of the emperor." They drafted legislation for the Diet, had access to cabinet ministers, and generally controlled the administration. As members of a career bureaucracy, they were immune from outside political influences, popular favor, or special interests. Therefore they were a stabilizing factor in society.

Military education was rigidly specialized and produced an officer corps with a distinctive outlook and experience that emphasized obedience, esprit de corps, and fanatical nationalism. Japanese officers viewed themselves as heirs of the nation's ancient military tradition, and since their education was narrowly limited, they tended to propose simple solutions to complex modern problems. The ordinary citizen, accustomed for generations to respecting rulers from the hereditary military class, or *samurai*, looked up to the military. Successful in war, the military provided the people with national heroes. Its image was also helped by government propaganda that placed great emphasis on loyalty and devotion to the imperial cause and to its champions, the army and navy.

For centuries the *samurai* had in fact ruled Japan, but after the Meiji Restoration all males were liable for military service. The end of the monopoly of the *samurai* class over the military by no means diminished the importance of the armed forces, which continued to dominate society and command respect. In an imperialistic age, the army and navy had no difficulty demonstrating their importance. The emperor was commander-in-chief of the armed forces under the Meiji Constitution. He was advised in military matters by ministers who were active senior officers of the army and the navy, nominated by their respective services. In time, the military establishment began to control the civilian cabinets and cabinet policy. If the army and navy leaders did not like a proposed cabinet, they refused to nominate men to serve in the army and navy posts. If a cabinet did not do the military's bidding, they ordered their respective ministers to resign. Since no cabinet could survive without army and navy ministers, the armed services in effect exercised veto power over the formation and survival of governments. In both absolute and proportional terms, military expenditures increased year by year, from about one-third of the national budget in 1894 to nearly one-half by 1913.

To strengthen the state's claim of unquestioning obedience and loyalty from its citizens, the Meiji Constitution made Shintoism Japan's official religion. Shinto means "The Way of the Gods," and is unique to Japan. Shinto creation myths tell of the divine origin of the imperial house. Until 1945, Shintoism was used to instill patriotism among the Japanese and in part to justify Japanese aggression.

The Transformation of Japanese Society

Industrialization and modernization depended on new skills, attitudes, and knowledge. Japan's success in these endeavors was due to farsighted leadership as well as to the responsiveness of millions of its citizens, who felt that Westernization was the wave of the future and were willing to make sacrifices to bring it about. Some of the copying was indiscriminate, such as the adoption of Western dress and hair styles, handshaking, and ballroom dancing. Many mansions of the rich began to sport "Western rooms" furnished in the Victorian manner.

On the other hand, some of the changes were fundamental. Legal reform was one: To win acceptance by the West, it was necessary to change Japanese legal institutions, which was done in the 1890s based on the German model. This paved the way for the end of unequal treaties and extraterritorial rights for Westerners. However, Western legal reforms brought with them the Western concepts and value judgments on which they were based. Although it was easier to understand and accept Western fashion and scientific techniques than morals and ideas, the latter also began to make inroads. Westernization was speeded along by the hundreds of Westerners hired to work in Japan as experts and teachers, by Christian missionaries and their schools, by the thousands of young Japanese men and women who went to the West to study, and by Western language books translated into Japanese.

The many rapid changes of the Meiji era were nothing short of revolutionary. Old legal class distinctions were abolished, old laws were replaced, and many old norms were regarded as obsolete. The old static but stable society was replaced by shifting populations and unstable social relationships in the dynamic new industrial cities. While there was no turning back, some social critics nevertheless lamented the passing of the old ways.

JAPAN BECOMES AN IMPERIALIST POWER

Leaders of Meiji Japan turned to imperialism when they saw that their modernization programs were successful and continued on that course until 1945. There were several reasons for this quest for conquest and empire. One was historical precedent. In the late sixteenth century, powerful Japanese warlords had dreamt of conquering China and invaded Korea as a first step. Other reasons were the prevailing mood of the late nineteenth century and the teachings of social Darwinism, which glorified imperialism as a symbol of international success and racial superiority. Having suffered humiliation by Western powers, Meiji leaders sought international recognition and equality with the great powers by demonstrating military prowess and by conquering colonies. Finally, economic motivation was also important; resource-poor Japan sought security in colonies that would provide secure raw materials and markets.

Japanese diplomatic efforts in the late nineteenth century focused on treaty revision or on the negotiation of new, equal treaties to replace the old, unequal ones. It was argued that the Meiji Constitution of 1889 had placed Japan among the modern civilized nations and further that the adoption of modern legal codes no longer justified the enjoyment of extraterritorial rights by citizens of Western nations in Japan. Japanese arguments were apparently persuasive, for Great Britain signed a new treaty in 1894 that ended extraterritorial rights for British subjects in Japan within five years and also restored tariff autonomy to Japan. Other nations, impressed by Great Britain's leadership and by Japan's resounding victory over China in 1895, followed suit. By 1911 all treaties between Japan and Western nations were based on equality.

Despite its formal treaty status, however, Japanese pride was continually rankled by Western racist attitudes toward Asians, especially toward Japanese living in Western nations. It was most hurt by the treatment of Japanese nationals as inferior people in the United States. When the governments of the United States and Japan began negotiations over Japanese immigration to the United States and the treatment of Japanese by Euro-Americans, Japan's foremost concern was that its people should not in any way be treated as inferiors to peoples of European background. The U.S. government pressured local governments to modify their anti-Japanese ordinances, but the Japanese government ultimately decided that the only way to avoid international humiliation was to forbid some of its own nationals to emigrate to the United States, and the United States agreed. The arrangement was called the Gentlemen's Agreement of 1908. Despite this, the U.S. Congress passed an Exclusion Act in 1924 that specifically designated Japanese immigrants as ineligible for citizenship.

Japan's First Victims: China and Korea

From the 1890s on, Japanese foreign policy had the twin goals of self-aggrandizement and the reduction of Western influence in East Asia. Japan defeated China resoundingly in the Sino-Japanese War of 1894–1895 and forced China to cede Taiwan (Formosa), which became its first overseas colony. Victory against China also brought Japan an indemnity, and Japanese citizens in China obtained the extraterritorial rights enjoyed by Westerners.

Japan was now gaining confidence to seek equality with Western nations. The main issue that had led to the Sino-Japanese War had been control of Korea, a Chinese vassal state that Japan coveted. The 1894–1895 war eliminated Chinese political influence from Korea, but the impotent Korean government could ward off neither Japanese nor Russian imperialistic advances. Russia was interested in Korea for its ice-free ports, its resources, and the prestige that control of that state would give. Similar reasons motivated Japan, except that Japanese industries were more in need of such Korean raw materials as iron ore and coal. Thus Japan regarded the possibility of Russian control over Korea as "a dagger pointed at her heart," which it must ward off at all costs.

Beyond Korea, both powers also coveted Manchuria, a sparsely populated part of northeastern China that was rich in both agricultural and mineral resources. During 1900, using suppression of the Boxer disturbances as an excuse, Russia poured 175,000 troops into Manchuria and refused to evacuate them after the Boxer Rebellion had been put down. In 1903, in a blatant gesture of imperialism, the Russian government created a new position of Viceroy of the Far East and gave its appointee authority to advance Russian interests in Manchuria and Korea. The proexpansion faction was definitely in the ascendant in the Russian court, and Russia seemed determined to have its way in East Asia.

Since Japan was equally determined not to concede, it began to prepare for war. Between 1893 and 1903 the Japanese military budget increased by more than 300 percent. Japanese leaders also realized the need for allies who could give it support in times of international crisis and found one in Great Britain. In the Anglo-Japanese Alliance of 1902, the two powers agreed to aid each other in their respective imperialist goals in East and South Asia. The treaty was the first modern military pact between a Western and a non-Western nation concluded on the basis of equality. It also provided for British neutrality if Japan went to war against one enemy, and British assistance should Japan become embroiled in war against two or more nations, and vice versa. This last provision, more than any other, strengthened Japan's hand in its rivalry with Russia.

The Russo-Japanese War: Japan Electrifies the World

While it was completing its military preparations, Japan negotiated with Russia. Since neither side offered any concessions, the talks bogged down. The Japanese navy then made a surprise attack and sank the Russian Far Eastern Fleet in its harbor at Port Arthur in southern Manchuria (a Russian sphere of influence in northeastern China). Two days later, Japan declared war.

Most of the battles of the Russo-Japanese War were fought in Manchuria. It was a measure of China's impotence that it could do nothing to prevent the two antagonists from conducting their campaigns on its territory. The Russians were divided by social unrest and felt no unity of purpose in waging the war, and the morale of Russian troops was low. Conversely, the war was popular in Japan and morale was high. Japan's modern military machine won spectacular victories on both land and sea. Russian troops were first expelled from Korea and then surrendered in Port Arthur after suffering a five-month siege. In March 1905, Japan captured Mukden, the chief city of Manchuria, after a battle in which about 400,000 troops were engaged on each side. In May, the Russian Baltic Fleet, which had sailed from Europe via South Africa, was destroyed in the Korean Straits by the Japanese navy under Admiral Togo Heihachiro. This last feat aroused admiration for the Japanese all over the world, as was evident in President Theodore Roosevelt's excitement as he wrote: "This is the greatest phenomenon the world has ever seen. Even the battle of Trafalgar could not match this."

Defeated on both land and sea, Russia sought peace. Japan, too, was exhausted. When President Roosevelt offered to mediate, both sides accepted eagerly, and the peace conference opened in August 1905 in Portsmouth, New Hampshire. Many of the negotiating sessions were held on a yacht loaned by banking magnate J. P. Morgan. Roosevelt was motivated partly by a desire to achieve a settlement before either side gained a complete victory, which would jeopardize the Open Door policy the United States was trying to uphold in Manchuria. Ability to host a major peace conference and mediate a peace treaty would also enhance U.S. international prestige. Although both China and Korea were to be vitally affected by the peace terms, neither was invited to the conference.

In the Treaty of Portsmouth, Russia acknowledged Japan's "paramount interests" in Korea and agreed to cede to Japan its railroad rights and sphere of influence in southern Manchuria. Russia also ceded to Japan the southern half of the island of Sakhalin but paid no indemnity. The Japanese people had expected more for their sacrifices, and riots broke out in many Japanese cities when the terms of the treaty were published. The Japanese negotiators had to sneak home to avoid physical harm from popular anger. Roosevelt received the Nobel Prize for Peace.

Japan interpreted its "paramount position" in Korea to mean control of key Korean government agencies, which it proceeded to force on the weak Korean government. Those Koreans who did not wish to be ruled by Japan protested and rioted. In 1907, the king of Korea secretly sent a delegation with an appeal against Japanese imperialism to the Hague International Peace Conference, then in session, but the conference refused to receive it. Next, Japan forced the Korean king to abdicate and placed his feebleminded son on the throne instead. In late 1909 a Korean patriot assassinated the Japanese resident-general in Korea. This event gave Japan the pretext it needed to annex Korea, which was done on August 22, 1910. Thus began a harsh colonial rule that lasted until 1945.

The Russo-Japanese War was a landmark conflict for both Japan and the world. There was now little doubt about Japan's great-power status. Its victory gave inspiration to peoples under or threatened by Western imperialism. As Jawaharlal Nehru, later prime minister of independent India, said in his autobiography, it was a "great pick-me-up for Asia." Territorial gains from both wars and the potential for more definitely set Japan on the path of imperialism that ended only with its defeat in World War II.

SUMMARY

Drawn westward by prospects for a lucrative Asian trade, the United States acquired Hawaii and other island bases across the Pacific. The United States also conquered the Philippine Islands, where it created a relatively enlightened colonial administration. U.S. merchants who had acquired a share of the Chinese market were anxious that their government act on their behalf to preserve and expand that share. The United States did not establish an exclusive sphere of influence in China but instead formulated an Open Door policy aimed at equal opportunity for all foreigners in that nation.

Japan was opened to the modern world by the threat of force by the United States. Failure of the government to defend the nation brought about a political revolution in Japan, called the Meiji Restoration. The new rulers of Japan, supported by the people, set out to learn everything they could from the Western world, which they did with astonishing success and great speed. In one generation, Japan was transformed from an isolated, traditional land to a modern nation with industries, a bureaucratic infrastructure, competent schools, Western-influenced law codes, and a constitutional government that gave a voice to the people. Its accomplishments inspired admiration, won for it formal international equality, and made it the inspiration for other peoples who also aspired to success.

Japanese leaders were first and foremost motivated by national security considerations when they embarked on their modernization program. Once they were secure, the nature of Japanese national goals changed: Japanese nationalism became imperialism. The Japanese believed that they had to control the raw materials and markets of Asia if their progress in industrialization and modernization was to continue. Japan went to war against China and Russia to achieve those goals and succeeded, acquiring Taiwan and Korea as colonies and securing extensive economic rights in resource-rich Manchuria.

The rapidity and success of Japanese expansion in Asia in general and its defeat of Russia in particular surprised and impressed the Western powers and was a matter of great pride for the Japanese. Asians admired Japan for defeating Europeans but feared its mounting aggressiveness. Initially the United States and Japan were primarily interested in competing with the imperialist European powers, already established in East Asia, but tensions between the two new imperialist nations heralded greater conflicts to come.

SUGGESTED SOURCES

BEASLEY, WILLIAM G., *The Rise of Modern Japan* (1990). A history of Japan since the Meiji Restoration.

BERNSTEIN, GAIL LEE, *Recreating Japanese Women, 1600–1945* (1991). A team of scholars wrote this richly varied book.*

CONROY, HILLARY, *The Japanese Seizure of Korea, 1868–1910* (1974). An account of Japanese imperialism at work in its early phase.*

CREIGHTON MILLER, STUART, *"Benevolent Assimilation": The American Conquest of the Philippines, 1899–1903* (1982). A colorful account of the Philippine-American War, drawing heavily from contemporary American newspaper materials.

GRISWOLD, A. WHITNEY, *The Far Eastern Policy of the United States* (1966). A well-written and comprehensive overview of U.S. action in the Philippines and China.

JANSEN, MARIUS B., *Japan and China: From War to Peace, 1894–1972* (1975). A survey of Sino-Japanese relations in modern times.

MICHENER, JAMES, *Hawaii* (1978). A saga about Hawaiians, missionaries, white traders, Chinese and Japanese settlers.* (Also a film.)

NEUMANN, WILLIAM L., *America Encounters Japan* (1969). A study of the ideas and attitudes that shaped U.S. foreign policy toward Japan.*

REISCHAUER, EDWIN O., *The United States and Japan*, 4th ed. (1978). A brief, interesting survey of the relationship between the two nations by a former U.S. ambassador to Japan.*

*Paperback available.

CHAPTER 8

The Origins of World War I

On June 28, 1914, a Serbian nationalist assassinated the Austrian archduke and heir to the throne, Franz Ferdinand, in Sarajevo, Bosnia. While Ferdinand was sitting in the open back seat of a car—it was a beautiful sunny day—a nineteen-year-old youth stepped out into the street and fired several shots. Before the archduke himself expired—after several times dismissing his wound as "nothing"—his wife Sophie had already died from a bullet in the stomach. The assassin was Gavrilo Princip, a Bosnian of Serbian nationality. Himself stricken with tuberculosis, he was fond of quoting Nietzsche's lines from *Ecce Homo:* "Insatiable as the flame, I glow and consume myself." Princip wished to see Bosnia break away from the Austro-Hungarian Empire and become part of a Greater Serbia. Austria-Hungary soon declared war on Serbia, and by August 4 most of the major European powers were involved in World War I. To understand how a major war could follow from the shooting of an Austrian archduke, it is necessary to investigate the combustible atmosphere that transformed the spark of an assassination into an all-consuming fire that would bring about the deaths of millions.

NATIONALISM

Nationalism was the first element at work. This passion was especially strong in the Balkans. Serbia had gained complete independence from the Ottoman Empire in 1878. In that year, major European powers at the Congress of Berlin allowed Austria-Hungary to occupy Bosnia and Herzegovina despite the fact that these provinces were still legally part of the Ottoman Empire and that most of the population in both provinces consisted of Serbians. After King Peter I came to the throne in 1903, Serbia stepped up its efforts to incorporate ethnic Serbian areas still outside its national borders; it was outraged when Austria completely annexed Bosnia and Herzegovina in 1908. Serbia made threats and appealed to Russia for help. Germany promised Austria its backing and sent the Russians a

Sarajevo, 1914: Austrian Archduke Franz Ferdinand and his wife in the rear of the automobile in which they would soon be assassinated.
(UPI/Bettmann Newsphotos)

note demanding that the tsarist government recognize the annexation and not support Serbia in the matter. Russia yielded, and without Russian support Serbia had to acknowledge the annexation. As a result of strong Austrian pressure, Serbia also promised to cease activities that were hostile to its northern neighbor.

Despite its promise, however, Serbia failed to curtail such actions. In fact, within a short period, several new nationalistic societies appeared. One of these was the conspiratorial group "Unity or Death," commonly referred to as the "Black Hand," which specialized in encouraging ethnic Serbs in areas such as Bosnia to work for unification with Serbia. It helped to smuggle men, guns, and propaganda to sympathetic individuals still outside Serbian borders. Led by the chief of intelligence of the Serbian army, the Black Hand organized Princip's bloody deed.

Although this act of Serbian nationalism had precipitated the crisis, the nationalism displayed by other powers widened it. Kaiser Wilhelm II and segments of the German public, including many intellectuals and politicians, believed in the superiority of the German nation and culture. Some Germans dreamed of uniting all Germans in a Pan-German state that would include large areas of Austria-Hungary.

Pan-Germanists were countered by Russian Pan-Slavists, who dreamed of politically uniting with Russia the many Orthodox Slavs who populated the Balkans. As the control of the Ottoman Empire in the Balkans weakened during the century preceding World War I, the Russians planned to exercise increasing influence in the area but instead suffered a number of disappointments. Russia lost the influence it once had in Bulgaria, and, along with Serbia, suffered a diplomatic defeat when Austria-Hungary annexed Bosnia and Herzegovina in 1908.

A quickening of French nationalism was also apparent. An anti-German disturbance in late 1913 in a French town in the German provinces of Alsace-Lorraine symbolized the painful loss of these provinces to Germany in the Franco-Prussian War. Ten-year-old Raymond Poincaré had watched the Germans march through his hometown in Lorraine in 1870. Elected premier of France in 1912 and president in 1913, he played an active role in leading France into war with Germany in 1914.

Nor were the Serbians, Germans, Russians, and French alone in their nationalism. As Winston Churchill later wrote about this period, "National passions, unduly exalted in the decline of religion, burned beneath the surface of every land with fierce, if shrouded fires." Not even the rival faith of socialism could compete with nationalism. For twenty-five years, the Second International Workingman's Association had preached the international brotherhood of the working class. It had also often criticized war, attributing it to capitalist forces. Yet the vast majority of its members supported their homelands in the crucial days of early August 1914.

IMPERIALISM

Imperialism was the second combustible element in the prewar atmosphere. The influential German historian Fritz Fischer has written of German imperialistic aims in Europe, Africa, and the Near East and identified them as a chief cause of the war. Although some historians have disputed his charges, what is undeniable is that imperialistic rivalries stimulated hostile feelings between some of the major European powers.

The first Moroccan crisis of 1905 serves as an excellent illustration. In 1904 Great Britain and France had concluded the Entente Cordiale, an understanding concerning their overseas spheres of influence. As part of the agreement, Great Britain recognized France's desire to control Morocco. Germany disliked the Entente and thought that a stiff challenge to the French position in Morocco might split it apart. In 1905 Kaiser Wilhelm II landed at Tangier and recognized the sultan of Morocco as a ruler independent of French control. Wilhelm also demanded an international conference, which assembled in 1906, to discuss the situation. Meanwhile, the British had become so alarmed at German belligerence over Morocco, as well as at the continuing German naval build-up, that they moved much closer to France. While not going as far as the French would have liked—a promise of British support in case of war with Germany—Great Britain's foreign minister, Sir Edward Grey, did authorize informal military conversations with the French. These conversations continued from time to time over the years and strengthened the impression among some French statesmen that Great Britain would back France in case of a war with Germany.

In addition to bringing Great Britain closer to France, the Moroccan crisis also helped to bring about the Anglo-Russian Entente in 1907. It was not an alliance but primarily a settlement over spheres of influence in Persia,

Afghanistan, and Tibet. Nevertheless, it brought Great Britain closer to Russia, France's ally. The entente increased the Germans' fear of encirclement and to some extent induced them to vigorously back the Dual Monarchy in the annexation crisis of 1908—itself a manifestation of Austro-Hungarian imperialism. Again in 1914, Germany's uncompromising support of Austria-Hungary reflected its fear of losing its only real ally.

MILITARISM

Militarism also contributed to the outbreak of World War I. European nations feverishly expanded their military forces and armaments in the years immediately before 1914. German and Austrian military spending doubled between 1910 and 1914, and other European nations increased their expenditures markedly. By 1914 both Germany and France had each assembled standing armies of 800,000 men, with a million more in the reserves. About 1.2 million Russians were under arms, although the Russian army was inferior in equipment, training, and leadership. By 1905 the British had begun construction on a new battleship, the *Dreadnought,* designed to be the most powerful ship ever built. Germany responded with increased naval expenditures of its own. From 1900 to 1911, German naval spending nearly tripled. Such contests did little to increase the security of either side; instead they heightened the hostility and mistrust already existing among nations.

Another manifestation of the militarism of the era was the failure of the peace conferences of 1899 and 1907. Most government and military leaders were more concerned with keeping up in the arms race and maintaining absolute national sovereignty than with achieving disarmament and arbitrating disputes. At the 1907 conference, the delegates quickly postponed the issue of disarmament and passed a resolution calling for further study of the question. The delegates then spent weeks thrashing out the guidelines for the proper conduct of warfare. It was as if they were saying to the world, "Disarmament is a fool's dream, but war will surely come. So let us agree on the rules."

In this militaristic era, the plans and advice of military leaders played an increasingly influential role in government decisions. Germany chose war in 1914 partly because it feared that if it waited, Russia's rearmament program would make Russia a stronger foe. Germany's Schlieffen Plan, which the French and Russian generals knew in broad outline, was a key factor in the peace options and war plans of several nations. In the plan, the German general staff had assumed that in a two-front war with France and Russia, Germany could not defeat both opponents simultaneously. Germany had therefore decided to knock out France first by an invasion through Belgium, while holding off the slowly mobilizing Russians. After defeating France, Germany would then concentrate its forces in the east and crush the Russians. For this plan to work, the German military could not give the Russians a significant head start in mobilizing their forces. Russia, on the other hand, reacting in part to strong French pressure, had to do just what the Germans hoped they could not do—

divert German troops to the Russian front before France could be defeated. Other nations had their own military plans that demanded lead time for mobilization and deployment of troops.

Thus, in those final hectic days, military considerations afforded diplomacy little time to reach a peaceful settlement. Because it included the military necessity of invading neutral Belgium, the Schlieffen Plan was also likely to bring Great Britain, which wanted nearby Belgium free from either French or German control, into the war.

That troops, weapons, and plans had such influence was partly a result of the continuing belief that war could be more beneficial than harmful. On the eve of World War I, most European leaders still expected a brief and not terribly destructive war—a "short, cleansing thunderstorm" in Winston Churchill's words.

THE ALLIANCE SYSTEM AND WAR PREPARATION

As the events of July and August 1914 clearly indicate, the two European alliance systems were the mechanisms that transformed a local conflict into World War I. After the shooting of Ferdinand, Austria was convinced that the Serbian government was implicated. The government in Vienna believed that, one way or another, it must crush the threat to its empire posed by advocates of Greater Serbia. Before acting, however, Austria sought to keep Russia from mobilizing to aid Serbia, or at least to ensure German backing against Russia should intervention occur. Germany granted almost unconditional backing—a "blank check"—to her ally in early July, and Austria sent an ultimatum to Serbia on July 23. Austria demanded an end to anti-Austrian organizations and propaganda, the removal of officers and officials accused by Austria of being hostile, Austrian participation in the investigation of the assassination plot, and the suppression of subversive movements directed against Austria-Hungary. The Serbian government was given forty-eight hours to reply.

Serbia was aware that Russia, its chief supporter, advised caution but would nevertheless ultimately back Serbia in case of hostilities. Russia supported Serbia because after the diplomatic defeat of 1908 it did not wish to lose further influence and power in the Balkans to Austria-Hungary. Serbia was Russia's last bastion of influence in the area. If Austria were allowed to crush Serbia, either diplomatically or militarily, Russia's hopes in the Balkans would be finally smashed. After hearing of Austria's ultimatum, the Russian foreign minister, Sergei Sazanov, declared: "It means a European war!" He accused Austria of "setting fire to Europe," and on July 25 his government approved preliminary military preparations. This was done in the hope that it would frighten Austria into arriving at some sort of compromise. Russia also wished to be prepared in case it was necessary to come to the aid of Serbia.

In addition to its concern about Austria, the tsarist government had also become increasingly troubled about growing German influence in the Ottoman Empire. It is not difficult, therefore, to understand why some Russian

Inflamed with Patriotism

To me those hours seemed like a release from the painful feelings of my youth. . . . Overpowered by stormy enthusiasm, I fell down on my knees and thanked Heaven from an overflowing heart for granting me the good fortune of being permitted to live at this time.

A fight for freedom had begun, mightier than the earth had ever seen; for once Destiny had begun its course, the conviction dawned on even the broad masses that this time not the fate of Serbia or Austria was involved, but whether the German nation was to be or not to be. . . .

As a boy and young man I had so often felt the desire to prove at least once by deeds that for me national enthusiasm was no empty whim. . . . Thus my heart, like that of a million others, overflowed with proud joy that at last I would be able to redeem myself from this paralyzing feeling. I had so often sung *"Deutschland uber Alles"* and

shouted *"Heil"* at the top of my lungs, that it seemed to me almost a belated act of grace to be allowed to stand as a witness in the divine court of the eternal judge and proclaim the sincerity of this conviction. . . . [I] was ready at any time to die for my people and for the Reich which embodied it. . . . [D]ays later I was wearing the tunic which I was not to doff until nearly six years later.*

———————◆◆◆◆———————

Adolf Hitler, describing his feelings at the start of World War I, when he was twenty-five and living an impoverished life in Munich. On August 3, 1914, he volunteered to enlist in the German army. See Chapters 13 and 18 for more on Hitler's youth and his dictatorship in Germany.

*From *Mein Kampf* by Adolf Hitler, translated by Ralph Manheim. Copyright © 1943 by Houghton Mifflin Company. Reprinted by permission.

officials perceived the demands placed on Serbia as part of a united effort by Austria and Germany to strengthen the "Germanic" influence in areas long considered of special interest to the Russians.

Partly because of Russian support, Serbia did not accept all the Austrian demands. Nevertheless, its carefully worded reply reflected a conciliatory spirit. Austria, however, despite some belated German qualms, would recognize nothing less than unconditional acceptance. On July 28 Austria declared war on Serbia and bombarded Belgrade, the Serbian capital.

Meanwhile, Russia's ally, France, had been giving strong support to the tsarist government. The French remembered the 1870 war with Prussia (Germany, 1871) and did not wish to be isolated again in a struggle with Germany. Accordingly, they were prepared to give full backing to their major ally, Russia. In addition, a war against Germany, if won, held out the hope of recovering the lost provinces of Alsace and Lorraine. From July 20 to 23 French President Poincaré and Premier Viviani were in St. Petersburg encouraging the Russians to stand firm.

After some indecisiveness about how to proceed, on July 30 Russia finally decided on a general mobilization of its troops. The French encouraged such an action because France knew of the general thrust of the Schlieffen Plan. If Russia mobilized substantially ahead of Germany, there would be less likelihood that Germany could swiftly defeat France.

Because of Germany's war plan, it was no surprise that after several warnings on previous days, Germany, on July 31, sent an ultimatum with a twelve-hour limit demanding that Russia end its war preparations along the German frontier. On the same day, Germany asked the French government what its position would be in case of a Russian-German war. On August 1, the French replied that France would consult its own interests. On the same day, the government in Paris ordered mobilization. Germany also mobilized on that day and, having received no reply to its ultimatum, declared war on Russia. Two days later, certain that France was preparing to aid Russia and unwilling to lose any more time, Germany declared war on France and directed its attack through neutral Belgium.

As a result of British-French friendship and military conversations that followed from their entente and the Moroccan crisis of 1905, Great Britain had already been moving toward support of France. A few days before, for example, the British cabinet had voted to give assurance to the French that the British navy would protect the French coast and shipping against any German attack. However, the invasion of Belgium made it much easier to decide on a declaration of war. The neutrality of Belgium, just across the English Channel from Great Britain, was considered essential to British interests. Great Britain, along with France, Germany, Austria, and Russia, had been one of the guarantors of

Serbia, Austria, Russia, Germany, France, and Great Britain in a cartoon suggesting how the alliance systems would work.
(*Brooklyn Eagle*)

that neutrality since the Treaty of London in 1839. Thus, on August 4, Great Britain declared war on Germany. "All for just a word—'neutrality'—just for a scrap of paper," lamented Germany's Chancellor Bethmann-Hollweg, who nevertheless had earlier in the day stated: "Whatever our lot may be, August 4, 1914, will remain for all eternity one of Germany's greatest days."

With the British declaration, almost all the major European powers that would enter the war were committed. Great Britain, France, and Russia opposed Germany and Austria-Hungary. The fear of being left without an ally helped ensure such a widespread war. Italy, the ally of Germany and Austria-Hungary in the Triple Alliance, did not enter the war at this time on the grounds that the alliance was a defensive one, and that Germany had taken the offensive.

SUMMARY

The assassination of Archduke Franz Ferdinand was the immediate cause of World War I, but four prominent background factors helped to explain how such an event could lead to a war as vast as World War I. As with the Boxer Rebellion of 1900, nationalism, imperialism, and militarism again all played a part. So too did a fourth factor: the alliance system.

Historians have debated and will continue to debate which nation was most at fault. In recent years, many historians have followed Fischer's lead in placing the primary blame on Germany. Yet none of the nations that went to war in the summer of 1914 had done all they might have done to prevent the conflict from occurring. Despite some late and relatively weak diplomatic efforts to slow the rapid escalation of events, each nation finally valued security, prestige, influence, and allies more than peace. Only after years of death and destruction did many realize that in 1914 they had undervalued the fruits of peace and vastly underestimated the human and material costs of modern warfare.

SUGGESTED SOURCES

DEDIJER, VLADIMIR, *The Road to Sarajevo* (1966). A detailed but fascinating account of the events leading up to the assassination of Archduke Franz Ferdinand; sympathetic with the idealism of the conspirators.

EVANS, R. J. W., and HARTMUT POGGE VAN STRANDMANN, Eds., *The Coming of the First World War* (1989). A series of essays that delineates the position of each major country that entered the war in July and August and also looks at the influence of public opinion.*

FISCHER, FRITZ, *World Power or Decline* (1975). A summation of the author's controversial case for primarily blaming Germany's imperialist aims for causing World War I.*

HERWIG, HOLGER H., Ed., *The Outbreak of World War I: Causes and Responsibilities* (1991). A new edition and editor of a title first published in 1958 in the Heath "Problems" series. Contains an introduction and sixteen short selections representing different viewpoints.*

JOLL, JAMES, *The Origins of the First World War* (1984). A concise overview of the causes of the war and a reexamination of differing historical interpretations of them.*

KENNEDY, PAUL M., Ed., *The War Plans of the Great Powers, 1880–1914* (1985). An excellent and comprehensive collection of essays on the war.*

LAFORE, LAURENCE, *The Long Fuse* (1981). A readable work on the origins of the war that while emphasizing Serbian-Austrian tensions also examines the concerns of the other major powers.*

LIEVEN, D. C. B., *Russia and the Origins of the First World War* (1983). A clear, well-balanced analysis of why Russia became involved in World War I.*

REMAK, JOACHIM, *The Origin of World War I: 1871–1914* (1980). A good, brief, balanced introduction to the subject.*

TURNER, L. C. F., *Origins of the First World War* (1970). A brief account of the origin and causes of the war, highlighting Russia's culpability; especially good on the significance of military considerations.*

*Paperback available.

CHAPTER 9

World War I

Those who lived during the conflict that broke out in July and August 1914 called it the Great War; later it became known as World War I. Both names are appropriate, for 65 million people from 35 nations served in the armed forces, hundreds of millions of civilians were directly involved, and fighting occurred on three continents and throughout the oceans. The main struggle, however, was on the continent of Europe and in the adjacent North Atlantic waters. The war was the ultimate expression of the intense nationalism and militarism of the period. It also taught a grim lesson in how rapidly developing technology can overwhelm its creators; in World War I it sometimes appeared that the submarine, the cannon, the shrapnel bomb, and the machine gun were the real commanders.

THE OPENING PHASE OF THE WAR

In the beginning, it was a popular war. The citizens of the participating powers, conditioned by years of nationalistic propaganda, greeted their nation's declaration of war with enthusiasm. Cheering crowds showered flowers and gifts on the proud troops departing for the front. Most thought it would be a short war; they expected an early rout of the enemy and a glorious and profitable peace settlement for their nation. "You will be home before the leaves have fallen from the trees," Kaiser Wilhelm told his departing troops.

Upon declaring war, Germany immediately carried out its Schlieffen Plan. The Germans concentrated the bulk of their powerful army against France while assigning limited forces to hold off the slowly mobilizing Russians. German planners had modified the Schlieffen Plan, however, placing proportionately fewer troops on the wing that was to attack through Belgium than had originally been specified. Still, the German high command was confident that there were enough men to move the bulk of the German army in a great arc through Belgium and northern France, swinging around west of Paris and crushing the enemy in a vise in eastern France. All through August, the German armies moved forward, persistently pushing back their French, British, and Belgian opponents. By early September, approaching Paris, the Germans had curtailed their arc to swing southward to the east of Paris. They were also behind schedule, fatigued, and plagued with supply problems.

Under the leadership of General Joseph Joffre, the French and British reorganized the front. Beginning on September 5, at the Marne River, they threw their last reserves, some of them rushed by taxicabs through Paris, into a series of counterattacks. Although the counterattacks made only a limited penetration, the Germans decided to pull back northeastward to the Aisne River. The Schlieffen Plan had failed; subsequently, both sides extended the battleline to the seacoast, digging in along the way. By the middle of October 1914, a heavily fortified trench system, the Western Front, meandered 450 miles across Belgium and France from the North Sea to the Swiss border.

As the Germans were advancing across France in August, the Russians attacked more quickly than the Germans had expected. Two Russian armies swept into East Prussia and defeated German forces on the Prussian frontier. The German command diverted troops from the Western Front, but they arrived in East Prussia too late. Meanwhile, German forces already in East Prussia recovered quickly. Maneuvering their outnumbered forces brilliantly, General Paul von Hindenburg and his chief of staff, Erich von Ludendorff, annihilated one Russian army at Tannenberg and routed the other at the Masurian Lakes. Hindenburg became a popular hero, and Ludendorff eventually went on to direct all German army operations. However, the Germans were not yet strong enough to follow up their victories and invade Russia. Meanwhile, the Ottoman Empire and Bulgaria, each for its own reasons, joined Germany and Austria-Hungary. These four nations are traditionally called the Central Powers, and their opponents, the Allies.

THE PERIOD OF STALEMATE

Other battlefronts opened up in Europe during 1915 and 1916, but for the most part they became bogged down like the armies on the Western Front. Lured by British and French promises of Austrian and Ottoman territory, Italy attacked Austria in 1915. The new battlefront, located in mountainous terrain, soon became deadlocked. In a major strategic move, an Allied expeditionary force attempted to seize the Dardanelles (the passageway between the Mediterranean and the Black seas) with the object of defeating the Ottoman Empire and opening a water route to supply Russia. Ottoman forces pinned down the attackers at Gallipoli near the mouth of the Dardanelles and forced them to withdraw. In the Balkans, where the war had begun, German, Austrian, and Bulgarian troops overran Serbia. The British and French, always sensitive to any potential threat to their Mediterranean supply lines, rushed forces to northern Greece, but no active front developed there.

For almost two years, there was considerable movement on the Eastern Front. In 1915 and 1916 both sides launched major offensives that seized ground and lost it again, but the Germans steadily gained the upper hand and eventually conquered the Russian provinces of Poland and Lithuania. In 1916, German, Austrian, and Bulgarian forces overran Rumania, forcing the Russians to enter eastern Rumania in order to prevent an invasion of southern Russia. The Eastern Front now extended 1,200 miles from the Baltic to the Black Sea. Most of the front consisted of lightly defended sectors interspersed with heavily fortified strong points. Some areas of heavy forests and extensive swamps were not defended at all. Germany did not have sufficient forces to launch a decisive invasion of Russia; in that sense, the Eastern Front also became a stalemate.

THE WAR OUTSIDE EUROPE

Between 1914 and 1918, fighting spread around the world, although nowhere did it remotely attain the magnitude of the struggle in Europe. In Africa, Allied colonial troops captured German colonies isolated by the blockade. Togo, Cameroon, and German Southwest Africa were quickly overrun, but a small German force held out in part of German East Africa until the end of the war.

In Asia, the outbreak of war gave Japan an opportunity to improve its position in the Far East and in the western Pacific, and it lost little time in making the most of it. Following the terms of the Anglo-Japanese Alliance, Japan declared war on Germany. Japanese and British military units cleared German forces from its sphere of influence in China before the end of 1914. While Australian and New Zealand (ANZAC) forces were occupying German colonies south of the equator, units of the Japanese navy seized German-held islands north of it. After these conquests, Japan became essentially a noncombatant.

Japan also took advantage of the war to advance its imperialist designs on China. On January 18, 1915, the Japanese presented to the Chinese government the Twenty-One Demands, which would have turned China into an economic protectorate. In effect, Japan insisted on virtually direct controls over Manchuria, eastern Inner Mongolia, and the Shantung peninsula, and demanded a monopoly of iron ore and coal mining in the Yangtze valley. Japan also "requested" the right to build railroads in southern China and to share control over Chinese police units and arsenals. China looked for outside support, especially from the United States, in vain; alone and feeble, China capitulated on nearly all points on May 15, 1915. Japan subsequently secured pledges from Great Britain, France, Italy, and Russia that they would back Japan's claims in postwar negotiations. The United States, however, in a joint agreement with Japan, assented only to the vague statement that "Japan has special interests in China, particularly in that part to which her possessions are contiguous."

In the Middle East, the Allies faced a more formidable problem. Unlike Germany, which could not adequately defend its African and Asian colonies, the Ottoman Empire could devote a significant portion of its military forces to defending its Middle Eastern territories. The Ottoman army was on the whole not particularly well trained or led, but it was initially able to keep the Rus-

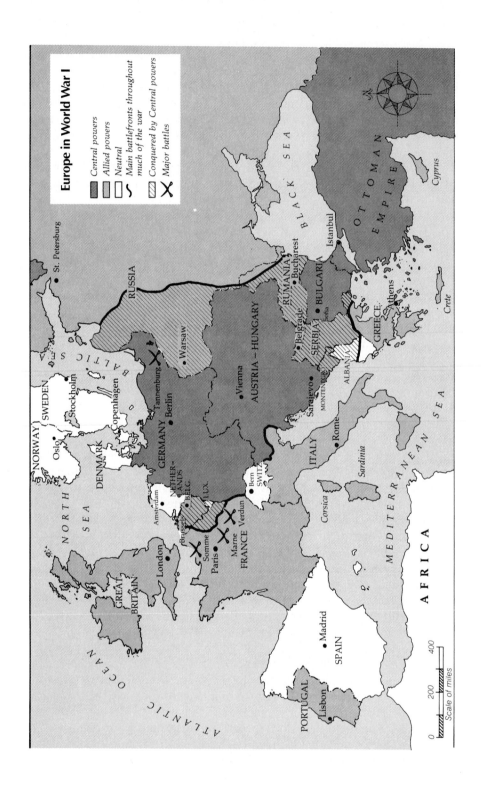

Europe in World War I

Central powers
Allied powers
Neutral
Main battlefronts throughout the war
Conquered by Central powers
Major battles

ATLANTIC OCEAN

NORTH SEA

BALTIC SEA

BLACK SEA

MEDITERRANEAN SEA

AFRICA

GREAT BRITAIN
• London

NORWAY
• Oslo

SWEDEN
Stockholm •

DENMARK
Copenhagen •

• St. Petersburg

RUSSIA

• Warsaw

GERMANY
• Berlin
Tannenburg ✗

NETHER-LANDS
Amsterdam •
Brussels • BELG.
LUX.

Verdun
Marne
• Paris
Somme
FRANCE

SWITZ.
Bern •

AUSTRIA – HUNGARY
• Vienna

ITALY
• Rome

Corsica

Sardinia

SPAIN
• Madrid

PORTUGAL
• Lisbon

RUMANIA
• Bucharest
Belgrade •
SERBIA
Sarajevo •
MONTEN.
ALBANIA
BULGARIA
Sofia •
GREECE
Athens •

Istanbul

OTTOMAN EMPIRE

Cyprus

Crete

0   200   400
Scale of miles

114

sians from advancing deep into Armenia, to repulse a British invasion of Iraq, to watch the British in Egypt, and to contain an Arab revolt in the Arabian peninsula. By 1917, however, Great Britain had assembled British, ANZAC, and colonial forces and begun driving into Palestine and Iraq. In addition, the romantic hero Colonel T. E. Lawrence, among others, helped the Arabs to mount a more effective revolt. By 1918 Ottoman control of the Middle East had collapsed and the region was fully in control of Allied and Arab forces.

In a reversal of recent European encroachment on the rest of the world, World War I saw military forces from the outside world appear in Europe. Contingents of troops from the British Empire, French colonial troops from Africa and Vietnam, and token units from Latin American nations saw service on the Allied side on the Western Front. A Japanese destroyer force patrolled the Mediterranean. In addition, the United States intervened massively. The presence of personnel from the other continents in Europe was a forewarning of the decline of European global power throughout the middle of the twentieth century.

THE WAR OF ATTRITION BECOMES "TOTAL WAR"

Bogged down in a stalemate, the leaders of the warring powers nevertheless refused to end the struggle and settle for "peace without victory," as President Wilson later advised. However, some leaders began to doubt that a major battlefront breakthrough would win the war and considered another approach to winning wars—attrition. In a war of attrition, instead of a decisive battlefield victory, a nation wins if it outlasts the other side's ability to carry on the conflict. There are two general ways, singly or in combination, to win a war of attrition. One is to bleed the enemy by causing so many casualties they can no longer sustain effective military operations and are finally forced to sue for peace. Another is to cut off supplies coming to the enemy from abroad, hampering the output of vital war materials. Such a cutoff also deprives the enemy's civilians of food, clothing, and fuel. Faced with mounting losses of loved ones on the battlefront and/or increasing deprivation at home, the civilians of the enemy power will force their government to make peace.

As the stalemate continued into 1915 and 1916 the struggle evolved into a war of attrition. Each government attempted to mobilize all the resources of its nation to win the war. In the process, the difference between the civilian population and the military forces became less distinct. Governments became more authoritarian, increasing their control over the economic, social, political, and cultural lives of their peoples. This process has been referred to by many historians as "total war."

The War on Land

Although there were extensive military activities elsewhere, both sides invested their main efforts on the Western Front, where six million troops were massed. The troops had fortified themselves in an intricate network of multi-

Death on the Western Front: A German patrol fires on a French patrol between the lines.
(Acme/UPI/Bettmann Newsphotos)

ple trenches, underground bunkers, barbed wire, and mine fields, all integrated with an extensive deployment of artillery, mortars, and machine guns. Elaborate support facilities, including railroad systems that reached back into the civilian support areas, supplied the front-line troops.

This combination of fortifications and weapons made it impossible for attacking infantry to break through to victory; frontal attacks produced enormous losses and insignificant gains. Throughout 1915, 1916, and 1917, the same grim scenario was played and replayed. The attackers would commence with a massive artillery bombardment along a front sometimes fifty miles wide. The bombardment might last for several days and was intended to clear out the mines and barbed wire, smash in the front-line trench system, and kill and wound many of the defenders, while others suffered shell shock and hysteria. The defenders would take refuge in their underground bunkers while reinforcements and artillery were rushed up and held ready in the rear. When the attackers' artillery barrage lifted and the attacking infantry surged forward, the defenders' artillery would rain shells on the attackers, and the defending infantry, reinforced, would come out of the bunkers, set up machine guns, and mow down the attacking infantry. The attackers would in their turn be reinforced, and occasionally penetrate a few miles or so, but eventually both the attackers and the defenders would become exhausted and break off the fighting.

As the war progressed, commanders would send their men into battle hoping for a breakthrough but willing to settle for killing and incapacitating more of the enemy's men than they lost of their own. "I am nibbling them," Joffre explained. Two of the most gruesome encounters came in 1916, when two million men were killed and wounded in battles at the Somme River and at Verdun. "Humanity . . . must be mad. . . . What scenes of horror and carnage! . . . Hell cannot be so terrible," wrote a French soldier at Verdun. Since the casualty rates were approximately equal, neither side "won." Other major offensives had the same results.

Between battles, men died from sniper fire, frontline patrols, random mortar fire, disease, exposure, and spoiled and adulterated rations. In Erich Remarque's novel *All Quiet on the Western Front,* the hero commented:

> Although we need reinforcement, the recruits give us almost more trouble than they are worth. They are helpless in these grim fighting areas, they fall like flies . . . a man must have a feeling for the contours of the ground, an ear for the sound and character of shells, must be able to decide beforehand where they will drop, how they will burst, and how to shelter from them.
>
> The young recruits of course know none of these things. They get killed simply because they hardly can tell shrapnel from high-explosives, they are mown down. . . . They flock together like sheep instead of scattering. . . . Some of them in a shell hole took off their gas masks too soon; they did not know that the gas lies longest in the hollows. . . . Their condition is hopeless, they choke to death with haemorrhages and suffocation.

Survivors had to endure crowded quarters, trench foot, rats, lice, mud, loss of comrades, and the probability of death during the next offensive. Under such conditions, men became living automatons. "We are not leading the lives of men at all," one British soldier wrote, "but that of animals, living in holes in the ground, and only showing outside to fight and to feed." Some deserted, and on occasions there were mutinies. Most of the troops, however, kept on fighting loyally.

In an attempt to find a way out of the stalemate, each side invented new weapons. They used poison gas and flamethrowers, but in particular, special hopes were pinned on developing effective airplanes and tanks that might help the infantry to break through entrenchments. Both sides used airplanes and dirigibles (propelled lighter-than-air craft) for observation and for attacks on the front lines and the rear support areas. Airplanes fought each other in spectacular "dogfights," and skillful pilots ("aces") became romantic heroes in an otherwise grim war of impersonal death. Airplanes and dirigibles also attacked cities behind the battlefronts, often for the specific purpose of demoralizing the civilian population. The phenomenon of civilians suffering the same grisly deaths as soldiers and sailors foretold the nature of wars to come. Tanks became a major supporting weapon for infantry attacks late in the war. When used in conjunction with airplanes, they gave the promise of breaking through entrenched positions and thus returning combat to a war of maneuver. However, neither the airplane nor the tank was fully developed during the war, and they were not decisive in bringing victory.

The War at Sea

While attempting to wear down the enemy on the battlefield, military leaders also pursued another goal of the war of attrition—cutting off supplies coming to the enemy by sea. Germany and particularly Great Britain depended on overseas sources of raw materials and food, and both nations were thus vulnerable to enemy navies. To protect its own trade and to cut off the commerce of any wartime enemy, Great Britain had built up the world's largest navy. Early in the war, the British mined the North Sea approaches to Germany and cleared German surface raiders from the sea. In addition, the British seized all merchant ships carrying contraband, which Great Britain in effect defined as any product that might help the enemy war effort. The British even seized neutral ships heading for neutral nations if the British suspected their cargoes would be reshipped to Germany. Neutral nations, including the United States, protested; but despite the seizures U.S. shipping to Europe continued. Since little could get through to Germany, U.S. trade benefited the Allies almost exclusively. Although some supplies continued to get through, as time passed it became clear that in the long run the British blockade would strangle Germany.

Germany could also play the blockading game. Great Britain depended on large numbers of ships daily docking at its ports to feed its people and to keep its factories running. If its supplies were cut off, Great Britain would crumble much faster than Germany, and if Great Britain dropped out of the war, France would not last long. To starve out the British, the Germans had developed the submarine, an effective new weapon labeled by a British admiral as "underhanded, unfair, and un-English."

Beginning in earnest in 1915, German U-boats fanned out over the western approaches to Great Britain, destroying shipping at a rapid rate. At first, even though their submarines were vulnerable to attacks by airplanes and destroyers when they surfaced, German commanders tried to follow the rules of war by warning British merchant vessels so that their crews could take to the lifeboats. To counter the submarine blockade, the British began to arm merchant ships, have merchant ships ram submarines, send war supplies and soldiers on passenger liners, fly the flags of neutral nations, and register British ships under foreign governments. In response, the Germans began sinking merchant ships without warning, killing many more seamen and passengers. These German actions, exaggerated by Allied propaganda ministries, provoked international outcries. The climax came on May 7, 1915, when a U-boat sank the British passenger liner *Lusitania*, with the loss of 1,198 lives, including 128 Americans. The Germans claimed, possibly correctly, that the ship was carrying munitions and soldiers, and there is some evidence that the vessel was armed as well. By 1916, after repeated incidents, the reaction of the U.S. government became so threatening that the German government restricted the aggressive tactics of its submarines. With the submarine campaign hampered, the German surface fleet steamed out in an attempt to break the blockade, but at the Battle of Jutland on May 31–June 1, 1916, the British fleet forced the German navy back into port, from which it did not emerge for the remainder of the war. Admiral John Jellicoe, "the man who could have lost the war in a single hour," had held on.

The War at Home

If a nation expected to outlast its enemy in a war of attrition, it had to mobilize its civilian population effectively and create a new war front—the "home front." Since the warring governments had believed the conflict would be short, none of them had stockpiled resources or made plans to allocate them in the event of a lengthy struggle. As a war of attrition emerged, the warring governments, whether authoritarian or democratic, took increasing control of broad facets of their society and their national economy. The men who planned the centralization of the home front now became the pivotal figures of the war. Some were technicians, such as Walter Rathenau in Germany and Bernard Baruch in the United States; others were political leaders, such as David Lloyd George in Great Britain and Georges Clemenceau in France.

The managers of the home front had numerous responsibilities, none more crucial than the allocation of manpower. General Kitchener contributed substantially to the Allied war effort when he transformed the small professional army of Great Britain into a force based on mass conscripts, without a notable

World War I war production needs eased restrictions on what activities were possible for "respectable" women.
(National Archives)

loss of efficiency. Eventually, all the major belligerents conscripted able-bodied men and in some cases took teenagers, the elderly, and the marginally disabled.

To replace these men in their civilian occupations, cultural tradition was swept aside as women were recruited for labor in the factories and offices and on the farms. In Germany, 702,000 adult women were employed in the armaments industry in 1917, an increase of 500 percent over 1913. In the German state of Prussia there were 100,000 female railroad employees in 1918, an increase of 1,000 percent over 1914. Also, many more adolescents worked in industry; the number of fourteen- to sixteen-year-olds working in German chemical plants increased 225 percent. Many of them were females.

Governments seized complete control of the production of industrial raw materials, and when key commodities such as food and natural nitrates were in short supply, governments financed research, development, and production of substitutes. Germany created many *ersatz* (substitute) commodities, such as artificial nitrates, cellulose clothing, bark coffee, and turnip bread. Civilians contributed to the war effort by working overtime, sending packages to service personnel, planting gardens, investing in government bonds, supplementing rationing with fast days and meatless days, and watching for spies and saboteurs.

Because of the tremendous strain on the civilian populations, government propaganda ministries became a crucial aspect of the war effort. These organizations incited citizens to work harder, love their government, and hate the enemy. Vivid propaganda posters portrayed opponents as slavering inhuman beasts fit only to be exterminated. At the same time, governments suppressed dissent through censorship and jailed critics.

THE BREAK IN THE STALEMATE

The decisive point in the war came in the winter of 1916–1917. Germany was staggering under the pressure of the British blockade and other factors, and its population was suffering severe deprivation. German leaders feared that unless something was done to break the impasse, Germany would lose the war. The German naval command pressed for permission to resume unrestricted submarine warfare, sinking all ships heading for the British Isles. The German leaders understood that such a campaign would probably bring the United States into the war, but it was already a virtual ally of Great Britain, providing millions of dollars of war materials to Germany's enemies. They derided the United States as a "disorganized and undisciplined" nation that would not be effective in the war, and some German officers pledged that "not one American will land on the Continent." Even the more cautious German leaders estimated that it would take a year for the United States to place substantial troops on the Western Front. Long before the Americans could effectively intervene, they reasoned, Great Britain would be starved out and would surrender, and the other Allies would subsequently collapse. Over the protest of the civilian leaders, the kaiser reluctantly gave his approval.

On February 1, 1917, the reopening of unrestricted submarine warfare marked the beginning of the final phase of the war. For two months, the submarine campaign was spectacularly effective, and by April the British found themselves without reserves of industrial raw materials and with only six weeks' supply of food. Meanwhile, on April 6, the United States declared war on Germany. President Wilson, while personally a supporter of the Allied cause, had been a sincere advocate of neutrality. However, the new submarine campaign not only cost U.S. lives, but also, in Wilson's eyes, demonstrated a malignant militarism that threatened liberal institutions all over the world. This last point had been brought home to Americans when they discovered that Germany had promised to return the southwestern area of the United States to Mexico if Mexico would attack the United States. Congress supported the president, and Americans entered the war believing they were going "over there" to "make the world safe for democracy."

Soon after the United States entered the war, it became apparent that the Germans had miscalculated. While the U.S. army did take many months to train and transport, the powerful U.S. navy was immediately ready to deal with the submarines. U.S. and British naval units created a convoy system, and both navies employed new antisubmarine weapons such as depth charges and hydrophone detectors. During the summer and autumn of 1917, the combined navies sank an increasing number of submarines, while more and more merchant ships got through to Great Britain and France. By the autumn of 1917, as U.S. supplies poured in, it was clear the U-boat offensive had failed. If the Germans could not win a quick victory on the battlefield, the Allies, reinforced by the Americans, would win the war.

In fact, the Germans in the autumn of 1917 believed that victory on the Western Front was still possible, even likely. Russia appeared to be on the verge of collapse; if it did, German troops could be rushed to the Western Front for a decisive breakthrough before the Americans could make a difference. Russia had held on grimly throughout 1915 and 1916, absorbing millions of casualties, yet saved by the fact that the Germans and Austrians were too committed elsewhere to undertake a decisive offensive across the vast spaces of western Russia. Finally, however, the government of the tsar became the first casualty of the war of attrition. War-weariness and privation spurred both civilians and soldiers to take to the streets and drive Tsar Nicholas from power in March 1917. The new provisional government attempted to carry on the war but was crippled by desertion at the front and political dissension at home (see Chapter 12). In November 1917, the Bolsheviks toppled the government, seized power, and immediately began negotiations for peace. On March 3, 1918, at Brest-Litovsk, Russia signed a humiliating peace treaty with Germany and dropped out of the war.

Russia's collapse allowed Germany to send its best troops in the east to the Western Front during the winter of 1917–1918. Fearing these soldiers might have been infected with Bolshevik propaganda, the German government set up "mental delousing stations" to reindoctrinate them with the correct loyal attitudes. Bolstered by this additional manpower arriving on the Western

Front, the Germans prepared to launch a decisive offensive. As Ludendorff put it, "Our general situation requires that we should strike at the earliest possible moment . . . before the Americans throw strong forces into the scale." Meanwhile, U.S. industry was pouring out an enormous quantity of war material to bolster the French and British armies, and U.S. troops began landing in France in numbers that eventually reached 250,000 a month. U.S. commander John "Black Jack" Pershing ringingly announced on his arrival in France, "Lafayette, we are here," in memory of France's contribution to rebel victory in the U.S. War for Independence.

In March 1918, the Germans commenced their do-or-die offensive. They successfully used a new technique of sudden, overwhelming onslaughts on a narrow front to achieve a breakthrough, followed by rolling up the flanks of the break. They drove the French and British back for miles in a series of offensives lasting into July. The Allies, increasingly reinforced by the Americans, did not allow a major breakthrough: "There is no course open to us but to fight it out. . . . each one of us must fight on to the end," read a typical headquarters command. As the Germans paused in exhaustion, Marshal Ferdinand Foch, the newly created commander in chief of the Allied forces, coordinated a series of counterattacks that steadily drove the Germans back through their main positions and out into open country. The increasing presence of U.S. troops at the front, plus a spectacular breakthrough on August 8 by British troops supported by large numbers of tanks, signaled the approaching end of the war. By September 1918 the German army, though not broken, had been pushed out of most of the territory it had conquered in France. On September 29, Ludendorff informed the kaiser that Germany could not win the war and recommended that the German government explore avenues for peace while its military forces were still formidable.

THE ENDING OF THE WAR

Feverish diplomatic maneuverings punctuated late September and October 1918. Wilson, convinced that demands of unconditional surrender would prolong the war, had brought forth his peace plan, the Fourteen Points, in January 1918. The proposal contained three broad goals. The first goal was to prevent future wars by eliminating practices that had helped to precipitate the current war: trade barriers, interference with freedom of the seas, secret diplomacy, colonial tensions, and arms races. The second goal, aimed at settling particular problems in Europe, was a series of specific proposals concerning territorial integrity, national boundaries, and ethnic nationalism. To Wilson, the third goal was the most important: a League of Nations to preserve peace in the future. In addition to the Fourteen Points, Wilson had another condition for peace—the end of authoritarian government in Germany. He did not call for harsh punishment of the Central Powers. The other Allies, which had suffered much more than the United States, were not particularly happy with Wilson's leniency toward Germany, but they eventually agreed, with some reservations.

As the Germans made overtures for peace on the basis of the Fourteen Points and tinkered with coalition governments that might satisfy Wilson that Germany was no longer an autocracy, the war wound down. Bulgaria surrendered on September 30, and Turkey on October 30. Ethnic minorities in Austria-Hungary began declaring their independence, and on November 3 Austria surrendered, with Kaiser Karl going into exile shortly afterward. On the same day, the German sailors at Kiel mutinied, running up the socialist red flag. Councils of workers and soldiers began springing up in the major German cities in imitation of the Russian Soviets. During the days that followed, socialist leaders encouraged wildcat strikes in many German cities, and the military leaders forced Kaiser Wilhelm II to abdicate and go into exile in the Netherlands.

When representatives of the new German republic arrived in France prepared to sign an armistice (cease-fire) on the basis of the Fourteen Points, they found to their dismay that the Allies had additional terms that would make it impossible for Germany to renew the fighting if the cease-fire agreement were violated. If Germany wanted to end the fighting, the German army must withdraw to the east bank of the Rhine so that the Allied armies could occupy the west bank and several bridgeheads. Germany was to surrender the bulk of its surface fleet, its submarines, its air force, much of its machine guns and artillery, and its motorized transport. Finally, Germany was to renounce the Treaty of Brest-Litovsk and make reparations for damages sustained by civilians in the occupied territories. The German representatives reluctantly and bitterly signed: "I saw[the German delegation leader] brandish his pen and grind his teeth, . . . the business was settled," Foch recalled. On November 11, 1918, at 11:00 A.M., the guns fell silent on the Western Front. World War I was over.

SUMMARY

World War I was fought primarily in Europe and the North Atlantic, although some fighting occurred in Asia and Africa and elsewhere on the world's oceans. The French and British halted the Germans at the Battle of the Marne, and both sides dug in. The military weapons on both sides were so equally deadly in effect that neither side could break through their opponent's lines, creating a stalemate on the Western Front. In the east, German forces routed invading Russian armies, but the Eastern Front also ended in a stalemate, as did secondary fronts in Italy and northern Greece. Elsewhere, Allied forces conquered German colonies in Asia and Africa and cleared German vessels out of the Indian and Pacific oceans.

As the stalemate persisted, each side attempted to wear down the opponent's armed forces and break the morale of the opponents' civilian population. The war of attrition on the Western Front entailed rituals of mass slaughter, as assaulting infantry was almost invariably turned back by entrenched defenders. Great Britain conducted a surface and mine blockade that slowly strangled the German economy and caused great deprivation among German civilians. Germany responded with a submarine blockade of Great Britain but temporarily ceased sinking neutral ships when threatened by the United States. Governments of the warring nations pushed the concept of nationalism to its limits, urging their "home front" populations to make greater and greater sacrifices for their country and to hate all the people of the opposing nations as the enemy.

In 1917 two major occurrences broke the stalemate. One was the German decision to resume unrestricted warfare, which brought the United States into the war on the side of the Allies. Anglo-American naval cooperation broke the submarine blockade, and U.S. war materiel and U.S. soldiers began to pour into Europe. The second major event was the revolution that knocked Russia out of the war and freed German troops to fight on the Western Front. In March 1918, the Germans launched their last offensive but were thrown back by Allied troops, who launched a counteroffensive that slowly drove German troops out of France. Unable to stop the Allied offensive, faced with social revolution, and deserted by its allies, Germany agreed to a harsh armistice, which went into effect on November 11, 1918.

SUGGESTED SOURCES

COBB, HUMPHREY, *Paths of Glory* (1935). A fictional account of the French army that attacks the high command. *(Also an impressive film.)

FALLS, CYRIL B., *The First World War* (1960). An extremely well-written account by a noted British expert in military history.

FERRO, MARC, *The Great War 1914–1918* (1973). A concise interpretive account stressing the overall economic, political, and psychological context of the struggle.*

FRIEDEL, FRANK, *Over There: The Story of America's First Great Overseas Crusade,* 2d ed. (1990). A heavily illustrated survey of the U.S. role in World War I. Extensive use of first-hand accounts.*

Gallipoli. An Australian film vividly recreating the bungled British operation against Turkey. Authentic scenes of trench warfare.

HOUGH, RICHARD, *The Great War at Sea* (1987). The best single-volume account of a crucial aspect of the war.*

LINCOLN, W. BRUCE, *Passage Through Armageddon: The Russians in War and Revolution, 1914–1918* (1986). A lively presentation of the Russian war effort.*

MIDDLEBROOK, MARTIN, *The First Day on the Somme* (1972). A vivid description of the ordinary soldier's plight during a major offensive on the Western Front.

REMARQUE, ERICH MARIA, *All Quiet on the Western Front* (1928). A classic novel about the nature of modern war, emphasizing the lives of the soldiers.* (Also a film and a television program.)

STOKESBURY, JAMES L., *A Short History of World War I* (1981). A well-written general survey of the conflict.*

TANSILL, CHARLES C., *America Goes to War* (1963). A survey of U.S. involvement.

TUCHMAN, BARBARA, *The Guns of August* (1982). A lively account of individuals and events at the opening of World War I.* (Also a film.)

*Paperback available.

PART TWO

The Era of Revolution and War

TIME CHART II
1918–1945

Year	South & East Asia	Middle East & Africa	Europe	Western Hemisphere	Trends in Culture, Science, Technology
				UNITED STATES PREDOMINANT IN LATIN AMERICA	
1918	Chinese Republican Revolution, 1911–26		Russian Revolution and civil war, 1917–20	Revolution and civil war in Mexico, 1910–24	
1919	PARIS PEACE CONFERENCE AND FORMATION OF THE LEAGUE OF NATIONS					Popularization of Freudian analysis
	GROWING NATIONALISM	Wafd party in Egypt, 1919–52	Rebellion and civil war in Ireland, 1916–23		
1920		Ataturk in Turkey			
1921					The Roaring Twenties
1922	Gandhi leads non-violent independence movement in India, 1920s–40s		Mussolini assumes power in Italy		
1923					Decade of the popularization of motion pictures and radio
1924			Lenin dies		Advent of surrealism
1925		Reza shah in Iran	Locarno treaties	U.S. military withdrawal from Latin America, 1920s–1930s	Scopes trial
1926	Chiang leads northern expedition in China, 1926–28	Ibn Saud in Saudi Arabia			

1927				
1928				
1929	Stalin begins collectivization and first Five-Year plan			

THE GREAT DEPRESSION BEGINS

1930		Stock market collapses		Decade of popularization of air travel
1931	Japan occupies Manchuria			
1932				
1933	Hitler assumes power in Germany	Roosevelt launches New Deal		Mexican muralist Rivera
1934	Communist Long March in China, 1934–35	Purges in U.S.S.R., 1934–35	U.S. Good Neighbor Policy, 1930s	
1935	Italy conquers Ethiopia, 1935–36	Period of appeasement, 1935–39		
1936		Spanish Civil War, 1936–39		
1937	Japan invades China			
1938		Munich Agreement		
1939		Nazi-Soviet Pact		

WORLD WAR II

1940	North African campaigns			
1941	Japanese conquest of Southeast Asia	German invasion of U.S.S.R.	Japan attacks Pearl Harbor	Tank and air warfare
1942		Battle of Stalingrad		
1943			U.S. war industries build-up	Amphibious warfare
1944		Normandy invasion		
1945	Atomic bombs dropped on Hiroshima and Nagasaki			Mistral – first Latin American writer to win Nobel Prize for literature

CHAPTER 10

General Trends in the Interwar Years

The global trends that characterized the opening of the twentieth century—nationalism, imperialism, political diversity, economic disparity, and social and cultural upheaval—continued to dominate events during the interwar years of 1919–1939. After World War I, nationalists intensified their struggles for self-determination, while many Western and Japanese leaders sought to maintain and increase their national empires. Some nations escalated their races for military supremacy, while at the same time individuals and organizations worked toward disarmament and the formation of meaningful international organizations. Many had fought in World War I believing that victory would lead to more liberal, progressive governments; however, after the war, authoritarian regimes steadily increased in both number and power. During the interwar years, it was by no means clear which forces would emerge victorious.

PROGRESS IN SCIENCE AND TECHNOLOGY

During the interwar years, scientists and technicians refined and expanded previous achievements in physics, biology, and engineering. Chemists and biologists took major steps toward understanding and explaining the structure and genetic composition of the cell. Medical researchers improved techniques for inoculating against disease, thereby further prolonging the span of human life. Ironically, such improvements in health care also contributed to the population explosion in the colonized world at the very time that increased use of birth control methods slowed or stabilized population growth in the industrialized world.

In engineering, structural designers created larger and taller buildings, and propulsion experts developed an infant rocket industry. The armament industries in many nations continued to prosper as their technicians developed bigger and more deadly weapons. Airplanes, submarines, and tanks, introduced during World War I, would play a major role during the coming world conflict.

In addition to these developments, during the interwar years more efficient mass production of consumer goods, especially in transportation and communication, profoundly changed how people lived. Henry Ford's mass production techniques and Frederick Taylor's labor efficiency studies dramatically increased the production of consumer goods that could be sold at cheaper prices and still make a good profit. The automobile and many other items came within the purchasing power of the average Western worker. By 1930 there were more than 5 million automobile owners in Europe. In Great Britain, there were seven times as many in 1930 as in 1913; in France, almost twelve times as many.

One category of "affordable" consumer goods, the automobile, ushered in a new epoch of mobility that helped break down isolation and parochialism. Driving the family's new Ford Model T, available only in black, on a Sunday afternoon to see what it was like in the next town epitomized the new era. The automobile fostered a number of new industries, especially rubber, asphalt, and concrete. A mass-market tourist industry came into being. The aircraft industry developed more slowly, but by the 1930s, commercial air travel, catering to wealthy vacationers and enterprising business executives, was well established. The transportation revolution took hold quickly in North America, Australia, and to a lesser extent, in Western Europe; in Africa, Asia, and Latin America, however, such consumer goods and changes in transport remained luxury items only the very rich could afford.

Widespread use of automotive and air travel created escalating demands for gasoline. To meet this demand, the petroleum industry increased its operations on a global scale. In the process, entrepreneurs created huge international corporations that monopolized petroleum resources. After World War II, these international corporations directly clashed with petroleum-producing nations in the Middle East, Africa, and Latin America, as these nations sought a more advantageous distribution of the profits from this vital industry.

The radio, another mass-produced consumer item, was a major breakthrough in the field of mass communication, with momentous effects on the culture of the twentieth century. Because of mass production, most Western families could afford a radio, which became the leading form of home entertainment. There were about 3 million radios in Great Britain and Germany by 1930. Such figures were small, however, compared to those for the United States, which far surpassed the rest of the world in producing and owning consumer goods.

Motion pictures also became popular: Millions flocked to see "movies" featuring Mary Pickford, Rudolph Valentino, Jean Harlow, Douglas Fairbanks, Edward G. Robinson, and others. These "stars" were featured everywhere, and the public avidly followed not only their professional careers but also their private lives. Radio, newspapers, films, and magazines fueled public interest in fashion, health, sports, society, and crime. Media coverage popularized personalities from the gangster Al Capone to Charles "Lucky Lindy" Lindbergh, the first person to fly solo nonstop across the Atlantic. In Asia and the Middle East, Tokyo, Shanghai, and Cairo also became centers of thriving movie industries.

Informational mass communication, such as radio news broadcasts and film newsreels had both positive and negative effects. The Western public, as well as a literate urban middle class in much of Asia and Africa, became more informed about national and international affairs and about the politicians and leaders who made decisions. Regional divisions inside nations were often reduced as citizens, especially the young, identified with the practices and ideals displayed in the national media. On the negative side, politicians sought to manipulate the media to present themselves in the most favorable light. As a result, the superficial media image of political leaders often became more important than substantive issues and programs. Thus, at the very time masses of people throughout the world were becoming better informed, they were also becoming more susceptible to manipulation of the mass media by charismatic individuals. Both Franklin Roosevelt and Adolf Hitler were adept at exploiting radio and motion pictures, although for very different reasons.

Toward the end of the interwar period scientists conducting theoretical research on the nature of the atom unleashed its immense power, with momentous consequences for humanity. After decades of prior research, scientists succeeded in creating a reliable "chain reaction" in uranium-235 and plutonium during World War II. By "splitting the atom," they were able to release and ultimately to harness the energy that had been "locked up" inside the atom. In this process, an atom that has been split (atomic fission) shoots out neutrons that strike and split other atoms, releasing immense power. When encased in a bomb, the chain reaction produces the blast effect of hundreds of conventional bombs, plus radioactive effects that kill and maim over an extended period.

ECONOMIC CRISES

After World War I, economic conditions varied widely from nation to nation. The United States emerged from the war with a huge industrial capacity, no wartime damage at home, and enormous amounts of capital owed to it from wartime loans to other Allied nations. U.S. business prospered; despite the unflattering portraits created by Sinclair Lewis in his novels *Main Street* and *Babbitt*, the businessperson became the ideal of Americans, compared by one enthusiast to Jesus. "The business of this country is business," summed up President Calvin Coolidge. War-generated demands also stimulated industrial growth in Japan and hastened industrialization in China and India.

In contrast, many businesses and industries in Europe never recovered the dynamism they had displayed before the war. Europe's share of world trade diminished; nations remained deeply in debt, particularly to the United States. In Great Britain and other European nations, unemployment remained almost constantly above 10 percent. Except in the United States, surging inflation was another global legacy of the war. By 1919 prices in Great Britain were three times as high as in 1913. By 1926 prices in France were at least seven times as high as in 1913. In Germany, the government tried to cope with the inflationary spiral by printing more and more money. Confidence in the German mark fell on the international exchange; however, because of attractive interest rates, U.S. creditors continued to advance money to German borrowers. At home, Germans attempted to invest in durable goods that would maintain their value. This only stimulated more price increases. By 1923 the German mark was worth only one-trillionth of its prewar value, and a loaf of bread could cost billions of reichsmarks. People demanded that they be paid every day so that they could rush to the stores to buy anything in sight before their money became even more worthless. Although the German statesman Gustav Stresemann took energetic steps to end the crisis, social and psychological scars remained, for the German people had witnessed the destruction of the value of their savings.

Many parts of the British and French empires also suffered economic difficulties. Western nations had fought the war not only with their own resources but also with those of their vast empires, enlarging the agricultural and industrial sectors of their colonial holdings to support the war effort. Once the war was over, there were surpluses of some goods, but these surpluses were often accompanied by scarcities of vital commodities such as bread and kerosene for cooking and heating. Mounting unemployment in rural areas forced peasants into cities in search of employment. There were few jobs in the cities, which were ill-equipped to provide even minimal services for this rapid influx of humanity. Asian, Latin, and African cities were soon plagued with the same kind of social and economic problems that Western cities had endured during the industrialization of the nineteenth century. Many of these problems continued to trouble societies to the end of the century.

The ravages of postwar inflation: German bank officials in 1923 carrying money that declined in value as they walked.
(*The Granger Collection*)

Through expansion of the mass media, even poor peasants became aware of the high standard of living in the West and in urban areas around the world. In poor agricultural areas, where the economy was still at a subsistence level, people began to demand an improvement in their daily lives. A widening gap existed between societies that enjoyed high living standards and those that remained relatively poor. Such a disparity had existed at the beginning of the twentieth century; the difference in the interwar years was that many had now become aware of these differences and therefore were impatient for change.

Many nationalist leaders in the colonized world believed that their particular economic woes—unemployment, inflation, poverty, scarcities of consumer goods—were caused by imperial domination. As a result, the middle-class elite in India, Egypt, and elsewhere concluded that their goal should be economic as well as political independence. Indeed, demands for more local participation in economic spheres often went hand in hand with demands for political autonomy. For example, Egyptian nationalists established an Egyptian bank (Bank Misr) and a locally owned cigarette factory and urged all patriotic Egyptians to boycott British goods and to "buy Egyptian." In India, nationalist leaders urged Indians to adopt *swadeshi,* that is, to buy only Indian-made goods. In China students and merchants organized boycott campaigns to resist political and economic encroachment of imperialist countries, particularly Japan.

However, total economic self-sufficiency, whether in poor or in rich nations, was an impossible goal in the twentieth century. The economies of nations had become much too interrelated through trade, credit systems, markets, and resource needs to be separated into individual independent entities. International corporations were only one evidence of the economic interdependency that surpassed narrow national interests. Like Latin American nations, most African and Asian countries ultimately secured political independence but remained economically tied to the industrialized nations who controlled the majority of the world's industrial might.

By 1929 the economic imbalances and problems of the global economic systems resulted in a worldwide economic depression. The Great Depression was a global economic crisis which lasted in many areas until World War II and which vividly demonstrated the interdependency of twentieth-century economies. There were several specific causes. Production far exceeded consumption. Staggering amounts of credit had been extended during the war. Individuals, businesses, and nations had become obligated to one another in a vast web of indebtedness. In addition, many individuals and nations had estimated their wealth, not by tangible goods or resources, but by paper assets such as money or stocks. Paper assets printed (as they were in postwar Germany) without real productivity or tangible assets such as gold to support them were in fact worthless. Finally, many gambled recklessly in the stock market.

The Great Depression began on October 24, 1929, when the U.S. stock market started to plummet; soon the economy began to crumble. By early 1933 the United States was deeply mired in business cutbacks, unemployment, and bankruptcies. Europe soon felt the impact of the economic disaster. In 1930, as the collapse hit Germany, five bankrupt Berlin businessmen committed suicide in one week. Chancellor Heinrich Bruning became known as "The Chancellor of Hunger." By the early 1930s, out of a population of 65 million, 1 million Germans were unemployed.

As a result of the economic crisis in Germany, the Allies were forced to postpone German reparations payments. The reparations issue had become one of the major sources of economic dispute among the major powers after World War I. In 1924, under the Dawes Plan, an initial foreign loan was promised and Germany's annual reparation payments were reduced. Again in 1929, under the U.S.-devised Young Plan, the reparations were further reduced. Finally, in 1932, the Allies admitted—albeit with great reluctance—that Germany would no longer have to pay reparations.

The economic crisis created by the Great Depression was felt in other European nations as well; by 1932, one man in four in Great Britain was on "the dole" (welfare), and production fell 28 percent in France and 33 percent in Italy. In early 1930, the Depression hit Japan. The Japanese public blamed the politicians, and many argued that the solution to the economic disaster lay in military expansion and the creation of a self-sufficient empire. Many Japanese viewed Germany's turning from democracy to authoritarian policies as a positive object lesson. Although Japan was the first major industrialized nation to

Unemployment was a problem in Japan through the 1920s and became worse with the Great Depression. Here, priests march through Tokyo soliciting money for victims of an earthquake and for the unemployed.
(The Bettmann Archive)

recover from the Depression, Japanese democracy and parliamentary government never really recovered.

The Depression also had devastating economic consequences on the largely agricultural economies of Asia, Africa, and Latin America, since most of the nations on these continents were linked to the industrialized world through imperial ties and trade. As industries in Europe and the United States slowed or shut down, demand for raw materials produced elsewhere in the world also plummeted. As most of the people in these nations were already living at the poverty level, the loss of even a few pennies of income per capita could mean economic ruin. Leaders of poor nations emphasized that when a man's belt was already pulled to the last notch, it was impossible to ask him to tighten it further.

SOCIAL AND POLITICAL TURMOIL

The interwar years also ushered in sweeping social changes. Continuing a movement begun before the war, suffragists mobilized growing support for equal political rights. During the 1920s women in most Western nations obtained the vote and gained influence in political circles. In Africa, Asia, and the Middle East, aristocratic and middle-class women were often in the vanguard of nationalist movements. They, too, struggled for political and social rights and joined the international women's movement. Women gathered at international meetings such as the Pan-Pacific Women's Conference to discuss women's concerns; in China new laws promulgated by the Nationalist government gave women legal equality.

As more and more women entered the labor force, old social patterns—already altered by the war and technological developments—changed. In most of the industrialized world, the birth rate continued to drop, and throughout most of the world, the average adult lived longer and the trend toward urbanization accelerated. To some extent, in Great Britain and elsewhere, upper-class privilege and its monopoly over the political and economic systems began to decline. During World War I many men and women, who had been full-time servants in upper- and middle-class homes, left their jobs for the battlefronts and wartime industries. Following the war, many never returned to menial jobs. The growing scarcity and rising cost of servants forced the wealthy to change their lifestyles by adopting fashions in housing, dress, and food that required less maintenance, washing and ironing, and cooking.

Superficially, the war ended in a victory for liberal, democratic forces. In reality, the conservatives on the Right and the socialists on the Left were far from destroyed. Struggles between socialist and conservative forces became particularly intense in defeated nations; in Italy and Germany, leftists and conservatives battled openly and violently in the streets of major cities.

Protracted political clashes and economic crises throughout Europe forced more and more people toward the extremes of the political spectrum, leaving fewer and fewer to support the center. Europeans became increasingly unwilling to compromise and grew more fearful of social and political anarchy. By promising easy, quick solutions, authoritarian forces under which individual freedoms were subordinated to the authority of the state generally dominated by forces from the Right, gained support. One by one, moderate or progressive governments in Italy, Portugal, Spain, Germany, and Eastern Europe fell to rightist dictatorial regimes. Through strict control over the media, education, and culture, dictatorial regimes sought to create so-called new men and women who would follow their leaders with unquestioning loyalty. It should be emphasized that these authoritarian regimes differed somewhat from subsequent totalitarian regimes in which all aspects of the society—culture, government, and economics—were dominated by a single party or dictator. See Chapter 18 for a further discussion of these regimes.

Faced with defeats in the heartland of Europe, Marxists redefined their immediate goals during the interwar years. In the first fervor of the 1917 revolution, Vladimir Lenin and Leon Trotsky had both argued that the Russian Revolution was merely the first link in a chain of revolutions that would soon sweep the world. Dominated by the Soviet Union, the Third International, or Comintern, aimed to hasten the advent of communism around the world by supporting local Communist parties in their fight against capitalism and imperialism. By the mid-1920s, with continued domestic problems and a new leadership under Stalin, the Soviets began to place less emphasis on international revolution and more stress on increasing the strength of the Soviet Union.

Before World War II, Marxist ideology had had little impact on the masses in Africa and Asia. The few Marxist leaders who did emerge generally came from the educated middle class, and they met severe opposition not only from the ruling classes and religious leaders in their own nations but also from the imperial powers. However, as demands for national autonomy were continually rejected by the colonial powers, some nationalist leaders began to turn to the Soviet Union for support. Some, like Sun Yat-sen in China, did not intend to institute Marxism but looked to secure Soviet assistance in ousting the imperial powers and internal enemies. Two Asian leaders, Mao Tse-tung in China and Ho Chi Minh in French Indochina, did seek to make Marxist states. However, both were faced with the task of converting Marx's ideas, which presumed an industrialized environment, to the needs of peasant societies.

The prewar politics of ethnic nationalism continued to be a divisive issue after the war. The delegates at Paris carved out new nations in Eastern Europe in an attempt to grant self-determination to peoples living within them. However, many of these new nations still contained minority groups inside their boundaries. The conflicts between these new governments and minority groups who wanted autonomy contributed to the next global confrontation.

INTERNATIONAL AFFAIRS: CONFLICTS AND THE SEARCH FOR PEACE

The Rise of Anticolonialism

One international trend during the interwar years was the increasing pressure applied by colonial nationalists for an end to imperialism. World War I had badly weakened the power of the great European nations relative to the rest of the world. As a consequence, the war also hastened the day when European colonial empires would disappear. Wartime statements in support of self-determination, particularly by Woodrow Wilson, had stimulated anticolonialism and demands for independence among the subject peoples at the same time that the war had weakened the colonial powers' ability to hold on to their possessions. For example, in China Wilson's statement on national self-determination was widely taken to mean an end to spheres of influence and an end to imperialist concessions. The seeds were thus germinating for the post-World War II breakup of colonial empires.

None of this was foreseen at the Paris Peace Conference, where old-fashioned imperialism was "business as usual." Western representatives, who controlled the conference, made it clear that self-determination applied to national groups in Central and Eastern Europe but not to demands from Arabs, Zionists, Chinese, Indians, and others under imperial control. In their last major effort to enlarge their empires, Great Britain, France, and Japan used the mandate system created after World War I to govern the colonies of the defeated powers. It was, however, at best a stopgap measure in the face of the mounting drive toward national independence throughout the world.

By the early 1930s, imperial powers, with varying degrees of reluctance, were beginning to make concessions to the rising pressures of antiimperialist nationalism. The British responded to the moves toward independence in their possessions by continuing the devolution process that was well underway before World War I in areas that had been settled and controlled by white Europeans, usually of British descent. These dominions—Canada, Newfoundland, Australia, New Zealand, and South Africa—had provided substantial financial and military assistance in the war effort. After the war, Great Britain acknowledged this support by agreeing to individual membership in the League of Nations for all of these dominions and for India as well. Later, Great Britain went further along the path of devolution. The Statute of Westminster in 1931 recognized these white-controlled dominions as "autonomous communities." Economic and military links to Great Britain were preserved through the Commonwealth, which was a loosely knit association of the dominions and Great Britain.

However, in the interwar period, Great Britain was willing to grant autonomy only to those parts of the empire with which it retained close racial and cultural ties. The more heterogeneous and less Westernized parts of the empire were kept under controls that were as tight as the British—given their weakened world status—could sustain. Similarly, the French fought tenaciously to maintain their far-flung empire. British and French determination to safeguard their empires provoked peoples living under their domination to increase their demands for freedom.

In another major example of the decline of imperialism, the United States began to moderate its interventionist approach in Latin America. The United States had intervened repeatedly in the affairs of nations in the Caribbean area, and by 1924 U.S. military and U.S. Treasury personnel directed fiscal affairs in ten nations. Many Latin Americans angrily resented this intervention by the "Colossus of the North." Mexican leaders sometimes bitterly complained that being a neighbor of the U.S. was like being a mouse sleeping next to an elephant. Realizing that a policy of direct interference was often counter-productive, the United States began to withdraw its forces, and after the marines left Haiti in 1934, no U.S. troops remained on Latin American soil.

The more relaxed policy of the United States was sharply tested in Mexico. President Lazaro Cardenas had moved to nationalize foreign petroleum com-panies, including U.S. corporation holdings valued by the companies at $500 million. The U.S. business community clamored for action against Mexico, but the Roosevelt administration was determined to pursue a "Good Neighbor" policy and chose to negotiate. As a result, the U.S. government agreed to lend the Mexican government $24 million to be used to pay off the petroleum com-panies. In a further retreat from imperialism, the United States recognized the political independence of Cuba in 1932; however, Cuba and many other Caribbean nations remained diplomatic and economic protectorates.

The Search for Collective Security and the Revival of Militarism

During the interwar years, extreme forms of nationalism developed that in turn encouraged the rise of militarism, particularly in Italy, Germany, and Japan. The rise of fascism in Italy and Nazism in Germany stimulated an up-surge of aggressive nationalism that in Nazi Germany was also based on be-liefs of racial and cultural superiority. In Japan, nationalism coupled with long-held beliefs of cultural superiority resulted in an aggressive, expansionist foreign policy aimed at acquiring an Asian empire.

Recognizing the problems inherent in a world of conflicting nationalisms, Wilson and others urged the formation of effective international organizations that would prevent future great wars. Wilson also spoke extensively about the need for disarmament. There was general agreement that stockpiles of arms had contributed to the martial spirit prevalent before 1914 and had prolonged the war.

The League of Nations represented the major postwar attempt to seek peaceful means of settling disputes and sharing responsibility for the protec-tion of its members from aggression. The League consisted of an Assembly (where all members participated), a Council composed of the great powers (Great Britain, France, Italy, and Japan) and four lesser nations elected to serve by rotation, and a Secretariat. The International Court was also established to settle disputes referred to it by member nations.

The League was fairly successful in settling border disputes between Latin American nations and between small European nations such as Sweden, Fin-land, Greece, Albania, and Poland. It also administered the free city of Danzig and the Saar district, both taken from Germany after the war. In addition, many noted humanists and philanthropists from around the world participat-ed in and lent their energies to League activities.

In matters concerning the interests of major nations, however, the League was a failure. Over and over again, nations refused to work collectively either to settle disputes or to stop aggression. The most powerful nations also re-fused to commit themselves to joint armed action against aggressors, nor would they act against their own self-interest for the larger good. The League was also hampered by the refusal of the United States to join and, in its early years, by the absence of the Soviet Union and the powers defeated in World War I. In the final analysis, the League's greatest achievements were its efforts in the fields of social welfare, its support of agencies for refugees and the poor, and its sponsorship of medical research.

Internationalism on a regional basis, in the form of a Pan-American Asso-ciation, was well established in the Western Hemisphere. Initiated in 1889 by the United States as a thinly disguised arrangement to facilitate its own goals in the region, the Pan-American Association met at five-year intervals; Pan-American conferences forged a number of agreements on, and created special organizations concerning, copyrights, labor codes, agriculture, child protec-tion, and arbitration procedures. However, these agreements were often ig-nored in practice.

In the interwar years, several international agreements addressing specific problems appeared to offer the greatest hope for lasting peace. The Locarno treaties (1925) addressed a number of European issues, and the Washington Naval Conference (1922) and the Kellogg-Briand Peace Pact (1928) were con-cerned with the difficult problems of arms limitation and war. Despite these limited arms agreements, most nations continued to stockpile weapons in order to be prepared for the next war. European and U.S. leaders spoke elo-quently of peace and disarmament during the 1920s, but they feared that, ex-cept for limitations on naval build-ups, their enemies were continuing the race toward armed superiority.

As had happened before World War I, only a few decades earlier, extreme nationalism contributed to military build-ups in the 1930s. In Japan, the mili-tary exercised substantial power within political circles, stockpiling arms and building up Japan's land and sea forces. As a defeated power, Germany's acqui-sition of armaments was strictly limited under the terms of the Versailles treaty. However, as it became evident that the Allies would not enforce their own treaty, the Germans moved to rebuild their armed forces. By the mid-1930s it was apparent that the Versailles treaty had failed to prevent Germany from be-coming, for a second time in the twentieth century, a major military power. The Soviet Union also expanded its military capabilities, preparing for the looming conflict that would again pit the major powers of the globe against one another.

After World War I, the total arms expenditures of Great Britain, France, and Italy actually increased. France refused to limit its armaments and subsi-dized arms for Central European nations as a safeguard against Germany. France also built, at great expense and effort, the famous Maginot Line, pur-ported to be an impregnable defense. Only the United States, far removed from the trouble areas of the world, greatly reduced its army. By 1932 fifteen nations, including Turkey and Rumania, had larger armies than that of the United States. In the final analysis, nationalism far outweighed the opposing movement toward international peace, dooming the League of Nations and other international agreements to failure.

IDEAS AND CULTURE

In the period between the wars, as people continued to search for a deeper meaning to life and the world around them, the works of thinkers such as Marx, Darwin, Freud, and Nietzsche exercised considerable influence. To some, the experiences of World War I made the ideas of these important intellectuals seem more relevant than ever.

The combined impact of these thinkers was particularly evident in the continuing battle between secularism and traditional religious beliefs. The most dramatic struggle took place in the Soviet Union. The new Marxist-Leninist government not only removed the Russian Orthodox Church from its exalted position as the state religion but also encouraged atheistic beliefs and in general persecuted and discriminated against religious believers.

In the United States and Western Europe, secularists and proponents of traditional religious teachings generally waged their battles in more democratic arenas, such as in law courts and on the pages of journals. One example was the spectacular Scopes "Monkey Trial" of 1925, where a high school biology teacher was found guilty of teaching Darwinian evolution instead of the Biblical account of creation. One of the leading and most influential opponents of organized religion in the United States was H. L. Mencken, a writer and editor, who as a young man had been greatly influenced by the ideas of Nietzsche. In color-

Defense attorney Clarence Darrow (left) and former Secretary of State William Jennings Bryan, who differed on the interpretation of the Bible at the Scopes "Monkey Trial." In the United States, the debate over teaching evolution in public schools continued into the 1990s.
(Historical Picture Services)

ful, exaggerated language, Mencken railed against theologians, censorship, middle-class values, and Prohibition—to name just a few of his favorite targets.

Secularists were also active in Latin America and in non-Western areas of the world. In 1917, Mexican revolutionaries pushed through a secular constitution which limited the power of the Catholic Church. In Asia, secularists, often strongly influenced by the West, challenged advocates of traditional religions such as Islam, Hinduism, and Buddhism. For example, Mustafa Kemal (Ataturk), head of the Turkish government through most of the 1920s and 1930s, set out to break, with some success, the centuries-old dominance of Islamic tradition over Turkish life.

Technological changes such as the motion picture and the automobile fostered challenges to traditional values in the United States and Europe, especially regarding sex and marriage. People became more familiar with the psychology of Freud, whose analysis of human psychological behavior was often misinterpreted by popularizers to mean that frustrating the sex drive was harmful. Anna Freud and Melaine Klein pioneered the application of Freudian ideas in the psychoanalysis of children.

Advocates of the new lifestyle spoke in the name of increased freedom. An affluent "smart set" stressed self-indulgent individualism through fast cars, "bathtub" gin, sex, and "hot" dance music. Many women began to discard the traditional demure female image and to wear short skirts, bob their hair, dance, drink, smoke, and "neck." A U.S. college president expressed feelings shared by many conservative Americans when he said, "The low-cut gowns, the rolled hose, and the short skirts were born of the Devil." Despite all these new challenges, however, most people continued to be heavily influenced by traditional religious beliefs. For example, Protestant fundamentalists were largely responsible for prohibiting the manufacture and sale of intoxicating beverages in the United States from 1919 until 1933.

Many of the new enthusiasms, often fed by newspapers, radio, and motion pictures, increased appetites for the novel and bizarre, while reflecting a nervous rootlessness and an attempt to escape from the harsh realities of the war years. Thus people turned increasingly to expending their energies on the enjoyments offered by the abundance of consumer goods and services: automobiles, radios, jazz records, movies, night clubs, and cabarets. In London, Paris, and Berlin, as in Chicago and New York, the 1920s often "roared." A penchant for new pleasures swept over many European cities. The Austrian writer Stefan Zweig noted that "all values were changed, and . . . Berlin was transformed into the Babylon of the world." He also wrote that "anything that gave hope of newer and greater thrills . . . anything in the way of narcotics, morphine, cocaine, heroin, found a tremendous market." For a girl "to be sixteen and still under suspicion of virginity," he added, perhaps exaggerating, "would have been considered a disgrace in any school of Berlin."

The rapid change in values and practices frightened traditionalists. A growing number of people throughout the world echoed U.S. President Warren Harding's cry for a return to "normalcy." The cry was echoed in Great Britain, where politicians called for a return to "tranquility" and "honesty."

However, in a transformed world in which so much had been destroyed, a return to a pre-1914 existence was impossible.

In the interwar years, people not only challenged traditional religious values and escaped into new pleasures and fads but also questioned a whole range of more traditional beliefs, such as loyalty to one's nation and faith in progress, science, reason, and civilization itself. For some disillusioned intellectuals, the experiences of the war underscored the validity of many of Nietzsche's earlier criticisms. One of the most popular books of 1919 was *The Decline of the West*, by Oswald Spengler, who thought of Nietzsche as Europe's greatest modern prophet. Spengler was an unknown former schoolteacher when his book was first published in the summer of 1918; in it he attempted to build upon Nietzsche's pessimistic view of the West and to construct a total survey (past, present, and future) of the rise and fall of Western civilization, comparing the destiny of the West with the fate of previous societies.

Even in the more down-to-earth, less rarefied intellectual atmosphere of the 1930s, the ideas of Nietzsche continued to appeal to some, especially in Germany, where his ideas of a superman were often selectively used to justify the new Nazi order. Hitler himself, although he lacked any sound knowledge of Nietzsche's ideas, was fond of quoting several of his lines, and on Mussolini's sixtieth birthday sent him the philosopher's complete works as a present.

Developments in art and literature paralleled those in philosophy. While fighting men were still in the trenches, a group known as Dadaists founded an artistic and literary movement in Zurich, Switzerland, which for a short time symbolized disenchantment with all the old values. One of the founders wrote, "I loathe fat objectivity and harmony" and "Logic was always false." After the war, the Dadaists returned to Paris and Berlin and resorted to displays such as reading poetry while ringing bells. When their actions created disbelief, they replied that their audiences were not the only ones who did not understand their actions—they themselves did not.

Dadaism soon gave way to surrealism, an artistic and literary movement begun in France. Influenced by Freud, surrealists expressed the belief that the unconscious world of dreams and fantasies represented a higher, more real and significant world than the external one of everyday life. In their writings, paintings, and films, they attempted to portray this unconscious dream world. Although surrealism as a distinct movement ended at the beginning of World War II, surrealist ideas continued to have an effect on writers, artists, and film directors wishing to go beyond traditional realism.

Two writers who reflected the 1920s spirit of challenging traditional forms and experimenting with new ones were James Joyce and Gertrude Stein. Joyce's *Ulysses* (1922) was one of the most significant novels of the interwar period. Its stream-of-consciousness technique reflected the author's interest in the subconscious life of his characters. The American writer Gertrude Stein, who had moved to Paris before World War I, experimented with language that at times seemed as nonsensical as that of dadaism. Stein was a patron of many artists and writers who made their way to Paris, and her writings were influenced by psychology, art, the new cinema, and her own unconventional personality.

From the beginning to the end of the 1920s, literature mirrored the disillusionment of the decade, as indicated by the title of T. S. Eliot's widely acclaimed poem "The Waste Land" (1922). Frederick Henry, a character in Ernest Hemingway's 1929 novel of World War I, *A Farewell to Arms,* came to the conclusion that "abstract words such as glory, honor, courage or hallow were obscene."

Following the Great Depression and the rise of Hitler, writers and artists in the West became more concerned with concrete social and political issues. The realistic style, more easily understood than that of Joyce or Eliot, regained some of the popularity it had lost in the 1920s. Writers like John Steinbeck, author of the novel *The Grapes of Wrath* (1939), expressed sympathy for the poor and stressed the fellowship of humanity. The Depression also led some Western writers to embrace Marxist ideas. For example, the Mexican artist Diego Rivera and the Chilean poet Pablo Neruda were influenced not only by European artistic ideas but also by those of Marx and Lenin, who helped to fuel their already critical view of a West that they perceived to be both capitalistic and imperialistic.

Cultural developments and conflicts in the West had only a limited impact on the non-West. The mass media helped to transmit Western cultural ideas to cities such as Cairo and Shanghai, where the upper and middle classes attempted to copy the example of those who "roared" in New York, Paris, and Berlin. On the other hand, despite some Western-oriented secularist leaders such as Jawaharlal Nehru, most Indian Hindus and Muslims regarded religion and religious customs as all-important. The traditional values advocated by Mohandas Gandhi dominated Indian culture. Although Gandhi worked with Nehru to obtain Indian independence and was tolerant of Islam and of some Western ideas, Gandhi's solutions for India's future were largely based on his own understanding of Hinduism, and he remained deeply suspicious of modern secularized Western states.

In China, as in India, people differed over the relative merits of synthesizing Western ideas with Chinese tradition. The older faiths of Buddhism, Confucianism, and Taoism did not generally exclude one another, and many Chinese practiced teachings from several faiths. Some tried to assimilate beliefs and ideas from the West. For example, Sun Yat-sen, the most outstanding leader of China until his death in 1925, was a Protestant who greatly admired Darwin's teachings and yet respected the Confucian tradition. His successor, Chiang Kai-shek, became a Protestant but retained respect for traditional Confucian ideas. The Chinese constitution of 1923 stated that a "citizen of the Republic of China shall be free to honor Confucius and to prefer any religion." By the early 1930s, the Chinese Communists were contesting Chiang for power, and their leaders had little respect for either Eastern or Western religious teachings. They agreed with another Western concept: Marx's statement that religion was "the opium of the people."

Some writers educated in Europe were torn, appreciating aspects of both the new Western culture and the traditions of their homelands. A good example was Leopold Senghor of Senegal, who spent much of the 1930s in France. A poet as well as a future politician, Senghor helped to develop and to popularize the idea of Negritude during the 1930s. The concept of Negritude was partly based on ideas adopted from Caribbean writers, including Claude McKay, who in the 1920s had become a prominent figure in the black or Harlem Renaissance in the United States. Senghor defined Negritude as "the sum total of the values of the African world." Although a Catholic married to a Frenchwoman, and admittedly influenced by European writers and thinkers, in his poetry Senghor praised the "Africanness" of his native land and people. Thus in the interwar years, artists, writers, and intellectuals from around the globe continued to exchange ideas and to be influenced by one anothers' cultures.

SUGGESTED SOURCES

BARRACLOUGH, GEOFFREY, *An Introduction to Contemporary History* (1968). A brief treatise on twentieth-century trends.*

The Blue Angel (1930). One of the great German films made in Berlin before Hitler's rule.

GALBRAITH, J. KENNETH, *The Great Crash, 1929* (1988). New edition of a readable work by a leading U.S. liberal economist; includes an introduction comparing the 1929 and 1987 crashes.*

Inherit the Wind (1960). A remarkable film about the famous Scopes "Monkey Trial," starring Spencer Tracy.

ISHERWOOD, CHRISTOPHER, *The Berlin Stories* (1979). A fictionalized reflection of the author's experiences during the Depression in Berlin.* The film *Cabaret* was based on Isherwood's Berlin experiences.

KOESTLER, ARTHUR, et al., *The God That Failed* (1950). A collection of six autobiographical sketches by U.S. and European writers who relate why they were attracted to communism in the interwar years.

LANDES, DAVID S., *The Unbound Prometheus* (1976). A work containing insights on technological, industrial, and economic developments between the wars.*

SOLOMON, BARBARA H., *Ain't We Got Fun* (1980). A collection of essays, lyrics, and stories that capture the cultural changes occurring in the United States during the 1920s.*

TAYLOR, A. J. P., *From Sarajevo to Potsdam* (1974). A lively, liberally illustrated survey of European affairs.*

*Paperback available.

CHAPTER 11

Postwar Settlements

The horror of World War I, prolonged by deadly military technology, was a shattering experience for European nations, both victors and vanquished. The international peace conferences after the war were conducted in an atmosphere of war-enflamed nationalistic hatred and fear. At these meetings, rejecting President Wilson's moderate "peace without victory" approach, the winning powers imposed severe terms on the defeated nations without consulting them. The Germans in particular considered these terms excessively harsh, and nationalistic resentment was stirred up. Some of the victorious nations, particularly Italy and Japan, were frustrated and humiliated when they failed to obtain all the treaty provisions they had expected. Several new European states were created in the hope of lessening ethnic nationalistic tensions in southern and eastern Europe, but many ethnic groups remained minorities. Western imperialist attitudes and actions overrode the aspirations for independence of Africans, Arabs, and others. The myriad of resentments engendered by the peace treaties heightened international tension in the postwar period. Many historians have claimed that the roots of World War II lay in the soil of these 1919 "peace" treaties.

THE DEVASTATION OF THE GREAT WAR

It has been estimated that about 10 million fighting men lost their lives in World War I, victims not only of their enemies but also of the advancing technology of warfare. Three-quarters of the dead were from Russia, Germany, France, Austria-Hungary, Great Britain, and Italy. Those wounded in combat numbered about twice the military deaths. One of every ten men in France was killed, and three of every ten between the ages of eighteen and twenty-eight. Since the United States had entered the war late, U.S. losses were numerically and proportionally less than those of any of the major European countries. For example, despite a population almost two and one-half times larger than that of France, U.S. combat losses were less than one-tenth of those suffered by the French. An extremely high percentage of well-educated young Europeans, many of them junior officers, lost their lives. The lack of vitality and leadership Great Britain and France displayed in the 1930s was in part a result of the war deaths of many potential leaders.

In addition to the military deaths, countless civilians died between 1914 and 1918 as a result of the war. Some estimates place the figure higher than that of military deaths. The Turks massacred nearly 1 million Armenians in 1915. Some civilians died as a result of shells or bullets, and many others, especially in eastern Europe, were attacked by the maladies that accompanied war: influenza, typhus, cholera, and malnutrition. Even after the war ended, many more millions of men and women continued to die in the chaos of the Russian civil war and the postwar worldwide influenza epidemic. The ravages of World War I contributed to both disasters.

Accompanying the loss of lives was a great loss of property, especially in Belgium, France, and eastern Europe. German property suffered little in comparison to that of France, where it was estimated that 300,000 homes, 8,000 factories and mines (including steel plants and coal mines, the basis of French heavy industry), 52,000 kilometers of roads, and 6,000 kilometers of railroads had been destroyed. About 7 million acres of arable land in France were also devastated.

The estimated overall direct cost of the war was $180 billion; the indirect cost was approximately $150 billion. The Carnegie Endowment for International Peace estimated that with the money spent on the war every family in England, Wales, Ireland, Scotland, Belgium, Russia, Germany, the United States, Canada, and Australia could have been provided with a home of its own. In addition, all the property and wealth of Great Britain and France could have been purchased, and a considerable sum would still have remained. From 1870 to 1914 Europe had been the world's banker, with major financial investments on every continent. By 1918, however, many of these investments had been lost or withdrawn to help pay for the war. In addition, Europe was now in debt, principally to the United States, which had now become the great creditor of the world.

THE PARIS PEACE CONFERENCE AND GERMANY

The Paris Peace Conference opened on January 18, 1919, with twenty-seven of the victorious nations represented. It was to be a gathering of only the victors; Germany and other defeated powers were not allowed representation at the conference. Nor was Russia; the victors resented the new Bolshevik government, which had made a separate peace with Germany, and a civil war then being waged in Russia provided a pretext for not inviting a Russian delegation to Paris. Originally, the victors made plans for a peace congress to follow the conference which would have included the defeated powers, but this idea was later dropped.

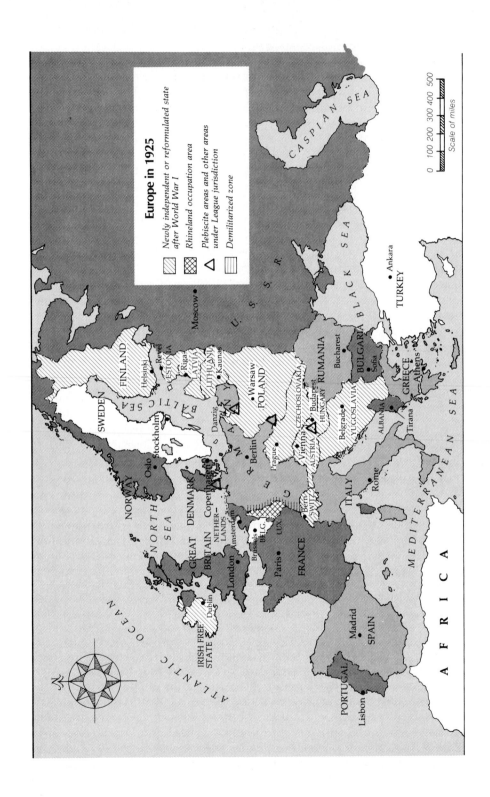

Europe in 1925

Newly independent or reformulated state after World War I

Rhineland occupation area

Plebiscite areas and other areas under League jurisdiction

Demilitarized zone

CASPIAN SEA

Scale of miles

0 100 200 300 400 500

• Ankara

TURKEY

BLACK SEA

• Moscow

U. S. S. R.

FINLAND

• Helsinki

• Revel

ESTONIA

• Riga

LATVIA

LITHUANIA

• Kaunas

SWEDEN

BALTIC SEA

• Danzig

• Warsaw

POLAND

G E R M A N Y

• Berlin

• Prague

CZECHOSLOVAKIA

• Budapest

HUNGARY

RUMANIA

• Bucharest

BULGARIA

• Sofia

GREECE

• Athens

• Stockholm

• Oslo

NORWAY

NORTH SEA

DENMARK

• Copenhagen

GREAT BRITAIN

NETHER-LANDS

• Amsterdam

• Vienna

AUSTRIA

YUGOSLAVIA

• Belgrade

ALBANIA

• Tirana

MEDITERRANEAN SEA

• Brussels

BELG.

LUX.

B E L G I U M

SWITZ.

• Bern

ITALY

• Rome

IRISH FREE STATE

• Dublin

• London

FRANCE

• Paris

ATLANTIC OCEAN

SPAIN

• Madrid

PORTUGAL

• Lisbon

A F R I C A

The important decisions at the conference were made by a Supreme Council made up of the heads of state and foreign ministers of the United States, Great Britain, France, Italy, and Japan. The dominant figures at the conference proved to be the scholarly U.S. President Woodrow Wilson, the colorful British Prime Minister David Lloyd George, and the French Prime Minister Georges Clemenceau, "The Tiger of France," who was in his late seventies and still a formidable figure. Since the three men had differing priorities, they had to make some concessions to each other in order to obtain at least some of their objectives. Wilson was primarily concerned with ensuring that agreement would be reached on a covenant for a League of Nations and that, to the extent possible, the peace would be based on his Fourteen Points. Clemenceau's main preoccupation was to ensure that Germany would never again threaten French security. Lloyd George was not as inclined as Clemenceau to be harsh toward the Germans, but he had just been returned to office after his party had promised to hang the kaiser and to "squeeze the German lemon until the pips squeaked."

Through the spring and into the summer of 1919, the conference moved at a rapid but often disorderly pace—"a riot in a parrot house," as one member of the British delegation described it. On June 28, exactly five years after the assassination of Archduke Franz Ferdinand, the attending nations signed the Treaty of Versailles with Germany. Germany had protested that the terms were too harsh and not in keeping with Wilson's Fourteen Points, on which basis Germany had agreed to lay down its arms. Undoubtedly, the German perception of the treaty was influenced by the fact that almost all the war had been fought on non-German soil, and to many Germans it seemed more a stalemate than a decisive Allied victory. However, Germany had little choice but to sign.

At the Paris Peace Conference: Lloyd George, Orlando (of Italy), Clemenceau, and Wilson.
(Brown Brothers)

According to the terms of the treaty, Germany lost Alsace-Lorraine to France, several small districts to Belgium, one to Czechoslovakia, and a large portion of eastern Germany to Poland. In addition, plebiscites were to be held in several areas, such as northern Schleswig on the Danish border; Germany eventually lost some of these territories as well. Several German areas, such as the Saar district and the city of Danzig, were to be put under the control of the newly formed League of Nations. The city of Memel was also taken away and eventually ceded to Lithuania. Many of the lost German territories contained only a minority of Germans. In the Saar, Danzig, and Memel, however, Germans predominated. Germany also lost all her overseas colonies, which came under the control of the victors. Despite these losses, Germany's population still outnumbered France's by more than a three-to-two margin and had been growing at a faster rate for some time—both causes of alarm in France.

According to the treaty, Germany and its allies were guilty of aggression in imposing a war on the Allies. The kaiser was to be tried for offenses against "international morality and the sanctity of treaties," and hundreds of German military officers were charged with war crimes. Although no significant individuals came to trial, Germany was assessed reparations to pay for war damages. The exact figure was not settled at the time of the conference, but the Allies stipulated that Germany would make payments totaling the equivalent of $5 billion by 1921. At that time the final sum, understood to be much higher, would be announced.

Germany also had to observe various strict limitations on its armed forces and weapons. As an additional safeguard for France, Allied forces were to occupy the Rhineland area west of the Rhine and control three of the river's bridgeheads, in both cases for periods ranging from five to fifteen years. In addition, the Rhineland and a thirty-mile zone east of the river were to be permanently demilitarized.

While Germany regarded the Treaty of Versailles as severe, the treaty would have been even harsher if French desires had been fully realized. Concerned for its future security, France had proposed, among other points, that the territory west of the Rhine be made into a separate buffer state under French influence. Wilson, however, was successful in reducing France's demands on Germany by agreeing, along with Great Britain, to guarantee France against any future German invasion, a guarantee that never became operative because of the U.S. Senate's later refusal to support Wilson's pledge.

ARRANGEMENTS FOR THE REST OF EUROPE

The Allies at the conference dictated terms to the other defeated powers: Austria-Hungary, Bulgaria, and the Ottoman Empire. All had to pay reparations, limit their armies, and acknowledge the loss of some territory. Punishment for Bulgaria was comparatively light in all these categories. To some extent, drafting treaties for the other defeated nations involved sanctioning the reformation of ethnic groupings that had already occurred in central and eastern Europe. By 1919 little was left of the old Austro-Hungarian Empire. Led by the able and respected Thomas Masaryk, the Czechs and Slovaks had appealed to Allied leaders to act on the basis of Wilson's principle of self-determination and recognize the independence of Czechoslovakia. Even before the November 1918 armistice was signed, the Allies had complied, and a separate government was already functioning there. A month before the convening of the Paris Peace Conference, the Kingdom of the Serbs, Croats, and Slovenes (or Yugoslavia, as it would later be officially known) had been proclaimed. It included, or soon would include, formerly independent Serbia and Montenegro, combined with the former Austro-Hungarian areas of Croatia, Slovenia, Bosnia, and Herzegovina. In addition, Rumania had seized the Transylvania region from Hungary.

The Poles also gained their independence. Poland had not existed as a nation since it had been divided in the late eighteenth century among Prussia (now part of Germany), Russia, and Austria. Woodrow Wilson's thirteenth point, proclaimed a full year before the convening of the conference, called for an "independent Poland, to include the territories indisputably Polish, with free and secure access to the sea." By the time the Allied diplomats assembled in 1919, a Polish republic had been proclaimed, and the Poles had already taken control of Polish segments of Austria-Hungary, as well as Polish-claimed portions of Germany and Russia. The key territory Poland annexed from Germany was the "Polish Corridor," primarily peopled by Poles. The corridor, along with Danzig (under the League of Nations' control), provided Poland with an outlet to the sea and severed East Prussia from the rest of Germany. The final Polish gains at the expense of Austria-Hungary and Russia were not determined until after Polish success in the Russian-Polish War of 1920.

The Allies ended the union of Austria and Hungary in the Treaty of St. Germain (1919) with Austria and the Treaty of Trianon (1920) with Hungary. Austria and Hungary recognized the losses to Czechoslovakia, Yugoslavia, Poland, and Rumania; in addition, Austria recognized the loss of territory to Italy. Fearing the possibility of German dominance over central Europe, the Allies also forbade Austria, now composed of only a German-speaking population, any future union (*Anschluss*) with Germany. Both Austria and Hungary agreed to reparations payments and to limitations on their armies.

In general, the conference delegates divided Austria-Hungary according to the principle of ethnic nationalist self-determination. But this principle was much more complex than it first seemed. It was almost impossible to create a new state comprised entirely of just one ethnic nationality. Some ethnic groups, for example, were thought to be too closely intermingled or too small to exist as an independent nation. Thus, some ethnic groups, willingly or unwillingly, became part of a larger state.

Earlier bargains also played a role in determining national boundaries. For example, the Allies had made promises to Italy and Rumania to bring them into the war. When the boundaries of Italy were drawn through the Alps in accordance with these promises, Italy was given control over several hundred thousand Germans in the South Tyrol and tens of thousands of Slavs in Istria.

When Italy further demanded the Adriatic port of Fiume, also claimed by the Yugoslavs, Wilson refused. At that point, Italy stormed out of the Paris Peace Conference. Rumania, too, was granted control over other ethnic groups. In the Transylvanian territory annexed by Rumania there were two Magyars for every three Rumanians.

Economic or strategic considerations also came into conflict with a strict application of the principle of ethnic self-determination. Both factors, for example, played a role in persuading Allied statesmen to recognize as part of Czechoslovakia a German-speaking area of the former Austro-Hungarian territory that the Nazis later claimed as the Germanic Sudetenland.

Like Austria-Hungary, the former Ottoman Empire (hereafter Turkey) was torn to pieces, mostly along ethnic lines. The Turks lost their Arab-populated territories in the Middle East, which came under either British or French control or, as with some of the Arabian peninsula, became independent. In addition, much of the Anatolian (Turkish) peninsula was put under temporary occupation by European nations.

As already noted, Russia was not invited to the peace conference, and neither the "Red" Bolsheviks nor the "White" anti-Bolsheviks were officially recognized by any of the Allied powers as the legitimate government of Russia. The fate of Finland, Estonia, Latvia, and Lithuania, all parts of the former Russian Empire, was not officially dealt with at the conference. Nevertheless, the conference diplomats were concerned by 1919 with the possible spread of communism. Their favorable treatment of Poland and Rumania in part reflected a desire to set up strong bulwarks against communism and to create a *cordon sanitaire*, or quarantine zone, to keep communism out of central and western Europe. Hence, between 1918 and 1921, European powers supported independence for the four Baltic nations as part of the *cordon sanitaire*.

EUROPEAN REFUGEES, EMIGRANTS, AND MINORITIES

Faced with new governments and changing boundaries, several million people left their homes and settled elsewhere. Some left their nation behind, as, for example, the Russians who left the new Soviet state to live in such cities as Berlin, Paris, and Shanghai. Some took up a new life in a nation for which they felt kinship, such as the Germans who moved inside the new borders of Germany from areas that had been part of prewar Germany but were now French or Polish.

Not all minorities, however, were able to move. Between the wars, minority problems, especially in central and eastern Europe, would remain a serious cause of tension. Of particular significance were the German minorities in Poland and especially Czechoslovakia, where more than one out of every five individuals was German. Other notable minorities were the Slavic and German minorities in Italy; the Hungarian (Magyar) minorities in Rumania, Czechoslovakia, and Yugoslavia; the sizable Ukrainian and White Russian minorities in Poland; the Ukrainians in Rumania; and the Great Russians in Estonia, Latvia, and Rumania. In Yugoslavia, made up of a variety of ethnic groups, dissatisfied Croats and Slovenes in particular threatened to upset a state dominated by Serbs.

Between the wars, ethnic minorities and the dominant national groups continued to view each other with hostility. In addition, separation from their home nation of some members of an ethnic group, such as the Germans of Memel and Danzig, provided a convenient grievance and excuse for one nation to interfere in the affairs of another.

EUROPEAN AND JAPANESE IMPERIALISM AT THE PEACE CONFERENCE

Although President Wilson had called for a peace without "annexations," the prewar imperialist drive to acquire new possessions showed up strongly again at the conference. Great Britain, France, South Africa, and Belgium divided up Germany's holdings in Africa. The conference also parceled out former German-held islands in the Pacific to Australia, New Zealand, and Japan. These former German territories and a large portion of the defeated Ottoman Turkish Empire were to be ruled by the victorious powers as "mandates" of the League of Nations.

The new mandates were divided into A, B, and C categories, and as such give a good indication of the attitude of cultural imperialism prevailing early in the twentieth century. Set up by the European and U.S. delegations, the classification was based on Western perceptions of the degree of inferiority of particular non-Western societies, that is, the degree of deviance from Western standards. Type A mandates, Middle Eastern areas formerly under the control of the Ottoman Empire, were considered to be almost ready for independence. Societies in Type B mandates, mostly African, would not be ready for independence for several generations. The peoples of the Pacific islands were judged not ready for independence in the foreseeable future and were assigned to Type C mandates. The League of Nations was to safeguard the interests of the peoples in the mandates, but in practice the powers that received the mandates exercised unrestricted authority and treated their mandates like colonies.

The proposed Middle Eastern mandates were strongly condemned by most Arabs. The mandates not only postponed independence for Arabs outside the Arabian peninsula but also artificially divided Arabs into different compartments, hindering the chances for a unified Arab nation in the future. Hopes for national self-determination had been fueled by Wilson's Fourteen Points and by wartime declarations by Great Britain and France favoring self-determination. Although a champion of self-determination as a general principle, Wilson was willing to back European interests in the Middle East instead of Arab aspirations to secure Allied support for the League of Nations and other parts of his program. Despite Arab objections, the British and the French were able to implement their territorial ambitions in the Middle East. Under the terms agreed on at the San Remo Conference in 1920, the British obtained mandated control over Iraq and Palestine, including what is today Jordan, and the French received mandates over Syria and Lebanon.

Although its participation in the war had been marginal, Japan also benefited at the Paris Peace Conference, especially when compared to China, which had no real voice in the proceedings. Japan and its delegates were accorded a special position on the Supreme Council and voiced three specific demands: (1) the transfer of the former German islands in the North Pacific (the Marianas, the Carolines, and the Marshalls) to Japanese control, (2) the confirmation of Japan's claim to former German rights in China's Shantung province, and (3) a declaration of racial equality in the Covenant of the League of Nations. Japan's first demand was essentially met when it received the German islands in the North Pacific to administer as mandates under the League of Nations. Because of Wilson's reservations, Japan was persuaded to drop its third demand. Japan considered this a particularly galling defeat, since the race issue was a symbol of discrimination. Defeated on the issue of racial equality, Japan threatened to walk out of the conference unless its second demand was met.

Sovereignty over the Shantung province was the one specific demand of the Chinese, who, like the Japanese, had participated marginally in the war. China also sought an international forum in order to air its grievances concerning the unequal treaties and to seek their abolition. In particular, the Chinese hoped Woodrow Wilson would champion their cause. The Japanese got their way, however, and as a result, Japan signed the peace treaty with Germany and China did not.

Although China lost on Shantung, and although its demand for a discussion on ending the unequal treaty system was ruled out of order, the balance sheet was not entirely negative. World War I had broken the solidarity of Western imperialism against China. The Soviet government had denounced tsarist Russia's unequal treaties with China and soon began to negotiate with China on the basis of equality. The Chinese also established equal treaties with the new governments of Germany, Austria, and Hungary.

THE UNITED STATES REJECTS THE TREATY OF VERSAILLES

When the U.S. Senate began its consideration of the Treaty of Versailles, one of the most dramatic struggles in U.S. political history occurred. The Republican Senate majority, led by Senator Henry Cabot Lodge, and some Democrats raised a number of objections to the treaty. Some senators criticized the peace as too harsh, a falling-off from the ideals of the Fourteen Points; others opposed the treaty from motives of partisanship and personal dislike of the President; still others denounced Wilson for the surrender of Shantung to Japan. Most senators, however, were apparently troubled by Article 10, which obligated members of the League of Nations to repel aggression against League members by means "the Council shall advise." They feared, incorrectly, that if the United States ratified the treaty and became a member of the League of Nations, the League could order the United States into wars around the world, even if Americans were opposed. Some shared the disdain of a former Senate colleague, Albert Beveridge of Indiana, who declared the League to be the work of "amiable old male grannies who, over their afternoon tea, are planning to denationalize America and denationalize the Nation's manhood." In order to preserve U.S. freedom of action in world affairs, many senators insisted that a number of reservations be added to the treaty. The reservation receiving the most support asserted that Congress must approve any U.S. involvement in League-sponsored actions to curb aggression.

President Wilson adamantly opposed any compromise that might curtail his fervent vision of a League of Nations to preserve the peace. He would not agree to any of the proposed reservations and was self-righteously shrill and partisan in dealing with doubters and opponents. While attempting to mobilize "grass roots" opinion, he suffered a stroke and was removed from an active role in the ratification struggle. When the treaty finally came up for a vote in November 1919, treaty supporters failed to muster the constitutional two-thirds majority, and it was not ratified.

In 1921, the United States signed a separate treaty with Germany that ratified most of the provisions of the Treaty of Versailles but forbade the participation of the United States in any international agencies created by the treaty without the consent of both houses of Congress. Americans were not yet ready for peace through collective security if that concept limited the U.S. tradition of unilateral action. The refusal of the United States to join the League was a blow to the League's prestige and to its effectiveness.

SUMMARY

World War I brought with it an unprecedented loss of life and property and the decline of European wealth and prestige. The postwar settlements pleased some nations, angered others, and left others with decidedly mixed feelings. The new nations of eastern Europe—Finland, Estonia, Latvia, Lithuania, Poland, Czechoslovakia, and Yugoslavia—gained the most from the conflict: their independence. Although Austria and Hungary were now also separate nations, they were not happy with their fate; nor were Bulgaria and Turkey. Many Africans and Arabs were upset that the principle of self-determination did not seem to apply to them. In Europe, Germany was the most aggrieved, having incurred various territorial losses, the payment of reparations, and other stipulations such as occupation of the Rhineland.

Each of the Allied powers, including Japan, achieved only part of its goals in the postwar settlements. While gaining Alsace-Lorraine, for example, France did not weaken Germany as much as it would have liked. President Wilson achieved his primary goal of establishing a League of Nations, only to have the U.S. Senate block his nation's membership in that body.

The postwar settlements, along with subsequent diplomacy, thus failed to foster security and stability. Whether as a result primarily of the attitudes and actions of the victors or of the vanquished, postwar resentment continued to exist, especially in Germany, and eventually helped lead to another war. The French writer Romain Rolland was more prophetic than he knew when on June 23, 1919, he wrote: "Sad peace! Laughable interlude between the massacres of peoples!"

SUGGESTED SOURCES

BIRDSALL, PAUL, *Versailles Twenty Years After* (1962). An interesting summary of the conference and of its long-term effects by one sympathetic with Wilson's goals.

HOUSE, E. M., and C. SEYMOUR, *What Really Happened at Paris* (1921). Includes accounts of the conference by various members of the U.S. delegation.

KLINGAMAN, WILLIAM K., *1919: The Year Our World Began* (1987). A vivid political, social, cultural narrative of the world's main events and personalities in 1919.*

LEDERER, IVO J., Ed., *The Versailles Settlement: Was It Foredoomed to Failure?* (1960). A collection of essays in the Heath "Problems" series representing various viewpoints.*

MAYER, ARNO J., *The Politics and Diplomacy of Peacemaking* (1968). A look at the political climate and especially the effects of the Bolshevik revolution that influenced decisions at the Paris Peace Conference.

MEE, CHARLES L., JR., *The End of Order: Versailles, 1919* (1980). A well-written, if not penetrating, account, critical of Wilson.

NICOLSON, HAROLD, *Peacemaking, 1919* (1933). The highly personal memoirs of a British participant.*

TILLMAN, SETH P., *Anglo-American Relations at the Paris Peace Conference, 1919* (1961). A thorough and scholarly study.

WALWORTH, ARTHUR, *Wilson and His Peacemakers* (1986). A first-rate, comprehensive narrative history of Wilson at the Paris Peace Conference.

*Paperback available.

CHAPTER 12

The Transformation of Russia, 1917–1932

In 1917 two revolutions occurred in Russia. The first overthrew Tsar Nicholas II and established a Provisional Government; the second (eight months later) brought the Bolsheviks (called Communists after March 1918) to power. Civil war and Allied intervention soon followed, but the Communist government survived and in 1921 instituted the New Economic Policy. This stabilizing measure was disrupted in 1928 when the government introduced the first Five-Year Plan and the collectivization of agriculture. These two measures greatly changed the everyday life of Soviet citizens. Although technological, economic, international, and cultural forces all played parts in Soviet life during this period, the most dramatic role was played by politics.

THE BACKGROUND TO REVOLUTION

World War I contributed to the instability that helped bring about the 1917 revolutions, and had it not been for the war it is possible that Russia could have avoided them. Even before that calamitous world conflict, however, the Russians and the empire's numerous other nationalities were becoming increasingly discontented, both in the countryside and in the cities. In the year before the beginning of the war, over 50 percent of the empire's industrial workers engaged in labor protests. Facing working and living conditions inferior to those of their counterparts in western Europe, they became more and more receptive to the ideas and ideologies preached by Russian radicals. From his distant throne, an aloof and ineffective Tsar Nicholas II, despite the scare of the 1905 revolt, remained virtually oblivious to the rampant dissatisfaction.

When war broke out in 1914, Russia was unprepared to meet the challenge. Once again, as in the Russo-Japanese War of 1904–1905, a combination of industrial-technological backwardness, governmental and military inefficiency, and corruption led to a series of military defeats. Nicholas II listened too much to the wrong advisors, including his wife, Tsarina Alexandra. At a crucial point in late 1915, he left the capital in her hands in order to assume personal command of the armies at the front. The tsarina was under the strong influence of the notorious Gregory Rasputin, a self-proclaimed holy man who specialized in seducing women. Thus, as one expert on Russia puts it, the fate of Russia was in the hands of "a narrow-minded, reactionary, hysterical woman and an ignorant, weird peasant—who apparently made decisions simply in terms of his personal interest, and whose exalted position depended on the empress's belief that he could protect her son from hemophilia and that he had been sent by God to guide her, her husband, and Russia."[1] Rasputin's death, on December 30, 1916—he was heavily poisoned, shot several times, kicked and beaten, and finally tied up and pushed through a hole in the icy Neva River—was not enough to restore popular confidence in the government. The tsar remained with the armies at the front, as ineffective as ever. In January 1917, the French ambassador wrote to his government: "I am obliged to report that, at the present moment, the Russian Empire is run by lunatics."[2]

THE REVOLUTIONS OF MARCH AND NOVEMBER 1917

Early in March[3] worker discontent in the capital of Petrograd sparked bread riots, demonstrations, and strikes. After subsiding in the first year of the war, the workers' dissatisfaction had been rising since 1915, triggered by inflation, a decline in real wages, deteriorating working conditions, and food shortages. Underlying these specific grievances was a seething resentment against the government and society for treating them so shabbily despite their important contributions to the war effort. On March 8, International Women's Day, women textile workers poured into the streets shouting, "Bread!" Other Petrograd workers quickly joined them, and within two days over 200,000 strikers brought everyday life to a standstill.

After being informed of the mounting chaos in the capital, Nicholas II telegraphed back that order should be restored. The city's military commander ordered police and troops to disperse demonstrators, shooting at them if necessary. But after some shooting, the key turning point occurred: Soldiers in one regiment after another refused to comply with orders and instead joined the demonstrators. After realizing he had lost control of Petrograd and the support of key military and political leaders, Nicholas II abdicated the throne on March 15.

Three days earlier leaders from Russia's legislative Duma had formed a Provisional Committee in an attempt to restore order. The committee now formed a Provisional Government. It was composed primarily of moderates with only one Socialist in its cabinet, the Minister of Justice, Alexander Keren-

[1]Nicholas V. Riasanovsky, *A History of Russia*, 4th ed. (New York and Oxford: Oxford University Press, 1984), p. 421.
[2]Quoted in W. Bruce Lincoln, *Passage through Armageddon: The Russians in War and Revolution, 1914–1918* (New York: Simon and Schuster, 1986), p. 312.
[3]Until 1918, Russia still used the old Julian calendar, which was thirteen days behind the Gregorian calendar in use in the West. All dates here, however, are from the Gregorian calendar.

sky. The power of the new government was challenged by a rival organization, the Petrograd Soviet (Council) of Workers' and Soldiers' Deputies. At first this body was led by the moderate Marxist Mensheviks and the peasant-oriented Socialist Revolutionaries, and it enjoyed the support of many Petrograd soldiers and workers. Encouraged by the Petrograd Soviet, radicals soon formed local Soviets throughout Russia, including some within military units. Despite their distrust of the Provisional Government, which many workers and soldiers thought represented upper-class society, both the Mensheviks and the Socialist Revolutionaries were reluctant to bring it down. For practical and ideological reasons, they were not yet ready to assume the burden of power. Some were influenced by the Marxist view of history, which held that a country could not initiate a socialist stage until it had first undergone a capitalist one. In their eyes, Russia had just overthrown a feudal order, and a lengthy capitalist period would have to ensue before this capitalist state could be replaced by a socialist one. When the Provisional Government continued the war, in part because of strong Allied pressure, the Soviets gave their support.

Although they had earlier spread their ideas among the Petrograd workers, the Bolsheviks did not play a major role in the opening weeks of the revolution. Their leader was Vladimir Lenin, born Vladimir Ulyanov in 1870, the son of a provincial school inspector. Young Lenin had been profoundly affected by the execution of his brother for revolutionary activities and had himself become an opponent of the tsar. By his twenties, Lenin had become a Marxist. He engaged in revolutionary activities that were punished by almost five years of prison and Siberian exile. Released in 1900, he spent most of the next seventeen years in western Europe. There, in 1903, he played a leading role in splitting the Russian Marxists into two factions: the Mensheviks and his own Bolsheviks. The Mensheviks favored a large, broad-based workers' party, while the Bolsheviks demanded a small, well-disciplined party of dedicated revolutionaries.

On April 16, 1917, Lenin returned by train from Switzerland to Petrograd. Knowing of his opposition to Russia's involvement in an "imperialist war," the Germans allowed him to pass through German territory but quarantined him from contact with any Germans, lest he infect them with his ideas. While Winston Churchill later compared the arrival of this short, balding, goateed, forty-six-year-old radical to that of a "plague bacillus," Lenin was not an alien infection but a Russian who well understood the volatile mood of the masses. He wanted a Marxist revolution to occur in Russia and to spread quickly from there to some of the more industrialized nations. These nations could in turn help Russia build up the industrial base necessary to construct Marxist socialism.

Following his return, Lenin immediately challenged the dominance of the Mensheviks and Socialist Revolutionaries within the Soviets. At the same time he called for "all power to the Soviets," anticipating that his own Bolshevik party could soon assume a commanding position within them. Lenin strongly criticized the war and called for peasants to seize the landed estates and for workers to take control of the factories. Although at first encountering strong opposition to his radical demands, as 1917 proceeded, his party gradually gained support. As early as May, representatives of the Mensheviks and Socialist Revolutionaries had become cabinet members in the Provisional Government; the Bolsheviks thus had the advantage of being the only major party of the Left not implicated in an increasingly unpopular government. Some peasant soldiers began to desert the front and go home, partly motivated by hopes of seizing property in the countryside. As Lenin later said, they "voted for peace with their feet." By October 1917 Bolshevik strength had substantially increased. They had gained a majority in both the Petrograd and Moscow Soviets; Leon Trotsky, who had returned to Russia in 1917 and decided to become a Bolshevik, was now the chairman of the Petrograd Soviet.

Late in October, Lenin returned to the capital after temporarily hiding in Finland and immediately called for a takeover of power. Lenin's urgings and Trotsky's persuasive and dynamic speeches to Soviet deputies, soldiers, and workers moved preparations steadily forward. On the evening of November 6 and the morning of November 7, troops under the control of the Bolshevik-dominated Petrograd Soviet took control of the bridges, railroad and electric stations, state bank, post office, and central telephone station. Finally, after a siege marked more by noise and confusion than by loss of blood, the revolutionaries broke into the Winter Palace during the early morning of November 8. Members of the Provisional Government (except for Prime Minister Alexander Kerensky, who had left the capital in order to seek out loyal troops) surrendered to representatives of the Petrograd Soviet.

Meanwhile, at a meeting of the Second All-Russian Congress of Soviets, deputies of the Mensheviks and many of the moderate Socialist Revolutionaries strongly objected to the armed takeover that was in progress, but they were outnumbered. Finally, in frustration, they stormed out in protest. Trotsky mocked those who left: "You are bankrupt. Your role is played out. Go where you belong: into the dustbin of history." On November 9, the delegates who remained approved a new government with Lenin as chairman of the Council of People's Commissars and Trotsky as commissar of foreign affairs.

Vladimir Lenin speaking to Soviet citizens during a May Day celebration.
(*Brown Brothers*)

CIVIL WAR AND ALLIED INTERVENTION

Although the Bolsheviks had an extensive following among workers and sol-diers, the peasant-oriented Socialist Revolutionaries remained more popular in the nation as a whole. When the previously scheduled elections for a Con-stituent Assembly took place in late November 1917, the Socialist Revolution-aries won more than twice as many seats as the Bolsheviks. When the Assem-bly met in January 1918, however, Lenin disbanded the Assembly after a day, and no major force was able to effectively challenge his action. As the year progressed, the Communists (Bolsheviks) used their newly founded secret po-lice, the Cheka, not only against conservative and liberal parties and groups but also against other radical parties such as the Mensheviks and Socialist Revolutionaries. Nevertheless, Communist control was primarily restricted to the ethnic Russian heartland. In other areas of the empire, many of the non-Russian nationalities refused to accept Soviet rule.

In March 1918, after months of diplomatic maneuvers to prevent it, the mil-itarily prostrate Russians signed the Treaty of Brest-Litovsk with Germany. The treaty recognized surrender of the huge, ethnically non-Russian parts of the tsar's empire west and southwest of the Russian heartland. Already, or soon to be, controlled by Germany, these lands—Finland, Lithuania, Estonia, Latvia, the Ukraine, and Poland—were now pronounced independent from Russia.

Although the Communists were willing, however reluctantly, to come to terms with Germany, Russia's former allies were not so inclined. One concern of the Allies was to see that the military supplies they had sent to such ports as Archangel and Murmansk did not fall into German hands. The Allies also wanted to prevent even greater numbers of German troops from being trans-ferred to the Western Front. They decided to send military forces into Russia, and eventually fourteen nations became involved, particularly Great Britain, France, the United States, and Japan. Allied intervention was also motivated by the Communists' call for "international socialist revolution" and their can-celation of several billion dollars of tsarist debt to Western creditors. Following the end of the war in November 1918, the Allies remained in Russia, support-ing the anti-Communist (White) forces that had organized during that year to challenge the Soviet government in a full-scale civil war.

The Whites were made up of various groups, including many former officers, Cossacks, and followers of political parties ranging from the conservative far Right to the leftist Socialist Revolutionaries. For two years, until the end of 1920, they fought on many fronts against the Communists, or Reds. (Nineteenth-centu-ry Europeans used the color red to symbolize radicalism, and the Communists adopted it for their new flag and other symbols like the "red star.") In Siberia, the Whites were supported for a time by a Czechoslovakian Legion of about 40,000 former Czech prisoners of war who had served in the Austro-Hungarian army. The point of greatest danger for the new Soviet government was probably in Octo-ber 1919, when White forces threatened both Moscow and Petrograd.

In April 1920, with the civil war still underway, Poland attacked Russia. After seesaw campaigning, Poland gained some Ukrainian and Byelorussian areas that it claimed by historical right. Despite losing the war with Poland, the Red Army pushed forward on all fronts against the Whites. In November 1920, Red troops in the south forced the last major White contingent to evacuate in Allied ships. Most of the Allied forces also withdrew, leaving only the Japanese in Siberia. Under increasing Soviet and U.S. pressure, the Japanese left the mainland in 1922 and the Russian part of the island of Sakhalin in 1925. All in all, Allied intervention against the Communists was a failure, leaving behind only a legacy of mistrust.

Despite Allied intervention, a war with Poland, and the opposition of powerful forces inside Russia, the Reds won the civil war for a number of reasons. They were more unified than their enemies, who found it almost impossible to work together. Despite differences among themselves—for example, between Trotsky and Stalin—party discipline and the leadership of Lenin kept the Communists working together. Trotsky, as head of the Red Army, displayed impressive organizational and leadership abilities, rushing in his specially equipped train from one front to another. The Communists also had the advantage of controlling the heartland of Russia, while their enemies were scattered around the periphery. Finally, a Red victory held out more hope to the peasants and the minority nationalities than did a White victory. While both sides forcibly requisitioned food from them, peasants feared that the Whites might try to restore the rights of landowners. Smaller nationalities feared that the Whites would reestablish the Russian Empire and that they would be dominated once again by the Great Russians. The Soviet leadership at least promised something better.

Yet the hopes of the non-Russian nationalities were almost immediately crushed. In 1920–1921 Bolshevik Russia restored control over most of the Ukraine not lost to Poland and over the Caucasian republics of Azerbaijan, Armenia, and Georgia. During the next few years the Bolsheviks also brought most of Central Asia back under Russian rule.

THE YEARS OF THE NEW ECONOMIC POLICY, 1921–1928

Although the Communists had won the civil war, they had inherited an exhausted and shrunken country. After heavy losses in World War I, millions more lives had been lost in the strife that followed. The drought, epidemics, famine, and starvation of the war years continued. Numerous cities and villages had been destroyed. Many factories sat idle, and the transportation system had almost ceased to function. Crop production had fallen off drastically. Not only had territory been lost to Poland, but in a series of 1920 treaties the Soviet government had also found it necessary to recognize the independence of Finland, Estonia, Latvia, and Lithuania. Parts of the Asiatic portion of the nation were still not firmly under Soviet control.

In March 1921 the sailors of the Kronstadt naval base, early supporters of the Communists who had grown tired of their authoritarianism, revolted; but the government crushed the uprising. The anarchist Emma Goldman, then in Petrograd, stated that the brutal slaughter of the sailors severed the last strand which had once united her with the Communist cause. Such expressions were

A Young Man in Lenin's Russia

I became a Bolshevik and a member of the Communist Party after the Revolution and a short time later joined the Red Army as a political worker and propagandist. As soon as I returned from the Front after the Civil War, the Yuzovka Party organization made me a deputy manager of the Ruchenkov mines. . . .

There was famine in the mines of the Donbass in 1922, and even isolated incidents of cannibalism. The villages were even more ravaged than the mines. My first wife, Galina, died during the famine in 1921. Her death was a great sadness to me. I was left with two children to look after, my son Leonid and my daughter Julia. In 1924 I married again to Nina Petrovna. Those first years of Soviet Power were years of struggle and hardship and self-sacrifice. But the people still believed in the Party; even the most illiterate of our citizens understood the Party's slogans and ral-

lying cries. The people knew that these hardships were being thrust upon us by the bourgeoisie—both by our own bourgeoisie and by the bourgeoisie of the world at large, which was instigating counterrevolution and intervention against us. We told ourselves that no matter how bad things were, they had been worse in the old days, before the Revolution.*

From the memoirs of Nikita Khrushchev, leader of the Soviet Union from 1953 until 1964. He was in his mid- and late twenties in the period described above. Although assistance from the American Relief Administration helped save many lives, at least 5 million people died in the Soviet famine of the early 1920s.

*From *Khrushchev Remembers*, vol. I, by Nikita Khrushchev, translated and edited by Strobe Talbott. Copyright © 1971 by Little, Brown & Co. Reprinted by permission.

commonplace by 1921 among many non-Communists who had enthusiastically backed the November 1917 revolution.

Faced with widespread economic and political unrest, Lenin decided to make concessions and in 1921 instituted the New Economic Policy (NEP). Following the revolution, the Communists had instituted war communism, which had nationalized industry and land, all but abolished private trade, and forced the peasants to turn over most of their crops to the state. Under the NEP, the state continued to maintain control over major industries, transportation, banking, foreign trade, and most wholesale trade. The new policy now allowed a measure of private enterprise in small industries and retail trade. In addition, the state no longer forcibly requisitioned peasant produce. After paying a tax, first mainly in food and later in money, peasants were free to sell what remained on the open market. Economically, the NEP was a notable success. By 1928 the total agricultural and industrial production had roughly reached 1913 levels. Given the devastation of the economy from 1914 through 1920, this was no small accomplishment.

From the beginning, the Communist party had dominated the state; and during the NEP years, despite easing economic controls, the party tightened its control over all levels of government. Inside the party, the hierarchy strengthened its hold on the rank-and-file membership. The constitution of 1924, proclaimed the nation a federation of republics, the Union of Soviet Socialist Republics (U.S.S.R.). Supreme power resided in an All-Union Congress of Soviets (after 1936 the Supreme Soviet). This body was to elect the Council of People's Commissars (after 1946 the Council of Ministers) and also an Executive Committee and a smaller Presidium that acted for the Congress between sessions. The Communist party, especially its Central Committee (sixty-three members in 1926), Politburo, and Secretariat, filled the government posts. Important central government figures were members of the party and followed the instructions of the central party leadership, this was true throughout all the republics. Claims of any truly autonomous powers for the republics were mere propaganda.

During the NEP years Joseph Stalin replaced Lenin as the most important Communist political figure. In 1922 Lenin suffered a stroke, and in January 1924 died. Although after his death Russian Communists revered him, before his death other leaders maneuvered to fill the power vacuum that resulted from his stroke. The man who seemed to be the frontrunner for Lenin's mantle was Leon Trotsky. Unfortunately for Trotsky, others united against him. Trotsky's main opponent was Joseph Stalin, who was forty-four years old when Lenin died. Born in Georgia in the Caucasus, Stalin was a long-time Marxist who had been made general secretary of the Communist party when the office was created in 1922. In 1923 Lenin concluded that Stalin "was too rude" and should be replaced in his position by someone "more patient, more loyal, more courteous, and more considerate of his comrades." Because of his stroke Lenin could not engineer Stalin's removal. After Lenin's death, Stalin used his position as general secretary to strengthen his control over the party, cleverly playing on the ambitions of others and making useful political allies when he needed them. By 1927 Stalin had Trotsky and a few of his other political opponents expelled from the party. In 1929 Trotsky was forced to leave the Soviet Union and eventually settled in Mexico. He watched from afar as "Stalinism," which he referred to as "the syphilis of socialism," was gradually imposed. In 1940 he was axed in the head by a Stalinist agent.

The NEP years were also ones of social and cultural experimentation. The power of husbands and fathers was curtailed. Divorces increased by 1927 to a ratio of one for every four marriages. The government legalized abortions, confiscated Church land and possessions, and, through the educational system and media, inculcated antireligious and pro-Communist propaganda. The state stressed technical, vocational, and adult education and also briefly experimented with progressive educational techniques. By 1939 about 81 percent of Soviet citizens were literate, compared with 51 percent in 1926.

Benefiting from the presence of some gifted writers and thinkers who remained in the Soviet Union, the NEP period was culturally richer than the Stalinist years that followed. Some "true believers" in the revolution, such as the film director Sergei Eisenstein and, for a time, the poet Vladimir Mayakovsky, shared with their audiences a sense of excitement about the new Communist era. Many others, such as the poet Boris Pasternak, who later wrote *Doctor Zhivago*, were not so enthusiastic, yet created works of merit. Censorship was not yet complete, and there was still room for experimentation; but under the increasing power of Stalin and the party, vital intellectual forces slowly dissipated.

Soviet foreign policy was yet another area of change during the NEP period. In 1919 the Communist International, or Comintern, was created amid hopes of establishing Communist governments elsewhere; it succeeded briefly in parts of Germany and Hungary (see Chapter 13). The Comintern eventually consisted of Communist parties of various nations that had, for the most part, split off from larger Socialist parties. Since the Comintern was managed from Moscow, other nations correctly perceived it as a force that encouraged Communist agitation and revolution outside the Soviet Union. In 1923, for example, Comintern agents attempted to take advantage of the unsettled conditions in Germany to encourage Communist takeovers.

While leaving such foreign activities to the nominally independent Comintern, the Soviet government sought to gain diplomatic recognition, trade, and credits from other nations. In 1921 it signed a trade agreement with the British; "One can trade even with cannibals," British Prime Minister Lloyd George once stated in defense of such trade. The Treaty of Rapallo with Germany in 1922 marked a further breakthrough, as the two nations agreed to restore normal diplomatic and commercial relations. In 1924 Great Britain, France, Italy, China, and a number of other nations also officially recognized the Soviet Union.

By the middle of the 1920s the Soviet government appeared to be becoming less revolutionary. In fact, Trotsky and a few others accused Stalin of a lack of enthusiasm for encouraging revolutions abroad. They accurately charged that Stalin's slogan of "socialism in one nation" deemphasized the policy of fomenting revolution abroad and stressed instead the construction of a socialist society within the Soviet Union.

In spite of a decline of revolutionary action on the part of the Comintern in the second half of the 1920s, Soviet foreign policy still continued to reflect its origins. In 1927 Great Britain broke off relations with the U.S.S.R. on discovering extensive Soviet espionage and propaganda activities in London.

COLLECTIVIZATION AND THE FIRST FIVE-YEAR PLAN

Despite the many changes Russia had experienced in the decade following 1917, the lives of Soviet peasants were not greatly changed from tsarist days. They still made up about 80 percent of the Soviet population; more than half of them were illiterate. Their communal work and leisure habits, social organization, and suspicion of authority had changed little. Many, especially the older peasants, also retained their prerevolutionary religious beliefs and, to the extent possible, their religious ceremonies and customs.

In 1928–1929 Stalin began to change the lives of the peasants profoundly. He inaugurated the collectivization of agriculture and the first Five-Year Plan, which emphasized the build-up of heavy industry. The reasons why Stalin introduced and continued these new policies are subject to debate, but five have been frequently mentioned: (1) More grain was needed to help feed the growing urban population, but peasants were not selling enough grain to the state at the low prices the government was willing to pay. (2) More rapid industrialization, especially in heavy industry, was necessary if the Soviet Union was to become a stronger military power. "If in ten years we do not cover the distance that other countries took fifty or a hundred years to traverse, we will be crushed," Stalin warned. (3) Marxist ideology based socialism on a developed industrial order, and therefore the continued development of a Soviet socialist state was thought by many to depend on the expansion of Soviet industry. (4) Both the Five-Year Plan and collectivization would increase the control of the party over the economy and over the lives of Soviet citizens. (5) If he now rejected the NEP approach, Stalin would at the same time discredit his remaining major political opponents, who had consistently supported it.

With the inauguration in late 1928 of the first Five-Year Plan, the Soviet economy took on the characteristics that would mark it for the next six decades. Government officials decided what should be produced in the Soviet Union and in what quantity; consumers' desires had relatively little effect. The government, following party orders as always, established target figures for the next five years, designed especially to increase metal and chemical production, electricity and petroleum output, new factory construction, and other industrial growth. The government obtained capital for expansion in these areas by squeezing high indirect taxes from its population. The purchasing power of Soviet citizens declined, and few consumer goods were available.

At the end of 1932 the government claimed that it had already met the goals of the first Five-Year Plan in a little over four years. While it is impossible to be sure of the exact figures, and while haste in meeting production quotas often caused shoddy workmanship, production did increase significantly in some areas. Most reliable estimates agree that iron and steel output went up at least 50 percent during the Five-Year Plan. The output of chemicals, machinery, equipment, fertilizers, petroleum, and electricity increased even more dramatically. New factories, industrial complexes, and cities sprang up, often located far in the interior, away from vulnerable borders.

The record in agriculture was not as impressive. Russian peasants in 1933 produced less food than before collectivization, and the amount of livestock markedly declined. In addition, famine occurred in 1932–1933. The poor record was largely due to the peasant's resistance to collectivization and the government's use of force. Stalin was determined to push most peasants into either collective farms or state farms. In the collectives, peasants worked the land collectively, and after meeting all other obligations, they divided what was left of their produce according to the percentage they had earned by their work. On a state farm, on the other hand, workers received wages directly from the state.

Both collective and state farms were unpopular with the peasants, and few were willing to give up their old ways. Peasants slaughtered their animals rather than turn them over to the collective farms. In response to such resistance, the government killed millions of peasants and sent additional millions to premature deaths in forced labor camps. Stalin waged war especially on those designated as "kulaks," who were supposedly prosperous peasants guilty of hoarding. Actually, almost any peasant who was in trouble with the authorities was apt to be included in this category.

Some of the millions of Soviet peasants who were deported from villages during the collectivization process.
(© *Illustrated London News*)

Stalin also deliberately kept food from the Ukrainians, who were always too independent-minded for his taste. Stalin's action, according to some estimates, caused 5 million deaths in the Ukraine alone during the famine of 1932–1933. The overall toll of deaths resulting from Stalin's collectivization policies and the famine has been estimated by the historian Robert Conquest at 14.5 million people.

Despite the resistance, however, Stalin succeeded in forcing many peasants onto collective or state farms. He granted only one noteworthy concession when he allowed collectivized peasants to maintain small private garden plots and a few animals. By the end of the first Five-Year Plan, more than 60 percent of the cultivated land in Russia was under the control of collective farms and about 10 percent under state farms. In subsequent years, the collectivization thrust continued, placing most of the remaining peasants and their produce effectively under the control of the party and state. At a time when Soviet peasants were starving to death, the government forced them to turn over grain to government agencies who used it to feed the expanding cities, to add to grain reserves, and even to export.

SUMMARY

The years 1917–1932 witnessed cataclysmic changes in Russian life. The overthrow of the tsar, the establishment of the Provisional Government, the Bolshevik revolution, the civil war, the NEP, and finally the first Five-Year Plan and collectivization all helped to greatly transform Russia. By 1932 it had changed from an overwhelmingly agrarian, religious, traditional empire with an autocratic government to a rapidly industrializing Marxist society. Its official values were atheistic and revolutionary, and the Communist party and Soviet government interfered more actively in the lives of the people than had the old tsarist government. Collectivization, in particular, transformed patterns of work. The increased use of education and the media as instruments of propaganda and the use of terror also made it increasingly difficult to ignore or oppose the desires of the authorities. In the immediate postwar years, the revolutionary nature of the government and its aggressive Marxist-Leninist ideas made it a threat to international stability. By 1932, however, it was more concerned with continuing the internal transformation of the Soviet Union than with causing Communist revolutions in other nations.

SUGGESTED SOURCES

ACTON, EDWARD, *Rethinking the Russian Revolution* (1990). An excellent historiographical overview of differing interpretations of the 1917 revolutions and the events leading up to them.*

CHAMBERLAIN, WILLIAM HENRY, *The Russian Revolution, 1917–1921*, 2 vols. (1935). A readable and still valuable overview of the revolution and civil war.*

CONQUEST, ROBERT, *The Harvest of Sorrow: Soviet Collectivization and the Terror-Famine* (1986). The appalling story of Stalin's policies which cost millions of Soviet lives.* (A fifty-five-minute documentary on the same subject, called *Harvest of Despair*, is available on video.)

FITZPATRICK, SHEILA, *The Russian Revolution, 1917–32* (1984). A clear, brief, and objective account.*

GOLDMAN, EMMA, *My Disillusionment in Russia* (1970). Recounts her experiences in Russia in 1920–1921 after she was deported from the United States.*

LINCOLN, W. BRUCE, *Red Victory: A History of the Russian Civil War* (1989). A comprehensive overview by a scholar who also writes excellent popular history.*

PASTERNAK, BORIS, *Doctor Zhivago* (1958). A great novel conveying the chaotic conditions of Russia during World War I, the revolution, and the civil war, and the reactions of a sensitive man to it all.* (Also a film.)

PIPES, RICHARD, *The Russian Revolution* (1990). A long account, full of interesting details, by a historian who believes that the Bolshevik revolution was one of the century's greatest tragedies.*

Potemkin (1926). One of Sergei Eisenstein's most famous films, it deals with a mutiny on a battleship during the revolt of 1905.

REED, JOHN, *Ten Days That Shook the World* (1919). A first-hand account of the Bolshevik revolt by the famous American Marxist.* (Several films have also appeared with this title: the first, an Eisenstein film, was originally called *October* and is now available on video tape under its original title; a more recent film narrated by Orsen Welles is also available on videotape.)

SUNY, RONALD, and ARTHUR ADAMS, Eds., *The Russian Revolution and Bolshevik Victory: Visions and Revisions*, 3d ed. (1990). Twenty-one essays representing a good cross section of scholarship on various aspects of 1917 revolutionary activities; part of the Heath "Problems" series.

THOMPSON, JOHN M., *Revolutionary Russia, 1917*, 2d ed. (1989). A brief and accurate book; a good introduction to the subject.*

*Paperback available.

CHAPTER 13

Europe in the 1920s

The period from the end of World War I up to the Great Depression of 1929 was one of economic, social, and political adjustments to the results of the war and to the Russian Revolution. From 1919 until 1923–1924, instability pervaded Europe and competing political forces struggled against one another. By the middle of the decade, there were signs that a more stable atmosphere was returning, both between European governments and in domestic affairs, but to some extent these signs were illusory.

1919–1923: A PERIOD OF FLUX

Economic and Social Adjustments

One of the greatest problems European governments faced after the war was how to reintegrate millions of returning servicemen into their peacetime economies. Some men were unable to find jobs and became part of a severe unemployment problem in Europe during the postwar decade. After years of combat, many also found it difficult to settle down into a civilian routine. They believed that those who had not been through combat were not in a position to hold themselves up as guides and teachers. Some veterans blamed their elders for the folly of the war, and some, especially in Germany and Italy, objected to the peace settlements. While many servicemen stayed out of politics or supported traditional political leaders, some of the early followers of Benito Mussolini and Adolf Hitler, both veterans themselves, were fellow veterans.

Europeans also found it difficult to adjust to inflation. It affected mostly old people on pensions, and clerks, civil servants, teachers, and others on fixed incomes. Many of these people had prided themselves on their "white-collar" middle-class status and now often saw their wages fall behind those of unionized "blue-collar" workers, who were in a better position to bargain for salary increases. Many feared that inflation would eat up their savings and that they would be destitute in their old age. Economic insecurities in Italy and Germany, later heightened in Germany by the Great Depression, led white-collar workers increasingly to doubt that moderate governments could find effective solutions. Fearful that the blue-collar parties of the Left would bring social disorder and loss of their status, many white-collar workers turned to the policies of Mussolini and Hitler.

The postwar period saw the gap between the aristocracy and the rest of society lessen. Ever since citizens had been encouraged to make sacrifices during the war, flagrant displays of wealth had gone out of style. The 1917 revolution had destroyed the aristocracy in Russia, and its status was in decline in Germany and Austria-Hungary with the collapse of the monarchies there. The aristocracy elsewhere in Europe often found its real wealth eroded by taxes and inflation.

At the other end of the social scale, the working class and its unions became more respectable. Most wartime governments had realized the need for cooperating with the unions, and this had conferred on the unions a new prestige. Immediately after the war, there was extensive labor unrest, but by the middle of the 1920s, the situation was more stable. In 1924 Great Britain acquired its first Labour government.

During the war, women had been permitted for the first time to engage in a number of occupations previously reserved for men. With the presence of so many men at the front, it had become more acceptable for respectable women to be seen in public without male escorts. Women had also secured the right to vote in a number of nations; Great Britain enfranchised those over thirty in 1918, and German women got the vote in 1919. During the 1920s it became more common to see women smoking and drinking in public. All these changes contributed to breaking down some of the traditional cultural distinctions between men and women.

Ethnic Nationalism and the Conflict in Ireland

During the immediate postwar period, the Irish, like many ethnic nationalities in Eastern Europe, struggled for their independence. The Catholic Irish majority on the island had long regarded the Protestant British rulers and Scots-Irish minority as exploiters and religious enemies. The Irish had already been agitating for the right to run their own internal affairs (Home Rule) for about fifty years. A Home Rule bill was enacted in 1914, but because of the outbreak of the war and resistance among Protestants in Northern Ireland, the British government decided not to put it into effect until the hostilities ended. After the British government executed fourteen ringleaders in 1916 for attempting an uprising, the radical Sinn Fein party, with Eamon De Valera at its head, became more popular among the Irish.

In December 1918 the Sinn Fein party won a smashing victory in the election of Irish members to the British Parliament. The next month, they organized an Irish parliament of their own and declared their independence from Great Britain. The British, supported by the Protestants, sent in forces to crush the rebels. A vicious cycle of terror and counterterror followed, marked by bombs, arson, and torture. In December 1921 the British government and rebel leaders signed a treaty that recognized the Irish Free State, a self-governing dominion comprising most of Ireland. Much of Ulster in the north, where the Protestants were dominant, remained a part of Great Britain.

The trouble was still not over. Some of the Irish nationalists, led by De Valera, were not willing to write off Northern Ireland or accept anything other than complete independence and continued to wage an unsuccessful civil war until De Valera's arrest in 1923. De Valera later returned and became the outstanding figure in Irish politics for decades. After World War II, the Republic of Ireland declared its complete independence. Northern Ireland, with its Protestant majority, continued to be united with Great Britain. The Catholic minority in Northern Ireland, however, opposed the union with Great Britain and wanted to be incorporated into the Republic of Ireland. The "Irish question" continued to be an unsettled problem.

Challenges from the Left and Right in Europe

With the collapse of the monarchies in Russia, Germany, and Austria-Hungary, champions of democracy hoped that the postwar period might be a golden age. They had been further encouraged by Woodrow Wilson, who had proclaimed in 1917 that the United States would fight "for the right of those who submit to authority to have a voice in their own government." The hope proved to be utopian. Instead, undemocratic movements of the Left and the Right, by challenging and at times overcoming fragile democratic institutions, contributed to the instability of the period.

The Marxist revolution in Russia not only helped to set off a chain of events that kept Russia in a chaotic condition until 1921 but also contributed to "Red Scares" in other European nations. In January 1919 disturbances involving leftists broke out in Berlin, after which two leading German Communists, Rosa Luxemburg and Karl Liebknecht, were murdered. Later in 1919, Communists established governments in Hungary and in Bavaria for a short time, until Rumanian troops helped to oust the first and German regular troops and Freikorps (free corps) volunteers the second. In 1920 German leftist forces were put down in the Ruhr mining districts.

There were also threats from the far Right during these early postwar years. In March 1920 Berlin was taken over for several days by rightist military forces during the Kapp Putsch. The putsch failed when the Socialist party and trade unions began a general strike. In 1923 in Munich, former army corporal Adolf Hitler unsuccessfully attempted to topple both the local Bavarian government and that of the German republic. In that same year, General Miguel Primo de Rivera took over the government in Spain in a military coup and established a dictatorship.

Fascist Italy

The most important and successful right-wing movement of the immediate postwar years was that of the Italian Fascist Benito Mussolini. Before the war,

A defiant-looking Mussolini with some of his followers before assuming power in 1922. *(The Granger Collection)*

Mussolini had been one of Italy's most prominent Socialists and the editor of the official Socialist newspaper. In addition to the ideas of Karl Marx, those of Nietzsche also strongly influenced him. "To comprehend Nietzsche," he wrote in 1908, "we must imagine a new race of 'free spirits,' strengthened in war . . . spirits endowed with a sort of sublime perversity, spirits that will free us from the love of our neighbor." Such macho statements were typical of Mussolini, who also thought of himself as a virile man—he reportedly had 169 mistresses during his lifetime. He also said that "war is to man as maternity to women," and that "the Italians must learn to grow less likeable and to become hard, implacable, and full of hatred."

Shortly after the outbreak of World War I, Mussolini's call for Italian participation on the side of France and Great Britain led the Italian Socialist party to expel him. He then became the editor of his own newspaper and continued a campaign for Italian intervention. Soon after Italy entered the war in 1915, Mussolini was sent to the front but did not see combat. After the war, he emerged as the leader of a group that soon came to be known as Fascists after they had labeled themselves *Fasci di Combattimento*, meaning "combat groups."

A number of factors explain how Mussolini was able to rise from the leader of a small group of malcontents to the legitimate head of the Italian government by late 1922. Although Italy possessed a parliamentary system, it did not have a strong democratic tradition. After the war, its prime ministers and the Chamber of Deputies had to deal with a number of serious problems, including an inflation rate that by 1920 had reduced the lira to one-fifth of its prewar value. Italy also faced, as did other nations, the difficulty of reintegrating veterans into its society and economy and of once again putting society on a peacetime basis. In addition, the government had to contend with the anger of those disappointed over the failure of Italy to gain more territory from the postwar settlements.

Mussolini and his black-shirted Fascists helped to magnify these problems and added others of their own. Aided by the alarm created by strikes and land seizures in 1919 and 1920, Mussolini played on the fears of communism and socialism that were shared by those afraid to lose their property and by those opposed to Marxist atheism. The Fascists attacked and at times killed their leftist opponents. Semilawlessness soon existed as violence countered violence. Many of the rich and powerful were willing to countenance Fascist brutality in the hope that it would destroy leftist forces. In the face of these difficulties, the various parties in the Chamber of Deputies found it increasingly difficult to work together. Finally, confronted with the threat of Fascist bands marching on Rome, Victor Emmanuel III, the constitutional monarch, asked Mussolini to form a new government in 1922.

Since his party still possessed only a small number of representatives in the Chamber of Deputies, Mussolini's first government included only four Fascists among the fourteen ministers. Undoubtedly, some Italians hoped that, once saddled with the responsibilities of government, Mussolini and his followers would become more moderate. Mussolini did consolidate his power cautiously, but his goal was still authoritarian government. For a short period, other parties continued to exist and to criticize the Fascists. In May 1924, for example, the Socialist deputy Giacomo Matteotti stood up in the Chamber of Deputies, amidst flying inkwells and insults, and accused the Fascists of rigging the recent elections and of resorting to murdering their political opponents. When he finished, he said to a colleague: "Now you may write the eulogy for my funeral." Eleven days later, he was stabbed to death by a Fascist gang. The public outrage that followed created the most serious crisis Mussolini had yet faced. Once again, however, the other political parties were unable to effectively move against Mussolini, and by 1925 all political parties except the Fascists were outlawed.

The Weimar Republic in Germany

In February 1919 a Constituent Assembly was convened at Weimar, Germany. By July it had adopted a democratic constitution, which was to remain in effect until Hitler began circumventing it in 1933. Both before and after adoption of the constitution, political conditions remained in a state of flux. Even more than the Italians, the Germans had no tradition of democracy. Parties on the extreme Right and Left opposed both the leadership of various moderate coalitions and the Weimar constitution itself. Political instability was partly a result of the Weimar system of representation: Parties in the Reichstag (lower house of parliament) received seats in proportion to the votes each had gained in general elections. This virtually ensured a multiplicity of parties and made coalition governments almost inevitable. As was often the case in other European nations with similar systems, Weimar coalition governments disintegrated quickly. The moderate Socialist Friedrich Ebert was president from 1919 until 1925, but cabinets under several chancellors changed on the average of once a year.

Stability was also difficult to achieve in Germany because of the resentment Germans felt toward the Treaty of Versailles. The Right, as well as many politically moderate Germans, believed their nation had not really been defeated but in fact had been tricked by the Allies or betrayed by their own leaders. Extreme right-wing enemies of the republic insisted that the military had been betrayed in World War I by some of the same politicians who now supported the new form of government and insisted that the Versailles treaty could have been resisted by again taking up arms. Partly in an effort to discredit further attacks from the Right, but also because most Germans were indignant regarding the treaty, most German politicians did their best to prevent it from being fully enforced. This undermining of the treaty fueled continual tensions with the Versailles "winners," which in turn further contributed to the unsettled conditions in Germany, especially before 1924.

The French Search for Security

In international affairs, France's search for security created tension and instability in Europe. France had fought two wars with Germany in fifty years and had twice seen German soldiers occupy its lands. The cost in lives and economic damage had been great. Yet Germany, despite its defeat in World War I, remained a potentially stronger nation, with a population considerably larger than that of France. Growing British and French differences over treatment of Germany, as well as other international issues, left the French in an especially difficult position. Great Britain's pledge to support France if Germany should attack in the future had lapsed when the United States had failed to ratify a similar commitment. Great Britain feared German resurgence less than France did and seemed more concerned with restoring prewar trade with Germany. Britain therefore was more willing than France to moderate the level of German reparations payments. Neither the League of Nations, dominated by the Europeans but with no real power, nor subsequent treaties signed with Eastern European nations offered much reassurance to French anxieties concerning German revitalization.

Meanwhile, France became increasingly frustrated by German attempts to evade the Versailles treaty. Because of opposition to the treaty at home, and because German statesmen also sensed a lack of Allied unity, Germany had no reservations about trying to subvert it. Germany attempted to evade full compliance with disarmament provisions, failed to comply with some boundary commission decisions, and failed to meet many of its reparations payments on schedule. In 1922, Germany's Rapallo Agreement with Russia, which reduced Germany's diplomatic isolation, caused further French fears.

Against the background of these events, and because of the insistence of the United States that Allied nations repay large wartime loans, France, Belgium, and Italy occupied the Ruhr industrial region in early 1923 when Germany failed to meet a reparations obligation. The Germans in the Ruhr responded with passive resistance, which inadvertently dealt a final blow to the already unstable German currency. As the economy faltered and inflation skyrocketed—paying a billion marks for a restaurant meal was not unusual—the Allies held firm, and the German government of Wilhelm Cuno collapsed. The French encouraged separatist movements in the occupied territories, and the Soviet-dominated Comintern helped stir up unrest in central Germany. Thus, in mid-1923, both German society and European international relations were still unsettled.

1924–1929: THE RETURN OF STABILITY?

By the middle of the 1920s it appeared that settled conditions had returned to Europe. By early 1924 the conflicts in Ireland and Russia had ended, and in that year a number of major powers recognized the Soviet government. In Germany, Chancellor Gustav Stresemann dealt with the threats by Hitler and the Communists in late 1923, reformed the ridiculously inflated currency, and began a foreign policy that appeared to be more accommodating than that of his predecessors. After being replaced as chancellor in November 1923—after only 100 days—he remained in various cabinets as foreign minister until his death in 1929. Stresemann helped Germany to improve relations with the former Allies and to scale down reparations payments. The latter accomplishment was aided by the Dawes Plan of 1924, which also provided for U.S. loans, and the Young Plan of 1929.

International Agreements: The Search for a Lasting Peace

One aspect of the apparent equilibrium of the middle and late 1920s was a series of agreements and adjustments in which some of the major European powers participated. The momentum for international accords that characterized the period began with a series of treaties signed in Washington in 1921–1922.

After World War I, the major naval powers feared that a new naval ship-building race would escalate tensions and increase expenses. In particular, many nations were concerned about the aggressive actions of Japan. The United States invited delegates from eight other nations to attend a conference in Washington, and during 1921 and 1922 several agreements were worked out. One agreement was the Five-Power Naval Treaty, which provided for scrapping seventy ships, a ten-year moratorium on new construction of capital ships, and a global tonnage ratio for capital ships (United States 5: Great Britain 5: Japan 3: France 1.75: Italy 1.75). The treaty also provided for a cessation of further naval fortifications in most of the Pacific area. Another agreement, the Four-Power Treaty, ended the Anglo-Japanese alliance and replaced it with an agreement between the United States, Great Britain, Japan, and France for mutual consultation in case of threats to the security of any territories belonging to any of them. The Nine-Power Treaty provided for continuation of the Open Door policy and preservation of China's sovereignty but continued the unequal treaties of the imperialist era. In addition, Japan agreed to make a compensated, gradual withdrawal from the Shantung peninsula in China and also to remove its troops from Siberia.

The agreements made in Washington in effect recognized that World War I had weakened the global power of Europe and augmented the military strength of the United States and Japan. In particular, in return for curbing aggressive tendencies on the Asian mainland, Japan gained de facto recognition as the dominant naval power in Asian waters.

For many, the Locarno treaties of 1925 represented the greatest sign of hope for a more tranquil era. The most important of these treaties confirmed the existing Franco-German and Belgian-German frontiers and was guaranteed by Great Britain and Italy. Germany, France, Belgium, Poland, and Czechoslovakia also signed a series of agreements promising to submit any conflict to arbitration. Finally, France signed treaties with Poland and Czechoslovakia providing for mutual assistance in case of a German attack.

While it might appear that the treaties signified no great gain for Germany, the rewards were significant. As the price for apparent German willingness to accept the western frontier imposed on it by the Versailles treaty, France agreed to give way on a number of points that considerably weakened its powers of coercion over Germany. The right of the Allies to inspect Germany's compliance with the disarmament provisions of Versailles now became almost meaningless. The evacuation of part of the Rhineland, which was scheduled to occur that year, went forward. Germany was also to join the League of Nations and to be given a permanent seat on its Council. Finally, it was significant that Germany refused at Locarno to confirm its eastern borders, a situation that increased the fears of Czechoslovakia and Poland and helped drive them into the arms of the French.

In 1926 Stresemann and the French and British foreign ministers, Aristide Briand and Austen Chamberlain, were all awarded the Nobel Prize for Peace for their Locarno efforts. Europeans talked of the new spirit of conciliation that was in the air. This "Spirit of Locarno" was further in evidence in 1928 when the U.S. Secretary of State, Frank Kellogg, joined Briand in creating the Kellogg-Briand Pact in which sixty-four nations renounced war as an "instrument of national policy." Paradoxically, the same nations reiterated their right to take up arms in self-defense.

Despite all these agreements, international stability proved illusory. Europe's economic recovery had in general been sluggish. Germany's economy and reparations payments were partly dependent on U.S. loans. Thus, a serious curtailment of the U.S. loans could have a ripple effect on Germany and the European Allies. Between a Germany bent on revision of the Treaty of Versailles and a France attempting to maintain its security, the potential for serious conflict remained. Germany's unwillingness at Locarno to agree that its eastern frontiers were permanent was also an ill omen.

Three foreign ministers, Gustav Stresemann (center, Germany), Sir Austen Chamberlain (left, Great Britain), and Aristide Briand (far right, France), discuss the future of Europe in 1928.
(Bilderdienst Süddeutscher Verlag)

In the case of the Washington Naval Conference agreements, there was no guarantee that the signatories would continue to honor them once they no longer felt it was in their interest to do so. The Kellogg-Briand Pact contained no provisions for dealing with aggression. In fact, it was little more than a pious wish, an "international kiss," in the words of one U.S. senator. Attempts in the late 1920s and early 1930s to deal with concrete issues of aggression and disarmament also proved fruitless.

European Governments: The Veneer of Stability

The ambiguous nature of international developments in the 1920s was also reflected in European governments, particularly in Germany. Despite the continuation of a multiplicity of political parties and coalition governments, the German governments following Stresemann from 1924 to 1929 appeared to be stable, as threats from the Left and the Right subsided. Nevertheless, important segments of German public opinion still criticized the new republican form of government or only grudgingly tolerated it. Despite the accomplishments of Stresemann as foreign minister, many nationalists believed that the government was moving too slowly in removing the shackles of the Versailles treaty. By 1929 such discontent took the form of organized opposition to the Young Plan and to continuing with reparations payments.

Part of the opposition to paying reparations came from Adolf Hitler and his small Nazi party. Although few guessed in 1929 how important Hitler would soon become, he had already come a long way from rather humble beginnings. Born in 1889, the son of a minor Austrian customs official, he failed to graduate from high school and had gone to Vienna hoping to enter art school. He was unsuccessful, but he remained in the Austro-Hungarian capital, living an impoverished life as a creator of advertising cards and small paintings. In 1913 he left Vienna for Munich in southern Germany. When World War I broke out, he enlisted in the German army. During the war he was wounded several times and was also cited and decorated for bravery on a number of occasions.

After the war, Hitler became involved with a small, rather insignificant nationalistic political group in Munich that called itself the German Workers' party. Within a couple of years he became its Führer, or leader. After leading the unsuccessful "Beer-Hall Putsch" in Munich in 1923, he spent nine months in prison. He used the time to write *Mein Kampf (My Struggle)*, a work he originally wished to call "Four and a Half Years of Struggle against Lies, Stupidity, and Cowardice." In it he spelled out his nationalism, anti-Semitism, racism, and totalitarianism. After his release from prison he continued to build up his party, by then called the National Socialist German Workers' (Nazi) party. In the 1928 Reichstag elections, the Nazis, now a party of some 108,000 paid members, won only about 3 percent of the total vote. By 1930, however, the onset of the Great Depression and continued national resentment over the Versailles treaty brought about impressive Nazi gains in the Reichstag elections; the Nazis gained 18 percent of the vote and became the second-largest party in that body. The illusory nature of the German stability of the late 1920s now became more evident.

In Great Britain, the Conservative party under Stanley Baldwin replaced a shaky Labour government in 1924 and remained in power for the next five years. Baldwin prided himself on being a plain and ordinary man, full of common sense. Under the Conservatives, the British appeared to be returning to happier times; the general standard of living went up, and the state provided even more benefits for the old, widowed, orphaned, and unemployed. But Britain's economic foundation was weak. Basic industries such as iron and steel, coal, cotton, and shipbuilding were in decline as a result of a combination of foreign competition, outdated business practices and technology, and legislation that prohibited general strikes and hampered the unionization of civil servants.

In France the government took longer than in Britain to stabilize. After Edouard Herriot, the leader of the Radical Socialist party, had governed for ten months, six successive governments followed each other in the period from April 1925 to July 1926, most of them brought down when they failed to deal with inflation. Only in July 1926, when Raymond Poincaré became prime minister of a broad-based National Union Coalition, was inflation brought under control. Poincaré's government lasted three years, a long time in French politics, and it was instrumental in bringing to France a measure of the calm that characterized the last part of the decade. Unfortunately for France, fundamental problems remained. The temporary equilibrium was largely a result of Poincaré's leadership rather than of change in the basically rickety French political system. In addition, French industry could not successfully compete with that of Germany, and both its industry and its agriculture remained inefficient compared to those of the United States.

While the larger nations of Europe struggled with their particular social and economic problems, two basic economic difficulties continued to lurk in the background of most of the smaller nations of Eastern and southern Europe: rural overpopulation and small markets for their exports, a problem exacerbated by rising foreign tariffs. Concurrently, there were signs of a movement toward the authoritarian Right in these nations. Right-wing seizures of power took place in Portugal and Poland in 1926, bringing about more ordered conditions than had previously existed, but at the cost of civil liberties and political freedom. In addition, a host of social and ethnic rivalries in Eastern Europe continued to simmer.

SUMMARY

The immediate postwar years presented the West with a number of problems: the reintegration of soldiers into a peacetime economy, reparations, the repayment of loans, unemployment and inflation, social and cultural adjustments, political conflicts in Russia and Ireland, and challenges from the Left and the Right to fragile democratic governments. For the time being, some governments were able to withstand the pressure, but others were not; the most notable case was that of Italy, where Mussolini came to power in 1922.

By the middle and latter part of the decade, most of the major powers appeared to be less troubled, as their economies apparently recovered. Agreements such as the Washington Naval Conference treaties, the Locarno treaties, and the Kellogg-Briand Pact all promised greater international equilibrium. Governments also seemed more stable. Stresemann remained Germany's foreign minister from 1923 to 1929, Baldwin was prime minister in Great Britain from 1924 to 1929, and Poincaré was prime minister in France from 1926 to 1929.

Underneath the apparent stabilizing developments of the late 1920s, however, there were problems. The economic underpinnings of many nations remained weak, and in Europe allegiance to democratic political forms was tentative. German resentment toward the Allies also was never far below the surface. All the international agreements in turn depended largely on the domestic stability and prosperity of the signatories, as well as continuing successful diplomacy. Beginning in 1929 and continuing into the 1930s, these problems became manifested in depression, aggression, and, finally, total war.

SUGGESTED SOURCES

FRIEDRICH, OTTO, *Before the Deluge* (1972). A portrait for the general reader of various aspects of Berlin life during the Weimar Republic.*

GRAVES, ROBERT, and ALAN HODGE, *The Long Week-End* (1936). An interesting portrayal of British life and customs from 1918 to 1939.*

KOLB, EBERHARD, *The Weimar Republic* (1988). A good overview by a German scholar.*

MACK SMITH, DENIS, *Mussolini* (1982). A well-written analysis by a leading scholar.*

MARKS, SALLY, *The Illusion of Peace* (1976). A brief and clear examination of international relations in the 1918–1933 period.*

Mussolini (The Twentieth Century Series). A twenty-seven-minute film dealing with the Italian dictator from the end of World War I until his death in 1945.

O'FLAHERTY, LIAM, *The Informer* (1925). A classic novel dealing with the Irish Civil War.* (Also an award-winning film directed by John Ford.)

SHIRER, WILLIAM L., *20th Century Journey* (1985). More than 300 pages are devoted to the 1920s in this U.S. journalist's account of experiences in the United States and in Paris, London, and other European cities.*

SILONE, IGNAZIO, *Fontamara* (1934). A leading Italian novelist's depiction of conflict in the 1920s between the village of Fontamara and Mussolini's Fascists.*

WAITE, ROBERT G., *The Psychopathic God: Adolf Hitler* (1983). A fascinating look at the personality of Hitler and the historical context in which he flourished; an example of psychohistory.*

*Paperback available.

CHAPTER 14

Economic and Social Upheaval in the United States and Latin America

During the 1920s and 1930s the Western Hemisphere was largely spared the horrors of war, but nonetheless the period was one of social discord and economic turmoil. The United States experienced social dislocations in the 1920s and plunged into the economic nightmare of the Great Depression during the 1930s. In Latin America the entrenched privileged classes were subject to challenges ranging from violence and social revolution in Mexico to more orderly reform movements in Chile. In international relations, the United States abandoned its policy of direct intervention in the Caribbean area. However, it still retained its political dominance there, and its economic exploitation of the resources of the area perpetuated the unequal distribution of income between an elite few and the impoverished masses. Nationalists in Latin America continued to regard their nations as victims of "Yankee Imperialism." By the late 1930s, however, there were hopeful signs of a recovering economy and more equitable social systems in both the United States and Latin America.

THE UNITED STATES: "BOOM" TO BUST

Postwar Discord in the United States

The United States, like Europe, found the postwar years unsettling. The Senate rejected the Versailles treaty, and the United States refused to join the League of Nations. Wilson spent his last months in office as a reclusive invalid. Warren Harding called for a return to "normalcy" upon taking office in 1921, but his administration was troubled by corruption, and soon after his death in 1923 a number of political scandals surfaced. In 1919 workers conducted widespread strikes; Attorney General A. Mitchell Palmer, playing on the fears of many Americans that the Communist revolution would spread to the United States, orchestrated a "Red Scare," jailing and deporting Marxists and anarchists. In Massachusetts in 1921, two anarchists, Nicola Sacco and Bartolomeo

Vanzetti, were convicted of robbery and murder and eventually executed. In view of the actions of the judge and others connected with the trial, many claimed that the men were convicted in part because of their beliefs. Anticapitalists around the world proclaimed that the trial was a symbol of capitalist repression.

U.S. ethnic and racial tensions, already on the rise before World War I, came to a climax after the war. Nativist Americans of northern European descent persuaded Congress in 1921 and again in 1924 to limit annual immigration to a low figure, to establish quotas that discriminated against Europeans from southern and eastern Europe, and to exclude the Japanese. Anti-Semitism continued, and race riots and lynchings of African Americans punctuated the scene. The revived Ku Klux Klan gained political control of several states across the nation. At its peak in the early 1920s, the Klan contested control of the Democratic party and staged a massive march in Washington before it collapsed from internal bickering. In addition to political and racial tensions, there was often a cultural hostility between advocates of the new values of the "Roaring Twenties," usually city dwellers, and those from smaller towns and rural areas who defended prohibition and conservative religious values.

"Prosperity"

During President Calvin Coolidge's years in office, from late 1923 until early 1929, the United States seemed to enter a quiet and secure period at the same time that stability was apparently returning to Europe. Many in the United States believed that normalcy had finally arrived. Coolidge himself claimed in 1928 that "in the domestic field there is tranquility and contentment. . . . In the foreign field there is peace." One measure of "tranquility" appeared to be a booming economy; industrial production doubled between 1921 and 1929. Republican administrations fostered business expansion by implementing a program of high tariffs and low corporate and income taxes. Many business corporations merged into larger and more efficient conglomerates, and new technology spawned an increasing array of consumer goods for Americans and for world markets. The growing middle class bought an enormous number of automobiles, telephones, radios, and electric appliances, taking advantage of an exciting new credit concept—the installment plan. Many Americans also found extra money to invest in the stock market, which moved ever higher.

Despite the apparent prosperity, however, there were grave problems in the U.S. economy. Railroads, textiles, and coal were depressed industries; many workers faced layoffs and wage cuts. Only those workers in the skilled trades benefited from union organization. In the South, children and women labored in textile mills for up to 60 hours a week for a few cents per hour.

Problems among the nation's farmers constituted another sign of impending economic trouble. Having expanded production in World War I to produce the bumper crops demanded by the Allies, U.S. farmers throughout the 1920s faced both a drop in demand and increased worldwide competition. As a result, crop prices plummeted and many farmers could not make enough money to pay their mortgages. Some of the larger landholders saved themselves by mechanizing their operations, but many sharecroppers and tenant farmers lost their jobs, and a growing number of marginal farmers had to abandon their farms. Farm belt politicians created a political furor, but Republican administrations failed to find any effective policies for relief.

By 1929, when Herbert Hoover became President, additional economic problems, largely unrecognized at the time, were present. Production far exceeded consumption; stockpiles accumulated as consumers lacked the money and even the credit to purchase the vast array of goods available. In addition, many individuals and banking institutions were speculating on the stock market. There were no laws controlling the amount of stock that could be purchased on credit; speculators could and did buy a maximum amount of stocks with a minimum amount of cash. When prices went high enough, speculators sold their stocks, paid their debt, and kept the remainder as a profit. However, if prices dropped or even remained steady, speculators could easily owe enormous sums of money they did not have. Few seemed worried. "Stocks have reached a permanently high plateau," commented a distinguished professor of economics on October 17, 1929.

On "Black Thursday," October 24, 1929, the stock market on Wall Street began to collapse, and the United States headed toward a full-fledged crisis. Within a matter of hours most speculators were ruined. Despite assurances from Hoover and other authorities that the worst was over, stock prices moved steadily lower until December 1932. During this three-year period a devastating downward spiral of business cutbacks, unemployment, and bankruptcies ensued. Many unemployed families lost their homes when they could no longer meet their mortgage payments. Other families lost their savings when their banks failed.

By early 1933 the U.S. economy was in a disastrous condition with industrial production cut back, 25 percent of the work force unemployed, and more and more banks going under. Hoover, a devout capitalist and a Constitutional conservative, believed that the best way to pull out of the depression was to let the economy alone to work its way through the crisis. In his view, the U.S. federal constitutional system placed responsibility for providing relief on the private sector and the states; the national government's role was limited to expanding public works, providing loans to big business (the benefits would "trickle down" to the average American), and raising tariffs to keep out competing foreign goods. Hoover's policies did not work; the economy continued to deteriorate, and he was defeated in his bid for a second term in 1932 by Democrat Franklin Roosevelt.

The New Deal

When Roosevelt took the oath of office on March 4, 1933, the United States faced its greatest threat since the Civil War. With the Republican party and its policies discredited by economic collapse and three years of failure to bring

President Franklin D. Roosevelt projects a cheerful image during the New Deal.
(*AP/Wide World Photos*)

about recovery, the American people had turned to the Democratic party. Roosevelt was a rather traditional politician from a wealthy family who wished to preserve U.S. capitalism, but he was willing to experiment with new programs to ensure that capitalism survived. Because state governments and the private sector had failed to cope with the economic disaster, Roosevelt was willing to extend the national government's regulatory power deep into the economic and social fabric of the country. "The only thing we have to fear is fear itself," he assured his fellow Americans. Roosevelt and the Democrats called their collection of programs the New Deal.

Roosevelt was concerned for the suffering of the poor and unemployed and was willing to run up large budget deficits to provide relief and stimulate recovery. "Our greatest primary task is to put people to work," he declared, and most of his relief programs focused on providing employment to put purchasing power back into the hands of U.S. families and to rekindle a sense of pride and worth. Various federal programs gave people jobs in reforestation and in constructing government buildings, schools, airports, hospitals, parks, and dams. Where possible, the government employed writers, musicians, actors, artists, and archivists in their own professions. The national government also provided grants-in-aid to states to supplement their relief programs. The government assisted tenant farmers, resettled farm families, and provided home loans to pay off mortgages.

Although the New Dealers were willing to spend money on relief projects for the short run, they were more interested in creating programs that would solve basic problems in the U.S. economy. Under Roosevelt's sponsorship, the U.S. government regulated the financial community, monitored the stock market, provided loans for banks to regain solvency, and insured savings deposits. When Roosevelt took the nation off the gold standard, Roosevelt's conservative director of the budget moaned, "This is the end of Western civilization."

In order to assist business, improve wages and working conditions, and protect consumer interests, the Roosevelt administration set up the National Recovery Administration (NRA), charged with creating codes to regulate production standards in business. In practice, the NRA codes often turned out to benefit big business; they were plagued with noncompliance, and they were eventually struck down by the Supreme Court. The government did succeed in regulating certain industries such as coal, petroleum, and trucking. In the interests of developing depressed regions, the government went beyond regulation. For example, in the Tennessee Valley Authority and in similar projects in the West, the government not only constructed dams to control floods but also produced cheap electric power, thus putting the government in competition with privately owned utilities.

To stimulate wage increases and thereby increase purchasing power, the federal government supported collective bargaining. The craft unions, long organized under the American Federation of Labor, grew stronger. After a period of strikes and violence, industrial workers, under the umbrella of the Congress of Industrial Organizations, established unions in the automobile, steel, mining, and other industries. Once unionized, workers made substantial headway in improving wages, working conditions, and grievance procedures. Labor leaders, such as the dynamic John L. Lewis of the United Mine Workers, became powerful national figures.

The Roosevelt administration also took strong measures to end the farm depression. Farmers limited production of certain basic commodities by voting to submit to government production and marketing quotas. In return, the government set a fair price level (parity) and guaranteed it would subsidize the difference or most of the difference if market prices fell below the parity level. With this approach and through related programs, farm income, especially for those with large holdings, began to rise steadily.

The New Deal also rapidly expanded the welfare state. The welfare state in the United States came later than similar modifications of capitalism in other industrialized nations, and it was less extensive. It was not a reflection of a coherent overall policy but a collection of specific programs, some administered by the national government and some by the states, which provided sketchy cradle-to-the-grave protection against personal catastrophes. It included aid to women with dependent children, aid to the blind and handicapped, unemployment compensation, workmen's compensation for injuries and illnesses sustained on the job, minimum wage and maximum hour limits, public housing, old age pensions, and limitations on child labor. Some Americans regarded the welfare state as socialism, but it proved to be popular with most of the U.S. public, even though benefits were low and many people were excluded.

By 1939 the New Deal had brought about a partial economic recovery. On the positive side, the percentage of families above the poverty level had increased and the percentage of the national income owned by the upper classes had declined, indicating a more equitable distribution of the national wealth. Middle-class Americans had been bolstered financially and psychologically, and lower-class Americans, especially minorities, had been saved from destitution. On the other hand, unemployment ran at 15 percent and real wages were still below those of 1929. Meanwhile, the budget deficit of the national government had risen from $7 million to $20 billion. It took the outbreak of the war in Europe, with the subsequent rise in military spending, to bring an end to the Depression.

While only partially successful in bringing back economic prosperity, the New Deal created substantial changes in the United States. Americans, through their national government, increasingly regulated capitalism and expanded the welfare state. Agriculture continued to be subsidized, and the trade union movement remained powerful in the basic industries. Roosevelt's aggressive leadership expanded the groundwork laid by Theodore Roosevelt and Wilson in strengthening the power of the presidency.

In politics, the Roosevelt coalition of white southerners, African Americans, union labor, ethnics, and urban voters made the Democratic party the majority party in Congress for most of the next 60 years. In the larger context, the people of the United States had strongly affirmed the historic democratic experience of their nation. Beset with heavy economic burdens, they worked out their problems inside the traditional democratic political system, rejecting totalitarian solutions of the Right and of the Left.

REVOLUTION IN MEXICO

By the early twentieth century many dictatorships, especially in the smaller and poorer nations, were essentially the same as in the nineteenth century. They were usually run by military "strongmen" or *jefes,* and the tone of these regimes varied with the personality of the leader.

Gradually, however, certain groups began to challenge the ruling order. Some members of the small middle class of entrepreneurs and professionals, traditionally subservient to the landlord families, wished to replace *caudillo* rule with representative government, hoping they would thereby be able to secure political power. They also wanted to reduce foreign investment and thus gain a greater share in the financial and industrial development of their nations. Some members of the elite and the middle class were idealistic and wished to improve the living conditions of the lower classes and bring them into the political system.

The rapidly growing masses of impoverished urban workers also challenged *caudillo* rule. Many workers were white immigrants from Europe who were often escaping from repression at home and had no tradition of obedience to the ruling elite. They were joined by peasants fleeing the poverty in the countryside, many of whom had abandoned their traditional passive subservience. The urban workers were interested in obtaining minimum wage and maximum hour laws, sickness and accident protection, health and safety regulations, and pensions, but they showed little interest in education or democratic political systems. They represented a volatile new force in Latin American politics, and traditionalists were uncertain whether they should suppress the urban masses if they became unruly or appease them with welfare legislation in order to obtain their political support.

The Díaz Dictatorship

Although the middle class and the urban workers appeared the most likely to bring social change to Latin America, the most radical social and economic revolution came in Mexico. The middle class furnished the catalyst for revolution, and the urban workers pitched in, but the Indian and mestizo peasants who had recently lost their land provided the driving force. In 1910, Mexico had been in the grip of a classic strongman, Porfirio Díaz, for 35 years. Díaz, a mestizo, was supported by Mexico's ruling families and foreign corporations. The Church also backed Díaz, as did the military. The mass of Indians and mestizos were considered fit to be only laborers. One element of Díaz's supporters claimed that Indians were inferior and that progress would come by attracting white settlement, in the pattern set by the United States, Argentina, Uruguay, Brazil, and Chile.

Díaz once said, "Poor Mexico, so far from God and so close to the United States." This was no doubt a vexatious situation, but most Mexicans found that their main torment was the dictator himself. Díaz used classic strongman tactics to perpetuate his regime. The *rurales,* his rural police, kept order in the countryside by shooting opponents and suppressing the riots sparked by angry Indians who had lost their land. The growing urban working class, especially in the new textile industry, was closely watched by the authorities; strikes were forbidden, and wildcat walkouts were crushed. Díaz conciliated some in the rapidly growing middle class by expanding the bureaucracy and giving them employment. Political opponents were watched, the press partially censored, and the judiciary controlled. Díaz manipulated the political process by nominating his allies to Congress and himself to the presidency and declaring everyone elected after votes were cast at the end of each term.

During the rule of Díaz, the great landlords of Mexico—a few thousand *hacienderos*—expanded their holdings, often at the expense of the Indian communities, in order to increase the production of staples for sale in the international market. Food production dropped, and food had to be imported; the standard of living for the majority of the population declined. In some states over 95 percent of the population were landless. Díaz encouraged foreign investors to build up the railroad system, to create electric power, and especially to develop the petroleum industry, which rose to the third largest in the world. He also invited them to become *hacienderos* by purchasing large tracts of mining, timber, and farmland. In 1910 Americans owned 22 percent of Mexican

---

Declaring against the Caudillo

[My college landlady boasted] that she had gone to the ball given for Porfirio Díaz. . . .

"He bears the stamp of the hero," she said.

"Of the assassin," I interrupted. . . .

Why my violent reaction against the Mexican caudillo? I had not thought it out. Perhaps I merely absorbed my hatred from my surroundings. He was never publicly attacked, but you breathed in the very air a violent dislike of him. . . .

The latent social distress of the country had at last taken form in the mind of . . . Francisco Madero. . . . He was looking for independent men, men of decision; he invited me to a meeting. . . .

Anything rather than Mexico under Díaz—corrupt, militaristic, murderous. Going home, I looked adoringly at my son, a few months old, smiling

and vigorous, and I thought, "I wish he might die if this does not change."*

◆◗◆◆

Thus the young Mexican philosopher José Vasconcelos discusses how his anti-Díaz sentiments were crystallized into action by the influence of Francisco Madero, the man who toppled Porfirio Díaz and launched the Mexican Revolution. Vasconcelos later became a leading, but controversial, politician and educator in revolutionary Mexico. As minister of education and head of the National University, he supported secularism and championed Mexico's Indian-mestizo heritage. Later, however, he repudiated this outlook and embraced the Catholic Church and the Spanish tradition of Mexico.

*From *A Mexican Ulysses: An Autobiography* by José Vasconcelos, translated and abridged by W. Rex Crawford. Copyright © 1963 by the University of Indiana Press. Reprinted by permission.

---

land. To outsiders, the Díaz regime appeared to be a stable and economically progressive administration. The United States and European nations extended their support. The U.S. millionaire Andrew Carnegie, for example, stated after a visit that "in every corner of the Republic reigned prosperity and peace."

Revolt, Civil War, and Revolution

Despite Díaz's dictatorial controls, his regime was overthrown. In 1910 Francisco Madero, a moderate liberal working for political freedom for the middle class, raised the standard of revolt. Madero was quickly joined by two charismatic leaders who became folk heroes of Mexico. In northern Mexico, Francisco "Pancho" Villa led a group of cowboys and small farmers who wanted to oust foreign property owners. In the south, Madero received support from Emiliano Zapata, who led a group of dispossessed peasants who wanted legal reforms and land. Díaz fled, reputedly remarking, "Madero has unleashed a tiger; let us see if he can control it." Madero and Zapata were both assassinated, and a bloody struggle between revolutionary factions raged across Mexico for ten years. Relations with the United States deteriorated in the wake of

A brief moment of unity in the Mexican Revolution: Francisco Villa (left) sits in the presidential chair with Emiliano Zapata beside him.
(Special Collections, University of Texas at El Paso)

Mexican border raids and two major punitive expeditions by the United States into Mexico. As many as 2 million Mexicans perished.

As the fighting raged on, it became apparent that what had begun as a relatively limited reform movement was changing into a broad-scale social, economic and political revolution. Some of the Indian and mestizo leaders wanted to destroy white rule in Mexico; secularists and religious reformers wanted to curb the power of the Catholic Church; Indian villagers wanted their communal lands returned; farm workers wanted land of their own; urban laborers wanted higher wages and improved working conditions; the middle class wanted a liberal republic, both for idealistic reasons and because of a desire to assume control of the political process. Nearly all agreed that foreign controls over the Mexican economy had to be rolled back. As the struggle continued, a new Mexico evolved as Mexican revolutionaries incorporated the reforms sought by the major contending groups.

The Constitution of 1917, the most radical constitution in the world at that time, laid out the goals of the Mexican Revolution. The aspirations of the Indian and mestizo middle and lower classes of Mexico dominated the document, which ended the rule of the predominantly white upper class. The constitution was traditional in its political provisions, setting up a typical Latin American government that coupled democratic process with a strong presidency.

On the other hand, the social and economic provisions of the constitution were revolutionary. It reduced the power of the Catholic Church in Mexico, stripping it of its remaining lands, removing the Church from primary education, and forbidding clerics to engage in politics. It empowered the government to take and redistribute private land, while at the same time it recognized Indian communal landholding. Petroleum, minerals, and water were declared common national resources, and foreign companies were made subject to government control. The constitution outlined a complete labor code, recognized the right to unionize and strike, called for minimum wage and maximum hour standards, and promised insurance and pension plans.

By 1921 order had been generally restored; as one general grumbled, "This revolution has now degenerated into a government." The men who controlled Mexico during the 1920s and 1930s were interested in restoring political stability. They wished to provide reforms at a moderate pace rather than stirring up new convulsions by immediately implementing the social and economic clauses of the Constitution of 1917. They brought the army and the church under civilian control and created what became essentially a one-party state. The new party, the Party of the Revolution, institutionalized the revolution and turned it away from violence. The party was pledged to carry forward the revolution; its support was so broad that it prevented effective opposition parties from developing in the interwar period. In time, the party organization became more important than individuals; party leaders agreed in advance on who would succeed to the presidency, thus providing for an orderly transfer of power at each election. Meanwhile, the government inaugurated a modest program of rural schools and slowly proceeded with land distribution. Such land redistribution expanded the small farmer class, which concentrated on producing badly needed foodstuffs.

The revolution bore its greatest fruit under President Lázaro Cárdenas (1934–1940). Remembering his roots in a grindingly poor village, Cárdenas was determined to improve the lot of his downtrodden compatriots. In a term in office paralleling the New Deal years in the United States, Cárdenas built up enormous popularity as he toured villages to learn of local problems and to make arrangements for relief. He accelerated the process of taking land from the *hacienderos* and giving it to landless peasants, placing particular emphasis on restoring land lost by the Indian communities. By 1940 the accumulated land reforms of 20 years had put almost half of the cropland of Mexico in the hands of small farmers. Cárdenas also ordered more schools built and supported improved working conditions and wage raises for urban workers.

To the widespread acclaim of Mexicans of all classes, Cárdenas also clamped down on foreign-owned companies. He nationalized the railroads, and after the petroleum companies ignored a Mexican supreme court ruling on paying minimum wages, he nationalized the petroleum industry. The national petroleum corporation was soon operating more efficiently than under the foreign owners, with petroleum earmarked for domestic development instead of foreign consumption. The United States and European nations were angry but eventually acquiesced.

In another major consequence of the Mexican Revolution, governments after Díaz began to recast the national image away from the Latin history of Mexico toward its Indian heritage. The mestizos, who now dominated Mexican affairs, encouraged books and murals about Indian history and culture. The new motion picture medium made a marked impression on the masses as they saw films about contemporary life in the Indian villages and about the Aztec and Mayan past. The population began to celebrate their Indian background and to identify with the nation and the new revolutionary party.

By the 1940s, however, revolutionary fervor began to fade, and Mexican society fell well short of fulfilling its revolutionary goals. *Hacienderos* still controlled half the productive acreage, and one-third of the population still worked as serfs. Graft and mismanagement dissipated the effects of many of Cárdenas' programs. Still, Mexico had come a long way from the days of Díaz.

The Mexican Revolution occurred at the same time as the Bolshevik revolution, but its ideology, pace, and results were quite different. The Bolsheviks had two successive long-term leaders, supported by a highly disciplined minority party determined to fulfill a blueprint for a new order. They gained control of their nation relatively quickly, and with clearly defined goals made profound changes in Russian society.

The Mexican Revolution was rooted in Mexican problems and worked its way toward a uniquely Mexican resolution. It had many leaders, none of whom had any significant connection with the revolutionary ideologies sweeping Europe. The civil war lasted for a decade, revolutionary goals varied widely among different groups, and a disciplined party and a consensus on goals were therefore slow to develop. Although substantial progress was made toward fundamental change, the revolution in Mexico was not pushed through to completion.

OTHER CHALLENGES TO THE CAUDILLO *IN LATIN AMERICA*

Mexico, with its partly realized social revolution and its one-party state, was unique in its overthrow of *caudillo* government in the interwar period. However, pressure from events outside Latin America, the influence of the Mexican Revolution, and developments inside particular nations brought about either threats to or modifications of the rule of the strongman.

In response to the great movements sweeping Europe, the authoritarian regimes were staunchly anti-Marxist, but some urban workers did join Marxist organizations. Some regimes flirted with fascism, but they did not become self-conscious ideological regimes like Hitler's Germany or actively indoctrinate the public through an extensive propaganda apparatus.

In some of the larger Latin American nations with a more complicated economic and social order, there was a movement toward a new pattern of authoritarian rule. These governments featured dynamic personalities, some influenced by Mussolini's fascism, who ruled by manipulating the vote and making concessions to the volatile masses of the urban centers.

Brazil is a good example of this trend. The largest Latin American nation and one with abundant natural resources, Brazil had a traditional plantation

South America
Before World War II

△ Major boundary or territorial dispute

⚔ Major War

FALKLAND ISLANDS (Br.) Claimed by Argentina as Islas Malvinas

0   200 400 600 800 1000
Scale of miles

economy in the nineteenth century but began to industrialize rapidly in the twentieth. Urban workers had been slow to unionize before 1930, but the Depression produced such disastrous effects that they quickly organized into unions and in some cases became involved in Marxist revolutionary activities. Getulio Vargas (1930–1945) moved quickly to win the support of urban workers by creating a welfare state with benefits such as minimum wages, pension plans, and guaranteed jobs. Vargas organized the workers into government-controlled unions that were forbidden to strike but had the benevolent support of the government when involved in negotiations with employers. With the support of the workers, Vargas kept the coffee planters, who had previously run the nation, at bay. He accommodated the planters to some extent by refusing to extend labor protection to rural workers. In effect, urban workers, in return for security, supported the rule of a strongman.

In a region characterized by authoritarian rule of one type or another, a few nations, particularly Chile, had managed to make democracy work during significant stretches of their history. In many ways, Chile displayed the same economic and social characteristics as other Latin American states. The nation was short on arable land, which was held by a few families who were inefficient agriculturalists; food supplies were often inadequate for the urban poor, which constituted an ever-growing—and hungry—segment of the population. Foreign companies controlled Chile's main exports, copper ore and nitrates, as well as its public utilities.

Still, Chile was different. Its population was more racially homogeneous than most Latin American nations, overwhelmingly mestizo at all social levels, making social mobility easier. The Church was relatively liberal, supporting programs to help the underprivileged. What made Chile unique, however, was that the nation had developed a democratic political tradition, later to be accompanied by a commitment to social welfare. During the late nineteenth and early twentieth centuries a multiparty parliamentary process similar to those in France and Italy had developed. This process was based on free elections and a tradition that the military ought not to intervene in civilian affairs. By and large this was a liberal era. Political leaders removed many Church controls over the state, enlarged the electorate, and inaugurated a few modest improvements in health services and education. Up through World War I Chile earned substantial income from taxes on large exports of nitrates and copper ore.

The interwar years, however, demonstrated that democracy and liberalism in Chile were shallow-rooted compared to its older traditions of authoritarian social patterns, class exploitation, and antagonisms between the various regions of the nation. The great mass of peasants and the growing numbers of miners and factory workers were still miserably exploited, living in rural slums and urban tenements with inadequate food and medical care; over half were illiterate. In the grip of strong tradition, the rural peasants were relatively quiet; but the miners, factory workers, and urban unemployed struck back through unionization, strikes, riots, and support for socialists and Communists. The government was paralyzed by infighting among a host of political parties representing narrow regional and group interests. Meanwhile, the bottom fell out of the nitrate market when World War I ended.

The result was twenty years on an economic and political rollercoaster. The economy gained ground in the 1920s, collapsed in the global depression of the early 1930s, and revived again in the late 1930s. Meanwhile, Chile began to squeeze out European holdings in transportation and nitrates but was able to put only a few weak regulations on U.S. business interests in nitrate and copper mining. Politically, a new constitution was established that promised more stability. It separated church and state and raised the office of president from that of a figurehead to that of coordinate power with the congress. On the other hand this was a period of military revolts and coups, juntas, rigged elections, dictatorships, and the rise of fascist and Nazi paramilitary forces.

The dominant figure of this period was Arturo Allesandri Palma, who led the nation three times between 1920 and 1938. A political chameleon who in many ways resembled Vargas in Brazil, Allesandri began as a liberal reformer and ended as a cryptofascist dictator. Allesandri and many other Chilean political leaders of this period, whether authoritarian or democratic, saw the need to make concessions to the miners and the urban masses. They instituted a number of social reforms, particularly a labor code similar to Mexico's that guaranteed the right to unionize and engage in collective bargaining, restricted child labor, and provided health insurance. The public school system was extended, and wages and government salaries increased. By World War II, in contrast to its tumultuous interwar period, Chile appeared to have stabilized. The economy had been revived, diversified, and modernized; there had been an advance in social justice; there was greater constitutional stability; and, as it turned out, the democratic tradition of free elections was in the process of being restored.

SUMMARY

The interwar period was one of social and economic disturbance in the United States and Latin America. The United States experienced an era of ethnic and racial discord, and although the upper classes profited from a major expansion of the industrial economy, some areas of the economy remained depressed and the purchasing power of the general public remained low. The stock market collapsed in 1929, triggering a massive depression which prostrated the nation by 1932. Roosevelt's New Deal introduced some reforms and relief and brought in the welfare state, but recovery was still incomplete in 1939.

In Mexico the initial political revolt of 1910 was followed by a decade of civil war before the revolution became institutionalized in an umbrella political party. The new revolutionary party was committed to implementing a broad spectrum of social, economic, and political reforms and made a significant start in this direction during the 1920s and 1930s before revolutionary fervor faded.

Traditional elite groups still ruled most of the nations elsewhere in Latin America, but new political patterns and steps toward social reform were making an appearance in some places. In Chile democratic institutions and social reforms were trying to survive a chaotic period. In Brazil the Vargas dictatorship rested in large part on the support of the urban masses, rather than on the large landowners.

SUGGESTED SOURCES

ALLEN, FREDERICK LEWIS, *Only Yesterday* (1931). A colorful history of U.S. fads and much more during the 1920s.*

AZUELA, MARIANO, *The Underdogs* (1962). A moving novel about the Mexican Revolution.*

BILES, ROGER, *A New Deal for the American People* (1991). The most recent brief survey.*

KNIGHT, ALAN, *The Mexican Revolution* (1986). Insightful and well-written.

LOVEMAN, BRIAN, *Chile: The Legacy of Hispanic Capitalism.* 2d ed. (1988). A sound general study.*

STEINBECK, JOHN, *The Grapes of Wrath* (1939). A powerful novel depicting the plight of an American farm family dispossessed by poverty and drought during the Depression.* (Also a film.)

WOMACK, JOHN, JR. *Zapata and the Mexican Revolution* (1972). An outstanding biography of an outstanding revolutionary.*

*Paperback available.

CHAPTER 15

East Asia between the World Wars

In the early twentieth century, China and Japan followed very different paths. The revolution of 1911 ended the world's longest continuous system of government, and republican China became absorbed in the search for an ideology and institutions to replace the discredited and outdated imperial order. As the Chinese made tentative advances toward a new society, including a modern sense of nationalism, they had to endure decades of disorder and civil war and the constraints of foreign imperialism. China's continuing quest for a modern replacement for the ancient order throughout the twentieth century would affect every part of that ancient civilization.

Japan, on the other hand, enjoyed continuing success; it had not only shaken off the shackles of inequality but had also emerged from World War I and the peace conferences as an undisputed great power. It continued to move forward in all fields with amazing speed and to close the technological gap between itself and the most advanced Western nations. In the initial postwar era Japanese politics moved toward greater democratization, following the trend that was also characteristic of the Western world. Japan's success in modernization, however, brought in its wake little-understood problems which led it along the path of disaster in the 1930s.

WAR AND REVOLUTION IN CHINA

From Dynasty to Republic

After the humiliation of the 1900 Boxer fiasco, the moral authority of the Manchu empire was shattered, and its hold on the people weakened. The imperial government, in a desperate attempt to win popular support, approved all sorts of proposals for change. A constitutional mission sent to Europe and the United States to study their forms of government recommended the gradual introduction of parliamentary government. A new educational policy called for Western-style schools and universities and a modern curriculum.

In spite of its eleventh-hour reform attempts, however, the dynasty was doomed as new forces emerged to challenge a government that had outlived its usefulness. The merchants and industrialists in the port cities opposed the Manchu dynasty because the unequal treaties it had granted to Western nations gave foreign products an unfair competitive edge over Chinese goods. Another opposition group was the Western-educated students, who wanted rapid modernization and resented the reactionary court. Opponents of the dynasty plotted revolution abroad or in the foreign concession areas in Chinese cities, which were outside the jurisdiction of the Chinese government. China was ready for revolution. All it needed was a catalyst.

The antidynastic forces found a leader in Sun Yat-sen. Sun was born in 1866 to a poor farming family near Canton in southern China. Thanks to an elder brother who had established a successful business in Hawaii, he was sent to school there and later studied medicine in Hong Kong, the British colony on China's southern coast. In his studies and travels, Sun was impressed with the progress of the West and correspondingly disgusted with China's backwardness. He gradually turned to revolution and after 1890 devoted himself to traveling, recruiting, and fund-raising to prepare for it.

Sun's ideology and the ways he proposed to put it into effect clearly showed Western political influence. He formulated a program known as the Three People's Principles. These principles were, first, nationalism, which stressed the overthrow of the Manchus (who were a minority ethnic-cultural group in China) as well as the recovery of China's rights from the imperialists; second, democracy, under a liberal republic where the people would be sovereign through representative government; and, third, livelihood, a combination of industrial socialism and land reform to ensure that cultivators owned their land.

In 1905 Sun organized a group of students, literati, and military officers into a political party that later adopted the name Kuomintang (the National People's party or Nationalist party, hereafter cited as the KMT). Between 1906 and 1911 Sun and his KMT followers attempted ten unsuccessful uprisings to overthrow the Manchus. The eleventh occurred on October 10, 1911 (hence called the Double Tenth in China), at Wuhan, an important industrial center. The revolt spread quickly across central and southern China. Sun was on a fund-raising tour in the United States and quickly made his way back to China, arriving in Shanghai on December 25. Four days later he was elected provisional president of the Chinese Republic by provincial delegates meeting in Nanking. Women also joined the Kuomintang, and women volunteer units fought in the revolution of 1911.

Frightened and leaderless, the Manchus were not prepared to fight the revolutionaries. They turned to general Yuan Shih-k'ai, organizer of the largest and best equipped Manchu army units. Yuan defeated the revolutionaries and then stalled further military moves in order to bargain a settlement that would satisfy his great ambitions. On February 12, 1912, the boy emperor abdicated the throne, and the ancient dynastic principle came to an end. China became the first republic in Asia, but Sun did not remain the president, resigning his position to Yuan Shih-k'ai in return for Yuan's promise to support the Chinese Republic.

The Era of Warlordism

Ineffectiveness and frustration marked the first years of the republic. Most of Sun's followers were satisfied once the Manchus had been overthrown and did little to fight for his other, little-understood, ideals. Yuan Shih-k'ai, not content with the title of president, proclaimed himself emperor in 1915; but the monarchical concept was now in disrepute and, faced with revolt, Yuan was forced to resign in humiliation.

The death of Yuan in 1916, shortly after his resignation, was the end of an effective central government in China, and chaos set in. The KMT remained an organization of politicians without political power. Force, now the main criterion for power in China, rested in the hands of local military leaders, or "warlords," who ruled parts of China alone or in coalition and fought frequent wars with one another. Warlords came in all descriptions. Manchuria, an area as big as France and Germany combined, was ruled by a former bandit; Szechwan, another huge province, was for years the battleground of two men surnamed Liu, uncle and nephew; parts of northwestern China were ruled for years by Feng Yu-hsiang, a poorly educated son of a bricklayer who was in succession a Christian, a Communist, and a member of the KMT. During his Christian phase, warlord Feng reputedly baptized his soldiers with a firehose. Associating cleanliness with godliness, he also personally inspected their fingernails. The capital remained in Peking, but obtaining the presidency after Yuan's departure became a game of musical chairs won by whatever group controlled Peking and its environs at the time. The government at Peking ruled little of the country and relied mainly on foreign loans for revenue.

Between 1914 and 1918 Western nations were too preoccupied with the war in Europe to meddle further in China. As Great Britain's ally, Japan declared war on Germany in 1914, but the Japanese, for their own reasons, kept China out of the war until 1917. At the end of 1914, a Japanese force landed in Shantung and expelled the German garrison from this province in northern China which was a German sphere of influence. China did not participate as a combatant in World War I, but 700,000 Chinese laborers were sent to work in Allied factories and mines in Europe and the Middle East.

World War I dealt drastic blows to European industries and trade in China and allowed native industries and trade to develop relatively unhindered by competition. All aspects of the Chinese industrial sector grew—textiles, iron and steel, coal, and flour mills, as well as modern banking. New industries and enterprises created new merchant and laboring classes in growing urban centers, where the new schools were located and where a new intelligentsia was emerging, all of whom were receptive to the calls of nationalism.

The Russian Revolution of 1917 and the U.S. role in World War I also profoundly influenced the Chinese nationalist movement. President Wilson's calls for national self-determination and the abolition of secret diplomacy appealed to many Chinese intellectuals. The Communist takeover in Russia, with its promise of world revolution, its antiimperialist ideology, and its initial promise to give up tsarist gains, made converts of others. Both stirred intellectual ferment in China, with far-reaching results.

Viewed as a period, the years between 1900 and 1918 brought both chaos and hope. Unrestrained by authority, all sorts of new theories were aired and experiments tried. Women did not win equality with men in the constitutions of the early republic. Confucianism, the official ideology of the empire, stressed the Three Bonds, which taught the duty of subjects to the ruler, the young to their elders, and wives to husbands. When the first bond was snapped as a result of the overthrow of the dynasty, the remaining two inevitably loosened. Henceforth modern educated young men and women would increasingly demand social changes that included the right of individual choice in careers and marriage. Upper-class women revolted against foot binding, and educated women demanded equality with men.

Modern educated youths became politically conscious and assertive in national affairs during this period. Increasing numbers of young men and women attended modern schools or went to the United States, Western Europe, and Japan to study. They formed a new social class of intellectuals who both represented and demanded change. They were nationalistic and were determined to create a strong China that could break free from the shackles of imperialism.

Intellectual Revolution: The May Fourth Movement

On May 4, 1919, students demonstrated in Peking to protest the awarding of Shantung to Japan at the Paris Peace Conference. This became known as the May Fourth Movement, a wide-ranging outburst of social and intellectual protest that had been fermenting for some time. This movement paved the way for the revival of the KMT and the rise of the Chinese Communist party (hereafter CCP), founded in 1921. The center of the intellectual revolution was National Peking University where a group of progressive faculty and bright students had set as their task the reexamination of old values and systems. In order to facilitate mass literacy, Hu Shih, a professor of philosophy at Peking University, began a movement to replace the difficult archaic classical written form of the Chinese language, used only by scholars, with the vernacular form that closely approximated everyday speech. Hu's language reform was so popular that by the 1920s the vernacular had become mandatory in school textbooks and commonplace in newspapers and popular journals. A new literature, influenced by Western trends, followed.

Immediately, the May Fourth demonstrations in Peking became a nationwide protest movement as students, merchants, and workers struck throughout China in sympathy with the Peking demonstrators. They forced the government to refrain from signing the Paris Peace Treaty and to dismiss blatantly pro-Japanese officials; more significantly, they showed widespread nationalist and antiimperialist feelings. The movement also inaugurated a new era of political and intellectual activism in China. Many of the young patriots of the May Fourth Movement joined and helped to revitalize the KMT, while others turned to the Soviet Union and Marxism. Female student participants also demanded better educational opportunities and won admission to previously all-male universities.

Nationalist Triumph

Deeply disappointed with the warlords, the Western powers, and the incompetence of his loosely organized KMT, Sun Yat-sen turned for help where he could get it—Soviet Russia. In return for aid in the form of Soviet advisors and arms, Sun agreed to admit the 300 members of the Chinese Communist party, as individuals, into the KMT and formed a United Front government with their participation.

After 1923 Soviet advisors assisted Sun in reorganizing the KMT and winning mass support for it. Sun sent his young ally, Chiang Kai-shek, to Russia for three months during 1923, where Chiang learned training methods from

Sun Yat-sen (seated), father of the Chinese republic, with his lieutenant, Chiang Kai-shek in 1924.
(Camera Press)

Organizing Peasants for Revolution

During my recent visit to Hunan I conducted an investigation on the spot into the conditions. . . . I called together for fact finding conferences experienced peasants and comrades working for the peasant movement, listened attentively to their reports, and collected a lot of material. . . .

All kinds of arguments against the peasant movement must be speedily set right. The erroneous measures taken by the revolutionary authorities concerning the peasant movement must be speedily changed. Only thus can any good be done for the future of the revolution. For the rise of the present peasant movement is a colossal event. In a very short time, in China's central, southern, and northern provinces, several hundred million peasants will rise like a tornado or tempest, a force so extraordinarily swift and violent that no power, however great, will be able to suppress it. They will break all trammels that now bind them and rush forward along the road to liberation. They will send all imperialists, warlords, corrupt officials, local bullies, and bad gentry to their graves.*

———◆◈◆———

Mao Tse-tung, a founder of the Chinese Communist party, contributed to the development of Marxism-Leninism by recognizing the importance of peasants as a potentially important revolutionary force in China, and, by implication, throughout the non-Western, nonindustrial parts of the world. In 1925 Mao was sent to his native province, Hunan, by the KMT-CCP United Front government, to investigate the conditions of the peasants there, and this report, partly reproduced above, was the result. Twenty-five years later he became head of the Communist government in China.

*From "Report on an Investigation of the Hunan Peasant Movement" by Mao Tse-tung (Zedong), quoted in William T. DeBary, Ed., *Source of Chinese Tradition.* Copyright © 1960 by Columbia University Press. Reprinted by permission.

the Red Army. Chiang also learned to distrust Communist aims in China. On his return from Moscow Chiang established a military academy to train and indoctrinate officers for the KMT army.

Sun died of cancer in 1925 and was afterward revered as Father of the Republic; Chiang Kai-shek emerged as Sun's successor. Born of a gentry family and trained in military academies in China and Japan as an army officer, he had taken part in the 1911 revolution. As commandant of the Nationalist military academy in Canton, he was responsible for creating the Nationalist army that he later commanded.

In 1926 Chiang was elected commander in chief of the KMT armies and began his Northern Expedition to unify China. By harnessing and riding the wave of a popular nationalist movement, Chiang's small army was able within a few months to conquer all the warlords in its path as it marched north to the Yangtze valley in central China. The KMT and CCP cooperated with each other so long as both were still weak. The Communist strategy was to help the KMT during the Northern Expedition, and, in Stalin's phrase, to drop it like so many "squeezed-out lemons" when victory was at hand.

In 1927, however, after conquering only half of China, Chiang squeezed first. Supported by the anti-Communist faction of the KMT, Chiang expelled the CCP from the KMT and killed as many of its members as he could. He also expelled Soviet advisors from China. In Canton, the Communists started a last-ditch uprising in December 1927. After it failed, Communists were identified by the red dye marks on their necks left by their discarded red scarves and many were summarily shot. The "purified" KMT resumed its march in 1928. In June, Peking surrendered, and in December the warlord of Manchuria declared his allegiance to the KMT government. With this act, all of China was nominally unified under the KMT.

For ten years between 1928 and 1937, Chiang Kai-shek's Nationalist government ruled China. Between 1928 and 1931 his enemies within the KMT rose either singly or in a coalition to challenge his power. One by one he defeated them, and in the process slowly expanded the power of the central government, the most modern government China had known. The Nationalists made significant advances in broadening and enlarging the modern sector during this period. They built factories, created new schools and universities for men and women, and improved road and railroad networks. New legal codes based on European models gave women equality for the first time. Women students accounted for about a quarter of all college students. In cities women entered government service and the professions. Traditions, however remained strong in the countryside; there women remained subservient.

A high priority of the KMT during and after the Northern Expedition was the "rights recovery" movement, an effort to end the unequal treaties and restore sovereignty. In 1928, under pressure from the Nationalist government, all powers except Japan recognized China's tariff autonomy (Japan was compelled to follow later). For the first time since 1842, China was able to set its own tariff rates. Except for those in Shanghai and Tientsin, all foreign concessions were restored to Chinese authority. After promulgating new civil and criminal codes based on Western models, China demanded an end to extraterritorial rights that nationals of some Western nations and Japan still enjoyed. While several small Western nations agreed to cooperate, Great Britain, the United States, France, Italy, and Japan refused. China then began to negotiate with these powers to provide for a gradual ending of extraterritoriality, which did not finally come until 1943.

With its very existence threatened by Japanese aggression after 1931, China deferred pressing Western powers on two additional remaining items that compromised its sovereignty: the right of Western powers to station troops and naval vessels in certain designated areas of China, and the right of Western naval vessels to patrol Chinese rivers. The Chinese also reasoned that a Western presence might deter Japan from becoming too blatantly aggressive and hoped that Great Britain and the United States might come to their aid against Japan. Clearly from the 1920s on the Chinese were much less fearful of Western European and U.S. imperialism, which was indeed in retreat, than of Japanese and Soviet imperialism. To non-Marxist Chinese, tsarist Russian imperialism had been replaced by Soviet Marxist imperialism. It is clear from the foregoing that in general terms the KMT government performed well in representing Chinese nationalistic aspirations and in recovering lost sovereign rights.

The Nationalist government failed decisively, however, to carry out Sun's principles of democracy and livelihood. Chiang's narrow military training limited his vision of China's needs and his choice of tactics to achieve reforms. The Nationalists made no real effort to train the people for the practice of democracy, which was an alien concept to the Chinese, and ruled in an authoritarian manner. No real effort was made to implement Sun's principle of livelihood through a redistribution of the land and other policies to revitalize the farm economy. Even where the KMT enacted rent control laws, it made little effort to enforce them, so that most farmers remained poverty-stricken. Chiang and his confederates feared the force of social and political change that any real economic reform would unleash. While they enacted reforms such as new marriage and inheritance laws and a law prohibiting foot-binding, enforcement was sporadic and confined to urban centers. Mass movements of the early 1920s such as the trade union movement, which had significantly helped to win popular support for the KMT, were now suppressed. Unwilling to tinker with the social fabric, the KMT let rising demands for reform pass it by.

The Resurgence of the CCP

Intra-KMT civil wars between 1928 and 1931 and major Japanese assaults against China after 1931 (see Chapter 19) gave the CCP remnants a chance to rebuild. Those who had survived the 1927 purges had either gone into hiding in the cities or taken to the hills in southern China, where Mao Tse-tung collected about 10,000 escapees in the winter of 1927–1928. Mao was the son of a prosperous farmer with a normal school education. He was a library assistant at Peking University during the May Fourth Movement, helped to found the CCP in 1921, and organized peasants during the Northern Expedition. Now, with the assistance of Chu Teh, father of the Chinese Red Army, Mao and others developed a guerrilla army and a Soviet-style government.

Since the Communists were hiding out in an economically backward area that contained no industries and therefore had no proletariat, Mao abandoned traditional Marxist concepts of reliance on the urban proletariat as the core of the revolution and turned to the poor peasantry as China's "revolutionary vanguard." During the late 1920s and 1930s, Mao wrote extensively to reinterpret Marxism and to apply it to the underdeveloped agricultural parts of the world. Since most of the world was populated by peasants, Mao's modification of Marxist doctrine would eventually give Marxism an enormous impact around the globe.

In CCP-controlled areas, land was redistributed by force in the name of class warfare. In November 1931 a Chinese Soviet Republic claiming control over 2.5 million people was proclaimed at Juichin, a small town in the mountains of Kiangsi province, with Mao as president. Between 1930 and 1933, KMT armies launched four successive "Extermination Campaigns" against the

Communists. In each case, Mao's guerrilla tactics and peasant support, among other factors, repulsed the better-equipped and numerically superior KMT forces. The tide turned in Chiang's favor in 1934 during the fifth Extermination Campaign, mostly as a result of the strategy of economic blockade carried out in conjunction with economic reforms for the people in the disputed areas. Defeat forced the CCP to flee. About 100,000 men and women of the CCP army and government broke through a poorly defended sector of the blockade and began a 6,000-mile march from southern China to the northwest, while constantly fighting off pursuing KMT forces.

The legendary Long March took 370 days to complete. In 1936 the Communists established their headquarters in Yenan in the remote, poor hinterland area in northern China. Of the 100,000 people who started, about 20,000 made it to Yenan, with Mao Tse-tung in control and his power consolidated. Most of the leaders survived. Mao's headquarters remained in Yenan until after the end of World War II. The main advantage of Yenan was its location, far from Chiang's army and bases. Chiang now had to rely on the unreliable troops of his Manchurian warlord ally to continue the fight against the Communists.

JAPAN IN THE 1920s

While China was preoccupied with domestic struggles, Japan consolidated its position as a great power. At the Paris Peace Conference, as one of the Big Five, Japan was allowed to take over German rights in Shantung province and received German islands in the North Pacific as mandates. In the newly formed League of Nations, Japan was the equal of Great Britain, France, and Italy, and at the Washington Naval Conference it had achieved naval supremacy in Asia.

Liberal Democracy Gains Ground

As its international status grew, developments in Japan itself after World War I reflected the intellectual, social, and economic changes within the nation and worldwide. Within Japan a new generation had come to maturity since the Meiji Restoration that was better acquainted with the outside world and more confident than its predecessors. The tremendous industrial and commercial expansion that took place in Japan during the war had made the business classes more important in Japanese life. As Japanese businesses expanded in Asia after the war, they offered the prospect of commercial growth unaccompanied by force of arms. The overwhelming victory of democratic Western powers in World War I and the defeat of the less democratic ones also convinced many Japanese of the merits of democratic government.

The 1920s was also the heyday of modern social trends. Even the physical appearance of Japanese cities was changing, brought about in part by the great earthquake of 1923 which flattened much of Tokyo and Yokohama. Downtown

Tokyo, rebuilt with wide boulevards and high-rise buildings, now resembled European and North American cities more than Asian ones. Other cities followed Tokyo's lead. Urban life also changed. Men and women office workers commuted to work on trains and trolley cars. In their leisure hours urban dwellers participated in the new mass culture of restaurants and cafes, movies, and sporting events. Baseball became a national sport, and tennis and golf were popular among the rich. Modish young women, called *moga* (abbreviation for modern girl) and young men, called *moba* (modern boy) demanded, though tentatively, independent choice in marriage and lifestyle. Highly literate, the Japanese public supported several mass circulation daily newspapers, each with a readership in the millions. New Western books were almost immediately translated into Japanese.

The ascendancy of liberal and democratic tendencies was evident in many ways. In 1926 the Diet enfranchised all males over twenty-five, increasing the size of the electorate from 3 to over 12 million voters. Another bill reduced the hereditary component of the House of Peers. The Japanese began to accept government by the political party that controlled the majority of votes in the lower house. Two important political parties emerged, providing considerable stability. In addition, many small political parties and groups were allowed to operate as long as they did not advocate changing the "national polity" or abolishing private property. As a result, a variety of political and social organizations mushroomed that campaigned for further reforms, including women's rights.

The Diet also enacted social legislation favorable to labor. It abolished an earlier law that restricted labor unions, and legalized union support of nonrevolutionary socialist movements. A revised Factory Law, a National Health Insurance Law, and a Labor Disputes Mediation Law improved the life of the worker.

In foreign policy, internationalism and international cooperation gained at the expense of militarism. At the Washington Conference in 1921, Japan joined the signing of a Naval Limitation Treaty and agreed to return many of its privileges in Shantung to China. The government reduced the military share of the budget from 42 percent in 1922 to 28 percent in 1928; four divisions were cut out of the army.

Underlying Weaknesses in Japanese Democracy

The progress toward democracy and liberalism in the postwar years was not, however, built upon firm foundations. Many deep problems, including those of rural tenancy and a dual economy of efficient modern industry and agriculture, and inefficient traditional handicrafts, were unresolved. Thus, when the world Depression hit Japan in 1930, the conditions it created easily undermined many of the progressive trends of the previous decade and finally led to the failure of the democratic experiment in the 1930s. Because of its newness, Japanese democratic constitutional government was not deeply rooted. With its deeply entrenched autocratic traditions, its traditional respect for the military, and its veneration of the imperial institution, Japanese society and politics were more akin to those of the German Empire than to the more liberal societies of Great Britain and the United States; the Meiji Constitution was closely modeled on that of imperial Germany.

Despite having several very able political leaders, most Japanese citizens, like many in Germany and Italy at this time, had little faith in or respect for elected party governments. The mud-slinging and often corrupt election campaigns did nothing to dispel the image of politicians as venal. The *zaibatsu*, or large conglomerates, contributed heavily to the political parties that they favored, and after an election the winning party returned the favor by awarding contracts to the *zaibatsu* that had supported it. Thus governments came to be called the "Mitsui cabinet" or the "Mitsubishi cabinet." Corruption under party governments came under slashing attack from both the Left and the Right after the onset of the Depression, when popular suffering made such behavior seem more blatantly immoral.

Even before the Great Depression changed the political and economic climate, and while party governments were in control, antidemocratic forces were at work which would later bring down the shallowly rooted liberal experiment. Some legislation reflected the strength of traditional authoritarian tendencies, even in an era of liberalism. An example of this was the Peace Preservation Law of 1925, amended in 1928, which stipulated heavy penalties for membership in the Communist party and for activities considered subversive. Attacking corruption in the political party system, antidemocratic groups demanded a government that was above parties and other interest groups.

A more important danger signal for Japanese democracy was a renewed tilt toward militarism and militaristic solutions to problems. Both inside and outside the armed forces, ultranationalists willing to use private force to gain political ends became glamorous. For example, in 1921 Prime Minister Hara Kei, a noted believer in constitutional government, was assassinated by an ultranationalist. In 1928, ultranationalist junior officers of the Japanese army in Manchuria blew up a train to assassinate the Chinese warlord of that region for fear that he would not be subservient enough to Japanese interests in the future. In the Manchurian case, the military blocked an inquiry that might have resulted in punishment of the guilty and caused the fall of the government that demanded it. Even when fanatical assassins were brought to justice, ordinary citizens increasingly sympathized with them as pure-hearted patriots opposed to venal politicians.

The Depression

The Depression of 1930 marked the watershed between the liberal decade of the 1920s and the militarism of the 1930s. Since a domestic depression in 1926, the Japanese economy had been on shaky ground. When the global Depression hit Japan in early 1930, it touched off a major catastrophe. The value of exports dropped 50 percent from 1929 to 1931; workers' real income dropped about a third, and unemployment rose to 3 million out of a total population of

64 million. The hardest hit, however, were the farmers, who could not recover production costs despite a bumper crop in 1931. This was followed by widespread crop failures in 1932, which brought conditions of near-starvation in several areas. Some tenants and poor farmers, who had few reserves even in the best of times, were reduced to begging and selling their daughters.

The politicians, the party government, and the *zaibatsu*, who composed the "parliamentary coalition," were blamed for the Depression, despite the fact that the party government acted effectively to counter it. Japan went off the gold standard in December 1931, an action that led to a boom in exports. Japan was thus the first major industrial nation to recover from the Depression, but the recovery did not benefit the political parties and democratic government. The Depression also called into question the validity of the postwar international economic order, which now lay in ruins. As nations erected protectionist tariff walls, the Japanese worried about their raw material and market needs in the future. The failure of the postwar international economy caused the Japanese also to doubt the international political order led by Western democratic nations. The rise of Nazism in Germany further discredited democratic forces in Japan and cast doubts on its parliamentary government because Germany had been Japan's constitutional model and was one of the Western nations the Japanese admired most.

Amidst the rough and tumble of political life and economic ups and downs, the armed forces alone retained an untarnished image. Those who opposed democracy and advocated a greater role for the army and navy in government argued that the military best expressed the will of the emperor and the interest of the people. They further argued that military expansion would ensure steady supplies of raw materials and markets for Japanese manufactured products. This was the background that permitted the Japanese army to act independently of civilian authorities in the 1930s and finally to topple them.

SUMMARY

China and Japan during this period were a study in contrasts. The Chinese revolution of 1911 overturned a discredited dynasty, but the Republic that replaced the Manchus was even less capable of preserving Chinese independence than its predecessor. Warlords struggled against one another and signed away Chinese rights to Japanese governments, who replaced Europeans as the primary imperialist nation against China. Sun Yat-sen, Father of the Chinese Republic, eventually turned to the Soviet Union to revitalize his political party, the Kuomintang. Shortly after his death, Sun's political heir, Chiang Kai-shek, led a military expedition that defeated the warlords and gave China its first effective, modernizing government in the twentieth century. Chiang's Nationalist government strove with success to realize Chinese nationalism and to recover rights lost to Western imperialists, but it neglected Sun's other principles, livelihood and democracy. Thus the Chinese Communists, who promised a drastic social and economic revolution, gained support which the superior military force of the KMT could not eradicate.

World War I enhanced Japan's international stature and boosted its industries and economy. Japan emerged from the war as the preeminent imperial power in East Asia. World trends that favored democratic and egalitarian political and social forces in the 1920s were also strong in Japan in the same period, evidenced by reforms that gave universal male suffrage, greater political freedom, and social betterment. However, the shallowly rooted democratic forces were fatally undermined by the Depression, which aided the triumph of militarism.

SUGGESTED SOURCES

BOSSE, MALCOLM, *Warlord* (1983). A historical novel set in China in the 1920s, where Nationalists, Communists, Soviets, White Russians, and others intrigued to secure their goals.*

DUUS, PETER, *Party Rivalry and Political Change in Taisho Japan* (1968). A study of Japan's experiment with democracy.

DUUS, PETER, RAMON H. MYERS, and MARK R. PEATTIE, *The Japanese Informal Empire in China, 1895–1937* (1989). On how Japanese imperialism supplanted Western imperialism in China.*

MCKENNA, RICHARD, *The Sand Pebbles* (1964). A novel set in the mid-1920s that pits American sailors on patrol along the Yangtze River against each other and against Chinese. (Also a film.)

ONO, KAZUKO, Ed. by Joshua A Fogel, *Chinese Women in a Century of Revolution, 1850–1950* (1989). First comprehensive history of women in modern China.*

PA CHIN, *Family* (1972). A translation of a novel first published in China in 1931 that deals with the conflict between forces of tradition and those of change.*

P'U-I, HENRY, *The Last Manchu: The Autobiography of Henry Pu Yi, Last Emperor of China,* Kuo Ying Paul Tsai, Trans., Paul Kramer, Ed. (1967). Pathetic story of the last Manchu emperor.* (Also a film.)

SHERIDAN, JAMES E., *China in Disintegration: The Republican Era in Chinese History, 1912–1949* (1975). Complete study of the republican era.*

WILBUR, C. MARTIN, *Sun Yat-sen: Frustrated Patriot* (1976). Evenhanded book.

WILSON, DICK, *The Long March, 1935* (1982). An account of the Chinese Communist Long March that is both scholarly and readable.*

*Paperback available.

CHAPTER 16

Nationalist Struggles in India and Southeast Asia

Although the movement for self-government in India and Southeast Asia had its roots in an earlier era, World War I and the years that followed accelerated its development. Before 1914 most nationalist movements of the area merely sought participation in the colonial government, but by the late 1920s many would be satisfied only with independence.

INDIA

India during World War I

India remained loyal to Great Britain throughout World War I. Most Indians realized that Great Britain and its allies were more liberal and democratic than the Central Powers. The Indian press was nearly unanimous in supporting the British war effort and in expressing shock at Germany's invasion of neutral Belgium. In any case, India and the self-governing dominions such as Canada had no choice in the matter of a declaration of war because George V, as king and emperor, declared war on behalf of the entire British Empire. India contributed substantially to the Allied war cause: 800,000 soldiers went to Europe and the Middle East, 500,000 noncombatant laborers worked in factories and mines in Europe, and many Indians made monetary contributions and war loans. In return, Great Britain appointed more Indians to high government positions, and an Indian delegation was allowed to participate in postwar peace negotiations.

In August 1917 the British government for the first time proclaimed its goal to be self-government for India, within the British Commonwealth, to be implemented in stages. Toward its eventual realization, the British Parliament passed the Government of India Act in 1919. By this act, an electorate of middle-class voters was permitted to elect representatives to provincial assemblies where the party with a majority formed a government that controlled a number of departments of the provincial administration. However, public security and the provincial budget remained under the control of the British-appointed governor. This system of sharing power in the provinces between appointed officers and the elected Indian representatives was called dyarchy. In the central government, a British-appointed viceroy retained supreme power and appointed a cabinet of Britons and Indians to assist him in the administration. The national assembly of elected Indian representatives could only advise the viceroy. At the insistence of Muslims, separate electorates, whereby Muslims and Hindus elected their separate representatives, were continued. The act of 1919 was intended to remain in effect for ten years, after which there would be evaluation for changes. Indian moderates welcomed these reforms, but radicals denounced them as inadequate. Because of the worldwide demand for women's suffrage and British women's enfranchisement after World War I, Indian women also won the right to vote on the same terms as men (based on literacy and property qualifications as in the Morley-Minto Reforms, but liberalized) in 1925.

In 1918 a government commission recommended legislation empowering provincial governments to jail suspected political subversives without trial and to try political cases without a jury. When the recommendations were enacted into law, known as the Rowlatt Act, Indian nationalists were outraged. The Indian National Congress launched public meetings to protest the law. The protests turned violent in Punjab province, where a mob murdered four Europeans in Amritsar. Shortly after this incident, about 10,000 people, without official permission, gathered in a large, enclosed square in Amritsar for a meeting. Without warning, the British commanding general in the city ordered troops to fire upon the assembled crowd. The official estimate of casualties was 379 killed and over 1,200 wounded. The Amritsar Massacre crystalized anti-British feelings and became a rallying point for the Indian independence movement.

The Rise of Gandhi

Mohandas K. Gandhi was commonly called Mahatma ("Great Soul" or "Holy One") by his followers. He was born in 1869 of prosperous, devout Hindu parents and was educated in law in London, where he also studied the New Testament and the works of Leo Tolstoy and Henry Thoreau. After a brief, unsuccessful attempt to practice law in India, he took his family to South Africa to represent some Indian clients. He quickly gained a reputation there as a champion of Indian immigrant workers against white South African bigotry and discrimination. He perfected techniques of nonviolent protest demonstrations and called his nonviolent movement *Satyagraha* (truth force). He taught his followers the tactics of noncooperation to protest unjust laws. Gandhi returned to India in 1915 after organizing an ambulance corps for noncombatants to assist in the British war effort.

The immediate postwar years were disturbed ones in India. There were severe economic problems associated with demobilization. There was also

A New Weapon in the Struggle for Freedom

News was received that the Rowlatt Bill had been published as an Act. That night I fell asleep while thinking over the question. Towards the small hours of the morning I woke up somewhat earlier than usual. I was still in that twilight condition between sleep and consciousness when suddenly the idea broke upon me—it was as if in a dream. Early in the morning I related the whole story to Rajagopalachari [a Congress leader].

The idea came to me last night in a dream that we should call upon the country to observe a general hartal. Satyagraha is a process of self-purification, and ours is a sacred fight, and it seems to me to be the fitness of things that it should be commenced with an act of self-purification. Let all the people of India, therefore, suspend their business on that day and observe the day as one of fasting and prayer. The Musalmans [Muslims] may not fast for more than one day; so the duration of the fast should be 24 hours. . . .

Rajagopalachari was at once taken up with my suggestion. Other friends too welcomed it. . . . I drafted a brief appeal. The date of the hartal was first fixed on the 30th March 1919, but was subsequently changed to 6th April. . . . The whole of India from one end to the other, towns as well as villages, observed a complete hartal on that day. It was a most wonderful experience.*

Mohandas K. Gandhi (1869–1948), a British-educated lawyer, became a leader of the Indian National Congress during World War I. He was responsible for changing its direction into a mass movement by such actions as the hartal described above. A hartal is a strike with a moral purpose, accompanied by fasting. Gandhi first employed it as a protest against the British-imposed Rowlatt Act, which cracked down on Indian protests. He won worldwide respect for his saintly lifestyle but was resented by some Indians for his moral scruples. He was assassinated by a Hindu fanatic soon after India won independence.

*From *The Story of My Experiments with Truth* by Mohandas K. Gandhi. Copyright © 1927 by Viking Penguin Company. Reprinted by permission of Navajian Trust.

widespread dissatisfaction with the slow pace of political reform and outrage over the Rowlatt Act and the Amritsar Massacre. In addition, Muslims were resentful about the fate of the Ottoman Empire and the humiliating treatment of Muslims in the Middle East by the Allies at the Paris Peace Conference.

It was at this critical juncture of the Indian nationalist movement that Gandhi entered the struggle for independence. In 1921 the Indian National Congress gave Gandhi sole executive authority. He immediately launched a campaign of civil disobedience against British rule. His ideas were simple. He argued that since fewer than 200,000 Britons ruled 400 million Indians, the maintenance of British authority had to be based on Indian cooperation. Consequently, if Indians withdrew their cooperation, British rule could not continue. Gandhi also realized that the nationalist movement, previously mostly middle-class, must be expanded to include the masses. Toward this end, he visited villages throughout India, dressed in simple homespun garb, where he identified with the poor, preached his message in simple terms, and taught the goal of national unity and the tactics of nonviolence to ordinary people.

Despite his upper-middle-class upbringing, Gandhi understood and sympathized with the ordinary Indian. He broadened the nationalist movement into one for the masses. He persuaded the Indian National Congress to lower its membership dues to a nominal sum to attract poor members and to publish its messages in Indian languages as well as in English. Women became politically active during this period. In 1926 the All-India Women's Conference was established, which became an unofficial auxiliary of the Congress. Thousands of women came out of the seclusion of their homes to join Gandhi's demonstrations. The most famous woman activist was Sarojini Naidu, a poet dubbed "India's nightingale." Later she became India's first woman governor. Gandhi also attempted to narrow the gap that divided Hindus from Muslims by such acts as endorsing Indian Muslim demands for lenient treatment of the Ottoman dynasty, but he opposed separate electorates.

Gandhi was not only interested in driving out the British. He also crusaded in favor of social reform to rid Hindu society of customs that oppressed and abused women and certain social classes. He spoke eloquently against child marriage, especially for females, the prohibition against widow remarriage, and, above all, the oppression of the untouchables. He spoke of independence as something one must deserve and implied that Hindus did not deserve self-rule when they oppressed whole categories of their own people. He renamed the outcastes, or untouchables, *Harijans,* which means "Children of God," to signify their common humanity with other Indians. He founded a

A protest march organized by the Indian National Congress against the British in 1928. *(BBC Hulton/The Bettmann Archive)*

journal named *The Harijan,* where his writings were published, and often insisted that he be quartered in the untouchable part of a town that he was visiting. In his *ashram,* or retreat, he made sure that all shared in doing unpleasant menial work such as sweeping and cleaning toilets that was otherwise the lot of the untouchables. He did not believe in legislating social change; rather, he emphasized changing people's hearts and minds. The name *Harijan* is still widely used today.

Gandhi mobilized the masses in repeated *Satyagraha* movements against the British. He organized peaceful demonstrations and strikes and told Indians to confront police brutality by "offering the other cheek." Thus, when Indians rioted and committed violent acts during demonstrations, a disappointed Gandhi would call off his *Satyagraha* and go on a fast to atone for the violence. He also fasted to persuade his British adversaries and his Indian followers to see the error of their ways and to change as a result of their own moral awakening. Some Indians who did not care about the means used so long as they achieved their desired end blamed Gandhi's moral scruples for delaying the attainment of Indian independence.

Gandhi's Salt March of 1930 was a good example of his method of protest. The government had a monopoly on the manufacture and sale of salt and taxed it for revenue. Gandhi chose to protest the salt tax as a burden on the poor and as a symbol of British laws that violated Indian civil rights. In March 1930 Gandhi led seventy-eight followers on a "Great Salt March." In a well-publicized media event, they slowly walked 200 miles to the seacoast. Daily, thousands turned out to cheer them on, and some joined the march. When he reached the coast, Gandhi waded into the water and drew out a pitcherful, which he boiled to extract the salt. In so doing, he defied the salt monopoly and the salt tax law. Indians responded with a general strike and with *Swadeshi,* a movement to boycott British manufactured goods, especially British woven cotton textiles, and to replace them with Indian homespun cotton cloth. The boycott put many British laborers out of work, thus placing additional pressure on the government to make concessions. Gandhi and 60,000 of his supporters were arrested, but the civil disobedience campaign persisted. Finally the government capitulated. Gandhi and his supporters were released from jail, the salt tax was reduced, and some restrictive laws were rescinded.

The campaign showed Gandhi at his most brilliant. As a humanitarian, he abhorred violence, and, as a political realist, he understood that his cause would most benefit by winning the sympathy of world public opinion. He further understood that democratic Great Britain was sensitive to public opinion and that the British government could be forced to make concessions in response to public pressure.

In many ways, Gandhi was a traditionalist. He loved Hindu customs and dreamed of an independent India true to its ancient heritage, one that turned its back on modern technology and industrial society. Gandhi advocated reviving cottage industries not only to support the *Swadeshi* movement but also for their intrinsic economic and social value. For several hours nearly every

Gandhi and J. Nehru in 1938: Both had discarded Western clothes in favor of Indian garb, Gandhi for homespuns.
(Nehru Memorial Library)

day, he spun and wove his own cloth, which he wore exclusively after he gave up wearing Western-style clothing. Millions of Indians, of high station and low, also took up the weaving of homespun cloth, so that the spinning wheel came to symbolize the Indian nationalist movement. At his insistence, the Congress required its members to spend a portion of their day working at a handloom, to the annoyance of some.

The Hindu-Muslim Communal Problem

Gandhi advocated a policy of generosity toward Muslims. He welcomed all, especially the Muslims, to join the Indian National Congress, which he sought to make into a body that represented all Indian nationalists. Thus he disapproved of separate electorates for Muslims or any other minority. Instead, he suggested that Muslims be given a guaranteed number of representatives on the Congress ticket. In this effort Gandhi failed, for several reasons. One was that militant Hindus in the Congress smelled victory in the elections and refused to set aside a percentage of seats for Muslim representatives. The other was that the Muslims were now largely represented by the All-India Muslim League led by M. A. Jinnah. League leaders, many of whom were British-trained lawyers, objected to Gandhi's nonconstitutional methods of protest and did not share his rejection of Western values. Moreover, the League relied on separate electorates to protect Muslim rights. Thus any Muslim who joined the Congress was not recognized as a representative of the Muslim community.

As a result, in the rancor that surfaced in the post-1919 election campaigns and competition for power, the relative communal peace of the war years quickly evaporated. Congress Hindus sought to capture and hold the power their numbers guaranteed to them. On the other hand, Muslims feared the potential tyranny of Hindu majority rule and demanded safeguards for their rights in any political negotiations.

From the late 1920s on, Great Britain stepped up the timetable for Indian independence in response to Indian demands. However, no proposal the British made was acceptable to both the Congress and the League, and neither accepted the other's suggested solutions. Whatever the specific issue at hand, both Hindus and Muslims looked at it in terms of power: who would dominate an independent India and who would be dominated. Mutual hatred between Hindus and Muslims (Muslim fear of Hindu numbers and Hindu fear of possible new Muslim inroads by conversion) came to outweigh hatred for the foreign ruler. In the final analysis, the inability of Indians to solve their communal problem delayed their attaining self-government.

The India Act of 1935

After several years of intensive consultations with the representatives of different interests, the British government concluded that India should become a federation that combined princely states and self-governing provinces. The Government of India Act of 1935 enlarged the electorate to 18 percent of the population, which would elect representatives to both provincial and federal legislatures. Each province was to be entirely self-governing; the party with a majority of elected representatives would form the government. The British-appointed provincial governor became largely a figurehead, except in emergencies when he could veto actions by the elected government. At the federal level, the British-appointed viceroy was advised by an Executive Council chosen from the elected members of the federal legislature. He also had the power of veto and emergency powers. At the Muslim League's insistence, separate electorates were retained for Muslims in all elections. In addition, the India Act provided that other minorities and special-interest groups such as Christians, untouchables, women, Europeans, laborers, and landlords would also have their own representatives in every assembly, in seats reserved according to a quota system. The more than 500 princely states were also given representation in the federal legislature based on their size and population. This act attempted to ensure that all Indians received representation and had a voice in the government. The federal form of government, in which each province had broad rights, was an attempt to satisfy Muslim demands that they should rule themselves in areas where they were a majority.

While the Indian National Congress criticized portions of the act as either insufficient or reactionary, it nevertheless set about to capture as much power as possible in the elections that the act mandated. Although the Muslim League won majorities in the few Muslim-dominated provinces in the provincial elections of 1936, the Congress captured a majority in all the remaining provinces. Greatly encouraged by its effective organization and vote-getting power, Congress leader Jawaharlal Nehru bragged: "There are only two parties in the country—the Congress and the British." Such statements only aggravated the fears of Muslims over their future in a Hindu-dominated India. The India Act also separated Burma from India and provided the Burmese with self-government comparable to that of the Indians.

NATIONALIST MOVEMENTS IN SOUTHEAST ASIA

In the Dutch East Indies, a Muslim-rooted nationalist movement had been active since the early twentieth century, but the Dutch government made only slow progress in accommodation to it. The Dutch-created People's Council, which began in 1918, initially had only advisory power. After 1929 half of the Council were elected Indonesians, and all legislation needed its assent. These reforms did not satisfy either the National Indonesian party led by Sukarno or the Indonesian Communist party, which vied for leadership in the independence movement.

In Indochina, French tactics of combining direct and indirect rule, cultivation of the native elite, and local ethnic diversity all retarded the nationalist movement. Among all Indochinese, the Vietnamese offered the greatest resistance to French rule. The failure of moderate Vietnamese nationalists to persuade the French to make concessions opened the way for the more extreme elements. Ho Chi Minh emerged during the interwar years as the most prominent nationalist leader. He went to France as a young man and helped to organize the French Communist party there after World War I. In 1925, he surfaced in Canton, where he worked for Soviet advisors who were then helping the KMT in China. It was not until 1930 that he drew together various dissident Vietnamese groups in Hong Kong and formed the Communist party of Indochina. In that same year, French authorities crushed all peasant and nationalist revolts in Vietnam. The repression that followed failed to eliminate a growing nationalist movement.

In the Philippines, in contrast, a bicameral legislature of elected representatives had taken over lawmaking since 1916. Only the governor-general, the vice-governors, and the judges of the supreme court were still appointed from Washington. In 1919 President Wilson promised complete independence, but it took the Depression of 1930 to hasten its realization.

Since the Philippines was a U.S. possession, both Filipino products (notably sugar, tobacco, and coconut oil) and Filipino immigrants could freely enter the United States. During the Depression, U.S. industry, in particular the sugar industry, and U.S. labor unions agitated in favor of granting independence to the Philippines so that its cheap products and labor could be shut out of the United States. Others supported Philippine independence because if it remained a possession its defense would be a military liability to the United States. The U.S. Congress passed the Tydings-McDuffie Act in 1934, whereby the Philippines immediately became fully self-governing except for control of its foreign policy by Washington for ten years. Complete independence was promised for July 4, 1944.

SUMMARY

Between the two world wars European imperialism was on the retreat and nationalism was on the rise throughout the colonial world in South and Southeast Asia. As before, India led the way. As a result of Indian contributions in World War I, Britain agreed to grant India self-government, which it proceeded to implement in the acts of 1919 and 1935. Sharp disagreements emerged, however, over the timing and over how Hindus and Muslims would share power in a self-governing India. Led by Mahatma Gandhi, who applied tactics of nonviolent protest that he had earlier developed in South Africa to the Indian independence struggle, the Congress developed grass-roots support but increasingly represented only Hindu aspirations. The prospect of a Hindu-dominated self-governing India led Muslims to cling to separate electorates and to follow the All-India Muslim League and its president, M. A. Jinnah, as their champions. In elections held in accordance with the India Act of 1935, the Congress won majorities in Hindu-populated states, and the League in Muslim ones.

By comparison, the Dutch East Indies was far behind in its nationalist struggles. In Indochina, likewise, French authoritarian rule continued supreme after successfully suppressing peasant revolts in 1930. In the same year, however, Ho Chi Minh organized the Indochinese Communist party in exile. The U.S.-ruled Philippines was the only colony in Southeast Asia where there was significant progress toward independence, as U.S. policy progressively associated Filipinos in the process of self-government. In 1934 the U.S. Congress passed an act that immediately granted autonomy to the Philippines, with full independence to follow in ten years.

SUGGESTED SOURCES

AUNG SAN SUU KYI, MICHAEL ARIS, Ed., *Freedom from Fear and Other Writings* (1991). Part one deals with Aung San, leader of Burma's struggle for independence and with British rule of Burma. The author is a daughter of Aung San and the winner of the 1991 Nobel Prize for Peace.*

BONDURANT, JOAN V., *Conquest of Violence: The Gandhian Philosophy of Conflict*, rev. ed. (1988). Good book on Gandhi's political thought and philosophy.*

EMBREE, AINSLIE T., *India's Search for National Identity* (1981). A brief, readable, and objective introduction.*

FASWELL, BYRON, *Armies of the Raj from the Great Indian Mutiny to Independence: 1858–1947* (1989). A good, colorful book.*

FISCHER, LOUIS, *Gandhi* (1983). A concise biography, full of human interest.*

Gandhi (1982). A sympathetic film portraying the powerful impact of the great Indian leader.

KHANH, HUYNH KIM, *Vietnamese Communism, 1925–1945* (1986). A description of the origins and development of Vietnamese communism and the role of the party in the anticolonial struggle.*

NEHRU, JAWAHARLAL, *An Autobiography* (1989, first published in 1936). A reflective account of his life and times written while in prison in 1934–1935.*

WOLPERT, STANLEY, *Jinnah of Pakistan* (1984). An objective study of the founder of Pakistan.

*Paperback available.

CHAPTER 17

Anticolonialism in the Middle East and Africa

As the anticolonial struggle swept India in the period between the wars, nationalists were also intensifying their efforts in the Middle East and Africa. The strength and extent of these nationalist movements differed widely from area to area. The Middle East was often in a state of turmoil, as Arab nationalists shifted their activity from resisting the Ottomans to opposing British and French control, and Jews attempted to establish a homeland in Palestine. Even those states that were nominally independent, such as Iran and Turkey, witnessed the stirring of a new nationalism. In both nations, dynamic leaders emerged who sought modernization and Westernization precisely in order to repel Western domination and to make their homelands independent in fact as well as in name. African nationalist movements developed later in the century than their Asian counterparts. Nevertheless, the interwar period witnessed the beginning of anti-Western independence movements throughout the continent.

NATIONALIST UNREST IN THE MIDDLE EAST

Allied political considerations during World War I aided nationalist movements throughout the Middle East. The British were generally willing to assist Arab nationalism, not because they necessarily believed in its aims but because they hoped that an Arab revolt would weaken Ottoman forces and thus help to protect the Suez Canal. Lord Herbert Kitchener of Khartoum, as British high commissioner in Egypt and later secretary of war, discussed the possibility of Arab independence with Abdullah, a son of Sharif Husayn (sharif is a title indicating both a religious and political leader). Sharif Husayn was the ruler of the Muslim holy city of Mecca. To implement their war and postwar plans, the British made three agreements involving the Middle East that sowed the seeds for a struggle—the Arab-Israeli conflict—that has yet to be resolved.

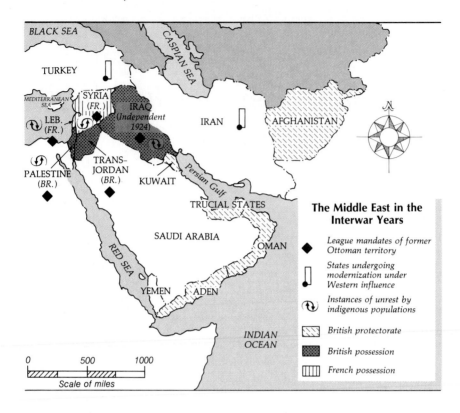

BLACK SEA

TURKEY

CASPIAN SEA

MEDITERRANEAN
SEA

SYRIA
(FR.)

IRAQ
(Independent
1924)

IRAN

AFGHANISTAN

LEB.
(FR.)

PALESTINE
(BR.)

TRANS-
JORDAN
(BR.)

KUWAIT

Persian Gulf

TRUCIAL STATES

SAUDI ARABIA

OMAN

RED SEA

YEMEN

ADEN

INDIAN
OCEAN

**The Middle East in the
Interwar Years**

♦ *League mandates of former
Ottoman territory*

▯ *States undergoing
modernization under
Western influence*

♨ *Instances of unrest by
indigenous populations*

▧ *British protectorate*

▨ *British possession*

▥ *French possession*

0   500   1000

Scale of miles

Conflicting Wartime Agreements

The first wartime agreement was the secret correspondence (1915–1916) between Henry McMahon, the British high commissioner in Egypt, and Sharif Husayn, acting in the self-appointed role of champion of Arab independence. The British promised to support an independent Arab state after the war in return for Arab support during the war. The negotiations were protracted because of the conflict over the boundaries for the proposed Arab state. Husayn originally demanded all of the Arab Middle East south of Turkey, including most of the Arabian peninsula. The British countered that they had interests in Iraq and that the French had religious and economic interests in the territory that is today Lebanon. While pointing out that all the territory was clearly Arab, Husayn finally agreed to compromise on Iraq and Lebanon. As a result, the Arabs raised the standard of revolt against the Ottoman Empire and fought on the Allied side, believing that after the war they would receive independence.

However, the British had made a second commitment, which in part contradicted their agreement with Husayn. In the Sykes-Picot Agreement (1916), the British and the French agreed to divide the Ottoman Empire among European nations. The Anatolian peninsula was to be partitioned, and the French were to secure Lebanon and Syria, while the British were to receive Iraq and Palestine and a sphere of influence over the Arabian peninsula. The British probably did not demand direct control over what is today Saudi Arabia because in 1916 the vast petroleum reserves in that nation had not yet been discovered. Because both European terms and Ottoman administrative divisions for these areas were used in both agreements, after the war there was some confusion and argument over the exact terms and borders.

The Balfour Declaration of November 1917 was the third British statement regarding the Middle East. To understand this pronouncement it is necessary to discuss briefly the Zionist movement, which was fervently supported by some Jews in Europe and the United States. The Zionists sought to establish a Jewish state in Palestine. Theodor Herzl, a Hungarian journalist and Zionist leader, had advocated in his book *Der Judenstaat (The Jewish State)* that Jews have a nation of their own in order to avoid anti-Semitism (anti-Jewish attitudes and behavior), which he believed was an evil inherent in Western civilization. The Dreyfus case in France and the pogroms in Poland and Russia had convinced Herzl and other Jewish leaders that Jews needed a state of their own. Herzl favored accepting any territory; parts of Argentina and Uganda were even suggested. However, Chaim Weizmann, a chemist of Polish origin, argued that Palestine, the location of the ancient Jewish state, was the only place in which the Zionists could realize their aspirations. In 1897, at the First Zionist Congress, Zionists pledged to work for the creation of a Jewish state in Palestine.

In November 1917, British Foreign Secretary Arthur Balfour wrote to a prominent British Zionist, Lord Rothschild, publicly stating British support for "the establishment in Palestine of a national home for the Jewish people." Balfour also stated that "nothing shall be done which may prejudice" the rights of the "non-Jewish" communities (the Arab majority) in Palestine or the rights of Jews in other nations. In such a manner, the British hoped to assuage those Jews, particularly in Great Britain, who opposed the Zionist idea of creating a Jewish state because they feared the existence of such a state would only increase anti-Semitism. Prime Minister David Lloyd George favored the Balfour Declaration because he wanted more support for the war effort. Zionists hailed it as a major step toward the realization of their dream. Although Balfour had not promised that Great Britain would support an independent Jewish state in Palestine, many Jews and non-Jews believed that an independent Jewish state would eventually be established.

Arab leaders promptly condemned the Balfour Declaration and vowed to oppose the creation of a Jewish state in Palestine, where about 90 percent of the population was composed of Arabs many of whom lived in rural villages. Many Westerners who knew little of the area concluded—on the basis of the Balfour Declaration, which had referred only to the "non-Jewish population"—that only a few nomads lived in what was otherwise a sparsely populated territory. Consequently, many Westerners failed to recognize that if Jewish settlements were supported, another group, the Palestinians, might

A Vision of Zion

In the winter of 1918 the American Jewish Congress held its first convention in Philadelphia. The main purpose was the formulation of a program (to be presented at the Peace Conference in Versailles) for the safeguarding of the civil rights of the Jews in Europe. To my astonishment . . . I was chosen to be one of the delegates from Milwaukee. It was a marvelously stimulating experience; I can still remember how proud I was to have been chosen to represent my own community and what it was like sitting with the rest of the delegation in the overheated train on our way to Philadelphia. I was (as always in that period) the youngest in the group and, in a way, everyone pampered me— except when it came to giving me assignments. Today when journalists ask me when my political career actually began, my mind always flashes back to that convention, to the smoke-filled hall in a Philadelphia hotel where I sat for hours listening, completely absorbed, to the details of the program being thrashed out, to the excitement of the debates and of being able to cast my own vote.*

◆◀◆▶◆

In her autobiography, Golda Meir remembers the exciting times in her early twenties when she was just beginning her political career. Born in the Ukraine in 1898, Golda Meir and her family immigrated to the United States where they settled in Milwaukee. While still in school, Meir became an ardent supporter of the Zionist movement for an independent Jewish state and moved to Palestine where she became a leading figure in the movement to create the independent state of Israel. As a key figure in the Labor party, Meir twice won in general elections, becoming one of Israel's most famous prime ministers. She died in 1978.

*From *My Life* by Golda Meir. The Putnam Publishing Group. Copyright © 1975 by Golda Meir.

well lose their homeland. This laid the foundation for the Arab-Israeli conflict.

The contradictions inherent in the three agreements became clear at the Paris Peace Conference. Sharif Husayn's son Faysal, Weizmann, and a host of other nationalist leaders appeared in Paris with their documents. Their hopes for national self-determination had been fueled by Wilson's Fourteen Points and declarations favoring self-determination. Although a champion of self-determination, Wilson was willing to back European interests in the Middle East instead of Arab aspirations in order to secure Allied support for the League of Nations and other parts of his program. As a result, the British and the French were able to implement their territorial ambitions in the Middle East. Under the terms agreed on at the San Remo Conference in 1920, the British obtained mandated control over Iraq and Palestine, including what is today Jordan, and the French got mandates over Syria and Lebanon. When it became clear that the Arabs were not to receive independence, one Arab leader remarked, "Independence is never given, it is taken." In fact, several decades were to pass before Arab national aspirations were realized.

Postwar Developments

Following the Paris conference, France immediately moved troops into Syria and Lebanon even though a General Syrian Congress had in March 1920 proclaimed Faysal as the constitutional monarch of a united Syria. However, in the face of superior French military force, Faysal was forced to flee from Syria, but the Syrian Arabs never accepted the French occupation and continued to fight against it. In Lebanon, the French created a more autonomous government by relying heavily on the Maronite Christian Lebanese, who were about half the total population. They also enlarged the nation by including within its boundaries several predominantly Muslim areas that had previously been under Syrian domination. By relying on one religious group, the French helped to intensify religious differences in Lebanon that persisted into the 1980s.

Meanwhile, Great Britain proceeded with its own arrangements. The British attempted to provide a facade of independence in Iraq by crowning Faysal king of a constitutional monarchy that was bound by treaty in a close alliance with Great Britain. British troops remained in Iraq, and the British continued as the major power behind the monarchy.

Great Britain divided the Palestinian mandate into two sections, making Abdullah the amir (prince) of the new state, Transjordan, in the interior, which historically had never been part of Palestine and which had been ruled under the Ottoman Empire from Damascus. (This state was later known as Jordan.) In the coastal area of Palestine proper, the British attempted to balance the conflicting Zionist and Palestinian Arab demands for independence. The 1920s and 1930s were marked by continued political confrontation and sporadic armed conflict between Zionists and Palestinian Arabs.

Meanwhile, the Zionists worked to translate their goals into reality through Jewish immigration, colonization, and Western support. The Palestinians opposed both Zionist and British activities; by the 1930s, Palestinian opposition was directed largely against the British. The British, responding in the old imperial tradition, sent out a series of commissions to investigate the problems. By 1937 it appeared to the British commission that the conflict was irreconcilable and that Palestine should be partitioned into a Jewish and an Arab state. The Palestinian Arabs, who viewed the territory as theirs, rejected the partition scheme, which allotted about 50 percent of the land to the Jews, who numbered only 30 percent of the population. Many Zionists also opposed the plan because it failed to allot to them all of the territory that had been part of historic Israel.

As a result of continued British controls and the mounting Zionist presence that the British had permitted and sometimes encouraged, the Palestinians launched a full-scale strike and armed opposition against British troops. From 1936 to 1939 the British retaliated with superior weapons and organization, and, after inflicting heavy losses, destroyed the Palestinian armed opposition. However, as World War II drew closer, the British sought to placate Arab leaders. The White Paper of 1939 proposed limiting Jewish immigration for five years, after which time immigration quotas were to be subject to Palestinian acquiescence. Further, British control over Palestine was to be discussed after ten years. The Zionists immediately rejected the 1939 plan, which they dubbed the "Black Paper." Thus the British wavered between the Zionists and the Palestinians, while both remained opposed to continued British domination.

In Mecca, Sharif Husayn, who had proclaimed himself king during World War I, was having troubles of his own. Throughout the war, Husayn had fought not only the Central Powers but also local rivals. Ironically, his major rival, Ibn Saud (a follower of the Wahhabi movement, which advocated the establishment of a puritanical Islamic government), had also received British subsidies during the war. Saud had the advantages of religious zeal, better organization, and military strength; by 1925, he succeeded in ousting Husayn. He then established a Saudi Arabian monarchy based on strict adherence to Islamic precepts.

SECULARISM VERSUS SPIRITUALISM

In the Middle East and the Islamic world in general, so-called modernizing leaders wanted to create secular nation-states largely modeled on Western ones. They sought to industrialize the economies of their nations while simultaneously adopting largely Western models in dress, culture, education, and behavior. More traditional or conservative forces in these societies argued against the wholesale adoption of Western institutions. They sought to preserve and reinforce traditional spiritual and societal values based on Islam.

After World War I, new, Western-looking leaders seemed to predominate, instituting sweeping changes in Turkey and Iran. To a much lesser extent, Afghanistan was also affected by similar conflicts between modernizing leaders and a largely conservative traditional populace. In both Turkey and Iran, largely Muslim and traditional nations, modernizing but authoritarian rulers sought to diminish the importance of religion and religious institutions and to force secularization based on the Western model. In both nations, changes were forced from above rather than from the grass-roots level. Perhaps nowhere else in the postwar world were the lines between the conflicting forces of religion and secularism more clearly drawn.

In Turkey, Mustafa Kemal, or Ataturk (Father of the Turks), emerged as the leader following the collapse of the old Ottoman government. A professional soldier by training, Ataturk embarked on an ambitious program of Westernization. He eliminated both the old Ottoman sultanate and the caliphate and created a parliamentary state with himself as the president. Using nationalism and his enormous personal popularity, Ataturk attempted to alter the entire structure of Turkish society. He banned the wearing of the veil by women, forced men to wear Western hats rather than the traditional fez, and even had a new alphabet created based on Western models. Ataturk often toured the countryside with a portable blackboard on which he personally taught the new alphabet, thereby turning Turkey into one vast classroom.

Turkey also managed to avoid imperial domination or foreign entanglements while steering a careful course of neutrality. Although Ataturk was certainly an authoritarian ruler, he bequeathed to Turkey a relatively effective legislative democracy which survived long after his death. In contrast, many of his reforms regarding religion and the status of women were not as permanent.

In neighboring Iran (formerly Persia), another military officer, Reza Khan, overthrew the Qajar dynasty and also moved to Westernize and secularize the nation. Unlike Ataturk, however, Reza Khan retained the monarchy, with himself at the helm. The Pahlavi dynasty that Reza Khan established lasted until 1979, when it was overthrown in a popular revolution. Reza Shah was able to avoid imperial domination by either the Soviet Union or Great Britain, but his personal ambition and his attempts to undercut the power of the clergy and religion eventually brought down the Pahlavi dynasty.

NATIONALIST STIRRINGS IN AFRICA

As in Asia, people throughout Africa had been swayed by Wilson's persuasive statements regarding self-determination. However, African nationalist movements did not generally reach maturity until after World War II. In general, the first generation of African nationalist leaders represented the educated elite, who often came from old established tribes and who had enjoyed positions of power long before the arrival of the Europeans. These leaders, while well-meaning, often failed to reach the masses of the people who lived in isolated, remote villages. Ironically, during World War II, there was a brief rapprochement, as both Africans and European settlers fought against Fascist and Nazi aggression. This cooperation ended after the war when the settlers moved to maintain their superior political and economic status and the black African majority struggled for independence.

Contrasting Imperial Policies

As previously indicated, the imperial policies of the European nations differed widely within Africa. For their African empire, the British had developed a system of working through the traditional political institutions, known as indirect rule. However, the application of this policy varied tremendously from colony to colony. It tended to be most successful in areas where there were identifiable tribal authorities, as in Nigeria and the Gold Coast (Ghana), and was less successful in areas where there were conflicting local leaders or where there were white settlers, as in Rhodesia and Kenya.

The British also continuously reaffirmed their intention to grant self-government as soon as they deemed the African peoples ready to assume the responsibilities of national independence. In British eyes, this would not occur, for the most part, for several more generations. During that time, members of the local African elite were to be exposed to and educated in the British system. Once they were educated, the local bureaucracies would be turned over to the African leaders. However, the British still planned to retain overall control for a period of time well into the future. In areas where there were white settlers, they anticipated turning over the government to them after an unscheduled period had elapsed. Anticipation of eventual self-government intensified African nationalism, causing open breaks between African nationalist movements and the British government.

In contrast to the British, the French claimed to be dedicated to a policy of maintaining close economic ties with their African colonies and of assimilating Africans into French society. Although the process of assimilation was never realized, it did seem to avoid the implication of African racial inferiority that was sometimes charged to the British approach of maintaining local and British systems in isolation from each other. Both approaches were, in the final analysis, based on the notion of cultural superiority.

In short, British policies seemed to be based upon the notion that Africans could never be like the British, and so there was no point in trying to assimilate them. On the other hand, French policies were based on belief in the superiority of French culture and the absolute assurance of the French that, given the opportunity, all people would in fact wish to become French. As a result of these conflicting policies, there tended to be greater nationalist political activity in British-held African territories than in those held by the French, Portuguese, or Belgians.

Revolts in North Africa

The French kept firm control over their North African empire of Morocco, Algeria, and Tunisia. Political movements organized by local nationalists were swiftly curtailed. In the 1920s, the Rif rebellion in Morocco, led by the Krim

Toward liberation: Moroccan fighters against Spanish colonial rule during the rebellion of 1924–1926.
(BBC Hulton/The Bettmann Archive)

brothers, was brutally crushed by Spanish and French forces. Likewise, the religious and nationalist movement in Libya was attacked and its followers bombed by the Italians. Throughout North Africa, nationalist leaders were closely watched and frequently jailed or sent into exile. In the Western world, nationalist forces and their opponents, such as the French Foreign Legion, were often pictured through the distorted lens of Hollywood cameras. The area became a favorite subject for romanticized tales of adventure like *The Sheik* and *Beau Geste,* two popular films of the era. These fictionalized accounts created a false impression that the peoples of North Africa were all either desert sheiks, living in exotic desert cities and oases, or poverty-stricken nomads. These stereotyped images distorted Western perceptions not only of North Africa but also of Arab and Islamic society in general.

In Egypt, Britain faced a fully developed nationalist movement. Encouraged by the Fourteen Points and Allied declarations, a group of Egyptians led by Saad Zaghlul formed a delegation, or Wafd, to ask for Egyptian independence after the war. However, Egyptian demands were thwarted by British determination to control the vital Suez Canal. The British rejected the Egyptian demands, which resulted in a full-scale revolution in 1919. Although Wafdist leaders were exiled, the Wafd party became the chief political and nationalist organization from 1919 to 1952, and nationalist revolts persisted. The interwar years saw a protracted tricornered conflict for political power among the British, King Fu'ad and his successor King Faruk, and the Wafd. As a means of maintaining their presence in Egypt while undercutting the nationalist move-

Egyptian women demonstrate against the British occupation and in support of Wafdist demands for independence.
[From *A Woman Tenderfoot in Egypt* by Grace Thompson Sexton (New York: Dodd, Mead and Co., 1923)]

ment, the British unilaterally proclaimed Egyptian independence under the constitutional monarchy of King Fu'ad in 1922. Some Egyptian nationalist demands were furthered under the Anglo-Egyptian treaty of 1936, but the British continued to hold the Suez Canal, to base soldiers on Egyptian territory, and to exercise widespread influence over Egyptian political life. As nationalist demands for complete independence failed, both the monarchy and the Wafd became increasingly corrupt and lost the support of the Egyptian population, which turned to more radical groups on the Left and Right and finally to the army for realization of their nationalist aspirations.

Agitation in West Africa

Although West African colonies had given loyal support to the Allied efforts in World War I, nationalist discontent became apparent immediately following the peace settlement, particularly in the British colonies. Groups from the Gold Coast (Ghana) led the first demands for greater autonomy. Under the leadership of Casely Hayford, educated Africans from the four British colonies in West Africa met in Accra, the capital of the Gold Coast, in 1920 to discuss the implementation of reforms that would lead to independence. This group formed the nucleus of the National Congress of British West Africa, which met periodically for the next decade; after Hayford's death in 1930, however, the congress withered away, its demands still far from realization.

Nigeria, the largest and one of the most important British territories, was one of the focal points for nationalist outbreaks. Women merchants led demonstrations and riots in 1919 and again in 1928 in opposition to British domination. Under the leadership of Herbert Macaulay, Lagos, the capital city, soon became the center of the well-organized and effective nationalist opposition. In 1923, Macaulay organized the Nigerian National Democratic party, which pushed for more Nigerian participation within the British-dominated political system. Similarly, Blaise Diagne, a customs official who became the first African to be elected to the French Chamber of Deputies, pushed for African national causes in French-held Senegal. However, following the same pattern as the rest of Africa, West African nationalists in both British and French territories faced an uphill battle, and their demands for independence were not met until after World War II.

Nationalists in the Belgian Congo faced even greater difficulties. Although the Belgians had established a local school system, few graduates went on to European universities, and, in general, the Belgians continued to pursue a highly paternalistic policy in the Congo. Not surprisingly, repressive tactics by the Belgians only increased the number of nationalist sympathizers, who in the Congo frequently used religious fervor to popularize their programs. The Belgian government responded by reinforcing its authoritarian system.

Multiracial Tensions in British East Africa

Nationalist fervor varied greatly in British-dominated East Africa. In Uganda, where British authorities worked through local leaders who exercised local government duties, nationalist demonstrations were rare. In contrast, Kenya was far from quiescent during the interwar years. The continued racial and class divisions among elements of the diverse population caused ongoing conflict. Indians from the subcontinent had settled in fairly large numbers in Kenya and in Uganda and had gradually become the dominant merchants. Owing to their superior social and economic status within the British imperial system, the Indians never assimilated with the indigenous African population. On the other hand, they were never fully accepted by white European settlers or by British officials. Consequently, the issue of Indian citizenship and national participation irrevocably separated the East African population from the Indian immigrants, who generally sought to attain British citizenship.

British policy in Kenya attempted to balance the rights of the Africans with the goal of furthering white settlement of the rich agricultural land in the Kenyan highlands. The Kikuyu, the largest tribe in the highlands, were particularly alienated by British policies. Not surprisingly, they resented the loss of their traditional landholdings and were also angered by British taxes. By the 1920s, Kenyan nationalists had established several groups, including the Kikuyu Central Association (KCA), formed in 1924. The British responded by arresting Kikuyu leaders, which only increased local hostility. Membership in the KCA grew as younger Kenyans joined the ranks. In 1928, a key Kikuyu leader, Jomo Kenyatta, became secretary of the KCA and presented Kikuyu grievances to the British government in London. Kenyatta remained in Europe until 1946, when he returned to take up the leadership of the Kenyan nationalist movement.

Southern Africa: Nationalism versus White Settler Rule

Nationalist movements in southern Africa faced many of the same problems as those in East Africa. In the Portuguese colonies of Angola and Mozambique, *prazos* (huge feudal estates) held by a very small white minority dominated agricultural and business activities. Like the *colons* in Algeria and the British settlers in Kenya, the *prazeros* clung tenaciously to these colonies and were the major force behind authoritarian Portuguese policies that were similar to those adopted in the Belgian Congo.

As in Mozambique and Angola, European settlers in British-held Rhodesia controlled economic and political power, placing the black African majority in a subordinate position and depriving them of effective political participation. The relative poverty and economic dependence of the Africans prevented them from forming effective nationalist organizations in the Portuguese colonies and in Rhodesia; the result would be protracted struggles for national independence after World War II.

The racial and political divisions in the Union of South Africa were complex. After winning a victory over the Boers in South Africa and enjoying considerable support by many European settlers in South Africa during World War I, the British government first incorporated Boer territory and then granted it Dominion status within the Commonwealth, a position which implied an equal partnership with the mother country rather than a role as a subordinate. The British also embarked on a program of economic rehabilitation and assimilation of the Boers. While the economic programs were fairly successful, attempts to assimilate the Boers failed, and a new brand of Afrikaner (white South Africans of Dutch origin) nationalism emerged.

The Afrikaners, as the Boers called themselves, formed political parties led by the military heroes of the Boer War. The Afrikaners moved to maintain their superior political and economic status through the United Party, which was established in 1934 by Generals Jan Christian Smuts and James Hertzog. By 1934 the segregationist policies which formed the foundation for apartheid ("separate development," a strict government policy of racial segregation) had already become apparent.

With vast natural resources, rich agricultural land, minerals, and water, the Union of South Africa, dominated by the white Afrikaners, prospered. However, the Bantu tribal peoples who constituted over 80 percent of the population were kept in subordinate positions as tenant farmers, manual laborers, or workers in the mines and factories. As they became increasingly disenfranchised from the political and economic centers of power, educated black South Africans responded in 1912 by forming the South African Native National Congress, the first political coalition of its type in Africa. In 1923 the party changed its name to African National Congress of South Africa (ANC) which became the major nationalist organization for black participation and self-determination in South Africa. As in East Africa, Indians formed a small but generally prosperous minority. Here too, white settlers, particularly the Boers, tended to discriminate against Indians solely on the basis of race. Indeed, it was in South Africa that Gandhi first began his struggle for equality and began to formalize his commitment to nonviolent struggle.

A small group of settlers of British origin attempted to liberalize the society of South Africa but failed, and the Afrikaners kept their dominant positions. To perpetuate their privileged status, the Afrikaners tried a policy of divide and rule, and encouraged intertribal differences. As a result of their tribal policies and their vastly superior economic position, the Afrikaners continued to subordinate the majority black African population and to ignore or repress nationalist demands.

THE EMERGENCE OF PAN-AFRICANISM

By the turn of the century, African leaders, who were increasingly alienated by European economic, political, and cultural domination, called for the unity of all Africans, or Pan-Africanism. Called by Henry Sylvester-Williams, the first Pan-African Conference was held in London in 1900. Later conferences, supported by African Americans in Latin America and the United States, were held in various European capitals. E. W. Blyden, a Liberian diplomat born in Trinidad, and W. E. B. DuBois, an African American who was also active in the NAACP, helped to popularize the Pan-African movement in the West.

The noted African American leader Marcus Garvey, who had been born in Jamaica, was another outspoken champion of black nationalism. In the United States, Garvey enjoyed enormous personal popularity among many African Americans. With slogans like "Africa for the Africans!" "Renaissance of the Negro Race," and "Back to Africa," Garvey attracted widespread support from African Americans in the Western Hemisphere; his Back to Africa movement had over 2 million followers. The Pan-African and Back to Africa movements tended to be dominated by educated Africans and African Americans who advocated an appreciation of African cultures, better education, and racial equality. However, the movement secured few concrete results before World War II.

SUMMARY

During the postwar era, British and French refusals to grant full autonomy assured continued nationalist upheavals in the Middle East. Nationalist leaders, generally from the middle class, persisted in their demands for political and economic power. Their demands, whether presented through diplomatic channels or in revolutions, were consistently rebuffed. The British and French governments were determined to control the Middle Eastern oil fields and the strategic Suez Canal and Persian Gulf. When the middle-class political parties and nationalists failed to secure national independence, as in Egypt and Iraq, masses of people in the region turned to more radical groups and often concluded that only military action would achieve national liberation.

As in India, nationalism in the Arab world was highly developed. Also as in India, nationalism was segmented, both as a result of Arab heritage and of circumstance and because of the division of Arab lands between the British and the French. The progress of Arab nationalism was further complicated by the extension of Jewish nationalism (Zionism) in Palestine.

Nationalist discontent in Africa also continued to mount during the interwar years. The first generation of African nationalists failed to achieve their goals, and in many parts of the continent, as in the areas under the repressive domination of Belgium and Portugal, mobilized only a small fraction of the local populations. Economically and politically, most Africans remained subordinated to the imperial powers and to the European settlers. In South Africa, as the minority Afrikaner population sought to perpetuate its dominant position, the political and economic gaps between the minority white population and the majority black population widened. However, the more repressive the settlers and Western imperial governments became, the more the opposition increased. After 1945, another generation of African leaders emerged to demand and ultimately to achieve national independence.

SUGGESTED SOURCES

AFIGBO, A. E., E. A. AYANDELE, R. J. GAVIN, J. D. OMER-COOPER, and R. PALMER. *The Making of Modern Africa*, vol. 2 (1986). Basic textbook survey of African political and cultural developments.*

ANTONIUS, GEORGE, *The Arab Awakening* (1976). A straightforward description of the growth of Arab nationalism.*

I Stand for Your Dreams (n.d.). Highly laudatory Turkish film on Ataturk's military and political career. Video available from the Turkish Embassy.

Lion of the Desert (1981). An action-packed film depicting the revolt of Libyan Arabs against the Italian invasions during the 1920s and 1930s.

MAHFOUZ, NAGUIB, *Midaq Alley* (1981). A novel by the Nobel Prize-winning Egyptian writer detailing lives of people living in Cairo during World War II.*

PATON, ALAN, *Cry, the Beloved Country* (1961). A compelling novel about the black experience in South Africa.* (Also a film.)

ROSE, NORMAN, *Chaim Weizmann: A Biography* (1986). An excellent introduction to Zionism and a sympathetic account of one of Israel's founding fathers.

YAPP, M. C., *The Near East Since the First World War* (1991). Thoughtful survey of an area swept up in change and crisis.*

*Paperback available.

CHAPTER 18

Dictatorship and Democracy in Europe during the 1930s

During the 1930s authoritarian government became increasingly prevalent in Europe. Democratic ideals, which Woodrow Wilson popularized at the end of World War I, had subsequently been buffeted during the 1920s by dictators such as Lenin, Stalin, and Mussolini, and by authoritarian movements on the Iberian peninsula and in parts of eastern Europe. After 1929 the devastating economic effects of the Great Depression posed another serious challenge to democracy throughout Europe. By 1932 unemployment was skyrocketing, and people were struggling both in cities and on farms. Such an atmosphere was conducive to the would-be dictators who promised people an end to their misery. Adolf Hitler, who came to power in 1933, was not the only authoritarian politician in the 1930s to benefit from people's misery and a longing for better times, but he was the most infamous. By 1939 democracy survived only in western and northern Europe.

HITLER AND THE CONSOLIDATION OF NAZI POWER IN GERMANY

By 1930 Hitler was a rising political leader. While his primary appeal to the German people was his outspoken nationalism and criticism of the Allied treatment of Germany, the Depression also contributed significantly to his rise to political power. Many Germans blamed their economic ills on the Allies and the imposition of reparations payments. Others agreed with Hitler that the Jews were somehow to blame. Hitler's extreme criticism of the Versailles settlement grew in appeal as the economic situation worsened. In the autumn of 1930, as the 107 brown-uniformed Nazi delegates goose-stepped into the Reichstag building, the Depression was still in its early stages. In the summer elections of 1932, by which time economic conditions had worsened considerably—about 30 percent of German workers were unemployed—the Nazis received 230 seats. This was almost 100 more than their nearest rival, but still only 37 percent of the

Reichstag seats. As the leader of the largest party in the Reichstag, Hitler was now a major political power. Despite a loss of 34 seats in an autumn election, the Nazis remained by far the largest party.

Although their most consistent support came from small farmers and lower-middle-class elements, by 1932 many young people (including a considerable number of university students), civil servants, and upper-class individuals also supported the Nazis.

After 1930 German governments, unable to command a parliamentary majority, increasingly resorted to ruling by emergency decrees signed by President Paul von Hindenburg. Such decrees were allowed by the Weimar constitution. Nevertheless, parliamentary government ceased to function as originally envisioned, and the situation became more chaotic. Finally, Hindenburg reluctantly bowed to pressure from some conservative politicians and men of property who were impressed by the size of the Nazi following. They convinced the aging president that they could use Hitler for their own purposes. Thus Hindenburg, who two years earlier had said contemptuously that the highest office Hitler could ever hope to obtain was head of the postal department, appointed him chancellor of Germany on January 30, 1933.

After assuming the office, Adolf Hitler moved quickly and skillfully to strengthen his control. First, he blamed a fire that had destroyed the Reichstag building on the German Communists. He then convinced Hindenburg to sign an emergency decree that indefinitely suspended basic liberties and the due process of law. Hitler also stepped up his accusations and bullying tactics against the Communists. In Reichstag elections in early March 1933, the Communist vote declined and the Nazi vote increased to 44 percent of the total. Many of the Communist deputies were imprisoned, and none was allowed to

Two of Europe's leading dictators, Hitler and Mussolini, at a German military review in 1937.
(Brown Brothers)

take his seat in the new Reichstag. Later that month, using threats and promises, Hitler convinced the Reichstag to agree to the Enabling Act, which transferred legislative power to Hitler and his cabinet and allowed him to suspend parts of the Weimar constitution. The other political parties had thus allowed Hitler to assume dictatorial powers. By the summer of 1933, all political parties except the Nazis were outlawed.

Hitler's next move was to deal with a potential threat within his own Nazi party. The Storm Troopers (SA), who had been the "street fighters" of the party, were under the leadership of Ernst Röhm. Röhm and others wanted the "Nazi revolution" to be a true revolution that would destroy the old aristocratic and conservative elements, including those within the army. Hitler, however, had perceived the desirability of using these groups for his own purposes. On June 30, 1934, the "Night of the Long Knives," he set his elite guard, the *Schutzstaffel* (SS or black shirts), on the SA. Röhm, other SA leaders, and some of Hitler's non-Nazi political opponents were killed.

As a result of Hitler's handling of the more radical elements within his party, the conservative army leaders became more cooperative. After President von Hindenburg died in August 1934, Hitler assumed the presidency. He then ordered the armed forces to swear an oath of personal loyalty to him as Führer (leader). Meanwhile, the Nazi party took control of state and local governments and the judiciary. The secret police (Gestapo) ferreted out the remnants of political dissent. Arrest, torture, imprisonment, and death were commonplace. Special concentration camps were set up to hold political opponents and other so-called undesirables.

Despite earlier Nazi attacks on capitalism, Hitler's economic program after he came to power was based on supporting big business while making labor happy and controlling both. Once in power, he allowed major industries and large businesses to dominate the economy as long as they supported his regime. Hitler's military rebuilding program, in particular, allowed German industrialists to enjoy favorable contracts and to make large profits. Meanwhile, Hitler put German workers back to work constructing public buildings and superhighways (Autobahns) and producing armaments for the German war machine. Already by mid-1935, two-thirds of the number of unemployed in January 1933 were once again working. Forbidding any threats to his authority, Hitler dissolved the old labor unions and prohibited strikes. Workers were enrolled in a powerless national labor organization and were pacified with better wages and working conditions, vacations, pensions, children's camps, and a Nazi ideology which preached overcoming class differences in the process of creating a harmonious racial community.

Nazism was by now a potent stew of half-cooked ideas of Darwin, Nietzsche, and the nineteenth-century German nationalist composer Richard Wagner, combined with anti-Semitism and anti-Communism. Hitler's most important idea, and one that would soon cause much misery in the world, was the theory of the superiority of the German race (Aryans). In 1927, he had said: "Man owes everything that is of any importance to the principle of struggle and to one race which has carried itself forward successfully. Take away the Nordic Germans and nothing remains but the dance of apes." In the mind of Hitler, who had been anti-Semitic since his youth, Jews had polluted the pure Aryan blood and were behind many of the evils confronting Germany: the Versailles treaty, democracy, communism, the Depression, and the threat to traditional German values. Although Hitler's ideas were bogus, he believed deeply in them, and their emotional appeal was great, especially when delivered by the master orator himself. At giant rallies, such as the one in Nuremberg in 1934 at which hundreds of thousands participated amidst 130 giant searchlights and 20,000 flags, Hitler stirred crowds to a frenzy by appealing to German romantic nationalism, asking his listeners to pledge themselves to put the *Volk* (the German folk or nation) above all.

In order to entrench Nazism in Germany in both the present and the future, Hitler and his party created an elaborate program to indoctrinate the German people with loyalty to the Führer and to Nazi ideology. A ministry of culture supervised art, music, drama, literature, architecture, radio, films, and the press to ensure that all media instilled the Nazi program. In public bonfire ceremonies the Nazis burned publications with opposing or "incorrect" views and silenced dissenters.

The Nazis concentrated particularly on indoctrinating young Germans. They attempted to inculcate Nazism and an almost godlike reverence for Hitler in the schools, while Nazi-approved professors taught college youth racial pseudoscience and other "correct" subjects. The party also trained adolescent boys in the Hitler Youth to fight and die for the Führer, while adolescent girls were taught that the home was their rightful place and that they should have many babies to propagate the "superior" German race. Hitler once said "a woman must be a cute, cuddly, naive little thing—tender, sweet, and stupid."

Meanwhile, Hitler began his special campaign to isolate and degrade the Jews of Germany—about 1 percent of the population. In the spring and summer of 1933, they were removed from the civil service and from leading positions in German cultural life. In September 1935 the Nuremberg Laws deprived German Jews of their citizenship and forbade marriages between Jews and those defined as Germans. The Nazis gradually increased the use of terrorist methods against them. On November 9 and 10, 1938, Nazi thugs and others destroyed or ransacked well over 10,000 Jewish shops, homes, and synagogues, killed scores of Jews, and arrested and sent tens of thousands of Jews to concentration camps. Despite Crystal Night (as the Nazis labeled the event), until World War II broke out, more Jews emigrated—close to half the total—than were imprisoned, including such notables as Albert Einstein. Only after the beginning of the war did Hitler begin a massive slaughter of Jews who fell under Nazi control.

Despite Hitler's many successes in a short time, not all Germans approved of his policies. Some leaders of the German Catholic and Protestant churches, for example, resented Hitler's attempt to foster and propagate Nazi ideals contrary to the spirit of Christianity. A papal encyclical of 1937 criticized Nazi racism and paganism. German clergymen and lay leaders who spoke out openly often suffered persecution.

Overall, however, bold opposition was scarce; the Nazi regime was popular in Germany. In a general sense, Nazi indoctrination was effective. It stimulated pride in the German past and promoted the determination to overcome Germany's humiliation and to become a great power in the future. The violations of the rights of Jews and of those who opposed Hitler's policies were less important to many Germans than were Hitler's apparent successes. While Nazi terror helped keep Germans in line, many apparently would have supported Hitler in any case, in appreciation for his restoration of German economic and political power.

THE CORPORATE STATE IN ITALY

By the time Hitler became chancellor of Germany, Mussolini had already been in power in Italy for a decade, and his Fascist state continued to evolve toward greater authoritarian controls. Until 1929 the Catholic papacy continued, as it had for almost sixty years, to have serious differences with the Italian state. In that year, Pope Pius XI and Mussolini came to an agreement, the Lateran Treaty, that recognized papal control over Vatican City and its political independence. At the same time, Catholicism was recognized as the religion of the Italian state. Catholic religious education was allowed in the public schools, and Catholic marriage laws were to become the norm for state law. While this pragmatic agreement by the atheist Mussolini and the Catholic pope proved quite popular among Italy's overwhelmingly Catholic population and greatly increased Mussolini's support, strains between the Italian state and the papacy soon reappeared. In 1930 the pope denounced the government's attempts to train the young in "a pagan worship of the State." While not causing Mussolini serious problems, relations with the papacy were strained for the rest of the decade.

In the 1930s Mussolini's "corporate state" became something of a reality. In theory, such a state would overcome class conflict by bringing representatives of employers, employees, and the government together in corporations to decide on such questions as wages and working hours. By 1934 twenty-two of these corporations had been established, representing such areas as the clothing trades and mining. Since only Fascist trade unions were allowed to exist and represent the workers in the corporations, the interest of the workers was sacrificed to that of the Fascist party and the employers. The party, appreciative of the financial and political backing of big business, allowed business to help run an economy more and more dominated by large firms and monopolies. When some businesses found themselves near bankruptcy during the Depression, the government invested in them to keep them afloat. As a result, by 1937 the government possessed the controlling interest in shipping, electricity, heavy machinery, steel, and telephones. In 1938 the Chamber of Deputies, a carryover from a more democratic Italy long since dominated by Fascists, was replaced by the Chamber of Fasces and Corporations. While no real power changed hands, this move symbolized Mussolini's dislike of liberal democracy and his fondness for his own type of "corporatism."

AUTHORITARIAN GOVERNMENTS ELSEWHERE IN EUROPE

At the beginning of the 1920s, parliamentary governments, democratic in form, existed almost everywhere in Europe west of the Soviet Union. By 1939 rightist authoritarian dictators had taken over most of the nations of Europe, and few republics remained outside western Europe and Scandinavia. However, none of the other governments was as oppressive as Hitler's.

On the Iberian peninsula, Spain and Portugal had already witnessed the collapse of democracy in the 1920s. In Spain, General Primo de Rivera, who took power in 1923, held it until 1930. In 1931 democratic forces succeeded in restoring democracy until civil war broke out in Spain in 1936 and General Francisco Franco eventually established a dictatorship (see Chapter 19). In Portugal, the military uprising of 1926 led to the eventual dictatorial control of Antonio de Oliviera Salazar, who became prime minister in 1932. Both Franco and Salazar would continue in power for over three decades.

The authoritarianism of Primo de Rivera, Salazar, and Franco had just as much in common with Catholic traditionalist ideas as it did with those of Mussolini, perhaps more. Papal encyclicals such as Leo XIII's *Rerum Novarum* (1891) and Pius XI's *Quadragesimo Anno* (1931) and the writings of Catholic intellectuals such as Gilbert Chesterton and Charles Peguy criticized modern individualism as well as some of the inequities and abuses of both capitalism and Marxism. They emphasized subordinating individual and economic interests and rights to the good of the whole, as understood in the light of Catholic teaching. The Iberian dictators felt they were best qualified to interpret how this was to be done. From 1933 until 1938 Austria pursued a path similar to that followed by the Iberian states: Englebert Dollfuss, sometimes referred to as "Mickey Mouse" because of his small stature, and his successor, Kurt von Schuschnigg, attempted to rule in an authoritarian fashion, which Dollfuss claimed was to be based on the *Quadragesimo Anno*.

In the eastern European nations, a variety of authoritarian governments appeared and disappeared during the 1920s and 1930s. In some nations, real power was exercised by kings, as for a time in Yugoslavia, Rumania, and Bulgaria. In other nations, it was held by men of military background, such as Marshal Joseph Pilsudski in Poland and Admiral Miklos Horthy in Hungary. The trend toward authoritarian right-wing regimes accelerated following the onset of the Depression, as did economic and political nationalism and hostility toward minorities, especially the Jews. The involvement of some Jews in the region's banking, industry, and trade made them convenient scapegoats at a time of economic misery. By 1938 only Czechoslovakia still maintained a viable democratic government in eastern Europe, but its German minority became increasingly troublesome as a result of the Depression and Nazi-generated propaganda.

STALINISM IN THE SOVIET UNION: 1933–1939

Aware of the rising power of Germany and Japan, Stalin knew that it was more important than ever for the Soviet Union to strengthen its industrial base and its armed forces. As a result, the Second Soviet Five-Year Plan, begun in 1933, continued to emphasize the build-up of heavy industry. While increasing Communist party and personal control over the nation, Stalin began to down-play some of the ideological innovations introduced after the revolution, especially if they appeared to interfere with industrial productivity. The Communist ideal of egalitarianism, for example, was increasingly ignored. Thus, in order to get workers and managers to produce more, the party introduced various types of wage incentives and established a variety of incentives on the collective farms. The wages and privileges of technocrats, party and government bureaucrats, and military officers were also increased. A new privileged class of leaders came into existence, but the life of the average agricultural or industrial worker improved little. During the middle and late 1930s, the Soviet people had to cope with cramped housing, food shortages, and a dearth of consumer goods. The regime also retreated from earlier innovations regarding family life and education, making divorce and abortions more difficult to obtain and introducing new incentives for having children. In education, some of the earlier progressive experiments were scrapped, and hard work, discipline, and academic standards were reemphasized.

As the German and Japanese danger became greater, Stalin increasingly appealed to a Russian patriotism that stirred many hearts more than Marxism did. Books, films, and other media now displayed more respect for such figures from the tsarist past as Ivan the Terrible and Peter the Great. Even the Orthodox Church, which was so intricately connected with the tsarist past, began to receive somewhat better treatment. There was, however, no relaxation of the party's attempt to control people's ideas; in fact, Stalin tightened the party's cultural controls.

As another tool to motivate the Soviet people to work harder for their nation, Stalin forced writers and artists to use the techniques of approved "Socialist realism" for artistic and literary expression. Basically, this meant that artists and writers were to portray reality as the party wished it portrayed, in a clear, simple form that the average worker could understand. To the party, "reality" during the 1930s often meant the image of pure, courageous workers overcoming all sorts of obstacles and enemies in order to help increase productivity and thereby make the Soviet Union stronger.

Although Stalin was very anxious to strengthen the Soviet Union, he became even more interested in increasing his personal power. After discovering that his fellow Communist Sergei Kirov was much more popular among the party elite than he was, Stalin apparently approved of his assassination. He then blamed it on many others, whom he charged with being involved in a massive conspiracy against the Soviet Union. The Kirov case marked the beginning of what Robert Conquest has called "The Great Terror." Arrest followed arrest. Imprisonment, exile to Siberian prison camps, and execution awaited many. Important former political figures were executed after staged trials at which the defendants often confessed to crimes they could not possibly have committed. Despite the need for a strong military, the overwhelming majority of generals and colonels in the army were imprisoned, exiled, or executed. Of the members of the Central Committee of the party in 1934, the most powerful governing group in the Soviet Union, about 70 percent had been shot by 1939. Even the head of the secret police, Nikolai Yezhov, who directed the purge for Stalin during its most intense phase, was removed in 1938 and eventually executed—only to be replaced by the infamous Lavrentia Beria, who once said: "[Give me someone] for one night, and I'll have him confessing he's the king of England." The flood of arrests did not abate until 1939.

While the purges of former leaders and party members were the most dramatic events, others also suffered in these years. Prominent among them were intellectuals and those minorities accused of "bourgeois nationalistic tendencies." At times the police arrested ordinary individuals for no apparent reason other than to fill "arrest quotas" and to terrorize Soviet citizens into becoming more docile. While estimates of the number arrested and killed from 1935 to 1940 still vary widely, recent findings suggest that at least 7 to 8 million were put to death then and slightly more than that lived on in prison and prison labor camps.

TOTALITARIANISM

In practice, German Nazism and Stalin's Soviet communism had much in common. Both Hitler and Stalin were dictators, and the respective parties they dominated exercised almost complete control over all phases of life: government, the judiciary, the military, police forces, the economy, ideology, education, the press, and cultural institutions. Massive propaganda, as well as terror and fear, were regular instruments of their policy. Before their deaths, Hitler and Stalin would be responsible for the execution of millions. While figures are far from exact, Hitler was responsible for the murder of perhaps 6 million European Jews and 7 million other Europeans; from 1928 to 1953, Stalin was responsible for the extermination of an even higher total number of Soviet citizens. "One death is a tragedy, a million just statistics," Stalin once said.

Systems such as those of Germany and the Soviet Union in the 1930s, where the government attempted to maintain total control over the hearts, minds, and actions of the populace, are commonly referred to as totalitarianism. The term was a favorite of Mussolini (although not of Hitler or Stalin), who thought of his Fascist Italy as a totalitarian state. In some ways it was, but in actuality his control was never as "total" as that exercised by the other two dictators. In general, other authoritarian regimes of this time could not be classified as totalitarian. Even though each was run by a dictator or a small elite group, its control over various phases of life did not approximate that of Hitler or Stalin. Nevertheless, some type of censorship, restriction of civil liberties, and limitation on political opposition was practiced in all these regimes.

Despite the similarities between Stalin's U.S.S.R. and other nondemocratic societies, some distinctions existed that were also important. When Communists came to power in Russia, they effected a social and cultural revolution and dealt harshly with the prerevolutionary upper and middle classes and with traditional religious beliefs and values. While Hitler certainly weakened the power of the old German aristocracy, he and men such as Mussolini and Franco benefited from the fear and support of conservative classes and individuals who saw the Communists as a much more serious threat to their status, property, and beliefs. Another difference was that though Stalin increasingly appealed in the 1930s to Russian nationalism, he continued to reconcile it, at least in theory, with the internationalist emphasis that had long characterized communist ideology. The right-wing authoritarian governments, especially those of Hitler and Mussolini, were aggressively nationalistic.

SOCIAL AND POLITICAL CHANGES IN THE EUROPEAN DEMOCRACIES

The Depression and the rise of Nazism greatly affected the European democracies during the 1930s. Unemployment and other hardships experienced by many during the 1930s produced numerous significant social consequences, including a decline in the birth rate in most of the western democracies and a corresponding proportional increase in the number of older people. Numerous couples were apparently unwilling to have children while they remained in precarious economic circumstances.

Another change was the increasing attraction of workers to more militant unionism and more radical political ideas than those that had appealed to them in the late 1920s. As the Depression threw more and more workers out of jobs, they demanded an end to the liberal laissez-faire policies of their governments. Some felt that the Depression had proved the failure of capitalism. In Scandinavia, where democratic Socialist parties had alternated in power with more conservative parties during the 1920s, Socialists became dominant in the 1930s. In France, support for the Socialist and Communist parties increased, and a leftist coalition Popular Front government was formed in 1936 under France's first Socialist premier, Léon Blum. Blum's government took a more active role in the economy by increasing public spending and helping workers gain salary increases. Like President Franklin Roosevelt in the United States, he hoped to help France out of the lingering Depression by stimulating purchasing power. Blum strengthened the rights of unions and helped workers gain a forty-hour work week and a two-week paid vacation every year. Like most French governments in the interwar years, however, Blum's coalition government was unstable. Its reforms had the effect of decreasing production in the area of armaments, which was significant, considering the Nazi threat.

In Great Britain, the socialist-oriented Labour party was already in power when the Depression hit the nation, and it did not cope effectively with the early stages of the downturn. In August 1931 the Labour government fell when half the cabinet refused to go along with cuts in government benefits, cuts that U.S. and British bankers insisted were necessary before further U.S. loans could be issued to stabilize the British currency. For the remainder of the decade, the Conservative party ruled with mixed success by dominating successive National Coalition governments. Despite being more cautious than the Labour party, the Conservatives were moved by high unemployment and the public mood to enact some welfare state provisions—for example, in regard to public housing and expanded social insurance coverage.

SUMMARY

Undermined by the Depression, democracy seemed an outdated concept to many in Europe during the 1930s. Right-wing dictatorial and authoritarian personalities such as Hitler, Franco, and many eastern European leaders joined the earlier victorious Mussolini in opposing democracy, individualism, and equality with ideas of national or racial superiority, the superiority of the state over the individual, and various forms of elitism. In Russia, Stalin praised democracy and equality; but no less than Hitler, he aspired to totalitarian control of his country's actions and thoughts. While democratic governments survived in Scandinavia, Great Britain, and France, these governments had to increase their control over economic life in order to combat the effects of the Depression. By 1939 governments that advocated traditional laissez-faire economic policies seemed outmoded. To many, either dictatorships or democratic welfare states represented the future.

SUGGESTED SOURCES

BULLOCK, ALAN, *Hitler, A Study in Tyranny,* rev. ed. (1971). An excellent introduction to Hitler and his domestic and foreign policies. Also available in an abridged edition.*

DANIELS, ROBERT V., Ed., *The Stalin Revolution: Foundations of the Totalitarian Era,* 3d ed. (1990). A collection of essays in the Heath "Problems" series.*

FISCHER, LOUIS, *Men and Politics* (1941). A lively account of politics and personalities in Europe between the wars by a leading U.S. correspondent.*

MITCHELL, ALLAN, *The Nazi Revolution: Hitler's Dictatorship and the German Nation,* 3d ed. (1990). A collection of essays in the Heath "Problems" series; special attention is devoted to Hitler's personality and Nazi relations with industry, the churches, the military, and groups like women, youth, and the Jews.*

PEUKERT, DETLEF, *Inside Nazi Germany: Conformity, Opposition, and Racism in Everyday Life* (1987). A scholarly work that examines the reactions of ordinary citizens to Nazi policies.*

RYBAKOV, ANATOLI, *Children of the Arbat* (1988). A Russian novel that captures well the spirit of Stalin and Stalinism in 1934 Moscow.*

SHIRER, WILLIAM L., *Twentieth Century Journey*, vol. II, *The Nightmare Years, 1930–1940* (1984). A foreign correspondent's account of the important events of the 1930s, many of which he witnessed firsthand.*

SOLZHENITSYN, ALEKSANDR I., *The Gulag Archipelago: 1918–1956*, 3 vols. (1973–1978). A fascinating collection of materials about the treatment of those whom the Soviet government considered "enemies" of the state.*

SPIELVOGEL, JACKSON J., *Hitler and Nazi Germany: A History* (1988). A blend of biography and history with special emphasis on social history and the Holocaust.*

Triumph of the Will. The infamous 110-minute propaganda film of the 1934 Nazi Nuremberg rallies. (Also available on video.)

TUCKER, ROBERT C., *Stalin in Power: The Revolution from Above, 1928–1941* (1990). A comprehensive treatment of Stalin in this period by a leading scholar.*

WISKEMANN, ELIZABETH, *Fascism in Italy* (1970). A short, well-written, scholarly treatment of fascism in Italy and of its ideological influence in other European nations.*

*Paperback available.

CHAPTER 19

Aggression in the 1930s

During the 1930s the fragile system of international order broke down as some of the major world powers resorted to force to achieve their national goals and to settle real or imagined grievances. The rise to power of Japanese militarists, Hitler, and other European dictators, coupled with the hardships of the Depression, brought on more aggressive policies. While Japan used military force in expanding its holdings at the expense of China, Hitler made advances by relying on a combination of diplomacy and implicit or explicit threats of force, up until the invasion of Poland on September 1, 1939. Both Japanese aggressions and the actions of Hitler and other European right-wing dictators were met with little more than empty protests and appeasement.

JAPANESE AGGRESSION AND CHINESE RESPONSE

Japan Seizes Manchuria

Witnessing the trade barriers erected following the onset of the Depression, the Japanese became more convinced than ever of the need for a self-sufficient empire. Dependent upon importing industrial raw materials and food from the mainland of Asia, particularly from China, Japanese leaders were now determined to seize those parts of Asia that would give Japan a secure supply of these commodities. In addition, ultranationalists in Japan saw their nation as the rightful ruler of Asia. By either measure, China was Japan's next target. During the same period, China was slowly inching toward modernization and national unity. Japanese militarists could not tolerate this since a strong China would preclude Japanese dominance on the Asian mainland.

In the 1930s the Chinese and the Japanese embarked on a collision course in Manchuria, as both intensified their efforts to control the area. Japan had been satisfied to maintain a facade of Chinese sovereignty in Manchuria as long as a disunited China allowed it to control the warlord there. Japan called

Manchuria its "lifeline" and relied on it for such vital resources as iron ore, coal, and grain. The Chinese called Manchuria the "granary of China," where poor peasants from north China migrated to pioneer the virgin land. The KMT had targeted Manchuria as a key area in its movement to recover sovereign rights lost to outside powers. After 1929 the pro-Chiang warlord of Manchuria began a program of economic development, which included the building of Chinese-controlled railroad lines and seaports in competition with those already established by Japan.

These KMT initiatives led militant Japanese to fear that unless they acted quickly, Chinese authority would be reestablished in Manchuria. On September 18, 1931, junior officers of the Japanese army in Manchuria, whose goal was to conquer Manchuria and then take over the rest of China, engineered the Manchurian, or Mukden, Incident. Late that evening, the Japanese army staged an explosion on the tracks of the Japanese-controlled South Manchurian Railway. Blaming the Chinese, the entire Japanese army in Manchuria swung into action. Within days, they had captured all the important cities in the region.

It was a critical moment for party government in Japan. A strong government might have restrained the army's action and postponed a reckoning with China, but the government in Tokyo was weak and dared not risk its existence by forcing a showdown with the army. The army ignored civilian calls for restraint and completed its conquest of Manchuria by the end of 1931. In March 1932 Manchuria, renamed Manchukuo (Land of the Manchus), was proclaimed an independent state headed by the last Manchu emperor, who had abdicated the Chinese throne in 1912 when he was a little boy. In reality, Japan controlled every department of the new government, which it ran as a de facto colony until 1945. These events led to the resignation of the Japanese prime minister and cabinet.

China appealed to the League of Nations and the international community for help. After debates and futile resolutions ordering Japan to cease its aggression, which the Japanese army ignored with contempt, the League appointed an international commission headed by a British chairman, Lord Lytton, whose report condemned Japan for aggression and called on it to withdraw from its conquests. The League Assembly unanimously adopted the report, and Japan withdrew from the League. The League did nothing further. This was the first major crisis of war and peace to confront the League of Nations, and it had shown itself to be ineffective. U.S. protests were also not successful in deterring the Japanese.

Japan Attacks China

In the years following the Manchurian Incident, the Japanese pushed farther into China, brushing aside ineffective Chinese resistance. In 1933 Jehol, a province that linked Manchuria to northern China, was conquered by Japanese and puppet Manchukuo troops. Japan's next step south was to form the five provinces of north China into a neutral zone and oust the Chinese central

Japanese troops overrunning part of the devastated Shanghai in the war against China. *(Historical Pictures Service)*

government from the region. In response, Chiang Kai-shek clung to the strategy of "unification before resistance." Translated, this meant that Chiang wished to eliminate the Communists and warlords first, to build up the military next, and finally to resist Japan. Meanwhile, he would trade space for time, negotiate, temporize, but not commit his ill-prepared army to battle. In conventional military terms, Chiang's strategy made sense, but he discounted the potential power of nonmilitary and guerrilla forces when mobilized in support of a conventional war.

Above all, Chiang was insensitive to popular opinion, which demanded active resistance to Japan. Chinese students took to the streets calling for an end to civil wars and for all Chinese to form an anti-Japanese united front. The CCP was quick to take up the student cause; hard-pressed as it was in Yenan, it wanted a united front, if only to relieve KMT pressure on itself. The Soviet Union also came out for a Chinese united front, because a Sino-Japanese war would take Japanese pressure off Soviet Siberia and allow the Soviet Union to concentrate on the German menace in Europe. In 1937, Chiang bowed to public pressure and began negotiations for a united front with the CCP.

Given their ambition to dominate China, the last thing the Japanese wanted was the creation of a united front in China to resist them, and they decided to strike before a more unified China could foil their plans. On the night of July 7, 1937, at an important railroad junction near Peking called the Marco Polo Bridge, the Japanese army attacked. Popular feeling in China was so strongly in favor of resistance that no government could have survived unless it complied. In Tokyo, the Japanese cabinet vainly attempted to halt the spreading conflict. It failed because it could neither restrain its men at the front nor offer terms the Chinese government could accept. By August, serious fighting had spread to several fronts in north and central China. This was the beginning of World War II in Asia, which in China would last a full eight years.

China during the War

From 1937 to 1941, China fought alone. Until mid-1941, the isolationist United States continued to sell the essentials of war, such as petroleum and iron, to Japan. Great Britain and France were too preoccupied with their own problems in Europe and elsewhere to come to China's aid. The Soviet Union assisted China in the first two years of war, supplying a volunteer air force and loans. Soviet aid ended in 1939, however, because of the threat of war in Europe between the Soviet Union and Germany.

With inadequate aid from abroad, China was no match for Japan. With its modern war machine, Japan had little trouble conquering major cities along China's coast and rivers. However, Japanese mechanized warfare was tied to an inadequate Chinese road and railroad system for logistical support, and eventually Japan's war effort bogged down. Its occupation of the countryside was ineffective, limited to forays and punitive expeditions. In spite of, or perhaps because of, the barbarous behavior of Japanese troops, China would not surrender.

The Chinese government retreated westward to the mountainous interior to get out of reach of Japanese tanks, although that area was still within range of Japanese planes. The retreating Chinese army used the "scorched earth" policy, destroying what it could not take with it. Stage by stage, the Chinese government retreated westward up the gorges of the Yangtze River, taking with it whole arsenals, factories, libraries, and groups of people, until it attained safety in Chungking. It was one of humanity's largest migrations. Despite enormous hardships, the war hastened modernization in China's interior provinces, bringing new industry and schools to the region. By 1945 free China had twice as many university students as in all China in 1937. On the other hand, education had all but stopped in Japanese-occupied China.

After 1939 a war of attrition began, as Japan was both unable and disinclined to occupy all of China. The Chinese government continued to hold on, convinced that in its fanaticism Japan would eventually widen the war and thus bring other nations to China's aid. In the occupied areas, Japanese-sponsored puppet governments emerged in northern and southern China, but they were unable to attract to them many men or women of stature.

The full-scale war with Japan compelled the KMT and CCP to form the United Front in September 1937. Under its terms, the CCP agreed to abide by Dr. Sun's Three People's Principles, abandon its Marxist policies and Soviet-style government in areas it controlled, and abolish its Red Army. In return, the KMT agreed to reorganize the 40,000-strong Red Army into the national army, in separate units under CCP command, and to recognize CCP control of Yenan and some other areas.

From the beginning, the CCP regarded the Sino-Japanese War as an opportunity to build up its strength while the Japanese destroyed the KMT. While Nationalist armies were preoccupied with the Japanese, the Communists greatly expanded their area of control in the northwest. Shortly after the United Front was formally proclaimed, the Central Committee of the CCP issued the following directive to its cadres: "Our fixed policy should be 70 percent expansion, 20 percent dealing with the Kuomintang, and 10 percent resisting Japan." Besides territorial expansion, the CCP attempted to increase its army to 1 million men and the party to 1 million members. During the next eight years, Communist units were very successful in slipping behind Japanese lines and organizing peasant guerrilla bands to harass the Japanese.

The United States Moves toward Confronting Japan

From the beginning, the United States strongly opposed Japanese aggression in China. Although Americans living in China enjoyed extraterritoriality and other benefits of Western imperialism, the U.S. public fancied itself as a longtime friend of China. Most Americans regarded Japan not only as a brutal attacker of a nation friendly to the United States but also as a threat to U.S. interests in Asia. When Japan seized Manchuria in 1931 the United States was opposed, but it was unwilling to intervene militarily or to deepen the Depression by imposing economic sanctions and had to content itself with a strong diplomatic protest. Secretary of State Henry Stimson announced that the United States would not recognize Japan's seizure of Manchuria because it impaired U.S. rights, violated the Open Door policy, and flouted the Kellogg-Briand Peace Pact. This statement, plus a U.S. threat to build up military strength in the Pacific, failed to deter the Japanese; meanwhile, normal business relationships continued.

When Japan invaded China in 1937, the United States again protested. Roosevelt stated that aggression was becoming "epidemic" and that a "quarantine" was needed. This time the United States government went beyond rhetoric. It arranged limited economic and military aid to the Chinese, placed an embargo on the sale of airplanes to Japan, and abrogated the Commercial Treaty of 1911. In order to increase military preparedness, Congress authorized the construction of aircraft carriers and battleships. None of these actions halted the Japanese in China or materially aided the Chinese, and extensive U.S. trade with Japan continued until 1941. This train of events rapidly soured relations between the two nations, and many officials on both sides of the Pacific believed that a direct confrontation might well occur in the near future.

THE NAZI THREAT TO PEACE AND THE ALLIED RESPONSE

During the 1930s Great Britain and France failed to deal effectively with the increasing aggressiveness of Nazi Germany and Fascist Italy. In the first half of the decade, before Hitler made his most conspicuous international moves, the major European democratic powers had already been unable to halt aggression. Following Japan's 1931 occupation of Chinese Manchuria, Italy attacked Ethiopia in late 1935. In the second case, as in the first, the British and French delegates to the League of Nations were critical of this aggression but put forward little effective response. Despite a personal appeal by Ethiopian Emperor Haile Selassie, the League imposed only halfhearted, short-lived, and limited economic sanctions on Italy. Nor did Great Britain and France take any meaningful action when, in early 1935, Hitler announced that, in violation of the Treaty of Versailles, he intended to reintroduce military conscription and increase the size of the German armed forces.

The German Occupation of the Rhineland

In March 1936 Hitler took the most daring gamble of his early years in power when he decided to send troops into the Rhineland, the German territory that according to the Versailles and Locarno treaties was to remain demilitarized. The French had removed their last troops from the area in 1930, but as long as the area was not fortified, a German attack on France was difficult. Many German diplomats, statesmen, and officers considered Hitler's gamble too risky. They believed French soldiers would be sent to turn back the Germans and feared that the German army was not yet ready for war with France. Hitler himself later stated: "If the French had then marched into the Rhineland, we would have had to withdraw with our tails between our legs." But he did not think the French would act. He was right; they did nothing.

There were a variety of reasons for the failure of France and Great Britain to take more decisive action. Among the most prominent were (1) a genuine hatred of war on the part of many who remembered the horrors of World War I, accompanied by a lack of enthusiasm for heavy military spending; (2) a feeling, more common in Great Britain than in France, that perhaps Germany had been dealt with too harshly in the Versailles treaty and that its desire for revision was understandable; (3) Hitler's ability to make some Allied statesmen believe he was a reasonable and peace-loving man with limited goals; and (4) a fear that if Hitler were overthrown in Germany, a worse situation might arise: a Communist government. In 1938 British Prime Minister Neville Chamberlain, prompted by a discussion of Hitler's possible overthrow, asked: "Who will guarantee that Germany will not become Bolshevik afterwards?"

Soviet Response to Japanese and German Aggression

Soviet policies toward Hitler zigzagged. First, Stalin helped Hitler come to power by preventing German Communists from cooperating with other leftists to prevent it. Stalin apparently realized that a Nazi government would be hostile to western European powers, and vice versa, a situation from which the Soviet Union could benefit. Despite Hitler's known hostility to communism, Stalin at first indicated a willingness to do business with him. After

Hitler displayed little inclination to reciprocate, however, Stalin began looking for assistance against this potential new threat. Already alarmed by Japan's movements near Soviet borders in Manchuria, the Soviet Union achieved diplomatic recognition in 1933 from the United States. In 1934 it joined the League of Nations, an organization that Lenin had earlier described as "an alliance of world bandits against the proletariat."

After 1934 Soviet delegates frequently attempted to arouse other nations to a realization of the dangers presented by Japan and Germany. In May 1935 the Soviet Union signed the Mutual Assistance Treaty with France, in which each party agreed to come to the assistance of the other in case of an unprovoked attack. That same year, the Soviet government concluded a similar treaty with Czechoslovakia, except in this case neither party was obligated to aid the other unless France first came to the aid of the attacked nation. Both treaties clearly reflected the Soviet Union's growing fear of Germany.

Another important step taken in 1934 and 1935 was that Moscow directed foreign Communist parties to cooperate with other political parties in nations that were willing to take steps to check German aggression. In both Great Britain and France, however, fear and suspicion of Communist aims hindered close cooperation against Germany. In France, conservative distrust delayed ratification of the pact with Moscow until February 1936.

The Soviet Union's apprehensions about Germany and Japan were increased when the two nations signed the Anti-Comintern Pact in 1936. The following year, Italy, which had been moving closer to Germany, also affixed its signature. Although the pact did little more than record the signatories' opposition to international communism, it did symbolize the growing affinity of the three powers.

Franco Triumphs in Spain

In the Spanish Civil War (1936–1939), dictatorship won a significant victory over democracy. In the summer of 1936 General Francisco Franco invaded Spain from Spanish Morocco, seeking to oust the shaky leftist coalition government of the Spanish Republic. Franco was supported by most of the army, conservative elements in the Spanish Catholic Church, and the middle and upper classes, especially in agrarian areas. The Republican government, on the other hand, relied on support from most urban areas, including the capital, Madrid, and from many of the lower class, especially from the industrial workers. Portions of the Spanish air force and navy also remained loyal to the government. It was a cruel war, with atrocities on both sides; an estimated 1 million people lost their lives.

From the very beginning, however, the Spanish Civil War was more than a domestic problem. Ideological forces in Europe seized on the conflict as a symbolic test whose outcome would predict the future direction of European affairs. By 1937 Mussolini was assisting Franco with about 70,000 troops and technicians, plus planes and mechanized equipment. Germany had at least 10,000 military personnel in Spain, including the dreaded Condor Legion, an air force unit that bombed Madrid and other Spanish cities, causing many civilian casualties. On April 26, 1937, the Germans bombed and destroyed the market town and Basque religious center of Guernica, killing and maiming much of the population. "We bombed it, and bombed it, and bombed it, and why not?" one aviator was reputed to have said. The bombings, a preview of World War II terror bombings, outraged world opinion and inspired Pablo Picasso to create *Guernica*, one of the major paintings of the twentieth century.

To counter Fascist and Nazi efforts in Spain, the Soviet Union sent aid and advisors to the Spanish Republic and worked through the Comintern to help drum up volunteers to fight Franco. Even without Soviet promptings, foreigners volunteered to fight on the side of the Spanish government. There were several "international brigades," including the Abraham Lincoln Brigade from the United States and the Canadian McKenzie-Papineau Battalion. The anarchist Emma Goldman also came to Spain to aid in the fight against the Franco forces. For many politically inclined intellectuals, it was a chance, in one way or another, to demonstrate their hatred of fascism and the Nazis. The French novelist and adventurer André Malraux, who flew fighter planes for the Republican side, and the U.S. novelist Ernest Hemingway, who served as correspondent and fund-raiser, were just two of the intellectuals who aided the Popular Front government. Leftist support to the Spanish government, however, was not as effective as that given by Italy and Germany to Franco. The Soviet Union appeared more concerned with using the war as an opportunity to control and expand the Spanish Communist party's role than with helping to win the war. Divided internally on the Left-Right political spectrum, Great Britain and France did little to counter outside support to Franco. Fearing that the civil war in Spain might spread, Great Britain and France ineffectually called on outside powers not to intervene in Spain. Thus Hitler and Mussolini once again witnessed the inability of Great Britain and France to check their actions. In 1939 Franco finally defeated the Republic and set up a repressive right-wing dictatorship.

German Aggression: March 1938 to March 1939

Hitler had indicated on the first page of his *Mein Kampf* that union with "German Austria" *(Anschluss)*, forbidden in the post–World War I peace treaties signed by Germany and Austria, should be a German goal. He also stated that all German-speaking people should be united in an enlarged German *Reich* (realm or empire). Territory or living space *(Lebensraum)* for such an empire could be obtained, conquered if need be, in eastern Europe. His activities during 1938 and 1939 were in keeping with these long-held beliefs.

In March 1938 Germany moved again. By pressure and bullying tactics, Hitler succeeded in bringing a Nazi to power in Austria and obtaining an invitation for Germany to occupy the nation. German troops marched in without resistance, and the forbidden *Anschluss* took place as Austria became a province of Germany. Once again, the French and British did nothing but protest.

In late 1938 Hitler demanded that Czechoslovakia cede what Hitler called "the Sudetenland" to Germany. This Czech territory, which bordered on Germany and the former Austrian Republic, consisted primarily of ethnic Germans. But the area had been a part of the former Austro-Hungarian Empire and not of Germany. On September 15 and again on September 22, the British prime minister, Neville Chamberlain, flew to Germany to see Hitler and try to avert an international crisis. After his first meeting, Chamberlain wrote to his sister: "In spite of the hardness and ruthlessness I thought I saw in his face, I got the impression that here was a man who could be relied upon when he had given his word." On September 29 Chamberlain returned to Germany, where at Munich he and Hitler were joined by Mussolini and the French premier, Edouard Daladier. Czechoslovakia was not invited to participate in the conference; neither was the Soviet Union, which had pledged to come to the aid of Czechoslovakia in case of aggression, providing France did so first.

France, on the other hand, although it had a defensive alliance with Czechoslovakia, agreed with Britain and Italy that the Sudetenland was to be given to Germany. Neither France nor Great Britain had kept up with German rearmament, and their intelligence services depicted Germany as even more powerful than it really was. Neither was yet ready to risk war. French military thinking was symbolized by the Maginot Line, a long series of defensive fortifications built on France's eastern front between 1929 and 1934; such defensive-mindedness ill prepared France to come to the aid of her Czechoslovakian ally.

Poland and Hungary also took advantage of the situation and within a few months seized portions of Czechoslovakia. Altogether, Czechoslovakia lost about a third of its population, much of its heavy industry, and important

After returning from the Munich Conference, British Prime Minister Chamberlain displayed a British-German declaration and predicted "peace for our time." (*Central Press Photos*)

defensive fortifications. When news of the Munich Agreement was received in Prague, people cried openly in the streets. Despite Chamberlain's claim that "peace for our time" had been achieved, the Munich Conference soon became a symbol of the dangers of "appeasement," and Hitler hardly seemed grateful. "If ever that silly old man comes interfering here again with his umbrella," Hitler said about Chamberlain, "I'll kick him downstairs and jump on his stomach in front of photographers."

The signatories of the Munich Agreement had promised to guarantee what remained of Czechoslovakia against aggression. In March 1939, however, Hitler took over most of what was left of that unfortunate nation except for an eastern portion, Ruthenia, that he allowed Hungary to add to its previous gains. A little later that month, Lithuania, faced with an ultimatum, allowed Germany to annex its Germanic city of Memel. Hitler then began putting pressure on Poland for return of the city of Danzig, with its overwhelmingly German population, while also demanding special rail and road rights across the Polish Corridor separating East Prussia from the rest of Germany.

By this time, however, the British and French governments had finally seen the light. Despite continuing doubts about their countries' military readiness, public opinion, especially in Great Britain, had been awakened by the events of March 1939. Appeasement was not working; Hitler always came back for more. On the last day of March, Chamberlain announced that he and the French leaders had agreed to back Poland fully if it were threatened. This awakening, however, came too late for the small nation of Albania, which, already under strong Italian influence, was formally occupied by Mussolini's forces in early April 1939.

The United States Remains Neutral

Like Great Britain and France, the United States had great difficulty creating an effective response to Hitler's and Mussolini's aggressive actions in Europe. The U.S. public viewed the upheavals in Europe with mixed emotions. On the one hand, there was some concern about the persecution of Jews in Germany and some fear of Hitler's threat to European democracy and to the United States. On the other hand, some Americans, like many Europeans, regarded a strong Germany as a bulwark against Soviet communism. Many New Deal liberals feared that involvement in European conflicts would distract energy and money from domestic reforms. An even larger number of Americans simply believed that intervention in World War I had been a mistake and opposed any actions that would involve the United States in another war.

Americans were thus, on balance, isolationists, and when Congress passed a series of Neutrality Acts, 1935–1937, it reflected public opinion. In this legislation, Congress prohibited U.S. vessels from transporting war materiel to belligerents, prohibited loans to belligerents, declared the United States neutral in the Spanish Civil War, and forbade U.S. citizens to travel on belligerent ships. By such action, Congress hoped to prevent U.S. trade from dragging the United States into war, as had happened in World War I. Roosevelt and his admin-

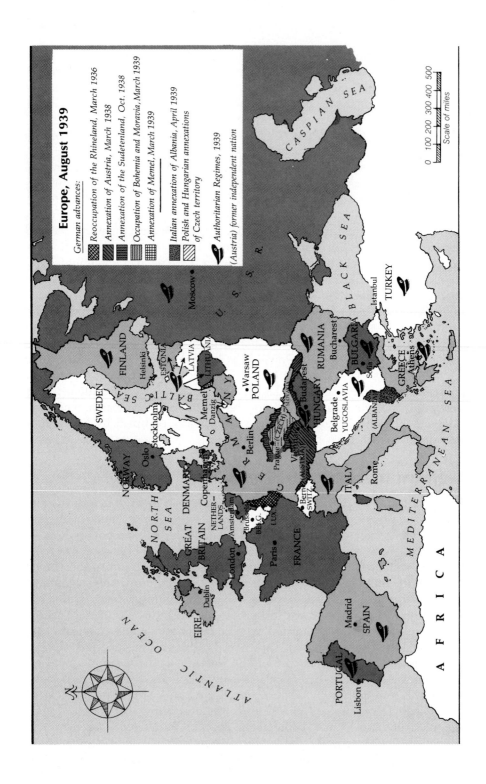

Europe, August 1939

German advances:

- Reoccupation of the Rhineland, March 1936
- Annexation of Austria, March 1938
- Annexation of the Sudetenland, Oct. 1938
- Occupation of Bohemia and Moravia, March 1939
- Annexation of Memel, March 1939

- Italian annexation of Albania, April 1939
- Polish and Hungarian annexations of Czech territory

- Authoritarian Regimes, 1939

(Austria) former independent nation

0 100 200 300 400 500
Scale of miles

ATLANTIC OCEAN

NORTH SEA

BALTIC SEA

CASPIAN SEA

BLACK SEA

MEDITERRANEAN SEA

AFRICA

U. S. S. R.

Moscow

FINLAND
Helsinki

SWEDEN
Stockholm

NORWAY
Oslo

ESTONIA
LATVIA
LITHUANIA

DENMARK
Copenhagen

GREAT BRITAIN
London

EIRE
Dublin

NETHER–LANDS
Amsterdam

BELG.
Brussels

LUX.

FRANCE
Paris

Memel
Danzig

G E R M A N Y
Berlin

Warsaw
POLAND

CZECH.
Prague
SLOV.

AUSTRIA
Vienna

HUNGARY
Budapest

SWITZ.
Bern

ITALY
Rome

YUGOSLAVIA
Belgrade

RUMANIA
Bucharest

(ALBANIA)

BULGARIA
Sofia

GREECE
Athens

TURKEY
Istanbul

SPAIN
Madrid

PORTUGAL
Lisbon

istration went along with Congress reluctantly, although the effect of the Neutrality Acts was to strengthen Hitler, Mussolini, Franco, and Japan.

As aggression in Europe mounted, the United States, distracted by Japanese advances in China and in hopes of preserving peace in Europe, pursued a policy of appeasement similar to that of Great Britain and France. Roosevelt raised little or no objection to Hitler's advances in the Rhineland, Austria, and the Sudetenland. However, Hitler's seizure of the rest of Czechoslovakia and Mussolini's conquest of Albania shocked Americans and began to bring them around to the belief that aggression in Europe should be stopped. Roosevelt appealed to Hitler to refrain from attacking a list of European nations, but Hitler (like the kaiser's advisors in World War I) viewed the United States as degenerate and incompetent and ridiculed Roosevelt's appeal. Despite Roosevelt's change of position, Congress refused to repeal the neutrality legislation, and the United States continued to remain a spectator.

Europe on the Eve of the War

Although the British, and to a somewhat lesser extent the French, were now more determined to oppose any further German advances, Hitler had no way of being sure that his opponents would not again back down. If France and Great Britain did support Poland against German aggression, however, he had to prevent the Soviet Union from becoming involved. If he could obtain a promise of neutrality from Stalin, perhaps Great Britain and France would once again retreat rather than support Poland alone. In any case, he did not want a war on two major fronts.

In 1939 the French government and many influential figures in Great Britain believed that a strong alliance with the Soviet Union was needed if they hoped to avert a war or defeat Hitler if one should come. However, despite their 1935 Mutual Assistance Treaty, France and the Soviet Union were suspicious of each other. Firm military arrangements in case of war, for example, were never worked out. Nor did France's other potential ally, Great Britain, have much faith in the Soviet Union. Chamberlain, especially, distrusted the Communist giant. Finally, Stalin's purges of the late 1930s, which had devastated the Soviet officer corps, had reduced British and French confidence in the Soviet military—and no doubt encouraged Hitler to become more aggressive.

Stalin, of course, had his own interests in mind, and when Hitler made overtures toward the Soviet Union, Stalin proved willing. Stalin had never trusted Great Britain or France and welcomed the possibility of their fighting Germany in a war that might exhaust and weaken all three.

On August 23, 1939, the Soviet government signed a Non-Aggression Pact with Germany. It stipulated that for ten years both sides would refrain from attacking each other and would remain neutral if the other became "the object of a belligerent action by a third power." A secret protocol, as later modified, divided eastern Europe into spheres of influence. Finland, Latvia, Estonia, Lithuania, eastern Poland, and Bessarabia (in Rumania) were to be in the Soviet sphere, while Germany's was to be western Poland.

With the Soviet Union now neutralized, Germany was ready to attack Poland, and as a result of the pact Hitler now had reason to hope that Poland might be deserted by Great Britain and France. He attacked Poland on September 1. Two days later, however, Poland's western allies declared war on Germany. World War II had begun in Europe.

SUMMARY

During the 1930s both Japan and Germany pursued aggressive policies designed to expand their territories. Interested in controlling its sources of supply in East Asia and worried about China's efforts to strengthen itself, Japan moved first in the decade, seizing Manchuria in 1931. Japan's pace of aggression thereafter accelerated; it attacked China in 1937 and subsequently conquered much of it.

In Europe, Nazi Germany and Fascist Italy committed similar aggressions. Between 1936 and 1939 Adolf Hitler tore up the Treaty of Versailles by remilitarizing the Rhineland and annexing Austria and later partitioned Czechoslovakia, all without effective opposition. Mussolini conquered Ethiopia, helped Franco win the civil war in Spain, and annexed Albania. Germany and Italy were aided, as was Japan, by the reluctance of Great Britain, France, and the United States to take stern measures to check aggression. Different ideologies and mutual mistrust on the part of the Soviet Union and the western democracies prevented them from forming an effective coalition against the aggressors. In August 1939, after years of denouncing Nazi behavior, Stalin signed a pact with Hitler, clearing the way for a division of Poland between the two. Allied appeasement of Germany ended when Hitler attacked Poland, bringing on World War II in Europe.

SUGGESTED SOURCES

BELL, P. M. H., *The Origins of the Second World War in Europe* (1987). A clear survey suitable for undergraduates.*

BUTOW, ROBERT J. C., *Tojo and the Coming of the War* (1969). An excellent study of Japanese policy before and during World War II.*

DIVINE, ROBERT H., *The Illusion of Neutrality* (1968). A general account of neutrality legislation in the United States.*

EUBANK, KEITH, Ed., *World War II: Roots and Causes,* 2nd ed. (1992). Up-to-date essays from a wide variety of scholars; part of the Heath "Problems" series.*

HEMINGWAY, ERNEST, *For Whom the Bell Tolls* (1940). A novel depicting the Spanish Civil War by a famous American writer who participated in it.* (Also a film.)

IRIYE, AKIRA, *The Origins of the Second World War in Asia and the Pacific* (1987). A clear introduction by a leading U.S. historian.*

LAFORE, LAURENCE, *The End of Glory* (1970). An excellent introduction to the individuals and events of the 1920s and 1930s that helped lead to World War II.*

MALRAUX, ANDRÉ, *Man's Hope* (1938). A novel dealing with the Spanish Civil War by a leading French writer who helped organize, and flew for, the Spanish Republican air force.*

MORTON, WILLIAM F. *Tanaka Giichi and Japan's China Policy* (1980). Tanaka was an important advocate of Japanese expansion in China.

TAYLOR, A. J. P., *The Origins of the Second World War* (1983). A controversial work that questions to what extent Hitler was "guilty" of beginning the war.*

WATT, DONALD CAMERON, *How War Came: The Immediate Origins of the Second World War, 1938–1939* (1989). The best book on the immediate origins of the war in Europe; well-written and comprehensive.*

YOSHIHASHI, TAKEHIKO, *Conspiracy at Mukden: The Rise of the Japanese Military* (1963). Details how the Japanese army flouted civilian control.

*Paperback available.

CHAPTER 20

World War II

Compared to World War I, World War II was a true global phenomenon. Spurred on by an inflammatory mixture of aggressive nationalism and virulent political ideology, the warring nations mounted major land campaigns in Europe, North Africa, and Asia, waged amphibious warfare in the western Pacific, and conducted extensive naval operations around the world. The weaponry used at the end of this war, particularly the airplane and the nuclear bomb, was so destructive that it appeared capable of destroying humanity itself.

HITLER'S CONQUESTS IN EUROPE, 1939–1941

In the first year of war, Germany dramatically demonstrated that it had tactically outstripped its opponents. To avoid the stalemate that had defeated them in the last war, the Germans waged *Blitzkrieg* (lightning warfare). In early September 1939 masses of German tanks, supported by airplanes, broke through the Polish infantry and pushed behind the lines, disrupting supplies and reinforcements. German infantry mopped up the isolated Polish remnants. The German air force bombed the Polish capital, Warsaw, and other cities, demoralizing the civilian population. The Polish campaign was over in three weeks; the entrenchment nightmare that had characterized World War I would not be repeated. Operating under a prior secret agreement with the Germans, Soviet forces moved in to occupy eastern Poland, whose ethnic makeup was predominantly Byelorussian and Ukrainian. The conquering powers divided Poland, which once again disappeared from the map of Europe.

Hitler offered peace to Great Britain and France if they would recognize his conquest of Poland; when they refused, he made plans to attack and defeat them in the spring and summer of 1940. As German preparations went forward, Great Britain contented itself with driving German surface vessels off the oceans, imposing a blockade, and sending a small army to assist France.

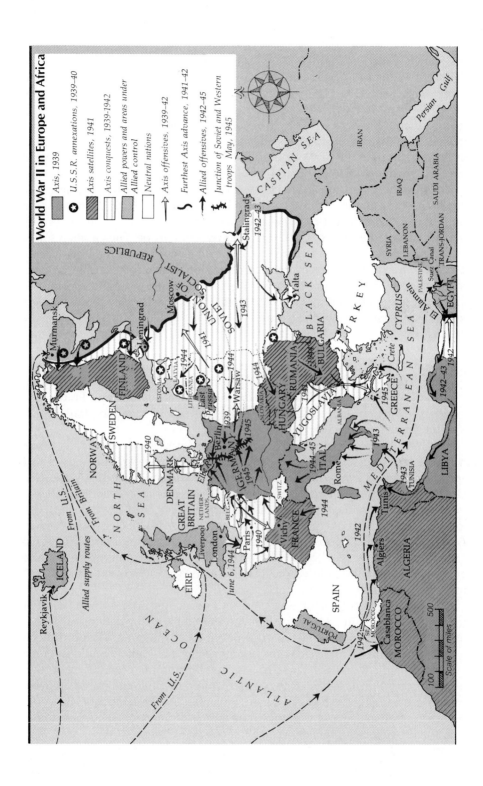

World War II in Europe and Africa

The French waited behind the Maginot Line for the German attack, a strategy observers scorned as "sitzkrieg." In April 1940 the Germans thrust northward rather than westward. They seized Denmark without resistance and conquered Norway in two weeks, expelling British forces that had attempted to hold northern Norway. Germany now controlled neutral Sweden's export iron ore and could use the Norwegian coast as a base for air and submarine attacks on British shipping. In Great Britain, the Chamberlain government collapsed and the dynamic Winston Churchill became prime minister.

In May the Germans struck in Western Europe, quickly overrunning the Dutch and the Belgians. Instead of wheeling in an arc as in the previous war, the Germans launched a massive armored attack through a gap at Sedan, France, in the center of the Allied front in Western Europe. The German forces broke through and dashed to the English Channel, cutting off the British army and some French troops from the main body of French forces. Using almost every craft in Great Britain that would float, the British staged a spectacular rescue operation at Dunkirk. They were able to evacuate most of the soldiers but had to leave behind their supplies and heavy equipment, leaving the British army gravely weakened.

In the face of the disaster, Churchill rallied the British people: "We shall fight on the beaches, we shall fight on the landing grounds, we shall fight in the fields and in the streets, we shall fight in the hills; we shall never surrender." In June the Germans drove southward and westward across France, bypassing the Maginot Line. The French army was unable to consolidate a front. With the French near defeat, Italy declared war.

On June 22 France surrendered. For the surrender ceremony, Hitler chose the same spot and same railroad car where the German representatives had signed the armistice in 1918. Under the terms of surrender, Germany annexed Alsace-Lorraine and occupied northern and western France, enabling Hitler to use the French coastline for submarine and air bases against Great Britain. Unoccupied France, with its capital at Vichy, became an ally of Germany. A small contingent of French troops in Africa and a body of French military refugees in Great Britain, led by General Charles de Gaulle, formed a government in exile and fought on at the side of the British. French underground "resistance" fighters harassed the Germans in France.

While Hitler was overrunning Western Europe, the Soviet Union was improving its position in Eastern Europe. It annexed the Baltic nations of Lithuania, Latvia, and Estonia, and a border province of Rumania; after a difficult war with the Finns, it annexed some border sections of Finland and a site for a naval base on the Baltic Sea. These moves, combined with its earlier incorporation of eastern Poland, enabled the Soviet Union to widen the buffer zone between Germany and the heart of the Soviet Union. At the same time, however, these actions alienated and frightened the authoritarian regimes in Eastern Europe and drove most of them to seek alliances with Hitler.

Meanwhile, Hitler turned his attention to his surviving enemy, Great Britain. He had never really been interested in fighting the British, and he made peace overtures to them based on the status quo. Great Britain rejected the German offers, although it was too crippled to attack Germany in Europe. Hitler then moved to invade Great Britain. He planned first to use his air force to destroy the British air force. With British planes destroyed, the Germans would be able to bomb or drive off the British fleet; the German army could then invade England. All through the summer and early autumn of 1940 a great air battle, the Battle of Britain, raged, but the Germans failed to destroy the British air force. "Never have so many owed so much to so few," said Churchill of the British airmen. The Germans turned to terror bombing the British cities, hoping to demoralize the British population who would then force the British government to sue for peace.

Despite extensive damage to some British cities and heavy loss of life, the British persevered. Churchill was an inspirational leader and effectively exhorted the British to fight on: "Hitler knows that he must break us in this island or lose the war. . . . Let us therefore brace ourselves to our duty and so bear ourselves that . . . men will . . . say, 'This was their finest hour.' " By the winter of 1940–1941, it was clear that Great Britain would continue in the war, although essentially on the defensive. Hitler hoped that a more intensive version of the World War I submarine blockade would eventually strangle them.

Although the British remained unconquered, Hitler turned to his long-standing dream of destroying the Communist government in the Soviet Union, enslaving its people, and colonizing the east with Germanic peoples. He planned to throw his army and air force against the Soviet Union in mid-May 1941 and to destroy Stalin's regime in five months, before winter set in. In preparation for the assault, Hitler forged alliances with Hungary, Rumania, and Bulgaria, reached an understanding with Finland, and moved German and allied troops toward the Soviet border.

Hitler's plans to invade the Soviet Union were disrupted, however, by the difficulties of his ally Mussolini. The British had conquered Italian East Africa, driven into Libya, sunk most of the Italian navy, and supported the Greeks in repelling an Italian invasion. In April 1941, with Yugoslavia on the verge of joining the British and Greeks, Hitler acted. German forces and their allies overwhelmed Yugoslavia, but guerrillas, especially Communist units led by Joseph Tito, fought the Germans there throughout the war. The British tried to hold Greece and Crete to protect their Mediterranean supply route but were driven out.

Meanwhile, Hitler dispatched the Afrika Corps under General Erwin Rommel to aid the Italians, and Rommel pushed into Egypt toward the Suez Canal. Desperate, the British called on Indian and ANZAC troops to hold Egypt and to protect the Middle East petroleum fields. The Soviets and British deposed the pro-German shah of Iran, Reza Pahlavi, and installed his young son Mohammed as ruler. Turkey, caught between German success in Europe and British and Soviet power in Asia, remained neutral.

In the meantime, Hitler prepared to invade the Soviet Union. The Balkan campaign had been highly successful, but it had delayed the invasion of the

Soviet Union for five precious weeks. Fearing British invasion, Hitler left a large number of troops and planes in Western Europe and launched the invasion of the Soviet Union with the bulk of his armed forces on June 22, 1941, exactly a year after the surrender of France. Throughout the summer, *Blitzkrieg* tactics brought spectacular successes to the Germans and their allies. They destroyed the Soviet air force and surrounded entire Soviet armies; 4 million Soviet soldiers surrendered. "The Russians are finished. They have nothing left to throw against us," Hitler chortled.

By November 1941 the Germans appeared to be on their way to victory. They surrounded Leningrad on three sides, and army units were less than twenty miles from Moscow. In the south, the Germans had reached Rostov-on-the-Don. Nevertheless, accumulated casualties, a shortage of transport, the climate, distance, and inadequate forces assigned to too many objectives caused the German offensive to sag. After an initial period of irresolution, Stalin rallied, directing a dogged defense of Moscow and Leningrad. In December Hitler called a halt to his campaign for the winter. He had lost three-quarters of a million men, his armies were short on supplies and warm clothing, and his equipment was breaking down under extensive wear and intensive cold—on December 2 the Moscow temperature reached 40 degrees below zero. By no means defeated, the Soviets counterattacked during the winter and drove the Germans back from Moscow. Hitler was confident, however, that he could finish off the Soviets in the summer of 1942.

HITLER'S "NEW ORDER" AND THE HOLOCAUST

By the autumn of 1941 Hitler was the master of the continent of Europe and used his control to carry out his demonic vision of a "New Order." At the center of Europe he created the Greater German Nation, consisting of an enlarged Germany, much of Poland and Czechoslovakia, and parts of Yugoslavia and France. This would be the homeland of the "superior" Aryan race. Germany stripped the nations under its military control for the benefit of the German war effort, often causing severe deprivation and hunger in those countries. Hitler ordered his allies to supply Germany with products on terms favorable to it and to follow its lead in foreign and military affairs. Germany directed commanders in the occupied areas and the governments of the client states to deport "undesirables" to Germany for slave labor; the number eventually reached 9 million. Farther east, Hitler planned to use the Soviet Union for future expansion of the Aryan race. Germans were to be settled there in increasing numbers as a "master class" that would control the vast raw materials in that region. The Slavs and Asiatics there, considered subhumans, would be reduced to serfs.

As a part of the New Order, Hitler's regime decided to implement "The Final Solution," a program to exterminate the Jews and Gypsies of Europe, now referred to as the Holocaust. The Final Solution is an example of genocide, a systematic process to destroy a particular national, ethnic, or racial

The Holocaust: After their uprising in the Warsaw Ghetto was crushed, surviving Jews are marched to the trains that would take them to extermination camps (above). The fate of these Jews, and millions like them, was to be gassed in batches and to have their remains burned in ovens (below).

(Above, YIVO Institute for Jewish Research; below, UPI/Bettmann Newsphotos)

Defying the Holocaust

We have been pointedly reminded that we are in hiding, that we are Jews in chains, chained to one spot, without any rights, but with a thousand duties. We Jews mustn't show our feelings, must be brave and strong, must accept all inconveniences and not grumble, must do what is within our power and trust in God. Sometime this terrible war will be over. Surely the time will come when we are people again, and not just Jews.

Who has inflicted this upon us? Who has made us Jews different from all other people? Who has allowed us to suffer so terribly up till now? It is God that has made us as we are, but it will be God, too, who will raise us up again. If we bear all this suffering and if there are still Jews left, when it is over,

then Jews, instead of being doomed, will be held up as an example. . . .

If God lets me live . . . I shall not remain insignificant, I shall work in the world and for mankind!

And now I know that first and foremost I shall require courage and cheerfulness!*

◆━◆●◆━◆

Anne Frank was a fourteen-year-old German Jew in hiding in Amsterdam when this diary entry was written on April, 11, 1944. Four months later she was arrested and sent to Auschwitz and later to the Belsen concentration camp where she died in 1945.

*Excerpted from *Anne Frank: The Diary of a Young Girl* by Anne Frank, © 1952 by Otto H. Frank. Used by permission of Doubleday, a division of Bantam, Doubleday, Dell Publishing Group, Inc.

group. History has recorded many instances of attempted genocide, such as the Turkish massacre of Armenians during World War I. In the east the Nazis and local police forces rounded up Jews, resistance fighters, and Communist party members; special execution teams shot them and dumped them into mass graves. This method was soon deemed to be too slow and expensive, however, and after 1941 local authorities in nearly every area of Europe under Hitler's control were ordered to send Jews to special extermination camps located primarily in Poland. Arriving packed in railroad boxcars, they were systematically gassed, then cremated, and their remains processed for soap and blankets. At Auschwitz, the Nazis daily killed an average of 12,000 people, including some non-Jews.

By one means or another, approximately 6 million Jews, about 75 percent of the European Jewish population, were put to death. Millions of other Europeans perished in slave labor camps from overwork, malnutrition, disease, and abuse. The Allies did little to aid the victims. How much and how soon they knew about the situation, and how much they could be accused of sharing the guilt for the Holocaust, has been the subject of historical debate. The horror of the Holocaust convinced many Jews to support the Zionist idea of setting up an independent Jewish state in Palestine. There Jews could control the government instead of being, as elsewhere, a minority group subject to the power and attitudes of the majority.

Hitler's New Order: Millions of slave laborers and political prisoners who were not Jews were beaten, tortured, starved, and worked to death in concentration camps throughout Europe.
(UPI/Bettmann Newsphotos)

THE UNITED STATES AND EUROPEAN AFFAIRS

As the power of Hitler spread across Europe, the U.S. government became increasingly concerned. President Roosevelt believed that, unless halted, Nazism and fascism would wipe out democracy in Europe and become a direct threat to the safety of the United States. The general public, however, opposed any action that might lead the United States into war. U.S. neutrality legislation was technically evenhanded, but its effect was to aid Great Britain, since the British could buy and transport U.S. goods to Great Britain while the British naval blockade prevented Germany from getting supplies.

While the U.S. public continued to hope for peace, U.S. leaders began to prepare for a possible war. By 1940 Congress was providing funds for a rapid increase in the armed forces and later in the year created the first peacetime conscription act in U.S. history. Meanwhile, the U.S. economy was booming with orders from the U.S. and British governments for war materiel.

Events in 1940 and 1941 drew the United States ever closer to the war in Europe. In September 1940 the United States agreed to supply Great Britain with fifty old destroyers in exchange for British bases in the Caribbean, Bermuda, and Canada. By 1941, with Hitler's power spreading south and east across Europe, the U.S. government became more assertive. Congress created a massive Lend-Lease program by making billions of dollars' worth of military equipment available to Great Britain and the Soviet Union. U.S. military forces began to take control of the western Atlantic, sending forces to occupy Greenland and Iceland and escorting convoys to the middle of the Atlantic. By the autumn of 1941, with U.S. destroyers suffering casualties in conflicts with German submarines, and with orders to arm merchant ships, the United States was only one step short of war with Germany.

CONFRONTATION BETWEEN JAPAN AND THE UNITED STATES

While Germany was conquering Europe, Japan was continuing to expand in Asia. By 1940 it had secured the coal and iron ore of Manchuria and north China and controlled the major industrial centers and seaports of China. Much of the Japanese army was bogged down in China, with the Japanese determined to fight on until they finally defeated the Chinese. The Japanese were equally determined to press on into Southeast Asia to wrest the petroleum, rubber, and tin located there from Western colonial control.

The United States continued to be the main opponent of Japanese plans for Asia. The United States, along with Great Britain, did what little it could to supply Chinese military forces. The United States also made it clear to the Japanese that it opposed Japanese expansion in Southeast Asia. Japan was prepared to attack the United States in order to control East and Southeast Asia.

Japan was aided in its expansionist plans by the war in Europe. In the summer of 1940, with France defeated and Great Britain beleaguered, Japan forced the British to close the Burma Road supply route to China and pressured the Vichy government to agree to Japanese occupation of northern Indochina, thus cutting off another source of supplies to China. The United States responded with an embargo on aviation fuel and scrap metal, although general trade continued. Japan countered by signing the Tripartite Pact with Germany and Italy, in which the three powers pledged to aid each other if any one of them was attacked by a new enemy, which in this case would have been the United States.

In the summer of 1941 the tension between the United States and Japan heated up. The Japanese moved into southern Indochina and appeared ready to launch a military conquest of Southeast Asia. The United States responded by expanding its embargo and freezing Japanese assets in the United States, while beginning discussions with the Dutch and the British concerning the mutual defense of Southeast Asia. Meanwhile, the Japanese government began a two-pronged program. On the one hand, Japanese diplomats were instructed to try to reach agreements with the United States that would guarantee Japan access to the raw materials of Southeast Asia and a free hand to deal with the Chinese. On the other hand, since the diplomats were likely to fail, the military laid plans for conquering Southeast Asia and eliminating U.S. power in Asia.

By the end of November, faced with the failure of negotiations, the new military-controlled cabinet of General Hideki Tojo decided to proceed with the military plans. Beginning on December 7, 1941, the Japanese attacked the British, Dutch, and Americans throughout Southeast Asia, an onslaught highlighted by a surprise attack on the U.S. Pacific fleet at Pearl Harbor. The United States declared war on Japan on December 8; Germany and Italy declared war on the United States on December 11, 1941. World War II was now to be a massive struggle in Asia as well as in Europe.

JAPANESE CONQUESTS IN ASIA AND THE PACIFIC, 1941–1942

Japan's program for waging war was a mixture of offensive and defensive strategies. Japan intended to seize Southeast Asia and the vital supplies there, defeat Chiang Kai-shek, and drive the U.S. forces from the Philippines and the western Pacific. Japanese leaders believed that once they were in control of East and Southeast Asia and dug in behind a wall of fortified islands in the western Pacific, the Western powers would be unable to fight their way back into Asia and would agree to Japan's having a free hand there.

In the five months following December 7, the Japanese secured most of their goals. The Japanese war machine either destroyed Western military forces or drove them out of East and Southeast Asia. The Japanese bombed the U.S. Pacific fleet into temporary impotence, although the fleet still had its vital aircraft carriers. Thailand was forced into an alliance with Japan, and the British were driven from Burma and Malaya, surrendering 60,000 men at Singapore. The Japanese quickly overran the Dutch East Indies and forced the U.S. army in the Philippines to surrender. They seized U.S. and British islands in the Western Pacific and secured a foothold in the Aleutian Islands and on New Guinea. Australia appeared to be Japan's next target, and Australians prepared for resistance. By April 1942 the Japanese had accumulated a vast land and water domain that geographically dwarfed the conquests of Adolf Hitler.

Japan's next step was to consolidate its conquests. It intended to eradicate the vestiges of Western colonialism and to exploit the conquered areas for its economic benefit. Toward these ends, Japan organized the Greater East Asia Co-Prosperity Sphere. Its ultimate aim was to make Japanese-controlled Asia an economically self-sufficient community that would blend into the rest of the Japanese Empire. In pursuing their goal, however, the Japanese made such heavy demands for manpower and materials and caused such hardship that they eventually alienated the local peoples. In the Philippines, where independence had been promised by the United States, resistance to the Japanese was strong and Japanese repression was especially brutal.

FORGING THE "GRAND ALLIANCE" AGAINST THE AXIS

By 1942 two conflicts of unprecedented magnitude were being waged simultaneously. In the Pacific and East Asia, the United States and China, with limited aid from the British Empire, made war against Japan. In Europe and North

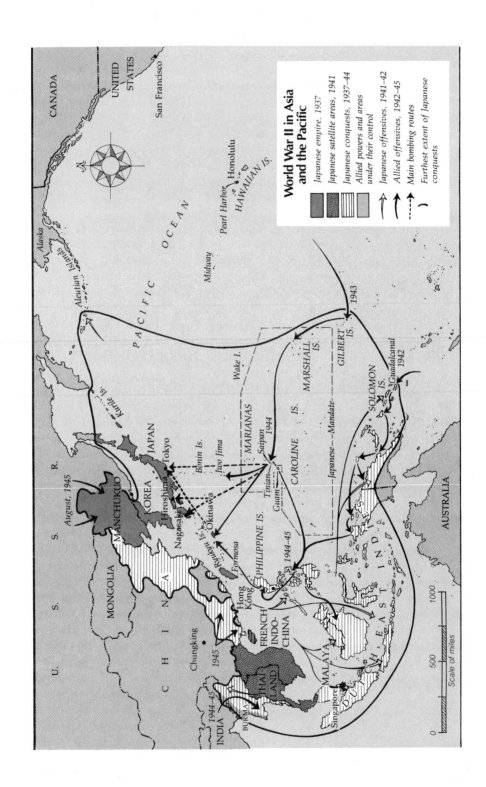

World War II in Asia and the Pacific

- Japanese empire, 1937
- Japanese satellite areas, 1941
- Japanese conquests, 1937–44
- Allied powers and areas under their control
- Japanese offensives, 1941–42
- Allied offensives, 1942–45
- Main bombing routes
- Furthest extent of Japanese conquests

CANADA

UNITED STATES

San Francisco

PACIFIC OCEAN

Honolulu
Pearl Harbor
HAWAIIAN IS.

Midway

Alaska

Aleutian Islands

1943

Kurile Is.

Wake I.

MARSHALL IS.

GILBERT IS.

Guadalcanal 1942

SOLOMON IS.

U. S. S. R.

MONGOLIA

August, 1945

MANCHUKUO

KOREA

JAPAN

Tokyo

Bonin Is.

Iwo Jima

Hiroshima

Nagasaki

Okinawa

Ryukyu Is.

Formosa

MARIANAS
Saipan 1944

Tinian

Guam

CAROLINE IS.

Japanese — Mandate

CHINA

Chungking

1945

Hong Kong

PHILIPPINE IS.

1944–45

AUSTRALIA

INDIA

1944–45

BURMA

THAI-
LAND

FRENCH
INDO-
CHINA

MALAYA

Singapore

DUTCH EAST INDIES

Scale of miles

0   500   1000

266

Yalta Summit Conference, 1945: Churchill, Roosevelt, and Stalin plan for the ending of World War II and for the postwar period.
(AP/Wide World Photos)

Africa, the Soviet Union, Great Britain, the British Empire, and minor allies were locked in combat with Germany and its allies, with the United States about to bring its armed forces into action.

Germany, Italy, and Japan (the Axis powers) did not coordinate their side of the two struggles. Their opponents, however, realized it was necessary to come to an agreement on strategic priorities. Before U.S. entry into the war, Roosevelt and Churchill announced in the 1941 Atlantic Charter that opponents of the Axis would fight to halt aggression and not to gain foreign territory, a position similar to Woodrow Wilson's during and after World War I. Stalin gave his qualified approval. From 1942 to 1945 Roosevelt, Churchill, and Stalin met at several conferences around the world to create a strategy for the defeat of the Axis powers. This was not easy; the Western Allies and the Soviet Union were suspicious of each other, and at times there were intense disagreements between the United States and Great Britain.

Despite their differences, but faced with a common peril, the leaders hammered out a series of broad agreements. The three men agreed that their nations would not make a separate peace but would fight the war through to the unconditional surrender of all the Axis powers. They concurred that Germany should be defeated because it was perceived to be a greater threat to the Allies than Japan and because the Allies were in a better position to assist each other effectively in Europe than in Asia. Stalin agreed that the Soviet Union would join in the war against Japan after Germany had been defeated. The leaders also decided to place all Allied forces in western Europe under U.S. General Dwight Eisenhower.

By far the greatest point of friction between the Allies was the time and place to attack German forces from the west. The Soviet Union demanded that the United States and Great Britain land in western Europe, presumably France, as soon as possible, creating a second front. This would take some of the pressure off the Soviet Union, whose people were desperately struggling against the main strength of the German armed forces. With an eye to postwar Europe as well as to the defeat of Germany, the British wanted to attack first what Churchill termed "the soft underbelly of Europe." This involved clearing North Africa, conquering Italy, and liberating the Balkans. This approach would fully open up supply routes to Great Britain and keep the Soviets out of the Mediterranean and eastern Europe, but it involved fighting on difficult terrain in Italy and the Balkans. U.S. leaders vacillated. As the war progressed, the United States supported clearing the Mediterranean but opposed landing in the Balkans. It eventually supported opening a front in France at the earliest opportunity.

INDUSTRIAL MOBILIZATION FOR TOTAL WAR

The awesome industrial and agricultural output of the United States, which made that nation, in Roosevelt's words, "The Great Arsenal of Democracy," was a crucial factor in the Allied defeat of the Axis powers. As in World War I, the wartime enemies of the United States had fatally underestimated U.S. economic power, with Marshal Hermann Goering sneering that Americans "only knew how to make refrigerators and razor blades." U.S. factories not only equipped their own military establishment of 12 million men but also underwrote part of the war effort of Great Britain, the Soviet Union, and other allies. During the war U.S. factories and shipyards produced 300,000 airplanes, 88,000 tanks, 2.5 million trucks, 17.4 million rifles, 315,000 artillery pieces, and 3,000 ships. Some ships were built in as little as seventeen days. U.S. farmers increased production by one-third, enabling the United States to send food to other nations. U.S. military output doubled the combined production of the Axis powers; when Allied industrial output, particularly that of the Soviet Union later in the war, is added to that of the United States, one key reason for the eventual defeat of the Axis is clear.

This massive military production, made possible by an ever-increasing alliance between government, industry, and the military, was one aspect of total war. Even more than in World War I, national governments closely regulated the production of raw materials, monitored labor, set production priorities, created manufacturing establishments where needed, and regulated the price and distribution of civilian and military products. Again, even more than in World War I, home front populations were exhorted by government propaganda organizations through pamphlets, radio, and motion pictures to hate the enemy, make sacrifices, and work harder. When World War II was over, the citizens of the Western democracies had become conditioned to function in a national environment in which the government was thoroughly integrated into economic and social life.

World War II, even more than World War I, brought women into roles traditionally dominated by men. Despite some discrimination and harassment, American women, personified as "Rosie the Riveter," took over many assembly-line industrial jobs. In embattled Leningrad, women eventually comprised 84 percent of the industrial workforce. Women in several nations served in auxiliary branches of the armed forces and fought in guerrilla forces in Europe and Asia. After their war experiences many women saw a greater variety of roles to aspire to than they had previously.

THE WAR AT SEA

Like World War I, World War II was largely one of attrition. In the new war, the airplane joined the submarine and the minefield as key weapons in the attempt to destroy the economy of opponents and to erode the morale of enemy civilian populations. Early in the war, as in World War I, the British navy mined the approaches to Germany, cutting off all supplies from outside Europe. This time, however, the British were unable to close off a corridor within Norwegian territorial waters, a gap exploited by German submarines and naval surface raiders. In any case, during World War II Germany could draw on the resources of most of Europe and was much less vulnerable to blockade than it had been in World War I.

Great Britain, on the other hand, was just as vulnerable to blockade as ever. Surprisingly, despite the proven effectiveness of its submarines during World War I, Germany had only a few of them ready for service in 1939. After the outbreak of war, Germany embarked on an intensive submarine-building program, and by 1942 it had built a large number of U-boats capable of long-distance travel. U-boats prowled the entire North and South Atlantic, operating from well-defended bases on the coasts of occupied Norway and France. Clusters of submarines, "wolf-packs," tore into Allied convoys as far south as Brazil and South Africa, while other U-boats operated along the Atlantic and Gulf coasts of the United States. Land-based aircraft from Norway assisted German submarines in attacking convoys passing around Scandinavia with supplies for the Soviet Union.

The Allies fought the submarines with increasing success, using the convoy system, destroyers, and submarine-hunting escort carriers, and by late 1943 the worst of the submarine threat was over. Submarines failed to sink any of the hundreds of transports that carried more than a million soldiers to Europe. Still, the Atlantic was a grim theater of war in which thousands of merchantmen and sailors were blown up, burned in oil fires, or drowned.

In the Pacific, the war at sea featured numerous encounters between elements of the surface fleets of the United States and Japan. The largest encounters introduced a new mode of naval combat: carrier warfare. Earlier in the century, naval combat had been decided by large battleships raining heavy shells on the enemy fleet. In the Pacific in World War II, the heart of naval task forces consisted of aircraft carriers, surrounded like queen bees by supporting craft bristling with antiaircraft batteries. Most battles were decided by the number of carriers sunk by the waves of dive bombers, high-altitude bombers, and torpedo planes launched by opposing naval squadrons hundreds of miles apart. The United States won the largest and most crucial naval battles, in part because it had cracked the Japanese naval code.

Submarine warfare was also extremely important to the Pacific, and here the roles were reversed. Even more than Great Britain, Japan was dependent on shipping to secure food and raw materials and to supply its armies on the Asian mainland and garrisons in the western Pacific. Realizing Japan's vulnerability, the United States mounted a campaign to sink Japan's merchant ships and thus strangle its war effort. By 1945 U.S. submarines and aircraft had succeeded in destroying the bulk of the Japanese merchant marine and had virtually cut off Japan from Asia and the Pacific islands.

THE AIR WAR

While there was extensive tactical bombing in support of ground operations, the war in the air was dominated by the strategic bombardment of the enemy's economic and military installations, accompanied by the terror bombing of civilian population centers. These operations, in which helpless civilians were attacked with the same weapons used against military combatants, was another aspect of the total war concept that typified World War II. The Germans had used both strategic and terror bombing in their attacks on Poland, western Europe, and Great Britain. After 1942 the air war began to turn against the Axis; Allied bombers probed deeper and deeper into Germany and central Europe. Allied fighters furnished protection for the bombers and shot down German planes faster than they could be replaced. As German air resistance weakened, Allied bombers became increasingly effective in destroying factories, dams, roads, canals, and railroads, although the Germans rebuilt their factories underground. The Allies also used terror bombing. Certain raids on Hamburg and Berlin and the raid on Dresden killed, as intended, hundreds of thousands of civilians.

To supplement their rapidly declining regular air force, German specialists in military technology developed a series of new weapons. Jet-propelled aircraft appeared in the skies late in the war, but too late to become effective. Germany produced V-1 jet-powered flying bombs ("buzz bombs") and used them to strike at southeastern Britain. They also developed V-2 liquid-fueled rockets. Because they traveled at a high speed and struck without warning, the V-2s had a particularly depressing psychological effect on British civilians. Nevertheless, these rockets were too few and too late to be decisive. Like the airplane and the tank in World War I, the jet and the guided missile pointed toward the nature of war in the future.

Strategic bombardment came late in the Pacific, but once underway it was devastating. Most of the war in the Pacific was centered around U.S. forces working into positions from which they could bomb the Japanese homeland. The bombardment of Japan was not effective until late 1944, when bombers began to fly over Japan from bases in the Marianas. The Japanese air force was effectively wiped out by 1945, and by the spring and summer of 1945, U.S. bombers flew at will over the cities of Japan, using incendiary bombs to create raging "firestorms" that consumed the wooden buildings of Japanese cities along with hundreds of thousands of Japanese civilians.

THE ALLIES DEFEAT THE AXIS, 1942–1945

Soviet Victories and Nazi Defeat

In 1942 the war in Europe centered on a titanic struggle in Russia. Here the bulk and the cream of the German armed forces were pitted against the capacity of the Soviet Union to fight on virtually alone and endure tremendous suf-

This gigantic statue in Kiev is one of the memorials to the suffering and heroics of Soviet citizens in World War II. (*Walter Moss*)

fering while it built up its own massive war machine. Like the Japanese in China the German army and air force found themselves bogged down on a 1,000-mile front inside an enemy nation of vast geographical dimensions and huge population. Unlike the Japanese, however, Hitler had not taken his primary objectives; Leningrad and Moscow in the north and the Caucasus petroleum fields in the south remained in Soviet hands.

The Germans added to their problems in the Soviet Union by making a calamitous mistake in dealing with the civilians in the areas they had conquered. Although many non-Russian ethnic groups in the Soviet Union initially greeted the Germans as liberators, and some fought on the German side, the Nazis regarded all Slavs as subhuman. They inflicted so many atrocities on the population that they unified most of the ethnic groups in the Soviet Union against them, stirring up a swarm of guerrillas who attacked German supply lines and installations. Another problem for the Germans was that their economy and their transportation system, increasingly disrupted by British and U.S. aerial bombardment, failed to keep the German armed forces effectively supplied. In the autumn of 1942 Soviet forces began to drive the Germans back and surrounded a German army at Stalingrad. After a ferocious struggle, the Germans surrendered in January 1943, having incurred 300,000 casualties, effectively ending Hitler's dream of destroying the Soviet Union.

By the summer of 1943 the Soviet Union, with some U.S. and British aid, had created an impressive armaments industry that now sustained a huge military machine—over 6 million men, more than double the German army. Soviet forces also outnumbered the Germans three to one in artillery, tanks, and airplanes. With this superiority, the Soviets could now attack along several sectors simultaneously. In July 1943 the Soviets destroyed the core of Germany's tank forces at Kursk and made advances all along the front. By the spring of 1944 Soviet troops had reconquered the Ukraine and pushed into Rumania and Poland. They also lifted the 900-day siege of Leningrad, but not before a million of its citizens had perished—one graphic example of the massive suffering the German invasion inflicted on the Soviet Union, where over 27 million died. The defeat of German forces in the east was now only a matter of time.

D-Day and the Final Phases

With the Germans fully occupied in the Soviet Union, the Western Allies struck in the Mediterranean. In November 1942 the Americans and British used the new technology of amphibious warfare to land on the coasts of Vichy-held Morocco and Algeria, quickly overrunning these areas and pushing eastward. At the same time British and Commonwealth forces pushed westward out of Egypt across Libya. Most of the German and Italian forces in North Africa were caught between the two drives and surrendered in Tunisia in May 1943. In July and August 1943 U.S. and British forces conquered Sicily. In September, Allied forces landed on the Italian peninsula, inducing the Italians to overthrow Mussolini and surrender. The Germans pushed troops into

Italy and dug in across the peninsula south of Rome, preventing further Allied advance. The armies bogged down in Italy in a scene of fortification and mud resembling the trench warfare of World War I.

In the summer and autumn of 1944 the Allies opened the crucial campaigns that were to end the war in Europe. On June 6, 1944—"D-Day"—U.S., British, and Canadian forces launched a massive landing on the Normandy coast in France, opening a major second front. For a month German forces held the Allies close to the beaches, but in July the Americans broke out and German resistance collapsed in France. By the autumn German forces had withdrawn to the fortified western border of Germany. In Italy, the central part of the peninsula, including Rome, fell to the Allies, but the Germans retained control of the north.

During 1944 the Soviets continued their relentless drive westward. By December the Soviet army had cleared most of the Balkans and advanced to the outskirts of Budapest and Warsaw. Anti-Communist Poles in Warsaw rose in revolt against the Germans. Soviet troops did not cross the Vistula River to aid the Poles, and the Germans smashed the revolt. Finland, Rumania, and Bulgaria surrendered, and Tito's Communist partisans made headway against the Germans in Yugoslavia. British troops entered Greece to finish securing the Mediterranean and to prevent Soviet expansion in that area.

By the spring of 1945 Germany was caught in a massive vise. Allied forces crossed the Rhine River and passed eastward, while Soviet forces moved in from the east and surrounded Berlin. Hitler committed suicide in his underground bunker in Berlin on April 30, as Western and Soviet forces met in the middle of Germany. By May 8, 1945, all German units in Europe had surrendered. The war in Europe was over.

Campaigns against Japan, 1942–1944

In mid-1942 the tide began to turn against Japan in the Pacific. The Japanese fleet was driven back from its advance on the Hawaiian Islands at the Battle of Midway, the first important reverse for the Japanese navy. In late 1942 and early 1943, in fighting centered at Guadalcanal, Allied forces gradually pushed the Japanese out of the islands northeast of Australia, diminishing the Japanese threat.

By 1943 the enormous U.S. war effort was turning out enough war material and training enough men to press the war in the Pacific as well as in Europe. In 1943 and early 1944 U.S. forces in the Pacific attacked selected islands in the Central Pacific, in a strategy called "island hopping." Once secured, these islands served as bases for attacks on the main objective: islands in the Marianas close enough to Japan to serve as bases for long-range bombing. Meanwhile, General Douglas MacArthur worked his way along the coast of New Guinea with the intention of seizing the Philippines and Formosa and using them as bases for invading Japan. The Japanese garrisons on the remaining islands in the perimeter, cut off from supply or reinforcement, were left to starve in isolation.

In June and July 1944 Admiral Chester Nimitz's forces seized Saipan and Tinian in the Marianas and set up major bases from which the new B-29 bomber could begin the regular bombardment of Japanese cities. MacArthur meanwhile began the reconquest of the Philippines. This, plus the destruction of the remainder of the Japanese fleet in a series of naval battles off the Philippines, effectively cut off Japanese forces in Southeast Asia from those in China and Japan.

THE ATOMIC BOMB: THE CLIMAX OF TOTAL WAR

In the spring of 1945, their Axis allies defeated, the Japanese were in full retreat across Asia and the Pacific. The Chinese were pushing forward, while the British and Indians were reconquering Burma. The U.S. command wanted air bases closer to Japan and captured the islands of Iwo Jima and Okinawa, sustaining heavy casualties.

The resolute Japanese defense of Iwo Jima and Okinawa, including the extensive use of kamikaze (suicide) air attacks, made it clear that invading the Japanese home islands would lead to a terrible loss of life for both sides. Meanwhile, Allied scientists had created two atomic bombs: one based on the power unleashed by splitting atoms and the other by fusing atoms. In July 1945 President Harry Truman, who had succeeded to office after Roosevelt's death in April 1945, authorized their use. On August 6 the U.S. air force

The devastation of the atomic bomb dropped on Nagasaki on August 9, 1945.
(UPI/Bettmann Newsphotos)

dropped one bomb on Hiroshima; it delivered the other one on Nagasaki on August 9. The bombs created tremendous explosive and radioactive effects that caused as much damage and death as hundreds of conventional bombs. They killed 200,000 Japanese, while radiation kept on killing and maiming long after the bombs had exploded.

Historians have subsequently argued about whether or not Japan would have soon surrendered without having been hit with atomic bombs. They have also debated whether the bombs were dropped primarily to end the war or to shape the postwar era (see Chapter 22). In any case, the fact that Truman did agree to drop the bombs, a decision which carried even further the trend of terror bombing masses of civilians, indicated how the "total war" concept now dominated the conflict. The huge, mushroom-shaped clouds towering over the doomed cities became the symbol of a new era: Humanity had pushed the concept of total war to the point where it had created the technology to destroy itself.

The detonation of the two atomic bombs quickly brought the war in the Pacific to its end. On August 8 the Soviet Union, as it had earlier agreed to do, declared war and attacked Japanese forces in Manchuria and Korea. The destruction caused by the bombs, coupled with the general military situation, convinced Emperor Hirohito that Japan had lost the war. On August 14 the Japanese announced their surrender, which was ratified at a ceremony on September 2, 1945, in Tokyo Bay. World War II was over.

SUMMARY

When World War II broke out in Europe in 1939 and in Asia in 1941 the Axis powers were far better prepared than their opponents. Using the new military technology of the improved tank and airplane effectively, German forces easily defeated and occupied Poland, Denmark, Norway, the Netherlands, Belgium, Luxembourg, and France. Great Britain held out despite submarine blockades and air bombardment, and the Germans and their Italian and eastern European allies turned their attention southward and eastward in 1941, conquering Yugoslavia and Greece, reinvading Egypt, and smashing into the Soviet Union. Although the Russians suffered immense losses, the Germans bogged down in front of Leningrad and Moscow in December 1941. Meanwhile, the Japanese decided that war was necessary to complete their designs on Southeast Asia. Accordingly, they invaded Southeast Asia and attacked U.S. naval forces in Hawaii in December 1941, quickly overrunning Southeast Asia and the western Pacific. German and Japanese administration of their conquered territories was brutal. In German-controlled Europe, mass enslavement and extermination campaigns led to millions of deaths and suffering for millions more.

In order to defeat the Axis powers, an effective alliance had to be forged by those nations allied against them, including—insofar as possible—common strategy and unified command. The United States became the economic and military backbone of the war against Germany from the west and of the war against Japan, while the Soviet Union engaged in a massive struggle with the main German forces. Extensive sea and air campaigns strangled the economies of Germany and Japan and inflicted heavy casualties on their civilian populations. The Allies finally defeated Germany by first clearing the Mediterranean and knocking Italy out of the war and then crushing Germany between massive advances from the east and west. The United States defeated Japan by isolating and ignoring the bulk of its armed forces in the Pacific and Asia and seizing selected islands in the Pacific. From these islands, U.S. fliers methodically bombed Japan. Japan surrendered after the United States dropped atomic bombs on Hiroshima and Nagasaki.

SUGGESTED SOURCES

BARBER, JOHN and MARK HARRISON, *The Soviet Home Front, 1941–1945: A Social and Economic History of the USSR in World War II* (1991). Shows the increasing contribution of women, peasants, and youth to the Soviet war effort.*

CLARK, ALAN, *Barbarossa* (1965). A lively account of the Soviet-German struggle in Europe during World War II.*

COSTELLO, JOHN, *The Pacific War* (1981). A comprehensive account of the struggle between the Allies and Japan, based in part on recently released documents.*

KUZNETSOV, ANATOLI V., *Babi Yar*, uncensored ed. (1970). A well-written, realistic novel of the German occupation of Kiev and the mass killing of Jews at Babi Yar.*

MONSARRAT, NICHOLAS, *The Cruel Sea* (1965). A stark novel about the destroyer-submarine struggle in the North Atlantic.*

SHAW, IRWIN, *The Young Lions* (1958). A novel depicting the war in Europe and North Africa as experienced by American soldiers and a Nazi.* (Also a film.)

Shoah (1985). A long but gripping film about the Holocaust, based on the testimony of the surviving victims and their persecutors. (Also available on video.)

TAYLOR, A. J. P., *The War Lords* (1979). A collection of descriptions of major leaders during World War II.*

TREGASKIS, RICHARD W., *Guadalcanal Diary* (1943). A first-hand account of jungle warfare in the Pacific.*

The World at War (1973). A BBC television series that provides an account of the conflict compiled from newsreels and documentaries. Emphasizes the British role. (Also available on video.)

WRIGHT, GORDON, *The Ordeal of Total War, 1939–1945* (1969). A broad overview, with attention to the war's impact on the home front and on ideas.*

YOUNG, PETER, *World War, 1939–1945: A Short History* (1966). A balanced survey of the war.

*Paperback available.

PART THREE

The Era of the Cold War and the Collapse of Empires

Time Chart III
1945–1992

Year	South & East Asia	Middle East & Africa	Europe	Western Hemisphere	Trends in Culture, Science, Technology
1945		THE UNITED NATIONS ESTABLISHED			The atomic age, 1945–present
1946	**ERA OF ASIAN INDEPENDENCE, 1946–67** First Indochina War, 1946–54		ORIGINS OF THE COLD WAR		
1947	India and Pakistan independent		Truman Doctrine Marshall Plan	The Peróns in Argentina, 1946–55	Antibiotic drugs
1948		First Arab–Israeli war	Berlin airlift	Organization of American States established	
1949	Chinese Communist victory		NATO		
1950	Korean War, 1950–53		First Soviet A-bomb tested		
1951		**ERA OF INDEPENDENCE IN NORTH, WEST, AND CENTRAL AFRICA, 1951–64**			
1952		Independence struggles in Kenya, 1952–56			Decade of the popularization of television
1953			Stalin dies		
1954	SEATO Geneva Agreement on Indochina	Algerian revolution, 1954–62		Arbenz government in Guatemala overthrown	Salk vaccine

1955			Warsaw Pact	Beginning of the civil rights struggle in United States	
1956		Second Arab–Israeli war	Hungarian revolt		
1957	Second Indochina War, 1957–75		Common Market founded		Sputnik launches the space age
1958			DeGaulle becomes president of fifth French Republic		
1959				Castro assumes power in Cuba	
1960	Sino-Soviet split				
1961			Berlin Wall	Bay of Pigs	
1962				Cuban missile crisis	
1963	Organization of African Unity founded				Vatican II convened

ERA OF INTERMITTENT DÉTENTE, 1963–79

1963					
1964	Tonkin Gulf Resolution	Khrushchev ousted		Era of rightist coups in Latin America, 1964–76	Era of Green Revolution, 1960s–1970s
1965				Decade of political and social turmoil in United States, 1965–75	
1966	Cultural revolution in China, 1966–76				
1967	Third Arab–Israeli war Civil war in Nigeria, 1967–70				
1968			Soviet intervention in Czechoslovakia		

Year	South & East Asia	Middle East & Africa	Europe	Western Hemisphere	Trends in Culture, Science, Technology
1969					Moon landing
1970	Bangladesh independent				Growing environmental concerns, 1970s–1990s
1971					
1972	Nixon visits China	Era of military coups in Africa	Strategic Arms Limitation Treaty (SALT)		
1973		Fourth Arab–Israeli war		Allende government overthrown in Chile	Era of women's activism
1974		**INDEPENDENCE STRUGGLES IN SOUTHERN AFRICA, 1974–90**			
1975	Vietnam unified		Helsinki Accords		Era of the popularization of computers
1976	Mao dies				
1977					
1978		Iranian revolution, 1978–present		Social revolution and cold war struggles in Central America, 1970s–present	Resurgent Islam
1979	Soviet invasion of Afghanistan, 1979–89	Egypt–Israel Accords	Thatcher becomes prime minister in Great Britain		Era of rising economic power of Asian Rim
1980	Deng Xiaoping in control of China	Iran–Iraq War, 1980–88			
1981			Martial law declared in Poland		
1982		Israeli invasion of Lebanon			
1983				Reagan conservatism in United States	
1984		Continued resistance against apartheid in South Africa			Drought and famine in Africa

1985	Gorbachev comes to power in U.S.S.R. — Chernobyl nuclear accident in Soviet Union
1986	Marcos ousted in the Philippines
1987	Intifada in Israeli-occupied territories, 1987–present — Civilian government restored in much of Latin America in 1980s
1988	Benazir Bhutto first woman head of a Muslim state (elected in Pakistan) — INF ratified
1989	Tiananmen Square massacre — Collapse of Communist governments in Eastern Europe
1990	Soviet withdrawal from Afghanistan — END OF THE COLD WAR
1991	U.S. gives up bases in Philippines — Persian Gulf War — Democratization of the Asian Rim — Reunification of Germany — Urbanization in Latin America intensifies — World population reaches 5.4 billion
1992	Movement toward black rule in the Republic of South Africa — Disintegration of the Soviet Union and of Yugoslavia — Democrats regain U.S. presidency — "Earth Summit" on environmental concerns at Rio de Janiero, Brazil

CHAPTER 21

General Trends in the Era of the Cold War and the Collapse of Empires

The era from the end of World War II until the breakup of the Soviet Union in 1991 was primarily one of a "Cold War" and collapsing colonial empires. The Cold War, marked by ideological hostilities and an arms race, was chiefly between the United States and the Soviet Union but also involved both countries' allies. The collapse of empires, with the "Soviet Empire" being the last to fall, resulted in well over 100 nations receiving their independence.

The policies of Mikhail Gorbachev, who took control of the Soviet Union in 1985, were primarily responsible for bringing the era to an end. They not only helped to end the Cold War but also, at times inadvertently, helped set off a chain of events that led first to the collapse of Communist rule in Eastern Europe in 1989 and 1990 and then, in 1991, to the breakup of the Soviet Union itself.

Although the Cold War and the collapse of empires were the chief trends of the era, there were other important ones. Scientists and technicians brought the world nuclear energy, television, and computers; they put humans in space and, by manipulating genes, produced new types of plants and animals. At the same time, scientific and technological advance was accompanied by environmental decline and the proliferation of thermonuclear weapons, both of which threatened to destroy life on our planet.

In the immediate postwar era, the United States emerged as the overwhelmingly dominant economic power; but in the decades that followed, a more balanced world economy developed as Western Europe, Japan, and other Asian nations became increasingly competitive. Although the standard of living of much of the world's population improved dramatically in the first three decades following the war, by 1991 the gap between the world's richest and poorest nations had grown wider. By then many countries, especially in Africa and Latin America, were worse off than they had been in the late 1970s.

Throughout the postwar era, the lower classes in many nations challenged the traditional political and economic controls that had held them "in their place." In poorer nations of the world, where ruling groups ignored or suppressed cries for reforms and supported authoritarian right-wing anti-Communist governments, Communist promises of land reform and economic justice had a considerable appeal and often led to guerrilla warfare. By the 1980s many leaders in both capitalist nations and Communist states were less ideological and more pragmatic in their handling of affairs.

In the realm of ideas and culture, the battle between traditional religions and secularist forces continued. Communications technology helped to spread Western ideas, fashions, fads, movies, music, and television programming; but some non-Western thinkers, both religious and secular, reacted against such influences. However, these influences persisted, and the world continued to become more homogeneous.

SCIENTIFIC-TECHNOLOGICAL ADVANCES AND ENVIRONMENTAL DECLINE

The postwar years witnessed a stunning display of scientific and technological achievements. One of the most important of these was the rapid development of atomic technology. By the 1950s scientists had learned how to fuse the atoms in hydrogen isotopes and had created the hydrogen bomb, which was a thousand times more destructive than the original atomic bomb. By the 1970s more than enough thermonuclear weapons existed to destroy all human life on the planet.

Splitting the atom also provided a significant opportunity to create energy for peaceful purposes. Atomic energy was inexhaustible and could beneficially transform life on earth and displace the world's reliance on shrinking and increasingly expensive supplies of petroleum and natural gas. By 1990 over two dozen nations operated a combined total of over 400 nuclear power plants. However, because of recurring accidents involving radioactive substances, extensive opposition to the development of a nuclear energy source persisted.

In the decades after World War II, scientists and technicians brought forth an array of other astonishing developments, particularly in transportation and communication. In 1947 a piloted jet airplane first flew faster than the speed of sound; jet propulsion eventually became the prime mode of civilian and military air travel. Ballistics technology generated the power to push rockets bearing either space capsules or atomic warheads through the earth's gravitational field into outer space at a rate of thousands of miles in a few moments. In 1957 the Soviet Union launched *Sputnik I,* the first of many artificial satellites. In 1969 U.S. astronauts traveled to the moon—about 240,000 miles—in just four days. Space technology also created manned space stations.

In the field of communications, television became a major phenomenon of the postwar era—contrary to the prediction of motion picture producer Darryl Zanuck, who said: "People will soon get tired of staring at a plywood box every night." In 1981 the average primary school child in Mexico City spent 1,460 hours a year watching television compared to 920 hours attending school. Polls in the United States reflected similar results. Television became an important instrument for entertainment, education, government propaganda, and business advertising. In 1986, for example, U.S. business concerns spent $22.6 billion on television advertising, which was more than the total spent by the national government on education and environmental protection combined.

During the postwar decades television news coverage increasingly influenced governments and citizens around the world. By the late 1980s the U.S.-based Cable News Network (CNN) was being viewed in some 150 nations, providing on-the-spot coverage of important events. World leaders came to rely on it for quick information and insight into how their decisions and actions would be portrayed around the world. In a related development, the invention of the transistor in 1947 eventually revolutionized radio communication, bringing broadcasts into the more remote areas of the world.

Information processing, as exemplified by the computer, was another dominant postwar development. Computers continually improved the storage, retrieval, and manipulation of enormous amounts of information, especially after the development of small silicon memory chips in the late 1950s. Combined with the most modern means of telecommunication, including communication satellites, computers could transfer data quickly from one part of the world to another. They brought about major changes in business and government practices, research and scholarship, military technology, and intelligence activities, and in general gradually transformed patterns of thought and behavior.

Despite their many advantages, computers also appeared to be a threat to privacy. Giant data bases available to creditors and advertisers included personal information on more than half of the people in the United States, and government data bases increasingly integrated the information they gathered concerning their citizens. The significance of the computer led some to speak of a new "Computer Age" or "Information Age."

Some of the most dramatic scientific advances related to the study of genes. Scientists declared that DNA (deoxyribonucleic acid) was the key to heredity, leading scientists and doctors to become increasingly optimistic about the possibility of preventing certain inherited diseases and dealing with defective genes. In 1988 Harvard University was granted the first U.S. patent on an animal: a type of mouse genetically engineered for use in cancer experiments. Genetic engineering also opened up a new realm of possibilities in regard to the breeding of plant and animal food sources, but it simultaneously aroused fears of unforeseen results.

Medical advances improved health care and decreased the world death rate while increasing life expectancy. Partly as a result, the population of the world increased from 1.6 billion in 1900 to 2.4 billion in 1950 and to 5.4 billion by late 1991. Even so, many chronic killers, such as heart disease and cancer, remained to be conquered, and a new incurable contagious disease, Acquired Immune Deficiency Syndrome (AIDS), caused a rapidly increasing number of deaths. By the end of 1991 it was conservatively estimated that in Sub-Saharan Africa alone, there were at least 6 million people infected with the HIV (human immunodeficiency virus) which causes AIDS. It was also rapidly spreading in other parts of the world.

During the 1960s and 1970s, many people, especially in advanced industrialized nations, became aware of environmental issues for the first time. One area of concern was the depletion of nonrenewable energy resources. Between the end of World War II and the late 1970s, the Western nations and Japan used more petroleum and minerals than had been consumed in all previous history; the United States was the biggest user, alone accounting for approximately 30 percent of world energy consumption during the 1970s. During the 1980s the democratic industrialized nations of the world became more energy-efficient. As a result of conservation efforts and a global economic recession, they actually decreased energy usage from 1980 to 1985, though it slowly rose thereafter. In the economically less developed nations of the world, energy use increased at a faster rate. From 1986 to 1990 petroleum demand among the poorer nations grew at about three times the rate of increase in demand from the more developed market economies. Even so, per capita energy usage in the richer nations of the world remained at least ten times greater than in poorer nations.

Just as population growth, industrialization, and urbanization all contributed to the need for more energy, so these factors also increased demand for a variety of other resources, such as food, forests, and water. To meet the growing need for food and fodder—also stimulated by an increased world demand for meat and dairy products—scientists and technicians developed new high-yield strains of wheat and rice. Other agricultural techniques, such as using more fertilizers, irrigating lands only marginally fit for agriculture, and reducing the periods in which land was allowed to rest, contributed to increased food supplies. Between 1950 and 1985, as world population doubled, global food production almost tripled.

Junked cars symbolize the heavy U.S. consumption of energy and world resources. *(EPA Documeria)*

In certain areas of the world, however, per capita food production decreased in the 1970s and 1980s. Africa's population increased almost twice as fast as its food production. Deforestation on the southern fringes of the Sahara and overgrazing combined with a series of dry years caused the desert to spread southward, contributing to famine and countless deaths.

In economically advanced nations, scientific and technological developments and increasing industrialization polluted the air and water. In 1975 alone, more than 10,000 petroleum spills were reported in U.S. navigable waters. In the Communist nations of Eastern Europe and the Soviet Union, pollution and ecological damage, although often unreported, was nevertheless extensive.

Western scientists had earlier discovered, at times belatedly, that many new chemical compounds, such as DDT, PCB, and PBB, had adverse effects on the environment and on people's health. Pesticides such as DDT introduced a special dilemma into a world hungry for food. By killing crop-threatening insects, DDT and a number of other pesticides increased crop yields, yet caused illness and death in humans and animals. In the 1970s in the United States, an estimated 90 percent of residents in the state of Michigan ingested some traces of PBB, a suspected carcinogen, after it had been accidentally fed to cattle.

The development of nuclear power plants in the United States and other nations led to increased concern about radioactive accidents and waste disposal that could damage the environment. In the 1950s and 1960s, hundreds of thousands of people were exposed to high levels of radiation resulting from three nuclear accidents in the Ural Mountain area of the Soviet Union, which remained unreported for decades. The worst accident occurred in 1986 at Chernobyl, near the Soviet city of Kiev, where a nuclear reactor exploded, spewing at least 50 tons of radioactive particles into the atmosphere. Winds then carried considerable contamination into other nations. Some experts believe the number of deaths caused by Chernobyl radiation exposure in subsequent years and the additional cancer deaths likely to occur in the future (in all nations affected) will be in the tens of thousands; others think it could be in the hundreds of thousands.

Several major fears about the environment grew rapidly during the 1980s, especially in economically advanced nations. As industrial smokestacks continued spewing sulfur dioxide into the atmosphere, more and more nations became alarmed at the destructive ecological effects of acid rain. Scientists also became convinced that heavy emissions of chloroflourocarbons were depleting atmospheric ozone and consequently increasing solar radiation, skin cancer, and damage to food crops. Another major concern was the "greenhouse effect." Many, though not all, scientists thought that the increased burning of fossil fuels like coal and petroleum was likely to cause an increase in global temperatures, possibly melting the polar ice caps, changing crop yields, and flooding low-lying parts of the world. Many of them also attributed the measurable rise in global temperatures in the 1980s to the greenhouse effect.

As a result of increasing environmental concerns, a number of governments took steps to reverse deteriorating conditions. The first clean air act was passed in Great Britain in 1955, and as a result London was less polluted by the end of the 1970s than it had been a quarter-century before. During the late 1960s and 1970s, the United States created a series of environmental protection laws, regulating in particular water and air pollution. At Montreal in 1987, 46 nations agreed to reduce chloroflourocarbon emissions 50 percent by 1999. Poorer nations, however, often perceived concerns about the ozone layer and the greenhouse effect to be a luxury compared to their need for economic development or for more pressing environmental concerns like safe drinking water.

RICH NATIONS AND POOR NATIONS COMPETING IN A GLOBAL ECONOMY

By the end of World War II the United States had emerged as the dominant economic force in the world. Europe, the prewar leader in producing goods and services, and the Soviet Union were now devastated, and much of their capital had been depleted. Japan lay in ruins, and China was on the verge of civil war. Toward the end of the war and shortly thereafter, the Allied powers agreed to encourage international economic growth and free trade by formation of the International Monetary Fund (IMF), the International Bank for Reconstruction and Development (World Bank), and the General Agreement on Tariffs and Trade (GATT). The United States played a leading role in the formation of all three institutions, but the Soviet Union declined to participate or to permit its satellite states in Eastern Europe to do so. GATT, which became a permanent organization, was especially created to reduce tariffs and other trade barriers, reductions which were particularly important to the United States, the nation with the greatest productive capacity.

For several years, much of Europe faced unstable economic and political conditions, but in 1947 the U.S.-sponsored Marshall Plan stimulated industrial and agricultural production and trade, while also stabilizing postwar inflation and unemployment. By the early 1950s Western Europe was well on the road to economic recovery. In Eastern Europe, which did not participate in the Marshall Plan, recovery was slower. The Soviet Union renewed its Five-Year Plans and once again squeezed economic sacrifices out of its people in order to rebuild heavy industry.

Between the early 1950s and the late 1980s, the unique postwar economic dominance of the United States slowly gave way to a more balanced world economy. By 1980 the United States produced only one-quarter of the value of the world's goods and services (gross world product), down from its 40 percent share in the early 1950s, but roughly equivalent to its 1938 portion. Within the same postwar period, Japan's share went from 2 percent to 10 percent, and Western Europe's also increased, although not nearly as dramatically as Japan's. From 1973 to 1981 members of the Organization of Petroleum Exporting Nations (OPEC) increased the price per barrel of petroleum tenfold, almost doubling their per capita gross national product (GNP). From 1981 to mid-

1990 however, petroleum prices fell by more than 50 percent, and the OPEC share of global wealth declined.

Meanwhile, during the 1980s, a number of other nations sharply increased their share of the global production of goods and services. From 1973 to 1986 China, Taiwan, South Korea, Singapore, and Hong Kong all saw their economies expand at about triple the U.S. rate. Although the growth of world output declined from 1988 to 1991, these nations along with others in South and East Asia produced the highest economic growth rate of any area in the world. One reason for the region's continuing strong economic growth was abundant Japanese investment. By late 1991 it was estimated that a new Japanese factory opened every three days in Thailand.

In the United States, foreign imports and investments (especially from Japan), an unfavorable trade balance, and large government budget deficits (an accumulated $3.5 trillion by late 1991) became major concerns of U.S. citizens. North American business leaders set up an increasing number of factories in poorer nations, where labor was cheaper and environmental restrictions less demanding. U.S. companies, including Ford, General Motors, General Electric, IBM, and Xerox, made up the overwhelming majority of over 1800 new plants established in Mexico between 1965 and 1991.

By the beginning of the 1990s U.S. citizens could no longer take overwhelming U.S. economic supremacy for granted. The postwar era ended with a much more balanced world economy than it had begun with. Japan and the European Economic Community (Common Market) of twelve nations, especially a reunited Germany, had emerged as major economic powerhouses.

In the first few decades after World War II, the economic status of most people in the world improved as their economies modernized, but the improvements were uneven, and economic modernization had its negative as well as its positive consequences. During the 1970s and 1980s many nations in the poorer areas of the world saw some of their earlier economic gains erode.

The twentieth-century trend toward disparity of income intensified during the postwar period. In 1960 the average income in the poorest one-fifth of the nations was about thirty times less than that earned in the most prosperous one-fifth. By 1990 it was about sixty times less. By then, the world's seven richest nations, possessing about 12 percent of global population, owned almost two-thirds of its wealth.

Several developments contributed to this broadening disparity. While richer nations generated more wealth, poorer countries produced much more rapidly increasing populations. From 1973 to 1981 poor countries found the steep price hikes for petroleum, manufactured goods, and some foods especially burdensome. Because of these increases, they had to borrow heavily abroad and incur excessive debt. When petroleum prices fell, some of the less affluent petroleum-exporting nations were also hard hit: They had borrowed large amounts of money in the expectation that healthy petroleum revenues would pay off their debts and now were more hard-pressed than ever to meet their obligations. The banks of rich nations continued to charge high interest rates, which raised the debts of poorer nations still further. By 1988, estimates of the debt of Latin American, Asian, and African countries totaled $1.2 trillion, up from $98 billion in 1973 and $575 billion in 1982. The debt was owed to banks, governments, and international lending agencies such as the IMF and the World Bank.

The debt became so staggering for many nations that a few suspended repayments. Even more shared the sentiment of Peru's President Garcia: "We reject the usurious terms of the foreign debt." In an increasingly interdependent international economy, however, outright refusal to repay loans meant no new credits and unfavorable treatment by the major global economic powers. Therefore, most debtor nations worked with the IMF to extend and restructure their repayment schedules. But the IMF frequently demanded domestic financial reforms of debtor nations as the price for restructuring debts or for any new credits. These demands were often resented by indebted nations because they included calls for politically unpopular austerity programs, balanced budgets, and more private enterprise. Some charged that the IMF (composed of 151 nations in 1988) was a tool of its major capitalist contributors, particularly the United States. In their view, the IMF was part of an overall system whereby rich nations controlled world finance and trade in order to maintain high prices for their exports to poor nations while paying low prices for basic commodities imported from these states. For poor nations, the only real answer to the debt problem was for lending agencies to reduce the overall debt.

While by the beginning of the 1990s some lenders had done just that for certain indebted nations, most poorer Asian, African, and Latin American nations were feeling increasingly neglected. Major economic powers, facing financial problems of their own at home, were little inclined to substantially increase foreign aid. Moreover, the collapse of communism in Eastern Europe and the Soviet Union was accompanied by economic hardships for the region's peoples, and the major industrial powers focused more on aiding that area's transition to capitalism than on increasing economic aid elsewhere. By 1991, Japan had replaced the United States as granter of the most foreign aid, and a number of other industrialized nations gave a larger percentage of their nation's wealth to other nations than did the United States.

The most essential need of poor nations after World War II was sufficient food. Although world per capita food production continued to increase, poverty and ineffective world distribution systems combined to deny enough of it to poorer peoples. During the early 1980s, for example, half the sugar, banana, and pineapple crops were exported from the Philippines, much of it by U.S. corporations, while most Philippine children were malnourished. Overall, experts contended that producer nations earned only about 15 percent of the final consumer costs of such tropical products.

Estimates varied widely on the extent of world hunger and undernourishment, but in the early 1980s, about 1 billion people a year suffered from serious malnutrition. During the 1970s and 1980s, millions of lives were lost as a result of famines in areas such as Bangladesh, India, Cambodia, the Sahel (the area immediately south of the Sahara), and eastern and southern Africa. During 1982, UNICEF estimated that about 40,000 children died each day in the

By the late 1980s over 1.2 million refugees in the southern
Sudan suffered from the effects of drought, famine, civil
wars, and government mismanagement.
(Sebastiao Salgado/Magnum)

poorer nations of the world as a result of hunger-related diseases, poor health,
and deficient sanitation practices.

Not only did the gap between rich nations and many poor nations widen
during the final postwar decades, but so did the difference between rich and
poor inside many countries. Peasants were often forced from land they once
farmed, as big producers converted it to the production of export crops. In increasing numbers, these peasants migrated to urban centers to swell the size of
city slums. In Latin America during the 1980s, 10 percent of rural landowners
owned 90 percent of all farmland, while a majority of rural inhabitants owned
none at all.

One of the most evident economic trends of the postwar period was that
the interdependence of the economies of the world continued to increase.

Part of the line waiting to get into Moscow's McDonald's, summer 1990.
(*Walter Moss*)

OPEC petroleum ministers during the 1970s, for example, greatly influenced the lives of Americans, and drought or bad harvest conditions in the United States affected the lives of millions of people dependent on U.S. food exports. The growing power of the multinational corporations also lessened the control of individual nations over their own economies. Businesses increasingly operated on a global scale. By 1991, for example, there were over 3,600 McDonald's restaurants in almost 60 nations outside the United States, with the one in Moscow being the world's biggest and busiest. The world's largest Kentucky Fried Chicken restaurant was in Beijing.

SOCIETY AND POLITICS: REBELLIONS AND CONFLICTING IDEOLOGIES

In the social sphere, the years after World War II witnessed a gradual but growing rebellion against the overwhelmingly dominant role that white adult males had held in the interwar years. African Americans in the United States and black Africans demanded equality. In Africa, as well as in Asia, the challenge to the authority of the white man was part of a broad anticolonial movement. In addition, by the 1960s youths in many nations were challenging the authority of societies dominated by older men and were becoming more aware of a "youth culture" of their own. This trend was especially noticeable in some affluent Western nations, where it was stimulated by media, music, and advertising that catered especially to youthful tastes.

Women, particularly in the same affluent Western nations, increasingly demanded equal rights. They gained the right to vote in some additional countries such as Japan (1946) and Portugal (1975). In democratic nations they gradually increased their political participation, both on behalf of issues of special interest to them and in politics generally.

One development of particular importance to women was the introduction and spread of the contraceptive pill, beginning in the early 1960s. Western European and U.S. feminists later became especially active in the struggle for abortion rights, which were generally recognized in the 1970s and 1980s. Even in conservative Catholic Spain—where before General Franco's death (1975) a married woman had to have her husband's permission to work outside the home or open a bank account—abortion became legal in 1985.

Although by then Communist governments in Eastern Europe had long allowed abortions and claimed that women enjoyed greater equality than in the West, the life of women in Communist nations was often difficult. It usually combined full-time work with the major household responsibilities. Women in such nations had fewer appliances and had to expend more time to obtain basic necessities than did women in the industrialized West. Generally the more economically advanced and democratic a nation, the better off were its women and the greater their political participation. But cultural traditions also played a part in determining their status. In Europe by the 1980s, Scandinavian women were most likely to have high status and hold high public positions. As Japan's economy and world position improved, so too did the position of its women in such areas as access to higher education. Yet, in part because of differing cultural values, Japan's women were still much less likely than U.S. women to hold important business or government positions.

In poorer regions of the world, most women combined heavy childbearing and family responsibilities with hard manual labor. In areas like Africa and India, they cultivated, gathered, and processed most of the food and cash crops—a Peace Corps workers' toast stated: "Here's to the African farmer and her husband." Women in poor nations were more likely than men to be poor, uneducated, and discriminated against because of cultural and family traditions, labor legislation, and inheritance laws.

Partly because of the increased use of contraceptive devices, families gradually grew smaller and households less traditional and more varied, especially in the industrialized world. Improved health conditions enabled people to live longer, and the percentage of older people in societies increased. Even in poorer nations, where the size of families and the percentage of younger people remained considerably higher than in rich nations, average life expectancy increased by fourteen years from 1950 to 1979. Increased urbanization and literacy were two other global trends, although here again significant gaps continued to exist among different states. By 1991 only about one-fourth of the 2 billion people in China and India lived in urban areas, whereas in the United

This African woman planting crops typifies the central agricultural role of women
in many parts of the world.
(Courtesy CARE)

States and Japan about three-fourths of the population did. More than one-
fourth of Chinese adults and almost two-fifths of Indian adults were still illiterate. In contrast, most of the richer industrialized nations reported that no
more than a few percent of their adults were so handicapped.

One of the characteristics of the twentieth century has been the persistence
of unrest brought about by dissatisfied ethnic and cultural minorities. Although influenced by demographic changes, these insurgencies were generally
more influenced by long-standing contention between ethnic groups. Some
minorities, like African Americans, sought simple equality. Others, like the
French in Quebec Province in Canada, agitated for autonomy or separation—
primarily through peaceful, legal, and constitutional means. Still others, such
as the Basques in Spain and the Tamils in Sri Lanka, with less hope for obtaining autonomy or independence through peaceful means, resorted to sporadic
terrorism and sometimes open rebellion. In Great Britain, the Irish Republican
Army in Northern Ireland carried on intermittent guerrilla warfare against
both British troops and armed Protestant paramilitary groups. In Africa, ethnic
disputes contributed to civil wars, almost splitting Nigeria apart in 1967. Toward the end of the postwar era, conflicts between ethnic nationalities in the
Soviet Union and Yugoslavia brought about the collapse of both states.

One of the most unfortunate minorities by this time was about 20 million
Kurds, dispersed over Iraq, Syria, Turkey, Iran, and the Soviet Union. Kurds in

Turkey, Iran, and Iraq were often repressed, although sometimes gaining outside support from regional and superpower nations.

In postwar Europe most right-wing governments were replaced with democracies in Western Europe and Communist dictatorships in the east. With Nazism, fascism, and the rightist authoritarian states in Eastern Europe destroyed, the only remaining European rightist governments were those of Salazar in Portugal and Franco in Spain. When these dictators died in the 1970s, both nations moved toward democracy. After seven years of military rule, democracy was restored in Greece in 1974–1975. By the late 1970s democracy prevailed in the non-Communist nations of Europe.

Compared to the period before World War II, politics in Western Europe was stable and pragmatic, dominated by moderate socialist or moderate conservative parties. As compared to conservatives, socialists favored more sweeping social welfare measures, were less hostile toward the Soviet Union, and were more willing to grant independence to colonies. Both moderate socialists and moderate conservatives in Europe continued to be heirs of the liberal tradition of support for civil rights and individual liberties.

In the United States, politics was primarily pragmatic, socialism was much weaker than in Europe, and the chief ideological split was between conservatives and liberals. The latter sought an expanded government role, especially on behalf of the poor and in protecting the civil rights of minorities, and tended to be more sympathetic than conservatives toward peaceful coexistence with the Soviet Union and China.

After a few brief attempts to establish postwar democracy, most notably in Czechoslovakia, Communism held sway in Eastern Europe until 1989. By 1948, in most cases as a result of Soviet power, Communist governments had come to power throughout that region. Immediately following the war, powerful Communist parties in France and Italy participated in coalition governments. Communism spread through much of Asia after World War II, and Marxist-influenced states appeared in Africa and Latin America in the 1960s and 1970s. On the other hand, after 1947, as Cold War tensions increased, Communists in general were excluded from cabinet participation in Western European governments.

After Stalin's death in 1953 world communism became less unified. In 1956, Soviet leader Nikita Khrushchev openly criticized the policies of the dead dictator. In the early 1960s accumulated disputes between China and the Soviet Union split the Communist world and divided Asian and African Communist parties into pro-Beijing and pro-Moscow factions. In Europe, especially in Western Europe, Communists began to display more independence from Moscow. For most Eastern European nations, however, there were limits on how far they could deviate from the Soviet interpretation of Marxism. In 1968 a Czechoslovakian attempt to create a more humane and democratic socialism was crushed by Soviet force. Earlier in Hungary (1956) and later in Poland (1981) attempts to create more democratic societies were also thwarted. Yugoslavian Communism developed along its own lines following its split from the U.S.S.R. in 1948.

After 1985 the Soviet leadership itself, led by the pragmatic Mikhail Gorbachev, liberalized its own institutions and government and called for more democratization, while at the same time encouraging similar steps in Eastern Europe. The Chinese Communists under Deng Xiaoping sought to prevent significant political reform, but beginning in the late 1970s they pushed through various measures that liberalized the Chinese economy.

For much of the postwar era the chief competing political forces in the Third World (nonaligned African, Asian, and Latin American countries) were Marxism and anti-Communist authoritarianism. Aided by the spread of the transistor radio, proponents of both forces broadened their indoctrination efforts, often reaching peoples living in remote areas. Linking capitalism with imperialism, Lenin had encouraged nationalist revolutions against the imperialist powers, thus building support for communism in areas that were in the grip of Western imperialism. In the Third World, leaders were often struck by the rapid industrialization that occurred in the Soviet Union and the planned economy that helped bring it about. As a revolutionary doctrine directed against the rich and powerful, communism also had an appeal in many nations where the disparity between the rich and poor was great.

Beginning in 1949 Marxist governments came to power in several nations outside Europe, such as China, Vietnam, Cuba, and Ethiopia. These governments were not carbon copies of the Soviet Union; rather, they were influenced by their own national traditions. Different interpretations of Marxism contributed to ideological conflicts in the Marxist world, especially after China and the Soviet Union began engaging in an ideological quarrel in the early 1960s.

Many anti-Communist leaders of Asia, Africa, and Latin America had little in common except their opposition to communism, democracy, and civil liberties. They were generally supporters of the status quo and opposed to social reforms and the redistribution of property. Some, however, like the Shah of Iran, were sympathetic to technological modernization, a force that greatly changed many non-Western societies. Many of these Third World anti-Communist nations were dictatorships or one-party states.

With a few exceptions, like India and Venezuela, democracy was uncommon in the Third World throughout much of the postwar period. In the 1980s, however, and especially from 1989 to 1991, many authoritarian governments, both of the Left and of the Right, were undermined or overthrown and the difficult transition to more democratic forms of government at least begun. This was true not only in Latin America, Africa, and Asia but also in Eastern Europe and among the fifteen former republics of the Soviet Union.

Some of the chief reasons for this shift were the increase of educated middle classes and the ever-growing interconnectedness of global communication-information technology and a global economy, both dominated by the major democratic powers of the world. Authoritarian rulers became more isolated. Their economic and human rights failures became more apparent. As their subjects increasingly contrasted their lives with the freer and generally more prosperous lives of those living in democracies, pressures from within joined demands from outside for reforms. These factors influenced Mikhail Gorbachev to seek to lessen Cold War tensions and support democratization, which in turn helped lead to communism's collapse in Eastern Europe and the Soviet Union. This collapse made communism—and authoritarian anticommunism—less appealing in other parts of the world.

After 1945 religion continued to play an important role in politics. In the Islamic world, politicians at least paid lip service to Islam, and some nations such as Saudi Arabia, Pakistan, and Iran based their laws on interpretations of Shari'a, the traditional system of Islamic law. The Catholic Church also played a political role in much of Latin America and Europe, where its leadership had been traditionally allied with conservative forces.

In the 1960s, however, Latin American Catholic clergy became increasingly critical of the social injustices perpetuated by right-wing governments. At times, they allied themselves with forces of rebellion. In the 1960s liberal Protestants, Catholics, and Jews in the United States became more active in civil rights and anti-Vietnam War protests and followed the nonviolent resistance tactics of Baptist minister Martin Luther King, Jr. By the early 1980s the momentum in U.S. Protestantism appeared to have swung back to conservative fundamentalists and evangelicals, who stressed the literal interpretation of the Bible and religious rebirth in Christ; they also became more active in politics.

INTERNATIONAL RELATIONS: COLLAPSING EMPIRES AND THE COLD WAR

During the three decades following World War II, the great majority of former colonial territories in Asia and Africa, and some in the Caribbean and the Pacific, became independent. The United States, Belgium, France, Great Britain, Spain, Portugal, and Italy relinquished control over more than one-quarter of the world's population. By 1980 the United Nations had welcomed over 100 new nations since its founding in 1945, and during the 1980s additional colonial areas, especially in the Caribbean and Pacific, gained their independence. Finally, in the 1989–1991 period, the collapse of the "Soviet Empire" brought real national sovereignty to satellite nations and independence to the former Soviet republics.

The decolonization of Western empires came about for many reasons. World War II had weakened Western imperialist control, especially in parts of Asia where Japan had temporarily taken over. Imperialistic controls were also weakened by growing disenchantment with imperialism within the Western nations, the economic cost of maintaining an empire on depleted resources, and increased resistance on the part of colonial peoples. Some powers departed from certain colonies in Asia and Africa only after years of bloody struggle, but in most cases imperial powers granted independence peacefully. Some Western powers continued to wield influence in their former possessions. France, for example, retained close associations with many of its African

"We have always loved the black ones as our own! But if they demand freedom and independence—they are no longer blacks, they are reds!"

A Soviet cartoon from the Khrushchev era indicates how independence and anticolonial movements could become involved in Cold War politics.
(Courtesy of Rodger Swearingen)

colonies, and Great Britain maintained a variety of ties with most of its former empire through the Commonwealth organization.

Developments in the colonies and former colonies were also affected by the Cold War between the United States and the Soviet Union that emerged immediately after World War II. At times, both the Soviet Union and the United States used economic and military aid, military advisors, and sometimes troops and covert operations to support friendly, newly independent governments. Many leaders of the new nations, despite vulnerability to superpower imperialism because of their economic poverty, were opposed to joining either camp. These leaders feared being trapped by a form of "neoimperialism" under which their nations would become the puppets of the superpowers. They also feared that their nations would become the battleground for superpower struggles. As an African saying goes: "When elephants fight, it is the grass that gets trampled."

To resist this danger, Third World leaders such as Nehru of India, Sukarno of Indonesia, Tito of Yugoslavia, and Gamal Abdul Nasser of Egypt, sought to form a movement of nonaligned or neutral nations. In 1955 leaders of twenty Asian and African states met at Bandung, Indonesia, and resolved to adopt the principles of nonalignment, coexistence, and cooperation. In 1961 representatives of twenty-five nations met in Yugoslavia for the first Conference of Non-Aligned Heads of State. In 1986, 101 nations took part in this group's eighth summit. Throughout most of the 1970s and 1980s the summits produced calls for a "new economic order" which would lessen the disparity between the rich and poor nations of the world. Although its members, including such nations as Cuba and Vietnam, declared themselves to be "against great power and bloc politics," the group was more critical of the United States and its allies, especially Israel, than of the Soviet bloc.

Although the Soviet Union encouraged nationalistic movements against Western imperialism, it enjoyed imperialist successes of its own. The Soviet Union and the Russian Empire before it had already been for centuries an empire of many nationalities. By increasing the size of the Soviet Union with World War II gains and by establishing Communist puppet governments in Eastern Europe in the late 1940s, this empire was greatly expanded, countering the postwar historical trend that witnessed the breakup of empires. The contiguous nature of this empire and the fact that it contained Communist "satellite states" in Eastern Europe instead of overseas colonies, distinguished it from other modern empires. Like the others, however, it fostered nationalistic resentment and was maintained by force—or the threat of it. Like other modern empires, the Soviet Union collapsed, primarily because its weakened central government was unwilling or unable to use enough force to hold down nationalistic forces that sensed the opportunity at hand.

Partly to counter Soviet influence after World War II, Western leaders encouraged regional and international economic and political cooperation. The Marshall Plan, the North Atlantic Treaty Organization (NATO), the Organization of American States (OAS), and the formation of the European Economic Community (EEC) and its subsequent broadening were examples of regional cooperation. Such continuing collaboration, however, often had to overcome nationalist obstacles such as the imposing General Charles de Gaulle, president of France from 1958 to 1969.

In Africa and the Middle East, as in the Soviet and Western blocs, some politicians promoted regional unity. Kwame Nkrumah of Ghana wrote a book entitled *Africa Must Unite,* and in 1963, the Organization of African Unity was founded. Islam was still another affiliation that transcended national boundaries. Many militant Muslims were critical of any nationalism that separated Muslims from one another. Secular Arab nationalism also transcended the boundaries of individual Arab states. Both forces competed for popular support in much of the Middle East, but both unifying forces were hampered by regional conflicts exacerbated by outside interference and the involvement of superpowers who had their own strategic, political, and economic interests in the area.

The major international organization of the postwar world, the United Nations (U.N.) was formed in 1945 by fifty-one nations to replace the League of Nations. It consisted of six bodies: the General Assembly (183 members as of 1993), the Security Council, the Secretariat, the Economic and Social Council, the Trusteeship Council, and the International Court of Justice. The Security

Council had five permanent members: France, Great Britain, the United States, the Soviet Union, and the People's Republic of China [after taking the place of the Republic of China (Taiwan) in 1971]. These permanent members could veto substantive Council action. In addition, the Council contained ten non-permanent members (six up until 1965) elected for two-year terms by the Assembly.

Under the secretary general, the Secretariat headed the administrative and civil service branch of the United Nations. The Economic and Social Council, elected by the General Assembly, coordinated various U.N. and autonomous commissions and agencies concerned with economics, social conditions, culture, education, and health. In 1945 the Trusteeship Council was given responsibility for eleven territories, most of which were earlier mandates of the League of Nations. By 1991 only the western Pacific island group at Palau, administered by the United States, remained as a U.N. Trust Territory.

The record of the United Nations was mixed. As a forum for international opinion and as an organization that called attention to the economic and social needs of underdeveloped areas, it was often effective. It helped to channel aid to these areas, dependent of course on the willingness of the richer nations of the world to offer assistance.

As a peacekeeping force, the United Nations had a better record than that of the League of Nations. In 1946, it helped pressure the Soviet Union into leaving Iran. In 1950, largely as a result of a temporary Soviet boycott of the United Nations, it condemned North Korea for invading South Korea and sent an international force to aid South Korea. Since the late 1940s, U.N. peacekeeping forces have served, in some cases for decades, in various parts of the world—for example, Kashmir along the India-Pakistan border, Zaire, Cyprus, and the Middle East. In 1988 the U.N. peacekeeping forces were awarded the Nobel Prize for Peace for their continuing efforts. As a result of heightened cooperation between the Soviet Union and the United States during the last years of the postwar era, the U.N. became even more effective. For example, in 1990–1991, following the lead of the United States, it condemned the Iraqi occupation of Kuwait and supported a successful military effort to end the occupation.

Despite U.N. efforts and the absence of another world war, smaller wars and protracted guerrilla warfare became increasingly common in areas like Asia, Africa, and Latin America. By one estimate, 25 million people lost their lives between the end of World War II and 1978 as a result of warfare. Civil war in China, Indo-Pakistani wars, the Korean War, Arab-Israeli wars, and the war in Indochina were just a few of the conflicts in that period. During the 1980s, the Iran-Iraq war and the war in Afghanistan were among the bloodiest conflicts, and civil wars in many African countries, such as Mozambique, spanned the 1970s and 1980s. In addition, there were many crises and near wars. The Berlin crises in 1948–1949 and 1961, the Cuban missile crisis of 1962, the Soviet-Chinese border skirmishes during the 1960s and 1970s, and a variety of Middle East crises throughout the postwar period all contributed to international tensions.

This chart demonstrates the world's nuclear firepower in the early 1980s (represented by all the multi-dot squares) as compared to the firepower of all the bombs dropped in World War II (the single dot in the middle).
(Courtesy Traprock Peace Center, Deerfield, MA)

Beginning in the late 1940s hostilities and suspicions also fueled a continuing escalation of global military spending and armaments. The United States and the Soviet Union, together with their European allies, easily accounted for the largest percentage of world military spending. From 1975 to 1987, the United States and the Soviet Union alone accounted for about 60 percent of the world total. By 1987 the combined nations of the world were spending an estimated $1.8 million a minute for military purposes. (See Appendix B for data on military expenditures by region for the years 1979–1989.)

The destructive power and proliferation of nuclear weapons increased dramatically after the explosion of the atomic bomb on Hiroshima. By the mid-1970s the United States and the Soviet Union had developed combined nuclear arsenals with over a million times the destructive power of the bomb dropped on Hiroshima, enough to kill the population of the earth twelve times over. By that time China, France, Great Britain, and India had also become nuclear powers, and a number of other nations, including India, Israel, Pakistan, and South Africa, were suspected of possessing nuclear weapons.

Amidst the spiraling military spending and developments, some superpower arms limitation treaties were signed, especially in 1972; and by 1988 the United States actually possessed fewer, though more sophisticated, nuclear weapons than it had had two decades earlier. These developments, however, did not prevent a significant increase in military spending in almost all regions of the world. Most leaders apparently continued to share Theodore Roosevelt's belief that a navy was an "infinitely more potent factor for peace than all the peace societies."

By the late 1980s military spending was becoming an increasingly difficult burden to bear, especially for Soviet citizens, who were much poorer than North Americans. In 1988 the United States and the Soviet Union ratified an intermediate-range nuclear forces (INF) treaty eliminating intermediate land-based missiles from Europe. By 1990–1991, as both sides began destroying some of the newly banned missiles and other disarmament treaties were signed, world military spending had begun to decrease. Especially noticeable was a small U.S. decline and a larger Soviet decrease.

TRADITION AND THE GLOBALIZATION OF CULTURE

In the postwar era, the challenge to traditional religious beliefs and values that was symbolized at the beginning of the century by Nietzsche continued throughout the world. As communism spread to Eastern Europe, China, and Southeast Asia, traditional religions in those areas were usually persecuted or at most grudgingly tolerated. Although in a few cases, especially Poland, the Catholic Church remained strong, in most Catholic nations of Europe the influence of the Church declined. Despite Church opposition, Italians legalized abortion in 1978; many Catholics in various parts of the world rejected papal teachings on birth control.

In the United States, local "blue laws" regulating Sunday work, amusements, and drinking were gradually eased or revoked. In the early 1960s the U.S. Supreme Court ruled against prayer and devotional reading of the Bible in public schools. In the 1970s it ruled that abortion was a woman's right under certain conditions. In the United States and Western Europe, censorship of pornography also eased, despite religious opposition. In the Third World, as urbanization, education, literacy, and mass media spread, more people became separated from traditional religious beliefs.

Secularism also strongly influenced many intellectuals. Some of them came to accept a view similar to that of the secular French existentialists, who were greatly influenced by Nietzsche. They believed that God did not exist, that the world was "absurd," and that the best one could do was try to live for the present in a responsible and honest manner. Writers such as Jean-Paul Sartre, Albert Camus, and Simone de Beauvoir helped make existentialism one of the most influential of early postwar movements.

Despite an overall trend in the world toward secularization, many traditional religions remained vigorous. After his elevation in 1958 Pope John XXIII worked toward a revitalization of the Catholic Church and encouraged ecumenical initiatives. The election of the Polish John Paul II as pope in 1978 helped to strengthen the already strong Catholic forces in Poland and, to a lesser extent, those in some other Eastern European nations. Protestant fundamentalism and Islam also displayed increased vigor during the late 1970s and the 1980s.

By the 1980s Communist values seemed increasingly unable to offer a meaningful alternative to traditional religious beliefs. Even the Soviet government under Gorbachev, concerned with Soviet alcoholism, corruption, and other signs of moral decline, spoke more favorably than in the past regarding religious values and displayed a growing toleration of religion. The collapse of communism in Russia was accompanied by a resurgence of interest in Russian Orthodoxy.

Some intellectuals supported traditional religions and their teachings. During the 1950s and early 1960s the influence of the Anglo-Catholic poet T. S. Eliot was still strong. In France, Catholic writers and thinkers like Gabriel Marcel and Pierre Teilhard de Chardin challenged the dominance of atheistic or agnostic existentialism. Beginning in the 1960s the much-acclaimed Russian novelist Alexander Solzhenitsyn increasingly celebrated the values of traditional Russian Orthodoxy. Protestant theologians such as Karl Barth and Paul Tillich and the Jewish thinker Martin Buber continued to have significant followings, and the controversial Catholic theologian Hans Küng appealed to many liberal Christians. Popularizers of Christianity such as the U.S. evangelist Billy Graham reached millions through various media.

In nations where authoritarian or totalitarian measures were imposed, culture often suffered and was made to reflect propagandistic purposes. In nations as diverse as the U.S.S.R., China, Turkey, the Republic of South Africa, Chile, and Guatemala, writers were censored and persecuted. Some writers in these nations smuggled their work out, and others wrote freely only in exile after having been encouraged or forced to leave their homelands.

Cultural pluralism, the coexistence of many different subcultures and beliefs in a society, became increasingly common in nations that allowed freedom of expression. Pluralism was encouraged by the tremendous expansion of various forms of media. The media often created instant fads and popularized new trends, a phenomenon first witnessed in the 1920s and now much accelerated. The average person in technologically advanced nations was able to select from an ever-increasing number of here-today-gone-tomorrow philosophies of life and role models. This was true not only in the West but also in many other parts of the world where Western culture had an impact. On the other hand, motion pictures, television, and transistor radios (especially valuable in areas of the world without electricity) also contributed to breaking down regional differences and to fostering standardization. Certain U.S. television programs, such as *Dallas*, seen in more than 100 nations, became commonplace throughout the world.

Non-Western ideas also played a growing role in world culture. For example, Zen Buddhism, Transcendental Meditation, the Hare Krishna sect, and various Muslim movements all had followings in the United States. In addition, many non-Western writers looked for inspiration within their own traditions. In Africa and the Caribbean, the Negritude Movement, founded between the wars, became increasingly popular after World War II. More non-Western writers and film makers achieved world recognition after 1945 than ever before, and their different perspectives exposed Westerners to non-Western viewpoints. Writers such as Chinua Achebe of Nigeria and Yasunari Kawabata of Japan, winner of the Nobel Prize for Literature in 1968, became international figures, as did the Japanese film director Akira Kurosawa, who directed such classics as *Rashomon*, *The Seven Samurai*, and *Ran*.

After 1945, when the poet Gabriela Mistral of Chile became the first Latin American to win the Nobel Prize for Literature, Latin American writers produced some of the most celebrated literature in the Third World. Four other Latin American writers in subsequent years were also awarded the prize:

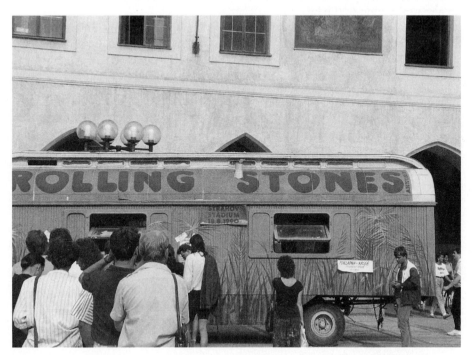

Rock music travels around the world: The Rolling Stones came to Prague in the summer of 1990.
(Nancy Moss)

Miguel Angel Asturias of Guatemala (1967), Pablo Neruda of Chile (1971), Gabriel García Márquez of Colombia (1982), and Octavio Paz of Mexico (1990). Márquez and Jorge Luis Borges of Argentina were especially influential for American and European writers who continued the attempt of many twentieth-century writers and artists to go beyond the techniques of literary or artistic realism. By 1981 Márquez's novel *One Hundred Years of Solitude* (1969) had been translated into thirty-two languages. Latin American women writers also began to achieve prominence. For example, the feminist Rosario Castellanos, who held important institutional and diplomatic positions in the Mexican government, achieved international recognition for her poetry, fiction, and essays.

Amid all these cultural currents, some individuals in various parts of the world felt uncomfortable and wished to stress traditional ways and values. Outside the West, for example in Iran, where Islamic fundamentalism manifested itself strongly in the 1980s, such feelings were often connected with anti-Westernism. Western, especially U.S., influences were perceived to be corrupting more traditional, cohesive, and religious-based societies. In the words of Iran's Ayatollah Khomeini, the United States was "the great Satan."

Most Third World intellectuals, however, rejected any simplistic attempts to return to past traditions, especially if they involved intolerance of modern ideas. They advocated expanding upon their own tradition in a creative way, in a manner open to the best ideas of other cultures.

By the beginning of the early 1990s, despite signs of an increasing standardization or globalization of culture, the world's peoples, both within nations and between nations, still displayed many divisions on fundamental values. In the 1930s, the poet T. S. Eliot wrote:

Where is the wisdom we have lost in knowledge?
Where is the knowledge we have lost in information?

A half-century later, many still doubted whether the new Information Age had led to any significant moral progress or made humankind any wiser.

SUGGESTED SOURCES

BARNET, RICHARD, J., *The Alliance: America, Europe, Japan, Makers of the Postwar World* (1983). An insightful account of how the major capitalist nations of the world became and remained allies.

BLAKE, DAVID H., and ROBERT S. WALTERS, *The Politics of Global Economic Relations*, 3d ed. (1987). A clearly written overview of global economic relations since World War II; presents contrasting points of view concerning major developments.*

BRANDT, WILLY, *Arms and Hunger* (1987). The former West German chancellor combines useful data and analysis in his reflections on two of the major problems of the postwar era.*

HARRISON, PAUL, *Inside the Third World*, 2d ed. (1987). A firsthand account and analysis of the poverty of many modern nations; 1987 printing contains an updated postscript.*

HYLAND, WILLIAM G., *The Cold War: Fifty Years of Conflict* (1991). A brief and readable overview by a former government official who subsequently became the editor of *Foreign Affairs*.

JACKSON, ROBERT, Ed., *Global Issues 92/93* (1992). A collection of forty-nine articles, forty-seven of which are from 1988–1991, dealing with such global problems as impoverished nations, energy resources, hunger, and pollution.*

MILLER, N., and RODERICK AYA, Eds., *National Liberation: Revolution in the Third World* (1971). A collection of incisive articles on Third World revolutions, primarily in the 1950s and 1960s.*

MEDVEDEV, GRIGORI, *The Truth About Chernobyl* (1991). A valuable work by a Soviet engineer who investigated the Chernobyl disaster.

RUBIN, BARRY, *Modern Dictators* (1987). An interesting examination of Third World dictators of recent decades in Asia, Africa, Latin America, and the Middle East.*

STROMBERG, RONALD N., *After Everything: Western Intellectual History since 1945*, 5th ed. (1990). A clear overview of Western political, cultural, philosophical, artistic, and scientific trends in the postwar decades.*

ULAM, ADAM B. *The Communists: The Story of Power and Lost Illusions, 1948–1991* (1992). A global overview by a leading expert on communism and the Soviet Union.

Writings on the Sand (1965). An engaging film on birth control programs in India.

*Paperback available.

CHAPTER 22

Postwar Settlements, Europe, and the Early Cold War

World War II was a catastrophe for the twentieth century. First, it brought about immense suffering, death, and destruction. Second, it was the catalyst for the onset of the Cold War, in which rivalry between the United States and the Soviet Union brought on a period of increasingly intense confrontation. When this rivalry was combined with the menace of atomic destruction at supersonic speeds, there began to be the distinct possibility of global holocaust, which in fact came fearsomely close in the Cuban missile crisis of 1962.

THE DESTRUCTIVE LEGACY OF WORLD WAR II

Because of its more lethal technology and the genocidal practices of some of its participants, World War II caused even greater carnage than World War I. Casualty estimates vary, but even modest ones are astronomical: 60 million military and civilian dead, 35 million injured, and 3 million missing. In this human disaster, the civilian losses were perhaps the most shocking: Possibly 40 million noncombatants died from starvation and disease or perished in battles, air raids, labor and extermination camps, and deportations. For some of the major nations in the war the figures were grim: 7 million Chinese, over 6 million Germans, 3 million Poles, and 2 million Japanese lost their lives. Six million Jews of all nationalities were killed. These losses, dismal as they were, paled in comparison to Soviet casualties: an appalling 27 million Soviet citizens died during the war. By comparison, British and U.S. losses were of a much lower magnitude, in combination numbering 600,000 killed.

In addition to the casualties, war and postwar dislocation uprooted 30 million Europeans from their homes, and the initials "D.P." (displaced person) became familiar. In many nations in postwar Europe, the ethnic majority in an area permanently expelled ethnic minorities; some 17 million Germans were driven out of Eastern Europe. In the Soviet Union, 20 million "unreliables," most of them ethnic minorities, were sent to Siberia. Greeks, Turks, Yugoslavs,

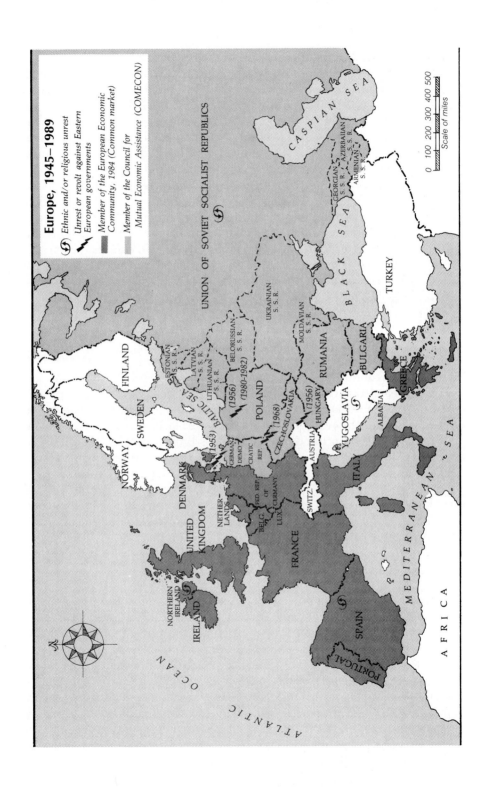

Europe, 1945–1989

⚔ Ethnic and/or religious unrest

⚔ Unrest or revolt against Eastern European governments

◼ Member of the European Economic Community, 1984 (Common market)

◻ Member of the Council for Mutual Economic Assistance (COMECON)

UNION OF SOVIET SOCIALIST REPUBLICS

CASPIAN SEA

GEORGIAN S.S.R.
AZERBAIJAN S.S.R.
ARMENIAN S.S.R.

BLACK SEA

TURKEY

UKRAINIAN S.S.R.

MOLDAVIAN S.S.R.

ESTONIAN S.S.R.
LATVIAN S.S.R.
LITHUANIAN S.S.R.

BELORUSSIAN S.S.R.

(1980–1982)

POLAND

(1956)

(1968)

CZECHOSLOVAKIA

(1956)

HUNGARY

AUSTRIA

SWITZ.

RUMANIA

BULGARIA

YUGOSLAVIA

ALBANIA

GREECE

ITALY

FINLAND

SWEDEN

NORWAY

BALTIC SEA

(1953)

GERMAN DEMOCRATIC REP.

DENMARK

NETHER–LANDS

FED. REP. OF GERMANY

BELG.

LUX.

FRANCE

UNITED KINGDOM

NORTHERN IRELAND

IRELAND

SPAIN

PORTUGAL

ATLANTIC OCEAN

MEDITERRANEAN SEA

AFRICA

N

0 100 200 300 400 500
Scale of miles

and Hungarians fled from other nations to their homelands, and about a million of the surviving European Jews immigrated to Palestine (later Israel). Over a million people had no homeland, and the United Nations struggled to resettle these refugees in Western Europe, the Western Hemisphere, and Australia. Five years after the war most ethnic boundaries in Europe, with some major exceptions in the Balkans, coincided with national boundaries, albeit at a terrible cost. Asia and Africa also suffered population dislocations, but most occurred during the decolonization process well after the war.

Vast stretches of Europe and Asia were physically devastated. Most of the principal cities in central and Eastern Europe had been bombed and shelled into rubble. The road, canal, and railroad systems of much of Europe had disappeared, and millions of acres of farmland had been damaged. In Asia, the cities of Japan had been obliterated, and many other Asian cities had been substantially destroyed. Much of rural China had also been damaged in eight years of war. The total cost of World War II, both in damages and in war expenditures, was estimated at $1.5 trillion.

THE POSTWAR SETTLEMENT

After the brutal conduct of the Axis before and during World War II the victors viewed the defeated nations with hatred and vengefulness. The Allied powers were resolved that neither Germany nor Japan would ever again threaten their neighbors. During the war the Allies had forged a broad consensus on the terms to be imposed on the defeated, but this broke down quickly after the war as antagonism among the victors intensified. Instead of settling affairs at a formal peace conference as after World War I, the Allies worked out most of the peace terms in military discussions immediately after the war and at a series of foreign ministers' meetings lasting until 1963. Some of these agreements were ratified through bilateral treaties; some de facto arrangements, particularly those dealing with Germany, were not ratified until 1975.

Europe

The territorial arrangements in Europe were not as extensive as those made after World War I. The single largest change involved the agreement that the Soviet Union would retain the areas originally acquired in 1939–1940 and again in their possession at the end of the war: Estonia, Latvia, Lithuania, portions of Rumania and Finland, and eastern Poland. In addition, the Soviet Union annexed a province of Czechoslovakia and the northern half of East Prussia. These acquisitions moved the Soviet border dramatically westward compared with 1939, but placed it at about the same place as the border of tsarist Russia in 1914. Although some nations refused to acknowledge the change, Poland received the eastern one-quarter of Germany in compensation for the loss of eastern Poland.

Boundary changes in the rest of Europe were relatively minor. Hitler's Axis allies—Finland, Hungary, Rumania, Bulgaria, and Italy—faced some territorial adjustments, reparations payments, and limitations on their military establishments; but the overall terms were not particularly harsh. The most notable change was Italy's surrender of the predominantly Slavic province of Istria to Yugoslavia. Alsace-Lorraine was returned to France, and the western boundary of Germany was set as it had existed in 1937. Austria was detached from Germany and occupied by the United States, Great Britain, France, and the Soviet Union. In 1955, the occupation forces were withdrawn and Austria regained its independence.

As at the Paris Peace Conference of 1919, the postwar status of Germany dominated the thinking of the victorious powers. During the war, Germany's enemies had considered permanently dismembering it or stripping it of industry and reducing it to a feeble agricultural region. By the war's end, the United States had changed to the belief that a healthy, united Germany would be essential to European recovery and to vigorous international trade. By 1945 the Allies had agreed to retain Germany as a single nation but hedged about with safeguards to prevent future aggression. To accomplish the latter, they agreed that Germany was to be disarmed and divided into four occupation zones: French, British, U.S., and Soviet. The occupying forces were to remain in place until they could be sure that the German people had been de-Nazified and would no longer be aggressive. At some future time, a German government acceptable to the occupying forces would be set up, a treaty would be concluded with this new government, and the occupying forces would withdraw. In 1945 most observers believed the occupation would be over in three to five years. Again, as after World War I, the victors were interested in reparations settlements and agreed that the heavily ravaged Soviet Union would receive the largest share. The Allies left the details concerning reparations for later resolution.

One feature of the arrangements for the German occupation zones became extremely important in postwar years. During the war, the Western forces had agreed to halt west of Berlin while Soviet forces captured the city; this put Berlin in the Soviet occupation zone. After the war, the Western Allies insisted on sharing in the occupation of the city, and an awkward arrangement was worked out. Berlin became a separate occupation authority divided into four zones. The Soviet Union agreed to set aside certain highways, railroads, and air corridors in their German occupation zone for the Western powers to use to supply their three sectors in West Berlin. This arrangement left the Western forces in Berlin cut off behind Soviet lines, a precarious military situation.

Finally, there was the matter of war crimes. The Nazis had caused such horror before and during World War II that this time the victorious powers were determined to punish the leaders. An international judicial tribunal assembled at Nuremberg during 1945–1946. The highest-ranking surviving Nazi leaders were put on trial for waging aggressive war and for committing crimes against humanity. Twelve were condemned to death, seven were imprisoned for terms up to life, and three were acquitted. While some attacked the process as "victor's justice," the precedent was set that brutal treatment of prisoners and noncombatants constituted a crime and that "following orders" was not a sufficient defense. Trials of lesser officials followed.

Asia

As in Europe, postwar arrangements in Asia devolved from basic agreements made at the midwar conferences. The victors stripped Japan of its empire, divided its possessions among themselves, and occupied Japan. They set Japan's boundaries as those of 1854, which restricted it to the four home islands. The United States, which had carried the great burden of the war with Japan, was to be the sole power occupying Japan and the Ryukyu Island chain with its important Okinawa air base. The United States also took over the western Pacific islands as a United Nations Trust Territory. The Soviet Union received the southern half of Sakhalin, the Kurile Islands, and railroad and seaport rights in Manchuria (all lost to Japan in 1905). China regained Taiwan (Formosa), which had been lost to Japan in 1895. Soviet and U.S. forces split Korea into two occupation zones until a mutually suitable government could be installed.

Defeated Japan received much the same treatment as Germany. Japan's armed forces were disbanded, and Japan, in a new constitution, was made to renounce war as an instrument of national policy. Japan was to be governed by a U.S. army of occupation under the direction of General MacArthur. U.S. forces would stay until the Japanese could demonstrate they were no longer an aggressive people, which they could do by creating a government acceptable to the United States. As at Nuremberg, Japanese leaders were put on trial in Tokyo and Manila for war crimes; seven were executed, and others were imprisoned. Unlike Germany, Japan retained its government, but it was purged of militarists. The emperor was also retained on the condition that he renounce his claim to divinity.

THE ONSET OF THE COLD WAR

As World War II approached its end, the alliance among the victorious powers began to dissolve. The United States, Great Britain, and the Soviet Union—nations very different in their political, social, and economic characteristics—had been united in a "shotgun marriage" against a fearsome enemy. Even as they were fighting the Axis, however, each of these allies intended to arrange the postwar world along lines that would be most beneficial to them. Great Britain wished to maintain its empire and retain its closed imperial economic system; the United States wished to retain its spheres of influence in the Western Hemisphere and Asia but also wished to construct a worldwide system of free markets; the Soviet Union was determined to dominate eastern Europe and to keep Germany militarily impotent in order to prevent another invasion out of the west. In addition, the Soviet Union was willing to exploit opportunities to advance Marxism and Soviet interests around the world if such opportunities did not embroil the Soviet Union in too much difficulty.

Reflecting such a diversity of interests, World War II, a "hot" war, was followed by the Cold War, a confrontation between the United States and the Soviet Union that persisted to one degree or another throughout most of the postwar period. Historians strongly debated its causes and the responsibility of each power for the outbreak.

Phase One: Eastern Europe and Germany

At the last two wartime conferences, Yalta in February 1945 and Potsdam in July and August 1945, it became clear that strong disagreements about the future of eastern Europe and the occupation of Germany were developing between the United States and Great Britain, on the one hand, and the Soviet Union, on the other. Soviet troops already occupied eastern Europe and eastern Germany. The Soviet Union, with approximately 27 million dead, was determined to weld eastern Europe into a buffer zone of friendly nations, presumably with Communist governments, that would protect it from future invasion. Stalin believed the Soviet Union was entitled to a sphere of influence in eastern Europe because the United States had spheres of influence in the Caribbean, Japan, and western Europe. Beginning in 1943 he began to organize Communist governments in exile for Poland and some other eastern European states. These organizations were primed to take over in their countries as Soviet troops moving westward ousted the Germans from eastern Europe. The United States wanted eastern European governments to reflect the will of their people through democratic elections, partly from principle and partly from confidence that such elections would create governments that would be friendly to the United States. It pressed the Soviet Union to permit the creation of governments based on a broad political spectrum, particularly in Poland, but the Soviet Union made only token concessions.

The wartime allies also clashed over German reparations. All the victors believed they were entitled to wring reparations from Germany, and they had talked about setting the figure at $20 billion. On the other hand, the United States was undamaged by the war and its economy had prospered mightily. American leaders also remembered the German experience after World War I and were more interested in rebuilding Germany as a trading partner than in burdening it with reparations. The Soviet Union on the other hand had been devastated during the war and wanted to rebuild its economy either through postwar loans from the United States or from reparations from defeated Germany, or both. To pressure the Soviets into opening eastern Europe, the United States cut off Lend-Lease and refused to make loans to the Soviet Union. In addition, in 1946, the Western powers ended shipments of industrial materials from their German zones to the Soviet Union, causing great bitterness in the Soviet Union. Meanwhile, the Soviets proceeded to strip their occupation zone in eastern Germany of materials useful to the Soviet economy.

The conflict between the United States and the Soviet Union stemmed from more than policy differences. In mid-1945 the two nations were led by Harry Truman and Joseph Stalin, men whose personalities contributed to the tensions. Truman's predecessor, President Roosevelt, a pragmatist, had tried to work in a cooperative spirit with Stalin. Truman was an intelligent, feisty politician who had come to the presidency by accident. He had little training in foreign affairs, but he had always been a critic of Stalinism; now that the war was over, he was temperamentally disposed to "get tough" with the Soviet Union.

Premier Stalin was also a clever, determined political leader, with limited contacts with the outside world. Possessed of an iron will and not overly concerned about the morality of the means he used, he had displayed an almost paranoid obsession with acquiring and maintaining political power. He harbored strong suspicions of the nations of the West, fearing that they were still determined to destroy the Soviet state, as they had tried to do following the Bolshevik revolution.

The atomic bomb also harmed postwar relationships. The political fallout in U.S.-Soviet relations matched the atomic fallout over Japan. Most historians claimed that the bomb was used because intense Japanese resistance threatened to prolong the war at a cost of over a million additional casualties. On the other hand, some took the view that the bomb was dropped primarily to prevent the Soviet Union from making gains in Asia and to make that nation more amenable to U.S. desires concerning Germany and eastern Europe. Whatever the case, U.S. possession of the atomic bomb made the Soviet Union fearful and suspicious, but it did not back down on matters concerning eastern Europe or Germany.

After Potsdam, relationships between the two superpowers deteriorated further. The United States blocked Soviet interests in Iran while strengthening its own interests in the area. The Soviet Union continued to suppress anti-Communist elements in Poland, Rumania, and Bulgaria and to tighten the grip of Communist parties there. In addition, the Soviet Union began to work for control in Czechoslovakia and Hungary, where free elections had been held and where, in each case, the Communist party was in a minority. Meanwhile, the United States presented a plan for the control of atomic energy, the Baruch Plan, which specified that all nations give up control of fissionable materials to an independent international agency, submit to international inspection of existing facilities, and cease making atomic bombs. Because the United States and its Latin American and western European allies controlled the United Nations, and through it would control the proposed international agency, the Soviet Union rejected the plan.

Meanwhile, the rhetoric escalated on both sides. In a speech at Fulton, Missouri, in 1946, Churchill charged that an "iron curtain" had fallen, dividing a Moscow-controlled entity, Eastern Europe, from "free" Western Europe. Actually, the situation was still fluid in parts of Eastern Europe. About the same time, Stalin told the Soviet people that the Soviet Union was ringed by enemies bent upon destroying it and that they would have to endure privations and return to Five-Year Plans to build up the economic and military strength needed to defend themselves.

Phase Two: The Truman Doctrine and European Developments

Late in 1946 and early in 1947, East-West tensions increased as the Soviet Union began to put pressure on Turkey and Greece. Interested in obtaining secure transit through Turkey's water passage from the Black Sea to the Mediterranean, the Soviet Union demanded joint Soviet-Turkish supervision of the waterway, but the Turkish government refused. Being much weaker than the Soviet Union, Turkey looked for help.

In Greece, the end of World War II had brought about a brutal, atrocity-filled civil war between the corrupt, authoritarian Greek government and Communist-dominated guerrillas. British army units backed the government, and Communist regimes in Bulgaria, Albania, and particularly Yugoslavia supported the guerrillas. Churchill had exacted from Stalin a promise not to support the guerrillas there, and Stalin, for reasons of his own, did not help them. In February 1947, unable to bear the cost, the British government announced it was pulling its troops out of Greece.

The Truman administration, faced with what it viewed as a Soviet threat to conquer smaller nations and break out onto the Mediterranean, responded by formulating an assertive policy that continued the intensification of the Cold War. Most U.S. diplomats and military leaders, assuming that the Soviet Union was out to destroy the "free" (non-Communist) world, viewed the crisis in the Mediterranean as the crucial test. If aggression against Greece and Turkey could be halted, the Communists would be unlikely to attempt aggression elsewhere. Instead of using atomic bombs, the Truman administration put emphasis on "containing" communism, preventing its advance until the people in the Communist nations tired of Marxism and overthrew their governments. The containment policy, as it came to be called, generally dominated U.S. strategic thought throughout the postwar period. As viewed in 1947 containment meant sending extensive economic and military aid to enable governments to defeat external or internal Communist threats through their own efforts. To carry out this policy, Truman and his advisors had to persuade the U.S. public and Congress to spend massive amounts of tax dollars for "peacetime" military aid.

In March 1947 President Truman called Congress into special session. He asked for money for military supplies and military advisors for Greece and Turkey, declaring, "I believe it must be the policy of the United States to support free peoples who are facing attempted subjugation by armed minorities or by outside pressures." Congress voted $400 million, and this policy became known as the Truman Doctrine. A naval squadron was already in the Mediterranean, and military aid and advisors were quickly rushed to Greece. Bolstered by the U.S. presence, the Turkish government continued to refuse to administer the waterway to the Mediterranean jointly with the Soviet Union.

A step into the Cold War: President Truman addresses a
joint session of Congress on March 12, 1947, calling for
military aid to Greece and Turkey in order to block
Communist expansion into the Mediterranean.
(UPI/Bettmann Newsphotos)

With U.S. aid, the reorganized and reequipped Greek army drove back the
guerrillas, and when Yugoslavia closed the border with Greece in 1949, cutting
off supplies and a place of refuge, the guerrillas laid down their arms.

Western Europe was another source of Cold War tension. Despite several
billion dollars in U.S. loans, by 1947 the economy of Western Europe had not
revived. France and Italy in particular were plagued with shortages, inflation,
unemployment, and inadequate housing. This situation, plus the fact that leftists had played an important role in the wartime resistance movement against
Nazism and fascism, induced many French and Italians to vote for Socialist
and Communist candidates. The only other major political party in Italy and
France that rivaled them in popularity was that of the Christian Democrats,
called in France the Popular Republican Movement. Christian democracy developed out of Catholic wartime resistance movements and was at first in-

clined toward a moderate Catholic leftist position. It had significant support in many European nations and in Latin America as well. However, under both the Italian and French multiparty political systems, no one party was able to obtain a parliamentary majority, and coalition governments were usually necessary. The Socialists and Communists were able to obtain cabinet posts along with the Christian Democrats, but no Communist had yet become prime minister in Italy or France.

The Truman administration concluded that the economic and political situation in Western Europe demanded effective U.S. economic intervention. In June 1947 Secretary of State George Marshall proposed that the nations of Europe consult with one another and with the United States to determine the amount of economic assistance they would need to rebuild their economies. Marshall's offer was technically open to every European nation, including the Soviet Union, although U.S. leaders expected—and hoped—that the Soviet Union would refuse. Western European nations accepted quickly, but the Soviet Union, suspicious that U.S. aid meant U.S. economic penetration, refused and prevented Eastern European nations from participating.

The U.S. Congress at first balked at the novel idea of giving money away as peacetime foreign aid rather than lending it in wartime. Soviet actions in Eastern Europe during 1947 and 1948 finally convinced Congress that the United States should undertake foreign aid; in 1948, Congress created the European Recovery Program, usually referred to as the Marshall Plan, with an initial outlay of $4 billion. By 1951 Marshall Plan aid totaled over $13 billion, most of it going to Great Britain, Germany, France, and Italy. The Marshall Plan was a success; the economy of Western European nations recovered rapidly.

Even before the Marshall Plan went into effect, Communist political power in Western Europe was already on the decline. Communists in both Italy and France were excluded from cabinet positions after mid-1947. In the Italian general elections in April 1948, Alcide de Gasperi's Christian Democratic party attained a near majority and the Communist-Socialist vote dropped to 31 percent. While no single party would again come as close to an absolute majority in Italy, Christian Democrats would remain the most influential of Italy's numerous parties. Communist-led general strikes in 1947–1948 in both Italy and France caused some disruption, but both were broken by government action. The popularity of the Italian Christian Democrats stemmed in part from the backing of more conservative elements who saw them as the only major alternative to the Socialists and Communists. During the late 1940s, this phenomenon also occurred in several other European nations, and it moved Christian Democratic parties toward more conservative policies than they had originally espoused.

In 1950 the United States extended the concept of foreign aid to the non-Western world in the hope that such aid would prevent new nations from turning to communism. The United States embodied this concept in the Point Four Program, which channeled millions and eventually billions of dollars into the economies of newly emerging nations.

At the same time that the United States was implementing the Truman

Doctrine and the Marshall Plan, the Soviet Union was tightening its grip on Moscow-backed Eastern European governments. In 1947–1948 Communist takeovers added Hungary and Czechoslovakia to the Soviet sphere, which already included Poland, Rumania, Bulgaria, and Albania. The takeover in Czechoslovakia, the only Eastern European nation with a solid interwar tradition of Western democracy, shocked the West and hastened Congress's approval of the Marshall Plan. In order to further control Eastern Europe, the Soviet Union created bilateral economic treaties, later followed by COMECON, a Soviet-controlled economic organization that integrated the economies of Eastern European nations with one another and with the Soviet Union. COMECON assigned some nations (such as Czechoslovakia) industrial goals and other nations (such as Bulgaria) agricultural goals. To reinforce the unity of Communist regimes in Eastern Europe, the Soviet Union created Cominform, a new organization containing most of the European Communist parties.

There was a hole in the Eastern European buffer zone, however: Yugoslavia, although Communist, took an independent, nationalistic course under Marshal Tito and, after a bitter confrontation with the Soviet Union, was expelled from Cominform in 1948. Because of other distractions Stalin did not attack Yugoslavia. Tito cautiously maneuvered his nation into a position of neutrality and eventually became important as one of the leaders of nonaligned nations around the world.

Although Stalin could do little more than expel Tito from Cominform, he was able to exert much more pressure on those he considered "Titoists" in other Eastern European nations. From 1949 to 1952 many of those so labeled were imprisoned, tried, and, on occasion, executed. Stalin also demanded that each government within the Eastern bloc follow the Soviet example more closely in such matters as centralized party control over the economy, acceleration of collectivized agriculture, persecution of religion, and establishment of a Soviet-style constitution. Nevertheless, these nations never became clones of the Soviet Union. For example, private agriculture and religion continued to be more significant forces in Eastern Europe than in the U.S.S.R., despite Stalin's efforts.

In a major application of the containment policy, the United States and its allies combined the three Western zones of occupation in Germany into a German national state. Although Germany had been a hated enemy and was still feared, particularly by the French, the West began to view a revived Germany as a buffer against the Soviet-controlled East. The Western powers united their zones in stages between 1946 and 1949, a process somewhat delayed because of French reluctance. By 1949 the Western powers were creating a national economic unit and a new currency in western Germany and building up the government from the local level. During 1948 and 1949, with Western supervision, the West Germans created a new constitution acceptable to the three occupying powers. The new Federal Republic of Germany put its capital at the university town of Bonn. Its first government was controlled by the Christian Democratic party, led by the anti-Communist Konrad Adenauer, who was already in his seventies when he came to power. His party held power for two decades. By September 1949 "West Germany" was operating as a sovereign state, although formal recognition would not come until later. Western troops remained, although less visible.

Of all the actions undertaken by the United States and its allies after World War II, the reestablishment of West Germany probably created the most hostility in the Soviet Union. After two devastating twentieth-century experiences, the Soviet Union hated and feared the prospect of a reborn Germany, armed by the West, to be used against the Soviet Union. The Soviets countered by transforming their occupation zone into the Democratic Republic of Germany.

The Soviet Union's main effort to derail the unification of West Germany centered on the spot where the West was most vulnerable: Berlin. In June 1948, the Soviets announced they had closed for repairs the railroads and highways in East Germany set aside to supply Western troops and the civilians in West Berlin. The Western governments immediately gathered all available cargo planes and used the air corridors to supply more than 2 million West Berliners and Western troops with food, clothing, coal, and other supplies. The Berlin Airlift, or "Operation Vittles," was a triumph of efficiency. At its peak, transport planes touched down at Berlin's Templehof airdrome every few minutes on an around-the-clock schedule. The blockade of Berlin lasted 300 days, until May 1949, when the Soviets conceded defeat and reopened the highways and railroads. The crisis was over, but Berlin remained a trouble spot for the future.

Cold War tensions were not confined to international diplomacy; they also affected the people at home. During the war, Americans had been friendly toward "Uncle Joe" Stalin and the Soviet Union. After the war, taking their cues from the government, they began to view the Soviet Union as heading an international conspiracy to overthrow capitalism. It was a short step from antipathy toward the Soviet Union to hostility toward those Americans who were perceived to be, or to have been, friendly to the Soviet Union. Americans were egged on by some leaders to worry about alleged "subversives," "Commie dupes," "parlor pinks," and "fellow travelers." Congress ran several investigations of alleged subversives in the United States and created legislation with such broad power to combat subversive organizations that it posed a threat to civil liberties. The executive branch created a government loyalty program designed to uncover subversives and unreliables in the federal government. Although there were indeed a few pro-Soviet Americans, most of the accused were innocent people, many of whom lost their jobs or saw their reputations tarnished. The climax of anti-Communist hysteria occurred from 1950 to 1954; it was intensified by the Communist takeover of China and the Korean War (see Chapter 24). Senator Joseph McCarthy made the term "McCarthyism" famous because of his unproven charges of subversion directed against a wide variety of Americans ranging from ordinary citizens to the army command.

As the economies of Western European nations recovered with the aid of the Marshall Plan, the influence of Communist parties continued to decline in France and Italy. West Germany under Adenauer recovered its full sovereignty. It also became increasingly prosperous, and in the 1950s there was talk of the German "economic miracle." Adenauer's relationship with a variety of French governments was better than that of any previous German leader of the century. He finally retired as chancellor in late 1963, but his Christian Democratic party continued in power for six more years. In 1951, aided at least in part by Cold War developments, the Conservative party in Great Britain returned to power after six postwar years of Labour party control marked by such social welfare policies as the institution of free medical care. The Conservatives, first under Churchill and then under Anthony Eden, Harold Macmillan, and Sir Alec Douglas-Home, remained in power until 1964. The Conservative dominance in Great Britain in the 1950s was symptomatic of a general European trend in that decade toward more conservative governments.

In the Soviet Union, Stalin tightened his hold over the nation. The enormous wartime loss of life and property necessitated massive economic reconstruction, and Stalin also distrusted the more friendly attitude toward the West that the war had generated in the Soviet Union. These factors, plus Stalin's continued concern with his own political power and Cold War tensions, all led to strict controls over the economic, social, and cultural life of Soviet citizens up to Stalin's death in 1953.

Phase Three: Global Nuclear Confrontation

The Cold War heated up further in 1949 as the United States abandoned its tradition of unilateral diplomacy and moved into a new era. After World War II both the Soviet Union and the United States had demobilized the bulk of their armies. However, postwar events culminating in Czechoslovakia and Berlin convinced U.S. leaders that the Soviet Union represented a permanent aggressive menace in Europe that must be confronted with a permanent U.S. military presence bolstered by an alliance system.

The era of alliances began in 1947 when the United States created the Rio Pact, a regional defensive alliance in which the United States and Latin American nations agreed to come to the aid of any member nation threatened with aggression. In 1949 the Truman administration set up the North Atlantic Treaty Organization (NATO), in which the United States, Canada, Iceland, Norway, Denmark, the Netherlands, Belgium, Luxembourg, Great Britain, France, Portugal, and Italy (and later Greece and Turkey) agreed to come to one another's aid if attacked. The alliance's goal was the eventual integration of the national armed forces of the member nations into a unified military command. In practical terms, NATO was dominated by the U.S. military establishment; a U.S. general (beginning with Eisenhower) was always the supreme commander. The United States Strategic Air Command (SAC) established air bases in Western Europe and the North Atlantic. The United States also began constructing air bases in non-NATO nations such as Spain and Libya, as well as developing bases in U.S.-occupied Japan and Okinawa. From all these bases, U.S. B-29s could drop atomic bombs on the Soviet Union.

Soviet reaction was twofold. First, the Soviet Union began to increase the size of its army in Europe until it heavily outnumbered the NATO forces opposing it, thus making it likely that the Soviet Union could overrun Western Europe if war broke out with the United States. Their vulnerability often prompted Western European nations to urge restraint during U.S.-Soviet crises. The Soviet's second move was to create its own bristling array of atomic weapons. Only five months after NATO was organized, the Soviet Union surprised the world by detonating an atomic bomb.

In the early 1950s the United States and the Soviet Union found themselves engaged in a fevered arms race, creating weapons of ever more destructive power. In 1952 the United States test-exploded a hydrogen bomb, followed in 1953 by the Soviet Union. The Eisenhower administration decided to base its military policy on "massive retaliation," the concept that in the event of any Soviet attack on the United States or its allies, SAC bombers would destroy the Soviet Union with atomic or thermonuclear bombs. Eisenhower's Secretary of State, John Foster Dulles, believed that U.S. military superiority would be an excellent backup for his "brinksmanship" policy of pressing selective issues with the Soviet Union to the limit. By 1955 both superpowers possessed bombers of intercontinental range that could hit the opponent's homeland. They carried four ten-megaton hydrogen bombs; each bomb was capable of substantially destroying a major urban center, such as Moscow or New York. The U.S. air force maintained a four-to-one lead over the Soviet Union in aircraft capable of delivering bombs on the enemy's homeland.

Meanwhile, the United States continued to tighten its containment noose around the Soviet Union. By 1954 the Cold War had spread to Asia (see Chapter 24), and the United States organized the Southeast Asia Treaty Organization (SEATO). This alliance supported anti-Communist nations in Asia while enlarging the string of SAC air bases surrounding the Soviet Union. In the Middle East, the United States stood behind but was not a member of the Baghdad Pact, allying Great Britain with Iran, Turkey, Iraq, and Pakistan. This alliance system collapsed because of Middle Eastern politics and other factors, but in 1957 President Eisenhower pressured Congress into authorizing him to commit U.S. troops to defend nations in the Middle East against "overt armed aggression from any nation controlled by international communism." Eisenhower used this policy to intervene briefly and unprofitably in Lebanon. The total result of these arrangements was that the United States could bomb the Soviet Union from virtually every direction, but the Soviet Union could bomb the United States only via the North Pole, and even that with difficulty because radar systems in Canada gave early warning of approaching Soviet aircraft.

Despite an extensive U.S. military buildup, the Soviet army, backed by medium-range missiles and bombers, still gave the Soviet Union a distinct advantage in Europe. In an effort to lessen the imbalance there, West Germany was admitted into NATO and permitted to rearm. To accomplish this, the United States had to pressure its reluctant NATO allies, who were caught between fear of the Soviet Union and suspicion of a rearmed Germany.

In 1955 the Soviet Union—with its own fears of a rearmed Germany—created a competing military alliance system, the Warsaw Pact, integrating the armed forces of Eastern Europe into a unified force under Soviet command. In addition, the Soviets recognized East Germany as an independent state. Although the hope of unifying Germany still remained in some quarters, as of 1955 Germany had become two separate nations, each integrated into the sphere of influence of a superpower.

Despite their intense integration into the Soviet Cold War bloc, Eastern European nations remained restless. Dissatisfaction with living conditions, plus the hopes raised by more liberal Soviet post-Stalinist policies (see below) led to riots and other convulsions in East Germany in 1953. The East German disorder was quickly suppressed, but in 1956 the Soviet Union faced two new challenges to its hegemony. Wladyslaw Gomulka, considered an unreliable Polish Titoist by the Soviet Union, was made the head of the Polish Communist party. The Soviet Union threatened to intervene in Poland but did not. In Hungary, the challenge was direct. Some police officials were lynched, and some army units went over to the people. Premier Imre Nagy announced that Hungary would cease to be a one-party state or a member of the Warsaw Pact. This was unacceptable to the Soviet Union, and Soviet troops poured in to suppress the rebellion.

The United States was caught in a dilemma. It had been the stated policy of the Eisenhower administration to "roll back the iron curtain" and to "liberate Eastern Europe." The Voice of America and Radio Free Europe had been beaming propaganda broadcasts into the region for years in an effort to stir up unrest there. Many Hungarian rebels expected that the United States would now intervene, but the Soviet Union made it plain that intervention meant war. The United States was not prepared to go to war over Eastern Europe; further, it was distracted at that time by a confrontation with its allies, Great Britain and France, over the Suez Canal (see Chapter 26). The United States did nothing, and the Soviet Union crushed the rebellion. About 25,000 Hungarians, including Nagy, lost their lives, and some 200,000 Hungarians fled to the West. Although the Soviet Union was, and would remain, supreme in Eastern Europe, there was to be no return to the policies of the 1949–1952 period. Conditions gradually improved as living standards rose moderately and repressive policies were slowly relaxed.

A Thaw in the Cold War

Although the Cold War intensified at times during the 1950s, the superpowers also made sporadic attempts to negotiate their differences. The death of Stalin in 1953 opened the door to a possible relaxation of tensions. After Stalin died, a scramble for leadership ensued in the Soviet Union, resolved by the accession of Nikita Khrushchev to power. In 1956 Khrushchev made a daring "secret speech" to a closed session of the Twentieth Congress of the Communist party of the Soviet Union; he criticized Stalin's policies, including his elimination of many innocent people during the 1930s. From then until his removal in 1964 Khrushchev used criticism of Stalin and Stalinist policies to weaken the

---

Stalin's Corpse

On March 5, 1953, an event took place which shattered Russia—Stalin died. I found it almost impossible to imagine him dead, so much had he been an indispensable part of life.

A sort of general paralysis came over the country. Trained to believe that they were all in Stalin's care, people were lost and bewildered without him. All Russia wept. And so did I. We wept sincerely, tears of grief—and perhaps also tears of fear for the future. . . .

I will never forget going to see Stalin's coffin. . . . The crowd closed tighter and tighter. I was saved by my height. Short people were smothered alive, falling and perishing. We were caught between the walls of houses on one side and a row of army trucks on the other.

"Get those trucks out of the way!" people howled. "Get them out of here!"

"I can't do it! I have no instructions," a very young, towheaded police officer shouted back from one of the trucks, almost crying with helplessness. And people were being hurtled against the trucks by the crowd, and their heads smashed. The sides of the trucks were splashed with blood. All at once I felt a savage hatred for everything that had given birth to that "I have no instructions," shouted at a moment when people were dying because of someone's stupidity. For the first time in my life I thought with hatred of the man we were burying. He could not be innocent of the disaster. It was the "No instructions" that had caused the chaos and bloodshed at his funeral.*

◆◀◆▶◆

The Russian poet Yevgeny Yevtushenko, who was nineteen when Stalin died, describes the general sense of grief and shock at Stalin's death and the tragic deaths of an untold number lining up to view his corpse in Moscow on March 6, 1953.

*From *A Precocious Autobiography* by Yevgeny Yevtushenko, translated by Andrew R. McAndrew. Copyright ©1964 by E. P. Dutton. Reprinted by permission.

---

power of his political rivals within the party hierarchy. While motivated largely by political concerns, Khrushchev's de-Stalinization campaign also led to less censorship. In 1962, for example, Khrushchev personally approved the publication of Alexander Solzhenitsyn's *One Day in the Life of Ivan Denisovich*, the story of a man unjustly sent to a prison camp during Stalin's regime. By the late 1950s the Communist party under Khrushchev's leadership had allowed millions of innocent people to be freed from the camps. Khrushchev also desired to improve living standards, including increasing agricultural output. In order to do this, he limited military spending more than some of his political rivals thought appropriate.

In 1953 there was also a change of leadership in the United States, as the moderate, easygoing Eisenhower ("Ike") succeeded Truman as president. Eisenhower and Khrushchev remained suspicious of each other, each determined to keep his country strong, but both were more willing than their predecessors to negotiate under appropriate circumstances. Concerned with the danger and cost of the escalating Cold War, and under pressure from world opinion, Khrushchev and Eisenhower met at a "summit conference" in Geneva during 1955. Although nothing of substance came from the meeting, enough momentum was established to lead to other meetings. In 1955 the occupying powers agreed to end the occupation of Austria, and the Soviet Union recognized the West German government. Selected groups of Americans and Soviet citizens began visiting each other's nations. At the same time, the U.S. media began to tone down its strident anti-Communist presentations. This thaw in the Cold War was limited in both accomplishments and duration, but neither superpower believed that it could bypass the opportunity for discussions. In the future, new discussions would accompany new alarms and distractions.

Phase Four: Missile Races

On October 4, 1957, the Cold War moved into a still more dangerous phase. On that day, the Soviet Union, using a powerful new rocket booster, launched a small satellite, *Sputnik,* into an orbit around the earth. The space age had begun. Two months later, the Soviet Union launched an intercontinental ballis-

The Great Kitchen Debate: Premier Khrushchev and Vice-President Nixon argue the merits of Soviet and U.S. ways of life at a U.S. exhibition in Moscow in 1959. *(UPI/Bettmann Newsphotos)*

tics missile (ICBM). The missile age had begun. The Soviets gloried in their achievements. "We will bury you," Khrushchev promised the West. His statement, probably a figurative assertion that Marxist concepts would triumph in the long run, was taken by some in the West to be a threat of imminent nuclear war. Shortly thereafter, in 1958, he pressed his advantage by putting pressure on Berlin. Terming Berlin "a bone in the throat," he warned Western powers that the multiforce occupation of Berlin must end in six months' time or the Soviet Union would turn over the responsibility for Berlin and the supply corridors to East Germany.

Sputnik, the ICBM, and the Berlin threat prompted several reactions in the United States. Americans took pride in leading the world in science and technology and were depressed by Soviet successes. One leading atomic scientist moaned, "[The United States] has lost a battle more important and greater than Pearl Harbor." Some feared attacks by Soviet ICBMs, and a political furor broke out. The Democrats charged the Republicans with having created a "missile gap," and made gains in the 1958 congressional elections. The scientific and educational community was blamed as well, with charges that "Johnny" was not measuring up to "Ivan."

In the face of public outcry, the Eisenhower administration moved quickly. It poured money into scientific research in the universities, tying them more closely to the military-industrial-political complex. The government sent up a satellite in 1958 and created the National Aeronautics and Space Administration (NASA) to advance American space exploration. The administration also spent vast sums of money to launch a major ICBM program and to build submarine-launched missiles (SLBM) that offered the advantage of a portable missile-firing platform that could not easily be detected. To further strengthen U.S. missile response to the Soviet Union, the United States offered to base intermediate-range and medium-range ballistics missiles in NATO countries; but only Great Britain, Italy, and Turkey agreed to set up missile sites. By 1962–1963 the United States had 450 missiles and 2,000 bombers capable of striking the Soviet Union, compared to 50 to 100 Soviet ICBMs and 200 bombers that could reach the United States. The "missile gap" had been reversed with a vengeance, and the U.S. margin widened monthly. Despite the U.S. lead, both sides could inflict enormous damage on each other, and a new phrase, "balance of terror," came into use.

Despite the missile race, diplomatic exchanges continued. Khrushchev repeatedly postponed the Berlin "deadline" and pressed for more summit meetings. In 1959, he traveled to the United States. While visiting American farms and hi-tech enterprises, Khrushchev took care to present himself as a jovial human being. Sometimes, however, differences in cultural outlook were difficult to bridge. He was upset that security problems prevented his visit to Disneyland. "Is there an epidemic of cholera there or something?" he asked. "Do you have rocket-launching pads there? . . . Or have gangsters taken hold of the place?" He was, however, able to visit Hollywood but was critical of the scantily clad chorus girls on the set of the movie musical *Can Can*. A meeting with Eisenhower at Camp David went well, and enthusiasts spoke of the "spirit of Camp David" while the Soviet premier explained away his threatening rhetoric. Nuclear disarmament talks were once again in the air, and the United States, the Soviet Union, and Great Britain (which now also had nuclear bombs) stopped testing nuclear weapons in the atmosphere.

Phase Five: To the Brink of Nuclear War

Beginning in 1960 the Cold War suddenly heated up into a confrontation in which the two superpowers teetered on the edge of nuclear holocaust. In May 1960, two weeks before a scheduled summit conference in Paris, Soviet forces shot down a U-2, a U.S. high-altitude supersonic spy plane that was violating Soviet airspace. Such planes were capable of flying from twelve to fourteen miles above the earth and taking photographs that could spot an object as small as a golf ball. The Soviet Union immediately turned that incident and the initial U.S. cover-up into a propaganda coup. In Paris, Khrushchev demanded an apology, plus punishment for those involved; when Eisenhower refused, he left the conference in a show of anger. The embarrassment of the Eisenhower administration and the missile gap controversy aided the election of John F. Kennedy, who promised new programs to restore U.S. prestige.

President Kennedy displayed many of the characteristics of President Truman. He was a tough political battler and a believer in the containment doctrine; he surrounded himself with advisors who were equally disposed to be "tough" with the Russians. His administration increased the defense budget and contributed notably to the U.S. surge in missile production. Kennedy was more aware than his predecessors of the necessity for dealing with struggles for independence and social reform in Asia, Africa, and Latin America, which Communists often supported as "wars of liberation." Kennedy therefore coupled to the old "massive retaliation" doctrine the new concept of "flexible response," which entailed building up the "conventional arms"—the army, navy, and marines—to fight in limited wars. As a part of this program, the United States stepped up commitments to train and supply the armed forces of allies in every quarter of the world. On the other hand, the Kennedy administration also created the Peace Corps, in which Americans volunteered to bring educational and technological skills to poorer nations.

Kennedy was soon tested by Khrushchev over the perennial trouble spot, Berlin. Berlin had become a double problem for the Soviet Union. In addition to housing a Western military garrison behind Soviet lines, it spotlighted the weaknesses of East Germany. The Communist regime in East Germany was so unpopular that masses of East Germans were fleeing annually, crossing from East Berlin into West Berlin and then to West Germany and beyond. In 1960, for example, 152,000 East Germans escaped via Berlin; on one day alone, August 6, 1961, 2,305 people arrived in West Berlin from East Germany.

The Soviet Union had to do something to stop the outflow of population or East Germany would collapse and communism would be held up to worldwide humiliation. At the June 1961 summit conference in Vienna, Khrushchev once again threatened to turn Berlin over to the East Germans if the city were

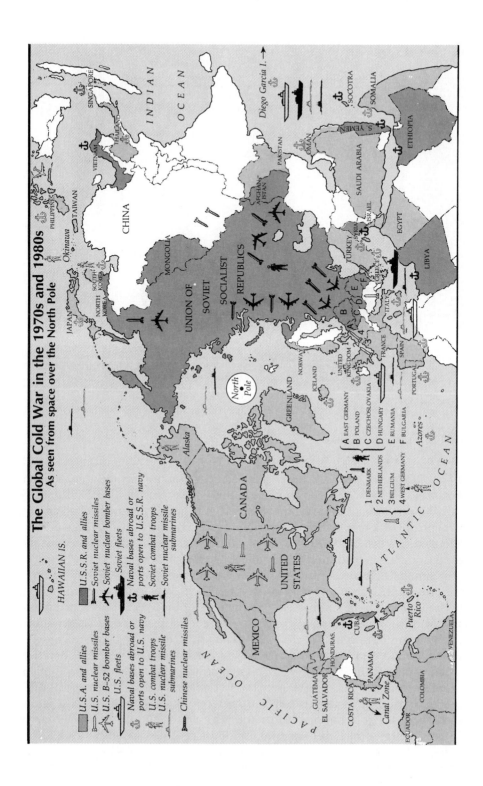

The Global Cold War in the 1970s and 1980s
As seen from space over the North Pole

HAWAIIAN IS.

- ▭ U.S.A. and allies
- ✈ U.S. nuclear missiles
- ⚓ U.S. B-52 bomber bases
- ⚓ U.S. fleets
- ⚓ Naval bases abroad or ports open to U.S. navy
- ⚓ U.S. combat troops
- ⚓ U.S. nuclear missile submarines
- ▬ Chinese nuclear missiles
- ▭ U.S.S.R. and allies
- ✈ Soviet nuclear missiles
- ✈ Soviet nuclear bomber bases
- ⚓ Soviet fleets
- ⚓ Naval bases abroad or ports open to U.S.S.R. navy
- ⚓ Soviet combat troops
- ⚓ Soviet nuclear missile submarines

A EAST GERMANY
B POLAND
C CZECHOSLOVAKIA
D HUNGARY
E RUMANIA
F BULGARIA

1 DENMARK
2 NETHERLANDS
3 BELGIUM
4 WEST GERMANY

INDIAN OCEAN

SINGAPORE
THAILAND
VIETNAM
PHILIPPINES
TAIWAN
Okinawa
CHINA
MONGOLIA
UNION OF
SOVIET
SOCIALIST
REPUBLICS
AFGHANISTAN
PAKISTAN
Diego Garcia I.
SOCOTRA
SOMALIA
S. YEMEN
OMAN
SAUDI ARABIA
ETHIOPIA
ISRAEL
SYRIA
TURKEY
EGYPT
LIBYA
GREECE
ITALY
SPAIN
PORTUGAL
Azores
FRANCE
UNITED KINGDOM
NORWAY
ICELAND
JAPAN
SOUTH KOREA
NORTH KOREA
Alaska
North Pole
GREENLAND
CANADA
UNITED STATES
MEXICO
CUBA
Puerto Rico
ATLANTIC OCEAN
GUATEMALA
EL SALVADOR
HONDURAS
COSTA RICA
PANAMA
Canal Zone
COLOMBIA
VENEZUELA
ECUADOR
PACIFIC OCEAN

325

U. S. and Soviet tanks confront each other in Berlin at a moment of heightened tension.
(*UPI/Bettmann Newsphotos*)

not demilitarized. Kennedy rejected the solution, but not firmly enough to impress the Soviet premier who apparently left Vienna with the idea that Kennedy could be pressured. Kennedy apparently also believed that he had left an impression of weakness. To dispel that notion, he announced that Berlin would be defended as a test of "Western courage and will." He called up reservists and asked Congress to institute a "civil defense" bomb shelter program.

Kennedy's clear resolve to remain in Berlin prompted the Soviet Union to authorize East Germany to stop the exodus. The East German government put up the Berlin Wall in August 1961; in the eyes of the West, it became a major symbol of repression and of the failure of communism. Tensions remained high in the months that followed. Additional U.S. troops and equipment were sent to Europe, and Kennedy went to West Berlin to underscore U.S. determination to protect the city, telling an excited crowd, *"Ich bin ein Berliner"* ("I am a Berliner").

Berlin had been a serious confrontation, but it was in Cuba that the world stood at the brink of thermonuclear war. This crisis grew out of the nature of U.S. relationships in Latin America. Traditionally, the United States had not been overly scrupulous about the nature of political regimes in postwar Latin America as long as they were "anti-Communist"—that is, anti-Soviet; the United States had previously toppled a government in Guatemala that it had suspected of becoming Communist (see Chapter 23). In the 1950s Cuba was controlled by the dictator Fulgencio Batista, an ally of the U.S. government and a friend of U.S. businesses ranging from sugar refining to gambling. In return, the United States backed the Batista regime. Under Batista, Cuban urban areas maintained a relatively high standard of living, but the rural peasantry suffered from seasonal unemployment, inadequate medical facilities, and lack of education.

In 1953 and again in 1956 Fidel Castro, a young lawyer, attempted and failed to overthrow the Batista government. After his second defeat, he went into the hills to build up a guerrilla army. In 1959 Castro had created enough support to topple the regime, and Batista fled. Between 1959 and 1961, defying increasingly hostile U.S. reactions, Castro rapidly moved Cuba toward a new society based on Marxist principles. During this period he consolidated his grip on power, becoming a leftist *caudillo* in tight control of a totalitarian apparatus. Accusing U.S. entrepreneurs and upper-class Cubans of exploiting the Cuban masses, Castro rapidly nationalized both domestic and foreign-owned corporations and instituted egalitarian social reform programs.

The Eisenhower administration, seeing Cuba heading out of the U.S. orbit, presumably toward the Soviet Union, reacted with increasing vigor. After its early protests were ignored, the United States organized an economic boycott and stopped buying Cuban sugar, measures designed to disrupt the Cuban economy and to bring Castro down. Faced with U.S. economic warfare, Castro accelerated his nationalization of U.S. business holdings in Cuba and began to build an economic relationship with the Soviet Union.

By 1960 the Eisenhower administration was convinced that the Castro regime was fast becoming a Soviet ally right in the heart of the U.S. sphere of influence in the Caribbean; such a government was to be overthrown and replaced with a reliable ally. The United States broke diplomatic relations with Cuba. In addition, Eisenhower, following the program earlier used successfully to overthrow the government of Guatemala (see Chapter 23), authorized the CIA (Central Intelligence Agency) to recruit and train anti-Castro Cubans to invade Cuba and provide a rallying point for the Cuban population to overthrow Castro. This plan was based on the belief that few people wished to live under communism, and that now that the Cubans had had a taste of it, they would be ready to rebel.

On entering office in 1961, President Kennedy authorized the invasion plans to proceed, with the understanding that the United States was not to be directly involved in the landing itself. In April 1961 the anti-Castro forces bombed Cuban air bases and landed at the Bay of Pigs, but the peasants did not revolt. Kennedy vetoed pleas for air support, Cuban militia moved in, and the invaders surrendered after two days.

The Bay of Pigs provoked a number of reactions that had a major effect on the Cold War. Castro, convinced that the United States would try to overthrow him again, quite possibly with a direct invasion, now sought the protection of the Soviet Union. In December 1961 he announced, "I am a Marxist-Leninist and will remain a Marxist-Leninist until the day I die." He also pledged that Cuba would work to spread Marxist revolution throughout Latin America.

More important to the future health of the world were the responses in Washington and Moscow. The fiasco was a sore blow to the prestige of the new young U.S. president. Kennedy, attacked for not supporting the invasion force, apparently decided to move with greater firmness in the future. Combined with Vienna, the Bay of Pigs incident apparently predisposed Khrushchev to consider Kennedy a weak leader; more ominously, it tempted Khrushchev to use Cuba to solve some of his own problems. The Chinese and some of his colleagues in Moscow had been criticizing Khrushchev for being insufficiently aggressive in Cold War confrontations with the United States. Some of his domestic policies, agricultural production in particular, were not working out, and he needed to distract attention. The Americans were clearly passing the Soviet Union in ICBM production, and, most pressing of all, Castro was calling for help.

These factors, plus the presence of fifteen U.S. Jupiter missiles in Turkey aimed at the Soviet Union, motivated the Soviet premier to make a daring, fundamental challenge to the United States by plunging into the heart of the U.S. sphere of influence. Khrushchev secretly began to send medium-range bombers and medium-range missiles to Cuba. These weapons could defend Cuba by hitting the southeastern United States, including Washington, D.C., but they could not hit most American ICBM installations or SAC bases. From Khrushchev's point of view, such a move would demonstrate that he could take a tough line, apply additional pressure to get the Western powers out of Berlin, and moderate the imbalance in the arms race. Above all, Khrushchev wanted to support Castro, who feared that a U.S. attack was imminent.

In October 1962 American U-2s discovered the missile sites in Cuba, some almost operational. The Kennedy administration sprang into action. In 1956 the Soviet Union had viewed the Hungarian uprising as a direct challenge to a vital sphere of influence and had launched an immediate, powerful response despite the potential risk of triggering a conflict with the United States, which was only indirectly involved. The Kennedy administration perceived the presence of missiles in Cuba as a similar but much more intense challenge to its Caribbean sphere of influence because the Soviet Union was directly involved. U.S. leadership in Latin America and its credibility in Western Europe were on the line. In addition, President Kennedy seemed to consider it a personal test.

Amid a flurry of pressures, including conflicting signals from Western Europe, the Kennedy administration worked out the U.S. position. The Soviet missiles and bombers in Cuba must go. The Soviet Union would be given the opportunity to remove them voluntarily. If the Soviet Union refused, the United States would destroy the missiles by air strike or invasion. If such an action meant a collision with the Soviet Union, the United States would go to war. The military command sent some SAC bombers into the air and put others on fifteen-minute alert, while placing ICBMs in a preliminary state of readiness to fire. The command also moved army units into position in the Southeast and reinforced Guantanamo Bay. Pressuring the Soviet Union to withdraw the missiles and bombers, Kennedy imposed a "quarantine," a peacetime naval blockade of Cuba (by international law an act of war) that prevented additional missiles from reaching Cuba. Latin American nations, at a meeting of the Organization of American States, supported the blockade. On October 22, Kennedy appeared on television to demand that the Soviet Union "halt and eliminate this clandestine and provocative threat to world peace."

The decision now lay with Moscow, and for six days peace or war hung in the balance. President Kennedy privately estimated the chances of war to be "between one out of three and even." Faced with U.S. resolve backed by U.S. nuclear superiority, the Soviet premier retreated. He ordered the Soviet merchant ships carrying missiles to turn back and avoid confrontation with the U.S. navy. In an exchange of notes, Khrushchev and Kennedy agreed that the Soviet Union would remove the offending missiles and bombers and that the United States would make a public pledge not to invade Cuba. Unofficially, Attorney General Robert Kennedy also informed the Soviet ambassador that the United States would remove its missiles from Turkey at some time in the future. The armed forces of the two nations were ordered to stand down, and the shadow of nuclear war passed over—for the moment.

SUMMARY

World War II caused a ghastly human carnage of tens of millions and destroyed much of Europe and Asia. The victorious Allies prescribed severe peace terms for both Japan and Germany; both nations lost territory conquered during the course of the twentieth century, and Germany lost one-quarter of its former homeland to Poland. The victors demilitarized and occupied Japan and Germany and imprisoned or executed some of their surviving leaders as war criminals. The Soviet Union was the chief beneficiary of the territorial changes, annexing a large area along its western border and additional territory in Asia.

Near the end of World War II, strains appeared between the Soviet Union and its allies, in part based on differing programs concerning the control and reconstruction of postwar Europe. These differences sharply increased immediately after the war, complicated in particular by U.S. control of the atomic bomb. The Soviet Union was determined to protect itself against any future attack out of the West, and the United States perceived the Soviet Union to be bent on a program of worldwide conquest. By the late 1940s the Soviet Union had installed friendly Communist governments in Eastern Europe, and the United States dominated Western Europe through the NATO military alliance and the economic ties of the Marshall Plan.

During the 1950s the Cold War further intensified. The United States pursued a policy of global containment of the Soviet Union and extended its network of agreements and alliances to Asia. As a consequence, by the late 1950s the United States had surrounded the Soviet Union with a circle of air bases and missile sites from which it could deliver nuclear warheads to the Soviet Union. The Soviet Union could respond by attacking Western Europe. Germany was in effect divided into two nations, with East and West Germany integrated militarily into the European power blocs. Despite the tension between the superpowers, their leaders attempted to moderate their differences by holding discussions to air grievances.

In the early 1960s, the superpowers had a frightening confrontation when the Soviet Union placed missiles in Cuba. The world stood at the brink of nuclear war, but the Soviet Union removed its missiles from Cuba, and the threat passed.

SUGGESTED SOURCES

BESCHLOSS, MICHAEL R., *Mayday: Eisenhower, Khrushchev, and U-2 Affair* (1986). A fascinating, dramatic, and well-researched work on the U-2 crisis and its background.*

BURLACHUK, FOKA FEDOROVICH, *Khrushchev and the First Russian Spring: The Era of Khrushchev through the Eyes of His Advisor Fedor Burlatsky* (1991). Burlatsky was a speechwriter for Khrushchev in the late 1980s who emerged as a leading reformer of the Soviet system.

GARTHOFF, RAYMOND L., *Reflections on the Cuban Missile Crisis*, rev. ed. (1989). Short, well-written discussion of the crisis. Gives fresh attention to the Soviet outlook.*

GELB, NORMAN, *The Berlin Wall* (1986). A complete study of a complex phenomenon, written in a fast-paced, journalistic style.*

LAFEBER, WALTER, *America, Russia and the Cold War, 1945–1990* (1993). A readable account that concentrates more on U.S. motives than on those of the Soviet government.*

LEUCHTENBERG, WILLIAM E., *A Troubled Feast*, updated ed. (1983). A concise and lively survey of U.S. history since 1945.*

MASTNY, VOJTECH, *Russia's Road to the Cold War* (1979). An excellent analysis of Soviet diplomatic aims from 1941 to 1945.*

PATERSON, THOMAS, *Meeting the Communist Threat: Truman to Reagan* (1988). A comprehensive account by a leading diplomatic historian.*

SCHALLER, MICHAEL, VIRGINIA SCHAFF, and ROBERT D. SCHULTZINGER, *Present Tense: The United States Since 1945* (1992). A solid survey of the period.*

SMITH, BRADLEY F., *Reaching Judgment at Nuremberg* (1979). A penetrating study of the corrupting effects of Nazism.* (Also a film, *Judgment at Nuremburg*.)

SMOKE, RICHARD, *National Security and the Nuclear Dilemma* (1993). A trenchant overview of the post-World War II arms race, from a U.S. perspective.

ULAM, ADAM B., *The Rivals: America and Russia since World War II* (1971). A stimulating treatment by an expert on the Soviet Union.*

*Paperback available.

CHAPTER 23

The United States and Latin America after World War II

After World War II the United States enjoyed twenty years of economic growth and social reforms. During the 1960s, however, the pace of change, the war in Vietnam, and other problems provoked social divisions. In Latin America, pressures against the elite establishment continued to build, not only from traditional reform groups but also from Marxist revolutionaries. The United States, acting from the Cold War presumption that if a nation became Marxist it would ally with the Soviet Union, returned to its earlier practice of intervention, this time to prevent Marxists from coming to power in Latin America, especially in the Caribbean.

THE UNITED STATES: FROM PROSPERITY TO SOCIAL CONVULSION

Economic Boom and the Attack on Poverty

In the two decades after World War II, Americans for the most part laid down the burden of wartime responsibilities and took advantage of rising economic prosperity. During most of this period, wages rose faster than prices, and goods and services were cheap. The Cold War kept defense and related industries humming, and unemployment was relatively low. American families enjoyed increased purchasing power and spent their money on appliances, television sets, automobiles, and other consumer goods, and also were willing to pay increased local taxes to build schools, parks, and cultural centers. Fewer people worked on farms and in factories; more Americans now held white-collar jobs in business and government. An increasing number of families moved out of the central cities to the new suburbs, where they could own a home with a yard and a garage and live near others of similar backgrounds. Auto-oriented suburban shopping malls sprang up, weakening central business districts in cities. By the early 1960s, as prosperity continued to increase, many families were purchasing second cars, vacation cottages, campers, and sporting equipment.

For almost twenty years after 1945 Americans supported the New Deal heritage but were not interested in major extensions of the welfare state. In Congress, a coalition of conservative Democrats and Republicans controlled the political process, no matter which party had a legislative majority or held the presidency. The Cold War abroad cast its shadow on domestic society. President Truman joined congressional conservatives in the Red Scare, a controversial campaign against internal subversives. Truman also had the support of both parties when he created the national security state, which included the first large peacetime army, the Department of Defense, the National Security Council, and the Central Intelligence Agency. When he tried to go beyond the New Deal by introducing federal aid to education and national health insurance, however, conservatives in Congress rejected his proposals. On the other hand, Congress maintained the welfare state by increasing Social Security benefits and the minimum wage and approving more public housing for the poor. Truman's successor, President Eisenhower, was a popular, genial war hero who generally left Americans alone to pursue their private goals. In the 1950s Congress, with bipartisan support, enacted public works programs such as the interstate highway system and the St. Lawrence Seaway through the Great Lakes.

By the mid-1960s economic prosperity, increased government revenue, and a resurgence of political liberalism prompted President Lyndon Johnson to launch the "Great Society." Johnson's program markedly expanded the welfare state, in which the federal government took the lead in providing opportunities for all Americans to have a better life. Congress made education a high priority, pouring money into every level. The administration supported mass transit systems and also created programs to fight decay in the central cities. Congress also enacted Medicare, a health insurance program for the aged.

A key element of the Great Society was the "War on Poverty." The federal government provided many of the poor with opportunities for legal aid, job training, youth employment, food stamps and school lunches, medical care, and special educational programs. In the first decade after the launching of the Great Society, the proportion of Americans living below the poverty level was cut by one-third.

Social Progress and Social Discord

While the United States was enjoying economic prosperity, it was also experiencing increased social tensions. Throughout U.S. history, white males of northern European extraction had controlled the economic, social, and political life of the country. Women and minority groups, particularly African Americans, faced discrimination, both legally and in practice. In the post–World War II period, this pattern began to crumble as African Americans, supported by a few white allies, began to press for equal treatment. Influenced by growing African American voting power in large cities, the Truman administration desegregated the armed forces and sponsored unsuccessful civil rights

---

Finding a Way to Attack Racism

[At Moorehouse College] I read [Henry David] Thoreau's *Essay on Civil Disobedience* for the first time. Fascinated by the idea of refusing to cooperate with an evil system, I was so deeply moved that I reread the work several times. This was my first intellectual contact with the spirit of nonviolent resistance.

Not until I entered Crozier Theological Seminary in 1948 . . . did I begin a serious intellectual quest for a method to eliminate social evil. . . . I came early to Walter Rauschenbusch's *Christianity and Social Crisis*, which left an indelible imprint on my thinking by giving me a theological basis for the social concern which had already grown up in me as a result of my early experiences. . . .

My study of Gandhi convinced me that true pacifism is not nonresistance to evil, but nonviolent resistance to evil. . . . It is rather a courageous confrontation of evil by the power of love. . . .*

Here the young Reverend Martin Luther King, Jr., shortly after his successful leadership of the Montgomery, Alabama, bus boycott, describes the ideas that influenced his technique of nonviolent group action to remove barriers to African American civil rights. The ideas of Reinhold Niebuhr and Hegel, and Marx's concern for the welfare of the masses, also influenced King. At first King was impressed with the power of Nietzsche's attack on Christian pacifism but came to believe that Gandhi's approach of nonviolent resistance overcame Nietzsche's position. King's outlook and tactics represent a blending of thought from all over the world; he applied these ideas while leading the civil rights movement in the United States in the 1950s and 1960s. He was assassinated in 1968.

*Excerpt from *Stride Toward Freedom* by Martin Luther King, Jr. Copyright © 1958 by Martin Luther King, Jr. Copyright renewed 1986 by Coretta Scott King, Dexter King, Martin Luther King, III, Yolanda King, and Bernice King. Reprinted by permission of Harper & Row, Publishers, Inc.

---

legislation. Meanwhile, federal courts outlawed restrictive covenants in housing and ordered the desegregation of graduate education in southern state universities. In 1954 the Supreme Court, in *Brown v. Board of Education of Topeka*, declared racial segregation in the public schools unconstitutional. White southerners responded with "massive resistance" to racially mixed schools.

In the decade following the Brown decision, African Americans mounted an increasingly effective civil rights movement. Led by Baptist minister Martin Luther King, Jr., they used nonviolent direct action and civil disobedience techniques similar to Gandhi's tactics in India. In the early 1960s African Americans staged sit-ins, freedom rides, and marches, particularly in the South. Their protests sought to end segregation in transportation, local businesses, and public buildings, and to win the right to vote in the South. White people resisted by means ranging from legal maneuvers to beatings, firebombings, and killings.

By the mid-1960s the national political establishment had conceded that the time for civil equality had come. After first trying to evade the matter,

President Kennedy endorsed the movement. On November 22, 1963, Kennedy was assassinated in Dallas, Texas, under circumstances that continue to be debated. His successor, Texas-born President Lyndon Johnson, appealed to Kennedy's memory in the campaign to move forward on civil rights. Quoting the song "We Shall Overcome," the symbol of King's movement, Johnson pressured Congress into enacting important legislation, particularly the 1964 Civil Rights Act, that banned legal inequality on the basis of race. These civil rights laws, supported by Supreme Court decisions, changed the South by eliminating segregated public accommodations and enabling African Americans to vote and hold political offices. In the North, however, the federal government was less vigorous in enforcing laws banning school segregation and bias in housing and employment.

Along with the African-American civil rights movement came an expansion of individual civil liberties. The Supreme Court, led by Chief Justice Earl Warren, restricted certain police and prosecution practices and extended the concept of due process of law so that the poor and uneducated would have access to fair trials. The Warren Court reduced the scope of censorship of printed and visual materials and broadened the rights of free speech. In addition the Court altered many traditional practices connecting church and state; for example, all state-sponsored devotional Bible reading and prayers in public schools were declared unconstitutional. The Supreme Court also promulgated

Civil rights leaders: Martin Luther King, Jr., Robert Kennedy, Roy Wilkins of the NACCP, and then Vice-President Lyndon B. Johnson meet in 1963. All are now dead, two by assassination.
(UPI)/Bettmann Newsphotos)

the "one man, one vote" doctrine in apportioning legislatures, increasing the political power of cities and suburbs, which had previously been short-changed by rural interests.

Meanwhile, the success of the African American civil rights movement inspired others, such as American Indians, Hispanics, gays, and women, to challenge discrimination. Indians tried to recover lost western land rights. Hispanics organized political groups and César Chavez's United Farm Workers. Feminists won federal bans against employment and credit bias and founded the National Organization for Women (NOW) to seek full legal equality. The more militant wing of the women's movement questioned traditional standards of appearance, sexual roles, and family structures.

By the early 1970s the reform impulse extended beyond civil rights. Many Americans became concerned about the deterioration of the environment and resulting threats to health. They celebrated "Earth Day," cut back on some sprays and plastics, and launched local recycling efforts. In response, Congress established the Environmental Protection Agency to monitor a network of new legislation designed to regulate strip mining, industrial and automobile contaminants in the air, and polluted water. Other legislation mandated automobile safety equipment and attempted to protect individuals from harmful additives in food and beverages. Governments at all levels also moved to preserve portions of the environment from industrial and residential development and exploitation.

Dissenting young people spearheaded several, often socially divisive, movements during the 1960s. American youth increasingly questioned the lifestyles and values of their parents. The "hippies" waged a cultural rebellion, trying to fashion a new society by the way they thought and lived. Often children of affluence themselves, members of the counterculture turned their backs on what they considered to be the materialism, competition, and emotional repression of mainstream society. Hippies glorified nature and leisure. They encouraged sharing and tried to shed their inhibitions and express their inner feelings. Their long hair, rock music, casual sex, and drug use shocked and angered elders, but the counterculture would soon leave its mark on adult society.

Although hippies often "dropped out" and ignored public issues, other young people became political activists. The "New Left," led by the Students for a Democratic Society (SDS), organized the poor, joined civil rights causes, and led campus protests. Rising opposition to the Vietnam War expanded the ranks of the New Left. Masses of young Americans marched in the streets, chanting, "Hey, hey, LBJ, how many kids have you killed today?" As draft calls passed 30,000 a month, students mobilized against the war, first holding teach-ins and sit-ins and then turning to draft resistance and evasion. As the SDS became more radical in ideas and tactics, it turned from peaceful to violent action against the war and nourished dreams of revolution. By the late 1960s government repression and internal factionalism had torn the SDS apart. Declining draft calls in the early 1970s lessened the urgency of antiwar protest. Meanwhile, the political establishment recognized the importance of the new generation by lowering the voting age in federal elections to eighteen. Many states lowered the age for marriage, contracts, and other adult privileges to eighteen as well.

Other movements seeking social change also added to the nation's frustration and division, often producing counterattacks. Environmental causes had broad support, but businesses and some unions complained about added costs and lost job opportunities. Many men and women, threatened by changing male-female relationships, ridiculed and attacked the women's movement. The Great Society and the Warren Court also drew heavy criticism. Many Americans believed that reforms in civil liberties favored criminals and stimulated crime. They complained that social welfare programs gave their tax money to undeserving people who refused to work. Furthermore, the challenge to traditional values by the counterculture and New Left horrified many. Both young people and adults from blue-collar families resented the cultural and political radicalism of youthful dissenters.

Meanwhile, the civil rights movement sparked explosive reactions among Americans of both races. Despite progress toward legal and political equality, poor African Americans saw little improvement in their jobs, housing, and public services. Their frustration boiled over in a series of riots, primarily in northern and western cities. As the civil rights movement met white resistance, a few African Americans mocked King's talk of love and peace. They turned to movements such as the separatist Nation of Islam (African American Muslims) and the radical Black Panthers. Each rejected the reformist style and goals of the civil rights movement, and each used confrontational language that frightened the white majority. Racial tension accelerated in April 1968 when a white assassin shot King. African Americans rioted and looted in scores of cities.

At the same time, the civil rights movement was shifting its focus from legal to economic issues and from the South to the North. These developments created a "white backlash." While many white Americans supported the idea of equality in general, they did not want to integrate their neighborhoods and workplaces, and they opposed busing to achieve racial balance in their schools. By the end of the 1960s opposition to the pace of social change had swelled so much that it overcame Johnson's Great Society vision. Appealing to the resentments of what he called the "silent majority," Republican Richard Nixon captured the presidency, defeating liberal candidates in 1968 and 1972.

SOCIAL CHANGE IN LATIN AMERICA

While revolution and war had swept much of the world during the first half of the twentieth century, Latin America, except for Mexico, had been relatively quiet. Most of the region had been officially independent for over 100 years and had therefore escaped the trauma of the independence struggle mounting in Africa and Asia. There had been only one major war between

South America Since World War II

(1975) Independent after W.W. II

 Leftist guerrilla warfare

Urban terrorism
1960s–1970s

Rightist military coups,
1960s–1970s

Scene of U.S. anti-
Communist involvement

CHILE Representative
government, as of 1993

Caracas
VENEZUELA

GUYANA (1966)
SURINAME (1975)
French Guiana

Bogatá
COLOMBIA

Quito
ECUADOR

Amazon R.

PERU

BRAZIL

Lima

BOLIVIA
La Paz
Sucre

Brasilia

PARAGUAY

CHILE
Asunción

Santiago

Buenos Aires

URUGUAY
Montevideo

ARGENTINA

ATLANTIC OCEAN

PACIFIC OCEAN

FALKLAND ISLANDS (Br.) Claimed by
Argentina as Islas Malvinas

0 200 400 600 800 1000
Scale of miles

Latin American nations in the twentieth century, and Latin America was only marginally involved in the world wars. During the postwar period, however, the region became increasingly caught up in social turmoil and enmeshed in the global Cold War. Most Latin American nations still retained the two-culture society, and the gap remained wide between the few rich and the many poor.

Meanwhile, the trend toward urbanization, underway earlier in the century, intensified after World War II. As the rural population kept growing in an area already suffering from a labor surplus, it appeared to many families that their only chance to survive would be to find work in the city. Consequently, swollen by a massive influx of *campesinos,* the cities of Latin America grew enormously after World War II. In 1930 only one city contained 1 million people; by 1991 twenty-nine cities had attained that size. Mexico City, with over 20 million people in 1991, was the second largest city in the world. Some of the arrivals from the countryside found employment in the new industries, but most found only part-time or marginal work and some found no jobs at all. As had happened earlier under the same circumstances in Europe and the United States, Latin American city administrators could not handle the massive influx of outsiders and were unable or unwilling to supply adequate housing, sanitation, transportation, water, schools, or police protection. *Villas miserias* (misery towns) that contained hovels constructed of scraps of tarpaper, wood, tin, and concrete sprang up around the cities, creating a stark contrast to the new luxury apartments and skyscrapers.

After World War II, Latin America remained an economically underdeveloped region, its standard of living trailing far behind that of the United States. Agriculture remained inefficient, and the region continued to import food. Even in those nations that expanded their economies, a rapidly expanding population often outstripped economic growth rates. Most were dependent on the fluctuating international market prices of such staples and raw materials as coffee, cocoa, bananas, sugar, cotton, wheat, meat, hides, wool, timber, copper, tin, and petroleum. After World War II the Latin American share of the world market actually decreased.

After the Depression of the 1930s staple prices dropped to a disastrous low, and leaders in larger Latin American nations sought to diversify the economies of their nations through industrialization. "Modernization" and "development" became key terms in Latin America, as they were in the newly independent states of Africa and Asia, and many nations rushed to develop factory systems. Latin American governments often accompanied their industrial expansion with the expropriation of foreign holdings. In the process, many nations ran into difficulties. Instead of developing basic industries such as iron and steel, textiles, and machinery, they concentrated on producing a spectrum of consumer goods ranging from automobiles to toothpaste. As a result, Latin American nations not only continued to import basic industrial products but also had to pay for the materials, machinery, technicians, and patents necessary to produce consumer products. They also found that such goods could not compete on the world market with those of the more efficient, established industrial powers and discovered further that their own populations were too poor to buy such products.

Argentina: Social Change from the Right

After World War II, several nations, following the lead of Mexico and Chile, instituted social reforms that narrowed the gap between the rich and the poor. One nation that moved in this direction, if somewhat unintentionally, was Argentina. Argentina was one of the larger and more industrialized nations of Latin America. In the early 1940s a conservative military clique controlled the government. One of the ruling group of officers was Juan Perón, a charismatic political adventurer who recognized, as had Vargas in Brazil, that the mass of urban workers, if organized, could become a powerful political force. As minister of labor under the military government, Perón wooed the workers with pay raises and bonuses and organized them into unions loyal to him. When Perón was placed under house arrest, massive demonstrations by the workers freed him, and in the election of 1946, with the backing of the *descamisados* (the shirtless ones), Perón swept into the presidency. Argentineans of every background rallied behind him as he nationalized foreign industrial and transportation holdings. He embarked on a massive program of social services, wage increases, pensions, and low-cost vacations for urban workers, who in turn rallied to him with intense gratitude and support.

In a broad sense Perón became a dictator, with personal characteristics reminiscent of Mussolini. He was genial instead of cruel, *muy macho* (a he-man) in image. A dynamic speaker at mass rallies, he harangued the crowds, who chanted back "Perón cumple!" ("Perón delivers the goods!") Perón did not hesitate to manipulate the media and the educational system and to rig his reelection. He often used mobs and arrests to intimidate political rivals. Perón was substantially aided by his former mistress and new wife, Eva Duarte Perón, an attractive and ambitious woman who had risen from poverty to become a radio star. She saw to it that women were enfranchised and headed a foundation that provided food, services, and jobs for the poor. "Evita" was widely beloved by the common people (but hated by most of the rich), and when she died in 1952 there was a campaign to canonize her. Juan and Eva together represented Latin American "personalist" rule at its ultimate.

Despite his personal dynamism and his intimidation of his opponents, Perón finally made too many mistakes and was driven from power. He ignored the *campesinos* and had little support in the countryside. His social programs and nationalization efforts were costly and created massive national debts and inflation. Late in his rule, he picked a useless quarrel with the Catholic Church. In 1955 the military, with the backing of the upper class, drove Perón into exile in Spain, but it did not tamper with much of his social legislation. Perón remained popular with many Argentineans, and returned to power in 1973 at the age of seventy-seven, remarking: "It is not that we are so good, but those who followed us were so bad that they made us seem better than we were." Now conservative, he served only a year before his death. Although his genuine commitment to reform was debatable, Perón's social programs remained deeply embedded in Argentina's national life.

Guatemala: Social Change from the Left

Until the late 1940s reforms in Latin America had been for the most part either inspired by the Mexican Revolution or liberalism, or engineered by rightist opportunists. In the 1940s, however, beginning with a secondary role in Guatemala, Marxism also began to play an increasing role in social change. A tiny foreign and domestic oligarchy controlled this small Central American nation. This group owned the land and the export crops of bananas, sugar, and coffee. The largest foreign enterprise in Guatemala was the United Fruit Company, owned by U.S. investors. The bulk of the population were Indian descendants of the Mayas—poor, illiterate peons destined to die young.

In the 1940s a movement toward social reform began in Guatemala. Reformers drew up a new constitution that prohibited great estates, permitted compensated expropriation, and created a new labor code to protect the rights of urban and rural workers. A small but well-organized labor movement, increasingly dominated by the Communist party, became active in politics. In 1952 Jacobo Arbenz became president and proceeded to accelerate the reorganization of Guatemalan society. He nationalized some foreign holdings and instituted a program for social security and improvements in education. He expropriated unused lands on private estates, sometimes encouraging Indians to occupy land not yet confiscated. After allowing a small compensation, Arbenz expropriated over 400,000 acres of unused United Fruit Company land, and he allowed no appeals to the courts. By 1954 Guatemala was a nation working its way toward social and economic justice.

THE COLD WAR COMES TO LATIN AMERICA

Although the Cold War began in Europe in the late 1940s, by the early 1950s it was spreading to other areas of the world, including Latin America. As noted previously, long before the United States had adopted its policy of containing communism in Europe and Asia, it had repeatedly intervened in the affairs of Caribbean nations to protect its economic and strategic interests there. Faced with mounting hostility in the region, the U.S. had by 1934 inaugurated a new policy of nonintervention, taking advantage of its established power in the Caribbean and the absence of any threat of European intervention. After World War II, however, a second period of interventionist outlook set in. U.S. leaders, worried about the spread of Marxism, scrutinized the Caribbean area for any signs of Communist penetration. From their point of view, Communists coming to power in the region constituted a threat to the United States and would have to be dislodged.

Guatemala: The Overthrow of Arbenz

Arbenz's program in Guatemala curtailing the power of U.S. businesses brought the Cold War to Latin America. Substantial property was at stake, and Communists were involved in the changes taking place. The United Fruit Company and conservative Guatemalans clamored for help and played up Communist strength in Guatemala. As a consequence, the Eisenhower administration decided to overthrow Arbenz. The United States trained and armed a small group of Guatemalan rebels in neighboring Honduras and Nicaragua. The rebels invaded in 1954; CIA-piloted planes assisted by bombing Guatemala City and other locations, and the Guatemalan army joined the invaders. Arbenz was driven from power and military-elite rule was reimposed. The new rulers canceled land reform and dispossessed the peasants, while Communists were jailed and murdered. Some leftists took to the hills and began a small guerrilla movement. Violence plagued Guatemala intermittently over the next decades.

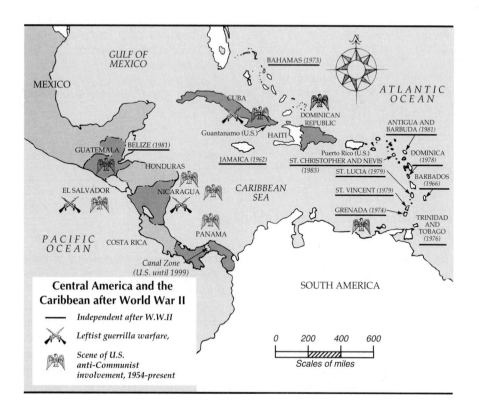

Central America and the Caribbean after World War II

—— *Independent after W.W.II*

✕ *Leftist guerrilla warfare,*

𓅯 *Scene of U.S. anti-Communist involvement, 1954-present*

Scales of miles
0   200   400   600

The Making of a Revolutionary Leader

I had been a political illiterate when I entered the university [of Havana]. As the son of a landowner, . . . I had brought nothing more than a rebellious temperament and the uprightness . . . they had inculcated into me in the Jesuit school. . . . [M]y first questionings of an economic and social kind arose when I was a student at the university, studying political economy and capitalist economics. . . . How could there exist overproduction of some goods, causing unemployment and hunger? . . . [Some concepts of Marx, Engels, and Lenin] seemed to me truly unquestionable: for example, the idea that society is divided into classes with antagonistic and irreconcilable interests. . . . [Such] intellectual interests inclined me more and more towards political struggle. . . . [B]efore the tenth of March [Batista's overthrow of the Cuban republic in 1952 and imposition of a dictatorship] I had been thinking of legal means, of using the Parliament as a point of departure from which I might establish a revolutionary platform and motivate the masses. . . .

When the coup d'etat . . . took place, everything changed radically.

. . . [W]hen none of [the established political] leaders showed they had either the ability or the realization of the seriousness of purpose or the way to overthrow Batista, . . . I finally worked out a strategy of my own.*

——— ◆◆◆◆ ———

In the passage above Fidel Castro, interviewed in 1965, reflects on his path to leadership of the revolutionary movement in Cuba. When Batista seized power in Cuba, twenty-five-year-old Fidel Castro, just two years out of law school, was one of many young radicals who were active in politics. After the takeover, Castro presented a brief to the Court of Appeals in which he demanded 100 years imprisonment for Batista for destroying the republic. After his brief was dismissed, he turned to insurrection. When the radicals led by Castro finally triumphed in 1959, they proceeded to bring about a social revolution along Marxist lines, but they created a political dictatorship instead of restoring the republic, with Castro still in power going into the 1990s.

*From *Castro's Cuba, Cuba's Fidel* by Lee Lockwood. Copyright © 1986 by the MIT Press. Used with permission.

Cuba: Marxist Social Change during a Cold War Struggle

In Cuba, despite Cold War harassment, Marxist revolutionaries brought about a thoroughgoing social transformation. In the 1950s under Batista, Cuba had been one of the more prosperous nations in Latin America. Cubans, especially in the cities, enjoyed—by Latin American standards—a high per capita income, high literacy and low death rates, and better-than-average life expectancy. Still, the per capita income of Cubans was one-sixth that of the United States. In the rural areas, where a few Cuban families and foreign businesses owned most of the land, many *campesinos* lived in poverty. U.S. investors owned 40 percent of the sugar crop and controlled sugar refining, mining, communications, and tourism.

In 1959 Castro came to power and began to transform Cuban society. The international confrontation that resulted has already been discussed, and while it was developing Castro continued his social revolution. Landholding was restricted to a maximum of 165 acres, and all holdings in excess of that were expropriated, a move that brought three-quarters of all the land in Cuba under government control. Most of the land was not redistributed to the peasants but held in large national cooperatives owned in theory by all Cubans and on which all rural Cubans found work. Former landowners, U.S. and Cuban, were offered limited compensation in the form of bonds. The Castro regime stressed the dignity of farm labor and discouraged migration to the cities.

Castro at first tried to diversify the economy, but his programs failed. By the 1970s the Cuban government had again begun to stress the importance of sugar production, but Castro failed to raise per capita sugar production above that of the 1950s. The United States and most OAS members refused to trade with Cuba, hampering Cuban economic growth. Loss of the U.S. sugar market forced Castro to sell sugar to the Communist bloc and anywhere else he could find buyers. Sugar prices fluctuated markedly, falling to a low level in the late 1970s but recovering somewhat in the 1980s.

In the meantime, Castro's government gave Cuba the most complete array of social services in Latin America. Cubans were provided with free medical care, and malnutrition was eliminated. Life expectancy rose to seventy years, the highest in Latin America, and close to that in the United States. The regime provided Cubans with free education and employed young Cubans to teach their illiterate elders to read and write. In 1980 the literacy rate stood at 94 percent, one

Latin revolutionaries Castro (center left) and Che Guevara (center right) review a parade.
(UPI/Bettmann Newsphotos)

of the highest in Latin America. The government constructed public housing projects, schools, and nurseries and inaugurated a complete pension plan. The new social programs were too expensive for a poor nation to afford, however, and the Soviet Union had to sustain them through massive infusions of aid.

Politically, Castro turned Cuba into a Communist totalitarian state. The government was altered several times over the years, with Castro's grip on power becoming ever tighter. Although his regime encouraged Cubans to participate in politics and instituted voting for a national assembly, the real power rested with the small, reorganized Communist party controlled by Castro and a small group of military leaders. The government molded the media and the education system into propaganda props for the state and encouraged Cubans to spy on one another. Castro banned opposition groups and expressions of criticism, and thousands languished in jails as political prisoners, although there were few executions after the initial purge. Approximately 700,000 Cubans, mostly from the middle and upper classes, representing about 8 percent of the population, fled the nation after 1959, disillusioned with life under Castro. Nevertheless, most Cubans apparently believed that Castro was interested in their welfare, and, despite shortages and other economic problems brought on by the boycott and the mistakes of the government, gave at least lukewarm support to the regime.

Besides appreciating the social benefits of Castro's regime, most Cubans, Marxist and non-Marxist alike, supported Castro in his roaring attacks on the Colossus of the North. He declared, for example, that "If there ever was in the history of humanity an enemy who was truly universal, an enemy whose acts and moves trouble the entire world, threaten the entire world, attack the entire world in any way or another, that real and really universal enemy is Yankee imperialism." Such denunciations engendered enthusiastic approval and made Castro popular throughout Latin America.

Castroism outside Cuba

While Castro was building a Marxist state in Cuba, his promise to export revolution caused enormous concern throughout Latin America. As the United States headed toward confrontation with the Soviet Union over Cuba in 1960–1962, it demanded support for its policy of isolating Cuba. This put most Latin American nations in a painful dilemma. Traditionally, most Latin American nations were hostile to U.S. pressure, but the conservative regimes in power in most of these nations were terrified of Castro-induced social revolution. Finally, most members of the Organization of American States reluctantly agreed to invoke economic sanctions against Cuba and to cut off diplomatic relations. Mexico, proud of its revolutionary tradition and of its independence from the United States, refused to go along, and Venezuela agreed only to limited measures.

During the 1960s Castro followed through on his announced intention to spread Marxist revolution to the rest of Latin America. Cuban guerrilla warfare experts went to Central America, Colombia, Bolivia, Venezuela, and Peru to encourage peasants to rise against their governments. Ernesto "Che" Guevara, a heroic symbol of Marxist revolution to radicals around the world, went to Bolivia in 1966 to revive the armed bands that had controlled Bolivia in the 1950s. The United States countered with military aid and advisors to the Bolivian government.

In the Dominican Republic, next door to Cuba, the United States went further. Fearing that Castro supporters were involved in political unrest there, President Johnson sent in U.S. troops in 1965, the first direct U.S. armed intervention in thirty years and a violation of the charter of the OAS. As it turned out, there was little Communist activity in the Dominican Republic, and a great hue and cry in opposition to U.S. intervention broke out both in the United States and throughout Latin America. The Johnson administration saved face by persuading the OAS to set up an international peacekeeping force headed by a Brazilian general; a year later, all foreign troops left the Dominican Republic.

In addition to military assistance and armed intervention, the United States also attempted to combat the turn toward communism in Latin America through the selective granting of economic aid. The Eisenhower and Kennedy administrations realized that impoverished Latin Americans might find communism attractive. They concluded that economic aid would be effective in forestalling communism only if it was used as a prod to Latin American governments to institute effective economic, social, and political reforms. The Eisenhower administration established the Inter-American Development Bank, which linked economic assistance to reforms. The Kennedy administration created the much-heralded Alliance for Progress, a ten-year plan with an initial funding of $1 billion. To receive this money, Latin American nations were to demonstrate progress in creating democratic institutions, improving health and education, and redistributing income.

The Alliance demanded too much from most Latin American regimes. Members of the upper and middle classes were generally not willing to make the sacrifices required, fearing that if significant reforms were undertaken to satisfy the United States, the lower classes would take over. Instead, Latin American governments, stressing the threat of Communist subversion, diverted the money to military buildups to combat real or potential guerrillas. By the early 1970s the Alliance was dead.

Castro's hopes for the triumph of Marxism through guerrilla warfare fizzled during the 1960s. American military aid and the lack of interest among the peasants led to the collapse of Castroite guerrilla movements in the countryside. Guevara was betrayed and shot in Bolivia in 1967. Castroites turned to terrorism in the cities, primarily in Brazil, Uruguay, and Argentina, committing kidnappings, robberies, bombings, and assassinations. Eventually, military forces also crushed these urban guerrillas. By the early 1970s it appeared that Cuban-inspired revolutionary forces had ceased to be a significant factor in Latin America.

No longer fearing Cuba, some Latin American nations began to drop their anti-Cuban stances and resumed diplomatic and trade relations with Cuba.

The U.S. government also lessened its hostile stance. It lifted passport restrictions and allowed limited U.S. tourism to Cuba. Americans and Cubans ranging from baseball teams to birdwatchers became the beneficiaries of the improved international climate. For a period in the mid-1970s, complete normalization of relations appeared to be at hand.

SUMMARY

After World War II, the United States enjoyed economic prosperity, and many went on a "buying spree" for a wide range of consumer goods. In the 1950s the nation was not interested in extensive political change, but by the mid-1960s the Johnson administration had embarked on its Great Society program, which greatly diminished poverty and expanded the welfare state. During this period, African Americans struggled for their civil rights, and by the mid-1960s had made substantial gains in eliminating segregated facilities and barriers to voting. At the same time, Supreme Court rulings curtailed government controls over the civil liberties of individuals.

Social problems arose in the United States as opposition to the Indochina war grew steadily and as militant African Americans rioted in the cities for improved economic and social conditions. Other minorities and some women began to apply pressure for an end to discriminatory practices. Environmental concerns mounted. Some young people protested against social injustices by peaceful means, but others resorted to violence and still others became hippie dropouts.

In many respects, Latin America after World War II was unchanged from earlier generations. Agriculture remained the dominant aspect of the economy, but many nations tried to diversify by supporting industrialization projects. Population increases swallowed up most economic gains, and Latin American cities grew so rapidly that they were beset by a number of social problems. The United States continued to dominate the region economically and resumed its interventions when Cold War interests dictated.

The region also experienced substantial changes. Its nations became more nationalistic, anxious to remove foreign economic controls and to steer an independent course in international relations. Some nations, even conservative ones, created extensive government controls over key elements in the economy. Perhaps the greatest change in Latin America was the movement in several nations toward ending the traditional two-culture society of the elite few and the impoverished masses. While the upper classes in many nations tried to repress the movements for social and economic change, some nations made efforts to provide social services, employment, and land. Change came sometimes from the right, as in Argentina; sometimes from the left, as in Guatemala. In Cuba, Castro created a new Marxist society, but his attempts to bring Marxist regimes to power elsewhere in Latin America were defeated. Acting from Cold War motives, the United States intervened in various ways throughout the Caribbean.

SUGGESTED SOURCES

BLUM, JOHN MORTON, *Years of Discord: American Politics and Society, 1961–1974* (1991). Readable history of the Kennedy, Johnson, and Nixon years.*

BREMNER, ROBERT H., and GARY W. REICHARD, Eds., *Reshaping America: Society and Institutions, 1945–1960* (1982). Historians' essays on social history topics, such as rural and urban life, women and families, business and labor, and crime and education.

CHAFE, WILLIAM H., *The Unfinished Journey: America Since World War II*, 2d ed. (1991). An outstanding one-volume history, notable for its lively style and its strong interpretive dimension.

DIGGINS, JOHN PATRICK, *The Proud Decades: American War and Peace, 1841–1960* (1988). A survey that treats social and intellectual history as well as politics and foreign policy.*

Evita (1979). A Broadway musical that gives a relatively realistic picture of the life and times of the Argentine cult figure Eva Perón.

GARCÍA MÁRQUEZ, GABRIEL, *One Hundred Years of Solitude* (1971). A novel giving an impressionistic view of life in Latin America.*

GOODSELL, JAMES NELSON, Ed., *Fidel Castro's Personal Revolution in Cuba, 1959–1973* (1975). A helpful introduction to the political, economic, cultural, and international aspects of Fidelismo.*

HAMBY, ALONZO L., *Liberalism and Its Challengers: F.D.R. to Bush*, 2d ed. (1991). Essays on leading political figures, covering most postwar presidents but also including Martin Luther King, Jr., and Robert F. Kennedy.

SKIDMORE, THOMAS E., and PETER H. SMITH, *Modern Latin America*, 3d ed. (1992). A concise and readable survey that provides the background for a better understanding of Latin American affairs.*

*Paperback available.

CHAPTER 24

Asia in the Aftermath of World War II

Besides its legacy of destruction and death, World War II also inspired many Asians to demand social reforms and freedom from outside controls. During its early phase, the triumphant Japanese army and navy had evicted every European colonial power from every colony in Asia east of India. The Japanese had tried to rally local popular support with the cry, "Asia for the Asians." Although the Japanese turned out to be harsher and more arrogant rulers than the Europeans, Asians were nevertheless in no mood for compliant acceptance of the return of European colonialism once the Japanese had been defeated.

World War II had also drastically altered the power equation in Asia. Japan, which had dominated East Asia for almost half a century, lay prostrate in 1945, its military and economy in ruins and its home islands under foreign military occupation for the first time in history. China, Japan's main target and victim, emerged a victor in the war, its international status enhanced. It had gained equality among nations after a century of unequal treaties and now stood as one of the Big Five victorious powers, a founding member of the United Nations and a permanent member of the Security Council. The United States hoped in 1945 that a friendly, strong, and united China under a KMT government would become the anchor of postwar Asia. However, the war had mortally weakened the Nationalist government, at the same time giving a new lease on life and unprecedented opportunities to the CCP.

The Soviet Union, which had entered the war against Japan at its very end, reaped many benefits as a victor. With a Communist government installed in North Korea by Soviet occupation troops and its Chinese Communist allies victorious in China in 1949, the Communist movement seemed poised to make new gains, and indigenous Communist parties in several Asian nations took heart. Threatened with the further spread of communism in Asia, a worried United States sought countermeasures. Asia thus became a key theater of the Cold War.

THE UNITED STATES REMAKES JAPAN

The Making of a Democratic Japan

The story of postwar Japan was that of the phoenix rising from its ashes, re-born and significantly changed. Wartime agreements between Allied powers stipulated that Japan be stripped of its conquests since 1895, which the emper-or's unconditional surrender implicitly accepted. Crushed in war, Japan in September 1945 was open to change to a degree that was unique in history. On the basis of its recent past, it had the potential to follow either a democratic or a totalitarian path, but U.S. occupation directed its political and social restruc-turing along democratic lines. By denying the Soviet Union a role in the occu-pation of Japan, the United States ensured that postwar Japan would follow a Western orientation.

The catalyst that sent Japan along the road to recovery and prosperity was the seven-year U.S. occupation of the islands. What happened to Japan after the war differed significantly from what happened to Germany. Unlike Ger-many, Japan was occupied by the United States rather than by forces from sev-eral nations. Although General Douglas MacArthur was Supreme Comman-der for the Allied Powers (SCAP), in reality he took orders only from the government of the United States. Unlike Germany, Japan was not directly gov-erned by the occupation forces; rather, it retained its emperor and its govern-ment, which was closely supervised by SCAP.

After their decisive defeat, most Japanese had no wish to return to their imperialist past. With their former sense of national mission shattered, they proved amenable to change and were cooperative with the occupiers whom they found surprisingly benevolent. With the Cold War spreading rapidly from Europe to Asia, the United States had an added impetus to rebuild Japan economically and to restructure its government along parliamentary and de-mocratic lines. It rightly assumed that a prosperous and democratically gov-erned Japanese people would not find communism attractive and would be less likely to disturb world peace again.

The immediate task for the U.S. occupation authorities was to help feed a large population that included 6 million repatriated soldiers and colonial per-sonnel. U.S. food aid prevented starvation until the Japanese could rebuild their shattered economy. The next task was to create a new political structure based on a new constitution. The emperor was retained as a stabilizing force but was stripped of his formerly divine status, which he renounced on January 1, 1946, in the Declaration of Humanity. In addition to a small number of lead-ers who were tried and punished for war crimes at the Tokyo International Court (similar to the Nuremberg trials for Nazi war criminals), about 200,000 former military officers, officials, and industrialists were forbidden to hold of-fice or continue in business. The removal of the old guard allowed older Japanese politicians who had opposed the militarists and eventually a young generation of Japanese to rise to power.

General MacArthur closely supervised the writing of the new constitution, which was promulgated in 1947, accompanied by a Bill of Rights. These documents contained elements from the Declaration of Independence, the U.S. Constitution, the Gettysburg Address, and the British parliamentary system. The constitution proclaimed the Japanese people sovereign, enfranchised women, and provided a bicameral legislature (National Diet), with members of both chambers elected by universal suffrage. The executive was made directly responsible to the Diet, and the judiciary was independent of the executive. The constitution renounced war and the right of belligerency forever and declared that "land, sea, and air forces, as well as other war potential, will never be maintained." This provision made the Japanese constitution unique among constitutions.

These reforms brought about changes in attitudes which shaped Japan for decades. On April 11, 1951, the Japanese were greatly shocked when President Truman dismissed General MacArthur in a dispute over the conduct of the Korean War. This event served as an important object lesson in democracy—that a message from a civilian leader could bring down a great and revered military proconsul who had seemed all-powerful, an event that would have been undreamed of in prewar Japan.

In the early 1950s Japan moved quickly toward independence. The United States had always assumed that it would occupy Japan for only a limited time. A Communist victory in China in 1949 and the outbreak of the Korean War in 1950 emphasized Japan's importance as an anti-Communist bastion and led the United States to end the occupation quickly so that Japan could take its place among the democratic nations of the world. In 1951 Japan and forty-eight victor nations of World War II signed a peace treaty in San Francisco. The Communist bloc nations refused to sign, and neither of the Chinese governments was included because each claimed to represent all of China. A separate treaty was soon signed between Nationalist China and Japan.

The occupation of Japan ended in 1952. The United States retained bases there and forbade Japan to grant military bases to any other power without its consent under the terms of a Mutual Security Treaty signed one day after the concluding of the Treaty of San Francisco. This treaty, which effectively made Japan a U.S. military protectorate, was as much the result of U.S. policy as that of Japan under Prime Minister Yoshida Shigeru. Yoshida, like most Japanese, welcomed the security provided by the U.S. nuclear umbrella in the Cold War. With U.S. protection, Japan did not need to change its constitution to allow it to spend large sums of money to ensure national security and could concentrate its resources on economic recovery. A small military, named the Land, Sea, and Air Self-Defense Force, well trained and equipped, was organized with encouragement from the United States but was sufficient only to defend Japan for one week under foreign attack until reinforcements from the United States could arrive. This force could not be deployed outside Japan or its waters. Until the late 1980s Japan never spent over 1 percent of its GNP on defense.

Just as Adenauer guided West Germany toward recovery and rehabilitation in postwar years, Yoshida Shigeru did the same for Japan during the decade between 1945 and 1955, called the "Yoshida Years." Yoshida served as a diplomat before World War II but opposed the imperialistic policies of the military, for which he suffered brief imprisonment. A staunch anti-Communist and a conservative, he worked well with SCAP to rebuild a new Japan, concentrating on economic recovery and efficient government. When SCAP restored free elections, the two major conservative parties of the prewar era emerged under new names as the Liberal party and Democratic party. Yoshida headed the Liberal party as prime minister. When various left-wing parties merged to form the Socialist party in 1955, the two conservative parties did the same thing, forming the Liberal Democratic party, which held power in Japan throughout the postwar period, relegating the Socialist party to the status of a permanent and ineffective opposition. The persistent domination of the Liberal Democratic party had led some to call the recent Japanese political system the "one-and-a-half party" system.

Laying the Foundations of Economic Recovery

Between 1947 and 1952 the United States gave Japan $2 billion in economic aid. It also instituted economic and social changes designed to promote economic equity among Japanese and to make the Japanese economy sound and viable. In a sweeping land reform program, SCAP sanctioned a drastic rent reduction, set a limit on land ownership, and sold excess holdings of landlords at a low price to existing tenants. Over a million families benefited from these sweeping but peacefully accomplished reforms.

Equally fundamental was the breakup of the *zaibatsu*. Ten family-owned holding companies and dozens of industrial and trading companies were dissolved and their stocks were sold to the public. The Diet passed laws modeled on U.S. antitrust legislation, established a Fair Trade Commission to police business practices, and abolished laws restricting the labor movement and trade unions.

Japan's economic miracle was partly the result of its excellent educational system. SCAP made fundamental changes in that system, first by ordering the Diet to extend compulsory education from six to nine years (later expanded to twelve). The Diet also changed the content of education, emphasizing democratic principles. Girls were given more educational and career opportunities, and all young people were given more chances for higher education.

U.S. military procurement orders during the Korean War helped send Japan on the road to economic recovery. Per capita income rose from $146 in 1951 to $395 in 1960; during the same decade, the GNP increased at an average annual rate of close to 9 percent. Japan's steady economic growth was helped by newly installed plants and equipment, a cooperative attitude between workers and government, government encouragement of business, and a determined work ethic. Since prosperity depended on its ability to export, the Japanese government supported an open and expanding world trading order. Japan agreed to pay reparations to several newly independent nations in Southeast Asia for World War II damages, which facilitated resumption of trade.

Japanese schools are strict and maintain high academic standards. Students in this class are attentive and well prepared.
(Michael Heron/Woodfin Camp & Associates)

Japan was the first Asian nation to bring population growth under control. Peace and better medical care brought about a baby boom in the immediate postwar years; between 1945 and 1950, the population increased 15.6 percent, from 72 to 83 million. In 1948, prodded by SCAP, the government legalized abortion for economic and medical reasons under the Eugenics Protection Law. As a result of the law and changing social mores, population growth tapered off, in a demographic revolution that only took a decade to accomplish. A low population growth rate enabled the Japanese to enjoy a rapid rise in standard of living.

THE TRIUMPH OF COMMUNISM IN CHINA

Eight years of war against Japan had devastated China. Seven million Chinese soldiers and civilians had perished, and 50 million people had moved into the interior. Chinese authorities in 1945 were faced with a shattered economy, galloping inflation, and millions of refugees awaiting resettlement.

As a result of these conditions, the KMT government was beset by troubles. War had destroyed its modern base in the coastal areas. Driven inland, it was forced to rely on the local conservative gentry for support, and as a result the government was unable to make needed reforms and became more conser-

vative. Wartime conditions and the overwhelming needs of the military reinforced existing tendencies toward authoritarianism and militarism, costing the
KMT support among the people, especially students and intellectuals.

While the situation for the KMT was deteriorating, the CCP was gaining
strength. During the Sino-Japanese War of 1937–1945, the CCP took advantage
of the widespread patriotic movement in Japanese-occupied areas and used its
expertise in guerrilla warfare to organize and control the resistance forces in
much of the nominally Japanese-occupied countryside. As Mao Tse-tung said
about guerrilla war, "The people are the water, the soldiers are the fish"; that
is, a successful war of resistance needed popular support. Whereas the CCP
had about 40,000 party members and 30,000 troops in 1937, at the end of the
war it claimed 1.2 million party members and over 80 million people, mostly
in northern China, under its control, plus a military force consisting of almost
1 million regulars and 2 million militiamen. These spectacular gains proved
Chiang Kai-shek right when he said during the darkest days of the war
against Japan that whereas the Japanese were a disease of the skin, the Communists were a disease of the heart threatening his government.

Communist Victory in the Civil War

The removal of the Japanese once again brought the competition for power between the KMT and the CCP to the forefront, and civil war erupted over control
of Japanese-occupied areas. The United States, which had become deeply involved in China during the war, was committed to a role in shaping postwar
Chinese politics. Initially, the United States aided the KMT by airlifting its troops
from south and west China to the major population centers in the north so that it
could take control before the CCP moved in from the northern countryside.

When the U.S. government later recognized how strong the Communists
were, it attempted to mediate a solution to the KMT-CCP conflict. Conditioned
by its own political tradition, however, it visualized the two parties in China
as similar to the two political parties in the United States and asked the two
sides to give up their independent armies and come together in a coalition
government. General George Marshall, with his great prestige as the architect
of Allied victory in Europe, was sent to China in December 1945 to mediate a
reconciliation between the two Chinese groups. However, neither party trusted the other, and neither would give up its hope of eventual total control. Marshall's mission ended in failure, and the United States stopped supporting the
Nationalist government.

In 1949 the CCP won the civil war, and the KMT government and part of
its military forces fled to the island of Taiwan. Many factors—military, economic, political, and psychological—contributed to this outcome. Militarily,
the KMT army, with about 3 million men in 1946, opposed approximately 1
million CCP soldiers and 2 million militiamen, but in taking over all areas formerly under Japanese occupation it had become overextended. Its strategic
doctrine was to hold cities and other strongly fortified positions. Conversely,
the CCP army resorted to guerrilla tactics, destroyed railroads, controlled the

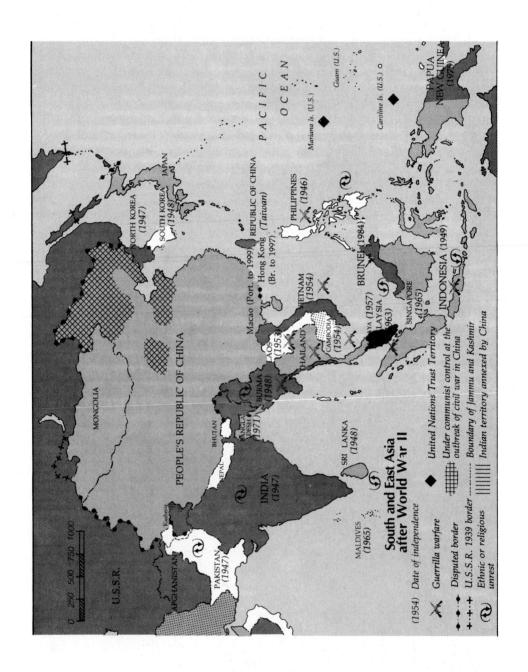

South and East Asia after World War II

(1954) Date of independence

◆ United Nations Trust Territory

▨▨▨ Under communist control at the outbreak of civil war in China

✕ Guerrilla warfare

◆ Disputed border

•–•–• U.S.S.R. 1939 border

----- Boundary of Jammu and Kashmir

|||||| Indian territory annexed by China

↻ Ethnic or religious unrest

U.S.S.R.

0 250 500 750 1000

MONGOLIA

PEOPLE'S REPUBLIC OF CHINA

NORTH KOREA (1947)

SOUTH KOREA (1948)

JAPAN

AFGHANISTAN

PAKISTAN (1947)

Kashmir

NEPAL

BHUTAN

BANGLA DESH (1971)

INDIA (1947)

BURMA (1948)

LAOS (1953)

THAILAND

CAMBODIA (1954)

VIETNAM (1954)

Macao (Port. to 1999)

Hong Kong (Br. to 1997)

REPUBLIC OF CHINA (Taiwan)

PHILIPPINES (1946)

MALAYA (1957)

MALAYSIA (1963)

SINGAPORE (1965)

BRUNEI (1984)

INDONESIA (1949)

SRI LANKA (1948)

MALDIVES (1965)

PACIFIC OCEAN

Mariana Is. (U.S.)

Guam (U.S.)

Caroline Is. (U.S.)

PAPUA NEW GUINEA (1975)

countryside, and avoided battle unless on terms favorable to itself. It put into practice Mao's dictum: "The enemy advances, we retreat; the enemy camps, we harass; the enemy tires, we attack; the enemy retreats, we pursue." The results were brilliant. The isolated KMT units, which also often suffered from corruption and poor command, either surrendered or were cut to pieces. Communist spies also infiltrated the KMT military command, leaking vital information to the CCP and contributing to its success.

The military debacle was partly caused by the collapse of the KMT government. Eight years of anti-Japanese war had taken a heavy toll. The loss or destruction of its economic base had forced the KMT to wage war against Japan by printing more and more paper money; at the end of the war, the volume of notes issued was 465 times that at the war's outbreak. After 1946 the need to finance a civil war led to continued deficit spending and runaway inflation that especially impoverished the urban middle class and caused chaos, corruption, and loss of confidence in the government. When the currency collapsed in late 1948, so did the remaining civilian support for the Nationalist cause.

On the other hand, the Communist cause exemplified strict military discipline, high morale, and coherent leadership. Although the CCP had carried out only moderate land reforms in areas it controlled during the war, it reverted to violent land reform tactics in its areas at the war's end and promised similar drastic programs for all of China. The poor and dispossessed backed the Communists because of this promise, and many students and intellectuals gradually came to support them, or at least withdrew support from the KMT.

The international situation, including, ironically, U.S. aid, also helped the CCP. To prevent Mao from taking over China, the United States sent over $2 billion in aid to prop up the KMT government. While U.S. arms equipped the KMT army, the U.S.-style reorganization of the army only furthered confusion and rivalry between units under different commands. When the United States withdrew support in 1948, it contributed to the rapid demoralization of the KMT government and sped its collapse.

The Soviet Union also contributed to the CCP triumph. During World War II, Stalin, after extracting concessions favorable to the U.S.S.R., recognized the KMT as the only legal government of China and promised to refrain from sending aid to the CCP. Stalin's low regard for the CCP was exemplified by his wartime characterization of the Chinese Communists as "margarine" (not the genuine article) or "radish" (red outside, white inside) Communists. Nevertheless, Stalin helped the CCP by timing Soviet withdrawal from Manchuria to ensure that the CCP captured all surrendered Japanese arms, by providing sanctuary to CCP units in North Korea and the U.S.S.R., and by rallying international support to the CCP cause.

On October 1, 1949, standing atop the Gate of Heavenly Peace in Peking, Mao Zedong[1] proclaimed the establishment of the People's Republic of China

---

[1]Hereafter in the text, the spelling of Chinese names will follow the pinyin system, adopted by the People's Rupublic of China, and the Wade-Giles system for Taiwan, in accordance with each government's convention.

(hereafter, China). China was immediately recognized by the Soviet Union and other Communist nations. Early in 1950 India and several other nations in Asia and Europe followed suit. Among the major Western powers, only Great Britain, concerned for its huge investments in China and the safety of its Hong Kong colony, extended recognition.

Although minor political parties acceptable to the CCP were allowed to exist, the People's Republic was a totalitarian state that carried out policies set by the Communist party. Nationwide mass organizations controlled by the Communist party, such as the All-China Federation of Trade Unions, paralleled the structure of the party and the government. Because everyone belonged to a union or mass organization, the government was able to reach and control all citizens in their professional or social roles.

China Fails to Modernize

Mao Zedong sought to reshape the thinking and behavior of everyone so that he could create a new society of "collective man." To do this, he initiated campaigns to abolish old loyalties and patterns of thought and to instill new values and obedience to the state. New marriage and divorce laws were enacted to eliminate the old patriarchal family and give women equality. The government required its citizens to attend frequent meetings to learn Marxist ideology and the party lines, and to criticize themselves and each other. To keep China on the "correct course" and to emphasize the importance of being "Red" rather than "expert," people were forced to attend frequent meetings

Mao Zedong reviews parade at Square of Heavenly Peace in Peking, celebrating the fourteenth anniversary of Communist victory in 1963. (*NCNA/Camera Press*)

where they studied Mao's thoughts and memorized his sayings, which they repeated on all occasions, for example, "All reactionaries are paper tigers." Children sang songs such as "The East is Red" in praise of Mao, rather than nursery rhymes, and at nursery schools the first words they learned to write were Mao's name. The government also used force to ensure obedience. It declared whole classes of people enemies of the revolution and between 1951 and 1953 exterminated or jailed millions of "landlords" and redistributed their land. The social and economic influence of the gentry-landlord class was totally destroyed. As in the Soviet Union, culture and the arts were strictly controlled. For example, the socialist realism style that showed heroic workers and happy collective farmers was approved in painting, while other styles were denounced as decadent.

In economic development, the party emphasized rapid modernization through Soviet-style planning and received massive technological assistance from the Soviet Union. The First Five-Year Plan (1953–1957) stressed building up heavy industry and collectivizing agriculture, but despite rapid progress in the first five years, vast problems remained. This led Mao, who believed that humans were the "decisive force in history," to ignore objective economic realities and instead of following the realistic goals of the Second Five-Year Plan, to embark in 1958 on a crash program called the Great Leap Forward. It involved the mass mobilization of labor, the establishment of communes, and the building of backyard furnaces to smelt iron, measures all pushed forward amidst an atmosphere of ideological frenzy.

Instead of instant development, the Great Leap Forward brought nothing but disaster. Most early statistics on initial gains made under the Great Leap were either wildly exaggerated or faked. Figures show that about 600,000 backyard furnaces were built, but the iron they produced was of such low quality that it was almost useless. By 1959 the economy had been crippled by the follies of the Great Leap, and the people were exhausted and demoralized. Bad weather exacerbated the man-made disaster, and starvation stalked the land. Economists estimate that the Great Leap caused a loss of $66 billion to the economy; demographers calculate that 26 plus million people died as a result of the mostly Mao-made famine. When the Central Committee of the CCP met in 1959, even Mao had to admit the magnitude of the disaster facing China. Many of his senior associates were disillusioned with the way he had run the country and eased him out of direct control of the party and the government, although he retained the title of Chairman of the Communist party. They preferred a pragmatic approach to China's problems, and they had their way between 1959 and 1966, as they repaired the damage that his policies had inflicted and began rebuilding again (see Chapter 30).

Alliance with the Soviet Union

China's foreign policy was based upon several factors. Still a weak nation and barely on its feet in 1949, China at first derived strength from its close ties with the Soviet Union. It needed both economic aid and protection from the Soviet

Union to forestall possible Western intervention, as had happened in Russia after the Bolshevik Revolution. To secure this, Mao went to Moscow in 1950, his first trip abroad. He paid obsequious tribute to Stalin in such statements as the following:

> Everyone knows that Comrade Stalin had an ardent love for the Chinese people and believed the might of the Chinese revolution to be immeasurable. To the problems of the Chinese revolution he contributed his sublime wisdom. And it was following the theories of Lenin and Stalin and with the support of the Soviet Union . . . that the Chinese Communist Party . . . won its historic victory.

As a result of the trip, a Sino-Soviet Treaty of Friendship and Alliance was signed in 1950, in which Stalin granted Mao a military alliance, provided credit, and promised tens of thousands of Soviet military and civilian experts to help China modernize its armed forces and industries. During the next decade, the Soviet Union, at a time when it had barely recovered from the devastations of World War II, transferred massive amounts of technology to China. It also returned to China the equipment it had looted from Manchuria at the end of World War II. Thousands of Chinese students went to study in the Soviet Union, which replaced Western nations as China's source of modern knowledge. Russian replaced English as the mandatory second language in schools and universities.

Understandably, in the light of China's century-long history of humiliation by Western and Japanese imperialism, the new government sought recognition as a great power. Mao proclaimed that in international affairs China would "lean to one side," that is, the Marxist side, in the Cold War. The Soviet Union surrendered its remaining privileges in China and accorded it the position of associate leader in the international Communist movement. In 1957 it promised to assist China in its nuclear development. For its part, China orchestrated its foreign policy to aid the international Communist movement, and in so doing enhanced its drive for leadership in Asia and major power status in world affairs. For example, in sending a million "volunteers" to aid North Korea in the Korean War and in assisting North Vietnam's struggles, China not only furthered the Communist cause in Asia but also reasserted its traditional role as the protector of the small states on its borders. In 1956 China mediated the disputes between the Soviet Union and its East European satellites, thus helping to maintain Soviet dominance in the socialist bloc while asserting its position as associate leader in the international Communist movement.

At the same time that it was strengthening its role in international Communist affairs, China sought to become the leader of all Asia and also of the Afro-Asian bloc of newly independent nations that was developing as former colonies became independent (see below and in succeeding chapters). Thus it championed the themes of coexistence and anti-Western imperialism. China won recognition as the leader of the Afro-Asian nations at the Bandung Conference held in Indonesia in 1955. Its successes became an inspiration to many underdeveloped nations.

The balance sheet of the first decade of the People's Republic showed considerable successes, not only in the domestic field (up to the Great Leap Forward) but also in world affairs, although at great human cost. China had not only thrown off the shackles of imperialist domination but was even reasserting its traditional role as the dominant power in its part of the world. In instituting the communes during the Great Leap Forward, it was attempting to put itself on a higher ideological plane than the Soviet Union and even gloated that it was ahead of the U.S.S.R. in its progress toward the Marxist utopia.

DECOLONIZATION IN ASIA

World War II ended not only Japan's dream of empire in Asia; the victorious Western nations discovered that they too had to divest their empires in the postwar era. Weakened by two world wars, the European colonial powers found that they could not hold back the rising tide of Asian nationalism, whether peacefully or violently expressed. Between 1946 and 1957 the people of every major colony in South and Southeast Asia became citizens of new nations. The United States led the way in 1946, granting full independence to the Philippines. Great Britain, however, demonstrated the full magnitude of the collapse of colonialism when in 1947 it departed from the most valuable possession of any colonial empire, the Indian subcontinent, leaving in its wake two new nations, India and Pakistan. One year later, it granted independence to Burma and Sri Lanka (Ceylon). In 1949 the Netherlands reluctantly left Indonesia rather than risk losing U.S. economic aid by trying to prolong a war of independence it could not win, and the French were driven from Indochina in 1954. In 1957 the British granted independence to Malaya, their last major colony in Asia, and combined it with several smaller neighboring British colonies to form the federation of Malaysia. This section will concentrate on events in India, Pakistan, and Indochina.

India's Continuing Struggle for Freedom

Since 1909, Great Britain had reluctantly but steadily granted ever-increasing measures of self-rule to India and Burma; this process led the way for the other nonwhite British possessions in Asia and Africa. Had World War II not occurred, India might have attained final independence before 1947. However, preoccupation with the war and the worsening relations between Hindus and Muslims during the war compelled Great Britain to postpone the final steps toward complete independence until the war was over.

Great Britain declared war against Nazi Germany in 1939 and against Japan in 1941, both on its own behalf and on behalf of India and its other possessions and dominions. While most Indian National Congress leaders supported British war aims against the Axis, they nevertheless objected to India's automatic entry into the war without prior consultation with Indian leaders. In protest, the eight Congress-controlled provincial governments resigned. The British government, maintaining that World War II was a life-and-death struggle, countered by taking control of the provinces and dissolving the India Act of 1935. Congress then began a new *Satyagraha* campaign throughout the land, for which the British arrested 1,400 Congress leaders including Gandhi and Nehru.

Muslim fear and dislike of Congress policies prompted Muslim League President Mohammed Ali Jinnah, called "Great Leader" by his followers, to declare the closing of Congress ministries in the eight provinces a "Day of Deliverance and Thanksgiving." The Muslim League and League-controlled provinces cooperated with the British administration throughout the war, fostering increased Muslim self-confidence and separate consciousness. Jinnah exemplified Muslim opinion when he said in a speech in 1940 at the annual meeting of the Muslim League:

> Hindus and Muslims belong to two different religious philosophies, social customs, literature. . . . To yoke together two such nations under a single state, one as a numerical minority and the other as a majority, must lead to growing discontent and final destruction of any fabric that may be so built up for the government of such a state. . . . The only course open to us all is to allow the major nations separate homelands for dividing India into "autonomous national states."

Following that speech, the League passed the "Pakistan Resolution," which called for a separate Muslim state. Pakistan, or the "Land of the Pure," was to consist of those areas of the Indian subcontinent where Muslims formed the majority of the population.

Most Indians actively aided Great Britain in fighting the Axis. Much more than during World War I, Indian troops fought in the Middle East, in Africa, and in Southeast Asia and defended India against a threatened Japanese invasion, acquitting themselves well. India formed part of the China-Burma-India war theater and was a vital link in the transport of U.S. Lend-Lease aid to China. Some Indians passively resisted the war effort, not so much out of pro-Axis feelings as out of frustration over India's political status. Some surrendered Indian troops fought on the Japanese side, a few Indians actively supported the Japanese, but they failed to gain a popular following.

A number of British missions came to India during the war years to offer concessions that would mollify the Congress. They suggested formulas for the transfer of more power to Indians during the war and also promised full independence immediately afterward. However, all British offers failed, either because of the Congress's intransigence on timing or because of the stumbling block of Muslim-Hindu communal hostility. The Congress now called on Britain immediately to "quit India"; the Muslim League responded by insisting that independence must result in the creation of two successor states, India and Pakistan. This was the deadlocked situation at the war's end.

Independence Comes to India and Pakistan

In July 1945, general elections in Great Britain brought the Labour party, which had never been sympathetic to imperialism, to power under Prime Minister

Clement Attlee. The new government declared its intention to grant independence to India immediately and appointed Lord Louis Mountbatten, a war hero and able diplomat, to accomplish that task. Even then, the final stages of British withdrawal were delayed by Hindu-Muslim antagonism. Communal riots in many parts of India took on the character of full-scale battles, and civil war threatened. Finally Gandhi and other Congress leaders agreed that it was preferable to let Muslims have a separate state formed by areas with a Muslim majority in the northwest and northeast of the subcontinent, rather than to engulf the whole land in civil war. Mountbatten appointed a Briton to head an impartial commission to draw up the boundaries, a very difficult task that pleased neither side. Indian princes, who had made separate treaties in the nineteenth century that put them under the protection of the British crown, were told that their states could join either India or Pakistan but could not become independent.

Compared to political transitions elsewhere in Asia, Indian nationalism triumphed with little bloodshed against the foreign ruler. At the stroke of midnight on August 14, 1947, India became a sovereign nation within the British Commonwealth of Nations. At the invitation of the Indian parliament and in gratitude for his efforts, Mountbatten stayed on for a year as governor-general (representative of the British sovereign) of India. At the same time, peoples of the predominantly Muslim northwest and northeast declared their independence as the new nation of Pakistan, also remaining a member of the Commonwealth.

Fearful of their fate in East and West Pakistan, Hindu minorities sought safety by crossing over into India, and many equally frightened Muslims from India fled into Pakistan. More than 15 million people took part in this massive human migration, with 9 million resettling in India and 6 million in Pakistan. Approximately 600,000 people died. Some were killed in riots and street battles in their towns and villages by members of the opposing religion; others died in attacks by hostile mobs as they were fleeing to their new nation; still others died of starvation or diseases during their grueling journeys. The disturbances immediately threatened to engulf the two new nations in war.

Gradually, the panic and frenzy diminished. Fifty million Muslims remained in India, and Prime Minister Nehru labored to ensure that they received protection. Similarly, Jinnah (who became governor-general of Pakistan) worked to protect the remaining 10 million Hindus in Pakistan. The wounds of partition never healed, however.

More heartsick than anyone over the carnage, Gandhi, the champion of nonviolence, undertook personal missions of peace to the disturbed cities and villages in India. He also began a fast for an end to communal hatred, which had a sobering effect on the violent mobs. On January 30, 1948, at a prayer meeting, he was assassinated by a Hindu extremist who believed that he had been too generous to the Muslims.

Prime Minister Nehru found the task of governing India an extremely difficult one, as indeed did the leaders of all newly independent nations, partly because most had had little prior experience in government and partly because of the many problems of nationhood. As one saying had it, before independence the British were blamed for everything that went wrong, even for too much or too little monsoon rain. No more. One problem was how to feed the inexorably growing population. Over 80 percent of Indians were rural, and most were desperately poor. With a high population density, primitive agricultural methods, and almost total dependence on monsoon rains, the land could not produce enough food for the population. Tragically, every improvement made in food production, sanitary facilities, and public health further boosted the population growth. In 1947 life expectancy for an Indian who survived infancy was thirty-two years; by 1969, it had reached fifty-two. Increased longevity put such a strain on Indian food resources that Nehru was led to remark, "India must run very fast just to stand still."

There was also the language problem. The 1950 constitution recognized sixteen official languages, including English, although there were many more. A government plan to make Hindi, a language common to northern India, the national language angered the majority of Indians who did not speak Hindi, and riots broke out. In retreat, the parliament passed a law, embarrassing to nationalist leaders, to retain English as the national language until the indefinite time when the non-Hindi-speaking peoples would accept Hindi; the matter remained unresolved.

Politically, Nehru and his Congress party favored democracy and believed the almost 600 princely states ruled autocratically by maharajas were anachronisms. After independence, all princely states were integrated, some by force, into seventeen states within the Indian federation, each with its own legislature. On the national level, the government was modeled after the British parliamentary system, with certain features of the U.S. congressional system added. The prime minister was India's political leader and presided over the Council of Ministers, or cabinet, which was chosen by the majority party in the parliament. India proudly counted itself as the most populous democracy in the world and living proof that democracy could thrive despite illiteracy and poverty. Because of high illiteracy, symbols such as the cow and plow were used on the Indian ballot to designate political parties.

Economically, the Congress governments encouraged industrial development as a solution to India's backwardness and abandoned the Gandhian ideal of traditional village handicrafts. To maximize development, Nehru and his successors opted for a "mixed economy," in which the government owned or controlled the basic industries but encouraged foreign investments and private enterprise. To develop industry, modernize agriculture, and stimulate trade, Nehru launched his first Five-Year Plan (1951–1956). Such plans were continued by successive governments. About 10 percent of the capital needed for these five-year plans came from foreign aid programs funded by the United States, the Soviet Union, other nations, and international agencies. Because of India's poverty and its importance to both sides in the Cold War, it became the largest single recipient of foreign aid in the post-World War II era. Between 1947 and 1980 India received over $9 billion in U.S. aid, and it became the tenth largest industrial power in the world.

The Indian government's main goal in its economic development program was to raise the pitifully low standard of living of the average Indian. The annual per capita income in 1951 was $53, and Indians had to spend up to 90 percent of their income on food, in contrast to U.S. citizens who spent 16 percent. The goal of improving the standard of living and literacy rate was constantly frustrated by the alarmingly fast growth of the population, which was in turn caused in part by illiteracy and poverty that perpetuated traditional values, including early marriages and a desire for many sons.

India chose a foreign policy of nonalignment with either power bloc in the Cold War. Its unwillingness to become a member of a bloc headed by the United States and Great Britain was a reaction to its colonial experience and an expression of its residual resentment against Great Britain, and by implication, its ally the United States. Nehru also hoped that India could become the leader of a bloc of neutral nations and could thereby mediate in disputes between the major powers. Nehru announced India's commitment to peace, which, however, did not prevent him from going to war against Pakistan or sending troops to evict the Portuguese from Goa, their colony on the Indian coast.

Pakistan was and remained India's primary concern. In addition to the bitterness created by the partition, India and Pakistan had problems over the distribution of water from the Indus River for irrigation. Kashmir, however, was the major bone of contention between the two nations. Both India and Pakistan claimed ownership of this area, which was a princely state with a population that was 80 percent Muslim. In 1947 India and Pakistan fought over Kashmir and continued to fight until the U.N. imposed a cease-fire in 1948, in effect partitioning Kashmir. A U.N. observer force remained there to monitor the cease-fire. Jinnah and his successors demanded a plebiscite, which Nehru and his successors rejected, since they feared that the Muslim majority would vote to join Kashmir with Pakistan. India and Pakistan fought again in 1965 over Kashmir but agreed to a cease-fire mediated by the Soviet Union, with no boundary changes.

Although Nehru encouraged good relations with Communist nations, he had no tolerance for native Communists and once remarked that India had more Communists in prison than any other nation. Nor was he successful in maintaining friendly relations with China. During the 1950s, Indians often professed in a slogan that "Indians and Chinese are brothers," but border disputes ended those good feelings when war broke out between the two nations in 1962. The Chinese soundly defeated the Indian army and occupied sections of disputed territory in the Himalayas. However, the Chinese did not press their advantage, withdrew from certain advanced positions, and called for negotiations. The border disputes were not settled, and Sino-Indian relations remained strained.

Pakistan after Independence

Most of the problems that plagued India also afflicted Pakistan, a wretchedly poor nation with primitive agricultural methods, little industry, many refugees, and one of the fastest growing populations in the world. Furthermore, Pakistan had an impossible geography. West Pakistan was located along the Indus valley, and East Pakistan was situated on the Ganges delta; the two were separated by almost 1,000 miles. From the beginning, the bizarre geopolitical structure of the state—two separate halves that had little in common except Islam—was the most serious threat to the survival of Pakistan. The capital city Islamabad was in West Pakistan, and West Pakistanis, who formed less than half of the total population, made up 70 percent of the civil service and 80 percent of the officer corps. Most of the foreign aid and export earnings went to develop industries and services in West Pakistan. Finally, West Pakistanis tended to regard the physically and linguistically different East Pakistanis as inferiors.

A year after independence, Jinnah, the father of Pakistan, died of cancer. In 1951, his successor, Liaquat Ali Khan, was assassinated. The deaths of these two leaders left Pakistan with a heritage of political instability. The military took control in 1958, dissolved the parliament, and instituted a system of modified and indirect elections that was termed "Basic Democracy." The military has controlled Pakistan for most of its life, with brief and generally chaotic interludes of elected civilian governments.

Pakistan's foreign policy was dictated by fear of its bigger neighbor, India; consequently, Pakistan maintained an inordinately large military establishment at a huge cost to ensure its safety. Since India had a neutralist foreign policy with a pro-Soviet leaning, Pakistan allied itself with the U.S.-led CENTO alliance and, after the war between India and China in 1962, maintained friendly relations with China.

The First Indochina War: France Is Forced out of Asia

Unlike Great Britain and the United States, France had done little to satisfy nationalistic aspirations in Indochina before World War II. Vichy France surrendered Indochina to Japanese occupation peacefully, but during World War II Nationalist China aided a broad spectrum of Indochinese nationalists who resisted Japan, among whom the Communists were the most effective. On Japan's surrender, the Communist Vietnamese leader Ho Chi Minh established his headquarters in Hanoi and declared the independence of all Indochina. France refused to accept Ho's claim, offered only limited reforms, and reoccupied Indochina. The nationalists totally rejected France's proposals, and war between the Indochinese and the French broke out in late 1945.

The struggle for independence centered in Vietnam. A pattern of French control in South Vietnam and Ho's control of the north soon emerged. Ho used his considerable influence as Vietnam's foremost nationalist leader to assimilate and dominate other Vietnamese nationalist movements. With his subordinate, General Vo Nguyen Giap, Ho perfected guerrilla warfare tactics to fight a war of attrition. They avoided open battles and concentrated on terrorist activities and sabotage. The French could not distinguish the peaceful citizen from the guerrilla fighter, who often worked at an ordinary job by day and took up arms at night. By 1954 French forces in Vietnam, including 200,000 Vietnamese soldiers plus Foreign Legionnaires, numbered 420,000. They confronted a Vietminh (short for The Vietnamese League for National Independence) army almost as large. For every Frenchman killed, perhaps ten Vietnamese on the opposing side died.

The climax of the war for independence came at the siege of Dien Bien Phu in 1954, in which 15,000 of France's best troops were hopelessly trapped in a strongly fortified strategic town by General Giap's forces, now heavily strengthened by arms from the Soviet Union and China. France appealed to the United States, which was already shouldering 80 percent of the cost of the war, to intervene with land and air forces. President Eisenhower, who had just extricated the United States from a deadlocked Korean War, refused to become involved. Without direct U.S. aid, Dien Bien Phu fell. By this time, the war-weary French public was ready to quit Vietnam and pressured its government to comply. France had already agreed to the independence of Laos and Cambodia and now departed from Vietnam.

THE PROBLEMS OF NEW NATIONHOOD IN SOUTHEAST ASIA

During the first decade of independence, the new nations of Southeast Asia faced similar problems of varying degrees of severity. A major problem for all was that their economies had been dislocated and devastated by World War II. The Philippines had suffered most from the fighting; only Warsaw was more war-damaged than Manila. Burma and Vietnam had also suffered from military campaigns. All the new nations needed outside economic assistance, but the source and amount of that aid were related to the foreign policies of the newly independent nations, in particular how they lined up in the Cold War. For example, the United States gave the Philippines large quantities of aid, both from a sense of responsibility for the islands' colonial past and because the new republic was willing to accept U.S. military bases on its land and to be allied with the United States.

Similarly, the British remained in Malaya until 1960 to clean up the remnants of rebel Communist guerrillas, even though Malaya had become independent in 1957. Great Britain and several Commonwealth nations also gave Malaya economic aid. Burma, however, opted out of the Commonwealth at independence and took a strictly neutralist and isolationist stand in international affairs; it rejected all economic aid from all parties. North Vietnam, on the other hand, received significant military and economic aid from the Soviet Union and from the People's Republic of China in its struggle against France.

The task of running a government was difficult in all cases, especially since many of the leaders had had no previous experience. Every nation had ethnic or religious minorities; in many cases these minorities were disaffected from the government, and some revolted to overthrow the government or to establish their own nations. Thus the Muslims of Mindanao Island revolted and waged civil war against the government of the Philippines, as did the non-Burmese hill tribesmen against the Burmese government.

In other cases, ethnic minorities in Asian nations were sometimes persecuted, as happened to the Indian minority in Burma and the Chinese minority in Indonesia. Even in Malaysia where there was relative harmony among the three racial groups—Malays, Chinese, and Indians—there were sporadic anti-Chinese riots. Political inexperience, poverty, and traditional attitudes also resulted in rampant corruption, which occurred regardless of the system of government and was as notorious in the democratic Philippines as it was in authoritarian Indonesia. While Malaysia and the Philippines continued with the democratic experiment, Burma's elected government was soon replaced by the military, and in Indonesia Sukarno became dictator under the guise of president for life of a "Guided Democracy."

Each Southeast Asian nation was also faced with severe social problems closely linked with economic ones. In all nations a wide gulf divided the rich from the poor, but the coming of independence unleashed energies that demanded social reforms, such as greater equality for women, and economic improvements that the new governments could not or did not wish to implement. In Muslim nations the demands for women's rights met in confrontation with the Muslim fundamentalist quest for return to traditional roles for women. Meanwhile, improvements in medicine and public health resulted in an inexorable population increase that wiped out most economic gains.

In North Vietnam, the problem of economic disparity was tackled by forced land reform accompanied by the killing and jailing of former landlords. In non-Communist Asian nations, social and economic inequities made the Communist call for revolt attractive to some. In the Philippines, where no reform took place, the desire of poor peasants for land caused a Communist-led uprising known as the Huk Rebellion. Although largely put down by 1954, the insurgency never died out because the conditions that caused it were never adequately remedied.

THE COLD WAR IN ASIA

After World War II Asia became one of the theaters of the Cold War. When the Communists emerged victorious in the Chinese civil war in 1949, President Truman initially did not consider the People's Republic a threat to U.S. interests in Asia; he appeared resigned to its conquest of Taiwan and considered recognizing it as the government of China. The outbreak of the Korean War in 1950 and Chinese participation in the war quickly altered U.S. perceptions of the goal of the Communist bloc in Asia. Later, as Communist insurgency movements cropped up in the Philippines, Malaya, and Burma and threatened their newly independent and unstable governments, the United States became increasingly concerned over the spread of communism across the continent, as it was over similar Communist expansion in Europe. These fears strengthened U.S. resolve to contain the spread of communism on both continents.

The Korean War and Its Aftermath

Allied leaders had agreed at wartime summit conferences to restore an independent Korea but had worked out no details for implementing their plan. When the Soviet Union declared war on Japan, Soviet troops immediately invaded Korea. As the Soviet Union and the United States had agreed, their representatives accepted the Japanese surrender north and south of the 38th parallel, respectively. As it turned out, they created two nations.

In the north, the Soviet Union proceeded to establish a state headed by a young Korean Communist named Kim Il Sung and an army guided by Soviet advisors. The government quickly implemented Communist policies and in the process drove 1 million of its citizens to seek refuge in the south. In the south, the United States hoped to help establish a democratic government with popular representative institutions, but it had no definite blueprints to realize its goals. It allowed exiled patriots to return home, among whom was seventy-year-old Syngman Rhee, a veteran opponent of Japanese imperialism. Rhee proceeded to organize an authoritarian anti-Communist government in South Korea.

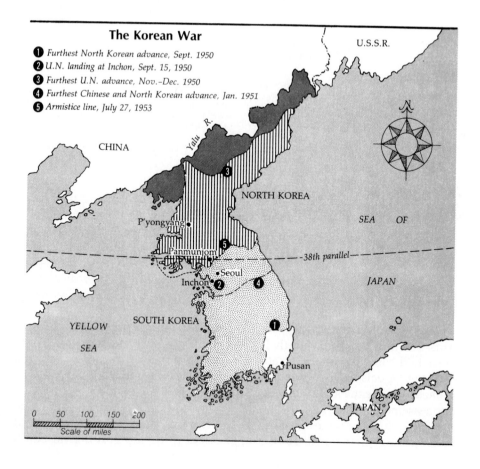

The Korean War

❶ *Furthest North Korean advance, Sept. 1950*
❷ *U.N. landing at Inchon, Sept. 15, 1950*
❸ *Furthest U.N. advance, Nov.–Dec. 1950*
❹ *Furthest Chinese and North Korean advance, Jan. 1951*
❺ *Armistice line, July 27, 1953*

U.S.S.R.

CHINA

Yalu R.

NORTH KOREA

P'yongyang

SEA   OF

Panmunjom

38th parallel

Seoul

Inchon

JAPAN

YELLOW

SEA

SOUTH KOREA

Pusan

JAPAN

0   50   100   150   200
Scale of miles

Inspiration from the West

It must be remembered that the great ambition which led me to the mission school was to learn English, and English only. This ambition I quickly achieved, but I soon discovered I was learning something of far greater importance than the English language. I was imbibing ideas of political equality and liberty. Those who know anything about the political oppression to which the masses of the Korean people were subject can imagine what a revolution took place in the heart of a young Korean Yangban [upper-class person] when he learned for the first time that people in Christian lands were protected against the tyranny of rulers. I said to myself, "It would be a great blessing to my downtrodden fellow men if only we could adopt such a political principle. . . ."

Let us gather all our powers and make our nation like the nations of wealthy, powerful and civilized people. Keep independence in your own hearts.

The most important part is to cast out hopelessness. We must become diligent workers. Our own individual dedication is the seed from which will grow the harvest of a sound nation.*

Syngman Rhee (1875–1965) was born into an aristocratic Korean family. He became a student activist when studying in a missionary school and founded the Independence Club, which opposed the government's submissive policy toward Japan and advocated modernization; for this he was imprisoned from 1897 to 1904. This passage comes from a book written by Rhee during the years he spent in prison. He became a lifelong crusader against Japanese rule over Korea and was the first president of independent South Korea after World War II. As president, he emphasized nationalism rather than democracy and ruled as a strongman. His government was overthrown as a result of student riots in 1960.

*From *Syngman Rhee: The Man Behind the Myth* by Robert T. Oliver. (Quoted from Syngman Rhee, *The Spirit of Independence*.) Copyright © 1954 by Dodd, Mead, and Company. Reprinted by permission.

In 1947 the United States placed the Korean problem before the United Nations, which appointed a commission to supervise elections. Rhee's party won the elections in 1948 and declared the establishment of the Republic of Korea, thus terminating the U.S. military government. Elections were also held in North Korea, but without the presence of the U.N. election commission, after which the Communist government proclaimed itself the Korean Democratic People's Republic. Soviet troops withdrew from North Korea but left in place a well-trained, well-equipped North Korean military force.

Both Korean governments were dedicated to unification, each on its own terms. On June 25, 1950, North Korea launched a surprise attack on South Korea. In the months before the attack, the United States government had sent confusing signals as to whether South Korea was inside the U.S. "defense perimeter." Once the attack occurred, President Truman, mindful of the lesson of appeasement of the 1930s in China and Europe—that unchecked aggression invited more of the same—decided to commit U.S. troops for the defense of South Korea against North Korean aggression. In deciding to defend South

Korea, Truman also was concerned about the security of Japan, Okinawa, and the Philippines. He also secured the support of the United Nations Security Council, which condemned North Korea for aggression against another sovereign state and called on member states to contribute military units collectively to repel the aggressors. The Soviet Union, which had been boycotting the Security Council for six months to protest the presence of Nationalist China on the Council, was not there to cast its veto.

South Korea contributed about one-half of the ground forces of the United Nations command in a war formally termed a "police action." The United States contributed the navy, air force, and two-fifths of the army; the remainder came from Great Britain, a number of Commonwealth nations, Turkey, and others—in all, fifteen nations. President Truman termed Korea "the Greece of the Far East," where the United States must contain Communist expansion.

United Nations Commander-in-Chief General Douglas MacArthur turned the tide of the Korean War in a brilliant maneuver by landing at Inchon in the rear of the North Korean forces. He then proceeded to drive the North Koreans out of South Korea and through North Korea toward the Chinese border.

President Syngman Rhee of South Korea thanks General Douglas MacArthur, commander in chief of U.N. forces, after the liberation of Seoul, capital of South Korea, from North Korean invaders in October 1950.
(UPI/Bettmann Newsphotos)

As the war changed from one of repelling aggression to one of conquering North Korea, Cold War tensions rose high. China became anxious as U.N. troops approached its border, partly because the remnants of the North Korean air force were still attacking U.N. troops from Chinese air bases. In October 1950, Chinese troops, allegedly "volunteers," began crossing into Korea and by December were driving U.N. forces back into South Korea. Soon a million Chinese troops, including Mao's son, were fighting in Korea. The front stabilized in 1951 close to the 38th parallel, the original boundary between the two Koreas.

During the retreat from North Korea, and as the war settled into a stalemate, MacArthur and his military and civilian supporters pressed to use Nationalist Chinese troops and U.S. air and naval power to attack and defeat the Chinese. President Truman and his civilian and military advisors, pressured by nervous European allies, decided that such proposals were unacceptable because they risked bogging down the United States in a major war against China that might widen into a conflict with the Soviet Union. When MacArthur began publicly to challenge Truman's decision, the President relieved him of his command for insubordination.

The stalemated war dragged on until an armistice was signed in 1953. The United States suffered 142,000 casualties, the fourth largest number in its history; South Korean casualties were estimated at 1.3 million, while combined North Korean and Chinese killed and wounded came to an estimated 2 million. Many Americans were indignant over the dismissal of MacArthur and were frustrated that the United States had not clearly won the Korean War. These two issues were added to the already acrimonious political debate in the United States over responsibility for the "loss of China." Together, they contributed to the election of Republican presidential candidate Dwight Eisenhower in 1952.

To clarify its intentions and instill confidence among anti-Communist Asian nations, the United States concluded a mutual defense treaty with South Korea in 1954, on which basis U.S. troops continued to be stationed in that nation. In addition, the United States committed large sums for the military buildup of the South Korean armed forces and the economic rebuilding of the terribly devastated land. To President Rhee's government fell the responsibility of postwar reconstruction. Autocratically inclined and still bitter over the brutal Japanese occupation, he put nationalism ahead of democracy in a state threatened by invasion and Communist subversion and used strong-arm tactics to bring dissidents into line. Rhee was toppled in 1960 by student demonstrations, but as the faction-ridden political parties were unable to produce unified leadership, the army seized power in 1961. The generals inaugurated a five-year plan for stimulating capitalist economic development. Successive economic plans, fueled in part by U.S. economic aid and investments, and after 1965 by Japanese investments, put South Korea on the road to prosperity. Although civilian rule was ostensibly restored in 1963, the elections returned a general to the presidency and the military continued to play a leading role in politics.

North Korea was one of the purest examples of a monocracy (government by one man)—Kim Il Sung concentrated in himself supreme power over the Korean Workers' party (Communist), the armed forces, and the government. It received large quantities of Soviet and Chinese aid and, until 1958, the continued protection of Chinese troops. North Korea had a smaller population than South Korea, but greater natural resources and more industries which the Japanese had built during its colonial occupation. Its economic buildup was accomplished under tight discipline imposed by Kim's government. By the late 1960s, however, South Korea had forged ahead of North Korea.

An uneasy truce continued, punctuated by incidents of sabotage, infiltration, and armed provocation by North Korea, along one of the most tightly guarded and tense borders in the world. Since the peninsula remained divided and provocations from North Korea continued, the U.N. command in South Korea remained, and the United States continued to maintain over 40,000 military personnel south of the Demilitarized Zone (DMZ). The governments of both Koreas remained committed to eventual reunification of the peninsula, and Kim, who still ruled North Korea in 1992, harassed South Korea time and again through assassinations and other terrorist acts. Much as it longed for reunification, South Korea appeared unlikely to start a war against the North. Nor did the United States wish a confrontation, showing restraint when North Korea captured a U.S. surveillance vessel, the *Pueblo*, in 1968, and killed two U.S. officers in the DMZ in 1976. Thus, while tensions remained high on the Korean peninsula, they did not lead to renewed war.

U.S. Anti-Communist Policies in Asia during the 1950s

By the early 1950s the United States was faced with the fact that communism was spreading fast in Asia. Mao Zedong had come to power in China in 1949, and in 1950 Communist North Korea had nearly wiped out South Korea, followed by a bloody stalemate between U.N. and Communist Chinese troops. Communist-led guerrilla insurgents were active in several newly independent nations of Southeast Asia, and Ho Chi Minh's guerrillas were getting the upper hand in Indochina. Some U.S. leaders believed that Stalin had a master scheme to make the world Communist, which he was now putting into effect in Asia with the aid of China. Asia had long been an area of U.S. imperialist and commercial interest, and many Americans were indignant over "losing" China and "not winning" in Korea.

Under these circumstances, the United States, determined that no more of Asia should be "given away," extended to Asia the containment doctrine that it had first applied to Europe in the late 1940s. A major aspect of containment was U.S. military and economic aid to friendly anti-Communist governments in Asia. In doing so, it failed to take into account an important difference between Western Europe and Asia and inadequately understood the force of nationalism and anticolonialism that dominated politics in most newly independent Asian nations. Most of them were beset by social upheavals, mainly from peasant demands for land ownership and other reforms. Since communism promised fundamental social and economic reforms, many Asians were attracted to local Communist movements. Motivated by Cold War fears, the United States gave support to what it perceived to be reliably anti-Communist governments in Asia, many of which lacked popular support because they opposed or were insensitive to needs for economic and social reforms. Thus in Asia, as in Latin America, the United States often became allied with governments that opposed reform, a position that would bring trouble in the decades to come.

Another goal of containment was to neutralize China. The Korean War had made the United States especially hostile toward China, and vice versa. The United States refused to recognize the government headed by Mao as the legitimate government of China and used its veto and other means to block Chinese admission to the United Nations. It also opposed a Chinese conquest of Taiwan (seat of the Nationalist government since 1949) and interposed the Seventh Fleet in the Taiwan Strait to prevent it.

As a further step to forestall Communist expansion and to prevent non-Communist nations from falling under communism like a row of dominos, the United States built up a network of alliances with anti-Communist governments in the region. Bilateral mutual defense treaties were concluded with Japan, the Philippines, South Korea, and the Republic of China on Taiwan (hereafter, Taiwan). These treaties were reinforced by the Southeast Asia Treaty Organization (SEATO), established in 1954, which tied Great Britain, France, Australia, New Zealand, Thailand, and the Philippines to a collective defense of the region. Another treaty (ANZUS) put Australia and New Zealand under U.S. military protection and gave U.S. armed forces access to military bases in the Southern Hemisphere. When SEATO and other Asian bases were linked with U.S. bases in Pakistan (under CENTO) and with NATO, U.S.-led alliances had ringed the Communist bloc. The U.S. attempt to halt the spread of communism in Indochina will be taken up in Chapter 30.

Both the Chinese Communist and Nationalist governments pursued a policy that there should be only one government of China. The Communist government, anxious to complete its victory, sought to destroy the Nationalists on Taiwan. In 1955 and 1958, China bombarded the tiny Nationalist-held offshore islands of Quemoy and Matsu, seemingly as a prelude to an assault on their 100,000 defenders. Since by their Mutual Defense Treaty the United States was obliged to supply the Nationalist garrisons, direct conflict between the United States and China became a distinct possibility. The United States stood firm in its commitment to support the Nationalists and threatened to use nuclear weapons should the Communists attempt to invade Taiwan, but it also ordered its supply boats to respect Chinese territorial waters by staying outside the three-mile limit. After the attempt to seize the islands had obviously failed, China ordered its artillery to fire only on alternate days, thus allowing U.S. supply ships to reach the islands. Hostilities were finally reduced to firing propaganda leaflets from both sides. The United States also pressured Chiang Kai-shek to renounce any intentions of attacking the mainland. Thus, the tensions over the Taiwan Strait gradually subsided.

SUMMARY

For seven years between 1945 and 1952 the United States occupied and remade Japan. War crime trials punished a small number of Japanese leaders responsible for waging aggressive war and for other crimes. The emperor was retained to facilitate reforms but lost his previous divine status. Thoroughgoing reforms, including political rights for women, a new democratic constitution that forbad waging war, land redistribution, and educational and economic liberalization, affected every aspect of Japanese society. U.S. aid prevented hunger in the difficult immediate postwar years and financed the initial rebuilding of the economy. A Eugenics Protection Law forestalled a population explosion so that Japanese could enjoy the fruits of their labors with a rising standard of living. By 1960 these reforms had laid the foundations for the Japanese economic miracle.

After suffering eight years of Japanese invasion, China was immediately engulfed in civil war after the victory against Japan. The Chinese Communists, despite preventive efforts by the United States, defeated the corrupt and demoralized Nationalist government, which fled to Taiwan. After 1949 Mao Zedong and other Communist leaders transformed the world's most populous nation into a totalitarian Communist state, the People's Republic of China, and placed it firmly in the socialist camp as an ally of the Soviet Union. It aided North Korea with a million soldiers in the Korean War and gave material and training aid to the Vietnamese Communists, but its economic backwardness and the domestic turmoil that Mao created with the Great Leap Forward prevented it from playing a larger role in the Cold War in Asia.

Between 1945 and 1960 most of the former colonies in Asia gained independence. Great Britain and the United States led the way, as they had done before World War II, and made peaceful and orderly transfers of power. They retained, for the most part, the good will of their former colonies. Most former British colonies remained in the Commonwealth, while the Philippines became an ally of the United States. France and the Netherlands were less attuned to a changing world and withdrew from Asia only when they had no other options.

In many cases, independence brought to the forefront ancient regional disputes and internal problems that had lain submerged and dormant during colonial rule. Thus Hindus and Muslims in India resurrected ancient rivalries that predated British control and remained smoldering. Several other newly independent nations almost immediately became embroiled in civil wars or insurrections by ethnic or religious minorities. Economic and social problems plagued most of the new nations and often defied both foreign aid and local efforts to find solutions, even when there was a will to do so. Ancient and modern local rivalries and nationalistic ambitions became entwined with Cold War politics, embroiling the new nations in alliances or leading them to policies of nonalignment.

As the leader of the non-Communist world, the United States became deeply involved in combatting the spread of communism in Asia. American forces were dispatched to Korea to prevent the Communist conquest of South Korea. On the other side, China entered the war to prevent the U.S. conquest of North Korea. The armistice that ended the fighting reflected a stalemate that continued into the 1990s. The United States also protected the Nationalist refugee government on Taiwan from invasion by China, sent aid to Southeast Asian nations to combat Communist guerrillas, and created a number of formal military alliances, collectively and individually, with nations of the area. When victorious Communist-dominated forces threatened to overrun all Vietnam and wrest it from war-weary France, the United States and other great powers intervened to partition the former colony and restrict the Communists to the northern half. Thus, on two major and several minor occasions, the Cold War in Asia erupted into hot wars and left a legacy of three divided lands.

SUGGESTED SOURCES

AKBAR, M.J., *Nehru, The Making of India* (1988). A well-respected Indian journalist assesses Nehru and his times.*

ANDERSON, DAVID L., *Trapped by Success: The Eisenhower Administration in Vietnam, 1953–1961* (1991). Balanced account of how Eisenhower's policy set the stage for later U.S. involvement.

CHANG, GORDON H., *Friends and Enemies, The United States, China, and the Soviet Union, 1948–1972* (1990). Well written and documented, it is the first book in the Modern America Series.*

COLLINS, LARRY, and DOMINIQUE LAPIERRE, *Freedom at Midnight* (1980). A gripping account of the last stages of India's struggle for independence.*

FIFIELD, RUSSELL H., *Americans in Southeast Asia: The Roots of Commitment* (1973). A survey of twentieth-century U.S. involvement in the region.

FITZGERALD, CHARLES, *Revolution in China* (1966). Focuses on the indigenous forces underlying the Chinese Communist revolution.

HARRIES, MEIRON, and SUSIE HARRIES, *Sheathing the Sword: The Demilitarization of Post-War Japan* (1987). Thought-provoking book on U.S.-Japanese relations since World War II.

JEFFREY, ROBIN, Ed., *Asia—The Winning of Independence* (1981). A concise summary of how each nation won its independence.

JOHNSON, KAY ANN, *Women, the Family and Peasant Revolution in China* (1983). Women remain unequal in China despite official profession.*

LEWIS, JOHN WILSON, Ed., *Peasant Rebellion and Communist Revolution in Asia* (1974). Explains the relationship between traditional peasant rebellions and twentieth-century Communist-led revolutions.

LIANG, HENG, and JUDY SHAPIRO, *Son of the Revolution* (1983). A poignant autobiography about growing up in Mao's China.*

Lord Mountbatten: The Last Viceroy (1984). TV series that dramatizes the people and events preceding the independence of India and Pakistan.

MEHTA, VED, *A Family Affair: India under Three Prime Ministers* (1982). A critical study of the politics and personalities of Indian leadership.

RUSS, MARTIN, *The Last Parallel* (1959). A marine's firsthand account of fighting in Korea.*

SINGH, ANITA INDER, *The Origins of the Partition of India, 1936–1947* (1987). Good book on problems of decolonization and nationalism.

WARD, BARBARA, *Women in the New Asia: The Changing Social Roles of Men and Women in South and Southeast Asia* (1977). An insightful description of social relations and changing roles of women.

*Paperback available.

CHAPTER 25

African Struggles for Independence

After World War II, Africa began to move from a continent of colonies to a continent of independent states. As in Asia, most European colonial nations, their strength eroded by two world wars, no longer had the power or even the will to hold on to their empires in the face of mounting nationalist pressure. In Africa, nationalist struggles for independence were often impeded or undercut by the complex mosaic of differing ethnic, linguistic, and religious communities, which made unification difficult. Frequently, as in West Africa, differing ethnic and religious groups had been grouped together under one imperial power. The artificial national boundaries devised by the European powers, often without regard to local populations, were to become the borders of newly emerging nation states whose fragile governments then had to deal with the problems of unification and cooperation among heterogeneous populations. For example, in Nigeria, one of the largest African nations, regional differences between the largely Islamic north and Christian or animist south caused resentment and threatened to destroy the federated structure of the republic.

During the years of imperial domination, rapid industrialization, urbanization, and increased contact with Western technology and culture caused radical alterations in the traditional patterns of African society; this accelerated the various movements toward independence. As the peoples of Africa loudly demanded control over their own political and economic destinies, it became evident that the small number of Europeans living in northern and eastern Africa could not hold back the forces favoring national self-determination. By 1963 virtually all of the northern two-thirds of Africa consisted of independent states. In southern Africa, however, white minorities still clung to power (see Chapter 32).

The struggle for independence took different forms throughout Africa. In some cases, as in Tunisia, Morocco, and Uganda, the imperial powers granted independence under predetermined conditions. In Libya, for example, the United Nations played a key role in establishing an independent political entity. In these instances, Africans secured independence with a minimum of

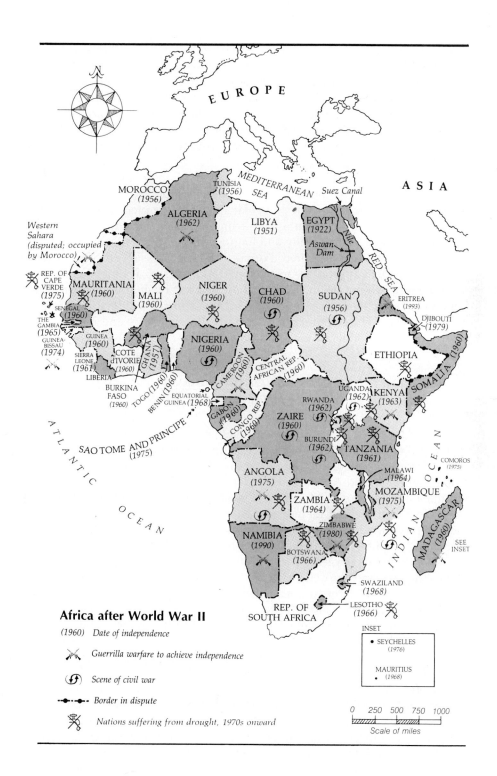

EUROPE

ASIA

MEDITERRANEAN SEA   Suez Canal

MOROCCO
(1956)

TUNISIA
(1956)

ALGERIA
(1962)

LIBYA
(1951)

EGYPT
(1922)

Aswan
Dam

Western
Sahara
(disputed; occupied
by Morocco)

REP. OF
CAPE
VERDE
(1975)

MAURITANIA
(1960)

MALI
(1960)

NIGER
(1960)

CHAD
(1960)

SUDAN
(1956)

ERITREA
(1993)

DJIBOUTI
(1979)

SENEGAL
(1960)

THE
GAMBIA
(1965)

GUINEA-
BISSAU
(1974)

GUINEA
(1960)

SIERRA
LEONE
(1961)

LIBERIA

COTE
d'IVOIRE
(1960)

GHANA
(1957)

NIGERIA
(1960)

CAMEROON
(1960)

CENTRAL
AFRICAN REP.
(1960)

ETHIOPIA

SOMALIA
(1960)

BURKINA
FASO
(1960)

TOGO (1960)

BENIN (1960)

EQUATORIAL
GUINEA (1968)

GABON
(1960)

CONGO REP.
(1960)

ZAIRE
(1960)

RWANDA
(1962)

BURUNDI
(1962)

UGANDA
(1962)

KENYA
(1963)

TANZANIA
(1961)

SAO TOME AND PRINCIPE
(1975)

ATLANTIC

OCEAN

ANGOLA
(1975)

ZAMBIA
(1964)

MALAWI
(1964)

MOZAMBIQUE
(1975)

COMOROS
(1975)

NAMIBIA
(1990)

ZIMBABWE
(1980)

BOTSWANA
(1966)

MADAGASCAR
(1960)

INDIAN OCEAN

SEE
INSET

SWAZILAND
(1968)

REP. OF
SOUTH AFRICA

LESOTHO
(1966)

Africa after World War II

(1960)   Date of independence

Guerrilla warfare to achieve independence

Scene of civil war

Border in dispute

Nations suffering from drought, 1970s onward

INSET

● SEYCHELLES
(1976)

MAURITIUS
(1968)

0   250   500   750   1000

Scale of miles

377

bloodshed. On the other hand, in areas where there were well-entrenched European white settlers or where the imperial powers were determined to maintain control, the struggles for independence were protracted and often violent. In Algeria and Kenya, and later throughout much of southern Africa, African nationalists were forced to resort to guerrilla warfare and armed attacks against the imperial powers. These guerrilla wars, or "wars of liberation," as they were often known in the Third World, followed the same pattern as that in Vietnam.

Just as the imperial powers had differed in their approaches to their African empires, so too did they adopt contrasting policies toward the newly independent nations. Some, in particular France, attempted with notable success to maintain close cultural and economic ties. Indeed, former French colonies remained economically and linguistically tied to France decades after independence had been secured. Former British possessions tended to adopt more independent approaches to economic and cultural development. Others, most notably Belgium in the Congo, abdicated responsibility for their former holdings. A selective look around the African continent will reveal in more detail how most of the colonies finally secured independence and how the various European imperial powers approached their former colonies.

NORTH AFRICA: INDEPENDENCE THROUGH NEGOTIATION AND WAR

In North Africa, nationalist sentiments had gained enormous popular support by the end of World War II. In the face of this groundswell for national liberation, France, after limited struggles, granted independence to Tunisia under Habib Bourgiba and to Morocco under King Mohammad V in 1956. Both Bourgiba and Hassan II, Mohammad's son, continued to rule into the 1980s. Similarly, Libya secured its independence under King Idris through the auspices of the United Nations. The traditional monarchy of King Idris was overthrown by a military coup led by Muammar al-Qadhdhafi in 1969. By the end of the 1960s, huge petroleum revenues transformed Libya from one of Africa's poorest nations into one of the richest.

In contrast, in order to obtain their independence, the Algerians, led by the National Liberation Front (FLN), fought a bloody war (1954–1962) against the French, who were unwilling to give up what the government had for a century considered an integral part of France. The French *colons*, who were about 10 percent of the Algerian population, were particularly vociferous and determined to keep Algeria as part of France. They even went so far as to establish their own secret army to fight the Algerians and those French who supported independence. The FLN used attacks on urban centers populated by the *colons* and other guerrilla warfare tactics similar to those employed in Vietnam; these included hit-and-run tactics and what has been called the "bombs in a basket" approach, whereby women and children would carry out attacks on the *colons* and the French military. The French retaliated by bombing villages, removing families from the countryside, and in some instances torturing Algerian suspects. General de Gaulle, who came to power in 1958, concluded that France could not win the struggle and should negotiate a settlement. After protracted negotiations, continued violence within Algeria, and assassination attempts on de Gaulle, Algeria finally achieved independence in 1962. Upon independence most of the *colons* left Algeria and settled in France or Spain. The Algerian war cost a million Algerian deaths and thousands of French casualties. In many ways, it divided French society much as the Vietnam War later split U.S. society.

Following independence, Algeria was in the vanguard of the revolutionary Arab states, but it later established more friendly relations with the United States. Although Algeria had substantial revenues from its petroleum resources, it also faced enormous economic problems. Unemployment was high among its youth, which, as in many of the newly independent nations, formed a large sector of the total population. All of France's former North African imperial holdings retained close economic ties with the former imperial power, with the majority of their imports and exports coming from and going to France. Following independence, Algeria became a leader of the Third World, and it often played a key role in mediating between Third World nations and Western superpowers.

DECOLONIZATION IN WEST AFRICA

As indicated previously, western Africa, particularly the Gold Coast (Ghana), had been in the forefront of African national movements. In 1949, Kwame Nkrumah formed his Convention People's Party (CPP), with its demand for "self-government now." Strikes and boycotts, accompanied by some violence, were directed against the British administration. As a result, Nkrumah was imprisoned, but internal unrest persisted.

Finally, in 1957, the British agreed to grant Ghana independence under the leadership of Nkrumah; in the view of many African nationalists, Ghana's independence was the first step toward independence for all of black Africa, but by 1960 the Ghanaian constitution had become authoritarian. Along with seeking further economic and educational development within Ghana, Nkrumah also portrayed himself as the leader of the Pan-African movement. As a result, he incurred the enmity of rival African leaders and, more important, alienated other Ghanaians who were more concerned over economic development. Consequently, Nkrumah was overthrown by a military junta in 1966. Attempts to return Ghana to stable civilian government met with varying degrees of success, and as in so many newly independent nations in the twentieth century, the army remained an important force. As a result of poor management and political instability, Ghana was plagued with economic problems, smuggling, and profiteering.

In Nigeria, one of the largest and most populous African nations, the British attempted to solve the problem of ethnic and cultural heterogeneity by

Struggling for Independence

In 1934 when I applied to the Dean for admission to Lincoln University, I quoted from Tennyson's "In Memoriam"

So many worlds, so much to do,
So little done, such things to be.

When I wrote that letter, however, I little knew that it would take ten years in America and two-and-a-half years in England, living almost as an exile, to prepare for the struggle. . . .

Those years in America and England were years of sorrow and loneliness, poverty and hard work. But I have never regretted them because the background that they provided has helped me to formulate my philosophy of life and politics.

Independence for the Gold Coast was my aim. It was a colony and I have always regarded colonialism as the policy by which a foreign power binds territories to herself by political ties with the primary object of promoting her own economic advantage. . . . There are few people who would not rid themselves of such domination if they could.

How was it possible, I asked myself, for a revolution to succeed without arms and ammunition? After months of studying Gandhi's policy, and watching the effect it had, I began to see that, when backed by a strong political or-ganization it could be the solution to the colonial problem. In Jawaharlal Nehru's rise to power I recognized the success of one who, pledged to Socialism, was able to interpret Gandhi's philosophy in practical terms.

I saw the whole solution to this problem lay in political freedom for our people, for it is only when people are politically free that other races can give them the respect that is due to them. . . . It is far better to be free to govern, or misgovern yourself than to be governed by anybody else.

————◆◆◆————

In his autobiography, Kwame Nkrumah describes how his experiences in America at Lincoln University, one of the first African American institutions of higher education, and the writings of Gandhi and other non-Western leaders contributed to his political philosophy. Born in 1912, Nkrumah became the leader of the Ghanaian national movement and was an outspoken advocate of closer relations among African, Arab, and Asian nations. Nkrumah led Ghana until his overthrow by the military in 1960; he died in exile in 1972.

*From *The Autobiography of Kwame Nkrumah* by Kwame Nkrumah. Copyright © 1957. Reprinted by permission of Zed Books Ltd.

forming a federated system that, in theory at least, was to give full local rights to the three main ethnic groupings within the nation. However, riots in 1953 demonstrated the major differences between the predominantly Muslim north and the predominantly Christian Ibos in the southeast. Attempting to reconcile these differences, the British declared Nigeria an independent nation in 1960. The carefully prepared constitution called for a federated nation, but the basic ethnic hostilities remained.

In 1967, the Ibos attempted to secede and to establish their own nation, which they called Biafra. The civil war that followed was characterized by bloody violence and extreme hardship; thousands died of starvation. The war dragged on until 1970, when war-weary and often starving Biafrans surrendered and the military regime of Colonel Yakubu Gowon reunited the nation. The Nigeria case demonstrated that African leaders recognized the difficulties posed by national boundaries that often grouped together under one government different and sometimes antagonistic ethnic, linguistic, or religious communities. However, they also realized that redrawing national borders could create even more complex and potentially violent problems. As a result, the borders generally drawn by the Western imperial powers continued as the borders of the independent nation-states.

In contrast to the British approach, the French tried to retain a close union with their West African empire. As early as 1944, General de Gaulle had promised a French union, which would respect indigenous societies while creating a more highly centralized version of the British Commonwealth. However, de Gaulle's attempt to keep some degree of French control over its empire failed to fulfill the national aspirations of West Africans.

Thus, in spite of the considerable financial benefits they received from the French government, nationalists continued to press for independence. After World War II, Felix Houphouet-Boigny played the leading role in forming a political alliance to fight for the independence of the Ivory Coast. Joined by nationalists from other French colonies in West Africa, the move triggered a series of violent confrontations. When de Gaulle returned to power in 1958, he proposed holding a referendum whereby West African nations could choose either to participate as autonomous units within a French union or to achieve complete independence. In the 1958 referendum, only Guinea, led by Ahmed Sékou Touré, voted for complete political and economic separation from France. Sékou Touré ruled Guinea until his death in 1984; subsequently, military officers led a takeover of the government and moved to restore civil liberties and revive the nation's faltering economy.

By 1960, France had granted the rest of its West African colonies full independence. Some, such as Senegal under the noted poet Leopold Senghor, proved remarkably stable. In the Ivory Coast, one of the most prosperous West African nations, a lively artistic heritage, particularly in the fields of ceramics, weaving, and metalsmithing, was continued and expanded. Other nations, such as Togo, Cameroon, and Benin, were plagued by continual military coups and countercoups. Indeed, military dictatorships became the predominant political force in most of West Africa and in some ways reflected traditional African respect for the "big man." As Yukubu Gowan, the military president of Nigeria, emphasized, "The trouble with military rule is that every colonel or general is soon full of ambition. The navy takes over today and the army tomorrow." Throughout Africa, military regimes were often able to put down regional disputes and tribal conflicts, but the costs were high. Many smaller ethnic groups were largely decimated by military leaders representing larger or more powerful forces. Military rule also meant that disproportionate amounts of already strained budgets were spent on armaments, high salaries for officers, and perks for the military.

After independence, Ghanaians proudly wore
clothes imprinted with pictures of their
nationalist leader, Nkrumah.
(Keystone Press)

Importantly, most former French colonies maintained fairly close economic and cultural ties with France. In contrast, the former British colonies often
went their own ways and established economic ties with other outside nations. Through organizations such as the Ghana-Guinea Union, some West
African nations attempted to form a nucleus for Pan-African unity on a continental scale. Nkrumah and Sékou Touré were both champions of this ideal.

CHAOS IN ZAIRE

All of the general patterns of African struggles for independence were apparent in the Belgian Congo (later Zaire). There was some violence and bloodshed; the superpowers became involved, and the United Nations attempted to
mediate the conflict. While both the British and the French had tried to prepare and to educate at least an elite to take over the governments of new independent states, the story was quite different in the Congo, because Belgian paternalism had kept the Congo under rigid controls. Much as they tried,
however, the Belgians could not isolate the Congo from the nationalist fervor

of its neighbors. A number of local nationalist movements developed, including one based in Katanga led by Moise Tshombe and another led by Patrice Lumumba.

In the face of growing nationalist sentiments, the Belgian government abruptly announced Congolese independence in 1960. The new state was immediately threatened by conflicting local rivalries. Tshombe announced the secession of the mineral-rich Katanga province, and Lumumba called for the intervention of the United Nations. The Congo became the arena for some private companies and the superpowers to meddle in African affairs. Hired mercenaries further complicated the situation.

Finally, U.N. police actions in 1963 reunited Katanga with the rest of the Congo, but the fighting continued even after the U.N. troops left in 1964. After Lumumba's assassination in 1961, the Congolese government was troubled with military threats and political instability. Following a relatively bloodless coup, General Joseph Mobutu became head of the government in 1965 and proceeded to change its name to Zaire. The government of Zaire used part of the capital earned from the nation's tremendous mineral wealth to build roads, lines of communication, and educational facilities. However, Mobutu also allocated substantial portions of Zaire's economic wealth to maintain a large army and to quell rebellions by groups opposed to the military or by those who had been systematically excluded from power. He also amassed a huge private fortune. Thus Zaire remained more divided and less wealthy than ever before.

PEACE AND WAR IN BRITISH EAST AFRICA

As in West Africa, the British moved toward granting *uhuru* (freedom) in East Africa after World War II. Unlike West Africa, however, East African nations came to independence through war as well through peace. Tanganyika, economically the least developed of British possessions in East Africa, secured its independence in 1961 after a decade of gradual steps toward autonomy. Unified with neighboring Zanzibar in 1964, it became the Republic of Tanzania. Tanzania emerged as a one-party nation led by Julius Nyerere's Tanganyika African National Union (TANU). Nyerere, one of Africa's leading champions of state socialism, promptly initiated a series of grass-roots development projects aimed at increasing agricultural output and providing better social services. China provided much technical and financial assistance for development, but most of the rural population remained poor.

In Kenya, the move toward independence was complicated by the presence of the white minority, most of them farmers in the Kenyan highlands. These white settlers, like the *colons* in Algeria, wished to keep their dominant position. In contrast, the British government had embarked on a gradual program of increased self-determination based on multiracial cooperation that would also include the Indians, Kenya's other minority. These concessions failed to alleviate African grievances, particularly among the Kikuyu, one of the largest of Kenya's ethnic groups. The Kikuyu had been the major victims of European colonizers who had confiscated large tracts of Kikuyu farmland in the highlands.

As white salaries and standards of living continued to rise, the economic position of blacks deteriorated. The Kenya African Union under Jomo Kenyatta persistently demanded that these inequities be eradicated and that black people be given a larger proportion of the important government positions. When these demands were ignored, the independence movement became more radical.

In 1952, there were widespread demonstrations as the Kikuyu organized a national resistance group to fight for "land and freedom." Popularly known in the West as the Mau Mau, the organization was centered mainly in the countryside. Guerrilla warfare lasted from 1952 to 1956, but the actual number of assassinations and violent acts perpetrated against Europeans by the Mau Mau was widely exaggerated in the Western media. In a futile effort to destroy the Mau Mau, the British imprisoned Kenyatta; in addition, at least 10,000 Kikuyu died in the struggle. Finally, the British and the white settlers admitted defeat, and Kenyan independence was proclaimed in 1963.

Kenyatta quickly emerged as the leader of a single-party state. Through a series of political maneuverings, and with the advantages of relative economic prosperity and his own charismatic appeal, he managed to unify the various Kenyan groups into a fairly cohesive nation. While many of the white settlers left Kenya, some remained as new Kenyan citizens. Under Kenyatta's leadership, the Kenyan government remained relatively stable and survived Kenyatta's death in 1978. Although the majority of political power certainly rested in the executive branch, Kenya was unusual in that it managed to retain civilian government and a cohesive national identity even after the demise of its first generation of nationalist leadership.

THE BLACK STRUGGLE FOR FREEDOM IN SOUTHERN AFRICA

Pressure on Southern Rhodesia and the Portuguese Colonies

In southern Africa, the Portuguese led by the dictator Salazar and the white-dominated regimes elsewhere in the area were far more determined to maintain their supremacy than were the colonial powers in the rest of Africa. In Rhodesia, for example, the white settlers announced their determination to retain their dominant political and economic position. On the other hand, the British government sought to avoid South African problems by agreeing to grant independence to Southern Rhodesia along the lines of equal representation. As British Prime Minister Harold Macmillan noted on a visit to South Africa, "The wind of change is blowing through [Africa] , and whether we like it or not this growth of national consciousness is a political fact . . . and our national policies must take account of it." Such an approach meant that the small white population would no longer enjoy the position of privilege it had had under the old regime. The white minority bitterly opposed the British plan and, in open defiance, unilaterally declared its independence as the state of Rhodesia in 1965. With the exception of the white-controlled Republic of South Africa, no nations recognized the new Rhodesian government under Ian Smith, and the United Nations declared an economic boycott of Rhodesia. However, Rhodesian tobacco and minerals continued to be channeled to Western markets, and the economic boycott seemed to have little effect.

As the pressure mounted, African states surrounding Rhodesia became involved. South Africa assisted the Smith regime, while black African nations supported the growing forces of revolutionary black Rhodesians. Armed insurrections became commonplace throughout the Rhodesian countryside. Both Great Britain and later the United States tried to mediate the dispute and to reach a settlement based on equal black participation in the government, with no success.

At the same time that Rhodesia was falling under siege, blacks in the Portuguese colonies of Mozambique and Angola increased their pressure for independence. Portuguese dictators Antonio Salazar and Marcello Caetano refused to grant independence or greater autonomy to the last vestiges of Portugal's 400-year-old colonial empire. Indeed, in 1955, the Salazar regime attempted to extend its centralized control by referring to the colonies as "overseas provinces," an approach that was similar to the French concept of Algeria as an integral part of France. Just as the concept of Algeria as French had failed, so too did the Portuguese attempts to incorporate its African colonies. Condemnations of Portuguese policies in Africa by the United Nations were ignored. As a result of nationalist sentiments and Portuguese repression, rebellion broke out in Angola and Mozambique in 1961 and 1964, and a decade of war followed.

Racial Repression in the Republic of South Africa

Much of the struggle for independence in the southern third of Africa focused on the Republic of South Africa. One of the richest and strategically important African nations, its society was still dominated by the conservative Dutch Afrikaners. During World War II, many Afrikaners, who had long chafed under British domination and attempts to liberalize the society, openly favored the Nazi regime. The Dutch Reformed Church reinforced the Afrikaners' philosophy of racial supremacy.

After the war, the Afrikaners in the Republic of South Africa enacted the policy of apartheid, a government-endorsed and -enforced system of strict racial segregation. By the early 1980s, the apartheid system had legalized the dominance of 4.5 million white Africans over 800,000 Asians (mostly Indian shopkeepers), 2.8 million "colored" people (those of mixed racial origin), and 22 million black Africans restricting their civil rights and allowing them no political power. In addition, it called for complete segregation of the races in

Resisting Apartheid

A short while later [1953] my first ban was served on me in terms of the Riotous Assemblies Act and the Criminal Law Amendment Act. In comparison with my later bans it was a mild affair. I was debarred from entry into all the larger centres of the Union. I was not allowed to attend public gatherings anywhere.

This last provision at once raised the question of attendance at public worship. My church took up the matter with the Department of Justice and told me that while they did not think that the police would interfere with my religious activities, I should apply for permission to be present at public worship.

In the winter of 1954, when the new battery of ruthless laws was freshly in place on the Statute Book, my ban expired. It was not immediately reimposed. I suppose I was being given a chance to go straight. I immediately misbehaved.*

Luthuli, the grandson of a Zulu chief, describes an episode in his struggle against apartheid in South Africa. He was President of the African National Congress and a leader in the Pan-African movement. He was awarded the Nobel Prize for Peace in 1961.

*From *Let My People Go* by Albert Luthuli. Copyright © 1962 by William Collins Sons & Company, Ltd. Reprinted by permission.

housing, education, religion, and government. It separated black Africans from Asians, both of these from colored Africans and all three from the white population. In many cases, it forced families who lived in areas designated as white, colored, or black to move if they were of the wrong color. Huge, largely black townships developed around the outskirts of largely white cities. Black people were permitted into these cities to work in industry or in white homes during the daytime, but they had to leave the cities during the evening hours. They had to carry identification cards at all times; to be caught without a card or after curfew in areas designated as white meant possible imprisonment or the loss of a pass to work in the cities, which meant unemployment and further impoverishment. The Afrikaner government justified these repressive measures on the grounds that they helped to suppress Communist activities.

In the decades after World War II, black society and white society moved further and further apart. Landless black Africans began to seek jobs in the growing industrial centers, which were profiting from South Africa's great natural wealth in diamonds, uranium, and gold. Here, too, skilled white workers held the highest-paying positions; black workers were given the lowest-paid jobs as manual laborers. Gradually, all white Africans even in unskilled jobs, were paid a higher wage simply because of skin color.

The apartheid policy and the repressive tactics that accompanied it provoked nonwhite leaders to resist. Initially, they stressed nonviolence after the pattern set by Gandhi, who had spent part of his early life in South Africa. Nu-

Black South Africans are massacred at Sharpeville in 1960.
(*Keystone Press*)

merous black leaders, including the Nobel Peace Prize winner Albert Luthuli, were imprisoned. Others, like white novelist Alan Paton, who was outspoken in his opposition to the regime, were censored and placed under virtual house arrest. The African National Congress (ANC), under Luthuli's leadership, sought a unified and racially integrated society in South Africa and led the struggle for nonviolent tactics and passive resistance against apartheid.

Black nationalists also initiated a series of strikes and demonstrations. These culminated in the 1960 Sharpeville incident, where police opened fire on the unarmed crowd, killing dozens and wounding many. Condemning the ANC as revolutionary, the white South African government declared the organization illegal in 1960. Nelson Mandela, one of the leaders of the ANC, evaded arrest but was ultimately caught and tried under the Suppression of Communism Act. Mandela, who was not a member of any Marxist party, and seven other nationalist leaders were sentenced to life imprisonment. Mandela was finally released from prison in 1990, by which time he had become the symbol of black nationalism in southern Africa. When Great Britain and other members of the Commonwealth criticized apartheid and the repression of black nationalist leaders, the white South African government retaliated by dropping its membership in the Commonwealth in 1961.

To alleviate growing internal and international criticism, the South African government in 1966 announced the creation of Bantustans, or black states, within South African territory. The Bantustans of Bophuthatswana and Transkei were, in fact, large black reservations. Permits were required for black Africans to leave the Bantustans and to go to any area designated as white. White South Africans argued that the Bantustans were created as a logical extension of the apartheid principle of separate development. However, the Bantustans were on only 13 percent of the total land area, generally exceedingly poor, territorially fragmented, and dependent for communication and transport lines on white South Africa. Their foreign affairs were also controlled by the South African government. In 1966, Prime Minister Henrik Verwoerd, a leading proponent of apartheid, was assassinated by a mentally disturbed Greek immigrant, but his successors continued the policies. As hopes for concessions faded, black nationalists began to turn to violence (see Chapter 32).

NEW MOVEMENTS TOWARD PAN-AFRICAN UNITY

Many African leaders, from Nkrumah to Nasser, saw Pan-Africanism, a concept born between the wars, both as a means to improve standards of living and as a way of giving Africans more political and economic clout in the international arena. African union was encouraged through various Pan-African conferences during the decades of the 1950s and 1960s. The Bandung Conference in 1955 gave enormous impetus to nonaligned movement of many African and Asian nations as they sought to steer a neutral path between the Soviet Union and the United States in the midst of the Cold War. Similarly, the First World Congress of Black Writers and Artists, held in Paris in 1956, was an important cultural event in bringing together English- and French-speaking Africans. The next logical step occurred in May 1963, when representatives of the newly independent African states met in Addis Ababa and created the Organization of African Unity (OAU). Much of northern Africa also considered itself part of the Arab world, and leaders such as Nasser in Egypt argued that the predominantly Muslim and Arab nations of Africa belonged to both the circles of Arabism and of Africanism.

However, in spite of their broad emotional appeal, both African and Arab unity appeared to be a distant dream. African union was verbally championed by most African leaders, but concrete attempts for unity generally failed, for a variety of political and economic reasons. Personal rivalries for dominant positions among conflicting African leaders drove wedges between African nations. Most of the educational institutions and economic relations of African states were plugged into Western nations; there was very little, if any, economic interdependence that would facilitate the movement toward political union. Thus, economic rivalries heightened political differences. The Western powers aggravated the differences among African states by economic and political interference and later occasionally by direct or surrogate military interference, as in Zaire.

SUMMARY

With the notable exceptions of Algeria and Kenya, independence came relatively peacefully in northern and central Africa in the 1950s and 1960s. By the 1960s all western and eastern African nations had become independent. Many of these new, struggling nations experienced political upheavals, and military dictatorships often became the norm. In Zaire, there were particularly bloody conflicts which were exacerbated by superpower involvement.

In southern Africa, levels of violence rose as colonial and white settler regimes in the Portuguese colonies and Rhodesia clung to power in the face of growing African discontent. The institution of apartheid widened the gulf between the races in South Africa. The white minority remained determined to keep the black majority out of the political system. In reaction to Afrikaner refusals to allow equality, black Africans turned first to nonviolent methods to force changes, but as the white minority clung to power, black activists turned to violence.

Independent African nations were troubled with economic crises and persistent political instability, which often led to military interference. Attempts at union, either political or economic, were impeded by cultural differences, outside interference, and political weaknesses.

SUGGESTED SOURCES

ACHEBE, CHINUA, *No Longer at Ease* (1963). A historical novel, a sequel to *Things Fall Apart*, where the hero returns to Nigeria after living in Britain.*

CALVOCORESSI, PETER, *Independent Africa and the World* (1984). A survey of Africa and superpower involvement since the 1950s.*

HARGREAVES, J.D., *Decolonization in Africa* (1988). Concise summary of independence movements.*

HORNE, ALISTAIR, *A Savage War of Peace: Algeria 1954–1962* (1979). A moving description of the Algerian revolution.*

OMER-COOPER, J.D., *A History of Southern Africa* (1987). Analytical study of origins of contemporary South African societies.*

PATON, ALAN, *Too Late the Phalarope* (1953). On the psychological dimension of apartheid, by a noted novelist.*

Winnie and Nelson Mandela (1986). Powerful biographical film about two of the most famous black South African nationalists.

*Paperback available.

CHAPTER 26

Conflict and Development in the Middle East

As with the rest of Asia and most of Africa, Middle Eastern nations achieved independence after World War II, but the region's vital petroleum fields and its strategic importance in terms of the Cold War meant that the superpowers constantly sought to secure allies and influence in the area. While the petroleum-rich nations were able to finance vast and far-reaching development programs, the poor nations without petroleum revenues continued to suffer the problems of underdevelopment. In addition, interregional rivalries and the ongoing Arab-Israeli conflict contributed to tensions and intermittent warfare. Finally, various Islamist parties in nations as diverse as Iran and Jordan, among others, gained popularity. Many people who supported these militant Islamic groups were disaffected with the spread of Western culture and approaches in their formerly traditional societies; they also concluded that their governments had failed to solve the economic and social problems in the region and that only Islamic regimes could rectify these problems. This tension between secular forces and religious, traditional forces reflected similar trends throughout the world during the twentieth century.

INDEPENDENCE AFTER WORLD WAR II

As war clouds gathered in Europe, Great Britain took steps to quell the growing nationalist storms in the Middle East. Great Britain wanted to ensure loyalty, or at least quiet, in the Arab world because of the area's vital strategic location. Consequently, the British tried to placate Arab nationalists, many of whom were prone to favor the Axis powers. Arab support for the Axis powers did not generally stem from ideological agreements with them but was based on the old expression "An enemy of my enemy is my friend." Encouraged by Nazi propaganda and hating the British presence in the area, Arab nationalists were encouraged to believe that if the Germans won the war, they would grant the Arabs complete independence.

In much of the Arab world, Great Britain attempted to secure its interests through censorship, military control, repression of Arab nationalists, and pro-

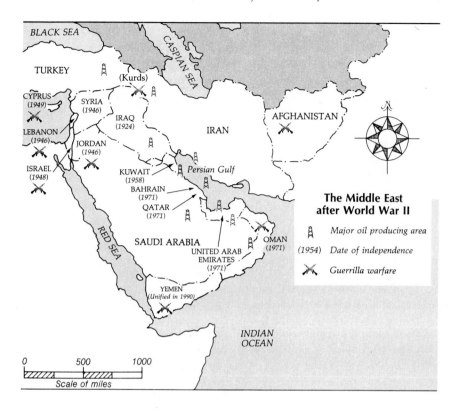

BLACK SEA

TURKEY ⌘
(Kurds)

CASPIAN SEA

CYPRUS
(1949)
SYRIA
(1946)
IRAQ
(1924)
IRAN
AFGHANISTAN

LEBANON
(1946)
JORDAN
(1946)

ISRAEL
(1948)
KUWAIT
(1958)
Persian Gulf

BAHRAIN
(1971)
QATAR
(1971)

RED SEA

SAUDI ARABIA
UNITED ARAB
EMIRATES
(1971)
OMAN
(1971)

YEMEN
(Unified in 1990)

INDIAN
OCEAN

**The Middle East
after World War II**

⌘   *Major oil producing area*

(1954)   Date of independence

⚔   *Guerrilla warfare*

0   500   1000
Scale of miles

Allied propaganda campaigns. After the fall of France and the creation of the pro-Nazi Vichy regime, Allied forces gradually occupied French-held Syria and Lebanon. In spite of French protests, the U.S. and British governments encouraged nationalist sentiments, particularly in Syria and Lebanon. By the end of the war, most Middle East nations had achieved national autonomy; however, the Western powers were still anxious to maintain their military and petroleum interests in the region. The problems involving the future of the British mandate in Palestine were particularly intractable and led directly to the ongoing Arab-Israeli conflict. Although this conflict was intrinsically intertwined with political, economic, and social developments in the region, it will be discussed at length in the following chapter.

To protect their vital interests in the Middle East, the British encouraged the creation of the Arab League in 1945. The League was designed to foster interstate cooperation, however, it was continually disrupted by feuds among the various independent Arab nations. After the war, interdynastic disputes among the Hashimites in Jordan and Iraq, the Saudi monarchy in Saudi Arabia, and King Faruk in Egypt were major stumbling blocks to Arab unification. After 1952 the Arab world was divided by rivalries between the conservative, generally promonarchy forces (Saudi Arabia and Jordan) and the so-called revolutionary forces in Egypt (under Nasser), Syria, and Iraq.

Attacking Imperialism

We, the whole generation, began to move towards violence. I confess . . . that political assassinations blazed in my inflamed mind.

I remember one night in particular. . . . We had prepared everything. . . . We selected one to put out of the way. . . . The plot was to shoot him as he returned home at night.

The appointed night came and I went out myself with the squad of execution. Everything went as we imagined. The person came and bullets were fired. . . .

I got home, threw myself on the bed, my mind in a fever, my heart and conscience incessantly boiling. . . . Suddenly I found myself exclaiming, "I wish he would not die." I rushed anxiously to the morning papers. I was happy to find that the individual whose assassination I plotted was destined to live.*

————— ◆◀◗▶◆ —————

Gamal Abdel Nasser describes how he and many other idealistic and nationalistic young people fought against the corrupt monarchy of King Faruk and British imperial control over Egypt in the years before World War II. Nasser became politically active in his late teens and as a military officer led the 1952 revolution that ousted Faruk. Between 1952 and his death in 1970, Nasser was the dominant political power in Egypt and a powerful charismatic force throughout the Arab world.

*From *The Philosophy of Revolution* by Gamal Abdel Nasser. Copyright © 1959 by Smith, Keynes, and Marshall, Buffalo, N.Y.

Mounting nationalist demands and the humiliating loss of the first Arab-Israeli war in 1948 led to sweeping changes in much of the Arab world. In Egypt the people blamed the corrupt monarchy of King Faruk for the loss of Palestine and the Israeli military victory in 1948. In 1952 a determined group of army officers ousted King Faruk in an almost bloodless coup d'etat. The officers, led by Gamal Abdel Nasser, announced plans for the eradication of imperialism and for massive economic and social reforms. The Aswan Dam, a huge development project to increase agricultural land and to provide hydroelectric power for villages and a new industrial base was the cornerstone of the economic program. The largest project of its kind in the world at the time, the Aswan project was originally supported by the West.

However, during the 1950s Nasser moved toward a stance of positive neutralism and improved relations with the Eastern bloc and China; as a result, the United States and its Western allies became increasingly hostile to his regime. Thus, as in Asia and Latin America, the Middle East also became a field for Cold War competitions. A highly charismatic personality and a brilliant public speaker in colloquial Arabic, Nasser was extremely popular throughout the Arab world. His support among Arab nationalists also caused Israelis to fear that he might be able to unify the Arab world and launch a successful military attack against Israel. As Nasser's popularity skyrocketed in the Arab world, he became increasingly unpopular in the West, and the Unit-

Egyptian President Nasser chats with Chinese Premier
Zhou Enlai in Cairo in 1965.
(UPI/Bettmann Newsphotos)

ed States ultimately decided to withdraw its support for the Aswan Dam,
thereby setting in process a chain of events that led directly to the second
Arab-Israeli war in 1956 (see Chapter 27).

THE ARAB COLD WAR AND DOMESTIC DEVELOPMENT

The second Arab-Israeli war resulted in another Israeli military victory but
again failed to achieve a peace settlement. The war also led to a wave of anti-
Western and pro-Nasser sentiments in the Middle East. Indeed, every Arab-Israeli war resulted in major political upheavals in the Arab world. After 1956
pro-Western Arab governments, particularly the conservative monarchies,
were severely threatened by pro-Nasser forces. This conflict between prorevo-
lutionary forces and conservative regimes was dubbed "The Arab Cold War."
After some delay, the Soviets agreed to lend financial and technical assistance
to build the Aswan dam. In 1958 revolutionary activity in the region reached
its peak. The conservative Hashimite monarchy in Iraq (see Chapter 17) was
overthrown by a military junta, which was in turn ousted in 1963 by an officer
group from the Ba'ath party, which espoused Arab unity and socialism. In the

following two decades, Ba'athists continued to rule in Iraq, while a more conservative Ba'athist group ruled in Syria under Hafiz al-Asad. The precarious throne of King Husayn, the Hashimite monarch of Jordan, was saved only by British parachutists.

In 1958 the U.S. Marines intervened in a civil war in Lebanon, acting under the proviso of the Eisenhower Doctrine that the United States would intervene in support of governments fighting communism. Actually, the Lebanese civil war was largely a conflict between conservatives and the leftist pro-Nasser forces; the war was temporarily settled by reestablishing another coalition government of Christian and Muslim Lebanese. However, the coalition perpetuated the problem of religious communalism in Lebanon.

Within the Arab world, Middle Eastern nations after World War II generally sought to create secular nationalist states similar to those found in the West; in non-Arab Turkey and Iran this continued a process begun under Ataturk and Reza Shah. Modernizing regimes often copied plans for agricultural and industrial development from the West and placed great emphasis on advanced technologies. The continued conflict between Israel and the Arab states, however, forced Middle Eastern nations to apportion increasing amounts of their gross national products to large armies and defense expenditures.

In spite of political problems and continued warfare, the Arab governments attempted, with varying degrees of success, to improve the standard of living of their people. They improved education—for girls as well as boys—and initiated other social welfare projects. By the 1960s and 1970s, when petroleum revenues became substantial, economic development surged dramatically, particularly in the petroleum-rich nations of Saudi Arabia, Libya, and the sheikdoms of the Arab/Persian Gulf. These areas, which previously had been among the poorest in the Middle East, were able with so-called petrodollars to embark on ambitious programs to build new hospitals, homes, schools, airports, and roads. Often, as in Kuwait, the governments provided its citizens free education through the university level, low-cost or free housing, free medical care, including dental and eye services, and even low-interest loans for starting new businesses. The Middle East tended to be divided between rich, relatively sparsely populated nations with conservative regimes and heavily populated, poor states often with socialist governments. Thus, nations without petroleum, such as Egypt, which had the largest Arab population, remained desperately poor and constantly had to struggle to provide even minimum services for their peoples.

MODERNISM VERSUS FUNDAMENTALISM: THE IRANIAN REVOLUTION

By the 1970s continued economic, political, and social problems had caused many people in the region to question and ultimately to reject the Western-based secular nationalist programs that their governments had instituted. As the governments, often military dictatorships, failed to satisfy the demands of the people, to solve the Arab-Israeli conflict, and to avoid entanglements with or dependency on the superpowers, many in the Middle East—as elsewhere in the world—began to turn toward religion. Increasingly, militant Muslims argued that the Western-based models, whether from the United States or the Soviet Union, were foreign, artificial imports that did not reflect the realities of Middle Eastern societies. They advocated the institution of Islamic governments ruled not by secular, essentially Western, legal codes, (as in Turkey or Tunisia), but by the Sharia, the Islamic law.

The move away from secularism was not limited only to Muslims; the Maronite Christians in Lebanon and some Jewish Israelis, particularly many new immigrants from the United States, pushed for increased religious participation in government and in society in general. Thus the ongoing trend of tension between the secular and the spiritual was brought into clear focus. This conflict would later break out into open warfare in Lebanon and would form the basis of sweeping revolutionary changes in Iran.

The modernizing state of Iran had become one of the cornerstones of U.S. foreign policy after World War II. The pro-United States ruler Mohammad Reza Shah built up a huge military complex using U.S. foreign aid and petroleum revenues that rose sharply during the 1970s. He also implemented the "White Revolution," which was to develop Iran agriculturally and industrially while improving living standards for all Iranians. Economic development seemed rapid, but it was accompanied by growing inflation, corruption in the highest levels of government, an actual decline in some agricultural sectors, and increased political repression. Disaffected Iranians from the political left and from the strongly entrenched Shia clergy on the right joined forces to launch a protracted and often bloody struggle which led to the overthrow of the shah in 1979. The shah and his family went into exile, and an Islamic republic based on strict application of Islamic law was instituted with the Imam (referred to in the West as the Ayatollah) Ruhollah Khomeini acting as the final voice of authority.

The new revolutionary government of Iran vowed to eradicate the abuses of the old regime, to champion traditional Islamic values, and to improve living conditions. Iranian leaders denounced the United States as "the Great Satan" for its support of the old regime and demanded that the shah be returned to stand trial for his alleged crimes. After the United States refused, the U.S. embassy in Iran was occupied in November 1979 and the staff taken hostage. For over a year there ensued threats, negotiations, and denunciations. The United States froze Iranian assets and attempted a rescue mission that proved abortive. Finally, in January 1981, a complex agreement was reached and the hostages were released.

The furor over the hostages often obscured the severe domestic problems faced by the new regime. Within Iran, there were open clashes as a number of different parties, particularly from the left and the right, sought to gain power. The religious right emerged victorious, with the mullahs (clergy) becoming the dominant political force in Iran. They championed the creation of Islamic governments, not only in Iran but throughout the vast Islamic world.

In 1978 massive demonstrations, boycotts, and strikes by thousands of Iranians helped to overthrow the Pahlevi dynasty. Many revolutionary women, as seen above, adopted "Islamic" dress as a symbol of their opposition to the shah. In much of the world, men and women wear Islamic garb to demonstrate their hostility to Westernization, particularly in cultural and social fields.
(*AP/Wide World Photos*)

The religious forces also pushed for the implementation of strict, traditional values in all aspects of society, including traditional dress and codes of behavior for women.

The victory of the Islamist forces in Iran gave moral support to other Islamist movements, particularly in the Arab world. By the 1990s Islamist parties had become enormously popular. In nations as widespread and diverse as Algeria, Egypt, the Sudan (where an Islamic regime already held power), and Jordan, militant Islamist movements demanded more conservative social legislation, particularly regarding women and the family. In many of these nations it seemed likely that were open and free elections to be held, the Islamist forces would easily win. As the century drew to a close, it was by no means clear whether the forces of secular nationalism or religious fundamentalism would emerge victorious.

CIVIL WAR IN LEBANON

Meanwhile, Lebanon became a battleground for both domestic and regional disputes. After 1970, Palestinian border raids from Lebanon into Israel increased, and the Israelis retaliated with ground and air strikes, including the bombing of Lebanese villages. The ongoing domestic tensions and border violence resulted in a protracted and bloody civil war that in effect divided Lebanon into several distinct sections. The Lebanese civil war, which continued intermittently after 1975, was partially caused by communal differences between Muslims and Christians. Political splits between the left and the right and the presence of many armed and politically active Palestinians also contributed to upsetting the fragile governmental balance. In addition, outside interference by Israel, Syria, and other surrounding Arab nations, and interventions by Western powers made acceptable compromises to reunite the nation almost impossible. Indeed, Lebanon became a surrogate battleground for wider conflicts. The war resulted in the Syrian occupation of parts of Lebanon, while the United Nations stationed troops along the border with Israel. Armed confrontations continued in southern Lebanon as Palestinian and leftist Lebanese forces fought with the Israelis and the Israeli-supported enclave in southern Lebanon. Clashes among the various forces also continued in Beirut. Mediation efforts by the United States, Saudi Arabia, and other nations from 1975 to 1981 failed to remedy the cycle of violence that turned Beirut, once one of the loveliest cities in the Middle East, into a scene of bombings, random assassinations, and extensive destruction. When Israel launched a massive invasion of Lebanon in 1982, the conflict exploded into the fifth Arab-Israeli war (see Chapter 27).

Israel won another military victory in 1982, but the conflict failed to resolve either the Arab-Israel conflict or the problems in Lebanon. In the aftermath of years of war, it appeared that Lebanon was moving increasingly toward a de facto partition, with separate Muslim and Christian governments. Although Israeli and Syrian forces continued to occupy large parts of the fractured nation, a fragile peace was achieved by 1991. However, Lebanon demonstrated the continued problems inherent in its confessional system, in which a citizen's religious affiliation forms the basis of national identity and participation in political, social, and economic institutions.

SUPERPOWER RIVALRY IN THE MIDDLE EAST

To complicate matters further, the Middle East, with its vast petroleum reserves and strategic location, was of major importance to both the United States and the Soviet Union. After World War II, as already noted, both nations periodically became directly and indirectly involved in various regional disputes. For example, in December 1979 the Soviet Union moved into Afghanistan. The collapse of the pro-U.S. Iranian regime and the unstable nature of the revolutionary Iranian government caused both the Soviet Union and the United States to reassess their positions in the region.

Since World War II, Afghanistan had remained one of the poorest and least-developed nations in the area, one in which numerous political factions constantly attempted to gain power. Following a cycle of coups and counter-coups, Babrak Karmal, backed by the Soviet Union, emerged as the leader of Afghanistan. To protect the dependent regime, the Soviet Union moved over

80,000 troops into Afghanistan. Political hostility to the Karmal regime and the presence of foreign troops led to an armed resistance movement dominated by militant Muslims, or Mujahedin. Many Mujahedin emulated the Iranian revolution and received military aid from the United States. As fighting in Afghanistan escalated, over a million refugees fled into Pakistan, which already had severe population problems.

Soviet involvement in Afghanistan largely isolated the Soviet Union from the Islamic world. The traditional governments in the Middle East, particularly in Saudi Arabia and the petroleum-rich sheikdoms of the Persian Gulf, fearing both the spread of the Iranian revolution with its particular brand of radicalism and the Soviet influence in the region, condemned the Soviet actions in Afghanistan. Because the mountainous terrain was ideal for guerrilla warfare, Soviet forces, even with superior military equipment, found it impossible to eradicate the Afghan opposition. In 1988 and 1989 the Soviets withdrew from Afghanistan, leaving the pro-Soviet Afghan government and the Mujahedin in a protracted struggle for control over the nation. Importantly, the war in Afghanistan further debilitated the fragile Soviet economy and contributed to the collapse of the Soviet Union (see Chapter 33).

Meanwhile, the United States moved to establish closer relations with Middle Eastern nations. During the Cold War, Turkey had become one of the cornerstones of U.S. military strategy against the Soviet Union. In Turkey, the United States built large military bases and supported Turkish entry into NATO (see Chapter 22).

However, the status of the strategic island of Cyprus off the Turkish coast was a major area of disagreement among Turkey, Greece, another U.S. NATO ally, and the United States. The population of Cyprus was comprised of a majority of people who were of Greek heritage and a minority who were of Turkish ancestry. Some Cypriots wanted an independent nation, and others wanted to merge with Greece. Following an attempted Greek coup d'etat and a Turkish armed invasion in 1974, a so-called Green Line manned by U.N. forces divided Cyprus into Greek and Turkish sectors. The U.S. government tended to favor Turkish claims because of the close military alliance, but public opinion in the United States was overwhelmingly pro-Greek. Consequently, Turkey gradually moved further away from the U.S. orbit, and Cyprus remained an area of heightened tension in the eastern Mediterranean. Even with the end of the Cold War, the island remained divided, and protracted U.N. mediation failed to resolve the differences among the Greek, Turkish, and Cypriot governments.

During the 1970s and 1980s the United States relied on the Arab states of Egypt and Saudi Arabia, on Israel, and on U.S. military strength in the Red Sea and the Persian Gulf to counter possible Soviet expansion into the Arab world and the region in general. Following Sadat's assassination in 1981, U.S. reliance on Israel and Saudi Arabia increased. The main thrust of U.S. military power in the region was through the Rapid Deployment Force, whereby armed units could be moved into the area. However, although the Saudis pressured for increased armaments (including sophisticated reconnaissance planes such as AWACs), most nations, both Arab and non-Arab, in the Middle East were reluctant to accept the permanent stationing of U.S. forces on their territories. Nonetheless, the United States created a substantial informal military presence in Egypt and Saudi Arabia.

The United States also concentrated on extending its military links with nations around the Persian Gulf. For the first time in its history, it established a permanent naval force in the Indian Ocean, with a new naval base at Diego Garcia; the United States also developed facilities in Somalia. Although the Soviets built up bases in South Yemen, in Ethiopia, and on the Indian Ocean, on balance, the United States, Great Britain, and France maintained military superiority in the region. Regional disputes, particularly over access to and control of the vital Persian Gulf, constantly threatened to upset the precarious military balance devised by the Soviets and the United States.

THE IRAN-IRAQ AND GULF WARS

The Islamist fervor of Iran threatened not only the secular Arab governments but also the Saudi monarchy, which, although it based its legitimacy upon Islam, maintained close relations with the West, particularly the United States. Islamist groups in Egypt, Tunisia, Lebanon, and elsewhere in the Muslim world were encouraged by the successes of the Iranian revolution and occasionally (as in Lebanon) even received direct support from Iran.

After Iran called for an Islamic revolution in neighboring Iraq, the Ba'athist government under Saddam Hussein moved to defuse the Islamic revolution and to settle old grievances by attacking Iran in September 1980. In a brutal power struggle, the war dragged on as Iran refused to compromise with the Iraqi regime, or what Iranians called the "Great Satan's Puppet Ba'ath party." By 1988, the eighth year of the war, there had been over a million casualties and the two nations had spent more than $450 billion—more than the United States had expended in all the years of fighting in Vietnam. Attempting to win the war, Iran used waves of men, some as young as fourteen, to clear mine fields, while Iraq used poison gas; the capital cities of both nations were periodically attacked by missiles. To continue this war of attrition, Iraq obtained military supplies from the Soviet Union, other Arab nations, and the United States, while Iran secured supplies from Korea, China, and Israel among others.

Owing to its opposition to the Iranian revolutionary regime, the United States tended, at least publicly, to support Iraq during this long war. It increased its military presence in the Gulf and agreed to arms shipments to Iraq. However, after the war, it became public knowledge that despite its public stance against the Iranian regime, which had been accused of supporting terrorism throughout the world, the United States had quietly continued negotiations with Iran. Through its ally Israel, the United States had also sold or approved arms shipments to Iran, thereby enabling it to continue the struggle. The Israeli government held that continued division within the Arab world

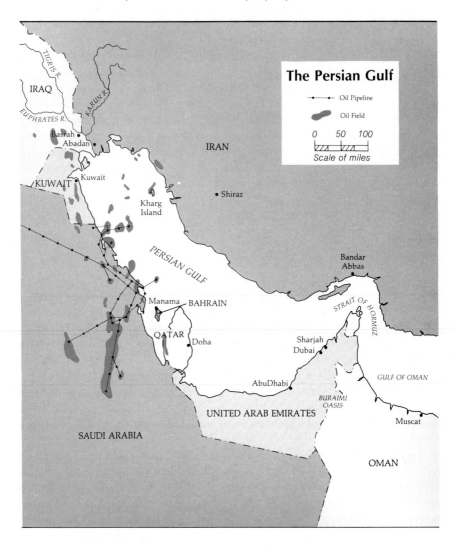

and diversions such as the Iran-Iraq war prevented the Arabs from directing hostilities against Israel. As one Israeli official said, "We don't want this war ever to end." Kissinger also noted that the United States did not want either side to win. Thus, as in previous instances, a local dispute became entangled with larger regional and international issues and with the unresolved Arab-Israeli conflict.

By the summer of 1988 the Iranian regime, which was finding it increasingly difficult to secure young volunteers to fight the war and which was suffering under continued Iraqi attacks, began negotiations through the offices of the United Nations and an uneasy armistice was arranged. Following Khomeini's death in 1989, the clergy (mullahs) retained power; although the new leaders tended to be more pragmatic in their relations with the West, they continued the conservative social policies initiated after the revolution.

Iraq emerged from the war with a large, battle-trained, well-equipped military, but its economy had been severely weakened; and it owed vast amounts of money borrowed during the war to Arab nations, particularly to Saudi Arabia and Kuwait. When these nations began pressing for the return of loans, Saddam Hussein angrily countered that Iraqis had fought and died in the war in part to protect the Gulf states from possible overthrow by the revolutionary Islamic government in Iran. Consequently, Iraq considered the money provided to buy arms during the war as payment by the Gulf states for having borne the burden of the war. In addition, Saddam Hussein was angry over what he perceived to be attempts to strangle Iraq economically. Western and petroleum-rich nations refused to grant loans for the rebuilding of Iraq, and Kuwait was allegedly slant-drilling into Iraqi petroleum fields, a practice that deprived Iraq of much needed petroleum revenues. Although Iraq had diplomatic relations with Kuwait, it had long-standing grievances with its neighbor and considered Kuwait an integral part of the historic borders of Iraq. Determined to maintain his total control over the Iraqi government and military, Saddam Hussein also sought to garner popular support by adopting an aggressive, strong stance against the West and Israel.

When negotiations among Arab regimes failed to resolve the differences, and relying on what appeared to be a lack of United States interest in the problem, Iraq invaded and conquered Kuwait in August 1990. The international community, including most Arab states, promptly condemned the aggression and demanded an immediate withdrawal by Iraq and the return of the Kuwaiti monarchy. With the Soviet Union in economic shambles, the United States had emerged as the sole superpower and it was determined to maintain its petroleum and political interests in the region. An international coalition under the auspicious of the United Nations, but fashioned by the United States, began a colossal military buildup in Saudi Arabia and the Gulf. When Saddam Hussein refused to withdraw Iraqi troops from Kuwait, the coalition forces, led by the United States, began a massive month-long aerial bombardment in January 1991. A short ground war in Kuwait followed in February with massive coalition victories on all fronts. The war ended in a clear-cut military victory for the coalition forces and the United States and the return of the pro-Western monarchy to Kuwait.

On the other hand, the Gulf war had mixed political results. Although there were uprisings among Kurds in northern Iraq and Shias in the south, Saddam Hussein's oppressive regime stayed in power. In addition, with the weakening of Iraq as the major Arab military power, Iran increasingly emerged as the regional force in Gulf. Nor did the war lead to democracy in the region. Although the monarchs in Kuwait and Saudi Arabia made some limited gestures toward opening up the political system, most of the regimes in the region appeared determined to retain absolute control and to thwart meaningful steps toward democracy. Jordan and Yemen were two exceptions. King Hussein in Jordan moved cautiously but steadily toward implementing increased political participation and open elections and Yemen also held open elections for members of parliament.

In contrast to the trend toward partition or Balkanization of the Arab world into even more small, separate nations, as in Lebanon and Iraq, northern and southern Yemen unified in 1990 and instituted sweeping democratic reforms. Many in the region feared that the possible partition of Iraq would create a snowball effect, paving the way for the collapse or division of unified nations like Egypt and Syria. The further partition of the Arab world might easily plunge the region into the sort of bloody civil strife seen in the Balkans, former Soviet republics in the Caucasus, and in the Horn of Africa. In addition, popular opposition to established political powers increasingly mobilized behind Islamist political parties that threatened the existence of both radical and pro-Western regimes. Thus, the Middle East remained one of the most volatile areas in the world.

SUMMARY

Regional differences, territorial disputes, and domestic problems made the Middle East a "hot spot." Like most of the Third World, it was an area of rapid change and uncertainty. The political fights between leftists and conservative forces within Middle Eastern nations and among the various governments of the region led to upheavals. The Arab-Israeli conflict also contributed to violence in the region. The emergence of various militant religious groups radically altered the nature of many Middle Eastern governments, particularly in Iran. Lebanon also became the surrogate battleground for many of these disputes. In addition, both superpowers had problems dealing with the new independent and dynamic nations and sought to establish alliances and military bases in the region.

Regional problems were further complicated by the geopolitical interests of the United States and the Soviet Union. Because of their strategic locations and their regional position as the world's largest producers of petroleum, Middle Eastern nations were of vital concern not only to the superpowers but also to the rest of the industrialized world. The Soviets suffered a defeat in Afghanistan, while the United States had continued problems in maintaining its petroleum and military interests in the area. The Gulf became a flash point for many of these conflicting interests and was the battleground in the long Iran-Iraq conflict and the far-shorter Gulf war of 1991.

SUGGESTED SOURCES

AROIAN, LOIS A., and RICHARD P. MITCHELL, *The Modern Middle East and North Africa* (1984). A concise textbook survey.

AWWAD, TAWFIQ YUSUF, *Death in Beirut* (1978). A novel tracing the political and religious divisions of Lebanese society before the civil war.*

FERNEA, ELIZABETH WARNOCK, Ed., *Women and the Family in the Middle East: New Voices of Change* (1985). Collection of firsthand accounts including poems and short stories by Middle Eastern women.*

GILMOUR, DAVID, *Lebanon: The Fractured Country* (1984). Balanced discussion of the causes and results of the Lebanese civil war.*

HALLIDAY, FRED, *Iran: Dictatorship and Development* (1979). An in-depth analysis of Iran before the 1979 revolution.*

HIRO, DILIP, *Islamic Fundamentalism* (1988). Incisive account of the role of Islam in culture and politics.*

HUNTER, SHIREEN T., *Iran and the World: Continuity in a Revolutionary Decade* (1990). In-depth analysis of Iran since the 1979 revolution.*

KORANY, BAHGAT, and ALI E. HILLAL DESSOUKI, *The Foreign Policy of Arab States: The Challenge of Change* (1991). Sophisticated discussion of complex political policies adopted by Arab governments during the Cold War.*

MARR, PHEBE, and WILLIAM LEWIS, Eds., *Riding the Tiger: The Middle East Challenge After the Cold War* (1993). Contributors focus on changing forces within the Middle East and the future U.S. role in the region.*

MOSLEY, LEONARD, *Power Play: Petroleum in the Middle East* (1973). Focuses on personalities involved in the development of the petroleum industry in the Middle East.*

WOODWARD, PETER, *Nasser* (1992). Incisive short biography of Arab nationalist leader.*

*Paperback available.

CHAPTER 27

The Arab-Israeli Conflict

As described in the previous chapter, the Middle East after World War II was swept by waves of nationalist fervor and became a region of enormous upheaval and conflict. Palestine was one of the major focal points of those changes. Before the war, Great Britain, in its Palestine mandate, had tried to pacify Palestinian Arab opposition by limiting Jewish immigration and by promising independence in the future. Because of the anti-Semitic basis of the Nazi regime, Great Britain knew that world Jewry would support the Allied war efforts. Thus assured of Jewish support, Great Britain felt safe in making friendly gestures toward the Arabs. This policy angered the Zionists, who believed all Jews in the diaspora (Jews scattered throughout the world) had the right to settle in Palestine.

THE CREATION OF ISRAEL AND THE 1948 WAR

When World War II ended, the Arab-Israeli conflict became the major political and military problem in the Middle East. After 1945, both the Zionists and the Palestinian Arabs pushed for the creation of their own individual nations; the problem was that each of these nationalist groups sought to express its independence within the same geographic territory. The Palestinians, who in 1945 were about two-thirds of the local population and owned about 80 percent of the land, believed the territory was theirs. On the other hand, the Zionists believed that through historical and religious involvement, the territory was theirs. In addition, Jewish national claims had enormous emotional support in the West and among Jewish survivors of the Holocaust, as a result of the tremendous suffering of the Jewish communities within Nazi-controlled Europe. The Holocaust, with its untold horrors, had caused many Westerners to conclude that the Zionists were correct in advocating a Jewish national state that would protect the religious and political rights of the Jewish people. In opposition, the Palestinians and the Arabs generally viewed anti-Semitism and the Holocaust as Western problems for which they were not responsible and for which they should not be forced to pay.

Jewish immigrants who fled Nazi persecution in Europe enter Palestine in 1939 despite British laws.
(*AP/Wide World Photos*)

In this situation, the British, who had played Palestinian and Zionist nationalisms against each other, were caught on the horns of a dilemma. If the British continued to support the creation of a Jewish state and the further immigration of survivors of the Holocaust to Palestine, Great Britain would lose support in the Arab world, with its petroleum resources and strategic locations. On the other hand, by attempting to limit Jewish immigration into Palestine, the British were placed in the untenable moral position of opposing and often imprisoning Jewish immigrants coming directly from the concentration camps in Europe. The British administration in Palestine also faced increased armed opposition by both the resident Zionists and the Palestinian Arabs. Furthermore, the British had severe domestic economic problems and were forced to cope with mounting nationalist demands throughout the empire.

The British solved their dilemma by washing their hands of it. In 1947, the year of Indian independence, Great Britain turned the problem over to the United Nations, which promptly formed a committee to investigate the problem. The U.N. committee (UNSCOP) recommended in its majority report that Palestine be divided into a Jewish state and an Arab state. Partition had been suggested on previous occasions but was not overwhelmingly popular. The Palestinians immediately opposed the UNSCOP plan, which allocated approximately 50 percent of the territory, including the more fertile coastal areas, to the Jewish state. The Zionists reluctantly accepted the idea of partition but were dissatisfied because the plan did not allot to them all the area of ancient Israel.

Despite the mounting violence in Palestine, in November 1947 the United Nations voted for the partition plan that was to be implemented when the British withdrew in May 1948. In the interim, violence spread throughout Palestine as both sides began to prepare for battle. On May 14, 1948, as the British hastily withdrew, David Ben-Gurion, who was fairly confident of U.S. and Soviet support, announced the creation of the state of Israel.

The surrounding Arab states and the Palestinian Arabs refused to recognize the new state, and the first Arab-Israeli war promptly began. The Arab forces, saddled with corrupt leadership, divided chains of command, faulty weapons, and no clear-cut military strategy, were no match for the well-organized, trained, and spirited Israelis. The Israelis won the 1948 war, expanding Israeli territory by approximately one-third more than granted under the original U.N. partition plan. The West Bank, which had been apportioned to the Arab state under the U.N. plan, was incorporated into Jordan. Jerusalem was divided between Israeli and Jordanian control, and the Gaza strip was administered by Egypt.

One way or another, all Palestinian Arabs found themselves under the control of others. Before and during the war, thousands of Palestinians, particularly peasants, fled their farms and homes. The Arabs maintained that the refugees, who clustered in southern Lebanon, the West Bank, and the Gaza strip, had been forced to leave because of Zionist terrorism and violence. The Israelis argued that they were not responsible for the refugees, who, according to Israel, had left as a result of Arab pressures or of their own free will. There are cases supporting both allegations, but there is no doubt that the 1948 war left almost a million Palestinians homeless. Receiving meager support from the U.N., these refugees numbered over 2 million by the 1990s, but they remained determined to return to their homeland. The guerrillas of the Palestinian liberation organizations that were active from 1967 onward came predominantly from the refugee camps.

With enormous domestic economic and political problems of their own, the Arab governments did little to solve the refugee problem and indeed often used the Palestinians for their own political aims. As the former Algerian leader Ahmed Ben Bella once remarked, "The Arabs in power bargain on the backs of the Palestinians." On the other hand, the Israelis generally refused responsibility and were reluctant to accept the return of the refugees, who they maintained would become a subversive presence within Israel. In addition, the Israelis stressed that the return of the Palestinians would alter the basic ethnic and religious structure of Israel and would thereby change its Zionist basis. Thus, although Israel won the 1948 war, no peace treaties were concluded, and the borders of Israel and the surrounding Arab nations remained tense.

DOMESTIC DEVELOPMENTS IN ISRAEL

On the domestic front, the newly created state of Israel concentrated on building new economic, political, and military structures while moving to assimilate large numbers of Jewish immigrants. By the 1970s Israel's multiparty system would lead to increased political divisions and infighting. Golda Meir, a leading Labor politician and prime minister, joked that if four Israelis met in a room they would create five political parties.

Economically, the kibbutzim, collective agricultural settlements created by the early Zionist immigrants, became less important as the nation's economy was increasingly geared toward manufacturing in the form of small factories, particularly those producing armaments and small cut diamonds. With huge expenditures devoted to the military, Israel remained heavily dependent on foreign assistance from Western nations, particularly France and later the United States, and donations from Jewish communities around the world.

THE 1956 WAR: THE COLD WAR SPREADS
TO THE MIDDLE EAST

Events in Egypt soon led to a second Arab-Israeli war. As previously discussed (see Chapter 26), a new regime under Nasser had come to power in Egypt in 1952. The new Egyptian government had announced a far-reaching development program with the Aswan (high) dam described as "more magnificent and seventeen times greater than the Pyramids," as its cornerstone. As previously noted, Nasser hoped to secure assistance from the West and the World Bank in order to build this massive project. When Nasser moved to improve Egyptian relations with the Soviet Union, China, and neutral Third World nations, Western support waned. In particular, U.S. Secretary of State John Foster Dulles was opposed to neutralism, which he believed was thinly disguised communism. After Nasser failed to receive military arms from the United States, he concluded an arms deal with Czechoslovakia. In light of these developments, Dulles abruptly announced the withdrawal of U.S. assistance for the Aswan Dam.

In Cairo, the refusal was correctly interpreted as an insult to Egypt and as a direct slap in the face to Nasser. In retaliation, on July 26, 1956, to the astonishment of many Western officials, Nasser nationalized the Suez Canal, which had previously been administered by the Suez Canal Company, whose stockholders were predominantly European. Furious, the British and French decided to take back the canal by force and to topple Nasser. The French government was also anxious to overthrow Nasser in order to end his support for the Algerians, who were fighting for independence. For political and military reasons, the Israelis were also willing to join in military actions with the French and British. The Israelis were being harassed by commando raids along their borders and feared Nasser's success in mobilizing Arab supporters throughout the region. An agreement was reached whereby Israel would launch an attack across the Sinai peninsula but would stop short of the Suez Canal. The British and French were then to intervene between the Israeli and Egyptian forces and occupy the canal. The scenario anticipated the immediate downfall of Nasser, followed by a more malleable or pro-Western Egyptian government.

In late October 1956 the Israelis successfully launched their attack and occupied the Sinai peninsula. After some delay, the British and French bombed Egyptian airfields and parachuted troops into positions along the Suez Canal. The tripartite collusion, which the British, French, and Israelis publicly denied for many years, was a military success but a political fiasco. Contrary to Western expectations, Nasser did not fall. In fact, the war strengthened his argument that the Western powers and Israel had imperial designs in the Middle East. The United States had opposed the use of military force and was placed in the awkward position of having to confront its closest allies, Great Britain and France; meanwhile, the Soviets played up the confrontation in order to divert attention from their invasion of Hungary. This divergence led to strained relations among the NATO allies.

Eventually, the British, French, and Israeli forces withdrew from Egyptian territory, but Israel secured free access through the Straits of Tiran to its southern port of Eilat. This acquisition, which the Egyptians and the Arab world never recognized, was to be the immediate cause of the 1967 Arab-Israeli war. As noted in the previous chapter, the 1956 war also led to widespread political changes in much of the Arab world.

THE 1967 "SIX-DAY" WAR AND AFTER

Because there had been no peace settlement following the 1956 war, both sides had continued to prepare for the next violent confrontation. In May 1967 Nasser, in an attempt to regain his preeminent position as leader of the Arab world, asked that the U.N. forces stationed on Egyptian territory, particularly those along the vital Straits of Tiran at Sharm al-Sheik, be withdrawn. Acting according to U.N. mandates that troops could be placed in sovereign territory only with the consent of the concerned nation, U Thant, the U.N. Secretary General, reluctantly agreed to withdraw the troops. After the 1956 war Israel had announced that it would consider any attempt to close the Straits of Tiran a cause for war. Quickly, both Israel and Egypt began to prepare for yet another confrontation. Syria and Egypt already had a mutual defense pact; although King Husayn of Jordan had been feuding with Nasser, he soon joined Egypt. Both the United States and the Soviet Union attempted to defuse the growing tensions, but while negotiations and talks were still in progress, Israel launched a preemptive strike against the airfields of Egypt, the major Arab nation, and other surrounding Arab nations, destroying Arab air strength within six hours.

The 1967 June war lasted six days but was really won by Israel within those first six hours. The Israelis, with complete air supremacy, soon defeated the Arab forces and occupied the Gaza strip, the entire Sinai peninsula, the

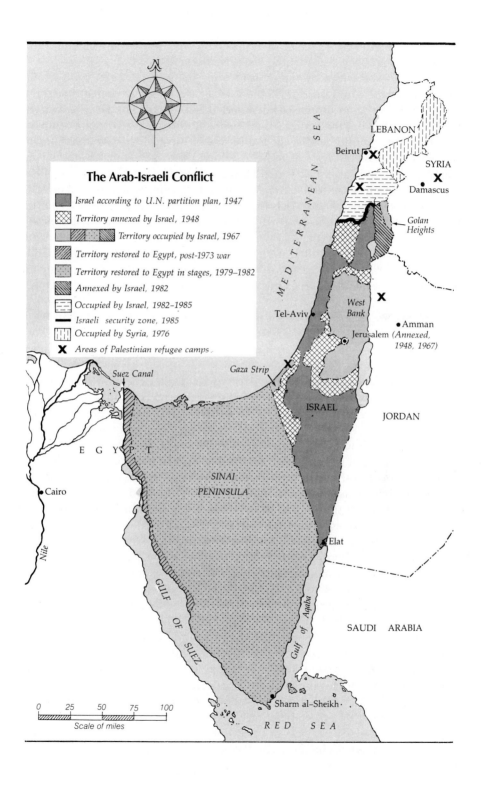

The Arab-Israeli Conflict

▨ Israel according to U.N. partition plan, 1947

▨ Territory annexed by Israel, 1948

▨ ▨ ▨ Territory occupied by Israel, 1967

▨ Territory restored to Egypt, post-1973 war

▨ Territory restored to Egypt in stages, 1979–1982

▨ Annexed by Israel, 1982

▨ Occupied by Israel, 1982–1985

━ Israeli security zone, 1985

▨ Occupied by Syria, 1976

✗ Areas of Palestinian refugee camps .

MEDITERRANEAN SEA

LEBANON

Beirut **✗**

SYRIA
✗
Damascus

Golan
Heights

West
Bank **✗**

Tel-Aviv

Jerusalem
●Amman
(Annexed,
1948, 1967)

Gaza Strip **✗**

ISRAEL

JORDAN

Suez Canal

EGYPT

●Cairo

SINAI
PENINSULA

Nile

GULF

OF

SUEZ

Gulf of Aqaba

Elat

SAUDI ARABIA

Sharm al-Sheikh .

0   25   50   75   100
Scale of miles

RED   SEA

West Bank (including the rest of Jerusalem), and the Golan Heights, from which Syria had been bombarding Israeli settlements.

The 1967 war was a dramatic victory for the Israelis and a complete humiliation for the Arab world. In the face of the massive defeat, Nasser resigned, but the Egyptian masses demanded his return. The Israelis were initially optimistic that their military victory would force peace negotiations. At first they were willing to discuss the return of most of the Occupied Territories, with the exception of Jerusalem, which they subsequently unified and proclaimed as the capital of Israel. However, the United Nations and the international community refused to recognize this gain, which was against the U.N. charter provision expressly forbidding territorial gains made through armed conflict. Israel refused to withdraw from the Occupied Territories until there were direct peace negotiations and full recognition of its existence by the Arab nations. The Arab nations refused to enter into direct negotiations or to accept Israel's right to any of the territory secured in the war. They also continued to demand the recognition of Palestinian rights to a homeland of their own.

The 1967 war also increased the refugee problem, since over 200,000 refugees crossed from the West Bank to the East Bank in Jordan. Only a small fraction of this number were permitted to return to the Occupied Territories after the war. Thus the stalemate was complete—no war, no peace. Various attempts were made to mediate the dispute, particularly by the United States, but all failed.

In the interim, the Palestinians concluded that no outside powers, including the Arab governments, would secure an independent Palestinian state. Consequently, a number of Palestinian guerrilla groups emerged from the disasters of the 1967 war and formed loose alliances under the umbrella of the Palestine Liberation Organization (PLO). The largest and most well-known of these groups was al-Fatah, led by Yasir Arafat. The PLO began a series of raids and attacks into Israeli territory; when these tactics failed to secure the objective of a Palestinian state, some Palestinians expanded the struggle to targets outside the Middle East and to those powers or individuals who supported Israel. These tactics included skyjackings, assassinations, and bombings. Some Arab leaders, including al-Asad in Syria and al-Qadhdhafi in Libya, also supported these tactics. Israel retaliated with raids and attacks into surrounding Arab nations and ultimately with assassinations of Palestinian leaders. Thus the cycle of mounting terrorism spread around the globe.

The PLO was particularly strong in Jordan, where about half the population was Palestinian. As it became clear to King Husayn that he was close to losing control of his government to the PLO, he launched an armed attack against Palestinian units in Jordan in September 1970. In the ensuing bloody war the Jordanian forces inflicted heavy casualties on the Palestinians. Nasser, in one of his last accomplishments before his death in September 1970, effected a settlement between the warring factions. Following the Jordanian civil war, the PLO moved its main base of operations to Lebanon, which then became the stage for armed clashes between Palestinians and Israelis.

EGYPT AND ISRAEL: WAR, THEN PEACE

Anwar Sadat, a fellow army officer with Nasser, succeeded as Egyptian president following Nasser's death. Most observers predicted that Sadat would not survive long, but their analyses were proven wrong as he revealed far more political acumen than had been anticipated. With strong fortifications along the Suez Canal, the Israelis were confident that the Egyptians could never cross. In October 1973, after several years of preparation, each of which he had termed his "year of decision" and which some Egyptians had dubbed his "years of indecision," Sadat launched a successful attack across the canal. Several weeks of tank and air battles in the Sinai followed and culminated in the Israelis making a countercrossing onto the western bank of the canal; Israeli and Syrian troops also clashed along the Golan Heights. The war caused a major confrontation between the Soviets who backed Syria and the United States who was the main supplier of arms to Israel. Following tense negotiations between the Soviets and Secretary of State Henry Kissinger, a cease-fire was implemented. Militarily, both sides claimed a victory.

Following the war, Sadat was hailed as the Arab leader who had taken the resolution of the Arab-Israeli conflict off the "back burner" and placed it at the forefront of international attention. Sadat also hoped to secure substantial economic aid from the United States in order to bolster the flagging Egyptian economy. With the limited 1973 victory, Sadat moved to enter into negotiations with Israel, with the United States as an arbitrator. The United States was anxious to secure a settlement of the conflict in order to maintain a balance with the Soviet Union in the region. The United States was also eager to ensure the continued free flow of petroleum that Arab oil producers, led by Saudi Arabia, had threatened to restrict for all nations that supported Israel. The United States feared a total "Arab boycott" of petroleum, but while supplies diminished, the cutoff never materialized.

Several years of negotiations followed, characterized by Henry Kissinger's shuttle diplomacy from Tel Aviv to Cairo to Damascus, and back again. The outgrowth of these protracted negotiations was the reopening of the Suez Canal and partial withdrawal of Israeli troops from the Sinai and the Golan Heights. Although further direct negotiations were held briefly in Geneva, the issue of Palestinian participation prevented a settlement. The Arabs demanded that the Palestinians, represented by the PLO, be participants in negotiations that were to deal with their vital national interests, and the Israelis refused to include them.

As discussions dragged on with no resolution in sight, Sadat, who was anxious for a settlement in order to spend substantial amounts of money, not on arms, but on domestic development projects in Egypt, decided to take matters into his own hands. In November 1977 he made a dramatic personal visit to Israel. During his speech to the Knesset, the Israeli parliament, he urged direct peace settlements. Sadat's visit, the first public visit by an Arab leader to Israel, altered the psychological atmosphere of distrust and led to direct nego-

In March 1979 President Sadat of Egypt, President Carter of the United States, and Prime Minister Begin of Israel signed a peace treaty ending the war between Egypt and Israel, but the treaty failed to settle the on-going conflict between the Israelis and the Palestinians.
(*UPI/Bettmann Newsphotos*)

tiations between Egyptian and Israeli leaders. With Sadat as leader of Egypt, Israel also saw a possible opportunity to reach a peace settlement with the major and most populous Arab nation. Egyptian-Israeli negotiations intensified during the Camp David meetings in the United States in the fall of 1978, when President Jimmy Carter directly mediated between Sadat and Israeli Prime Minister Menachem Begin.

The Camp David talks culminated with the signing of a peace treaty between Egypt and Israel in the spring of 1979. The settlement provided for a full peace between Israel and Egypt and a gradual return of the Sinai peninsula to Egypt, but it did not address the issue of Palestinian self-determination or the continued Israeli occupation of the Occupied Territories (the West Bank and the Gaza strip). Likewise, the treaty contained no agreement on the status of Jerusalem, a city with sacred meaning for Jews, Christians, and Muslims.

The rest of the Arab world, particularly the Palestinians, opposed the peace treaty. Arab nations refused to recognize Israel until Palestinian demands for a homeland were fulfilled, and Israel refused to negotiate with the PLO, which Israelis considered a terrorist organization.

Following the separate peace treaty with Israel, Egypt was ostracized from the Arab world. Many Arabs, particularly militant Muslims, held Sadat personally responsible for the treaty and the failures to secure Palestinian national rights. As he instituted repressive political controls and ignored or failed to address growing corruption in both government and economic arenas, Sadat also became increasingly unpopular in Egypt.

To demonstrate their hatred of Sadat's national and foreign policies and in hopes of fomenting an Islamic revolution, Egyptian Muslim radicals assassinated Sadat in October 1981 during the anniversary celebration of the 1973 war. Although the assassination indicated the widespread support of Muslim militants in Egypt, the expected revolution did not occur and Husni Mubarak managed to steer a middle-of-the-road course between secular nationalist and Islamist forces. President Mubarak's subsequent attempts to resume good relations with the Arab nations and the Soviet Union turned the settlement between Egypt and Israel into what has been called a "cold peace." However, Egypt remained a primary example of a society and a nation torn between the conflicting forces of secularism and religious political fundamentalism. By the 1990s it was still not clear which side would emerge victorious.

THE 1982 WAR IN LEBANON

As noted in Chapter 26, Lebanon had become a battleground for both domestic and regional disputes. During the 1970s, the PLO had used southern Lebanon as a base from which to launch attacks on Israel. Israel retaliated by raiding southern Lebanon in an attempt to eradicate Palestinian power. Hundreds of Lebanese and Palestinians died in the raid and counterattacks. By the 1980s Israel made it clear that it would not tolerate the continued presence of the PLO in Lebanon, where owing to the disintegration of a unified Lebanese government, the Palestinians had succeeded in establishing something of a "state within a state." In June 1982, Israel launched a full-scale invasion of Lebanon with the primary intention of destroying the PLO military presence there. In the ensuing war, Israel bombarded Lebanese cities by land, sea, and air. Thousands of people were killed, injured, and made homeless. After bloody combat with the Palestinians and their Lebanese allies, the Israelis and their Lebanese Christian allies besieged West Beirut.

Following weeks of protracted Israeli bombings of the city, the PLO fighters and leaders were evacuated under the auspices of international peacekeeping forces. Bashir Gemayel, son of one of the leading rightist Lebanese Christians and leader of the largest private militia, was elected president of the war-torn nation. His assassination in September led Christian militiamen to massacre hundreds of Palestinians in Sabra and Shatila, the large Palestinian refugee camps in West Beirut under Israeli control.

After 1982, as Israeli and Syrian forces remained in occupation of the southern and eastern sections of the small nation, Lebanese religious and political militias continued to fight among themselves. When international peacekeeping forces, including U.S. marines, failed to keep the peace and attacks against Israeli occupying forces by Lebanese Shia groups intensified, Israel withdrew from much of southern Lebanon in 1985. However, Israel continued its occupation of a ten-mile so-called security zone in Lebanon; likewise, the Syrians continued to maintain a large military force in Lebanon. Thus it was evident that until solutions for the problem of Palestinian self-determination and a settlement of the wider Arab-Israeli conflict were devised, there was little likelihood of a resolution to the warfare in Lebanon, which constantly threatened to expand into a full-scale Middle Eastern war.

ISRAELIS AND PALESTINIANS

The 1982 war was a severe blow to the Palestinian liberation movement, but it also caused serious political divisions within Israel. The ultimate status of the West Bank and the Gaza strip, which had remained under Israeli occupation since the 1967 war, became the focal point of the controversy. Israelis were widely divided on the issue. The Likud, the conservative party of the right, generally aimed to keep all of the Occupied Territories; the Labor party generally advocated a "land for peace" solution in which some of the territories would be traded for a settlement of the ongoing conflict with the Palestinians. However, the Palestinians demanded that the PLO be their sole representative, and the Israeli government absolutely refused to deal with the PLO. Meanwhile, the number of Israeli settlements in the Occupied Territories continued to increase, and the 1.4 million Palestinians in the Occupied Territories became increasingly disenchanted with Israeli military control.

After intermittent confrontations, the conflict broke out in a full-scale uprising (Intifada) in December 1987. Palestinians, particularly the young people, demonstrated, went out on strike, boycotted Israeli goods and services, and threw stones. The Israeli army retaliated with an "Iron Fist" policy, in an attempt to repress the uprising. By 1991 more than 1000 Palestinians and dozens of Israelis had been killed; although there were fewer massive demonstrations, the conflict and Palestinian opposition to continued Israeli occupation showed few signs of ending.

The uprising caused political debates within Israel and among Jewish-Americans over possible solutions. The Israeli elections in the 1980s failed to give either the conservative Likud party or the Labor party a clear-cut majority, and they were therefore forced to create a kind of dual government in which both shared power. By 1988 it was clear that the Israeli population was fairly evenly divided between those who wished to keep the Occupied Territories and those who wished to reach a settlement with the Palestinians and return at least portions of the territory.

In a sweeping move, the PLO in 1988 declared the independence of Palestine (the West Bank and Gaza), recognized the existence of Israel, and called for a negotiated settlement of the conflict. Dozens of nations recognized the new Palestinian state and lauded the move toward peace. The United States agreed to negotiate, and in 1991 in a precedent-breaking move, all the parties involved agreed to public, face-to-face meetings in Madrid. These negotiations centered on the withdrawal of Israel from the Occupied Territories, self-

Following the Madrid peace conference in 1991, the Palestinian delegation, including Hanan Ashrawi (left center) and Faisal Al-Husseini (with microphone) were greeted by crowds waving olive branchs upon their return to the West Bank. The Madrid conference, supported by the United States, marked the first direct, official meetings between the Palestinians and the Israelis.
(Lagerquist/SIPA)

determination for the Palestinians, and security for Israel. However, Israel continued to build new settlements and to maintain its military control over the Palestinians in the Occupied Territories. These policies guaranteed the continuation of Palestinian opposition. Consequently, it was clear that the conflict would continue until the two major parties—the Israelis and the Palestinians—were able to reach a compromise or some negotiated settlement.

SUMMARY

The creation of Israel in 1948 resulted in the first Arab-Israeli war, the displacement and loss of self-government for the Palestinians, and the opposition of the Arab nations. The 1948 war and the subsequent four wars were military victories for the Israelis, but all failed to secure resolutions of the conflict. In the 1967 war Israel expanded considerably the amount of territory under its control, ultimately annexing East Jerusalem and the Golan Heights, Syrian territory. Following the 1973 war the Egyptians and Israelis, with substantial involvement of the United States, negotiated a territorial disengagement and peace treaty in 1979; however, this treaty did not resolve the root causes of the conflict. The continued Israeli occupation of the West Bank and the Gaza strip remained the focal point of conflict between the Israelis and the Palestinians. Although the Israelis and the Palestinians began direct negotiations in 1991, they have yet to resolve their differences. The Arab-Israeli conflict and the failure to achieve a solution to Palestinian demands for self-determination have proven to be two of the most intractable issues of the twentieth century.

SUGGESTED SOURCES

FERNEA, ELIZABETH WARNOCK, and MARY EVELYN HOCKING, Eds., *The Struggle for Peace: Israelis and Palestinians* (1992). Good for course study on conflict resolution in coordination with PBS film of the same name.*

HILTERMANN, JOOST R., *Behind the Intifada* (1991). Study of causes and motivations behind Palestinian uprising in the Occupied Territories.*

KHOURI, FRED, *The Arab-Israeli Dilemma,* 3d ed. (1985). A factual narrative of a complex conflict.*

NEFF, DONALD, *Warriors at Suez* (1981) and *Warriors for Jerusalem* (1984). Highly entertaining yet informative descriptions of personalities behind the 1956 and 1967 wars.*

RUBINSTEIN, ALVIN Z. *The Arab-Israeli Conflict,* 2d ed. (1991). Short overview with articles by a wide variety of authors.*

SADAT, ANWAR, *In Search of Identity, An Autobiography* (1979). The Egyptian leader describes his political life and beliefs.*

SHIPLER, DAVID, *Arab and Jew: Wounded Spirits in a Promised Land* (1986). Readable and moving account of the conflict with a focus on human dimensions.*

YOUNG, ELISE G., *Keepers of the History: Women and the Arab-Israeli Conflict* (1992). Provocative account focusing on Israeli and Palestinian women.

*Paperback available.

CHAPTER 28

Détente and Europe, 1963–1984

Following the Berlin crisis of 1961 and the Cuban missile crisis of 1962 the superpowers pulled back from confrontation and there was a movement toward détente (a lessening of tensions) in the Cold War. Beginning in the 1960s Western European nations, especially France, became less dependent on the United States. Eastern European nations, thanks in part to the Sino-Soviet split, were able to achieve more autonomy than the Soviet Union had previously allowed. During the 1970s U.S. diplomatic initiatives toward Communist China further contributed to transforming the bipolar U.S.-Soviet global rivalry into a multipolar global balance of power. Events in Czechoslovakia in 1968 and in Poland in 1981, however, indicated that the Soviet Union was still determined to keep Eastern European countries firmly within its orbit. In the late 1970s and early 1980s, tensions between the superpowers again intensified.

THE DAWN OF DÉTENTE

The Cuban missile crisis had been frightening, and in its aftermath many world leaders became interested in lessening tensions and thus reducing the chances of nuclear war. In 1963 the major atomic powers, joined by over 100 nations, signed the Nuclear Test Ban Treaty, which prohibited testing in outer space, in the atmosphere, and underwater. France and the People's Republic of China refused to sign; the French wished to do more testing to catch up with the advanced nuclear powers, and the Chinese needed tests to complete the development of their first atomic bomb. In 1964 the People's Republic exploded a bomb and became a new and potentially powerful member of the atomic club.

The Chinese bomb spurred international action to deal with the growing threat of nuclear proliferation. The established atomic powers took the position that the world would be safer if no more nations created their own atomic bombs. The United States, the Soviet Union, and Great Britain prepared a draft treaty for the United Nations in which the signatories agreed not to develop atomic weapons. Eventually, ninety-eight nations signed the Nuclear Non-Proliferation Treaty. Again, France and China refused to sign; India, Pakistan, Israel, and other nations undertaking nuclear weapons research also refused.

Meanwhile, the United States and the Soviet Union proceeded with a number of bilateral agreements. Taking a lesson from the Cuban missile crisis, they agreed to install a "hot line," a direct personal telephone connection between the U.S. president and the Soviet premier that might defuse a developing crisis. A new trading era began between the two nations when the United States agreed in 1963 to sell large quantities of wheat to the Soviet Union at a time of shortage. Soon the United States was regularly selling a wide variety of products to the Soviet Union. Tourism was encouraged, and ordinary U.S. citizens found themselves looking at Lenin's Tomb in Moscow or visiting the Hermitage Museum in Leningrad, while Soviet officials viewed New York from the Empire State Building or visited the Lincoln Memorial. There were also cultural exchanges, as the Bolshoi Ballet and Louis Armstrong crossed the Atlantic to perform.

THE COMMON MARKET AND DE GAULLE

In 1967 the European Economic Community (EEC or Common Market), founded in 1957, joined with the European Coal and Steel Community and the European Atomic Energy Community to form the European Communities (EC), later the European Community. In 1968 the EEC, which continued to exist within the EC, attained its goal of ending tariffs between member nations (France, West Germany, Italy, Belgium, the Netherlands, and Luxembourg). A completely free flow of trade, however, remained elusive because of factors such as differing product standards and government contracts. In 1973 Great Britain, Ireland, and Denmark became members of the EC; and in 1981, Greece. As the organization grew, its departments, including a Council of Ministers and a European Parliament, also increased in significance.

Members of the EC and other European nations continued their postwar economic recovery. West Germany, especially, impressed the world by its strong postwar economic performance. The U.S. government bargained strenuously to reduce EC tariffs, fearing that U.S. products would be undersold in Europe by comparable goods from EC nations. At the same time U.S. families purchased an increasing number of European automobiles, television sets, and other products. Coupled with U.S. military expenditures in Europe, such spending helped to bring about a U.S. balance-of-payments deficit in Europe's favor that increased throughout the 1960s. The devaluation of U.S. currency in 1971 and 1973 against European currencies clearly indicated that the U.S. dollar no longer dominated Europe as it once had.

If the European Community was the symbol of growing economic independence, General Charles de Gaulle personified another: the desire to end European political dependence on the United States. He came to power in 1958, after the French Fourth Republic had produced twenty-seven govern-

General Charles de Gaulle in French Africa shortly before being elected president of France in 1958.
(UPI/Bettmann Newsphotos)

ments in thirteen years. In the midst of a governmental crisis revolving around Algeria, de Gaulle was invited by the French Assembly to rule while a new constitution was drawn up. The new constitution provided for much stronger executive powers than in the past. It created a president elected for a seven-year term, who appointed the prime minister; the president was given other powers that clearly made him the dominant figure in the government. De Gaulle was elected to the post in 1958 and remained the president of France until he resigned in 1969.

De Gaulle was an aloof and haughty figure—he once said: "When I want to know what France thinks, I ask myself." Roosevelt had stated that de Gaulle imagined himself another Joan of Arc. A nationalist in every inch of his imposing frame, he was continually concerned with the greatness and prestige of France. One of his first priorities was resolving the costly Algerian war, and by 1962 he had finally persuaded the French to acquiesce to Algerian independence. From the beginning of his presidency, de Gaulle encouraged France to develop its own atomic capability, and in 1960 France tested its first atomic bomb.

Another major goal for de Gaulle was to extricate France from the grip of the United States. He began to remove French troops from the U.S.-dominated

North Atlantic Treaty Organization (NATO) as early as 1959, and by 1967 he had withdrawn all French forces from NATO. Since the United States would not allow the French to control U.S. nuclear weapons, de Gaulle no longer allowed such weapons in France and had all NATO forces leave French soil.

De Gaulle envisioned France as the head of a Third Force that would stand between the United States and the Soviet Union. He hoped that most Western European nations would follow his lead; in part, that meant a leading role for France in the Common Market. During the 1960s he blocked British entry into the organization because he feared the rivalry of Great Britain and its close ties with the United States. He also tried to improve relations with the Soviet Union and the Eastern European nations, recognized the People's Republic of China, and traveled to such areas as Latin America and Canada in an effort to exercise global statesmanship. Although France did not gain the leading role he envisioned, de Gaulle did make a major contribution to the growing sense of independence in Europe.

In May 1968 students at several campuses of the University of Paris openly revolted against authorities, the police, and the French government. The student revolt in Paris was matched by student demonstrations in the United States, Great Britain, Italy, West Germany, and other nations during the late 1960s. Causes for Western student unrest varied: the boredom bred by an affluent, technological civilization; the impact of New Left ideologies influenced by Mao Zedong and Castro; the opposition to the Vietnam War; local student grievances; and a whole host of others. In Paris, the students were soon joined by leftist political leaders and by a large number of workers who went on strike. De Gaulle's regime was at first threatened with chaos, but wage concessions to workers, promises of university reforms, and support from French citizens opposed to the unrest helped him restore order. Nevertheless, the events were a blow to his prestige; and when the nation refused to approve an administrative reorganization referendum in 1969, de Gaulle resigned.

THE SOVIET UNION: BREZHNEV TO CHERNENKO

In October 1964 Nikita Khrushchev's colleagues ousted him from power, sent him into retirement, and kept him under close supervision until he died in 1971. He was forced out for a number of reasons: a poor harvest in 1963, along with a sluggish economy; foreign policy failures, including the Cuban missile crisis and a growing split with China; an increasingly abrasive, authoritarian, and incautious political style; and a backlash against his attack on Stalinism and attempts to reform the Communist system and bureaucracy. Leonid Brezhnev replaced Khrushchev in the key position of first secretary of the Communist party, while Alexei Kosygin took over as premier. After 1964 Brezhnev was the dominant figure in Soviet politics. Like Khrushchev, he was not a dictator but the most prominent of a small group of political leaders in a one-party state. Like most of them, Brezhnev had a technical background and a long history of party work.

During the Brezhnev era, the Soviet Union in some areas continued to follow the path marked out by Khrushchev. Throughout most of the late 1960s and the 1970s military spending remained the top priority, but the government also gradually improved the living standard of the average Soviet citizen. The government continued to develop the nation's rich resources of petroleum, gas, and minerals at a slow but steady pace. On the other hand, agriculture remained the most troubled area of the Soviet economy. Crop failures in 1972 and 1975 forced the Soviet government to make large grain purchases from the United States. From 1979 through 1982 the U.S.S.R. experienced four poor harvests in succession, the Soviet economy stagnated, and the standard of living declined. Despite some experiments in economic liberalization, the party and government kept tight control over the economy.

A major difference between the two eras was that Brezhnev put an end to Khrushchev's "de-Stalinization" campaign. Khrushchev's overall record on literature and intellectual life was considerably more liberal than Stalin's had been, and once writers experienced this thaw, the party discovered it was difficult to contain them. Nevertheless, in 1966, Brezhnev and his colleagues apparently decided matters had gone far enough: Andrei Siniavsky and Yuli Daniel were put on trial for "anti-Soviet propaganda," although their only crime had been to send literature to the West for publication. They were, respectively, sentenced to seven and five years in Soviet labor camps. But their trial and sentences sparked even greater opposition from Soviet intellectuals and helped launch a full-blown dissident movement which continued into the 1970s.

Other trials and the realistic fears of increased official sympathy for the Stalinist past continued to fuel opposition to the government. Underground literature and the number of manuscripts sent abroad increased. The underground *Chronicle of Current Events,* published regularly from 1968 to 1972 and sporadically thereafter, reflected the opposition of scattered intellectuals, religious groups, and ethnic minorities. While the party continued to sentence dissidents to prison, labor camps, and mental institutions, it also allowed or forced some of the more prominent ones to leave the U.S.S.R., as Alexander Solzhenitsyn did in 1974. In January 1980 one of the country's few remaining free dissident leaders, the prominent physicist Andrei Sakharov, was exiled to the city of Gorky.

Meanwhile, the vitality of the aging Soviet leadership was also declining. Brezhnev suffered a stroke in 1976 and, in the words of the Russian historian Roy Medvedev, "He gradually found it more and more difficult to carry out the most simple protocol functions and could no longer understand what was going on around him." He finally died in 1982. By then the Soviet people also seemed less vital and optimistic. Economic and political decline had taken their toll. Corruption, favoritism, and alcoholism were on their way up; life expectancy and belief in communism were moving in the other direction. Between late 1982 and early 1985 the party had two more leaders whose health was poor and who soon died in office: Yuri Andropov and Konstantin Chernenko.

EASTERN EUROPE IN THE 1960s: THE PURSUIT AND LIMITS OF AUTONOMY

If de Gaulle and some other Europeans resented early postwar U.S. domination of Western Europe, Eastern Europeans were even more hostile to Soviet hegemony over them and sought ways to reduce it. The Sino-Soviet split of the early 1960s encouraged this desire; but only small Albania, which sided with China, was able to leave the Soviet orbit. While Rumania remained a politically oppressive Soviet ally, its government insisted on a measure of independence in economic and foreign policies. In 1963, when COMECON attempted to hamper Rumanian industrial advancement, Rumania refused to cooperate. In its foreign relations, Rumania was on better terms with China and Israel than was the Soviet Union; on occasion it also voted differently at the United Nations.

Some Eastern European nations also pursued policies that were more liberal than those in the U.S.S.R. In Hungary, the János Kádár regime improved economic conditions by relaxing centralized economic planning and allowing more local initiative. The government also permitted more personal freedom; in 1964, for example, more than 100,000 Hungarians were allowed to visit Western nations. In Poland, most of the farmland, unlike that in the Soviet Union, remained in private hands. Poland and Rumania, as well as Hungary, also allowed more religious freedom.

There were, however, limits to how much autonomy the Soviet Union would allow its satellites, and in 1968 Czechoslovakia passed those limits. During the mid-1960s, discontent spread in Czechoslovakia under the Stalinist Antonin Novotny. In December 1967–January 1968, he was replaced by Alexander Dubček as first secretary of the Czechoslovak Communist party. Soon afterward, encouraged by public opinion, Dubček and his colleagues began to carry out a policy of liberalization. They greatly reduced censorship, recognized civil liberties, rehabilitated victims of past party injustices, and allowed autonomous political groupings to emerge. Relations with Western nations grew warmer, and Dubček displayed a desire to place Soviet-Czechoslovakian ties on a more equal footing.

Soviet leaders became increasingly alarmed about the liberalization policies and feared that they might spread like a virus to other Eastern European nations. Dissent in the Soviet Union, already a problem for the regime, might also be encouraged if the Czechoslovakians were allowed such freedoms. In addition, Czechoslovakia's strategic position between the U.S.S.R. and West Germany undoubtedly magnified Soviet fears. The Soviet Union began to pressure the Czechoslovakian leaders to rescind their reforms, but they refused to give way. On August 21, 1968, Soviet, East German, Polish, Hungarian, and Bulgarian troops invaded Czechoslovakia. Believing it would be suicidal to offer armed resistance, the nation's leaders and people simply offered a sullen and passive noncooperation. Dubček was soon forced out of office, and Gustav Husák became head of the party. The "Prague Spring" of 1968 and the accompanying hopes for a more humane socialism were dead.

Prague, Czechoslovakia, 1968: Soviet tanks and troops suppress the liberal Communist regime of Alexander Dubček.
(Keystone Press Agency)

Following the invasion, Husák restored Czechoslovakia to the status of a "police state" on which the Soviet Union could rely, and Soviet leaders elaborated their justification for interference—Western observers would label it the "Brezhnev Doctrine." It stated that "every Communist party is responsible not only to its own people but also to all the socialist countries," and that "the sovereignty of individual socialist countries cannot be counterposed to the interests of world socialism."

THE FLOWERING OF DÉTENTE

Despite the strained feelings stimulated by the Vietnam War and the 1968 invasion of Czechoslovakia, the "spirit of détente" was well under way when Richard Nixon became president of the United States in 1969. Nixon had been a hard-line anti-Communist "Cold Warrior" in the 1940s and 1950s but now shifted his position and intended to make his mark in history by easing Cold War tensions. In particular, he expected to improve relationships with both the Soviet Union and China. These two nations had become antagonists, and Nixon hoped to take advantage of the distrust between the two powers to improve relations with both. To carry out his initiatives, Nixon relied on the diplomatic skills of the dynamic Henry Kissinger, who sought to replace the Cold War with a more complex multipolar balance of power.

The core of the Cold War lay in the nuclear arms race, and both the United States and the Soviet Union were ready to consider means to slow it down.

The Soviet Union had, at great cost to its economy, achieved a rough parity with the United States in tonnage of deliverable atomic destruction but was increasingly distracted by its split with China. The United States was staggering under the economic burden of the Vietnam War, and its society was distracted by social unrest. In addition, both nations were faced with the costs of implementing two major new weapons systems now deemed necessary to keep abreast or ahead in the arms race. One was the antiballistic missile (ABM), a defensive missile designed to destroy incoming missiles. The special attraction and also danger of this weapon was that the first nation that believed itself fully protected by its ABMs would be tempted to launch a successful attack on its less well-defended adversary. To increase the sophistication of the offense against the ABM, military technicians had created another weapons system, the multiple independently targeted reentry vehicle (MIRV). The MIRV consisted of several warheads, each programmed to hit a different target, all mounted on a single rocket. The cost of fully implementing these systems promised to be a crushing burden on both nations.

In 1969 Nixon and Brezhnev agreed to arms limitation talks. By 1972 the basic agreement had been hammered out, and Nixon traveled to Moscow to sign the Strategic Arms Limitation Treaty (SALT). The treaty suspended the building of ICBMs, capped the number of missile-firing submarines that could be employed, and limited the deployment of ABMs. Even with these limitations, both nations remained capable of "overkill," that is, destroying their opponent many times over. The spirit of accord was enhanced in 1973 when Brezhnev visited Washington; some commentators claimed that the Cold War was over. Meanwhile, a number of bilateral and multilateral agreements were hammered out, including a pact not to deploy nuclear weapons on the ocean floor and one not to manufacture bacteriological weapons. In 1974, at Vladivostok in the Soviet Far East, President Gerald Ford and party leader Brezhnev signed a preliminary agreement designed to extend strategic arms limitations into the 1980s. The same year, the two nations also agreed not to conduct underground nuclear tests of more than 150 kilotons.

The series of agreements between the United States and the Soviet Union were important for world peace, but it was the sudden rapprochement between the United States and China in 1971–1972 that startled and excited the world. Since 1950, there had been a "bamboo curtain" between the United States and China; they had no diplomatic, economic, or cultural relations, and the two governments constantly attacked each other in public statements. The Chinese had conducted a relentless propaganda campaign against "the paper tiger of American imperialism," while the U.S. government encouraged anti-"Red China" attitudes among Americans.

Both nations, however, had reasons to change their policies. China feared the Soviet Union and also feared that improved U.S.-Soviet relations would isolate China and reduce its influence. China was also worried that if the United States lessened its involvement in Asia, the vacuum would be filled by Japan and the Soviet Union. All these factors crystallized at a time when China was emerging from the turmoil of the Cultural Revolution (see Chapter 31). At the same time, the United States was extricating itself from a disastrous war in Indochina, attempting to negotiate a settlement on some basic issues with the Soviet Union, and rethinking some of its belief that an expansionist China must be "contained."

Late in 1969 secret negotiations began toward the "normalization" of Sino-U.S. relations. In 1971 the United States refrained from employing its veto when the United Nations expelled Taiwan and seated the People's Republic in the General Assembly and in China's permanent seat in the Security Council. In 1972, amid mixed feelings both at home and around the world, Nixon traveled to Beijing, where he received a polite but restrained welcome. Nixon met briefly with Mao and participated in discussions with other Chinese leaders. At the Great Hall of the People, Nixon and his hosts banqueted, toasted one another with potent mao tai cocktails, and before departing exchanged gifts— Nixon received two giant pandas, Hsing-Hsing and Ling-Ling.

The Americans and Chinese did not come to any major agreements, being satisfied at that time to air their differences. The final communique ambiguously noted that "the United States acknowledges that all Chinese on either side of the Taiwan Straits maintain there is but one China and that Taiwan is part of China." Shortly thereafter, the two nations agreed to establish cultural and economic contacts to open China to U.S. tourists and to open "liaison offices" (embassies in all but name) in each other's capitals. The momentum established by the Sino-U.S. rapprochement quickly extended to China's relations with Japan, and later that same year Japan recognized the Communist government of China and established normal diplomatic relations.

After 1972 the main obstacle to complete normalization of relations between the United States and China continued to be China's insistence that the United States withdraw its recognition of Taiwan and abrogate its mutual defense pact with that island's government. The United States feared that China would attack Taiwan if the United States withdrew its pledge of military support. In 1978 the administration of President Carter, apparently receiving tacit assurances that China would not attack Taiwan, agreed to China's two principal conditions. On January 1, 1979, the two nations opened embassies in Beijing and Washington. Normalization was now complete, although the United States and China remained wary of each other. The United States continued to retain economic and cultural ties with Taiwan. In 1984 President Reagan visited China. As a result, the United States increased its technical aid and agreed to sell China certain weapons.

The spirit of détente in the 1970s also extended to settling lingering disputes in Europe, most of them centering on Germany and some of those going back to the end of World War II. Much of the credit for this, and a Nobel Prize for Peace, went to Willy Brandt, head of the Social Democratic party and since 1969 the chancellor of West Germany. Brandt urged the creation of an *Ostpolitik,* "a hand offered to the East." In 1972 the two German nations formally recognized each other. The United States recognized East Germany, and the Soviet Union pledged not to block access to Berlin. That year, both Germanies were admitted to the United Nations. At Helsinki in 1975 the process of détente expanded to Europe as a whole. In addition to affirming respect for human rights, thirty-three European nations plus the United States and Canada agreed in effect that the existing boundaries in Europe, including the German-Polish border, were "inviolable." The results of World War II had finally been ratified.

During the 1970s the arms race expanded, despite the easing of political tensions and despite a series of agreements on nuclear testing and proliferation and on strategic arms limitations. Nuclear powers continued to test underground frequently, and China still tested above ground. Even though the 1972 SALT treaty limited the number of nuclear weapons, the Soviet Union and the United States continued to improve their nuclear weapons in speed, range, accuracy, and, above all, power. By 1978 the two nations were in a state of approximate nuclear parity. They possessed over 40,000 strategic nuclear warheads with a total destructive force equal to 1.5 million bombs of the magnitude that fell on Hiroshima. Experts pronounced the arms race at the stage of Mutually Assured Destruction (MAD).

In addition to the potential for nuclear devastation from the "limited" bombs and missiles, military scientists had developed or were developing weapons not limited by treaty. Such weapons included low-flying "cruise" missiles and Stealth bombers that could escape radar detection; the neutron bomb, which killed people with little damage to property; laser beams, the "ray gun" of science fiction now become reality; and space satellites and platforms that could fire missiles and lasers.

WESTERN EUROPE, 1970–1984: ECONOMICS AND POLITICS

Western Europe entered the 1970s after several decades of economic growth. Of the major powers, only Great Britain continued to have serious economic problems; a sluggish economic growth rate, balance-of-payments deficits, labor unrest, and inflation all troubled the Labour party government that had taken over from the Conservatives in 1964 and continued in power until 1970. Nevertheless, even in Great Britain, the standard of living of most individuals continued to improve.

In 1974 and 1975, however, increased food and petroleum prices and an economic recession temporarily shook Western European nations that had become used to prosperity. West Germany's inflation rate had been under 2 percent in 1969 but by 1974 had risen to 7 percent. Great Britain's was a little under 6 percent in 1969, but by 1975 it was close to 25 percent. Italy's inflation and unemployment rates in 1974 were among Europe's highest. It was perhaps no accident that the men chosen to head the French and West German governments in 1974, Valery Giscard d'Estaing and Helmut Schmidt, had both been finance or economics ministers in previous governments. In Great Britain, after four years out of power, Labour party chief Harold Wilson, an economist by training, was also voted back into office in 1974.

Parodox: During the 1970s the superpowers pursued a policy of détente while at the same time continuing their post–World War II arms race. Above, Soviet President Brezhnev plants one of his trademark kisses on the cheek of U.S. President Carter at the 1979 SALT II conference in Vienna; below, Soviet missiles on parade through Moscow. (Top: *AP/Wide World Photos*, bottom: *Lee Lockwood/Black Star*)

By the late 1970s Western European nations gradually had begun to recover from the economic shock of the earlier part of the decade. By 1978 the inflation rate in Great Britain had fallen to about 9 percent, and in West Germany, to 2 percent. Although the British continued to be plagued by long-standing economic problems, they increased production of North Sea petroleum, reducing dependence on foreign sources. By 1981 several Western European nations were listed among the wealthiest in the world. Switzerland, Sweden, Denmark, West Germany, Norway, and Belgium all had a higher per capita GNP than the United States; the Netherlands and France were not far behind. During the early 1980s, however, the global recession brought to Western Europe its highest unemployment since World War II.

Despite economic ups and downs, Western European politics remained fairly stable, with moderately conservative and moderately socialist parties dominating. Italy's frequent changes of government—averaging slightly over one a year in the postwar decades—became so common that they seemed almost routine. In Portugal and Spain, where right-wing governments had long ruled, the people restored democracy in 1975–1977 and maintained it with less difficulty than many had predicted. By 1984 both countries had moderate socialist governments, as did France, Greece, and Sweden. The most important socialist leader was French president François Mitterrand, elected in 1981 and reelected to another seven-year term in 1988.

Two other important political figures were the Christian Democrat (moderately conservative) Helmut Kohl, who replaced the Social Democrat (moderately socialist) Helmut Schmidt as West Germany's chancellor in 1982, and the British prime minister Margaret Thatcher, elected in 1979. Sometimes compared to President Reagan because of her conservatism, she pursued a policy aimed at reducing Great Britain's welfare state and turning more and more of its functions over to free enterprise (privatization). Her supporters claimed that she revived the British economy, and her opponents charged that she benefited the rich at the expense of the poor. Regardless of differing political views, however, conservatives like Thatcher and socialists like Mitterrand all worked in the 1980s to augment European prosperity.

Although most Western Europeans were content with their governments, not all was calm in the political waters. Radical leftist terrorists plagued Germany and Italy in particular with sporadic bombings, kidnappings, and assassinations. In 1981 Pope John Paul II was wounded by a Turkish terrorist with apparent connections to the Bulgarian secret police. Basque separatists in Spain also committed acts of violence in their campaigns for independence, as did members of the radical Irish Republican Army (IRA), which struggled to separate Northern Ireland from the United Kingdom and join it to the Irish Republic. In 1981 several IRA prisoners gained wide attention as they starved themselves to death as a protest against British policy in Northern Ireland.

EASTERN EUROPE, 1970–1984: COMMUNIST REGIMES AND ECONOMICS

In the 1970s and early 1980s Eastern European nations continued efforts to become something more than mere puppets of the U.S.S.R. Some, such as Hungary, experimented with economic reorganization, and in general, Eastern European governments made greater attempts to appease their citizens through improving living standards than did the Soviet Union. While adequate housing remained scarce, personal incomes rose, and television sets, washing machines, and refrigerators became much more common. By the beginning of the 1980s one family out of four in Hungary and two out of five in East Germany owned an automobile. Travel to other nations, primarily within the Eastern bloc, continued to increase significantly. The process of urbanization and industrialization also proceeded at a rapid pace. By 1980 only Albania and Yugoslavia were more rural than urban. East Germany and Czechoslovakia had a higher percentage of urban population than did the Soviet Union. Improved living standards, however, were in large part dependent on stable prices, large loans from the West, and favorable trade relations with the U.S.S.R., which furnished energy and raw materials below world prices. Better short-term conditions also came at the expense of more long-term environmental damage. The increased prosperity of the 1970s—growth was especially strong in the first half of the decade—was thus based on an unstable foundation.

The fragile economic and political status of Eastern Europe became especially evident in the early 1980s during the development of an extended crisis in Poland. In 1980, the Polish government attempted to increase meat prices, and disturbances broke out. Earlier, in 1970 and 1976, price increases had also led to strikes and riots, the 1970 turbulence even driving Gomulka from power. This time, however, the unrest was more widespread and coordinated, and the government was forced to recognize Solidarity, a powerful new independent labor union. The government agreed to salary increases and made concessions regarding political prisoners, censorship, additional religious access to the mass media, and a number of other worker demands. Communist party leader Gierek was replaced by Stanislaw Kania, and for the next year liberalization proceeded at a rapid pace, as Solidarity, under the leadership of Lech Walesa, prodded the government. The Catholic Church, headed by the Polish Pope John Paul II, was sympathetic to the union and supported the push for liberalization.

As the Poles gained more freedom, Soviet leaders became increasingly alarmed and resorted to a variety of measures to express their displeasure. In an effort to appease Soviet leaders and to bolster the declining prestige of the party, in October 1981 the Central Committee of the Polish Communist party replaced Kania as first secretary and put in his place General Wojciech Jaruzelski. In December 1981 Jaruzelski, without warning, declared a state of national emergency, established martial law, and set up a Military Council of National Salvation to run the nation. Armored units appeared in the streets of Warsaw and other cities. Solidarity leaders were arrested, and union activities suspended. A few months later, the Polish government increased food prices.

Alarmed by Poland's precarious economic position and upset by the crackdown on Solidarity, Western governments became either hostile to or cautious about providing further credit. Already worried about rising worldwide indebtedness, Western governments became increasingly concerned about the large debts of Eastern European nations. By early 1982 the six Soviet satellites owed over $50 billion to Western governments and banks. At about the same time, the Soviet Union, beset by its own economic problems and debts to the West, began to reduce its energy deliveries to Eastern Europe and to charge prices more in line with world prices. As a result of these factors, as well as a global recession, the rate of increase in living standards leveled off sharply in the early 1980s. In some cases, living standards declined. While the Soviet Union encouraged its satellites to meet the situation by becoming less dependent on the West, some Eastern bloc leaders believed that the best solution was more economic reform and better relations with the West. By late 1982 the Polish government had freed most of those who had been arrested in December 1981 and had lifted many of the restrictions imposed at that time. Partly as a consequence of these actions, Western governments and banks agreed to the rescheduling of Polish debts.

THE FADING OF DÉTENTE

By the late 1970s earlier optimism that the Cold War had virtually ended had begun to fade. President Carter's emphasis on human rights—he once called it "the soul of our foreign policy"—and his sympathy for Soviet dissidents irritated the Soviet leadership. The continued Soviet military buildup of the 1970s alarmed some U.S. political leaders, and the movement toward international accords lost momentum rapidly as Cold War discord flared in the Middle East, Africa, and Latin America. The movement of Soviet troops into Afghanistan in late 1979 especially soured relations. In the United States, hostility and suspicion toward the Soviet Union claimed a major casualty when the 1979 SALT II agreement was not ratified. In the summer of 1980, as a response to the Soviet presence in Afghanistan, the United States boycotted the Olympic Games in Moscow and placed an embargo on U.S. grain shipments to the Soviet Union.

During the presidency of Ronald Reagan in the early 1980s, a number of events contributed further to the decline of détente. Soviet fears were nourished by Reagan's determination to increase U.S. military spending and by Reagan's harsh words, such as his calling the Soviet Union an "evil empire." In the face of recent Soviet deployment of SS-20s and other missiles threatening Western Europe, the United States proceeded with the previously scheduled deployment of Pershing II and cruise missiles in Western Europe. In reaction to the new missile deployments, the Soviets broke off arms talks in Geneva in late 1983. At the same time, Soviet leader Andropov had angry words for President Reagan's newest weapons plan: the Strategic Defense Initiative (SDI), often referred to as "Star Wars." Andropov charged that by advocating a space-based defense system that would destroy Soviet missiles before they could reach U.S. territory, Reagan hoped to prevent the Soviets from launching any type of retaliatory strike if the United States decided to attack the U.S.S.R. first.

The United States, on the other hand, was angered by the major role that the Soviet Union had played in turning back the Solidarity movement in Poland. It responded with limited sanctions not only against Poland but also against the

Soviet Union, which the United States charged bore a "heavy and direct responsibility for the repression in Poland." In 1983 over Soviet territory, the Soviet air force shot down a Korean civilian jetliner, which the Soviet military apparently believed was a spy plane. Although later U.S. intelligence information appeared to contradict him, President Reagan declared that "there is no way a pilot could mistake this for anything other than a civilian airliner." He condemned the act and cited it as evidence of the barbaric nature of the Soviet system.

Other areas of interaction and cooperation fostered by détente suffered as relations deteriorated. U.S.-Soviet trade and Jewish emigration from the Soviet Union, both of which had increased during the 1970s, declined in the early 1980s. Partly in retaliation for the U.S. boycott of the 1980 Olympics, the Soviet Union and many other Communist nations friendly to the Soviet Union refused to take part in the 1984 summer Olympics in Los Angeles.

SUMMARY

From the Nuclear Test Ban Treaty of 1963 through most of the 1970s, superpower relations were generally characterized by a spirit of détente. Both the United States and the Soviet Union attempted to find points of agreement and succeeded in expanding trade and cultural contacts and agreeing on a strategic arms limitation treaty. In the 1970s the United States and China ended a long period of hostility and established diplomatic, cultural, and economic relations with each other. Most of the international community, which displayed an increasing tendency toward multipolarity, joined in signing a number of treaties designed to limit the testing and proliferation of nuclear weapons. Meanwhile, however, the uninterrupted postwar arms race produced ever more destructive weapons. From time to time, international events, such as the war in Indochina and the Soviet invasion of Czechoslovakia in 1968, stalled progress toward improved relations. The appearance of Soviet troops in Afghanistan in December 1979 and events of the early 1980s signaled that the spirit of détente had faded and that the arms race was accelerating.

From the 1960s into the 1980s some of the European allies of the two superpowers made attempts to lessen their dependence on the United States or on the U.S.S.R. The Common Market, Western European economic prosperity, and de Gaulle all encouraged this trend in the West, while the "Prague Spring" of 1968, certain Rumanian and Hungarian policies, and the activities of Poland's Solidarity union reflected the desire for more independence in Eastern Europe.

While Europe remained, in general, economically and politically stable, there were some serious problems. The economic recessions of 1974–1975 and 1981–1982 shook Western European nations. Unstable governments, youth unrest, and outbursts of terrorism also plagued some of these nations for various periods during the 1960s and the following decades. The early 1980s also displayed a number of Eastern European economic shortcomings, including heavy indebtedness to Western governments and banks.

SUGGESTED SOURCES

ASH, TIMOTHY G., *The Polish Revolution: Solidarity* (1985). An excellent discussion of the events in Poland in the early 1980s.*

CRAIG, GORDON A., *The Germans* (1991). An examination of the German people in the 1980s from a historical perspective; contains an afterword on the German events of 1989–1990.*

DORNBERG, JOHN, *Eastern Europe* (1980). A look at Eastern Europe in the 1970s.

EDMONDS, ROBIN, *Soviet Foreign Policy: The Brezhnev Years* (1983). An insightful, brief account.*

HYLAND, WILLIAM, *Mortal Rivals: Superpower Relations from Nixon to Reagan* (1987). A good overview by a leading U.S. expert on foreign affairs.*

JENKINS, PETER, *Mrs. Thatcher's Revolution: The Ending of the Socialist Era* (1988). A distinguished British journalist offers his insights into a decade of "Thatcherism."*

KONWICKI, TADEUSZ, *A Minor Apocalypse* (1979). A novel by one of Poland's leading writers which captures well the anguished condition of the nation under communism.*

LACOUTURE, JEAN, *DeGaulle: The Ruler, 1945–1970* (1991). The second volume of a comprehensive and distinguished biography.

LAQUEUR, WALTER, *Europe in Our Time: A History, 1945–1992* (1992). A description of economic, social, political, and cultural developments in the postwar era by one of the most prolific historians of modern times.*

LEWIS, FLORA, *Europe: Tapestry of Nations* (1988). A U.S. journalist looks at the similarities and differences between European nations, both east and west, in the early 1980s and mid-1980s.*

SHIPLER, DAVID K., *Russia: Broken Idols, Solemn Dreams* (1984). An observant account of Soviet life in the early 1980s by a *New York Times* correspondent.*

SMOKE, RICHARD, *National Security and the Nuclear Dilemma*, 2d ed. (1987). A concise and informed history of the U.S. role in the arms race and in détente.*

*Paperback available.

CHAPTER 29

The United States and Latin America in Recent Years

In the 1970s and 1980s several broad patterns emerged in the United States and Latin America. In the United States, a conservative era set in as Americans cut back on the welfare state and lost interest in reforms and change. In Latin America, there were contradictory trends. Conservative military regimes were in the ascendancy in the 1970s, but largely gave way to civilian governments in the 1980s. Revolutionary Marxism gained ground in the late 1970s and early 1980s, but U.S. opposition and the withdrawal of Soviet support weakened Marxist forces in El Salvador and Nicaragua by the 1990s.

THE CONSERVATIVE PERIOD IN THE UNITED STATES

The Troubled 1970s

During the 1970s, as the United States gave up on the war in Indochina, the economy faced increasing difficulties. Already drained by the expense of the war, it suffered from low worker productivity, nagging unemployment, and, most destructive of all, a steadily increasing rate of inflation. One source of inflation was a rising national debt resulting from spending large sums on both the Vietnam War and on expanded social programs at home. Another cause of inflation was a sharp rise in the cost of imported petroleum, accompanied by a relative decline in the amount of petroleum available. This in turn stemmed from price fixing by the petroleum-producing nations and from the refining and distribution practices of the major petroleum companies. The era of cheap fuel for Americans ended as they faced long gasoline lines and skyrocketing heating bills. The automobile industry, long a mainstay of the domestic economy, sagged as consumers switched from large U.S. cars to small, energy-efficient imports from Japan. Because of inflation, many families found their real incomes dropping and their prospects for the future narrowing. They were not able to attain the higher standard of living they had hoped to achieve and in many cases found themselves compelled to give up luxuries they had come to expect.

Government struggled unsuccessfully with the economic problems of the 1970s. President Nixon put aside his conservative instincts when he adopted a planned budget deficit to stimulate the economy and a wage-price freeze to control inflation. Gerald Ford, Nixon's successor, tightened spending and credit; the resulting recession may have cost him the 1976 election. The victor, Democrat Jimmy Carter, did no better. An Iranian oil embargo worsened the existing energy crisis.

High inflation, high interest rates, and persistent unemployment contributed to a "misery index" that the Republicans used as one of their political weapons to take back the White House in 1980. The existence at the same time of inflation, slow growth, and a high jobless rate was unprecedented and baffled politicians and economists alike. Their failure to master the economy increased public mistrust of those in high places.

Already alienated from government by the war and economic stagnation, the public grew more cynical still as a result of the political and constitutional firestorm of the Watergate affair. Evidence indicated that President Nixon and his chief administrative aides had engaged in a criminal conspiracy to obstruct

Watergate: Senators Howard Baker and Sam Ervin examine a witness during Congressional hearings pertaining to the break-in of the national headquarters of the Democratic party. This investigation led to the resignation of President Nixon and the jailing of several Republican administration leaders.
(*George Tames/The New York Times*)

justice by attempting to cover up a Republican party break-in of Democratic party headquarters. When the House of Representatives Judiciary Committee voted bills of impeachment, and it appeared that both Democrats and Republicans would vote to convict him, Nixon resigned the presidency on August 9, 1974. His successor, Gerald Ford, pardoned him, and Nixon went into seclusion. The Watergate affair, Nixon's misuse of intelligence and internal security agencies, and the controversy surrounding the conduct of the war in Indochina convinced many that an "imperial presidency" had evolved that had gotten out of control. Congress created legislation, supported by Ford and Carter, that gave it more effective oversight of the conduct of foreign and military policy and brought the intelligence agencies under more supervision.

Meanwhile, economic uncertainties helped bring about a changed social mood. The Americans of the 1970s "me decade," preoccupied with their own employment and security concerns, were little interested in social change and gave scant attention to national or international issues. Meanwhile, trendsetters among affluent Americans stressed personal development, physical fitness, and a "laid-back" life of self-indulgence that in some ways echoed the counterculture of the 1960s. College students, once in the vanguard of political activity, now concentrated on compiling good grades to give them an edge in getting jobs in a tightening economy.

Meanwhile, conservative forces were gaining strength. Economic conservatives called for lower taxes on, and less regulation of, business. Increasing numbers of Americans objected to high property and income taxes, called for an end to "throwing money" at social problems, and advocated cuts in welfare programs. Interest in social reform faded as more Americans became skeptical that government regulations could solve social ills. The proposed Equal Rights Amendment guaranteeing equal legal treatment for women, at one time seemingly destined for ratification by the states, failed twice. Social conservatives called for an end to abortions, the return of prayers to the schools, the censorship of pornographic and literary materials, limitations on the social and occupational roles of women, and more jails and tougher punishments for criminals.

Public policy reflected the conservative forces that gained strength in the 1970s. Nixon's revenue-sharing program illustrated the new drive to reduce the role of the federal government. In this instance, the U.S. government turned over a small portion of its revenues to the states to be spent under loose federal guidelines as each state determined. The movement away from big government found support from both parties. During the Democratic Carter administration, Congress reduced regulation of airlines and truckers, allowing carriers to compete in the marketplace. Beginning in 1969, a series of appointments to the Supreme Court made that body less likely to continue the innovative role it had had under Earl Warren. While the Court broke new ground when it upheld the constitutionality of abortions under certain conditions, it slowly reduced procedural protections for persons accused of committing a crime.

The Reagan Era

In 1980 conservative forces won their greatest triumph, putting Republican Ronald Reagan in the White House and gaining effective control of Congress. Once a New Deal Democrat, Reagan was a former movie star and California governor who united traditional economic conservatives with cultural conservatives of the "New Right." Unlike Carter and Ford, Reagan left a firm imprint on public policy. Declaring that government was the problem, not the solution, Reaganites did some pruning on the extensive welfare state that had grown out of the New Deal. While programs with a strong middle-class following like Social Security escaped the budget axe, Congress slashed Great Society supports for the poor, such as food stamps, school lunches, and Medicaid. In addition, Congress enacted the biggest tax cut in the nation's history, with the wealthy reaping the greatest benefits. Moreover, Reagan ordered a major increase in military spending but at the same time curbed environmental and occupational safety programs.

Economic results were mixed. Inflation, a vexing problem for a decade, plunged sharply. Interest rates also fell. These gains, however, came at considerable cost. The percentage of the population living in poverty moved upward. The worst economic tailspin since the 1930s pushed jobless rates above 10 percent in 1982. Although the economy recovered and the unemployment rate declined significantly, many Americans never returned to high-paying jobs in basic industry. Increasingly, the United States moved toward becoming a service economy in which many Americans were in non-union, low-paying jobs with few or no fringe benefits. Many college graduates found themselves overeducated for the jobs available, and many young persons remained in their parents' homes because they lacked the income to set themselves up independently. For the first time in modern memory, there were indications that the youngest adult generation would have a lower standard of living than that of their parents.

In the conservative era of deregulation, market dynamics held sway, with attendant social consequences. Corporations also invested their capital in a series of "takeovers" of smaller firms, encouraged by the government's green light for business mergers. Meanwhile, the combination of tax cuts and accelerated military funding caused the national debt to climb to unprecedented levels. The "rust belt" states of the Midwest and Northeast decayed as corporations "outsourced," shifting the manufacture of autos, clothing, electronics, and other products to low-wage labor markets outside the United States. By the early 1990s Americans were buying so many products from the Asian Rim and Western Europe that a huge trade deficit joined the budget deficit. The government's debt burden grew, and the value of the dollar on world money markets sank. Foreign investors bought ever larger shares of U.S. economic assets. Once the world's economic giant, the United States watched as Japan and other East Asian nations seized the economic initiative.

Social trends of the 1980s continued to follow the conservative paths of the 1970s. The earlier "me decade" had its counterpart in the "Yuppies," or young urban professionals. Whereas earlier popular songs had celebrated social changes "blowin' in the wind," a widely admired singer of the 1980s claimed that she was "a material girl." Concerned with their private lives rather than public issues, Yuppies spent freely on possessions and pastimes. For many, a comfortable, upper-middle-class standard of living depended on both husband and wife holding full-time, long-term, well-paying employment.

Still another mark of the conservative mood of the 1980s was the continued growth and assertiveness of the nation's fundamentalist Christians. Although by the late 1980s they had not enacted their program of school prayer, "creation science" in the classroom, and an end to abortions, they entered politics in increasing numbers and set the political agenda. Evangelists, using television and mass mailing, built large followings and raised substantial sums of money. In the late 1980s, however, sexual and financial scandals tarnished the "televangelists'" image in the eyes of some.

Health, substance abuse, and crime were major intertwined concerns of the 1980s. The mid-decade saw the appearance of a deadly incurable disease, AIDS. At first striking down mainly homosexuals and intravenous drug users, the AIDS epidemic provoked a tangle of highly emotional concerns, among them sex, drugs, medical research, and the right to privacy. By the early 1990s AIDS was beginning to spread among the heterosexual population, with a consequent impact on social relationships.

Although AIDS was a major concern, opinion surveys ranked drugs as one of society's chief problems. The use of highly addictive cocaine spread rapidly, ensnaring victims of all races and social classes. First Lady Nancy Reagan urged the public to "just say no," while the authorities tried both suppression and treatment. Substance abuse counseling and treatment programs ballooned, and government pushed through ever harsher enforcement legislation—all with little success. Attitudes toward liquor underwent change as well. Social drinking declined in some circles, and state and local punishments for drunk driving intensified, partly in response to lobbying by groups like Mothers Against Drunk Drivers. Tobacco smokers found themselves increasingly on the defensive. Federally required health warnings had already appeared in advertising and on packaging; now employers and state and local governments banned or restricted smoking in workplaces, public buildings, and public carriers.

Although some reports showed lessening crime rates due to the declining youth population, crime remained a major public concern. States built more prisons and carried out the death penalty more frequently. A vigorous gun lobby used fear of crime to block federal handgun restrictions, even in the wake of an attempt on President Reagan's life.

The most notable social development of the late 1980s and the early 1990s was the reemergence of a wide-ranging controversy concerning the role of women in U.S. society. As in the 1970s, both men and women were divided on the issue of whether or not to change traditional roles and currents of behavior. An increasing number of women, however, began to demand freedom from what they considered long-standing patterns of male physical and psychological abuse and intimidation in their daily lives and from equally long-standing patterns of economic, political, and social discrimination. The abortion issue was intense, focusing especially on sit-ins at abortion clinics and on the attitudes of the justices of the Supreme Court. During hearings on the nomination of Judge Clarence Thomas for a seat on the Court, the patronizing and abusive grilling of Professor Anita Hill by an all-male Senate committee struck a deep chord of resentment in many women and spurred them to elect more women to Congress. A wide variety of issues affecting women was brought to the attention of the American public, including protecting wives from abusive husbands, allowing women in the military to go into combat, receiving equal pay for equal work, gaining equal access to employment in the skilled trades and to high corporate positions, and securing a more equitable division of housework.

As the decade neared its end, the 1988 election sustained the conservatives as Reagan's vice-president, George Bush, won the presidency. On the other hand, the Democratic party increased its number of seats in Congress and in state governments. Americans continued to be political pragmatists, putting their conservative political, social, and economic instincts in the hands of Republican presidents and their support for a slimmed-down welfare state in the hands of a Democratic Congress.

President Bush did not have a strong vision of the future, and much of his administration was marked by a number of political clashes and impasses with the Democratic Congress, increasingly referred to as "gridlock." His first three years were marked by fine-tuning the welfare state, in the course of which he defected from his "no new taxes" campaign pledge, alienating many conservative voters. In 1991 the economy plunged into recession, as sales and production fell and unemployment rose. The national debt soared to $4 trillion, three-quarters of which had accumulated under Reagan and Bush. Bush's popularity, mostly built on foreign policy successes and on his support for conservative social values, began to erode as many Americans looked to him in vain for public policy initiatives that would put them back to work.

The Republican President and his executive officers were not the only national politicians in trouble. By 1991 the Democratic-controlled Congress was embarrassed by controversies revealing that many of its members were increasing their "perks," raising their pay, bouncing checks, and in general giving the impression of arrogant abuse of power. In addition, many Americans believed that Congress had caved in to powerful financial interests by pledging billions of tax dollars to rescue inefficient and in some cases corrupt savings institutions and stockbrokers.

In the early 1990s the political mood in the United States soured rapidly. For over a decade, an increasing number of Americans had been losing faith in traditional party politics, believing it to be sham battles designed to perpetuate the power of an entrenched elite. Interest groups were perceived to have more influence on the president and Congress than the general public did. Traditionally such disenchantment had been expressed in apathy: In 1988 only 50 percent of those eligible to vote cast their ballots, an all-time low for the modern era. By 1991, however, there were signs that voters were angry enough to take an active role in changing the system, not only by voting incumbents out of office but also by demanding direct and more frequent communication with their leaders through television and radio.

STAGNATION IN MEXICO

While social change was sweeping through much of Latin America after World War II (see below), Mexico—the model for many Latin American reformers—had stagnated, its revolutionary fervor dissipated. The modest social and land reform programs inaugurated before World War II had been eroded by a huge increase in population, and wage increases had been eaten up by inflation. The nation, particularly its swollen cities, teemed with unemployed and marginally employed citizens. In the early 1970s, abundant petroleum reserves encouraged Mexico to borrow money to build steel mills and power plants and to make other capital improvements. Many U.S. corporations took advantage of the low wage levels in Mexico to set up manufacturing and assembly installations, thus adding to the nation's income. The profits from these projects mostly benefited the rich, however, and the large gap between the rich and the poor remained unchanged. The drop in petroleum prices in the late 1970s prevented Mexico from earning enough money to reduce the principal on its debt, which stood at $100 billion by mid-1989. The government was forced to institute austerity programs, to devalue the currency, and to dedicate the bulk of its petroleum earnings to paying interest on the debt. By 1991 the government had reduced the debt slightly to $95 billion.

Relations between Mexico and the United States remained uneasy. Millions of illegal Mexican immigrants and hundreds of thousands of seasonal workers crossed into the United States. A huge drug traffic from Mexico to the United States flourished. Proud of being an emerging world economic power, Mexicans remembered historic wrongs by the United States and resented being the butt of patronizing stereotypes about bandits and siestas. On the other hand, Mexico was interested in selling its staples to the United States and in encouraging trade and tourism, and the United States was interested in buying Mexican petroleum and natural gas. Frequent meetings between the leaders of the two nations helped to avoid serious ruptures in political and economic relations.

During the 1980s the economic and social problems of the Mexican people began to change their political behavior. Since the 1920s, the government had been in the firm grip of the Party of Revolutionary Institutions, many of whose leaders were accused of enriching themselves while in office. Opposition parties and a free press were tolerated as long as they posed no real threat to the control of the PRI, but any signs of violent opposition, such as student unrest or illegal strikes, were quickly smashed by the government.

By the 1980s, however, many Mexicans had become tired of the graft and inefficiency of the PRI. In the July 1988 presidential elections, the PRI faced formidable opposition for the first time. Strongly opposed by parties from the left and right, the PRI presidential candidate Carlos Salinas de Gortari lost the cities, but with support from the rural peasants who had benefited from land reform squeaked through with a bare majority amid cries of fraud. The once overwhelming PRI majority in the national legislature was sharply reduced.

The PRI responded to the political scare by improving relations with the Catholic Church, selling off some state-owned corporations, cutting welfare state funds to balance budgets, and instituting other measures designed to please the center-right voters in Mexico. Whether Mexico would someday have a true multiparty political system in which the PRI would surrender power if defeated at the polls remained to be seen.

MILITARY AND CIVILIAN GOVERNMENT IN LATIN AMERICA: A PENDULUM

By the 1960s the established elite in many Latin American nations, including some practicing democracies, had become alarmed by high inflation, sporadic violence associated with social reform programs, and Castroite subversion. They also feared that reforms might embolden the lower orders to rebel and destroy their privileges. As a consequence, they often turned to the military for security. In the process, representative government disappeared in many nations. By the early 1990s, however, the military of most Latin American nations, faced with economic problems they could not solve, had turned over the government to elected civilian leaders. Civilian governments, however, while more supportive of constitutional rights, were almost as ineffective as their military predecessors in combatting the economic woes of their nations.

The Pendulum in Brazil and Argentina

In 1964 the Brazilian military ousted a leftist president and terminated the civilian government. These officers did not make the promise often made by the instigators of twentieth-century military *golpes* (blows, or coups) that they would return Brazil to democracy after immediate problems had been solved. Rather, they were prepared to rule the nation indefinitely, proclaiming themselves the embodiment of the whole Brazilian people and promising a program of revolutionary changes to benefit all citizens. Military officials abolished political parties and tinkered constantly with the organization of the government until they were satisfied that they had created an arrangement that would give them tight control over the nation. They muzzled political opposition and repressed scattered violence from the Castroites. Private right-wing death squads killed individuals believed to be subversive. Brazilian officers intensified industrial development, presuming that the benefits of this would trickle down to the impoverished masses. They did not make social reforms or redistribute the land. Their economic program was apparently successful; production increased sharply, as did per capita income. Other nations hastened to copy "the Brazilian miracle."

By the late 1970s, however, the "miracle" in Brazil had faded. The industrialization program emphasized the production of consumer goods, but the cost of providing raw materials, machinery, technicians, and other supporting elements led to inflation. The increase in per capita income masked the fact that profits from industrial expansion were going to the rich and that the gap was widening between the rich and the poor. The illiterate rural and urban workers continued to live in abject poverty, with one of the lowest life expectancy rates in Latin America. They could not buy the consumer products manufactured by the new industries.

Despite these failures, the military continued in power with the support of the upper classes until the 1980s, when many Brazilians, including influential officers in the military, became disillusioned with the regime's floundering economy and a massive debt ($124 billion in mid-1989). Faced with the increased unrest among the middle class and workers, and under mounting pressure from foreign creditors, in 1985 the ruling officers began to turn the government over to elected civilians in stages. Unable in turn to cope with the huge debt, the Brazilian government in 1987 unilaterally suspended interest payments to foreign commercial banks. In 1990 Fernando Collor de Mello became the first civilian elected in twenty-five years. Collor moved to reduce the foreign debt by making budget-cutting austerity moves, privatizing some state-owned corporations, and encouraging foreign trade and investment. Although the debt dropped to $115 billion by 1991, Brazil still was devastated by hyperinflation (prices rose 450 percent in 1991), and evidence accumulated that officials of the Collor administration, through systematic influence peddling, were enriching themselves to the tune of tens of millions of dollars. Masses demonstrating in the streets called for Collor's resignation and impeachment.

In Argentina, the second Perónist government, headed by Perón's second wife, Isabel Perón, who had taken over after the death of her husband, was overthrown in 1976. The armed forces and right-wing death squads suppressed sporadic violence by leftist guerrillas and proceeded to imprison, torture, and execute those believed to oppose the new military regime.

After several years in control, the Argentine junta, like the military in Brazil, found itself unable to grapple with an array of economic and social problems. Hoping to regain popular support, the government embarked on a military adventure that in fact backfired and destroyed the regime. Since 1820 Argentina had claimed the Islas Malvinas in the South Atlantic, but Great Britain had taken these islands in 1833 and had held them ever since as the Falkland Islands dependency. In 1982 Argentine forces seized them in a surprise attack. British forces recaptured the islands, in the process smashing the Argentine navy and air force and capturing thousands of soldiers. The discredited junta arranged for free elections in 1983; Raul Alfonsin, whose centrist party defeated the Perónistas, won in an upset. The Alfonsin government put on trial some of the officers who had been responsible for the reign of terror, but his government had to move cautiously because the army was restive, and military revolts occasionally occurred. Alfonsin's other major task was to cope with Argentina's many economic woes, including inflation and a large national debt. In 1987 Alfonsin was able to refinance the debt, then standing at $53 billion, but economic problems continued.

By 1991, with the national debt at $61 billion and food riots and hyperinflation racking the nation, the Perónist party was returned to power with the election of Carlos Saúl Menem to the presidency. Menem was harassed by military coups, corruption scandals, and criticism for pardoning some of the officers accused of human rights violations. Nevertheless, he was able to lower inflation and turn the debt problem around by a combination of austerity cuts in the budget and the sale of state-owned corporations. Argentina's credit rating improved enough to enable it to get a new loan from the IMF and to advance the prospect of reconsolidating and reducing Argentina's foreign debt. New fears arose, however, that Menem's penchant for ruling by decree might be bringing in a new Perónist dictatorship.

The Death and Rebirth of Democracy in Chile

In Chile, multiparty democratic politics, which had been the rule since 1938, existed in uneasy conjunction with widespread poverty, a traditional social elite, and economic domination by a few families and foreign investors. Although the Mexican Revolution had already produced a rather strong social welfare program by Latin American standards, Castro's domestic program in Cuba inspired Chile's reformers, particularly its Marxist political parties, to press further. In 1970, despite CIA efforts to prevent it, Marxist Salvador Allende, supported by a coalition of leftist parties, was elected president in a divided field with 36 percent of the popular vote. Allende's government proceeded to nationalize foreign holdings without compensation, justifying the act with the claim that the companies owed back taxes to the government. He also greatly accelerated the land reform program, but not fast enough for Chilean radicals who encouraged *campesinos* to seize land not yet expropriated. Allende expanded the social welfare program and sold food to the poor at low prices. Wages rose and unemployment dropped. In the 1973 legislative elections, Allende's party, although still without a majority in Congress, gained ground. By 1972–1973 it appeared that Chile was becoming the world's first democratically elected Marxist state.

During 1973, Allende's program ran into trouble. Agricultural production dropped, and more food had to be imported. A decline in copper production, coupled with a drop in the price of copper on the world market, limited national income and drove the government further into debt. Landless peasants continued unauthorized and sometimes violent land seizures. At the same time, the Nixon administration, believing that Chile was controlled by pro-Cuban and pro-Soviet enemies of the United States, embarked on a program to "destabilize" Allende's government. The CIA spent over $13 million to foster opposition inside Chile, and the United States cut off aid and discouraged private investment there. Meanwhile, the Chilean middle class, fearing social revolution, fought back against Allende, mounting an increasing number of strikes and demonstrations as truckers refused to haul freight and shopkeep-ers closed their stores. In September 1973 the military moved in and Allende was killed in the takeover.

Like the military in Brazil and Argentina, the military government that ruled Chile in the 1970s and 1980s rested on the firm support of the upper and middle classes. Led by General Augusto Pinochet, the new rulers eliminated the legislature and political parties, censored the press, and became one of the most repressive regimes in Latin America, imprisoning, torturing, and killing thousands of Chileans. Pinochet halted land redistribution, canceled wage in-creases, and returned some nationalized business to private ownership. Dur-ing the early 1980s pressure on the military junta mounted. As the declining price of copper brought on an economic depression, various groups began to demonstrate and strike. Pinochet's government stood fast. By the late 1980s an increase in consumer goods production and copper output and a flourishing foreign trade brought prosperity to the upper classes, but the standard of liv-ing for the lower classes fell.

Meanwhile, the junta began to work on building up a long-term basis for conservative rule. In 1980 it created a new constitution, approved by plebiscite, that provided for a strong president with a single eight-year term and put severe limitations on freedom of expression, political activity, and the right to strike. Marxist groups and other organizations "contrary to public morality, order, or national security" were banned. Pinochet was to be presi-dent until 1990; meanwhile, presidential and congressional elections were to be held in 1989 and civilian government restored in 1990.

Despite economic prosperity for the upper classes under the military junta, Chileans nevertheless apparently wished to return to civilian govern-ment, and in 1988 they delivered a severe blow to the regime. The military government called for a plebiscite to determine if Pinochet would be the first president under the fully enacted constitution, and in a fair election 55 percent of the voters voted against him. Constitutionally mandated elections were held in 1989, and civilian government was restored in 1990.

URBAN POVERTY: A GROWING SPECTER

During the last decades of the twentieth century, the movement of *campesinos* into the city sharply escalated, turning Latin America into the most urbanized of the three impoverished world areas (73 percent; Asia, 33 percent; Africa, 34 percent). By the twenty-first century, 90 percent of all Latin Americans will live in cities; Rio de Janeiro will be connected to Sao Paulo in a 350-mile strip con-taining 40 million people. Mexico City, already the world's largest metropolis, had passed 20 million and was still growing.

For awhile, migrants to the city often found some minimal employment in the public or private sector, but the austerity programs employed in many na-tions to cope with their foreign debt problems had dried up the job market, leading to massive unemployment and the collapse of sanitation and of med-

Wealth and poverty in Latin America: shantytown suburbs and downtown office buildings in Caracas, Venezuela.
(Peter Menzel/Stock, Boston)

ical, educational, and transportation services. The *villas miserias*, shantytowns on the edge of Latin American cities, had rapidly expanded with teeming masses of the impoverished, while the middle class and the elite barricaded themselves in the city centers. This volatile situation posed a threat to the stability of most Latin American regimes, especially the civilian democracies.

In some nations such as Venezuela and Brazil, the situation was intensified by the fact that returning prosperity was uneven, adding to the wealth of the upper classes while inflation reduced the meager income of the masses; this situation was clearly conveyed to the average citizen by television and other media, adding to the frustrations of the populace and eroding support for the government.

THE COLD WAR RETURNS TO CENTRAL AMERICA AND THE CARIBBEAN

In the early 1970s it had looked as though revolutionary Marxism in Latin America had faded away outside Cuba. During the middle and late 1970s, however, guerrilla warfare led by leftist forces began to break out in Central America. The unrest generally stemmed from wretched living conditions in a region that was generally the poorest in Latin America. The insurgents were dedicated to ending the privileges of the few and were generally hostile to the United States. The guerrilla movements increasingly came under the influence and leadership of Marxists, although it was not always clear to what extent these groups considered themselves allies of the Soviet Union.

In the 1970s and 1980s opinion in the United States was divided over how to respond to the unrest in Central America and the Caribbean. On the one hand, politicians in both parties were more likely than in earlier decades to realize that poverty often brought about revolution and war in poor nations. Also, there was more understanding among U.S. politicians of the hostility engendered in Latin America by perceptions of "Yankee imperialism" held by many there. These attitudes led the United States to once again step up economic aid to relieve poverty and to pressure conservative governments into instituting reforms. On the other hand, as already discussed, U.S. leaders continued to be extremely sensitive about the presence of Marxism in the Caribbean and Central America and remained ready to take whatever actions they deemed necessary to keep Marxists out. For example, in 1983 the United States invaded the tiny island of Grenada, toppling a pro-Castro Marxist regime there.

By the late 1980s, however, the Cold War in the Caribbean area appeared to be on the wane. The Soviet Union, concerned with economic and political change at home (see Chapter 33), began to scale down its military aid for revolutionary movements in Central America and economic aid for Cuba. Castro's regime, facing an economy straining to support Cuba's effective but expensive social programs, itself gave only modest support to the Central American guerrillas. By the 1990s the Cuban economy, no longer propped up by Soviet aid, was increasingly in disarray, beset by shortages in basic commodities. The aging Fidel Castro's tattered Communist dictatorship, once a significant power in Latin American and even in global affairs, was increasingly perceived to be a historical anachronism.

Panama: Phasing Out and Bringing Back Imperialism

The situation in Panama was primarily one of resentment of U.S. imperialism. After World War II nationalist Panamanians had increased pressure on the United States to cede the Canal Zone to Panama and to surrender control of the canal itself to Panama. During the 1970s the Panamanian dictator Omar Torrijos stressed that the Panama Canal complex was a flagrant example of outdated Yankee imperialism. He also asserted that frustrated nationalism might become radical and endanger the canal itself. The canal was partly obsolete, since it could not handle the new petroleum supertankers, and was difficult to defend against sabotage and guerrilla attacks. With one eye on the situation in Nicaragua (see below), the Democratic administration of President Jimmy Carter concluded an agreement with Panama in 1978 that provided that the United States would complete a phased withdrawal from the Canal Zone by the year 2000, after which Panama would operate the canal as a neutral waterway. The United States reserved the right to intervene militarily to keep the canal open. With great reluctance about losing a prized symbol of U.S. power, the United States Senate ratified the treaty in 1979.

Although many Panamanians realized that they had economically benefit-ed from the presence of the United States, they remained very sensitive to the history of U.S. controls over Panama. In 1988 and early 1989 the United States tried to oust strongman Manuel Noriega from his dictatorship, indicting him on charges of criminal involvement in the international drug traffic. Noriega stood fast, claiming that Panama was faced with yet another instance of Yan-kee imperialism. In 1990, in a scene reminiscent of the early twentieth century, U.S. forces invaded Panama, and after light resistance captured Noriega and brought him to the United States where he was imprisoned and subsequently tried and convicted on drug charges. A government that would cooperate with the United States was installed in Panama.

Nicaragua: The Rise and Fall of Revolutionaries

The revolutionary struggle building in Central America in the 1970s achieved success in Nicaragua. A poor, thinly populated nation, Nicaragua was under the control of Anastasio Somoza, the latest in a family line of dictators. So-moza's rebel adversaries called themselves "Sandinistas" in honor of Augusto Cáesar Sandino, a Nicaraguan rebel who opposed the U.S. occupation of Nicaragua in the 1920s and 1930s. The Sandinistas were composed of a spec-trum of Somoza opponents ranging from moderates to Marxist revolutionar-ies; Cuba supplied them with some arms. Many were given sanctuary in Costa Rica, a neighboring democracy that had previously suffered harassment from Somoza. In 1979 the Sandinistas drove Somoza out and installed a leftist gov-ernment which instituted land reform and built schools and hospitals. The Carter administration, sensitive to charges of past U.S. overreaction in Cuba, the Dominican Republic, and Chile, concluded that the Sandinistas were not Communist allies of the Soviet Union and extended recognition and aid to the new government.

In the years that followed their triumph, however, the ruling Sandinista junta, led by Daniel Ortega, moved steadily to the left, bringing in teachers, doctors, and military training personnel from Cuba. The Sandinistas became increasingly anti-United States in tone, while harassing political opponents, censoring the press, and heavily regulating private business. Beginning in 1981, the Republican administration of Ronald Reagan took the position that guerril-la warfare in Central America, while in part a product of repressive economic and social conditions, was also the result of a plan by the Soviet Union to spread communism throughout the region by funneling arms and advisors from the U.S.S.R. through Cuba and then through Nicaragua to the guerrillas in El Salvador (see next section). The Reagan administration considered Nicaragua a Marxist ally of Cuba and the Soviet Union, and, despite resistance by some in Congress, employed the "destabilization" approach used against Guatemala, Cuba, and Chile. The United States applied economic pressures, such as refusing to buy Nicaraguan sugar, cutting off foreign aid, and opposing loans to Nicaragua by international financial agencies. Anti-Sandinista Nicaraguans, called "Contras," many of them supporters of the deposed dictator Somoza, were trained and supplied by the United States in neighboring Honduras and sent into Nicaragua to drive out the Sandinista government. The United States encouraged another set of anti-Sandinistas to attack Nicaragua from neighboring Costa Rica. U.S. land and air forces went on maneuver in Honduras, while U.S. warships and observation planes watched traffic in and out of Nicaragua. The CIA and other covert organizations harassed Nicaragua with sabotage, air raids, and mining of harbors. The Sandinista junta responded by obtaining economic and military aid from the Soviet Union.

During the 1980s the Contras made little headway against the Sandinistas, and congressional political and economic support for them wavered. Meanwhile, U.S. economic and military pressure, together with the ineffective economic programs of the Sandinista government, brought increasing hardship to the Nicaraguan people. In 1988 hyperinflation reached an astounding 20,000 percent, and by 1989 the junta was forced to announce a 44 percent cutback in the public sector of the national budget. Thousands of public employees were fired, and money outlays for land reform, housing, public health, education, and food subsidies were cut.

As domestic support for the regime eroded and the United States remained a powerful adversarial presence, faced with increased signs of ebbing Soviet support, the Sandinistas began to support a comprehensive agreement covering the region's insurgency problems. At one point the most hopeful sign for eventual peace in the area was the proposal put forth in 1987 by Oscar Arias, the president of Costa Rica, who received the Nobel Prize for Peace. Signed by the presidents of Guatemala, El Salvador, Honduras, Nicaragua, and Costa Rica, the plan called for negotiations between each government and its unarmed internal opposition groups, cease-fires with guerrillas, cessations of states of emergency, the restoration of civil rights, and an end to outside aid to insurgent forces. In 1989 the five presidents of Central America signed an accord in which the Contras' bases in Honduras would be dismantled in return for guarantees of free elections in Nicaragua, monitored by outside observers. In February 1990 President Daniel Ortega lost to Violetta Barrios de Chamorro, the leader of the newly formed National Opposition Union, in an election based primarily on economic issues. In subsequent negotiations the Sandinistas agreed to surrender control of the army and the police after the Contras had been disbanded, and the United States agreed to lift all trade embargos and provide economic aid. In April 1990 Chamorro was inaugurated president, the Contras subsequently laid down their arms, and an uneasy peace followed for the citizens of Nicaragua.

Guerrilla Warfare in El Salvador and Guatemala

In the early 1980s, it appeared as though revolutionary forces might repeat their Nicaraguan triumph in other Central American locations. Communist guerrillas became a formidable force in El Salvador, where tens of thousands of civilians died. Some were killed by guerrillas, but most died in army

---

Fighting against the Repression of the Indians

So I said, "I'm going away." I went because they hadn't kidnapped anyone, or raped anyone, in our village. . . . I was ashamed to stay safely in my village and not think about the others. . . . My father knew and he said: "Where you are going you may not have control over your life. You can be killed at any time." . . . But I knew that teaching others how to defend themselves against the enemy was a commitment to my people and my commitment as a Christian. I have faith and I believe that happiness belongs to everyone, but that happiness has been stolen by the few. I had to go and teach others. That's why I went to the villages most in need, the ones most threatened.

◆◀●▶◆

In her autobiography, Rigoberta Menchú, a Quiché Indian, tells of her decision as an eighteen-year-old to take an active role in defending the Indians of Guatemala against the repression of the Guatemalan government (see main text above). Menchú gives a harrowing view of

the exploitation of the Indian peasants throughout Central America. Two of Menchú's brothers died young of malnutrition; her father, an antigovernment organizer, died in a takeover incident in Guatemala City; her twelve-year-old brother was tortured and then burned alive; and her mother was slowly tortured to death. Menchú went into self-imposed exile in Mexico. There she publicized the plight of the Indians of Guatemala and championed Indian cultures throughout the Western Hemisphere. She worked to organize the Indians so that they could not only defend themselves and their culture from attacks but also demand human rights and social and economic improvement. Although willing to use force in self-defense, Menchú advocated negotiation with the government in the hopes of bringing in peaceful reforms. In 1992 she was awarded the Nobel Prize for Peace.

*From *I, Rigoberta Menchú: An Indian Woman in Guatemala* by Rigoberta Menchú. Edited and introduced by Elisabeth Burgos-Debray and translated by Ann Wright. © 1984 by Verso, London.

---

sweeps through the villages and at the hands of right-wing death squads that eliminated those suspected of supporting the guerrillas or of working for land reform. Those killed or missing included leftist politicians, labor organizers, and individuals working for the Peace Corps and for the Agency for International Development. In El Salvador, the Roman Catholic Church, which supported moderate reforms, was particularly hard hit. Victims included U.S. nuns, Salvadoran priests, and the archbishop of San Salvador, murdered in the cathedral chapel.

The United States, perceiving another instance of Communist subversion, acted. Operating under the principle of the Truman Doctrine, it provided military supplies and advisors to El Salvador during the 1980s to assist the Salvadoran army in defeating the guerrillas. At the same time, the United States attempted to eliminate domestic conditions fostering guerrilla warfare in El Salvador by stepping up economic aid, denouncing the death squads, and supporting moderate politicians such as José Napoleon Duarte, who was elected president in 1984. Most of the U.S. public, however, still mindful of the

Vietnam experience, appeared reluctant to have the United States intervene directly. Meanwhile, the guerrillas received military aid from Nicaragua and apparently from Cuba.

As the war dragged on into the late 1980s, the government emphasized bombing villages presumed to be in sympathy with the rebels; the guerrillas attacked military installations, blew up utilities, and assassinated village officials. By 1988 the war in El Salvador was at a stalemate; over 60,000 civilian and military personnel had been killed in the struggle, and the standard of living in the tiny, densely populated nation was the lowest of the century. Neither side was able to defeat the other, and in September 1991 U.N. Secretary General Javier Perez de Cuellar, a Peruvian, succeeded in extracting an agreement between the government of El Salvador and the rebels in which the insurgents agreed to cease fighting in return for keeping the land they already occupied and integration into the army and police.

In a less publicized Marxist insurgency in Guatemala, over 100,000 persons had been killed since 1972 and 60,000 were missing. Most of the killing centered around the attempts of the Guatemalan government and right-wing death squads to intimidate the Indians, who comprised the majority of the population, so that they would not join a minor but persistent Marxist insurgency. Villages were often destroyed and their inhabitants massacred with the utmost savagery as an example to other villages.

SUMMARY

During the 1970s and 1980s, the United States moved away from the expansion of the welfare state and from the social turmoil that characterized the preceding decade. Americans of the 1970s were harassed by fuel shortages, inflation, political scandal, and the distasteful aftermath of the Indochina war. Liberal causes, such as equal rights for women, fared poorly as political and social conservatism grew stronger.

During the "Reagan era" of the 1980s, conservatives curbed inflation, cut taxes, built up the military, and trimmed back the welfare state, but the United States also faced a huge budget deficit and a large imbalance in foreign trade. Social conservatives were unable to make much headway in their particular causes. U.S. society as a whole, as in the 1970s, appeared to put its emphasis on material success rather than on social reform. By 1990, however, economic recession threatened to erase the popularity that George Bush, Reagan's successor, had garnered through success in foreign policy. Meanwhile, the role of women in U.S. society became a major focus of national attention, as did voter hostility to what they perceived as abuse of power by public officials.

In the 1970s and 1980s the success of movements toward social justice and political democracy fluctuated dramatically in Latin America. By the 1970s, military governments supported by groups fearful of social change dominated Latin America. Meanwhile, in Central America, frustrated proponents of change turned to guerrilla warfare to achieve social and economic change for the masses.

By the 1980s failure to solve social and economic problems had put several South American military regimes into retreat. By 1990, nearly all Latin American nations had civilian governments. There were also signs that Mexico's traditional one-party state might be on the road to a competitive party system.

After World War II the Cold War shaped much of the history of the Caribbean and Central America. The United States, fearing the growth of Soviet influence in the region, agreed to return the Panama Canal to Panama to lessen antiimperialist hostility in the region. This was counterbalanced, however, by the U.S. invasion of Panama in 1990, which deposed its defiant strongman, Manuel Noriega. The United States responded to the presence of Marxism in Latin America by intervening in Chile in the 1970s and in Grenada and throughout Central America in the early 1980s. Leftist revolutionaries triumphed in Nicaragua and held on for a decade in the face of formidable pressures from the United States but lost power in a free election in 1990. The U.S.-backed government in El Salvador ended its civil war with Marxist forces with prospects of creating a coalition with the insurgents. Whatever the political characteristics of individual nations, however, the gap between the rich and the poor in Latin America, especially in the swollen cities, was greater than anywhere else in the world.

SUGGESTED SOURCES

ANDERSON, THOMAS P., *Politics in Central America* (1982). An examination of the social and economic context for political developments in El Salvador, Guatemala, Honduras, and Nicaragua.*

ARGUETA, MANILO, *One Day of Life* Bill Brow, trans. (1983). A novel set in El Salvador that captures well the peasants' daily struggle for existence and their dealings with church and state.*

BREMNER, ROBERT, et al., Eds., *U.S. Choices: Social Dilemmas and Public Policy Since the 1960s* (1986). Historians' essays on major social issues spanning the 1960s and 1970s, including poverty, women's issues, civil rights, the environment, and the economy.

CARROLL, PETER N., *It Seemed Like Nothing Happened: The Tragedy and Promise of America in the 1970s* (1982). A comprehensive and lively overview of the era, covering both politics and social trends but giving greater attention to the latter.

EDSALL, THOMAS BYRNE, and MARY D. EDSALL, *Chain Reaction: The Impact of Race, Rights, and Taxes on American Politics* (1991). A survey of the collapse of liberalism and the rise of conservatism since the 1960s.*

LEWIS, OSCAR, *Five Families* (1976). A study of Mexican families from the poorest to the richest.*

MAYOR, JANE, *Landslide: The Unmaking of the President* (1989). An overview of the Reagan presidency, designed for the general public.*

WESSON, ROBERT, Ed., *New Military Politics in Latin America* (1982). A collection of essays dealing with the long-lasting military dictatorships in Argentina, Brazil, Chile, and Uruguay.

*Paperback available'.

CHAPTER 30

South and Southeast Asia in Recent Decades

This large, diverse region suffered several wars after the 1960s. Conflicts that remained unsettled after France left the region in 1954 and old war rivalries brought on another war in Indochina. After U.S. withdrawal from Vietnam two additional wars, one caused by Vietnam's invasion of Cambodia and the other by a Chinese invasion of Vietnam, reflected regional antagonisms and power struggles among Communist nations. Short wars between India and China, and between India and Pakistan, were the result of regional rivalries and did not directly draw in the superpowers. Many governments in the region also battled insurgency movements caused by ethnic, religious, or economic discontent.

Newly independent nations in the region also struggled against problems associated with economic development, population explosion, unfulfilled and conflicting social aspirations, and political instability. While some nations maintained democratic political systems, others became battlegrounds for democratic versus authoritarian forces.

THE CONTINUING COLD WAR IN SOUTHEAST ASIA

The Great Powers Partition Vietnam

The economic, political, and international relations of all nations of Asia were profoundly affected by the intrusion of Cold War superpower interests into Indochina after France's withdrawal in 1954. The mixture of communism and nationalism in Indochina also ensured that the major powers would become embroiled in the decolonization process.

Where communism was not an issue, the United States supported independence for Asian peoples. Thus it had pressured the Netherlands to relinquish control over Indonesia. However, it opposed the Communist-led independence movement in Indochina, first by supporting the French. After France's defeat in the First Indochina War, the United States endorsed a 1954 international conference, convened at Geneva, Switzerland, where representatives of the United States, Great Britain, and France met with those of the Soviet Union and China and with Vietnamese leaders.

At the conference, the great powers agreed to partition Vietnam temporarily at the 17th parallel, the north to remain under Ho Chi Minh's control and the south to be under a non-Communist government that France had installed. They also agreed that elections, to be held within two years of the agreement in both parts of Vietnam, should determine the future of the land and asked the United Nations to supervise the elections. Laos and Cambodia became independent, neutral nations. The United States and South Vietnam did not sign the Geneva Agreement because Ho Chi Minh's Communist government was allowed to control the north, but the agreement nevertheless went into effect and France withdrew from Indochina.

The two halves of Vietnam quickly polarized into a Communist and an anti-Communist nation. North of the 17th parallel, Ho Chi Minh established the Democratic Republic of Vietnam, with its capital at Hanoi. With economic and military aid from the Soviet Union and China, Ho proceeded to build an effective totalitarian regime based on the Chinese model. His brutal land reform and other policies led to the flight of a million northern-born Vietnamese, many of whom were Catholics and ethnic Chinese, to the south and triggered a peasant revolt that had to be suppressed with troops.

In the south, the Republic of Vietnam established its capital at Saigon. After 1955 President Ngo Dinh Diem, a Catholic in a predominantly Buddhist land, ruled there autocratically. About 90,000 supporters of Ho fled north, which made Diem's task of consolidating the south easier. With the support of the French-trained army, Diem suppressed various armed religious sects and in 1956 promulgated a constitution which gave him extensive powers. Diem was a nationalist, but his regime became increasingly unpopular because it was corrupt and authoritarian and because he blatantly favored the Catholic minority. The United States supplied economic aid to South Vietnam and, fearing a Communist victory, encouraged the South Vietnamese government, which readily agreed, not to hold elections mandated by the Geneva Agreement.

The Second Indochina War

In chaotic South Vietnam, several religious and political groups challenged the government in revolts. The strongest and most coherent rebels were the South Vietnamese Communists (Viet Cong), who launched a revolt in 1958. They were strengthened by Communist southerners who had gone north in 1954 and now infiltrated back into their homeland as well-trained cadres. By 1960 the Communist cadres had fused together the disparate anti-Diem rebels into the National Liberation Front of South Vietnam (NLF). Meanwhile Laotian and Cambodian Communist guerrillas had also launched revolts against their governments, turning the hostilities into a general Indochina war.

The superpowers soon turned these local and civil wars, especially the one in South Vietnam, into a Cold War conflict. The Soviet Union and China hailed

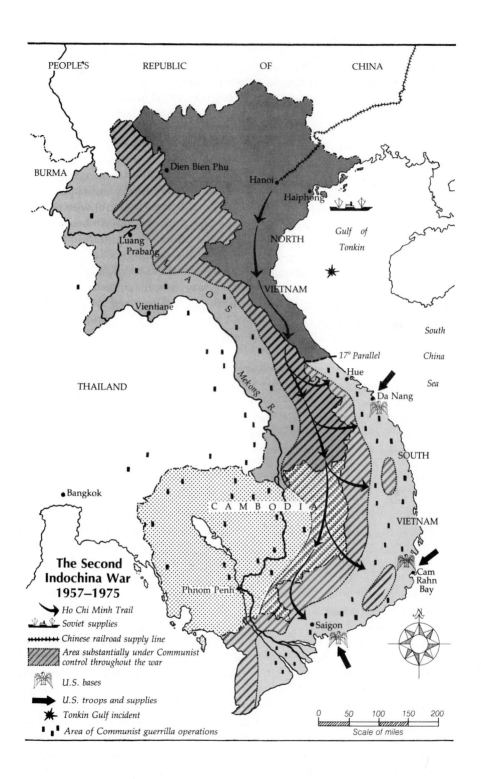

PEOPLE'S   REPUBLIC   OF   CHINA

BURMA

Dien Bien Phu

Hanoi

Haiphong

Luang
Prabang

NORTH

Gulf of
Tonkin

Vientiane

L A O S

VIETNAM

Mekong R.

THAILAND

17° Parallel

Hue

South

China

Da Nang

Sea

SOUTH

Bangkok

C A M B O D I A

VIETNAM

**The Second
Indochina War
1957–1975**

Phnom Penh

Cam
Rahn
Bay

Saigon

Ho Chi Minh Trail
Soviet supplies
Chinese railroad supply line
Area substantially under Communist
control throughout the war
U.S. bases
U.S. troops and supplies
Tonkin Gulf incident
Area of Communist guerrilla operations

0   50   100   150   200
Scale of miles

their side's goal as a "war of national liberation," but initially gave little more than moral support. President Eisenhower, however, viewed the NLF-led revolt as a Communist bid to topple a friendly government. To counter it he invoked the Truman Doctrine and began to send United States military aid and advisors to build up the South Vietnamese army (ARVN). President Kennedy continued this policy, expanding aid to South Vietnam and also giving aid to anti-Communist forces in neighboring Laos in what he called a "flexible response" policy.

As the United States became more involved in South Vietnam, the Soviet Union, China, and other Communist bloc nations countered by supplying North Vietnam with weapons, economic aid, and technical advisors. China also sent labor battalions to replace North Vietnamese who had been drafted into the army. Not only supplies, but also North Vietnamese troops were funneled through Laos and Cambodia into South Vietnam along the Ho Chi Minh Trail, a network of roads and paths that wound through Vietnam, Laos, and Cambodia. In South Vietnam, the Viet Cong fought a war of ambush and assassinations while they controlled peasants in the countryside by intimidation and won their support through land reforms.

Meanwhile, Diem's anti-Buddhist policies led the Buddhist clergy to head widespread protests; several monks shocked the world by publicly setting themselves afire. Late in 1963 the United States gave tacit approval to a plot by disaffected ARVN generals to overthrow the Diem government. In the resulting coup, Diem and his hated brother, the security chief, were both killed. Political instability followed as a succession of generals tried and failed to organize governments that enjoyed widespread public support.

Lyndon Johnson, who succeeded Kennedy as president in 1963, sharply escalated U.S. involvement in Indochina. Johnson used an engagement between U.S. naval vessels and torpedo boats of North Vietnam to maneuver Congress into passing the August 7, 1964 Tonkin Gulf Resolution which authorized the president to "take all necessary measures to repel any armed attack against the forces of the United States in order to prevent further aggression." After Johnson won election to a full term in 1964 he sharply increased U.S. troop levels until they reached one-half million in 1968. He also authorized air strikes against military targets in North Vietnam and along the Ho Chi Minh Trail. Australia, Thailand, South Korea, the Philippines, and several other U.S. allies also sent troops.

It was extremely difficult for U.S. forces, despite better arms, equipment, and supplies, to fight disciplined guerrillas in an oppressively hot climate among peasants of an alien culture. The United States was further hampered by having to work in tandem with a poorly led conscript South Vietnamese army and with an inexperienced and chronically unstable South Vietnamese government. By 1968 the United States and North Vietnam were shouldering the main burden of the fighting in South Vietnam. Although the United States and its allies were engaged in war with a Communist state supported by the senior members of the Communist bloc, the major powers tacitly agreed that the conflict should not be enlarged into a nuclear war.

A Buddhist monk burns himself to death in Saigon in 1963 in protest against the Diem regime.
(UPI/Bettmann Newsphotos)

The Tet (lunar new year) offensive of 1968 was the turning point in the war. Taking advantage of a traditional holiday when their adversaries were off-guard, the Communists launched heavy simultaneous assaults on all important towns in South Vietnam and inflicted heavy casualties, although they were eventually driven back with severe losses. The Tet offensive dashed hopes of a quick, victorious end to the war, and many war-weary Americans and their leaders began to look for a way out. In 1968 the United States and North Vietnam began discussions to end the war.

Unpopular because of his role in leading the United States into a wider war, Johnson did not seek reelection. Richard Nixon, the Republican candidate in the 1968 presidential election, announced that he had a plan to end the war "with honor." President Nixon ended U.S. involvement in the war by improving relations with the Soviet Union and China, heavily bombing North Vietnam to persuade it to negotiate seriously, increasing aid to strengthen the ARVN, and slowly withdrawing U.S. troops from South Vietnam.

On January 27, 1973, the United States and North Vietnam signed an agreement that called for a cease-fire, the complete withdrawal of U.S. troops in sixty days, and U.S. aid to both North and South Vietnam. Chief negotiators Henry Kissinger and Le Duc Tho were awarded the Nobel Prize for Peace in 1973.

Fighting continued in South Vietnam until 1975, when the North Vietnamese and Viet Cong crushed the South Vietnamese government. The thirty-year struggle for a united, independent Vietnam was over, on Communist terms. In 1976 representatives from North and South Vietnam voted to create the unified Socialist Republic of Vietnam; Saigon was renamed Ho Chi Minh City (Ho had died in 1969). Communist governments also took over in Laos and Cambodia.

After the Second Indochina War the Communist states of Indochina maintained one-party totalitarian rule, as elsewhere in the Communist world. The Vietnamese Communist party proved remarkably cohesive, dominated by northerners, who tended to treat newly integrated southern Vietnam with suspicion and as second class. Remarkably resilient and capable in war, they were inept at ruling and developing their nation in peace. The Marxist economic policies applied by Vietnam's leaders, carried out with a war mentality, brought hardship and stagnation to the country. Vietnam's economy was further weakened by the expense of its Cambodian adventures and a U.S. embargo. Millions of Vietnamese refugees, "the boat people," fled their country in leaky boats and risked the elements and pirates for economic and political haven anywhere else. Many boat people were members of the former middle

Vietnam opened its economy to foreign investment in 1987. This Export Processing Zone is run by an investment group from Taiwan.
(*Rachel Lee*, The Free China Journal)

class and were ethnic Chinese. In 1987 Vietnam began to return to some private enterprise to revive its economy and attract foreign investment. It has continued to move to a market economy. It agreed to accept back some of its people who had fled to Hong Kong on payment of money for each returnee.

In Cambodia, Communists were murderously intolerant of each other after assuming power. Fanatical Cambodian Communist leader Pol Pot and his supporters butchered over a million of their compatriots with genocidal fury and ruined the Cambodian infrastructure and economy. In 1977 Vietnam invaded Cambodia, ousted Pol Pot, and put its puppets in power. Pol Pot's supporters and other Cambodians opposed to Vietnamese imperialism then fought a guerrilla war against the Vietnamese-installed government and tied down a large portion of the Vietnamese military for a decade, in a replay of what had happened in Vietnam during the Second Indochina War, but with the roles reversed.

Communist Quarrels after the War

Contrary to fears engendered by the domino theory, communism spread no further in Asia after 1975. Instead, the Communist nations of Asia began to fight one another, demonstrating that nationalism and imperialism were often stronger impulses than common political and economic ideology. Historical Vietnamese imperialism, which had been halted by French colonialism and U.S. intervention, now triumphed across Indochina. In addition to invading Cambodia in 1977 to expel one set of local Communist leaders and install their puppets, Vietnam also established control over Laos. The Vietnamese military, fifth largest in the world, battle-tried and well armed with Soviet and Chinese weapons and captured U.S. armor, became widely feared by the militarily weak non-Communist nations of Southeast Asia. Many Southeast Asian nations, once afraid of the giant presence of the United States, now rued the day of U.S. withdrawal.

Vietnam's ambitions were checked by its erstwhile ally and mentor, China. Sino-Vietnamese enmity was a historic fact of long standing that was especially felt by the Vietnamese, who feared the long shadow cast by the much larger and historically dominant China. (China had ruled northern Vietnam for 1000 years until circa 900 C.E. and was Vietnam's overlord state until 1885.) To counter China, Vietnam cultivated close ties with the Soviet Union. For its part, China feared that Vietnam, and by inference the Soviet Union, would extend its influence in Southeast Asia. Alleging Vietnamese mistreatment of ethnic Chinese in Vietnam and accusing Vietnam of imperialism in its control of Cambodia, China launched a punitive campaign against Vietnam in 1978, but the inexperienced Chinese units did not perform well against the battle-hardened Vietnamese. In any case, after a limited invasion, China declared that it had punished Vietnam and withdrew, but it threatened to return should Vietnamese behavior require it in future.

The Chinese incursion put Vietnam squarely in the Soviet camp. Numerous Soviet technicians were sent to Vietnam, and large amounts of Soviet aid poured in to keep the inefficient and war-damaged Vietnamese economy afloat. In return, the Soviet navy obtained Camranh Bay, with its excellent natural harbor and U.S.-built installations, as a base from which it could challenge the U.S. navy at Subic Bay in the Philippines and exert power in Asian and western Pacific waters. U.S.-Vietnamese relations remained strained because until 1992 Vietnam would not cooperate in accounting for U.S. military personnel who had been missing in action since the 1960s. As a result, the United States refused to give aid to Vietnam and continued a trade embargo.

Throughout the 1980s Chinese-supported Cambodian guerrillas battled Vietnamese soldiers and their Cambodian allies in persistent warfare that sometimes spilled over the Thai border. Cambodia was terribly devastated. Vietnamese troops finally withdrew from Cambodia in 1989, followed by the formation of a coalition government that included several former guerrilla factions in 1991. Indonesia and Japan played major roles in the negotiations, and Japanese troops assumed their first post-World War II overseas mission as peacekeepers. Peace, however, remained elusive as former adversaries continued sporadic hostilities.

The Search for Stability

As the postcolonial era began, all newly independent nations in South and Southeast Asia faced massive economic and social problems which made the task of maintaining political stability extremely difficult. The problems varied from nation to nation. Great Britain and the United States had given their former possessions some training in the democratic process and decolonized in an orderly and peaceful manner. Upon independence these new nations possessed democratically elected governments and relatively well-developed political infrastructures. Their record as independent nations differed.

RACIAL, ETHNIC, AND RELIGIOUS CONFLICTS IN SOUTH ASIA

The story of the nations of South Asia in the last decades of the twentieth century continued to be shaped by a legacy of hatreds that long preceded independence. Every nation had suffered from sporadic outbreaks of ethnic or religious violence. They ranged from the breakup of Pakistan and major threats to the survival of Sri Lanka to persistent communal outbreaks among Hindus, Muslims, and other religious and ethnic groups in India.

Communal problems in India between Hindus and Muslims had delayed its independence and resulted in the partition of the subcontinent into India and Pakistan. In postindependence India, Hindu-Muslim communal antagonisms persisted and occasionally flared into rioting, most recently in Kashmir. Other minority groups, such as the Gurkas, who lived near Nepal, and the tribal people in Assam, agitated or revolted for special treatment or autonomy. In the 1980s serious troubles with the Sikhs, a religious minority of about 16 million people who lived in the northern state of Punjab, erupted into violence. The Sikhs were a successful people who had done well in the government and the military, and their state was one of the richest in the land. However, when the Indian government refused special recognition for their religion and greater autonomy for Punjab, extremists resorted to armed terrorism and began to store arms in the Golden Temple in Amritsar, Sikhism's holiest shrine. In 1984 Prime Minister Indira Gandhi ordered the Indian army to oust Sikh terrorists from the Golden Temple, and in the course of the action hundreds were killed and the temple damaged. After her assassination by her disgruntled Sikh bodyguards, her successor Prime Minister Rajiv Gandhi negotiated an accord with moderate Sikh leaders that included greater autonomy for Punjab and other concessions. The extremists, however, who would have been satisfied only with an independent Sikh state, were not mollified, and sporadic acts of terrorism continued. A multiethnic nation, India's many religious and linguistic groups continued to live in uneasy peace.

Despite ethnic problems, India enjoyed elected governments except between 1975 and 1977 when Prime Minister Indira Gandhi (daughter of Nehru and no relation to Mahatma Gandhi) suspended the constitution and ruled under emergency laws. When she allowed free elections in 1977, the Indian electorate demonstrated its political savvy and commitment to democratic principles by throwing Gandhi and her Congress party out of office. The Janata party that replaced her was ineffective and unstable, however, and Gandhi was swept back to power in the 1980 election. When Gandhi was assassinated in 1984 leaders of the Congress party quickly elevated her son Rajiv to the prime ministership. Rajiv Gandhi was at first popular because he was young, not corrupt, and supported modernization, and above all because of the circumstances of his succession; but he was handicapped by political inexperience.

Rajiv Gandhi's elevation to prime minister by the majority Congress party despite an almost total lack of political experience reflected the strong family-dynastic tradition in much of Asia in general and in India in particular. (He had been a pilot for India Airlines and became his mother's political heir after the accidental death of his politically active brother Sanjay.) He resigned as prime minister in 1989 because of electoral losses suffered by the Congress party. While campaigning for the 1990 general election Gandhi was assassinated by a Tamil extremist group from Sri Lanka (see below), whose secessionist fight he had initially supported and then abandoned. V. P. Singh of the National Front became prime minister of India. For only the second time since independence India was headed by a non-Congress government and was not led by a member of the Nehru-Gandhi family.

Economic policy in India has exhibited a steady movement away from Marxist approaches toward capitalist practice. The Indian leaders who won independence preferred socialism in economics. Throughout Indira Gandhi's tenure of power India's economy combined state planning and private enterprise. Many economists thought state planning mired the Indian economy in corruption and red tape and that the application of doctrinaire economic theories stymied progress. The economy began to grow faster after Rajiv Gandhi became prime minister because he favored private enterprise, deregulation, and high technology. As a result, India's middle class (defined as people with disposable income after paying for the necessities of life) grew to become larger than the total population of the United States. This trend accelerated under Prime Minister Singh; deregulation immediately resulted in rapid growth in the revitalized private sector. India changed economic policy partly as a result of the fall of communism in the former Soviet Union and Eastern Europe and the discrediting of planned economic systems. Itself in deep economic trouble, the Soviet Union/Russia stopped giving aid to India.

Despite India's own troubles with minority separatism, it intervened in the ethnic conflict in neighboring Sri Lanka. The Buddhist Sinhalese majority politically controlled that island, and the Hindu Tamil minority there resorted to terrorism to gain autonomy or to secede. India at first allowed the Tamil rebels to use southern India for training and refuge and supplied them with arms. It did so to assert its claim as the regional power of South Asia and because the large population of Tamils in southern India sympathized with the plight of their kindred in Sri Lanka. In 1987 the Indian government forced a mediated settlement and landed troops to enforce its terms, but it became mired in Sri Lanka battling the Tamils who were dissatisfied with the terms of the settlement and blamed India for betraying them. India withdrew its troops without having achieved its goals, and Rajiv Gandhi paid for the involvement with his life.

While Sri Lanka was trying to ward off secession, ethnic divisions succeeded in splitting Pakistan apart. In the 1970 Pakistani elections, the more populous East Pakistan won a majority, whereupon the generals, who came from West Pakistan, decided to postpone convening the National Assembly. This was the last straw for the East Pakistanis, who had long resented their second-class citizenship. Led by Sheikh Mujibur Rahman, leader of the winning political party called the Awami League, East Pakistan declared its independence and renamed itself Bangladesh in 1971. A bloody war between the segments of Pakistan ensued in which over a million people lost their lives as the army sent from West Pakistan sought to crush the rebellion. Ten million fled to seek refuge in neighboring India. India seized the opportunity to humble its enemy Pakistan, and Indian troops entered the war to help Bangladesh. This forced Pakistan to give up its attempt to reconquer the east. The military ruled Bangladesh for most of its postindependence years, but elections were held in 1989 that brought Kaleda Zia to power as prime minister. The only two women leaders in Muslim countries, Benazir Bhutto of Pakistan and Zia, came from the Indian subcontinent.

Pakistan had had some early episodes of parliamentary governments, but after 1964 was for long periods under either direct or veiled military control. In 1977 General Mohammad Zia ul-Haq seized power in Pakistan from the elected prime minister Zufilkar Ali Bhutto. After ruling for twelve years, Zia was killed in an airplane crash in 1988. In elections held in late 1988 the People's party, headed by Benazir Bhutto (daughter of the former prime minister), won a handy victory. As a result she was named prime minister, the first woman head of government in a Muslim country. Bhutto was dismissed from office by Pakistan's president in 1990 after charges of corruption by her party, and the People's party lost the subsequent general election. Although politics remained frequently violent and social and ethnic unrest portended a military takeover, elected civilian rule continued.

UNSTABLE POLITICS IN NON-COMMUNIST SOUTHEAST ASIA

As in South Asia, the newly independent nations of Southeast Asia had ethnic, racial, and linguistic minorities bent on autonomy or secession. In addition, many states had unassimilated minorities from recent immigration. Nonetheless, the governments of these states succeeded in keeping ethnic nationalism from breaking them up. Chinese minorities presented a special problem in Southeast Asia. There were Chinese populations in every nation who were numerically small but economically very influential. The success of the Chinese excited envy and often brought retaliation and victimization. For example, it was customary for Filipino politicians to shake down Chinese-Filipinos; and during the army countercoup in Indonesia in 1965, many of the victims were local Chinese who were killed because of their wealth. The recent rise of militant Islam among the Malays in Malaysia added to the disquiet of the Chinese and other minority groups and threatened the political stability that characterized Malaysia's postindependence years. Similarly, Indian minorities were victimized in Malaysia and Burma.

Despite ethnic problems, Malaysia and Singapore maintained uninterrupted democratic parliamentary governments since independence. Singapore briefly joined with Malaysia but seceded to form a separate ministate in 1965. Its almost 80 percent ethnic Chinese population was guided by the elected prime minister Lee Kuan Yu, who oversaw his orderly and prosperous nation in the manner of a family patriarch. Although Lee retired, his political party continued to rule Singapore through electoral victory. After Singapore's secession Malaysia had a slight Malay ethnic majority which ruled with unabashed bias in favor of Malays.

Indonesia and Burma were ruled by authoritarian military governments. Sukarno ruled Indonesia in an eccentric fashion as president for life under the guise of a "Guided Democracy" until 1965. In the face of deteriorating health, he held onto power by playing off the army against the Communist party of Indonesia (PKI) and its front organizations, which he seemed to favor increasingly. In a sequence of events that remained unclear afterward, the PKI staged a coup against the army in 1965 and killed a number of senior officers. It failed to capture several key leaders, one of whom, general Suharto, seized leadership and crushed the rebellion, killing between 150,000 and 500,000 people in the process. Sukarno was stripped of power and died in 1970. Suharto remained in power, heading an authoritarian and military-dominated regime, although several general elections were held. Suharto's government emphasized political consensus, a tradition highly regarded in Indonesia.

A spellbinding speaker, President Sukarno of Indonesia addresses a giant rally.
(*AP/Wide World Photos*)

Burma changed its name to Myanmar in 1989. It had become a parliamentary democracy upon independence, but in 1962 the elected government was overthrown by a military coup led by the commander-in-chief. Under repressive military governments Burma's economy stagnated and the people's standard of living deteriorated. Widespread demonstrations led by students and the Buddhist clergy forced the ruling junta to call elections in 1990. Aung San Suu Kyi, daughter of Burma's foremost independence fighter and then under house arrest, organized an opposition party that handily won the elections. However, the generals refused either to free Aung San Suu Kyi or to hand over the government to elected civilian leaders.

Thailand was a constitutional monarchy that had retained independence throughout its modern history. Like neighboring Burma it had had a checkered course for democracy and was frequently under corrupt military rule. Unlike isolationist Burma, Thailand actively participated in international alliances and organizations, and its economy prospered and neared the takeoff point. Rising prosperity and openness to the world had led to the growth of a middle class and a civil society in Thailand in past decades that recently showed unwillingness to continue to knuckle under autocratic rule.

The Philippine constitution established a U.S.-style democratic government that worked turbulently under a two-party system through the 1960s.

Continuing Her Father's Legacy

Many people ask me how I came to be involved in this nationwide movement for democracy. As the daughter of the man regarded as the father of modern Burma it was inevitable that I should have been closely attuned to political currents in the country. From childhood I was deeply interested in the history of the independence movement and in the social and political development of the Union of Burma. . . . [My father had been] an upright man who put the welfare of his country above his own interests. . . . [Studying his life I too] came to feel such a deep sense of responsibility for the welfare of my country. . . .

My years abroad provided me with the opportunity to assess Burma's problems from the broad perspective of the international scene, while my frequent visits home kept me in touch with developments within the country. It was not difficult to recognize that the nation was inexorably deteriorating under the government of the BSPP [Burma Socialist Programme Party—the ruling party dominated by military men]. But I could not see any signs of a popular opposition movement which I could support whole-heartedly until I came to Burma last April [1988]. Then I found that the mood of the people had changed and that the time for a popular anti-government movement was fast approaching. The massacre of peaceful demonstrators last August precipitated such a movement and decided me to come out in support of the people's aspirations. This decision was prompted partly by the belief that as my father's daughter I have a responsibility towards my country.

—◆◀◆▶◆—

Aung San Suu Kyi is the daughter of Aung San, leader of Burma's independence movement who was assassinated by political opponents in 1947, just before Burma achieved independence from Britain. On a continent where family rule often resulted in massive corruption and abuse of power, Aung San Suu Kyi represented the tradition where a parent's fame left an obligation on the children to give further service to their country. She married an Englishman and lived in Great Britain until her mother's serious illness called her home in 1988. There she found a budding democracy movement against Burma's oppressive military rulers and plunged into organizing a National Coalition that swept the elections in 1990. The generals placed her under house arrest and would not allow the elected representatives to form a government. Aung San Suu Kyi won the Nobel Prize for Peace in 1991 for her courage in defending democracy and human rights. She was not allowed to leave her country to receive it.

*From "In the Eye of the Revolution" by Aung San Suu Kyi, in Michael Aris (Ed.), *Freedom from Fear*, New York: Penguin Books, 1991, pp. 211–212.

Ferdinand Marcos was elected president in 1965 and reelected in 1969. In 1972, masking his quest to perpetuate his personal and family rule by asserting that he needed more power to put down a Communist revolt, Marcos suspended the constitution and declared martial law, which continued until 1981. During the 1980s, an ailing Marcos shared power with the military and with his wife Imelda. Meanwhile, separate long-active Communist and Muslim (mostly on Mindanao) insurgencies continued. Under mounting U.S. and domestic pressure, Marcos held presidential elections in 1986. He was opposed by Corazon Aquino, widow of an opponent who had been assassinated. Massive fraud allowed Marcos to declare himself the winner, but by then the United States had switched its support to Aquino. A military coup led by reform-minded officers finally toppled Marcos; Aquino was inaugurated president, and democracy was restored to the Philippines. Although personally upright, Aquino was surrounded by rich landowners who opposed economic reforms; politically inexperienced, her government was plagued by many coup attempts. Free elections were held in 1992, Aquino did not run, and former defense minister Fidel Ramos was elected president.

THE QUEST FOR ECONOMIC DEVELOPMENT

Economic development followed an unsteady course in South and Southeast Asia. As a result, the region boasted on the one hand the economic miracle of Singapore, while on the other Bangladesh remained one of the poorest nations of the world. The reasons for the disparity were complex, ranging from the quality and quantity of natural resources to ideology and religion, political leadership and stability, and Cold War alignments.

Population growth was a key factor that hindered development in most nations. The government of Singapore carried out a highly successful policy of family planning and population control. By the late 1980s it had achieved almost zero population growth (1990 estimates had the population increasing at 1.1 percent per year and a birthrate of 16 per 1,000 persons). As the result of an economic policy that fostered growth through free trade, and a highly competitive educational policy that produced a skilled labor force, in Asia Singapore trailed only Japan in standard of living. It was the only nation in South and Southeast Asia (aside from the oil rich ministate Brunei on Sumatra) whose per capita GNP exceeded $10,000.

Bangladesh was at the other end of the spectrum, where the birthrate stood at 43 per 1000 persons and the natural population increase was 2.8 percent per year. This Wisconsin-sized nation, which had few industries and depended almost solely on farming in perilously flood-prone delta land, had 118 million people in 1990. Only 29 percent of them were literate, and 75 percent lived in absolute poverty by United Nations standards. Per capita GNP stood at a pitiful $70 per year. Pakistan had 32 million people in 1947 in what was then West Pakistan; by 1990 the population had increased to 118 million. India had 350 million people in 1947, and 844 million in 1990. Similar rates of increase also held true for Indonesia and the Philippines.

Several factors explained this unprecedented and catastrophic population explosion. One was improved public health and medicine that eliminated epidemics and vastly decreased infant mortality, allowing those who survived infancy to live longer. While life expectancy was just over thirty years at independence in 1947, the average life span had increased to fifty-seven years for

Indian Prime Minister Indira Gandhi meets leader of Bangladesh,
a nation that owed its independence to India.
(Keystone Press)

men and fifty-eight years for women in India by 1990. A similar though slightly lower life expectancy was true for Pakistan and Bangladesh.

Outside of Singapore, none of the nations of the region had achieved
much success with population control; some had not seriously tried. Reasons
for population explosions were generally interrelated. One was lack of resources to set up family-planning clinics and train personnel; another was the
low educational level of the people. Uneducated people were generally ignorant about birth control and in any case supported traditional values that
taught the merits of early marriages and large families, in which a woman
gained respect by bearing many children, especially sons.

Even where governments had the will, they still had a most difficult
task in convincing very traditional people to desire small families. Prime
Minister Indira Gandhi tried in India in 1975 with the slogan "Stop at two
(children)." (Indian upper- and middle-class families needed no such re-
minders.) Her government also tried to force some Indians to undergo ster-
ilization during 1975–1977 when she suspended the constitution and took
away legal due process. This policy and these tactics so outraged tradition-
minded Indians, especially the Muslim minority, that they contributed to
her electoral defeat in 1977. Her successor governments have soft-pedaled
this issue ever since.

Despite the huge population increases there had been no famine in postindependence Asia, as there had been in Africa. However, most of the people on the Indian subcontinent were desperately poor by Western standards and subsisted on only two-thirds of the calorie intake of Westerners. A key factor in preventing starvation was effective international relief and humanitarian efforts, particularly in crisis-ridden Bangladesh. Another was the Green Revolution, begun in the 1960s, which introduced high-yielding hybrid seeds and increased food production. It allowed India, which since earliest times had suffered from sporadic famines, to produce enough food to feed its huge and expanding population. Other factors were the clearing of virgin lands to increase the acreage under cultivation and large new irrigation projects which made possible double- and triple-cropping. However, progress brought pollution and erosion. There was also a widening gap between the rich and poor, as many small farmers who could not afford the necessary capital to invest in farm machinery, chemical fertilizers, and pesticides were squeezed out.

Burgeoning populations have stymied efforts to improve education and standard of living. India's per capita GNP remained low at $330 per year in 1988, and that of Pakistan at $350; even resource-rich Indonesia's per capita GNP remained low at $430 because of a rapid increase in the population, which stood at 191 million in 1990. Compared with Singapore's at more than $10,000, the contrast is startling.

All nations in the region have benefited from foreign aid. Cold War rivalries helped neutralist India to obtain aid from both the Eastern and Western blocs; it received over $9 billion from the United States between 1947 and 1980, and billions from the Soviet Union. The Philippines and Thailand also received huge sums of aid from the United States. Great Britain, Canada, and Australia gave aid to other Commonwealth nations. Since the 1980s Japan has supplanted the United States as the chief aid giver and investor in Southeast Asia. In addition, international agencies such as the World Bank and the Asian Development Bank have provided aid.

Inept and corrupt governments throughout the region crippled development. For example, the Philippines, despite massive and continuing U.S. aid, remained on the verge of economic ruin partly because of mismanagement and corruption during the Marcos decades. Marcos rewarded members of his family and supporters and created a system dubbed "crony capitalism" in which wealth wound up in the hands of a small group of families and individuals. While peasants were pushed off the land, large estates thrived on producing crops for export. Lacking petroleum deposits, the Philippines imported petroleum at increasingly high prices and, despite extensive U.S. aid, chalked up a huge foreign debt of $26 billion. After 1986 the Aquino government barely checked the downward spiral because it was unstable and did not initiate land reform, reduce corruption, provide security, or generate enough confidence to attract investments. As a consequence, the Communist insurgency continued. Burma was a dismal example of a nation of rich natural resources ruined by an inept and corrupt military government that supposedly had a "Burmese road to socialism." The result was a bankrupt and barely functioning nation in a land that used to export food.

Large military expenditures were also to blame for the slow rate of development. Nearly all nations in the region either had grandiose imperialistic dreams or feared real or imagined enemies. All allocated large amounts of scarce resources to arms and military forces. India, for example, committed a large part of its resources to its military in order to guard against China, watch Pakistan, and sustain its pretensions to being the regional power of South Asia. Thus India became a nuclear power, maintained an aircraft carrier in its naval fleet, and under Prime Minister Rajiv Gandhi committed Indian troops to Sri Lanka's civil war. Fearful of the much larger India, Pakistan also maintained a strong military and secretly began to develop nuclear weapons.

A positive trend was the Association of Southeast Asian Nations (ASEAN) formed in 1967 by Thailand, the Philippines, Indonesia, Malaysia, Singapore, and (later) Brunei. Member nations held regular consultations on economic and other issues of mutual concern and worked to coordinate economic and trade policies and to foster cooperation. With regional economic unions in Europe and North America gaining ground, ASEAN members, too, created a customs union scheduled to be operational in the 1990s. Hoping also to benefit, Communist Vietnam and Laos showed interest in joining. Starting in the 1980s Malaysia, Thailand, and Indonesia began to chart significant economic progress and rapid growth rate. Many economists predicted that they would become the "Little Japans" of the future.

SOCIAL TRADITION AND SOCIAL CHANGE

Throughout South and Southeast Asia a wide chasm has separated the rich from the poor, the modern from the traditional, the educated from the illiterate, and the secular from the religious. Against such a background social progress has at best scored a mixed record. On the positive side, there had been regionwide improvements in life expectancy, medical care, and the literacy rate. Mass communication had reached even remote villages. On the other hand, television had shown impoverished villagers the lifestyles of the rich in their own nations and overseas, stirring up hopes and expectations for a better life that were too often unrealizable or that were met too slowly.

Social change affecting women made slow headway in the region. Politically women have made tangible gains. In nations where elections were held, women secured the vote and voted in numbers equal to men. India, Pakistan, Bangladesh, Sri Lanka, and the Philippines had women heading their governments, an achievement unmatched in most Western nations. Women also held numerous high diplomatic and government positions. As the urban middle class increased in size, more women asserted their rights.

The Indian parliament passed laws soon after independence that made women politically equal to men, enforced monogamy among all but Muslims, and granted Hindu widows the right to remarry, wives the right to obtain a divorce, daughters equal rights in inheritance with sons, and so on. However, among all but upper-class Hindus few women either understood their rights or felt confident enough to exercise them. Thus laws that protected women tended to be unfulfilled, and girls continued to marry early (sometimes younger than the legal age of fifteen), and those without sufficient dowries suffered harsh treatment by their in-laws. Women tended to have higher illiteracy rates than men, in some countries to have shorter life expectancy than men, to hold low-paying jobs, and to be left in the countryside while men went to the cities to seek higher-paying work.

In Pakistan, Bangladesh, and Malaysia, a resurgent Islamic fundamentalist movement sought to rescind civil and criminal codes introduced by Britain and to go back to traditional Islamic law, and succeeded in some areas. Fundamentalist vigilantes became emboldened to insist on the veiling of women and to intimidate modernized Muslims, especially women, to give up freer lifestyles. So as not to alienate Muslims, the Indian constitution allowed the Muslim community to remain under the rule of their religious laws and Muslim men were allowed more than one wife.

In the Philippines *macho* males also demanded the maintenance of female subordination. The Catholic Church contributed to the ethos of the homebound woman by encouraging large families. Only in economically prosperous Singapore did women win economic independence. In other nations, real equality either did not exist or remained only partially realized.

COLD WAR ALLIANCES AND NEUTRALISM

The foreign policy of every nation in South and Southeast Asia was affected by the continuing Cold War, and each nation's place and policy in the Cold War was in turn the result of its domestic characteristics, ideology, colonial experience, and relationships with its neighbors. Some nations chose alignment with one of the superpowers, while others chose neutrality or nonalignment.

As discussed in Chapter 24, India professed neutrality in superpower politics but in practice tilted toward the Soviet Union. When India's initially friendly relations with China deteriorated into war in 1962, the Soviet Union rewarded India with weapons and diplomatic support. In return India refused to criticize the Soviet Union for invading Afghanistan in 1978, even when the U.S.S.R. conceded its genocidal intervention in Afghanistan a failure and withdrew. India continued to receive military and financial aid from the Soviet Union until its dissolution. In 1961 India, together with Egypt and Yugoslavia, sponsored the Nonaligned Movement. Its Asian members included Bangladesh, Indonesia, Malaysia, and Singapore. Whereas India could not have aspired to leadership in either camp of the Cold War, its leadership was assured among the Neutralist bloc. Thus it suited India's national interest to be neutralist. India and Pakistan continued to be each other's worst enemy, intermittently threatening each other with war.

Confronted with neutralist but pro-Soviet India, Pakistan chose a pro-Western stance, and after 1962 also became pro-Chinese. When India detonated a nuclear device in 1974, its eventual target was undoubtedly Pakistan. The

Indian threat motivated Pakistan to develop its own nuclear capability, which it reputedly achieved in 1986. Although the United States opposed nuclear proliferation, it continued to assist Pakistan because that nation played the leading role in supporting the anti-Soviet guerrilla fighters in Afghanistan. Pakistan gave refuge to over 3.5 million Afghans who had fled their homeland, allowed its territory to be used as a staging ground for the Afghan guerrillas to strike back into Afghanistan, and became a conduit for U.S. military and economic aid to the insurgents. Anxious to continue receiving U.S. aid after Soviet withdrawal from Afghanistan, Prime Minister Benazir Bhutto announced in 1989 that Pakistan would not build nuclear weapons, but her successor government later fudged on that pledge.

The remaining non-Communist states of southeastern Asia, with the exception of neutralist Burma, tended to tilt toward the West in the Cold War. However, after the United States withdrew from the Indochina war, some of them, for example, Thailand, became fearful of antagonizing their powerful Communist neighbors and so began to distance themselves from the United States. Most were fearful of the Soviet Union's expanding naval presence in the region, centered on its naval base in Vietnam, apprehensive about Japan's economic clout lest it would also become military, and hoped the United States would retain a military presence in the region.

An uneasy relationship also developed between the United States and the Philippines. The two largest U.S. overseas bases, Clark Air Force Base and Subic Bay Naval Station, were located in the Philippines. The United States paid the Philippine government handsome, ever-increasing rent, plus an economic aid package, for use of the facilities, and the bases generated much-needed income for the Filipino economy. Nevertheless, many Filipinos resented the massive U.S. presence in their nation as a symbol of its residual colonial status and agitated for its termination. In the middle of negotiations for lease renewal in 1990, Mount Pinotubo burst into violent volcanic eruption. Ashes poured onto nearby Clark Air Force Base and destroyed the facility. With the disintegration of the Soviet Union, the strategic value of the bases had declined. With an economic recession in the United States, paying high rent for the bases seemed wasteful, and with the host nation resenting continued U.S. presence, the United States decided not to renew its lease on either base.

SUMMARY

The Cold War once again became a hot war in former French Indochina. The United States failed to stem the advancing tide of communism in Indochina, which after 1975 was ruled by Communist governments and dominated by Vietnam. However, the domino theory did not prove applicable beyond Indochina. In Communist-ruled nations regional imperialism resurfaced as Vietnam attempted to dominate Laos and Cambodia, and China to check Vietnam.

Political stability was another regionwide problem. Newly independent nations that often lacked experienced leaders tackled the problems of nationhood. Some maintained good records of democracy, but others succumbed to military or strongman rule. Everywhere people sought democratic rights, which recently even spread to isolated Burma. Internally each nation also faced conflicts between dominant majorities and ethnic and religious minorities. Old ethnic and religious hostilities submerged under imperialism arose to demand attention, frequently defying solution. New enmities created additional bitter feelings between states. Different value systems also battled for preeminence.

All the newly independent nations found themselves beset by common problems, especially population explosion, poverty, and economic backwardness. Economic progress was uneven. Most received foreign aid, and some, like India, received aid from both the United States and the Soviet Union. Burma rejected foreign aid in favor of isolation, while the Philippines received massive aid from the United States; both had mismanaged themselves into near-bankruptcy, while economists despaired that Bangladesh could ever progress beyond its desperate poverty. Tiny Singapore alone developed a strong economy, although Thailand, Malaysia, and Indonesia seemed poised to follow.

Women in all nations struggled for equality, and spectacular successes were scored. Most nations enacted laws to protect and advance the status of women, although in all countries poor women remained second-class citizens. In Muslim countries Islamic fundamentalism clashed with secular lifestyles and women's liberation.

Almost all nations, even those that professed neutrality, played some role in or were affected by the continuing Cold War. India led the neutralist nations but tilted toward the Soviet Union. Pakistan, on the other hand, joined a U.S.-headed alliance, in part motivated by fear and enmity toward India. Emphasizing economic advancement, ASEAN is an example of regional cooperation in Southeast Asia.

SUGGESTED SOURCES

BHUTTO, BENAZIR, *Daughter of Destiny, An Autobiography* (1989). A moving book by a courageous woman.

CAPUTO, PHILIP, *A Rumor of War* (1977). A thoughtful account of the war in Indochina by a marine who fought there.*

DANDEKAR, HEMALATA C., *Men to Bombay, Women at Home: Urban Influence on Sugao Village, Deccan Maharashtra, India, 1942–1982* (1986). Effects of modernization on urban and village life.*

FITZGERALD, FRANCIS, *Fire in the Lake* (1972). Excellent overview of the culture and politics of Vietnam and of the nature of the war there.*

GOODNO, JAMES B., *The Philippines: Land of Broken Promise* (1991). This book deals with many subjects; it is partly based on interviews and partly on the author's firsthand knowledge.

GREY, ANTHONY, *Saigon* (1982). An epic novel that intertwines French, American, and Vietnamese lives from 1925 to 1973.

GUPTA, PRANAY, *Mother India, A Political Biography of Indira Gandhi* (1992). A candid, sweeping biography.

HERRING, GEORGE C., *America's Longest War: The United States and Vietnam, 1950–1975* (1979). A concise, well-written narrative.*

KARNOW, STANLEY, *Vietnam: A History* (1983). A balanced account of the war. (Also a thirteen-part television series.)

LAPIERRE, DOMINIQUE, *The City of Joy* (1985). About Mother Theresa's Calcutta.*

ROMILOS, BETH DAY, *Inside the Palace: The Rise and Fall of Ferdinand and Imelda Marcos* (1987). An insider's look at the Marcos regime by the American journalist wife of a prominent Filipino.

*Paperback available.

CHAPTER 31

Competing Political, Economic, and Social Systems in East Asia

In recent decades East Asia has continued to be divided politically, economically, and socially. Wars and near-wars resulted from these hostilities and caused nations in the region to maintain large armed forces and join alliances. Two conflicts, the Korean war and the Indochina war, involved one superpower (the United States) directly, while the other, the Soviet Union, was represented by its proxies (North Korea and North Vietnam) and a sometime ally, China. North and South Korea remained intensely hostile after the cease-fire that ended formal hostilities in 1953. The Chinese civil war continued in a formal sense as the governments of both China and Taiwan professed to represent the entire nation, and China had not disavowed the use of force to compel Taiwan into its fold.

Two quite different political systems coexisted uneasily. China and North Korea were ruled by Communist governments. Japan remained a democracy as a result of U.S. occupation-mandated reforms. South Korea and Taiwan were ruled by authoritarian and staunchly anti-Communist governments but began moving rapidly toward pluralistic and democratic political systems in the late 1980s.

While Japan, South Korea, and Taiwan became industrialized and wealthy nations, a command economic system dictated by Marxist theories and by centralized planning failed to bring prosperity to the Communist nations. After 1978 China resurrected the private sector to revive its moribund economy, but North Korea did not budge from its orthodox Marxist economy. Improvements brought about by privatization, and the restoration of incentives inevitably led Chinese citizens to demand political and social reforms, but the government forcibly suppressed the reformers.

COMPETING POLITICAL SYSTEMS

A great ideological divide separated the Communist from the non-Communist nations of East Asia. The seven-year U.S. occupation had transformed Japan

472

into a democracy and a pluralistic society. The parliamentary democracy established in the 1947 constitution continued to function; no competing political system mustered enough support to change it. The Liberal Democratic party retained power through 1992, with the Socialist party relegated to permanent and ineffective opposition. During the 1980s democracy progressed impressively in South Korea and Taiwan. In contrast, the Communist party clung to totalitarian power in China and North Korea. While North Korea remained stable under one-man Communist rule, China was repeatedly rocked by massive disturbances in power struggles within the Communist party and by prodemocracy movements. With the fall of communism in the former Soviet Union and Eastern Europe, continental East Asia was the remaining bastion of communism by the end of 1991. Communist regimes there retained a monopoly of power through repression, but the long-term trend in Communist nations seemed to favor change.

Political Evolution in Taiwan and South Korea

Deeply scarred by defeat on the mainland and fearful of invasion by China, Chiang Kai-shek promulgated emergency laws and maintained an authoritarian government on Taiwan until his death in 1975. His son Chiang Ching-kuo assumed the presidency on Taiwan in 1978, following a pattern of family rule often seen in Asia. Chiang Ching-kuo continued and accelerated the economic development begun by his father, and he also inaugurated political reforms. In the late 1980s he declared that none in his family would succeed him and picked Taiwan-born and U.S.-educated Lee T'eng-hui as vice-president. Chiang died in 1989, but the reforms he had begun transformed Taiwan's political system into an open and democratic one. As a journalist who covered China said, "Other countries ranging from Albania to Paraguay have also cast off their repressive governments, but one would be hard pressed to find any place on earth that has so successfully combined an economic with a political miracle." By 1991 all repressive laws that abridged civil and political rights had been rescinded. Nationwide elections were held in 1991 and 1992 that international observers pronounced fair. Although the KMT won strong majorities in both elections, a two-party political system appears to be emerging on Taiwan.

South Korea's government was for long periods dominated by the military. Student-led demonstrations in 1988 resulted in democratic reforms and free elections in which several political parties participated. Students have continued to demonstrate sporadically in favor of unification with North Korea. The threat of political instability caused by the student demonstrations have had an adverse effect on South Korea's economic growth.

China's Continuing Political Tumult

Pragmatists in the regular party structure and bureaucracy led by Liu Shaoqi and Deng Xiaoping ruled China between 1960 and 1966 and repaired the deep economic damage wreaked by Mao's discredited Great Leap Forward.

Seething with resentment at his ouster from power, Mao plotted to end his forced retirement. Mao, his wife Jiang Qing (a former actress who until then had played only a minor public role), and some allies went to the campuses of universities and secondary schools where they enrolled millions of young people in the Red Guards and used them to oust the party cadres and bureaucrats from power. Mao called his campaign to seize power and implement his radical vision for China the Great Proletarian Cultural Revolution. He dreamed of a China in which material incentives played no part and in which ideological purity counted for more than expertise. An old man, he had little time left in which to attempt to realize his dream.

Between 1966 and 1968 China was thrown into a frenzy of turmoil as Red Guards shut down the schools, government offices ceased to function, collective farms were thrown into chaos, and factories stopped producing. Mao especially hated intellectuals, whom he derided as "swollen in head, weak in legs, sharp in tongue but empty in belly." His supporters humiliated, tortured, and jailed millions of party officials, bureaucrats, teachers, and managers, including chief of state Liu Shaoqi and party general-secretary Deng Xiaoping. Many of his victims were killed, and others committed suicide in despair. Mao returned to power, elevated in a personality cult that even Stalin might have envied. By 1969 China was in utter chaos as rival Red Guard units battled one another in power struggles. Mao then called in the army to put down the Red Guards, after which many young people were sent to the countryside to work on farms. Although normality began to return slowly after 1970, power struggles within the top ranks of the Communist party continued unabated.

Frail and senile, Mao died in September 1976. His death was followed shortly by the downfall of his widow Jiang Qing and her radical supporters who had risen to power during the Cultural Revolution. Deng Xiaoping and other surviving pragmatists, now rehabilitated, returned to power. In 1981 China's new rulers held a show trial that condemned Jiang and the other three members of the "Gang of Four" for prosecuting three-quarters of a million people and executing 34,375, and for other crimes. Although Mao was not on trial, the convictions of the Gang of Four made him guilty by implication. Later in 1981 a special meeting of the Central Committee of the Chinese Communist party passed a resolution that said: "The 'Great Cultural Revolution' from May 1966 to October 1976 caused the most devastating setback and heavy losses to the party, the state, and the people in the history of the Peoples' Republic, and this 'Great Cultural Revolution' was initiated and led by Comrade Mao Zedong." One of his colleagues added:

> Had Chairman Mao died in 1956, there would have been no doubt that he was a great leader of the Chinese people. . . . Had he died in 1966, his meritorious achievements would have been somewhat tarnished. However, his achievements were still very good. Since he actually died in 1976, there was nothing we can do about it.

Without doubt Mao was a hugely successful revolutionary, but he lived too long for his own or his party's good. With these assessments of Mao's final years, the Maoist era finally came to an end.

Deng Xiaoping placed his proteges in top positions in the government and the party. A tough Marxist, Deng had headed the purge of intellectuals in the Hundred Flower Campaign in 1957. A pragmatist on economic policy, he had been denounced during the Cultural Revolution for saying that it did not matter what a cat's colors were so long as it caught mice. Thus he was willing to make far-ranging economic reforms to improve the people's standard of living; but he adamantly opposed political reforms that would abridge the Communist party's monopoly of power.

Mao's closing of China's doors had resulted in economic stagnation while the rest of the world had forged ahead. Economic improvements necessitated the opening of China to outside contacts. During the 1980s China sent ever-larger contingents of scholars and graduate students to universities in the United States, Canada, Japan, and Western Europe. By 1989 there were about 40,000 Chinese studying in the United States alone. While China needed the knowledge and skills its students acquired in the West to sustain progress and modernization, the opening process inevitably brought about a yearning for political reform and democratization, especially among students and intellectuals. Many intellectuals believed that the economic modernization Deng sought could not be fully realized without political modernization through the introduction of democracy. The pace, scope, and direction of the reforms heightened public expectations and exposed the Communist party's shortcomings and corruption. Herein lay Deng's dilemma: While he wanted Western science and technology, he labeled Western values "spiritual pollution" which he sought to exclude.

Several episodes before 1989 in which the Communist party under Deng cracked down on popular demands for liberalization indicated Deng's outlook. During 1978 and 1979 a "Democracy Wall" came into being in Beijing where citizens could post their views. Because the posters often denounced the party and the government's wrongdoings, the government abruptly closed down the wall in 1980. Several dissidents were tried and given harsh sentences in labor camps. After the Communist party partly denounced Mao in 1981, no further denunciations were allowed. In 1986 students became frustrated with the gap between reality and promise and took to the streets in demonstrations. They were sternly put down, and some educators and journalists who had spoken out for greater freedom were disciplined. Deng became disillusioned with his protege Hu Yaobang for advocating a freer political climate and a faster pace of economic reforms and engineered his ouster as party general-secretary at the Thirteenth Communist Party Congress in the fall of 1987. Hu was replaced by a new protege Zhao Ziyang.

In 1989 to commemorate the seventieth anniversary of the May Fourth Movement and to protest pervasive corruption by Communist bureaucrats, students in Beijing marched in peaceful protest to petition the government to crack down on widespread corruption and to grant reforms such as freedom of speech. Like Mao, Deng was contemptuous of intellectuals, and like Mao, he believed that power emanated from the barrel of a gun. In June 1989 he refused to discuss student demands and issued an ultimatum for the unarmed students and their sympathizers to disperse. Before they could do so, the government ordered tanks and soldiers to mow down protestors in Beijing's Tiananmen Square and in many cities across China. Heavy censorship was imposed, and a widespread crackdown took place that especially targeted students and intellectuals. Communist officials who supported lenient treatment of students were purged and jailed, most notably Zhao Ziyang, who had voiced sympathy for student demands. Zhao remained under house arrest. Deng and his allies replaced them with hard-liners willing to implement his repressive policies.

Students led peaceful demonstrations in Beijing and other Chinese cities in 1989 to protest Communist rule and to demand democratic reforms. They were bloodily put down by troops.
(Robin Moyer/Time Magazine)

The "Goddess of Democracy" became the symbol of Chinese defiance against Communist rule and demand for reform before the bloody crackdown at Tiananmen Square in 1989.
(Peter Charlesworth/JB Pictures)

For a moment in Beijing in 1989 this young man slowed down the column of army tanks that bloodily put down a peaceful student-led demonstration for reform against Communist rule.
(Reuters/Bettmann Newsphotos)

Deng and his supporters were willing to ignore world censure when they bloodily repressed dissent to hold onto power. They felt vindicated by events in the Soviet Union which led to the unraveling of that Communist superpower in the wake of Mikhail Gorbachev's political reforms (see Chapter 33). With the toppling of communism in the former Soviet Union and Eastern Europe, they felt sure their crackdown had saved them from a similar fate. The future of political reform in China remained in suspended animation. Although Deng and his aged colleagues and rivals had ostensibly retired from party and government positions, they continued to rule through their proxies. China had not solved its problem of political succession.

COMPETING ECONOMIC SYSTEMS

Just as East Asian political systems were divided along ideological lines, so also were the economic systems of the region's nations. Japan's economy continued to expand on the foundations built during the U.S. occupation. Similarly, the capitalist economies of South Korea, Taiwan, and Hong Kong forged ahead in these three lands. Conversely, the doctrinaire application of Communist economic theories and centralized economic planning based on the Soviet model held back progress in China and North Korea. The magnitude of China's economic distress forced its Communist government to embrace limited free enterprise after 1978 in a successful attempt to revive its stagnant economy. Only North Korea retained its straitjacket Communist economic practices and was left behind even by Communist standards. Thus the ideological division of East Asian nations along economic lines has blurred, with capitalism in the ascendant.

Japan's Continuing Economic Miracle

Politically stable and secure under U.S. protection from foreign enemies, an increasingly confident Japan scored one economic success after another. All the things that contributed to Japan's initial economic recovery continued after 1960. A German industrialist who visited Japan in the late 1960s remarked that the Japanese worked the way Germans used to work. Even in the 1990s Japanese company managers frequently had to force their workers to take the annual vacations that were their due.

Since exports were key to Japan's prosperity, it attempted to follow a "no enemies" foreign policy in furtherance of trade. It maintained diplomatic relations with most nations and gave loans, credit, and economic aid to many. By the 1980s Japan had become the largest investor and the largest supplier of foreign aid throughout Asia. As labor costs soared in Japan, Japanese manufacturers built plants in Southeast Asian nations, where labor costs were lower.

Japan's economy suffered several severe shocks in the early 1970s. Two came from the United States in 1971 which the Japanese dubbed the "Nixon shocks." To counter an adverse balance of trade, mainly against West Germany and Japan, the United States placed a 10 percent surcharge on all imports and devalued the dollar. Later that year, without prior notice to Japan, President Nixon, motivated by rivalry with the Soviet Union, announced that he was planning to visit China to mend Sino-American relations, which had been marked by hostility since the Korean War. Following the lead of the United States, Japan had maintained diplomatic relations with Nationalist China on Taiwan until 1972, becoming an important trading partner. Following the new U.S. initiative, Japan quickly switched formal diplomatic relations from Taiwan to China, establishing a beachhead for profitable trade with that giant nation. High-volume trade continued between Japan and Taiwan.

The "petroleum shock" occurred in 1973 as OPEC nations raised oil prices by 450 percent and some refused to sell petroleum to Japan because of its friendly relations with Israel. Since Japan imported all its oil, 80 percent of which came from the Middle East, the shock was considerable. Although the problem of supply was solved quickly, Japan suffered from double-digit inflation in 1973 and 1974. Moreover, OPEC action raised the possibility that other producer nations might form similar cartels, a frightening prospect for resource-poor Japan which imported 100 percent of its iron ore, bauxite, wool, rubber, and phosphates and high percentages of other industrial raw materials.

Japan responded in several ways. One was quickly to establish diplomatic relations with China because China produced petroleum and other valuable raw materials Japan needed and in turn desperately needed Japan's machinery and technology. It also developed a "raw materials diplomacy" of befriending potential trading partners, negotiating long-term agreements with them, and supporting global free trade.

The crises of the 1970s also led to a larger debate in Japan over long-term national policies and goals. The Japanese decided to favor a slower growth rate than they had pursued in the preceding decades and to shift from smokestack industries such as steel and chemicals to "clean" industries such as computers, opticals, and high technology. After debating how to distribute the fruits of future growth, the Japanese agreed increasingly to divert profits and revenues to higher wages, better living conditions, and actions to protect the environment.

Differing priorities and perceptions have resulted in clashes between Japan on the one hand and the United States and other countries over environmental, ecological, and other issues. While fuel-efficient Japanese-made cars consumed less petroleum, a nonrenewable resource, and caused less pollution than larger and more wasteful U.S.-made cars, Japan supported whaling and drift-net fishing that threatened marine life that the United States and most European nations were anxious to protect. Lacking coal and petroleum, Japan committed itself to nuclear plants for energy generation and stockpiled plutonium for that purpose, which the United States opposed because of the danger of nuclear accidents and because plutonium can be used to build nuclear weapons.

Japan weathered the economic crises of the 1970s, and during the 1980s continued to sustain an impressive growth rate. With the second largest GNP (it surpassed that of the Soviet Union in 1987), Japan had become an industrial giant and a global trading and investing nation. The Liberal Democratic party (LDP) continued to win every election, so that although the premiership rotated among LDP factions and leaders, Japan experienced political stability and a continuity of economic policy.

Japan's economic strength, however, continued to provoke international problems. It chalked up enormous trade surpluses against most nations, especially its largest trading partner, the United States. Both governments worked to redress the imbalance by such measures as a sharp upward revaluation of the yen and the removal of many import restrictions; Japan significantly lowered tariffs (except on some agricultural goods, so that it could remain self-sufficient in the production of basic food such as rice). The United States also prodded Japan to play a larger role in international monetary institutions and to finance a greater share in such ventures as international peacekeeping.

Despite these measures, Japan continued to enjoy a huge trade surplus, mostly against the United States. In 1987 the Diet overcame a great psychological block and voted to increase defense spending over the previous limit of 1 percent of the GNP. Japan became worried about rising protectionist sentiments in much of the world, exemplified by a protectionist trade bill passed by the U.S. Congress in 1988. Japan was also worried by the expansion of the European Community and the forthcoming North American Free Trade Agreement, from both of which Japan would be excluded.

To maintain its competitive edge, Japan encouraged research that placed it well in the forefront of advanced technology, where its main competitor was the United States. It was in a race with the United States to develop a "seventh-generation" artificial intelligence machine, a ceramic engine, and ever more sophisticated computers. With an average per capita GNP of over $23,000 in 1989, Japan was a high-income and high-cost labor nation that had to resort to robots at home and in overseas manufacturing plants to keep the cost of its products competitive.

Booming Economies of Taiwan, South Korea, and Hong Kong

From the 1960s on, Taiwan, South Korea, Singapore, and Hong Kong followed Japan's path in economic advancement and became global trading nations. They were variously dubbed "the Little Japans," "the Four Dragons," or "the Four Tigers." (Singapore has been discussed in Chapter 30.)

Taiwan had within a generation been transformed from a poor agricultural nation to an industrial power. After arriving on the island in 1949 the Nationalist government initiated peaceful land reforms and introduced technological innovations that increased farm production. Taiwan also built up the physical and social infrastructure. Resource-poor, it had to rely on trade. Taiwan first developed labor-intensive and export-oriented light industries in the 1960s, followed by heavy industries in the 1970s and sophisticated high-technology industries in the 1980s.

The modernization program required capital, qualified personnel, and scientific management. U.S. economic aid provided much-needed capital until the early 1960s, when it was phased out. Political stability and favorable investment conditions attracted foreign capital. Taiwan created an excellent educational system, with nine years of free, compulsory education (soon to be increased to ten), although most students went on to finish twelve grades. Over 25 percent of post-secondary school young people were in colleges and universities, thus producing a qualified work force for development. Many of the brightest youths went on to graduate schools on the island and abroad, providing the necessary personnel for research and management.

Taiwan enjoyed an unemployment rate of less than 2 percent, low inflation, and fast growth. Its economy grew at a 9 percent annual rate, to be forty times as large in 1987 as it had been in 1969, and its foreign trade grew from twenty-first in the world in 1978 to thirteenth in 1990. In 1992 it was first in the world in foreign currency reserve holdings of about $84 billion. It was almost unique in its simultaneous achievement of rapid economic growth and equitable distribution of wealth (the ratio of the highest and the lowest 20 percent of wage earners in 1991 was 4.88:1, a smaller gap than in the United States). Per capita GNP for its 20 million people surpassed $10,000 in 1992 (from less than $145 in 1951). By all criteria, Taiwan was almost a fully developed nation. Economists referred to its rapid development as a miracle.

Like Taiwan, South Korea progressed from a poor agricultural nation, ravaged by war and flooded by refugees, to an economic power, despite heavy defense expenditures (5.8 percent of GNP in 1987). Similarly, it received economic aid from the United States until the economy reached a takeoff point. Again like Taiwan, South Korea implemented successful land reform and followed that by developing the agricultural sector and light industries. After 1962 it built up heavy industry and export-oriented industries. Despite a lack of petroleum and many mineral resources, South Korea's economy grew by leaps and bounds; and in the 1980s some of its products, for example, Hyundai automobiles, competed with those of Japan in foreign markets. Shipbuilding skyrocketed from almost nothing to third in the world. As time went on, the prospect of reunification of the more populous South (44 million in 1990) with the impoverished North (24 million) became less and less attractive, except to some radical students. (Based on Germany's expenditure in integrating former East Germany, some economists estimate that South Korea would need to spend $800 billion to bring North Korea up to its standard of living.) In the early 1990s South Korea and Taiwan ran neck-and-neck in their GNP, their export share, and the upward revaluation of their currencies. Both had opened their markets to imports, and both were keenly apprehensive about how outsiders might be harmed by the 1988 U.S. trade bill, the new tariff policy of the European Community, and the North American Free Trade Agreement bloc. Unlike Taiwan, however, South Korea had a substantial foreign debt.

Hong Kong, Great Britain's last imperial outpost in Asia, built up a bustling and thriving capitalist economy after World War II. Great Britain's

Hyundai shipyards and others make South Korea the world's third largest shipbuilding nation.
(Reuters/Bettmann Newsphotos)

rule of law and its free trade policy made that possession a showcase of capitalism. Most of Hong Kong's over 5 million people were refugees who had fled from Chinese communism. It had replaced Shanghai as the premier trading city along the China coast after China became Communist. Hong Kong's capital, know-how, and infrastructure were essential to the success of the "free enterprise zones" established by China after Mao's death to attract foreign capital and thus lift and revitalize its lagging economy. The bright lights and free lifestyle of Hong Kong were the envy of millions of Chinese across the colony's border and the destination of tens of thousands of refugees from China and Vietnam every year.

In 1984 Great Britain signed an agreement with China to return the colony of Hong Kong and adjacent leased territory in 1997. In the agreement China promised Hong Kong a separate administration and respect for its economic and social systems for fifty years after 1997. Many Hong Kong residents hoped that China would not overly interfere in the colony's affairs after 1997 so as not to kill the goose that lays the golden egg. However, China increasingly exerted pressure to thwart Hong Kong's progress toward representative democracy and to restrict freedom of the press. In light of repressions in China after the Tiananmen Square massacre, Hong Kong citizens, already jittery, became even more fearful of what would happen to them after 1997. As a result emigration from Hong Kong accelerated. About 60,000 of the colony's most able residents emigrated annually to any non-Communist nation that would take them, preferably a Western nation.

China's Search for Prosperity

In contrast to the rapid progress that marked Japan, Taiwan, South Korea, and Hong Kong, China's economy was characterized by chaos and lurches. No sooner had the pragmatists repaired the damages inflicted by the failed Great Leap Forward than Mao Zedong unleashed his teenage Red Guards to disrupt the economy. By Mao's death in 1976 the Chinese economy was in shambles. Industries were outdated and unproductive, and collective farmers had no incentive to produce, with the result that the nation was on the verge of bankruptcy and many people were near starvation.

When Deng Xiaoping came to power in 1978 the Communist party changed emphasis from ideology to "economics in command." Because China was near bankruptcy and compared unfavorably with the economic miracle that was Taiwan, there was enormous pressure for reform. Among socialist nations, Hungary and Yugoslavia had made economic strides with decentralization and capitalist incentives that compared favorably with China's Soviet-derived system of centralized planning, marked by institutionalized corruption, irrational prices, disjunction between supplier and consumer, and low quality.

Deng's attempt to revive the socialist economic system was called *gaige*, which means "restructure." It began tentatively in 1978 with rural reform in Sichuan province, a rich agricultural region whose 100 million people were close to starvation because of mismanagement. Individual plots of land were

Deng Xiaoping's reforms have allowed Chinese peasants to sell their produce in free markets like this one, near Canton.
(Jiu-Hwa Upshur)

offered to Sichuan farmers, who were still obliged to deliver to the state stipulated amounts of grain but who could then produce what they wished to sell on a free market. The results were so good that by 1984 all of China's 54,000 communes had been abolished. Farmers were offered land-use contracts of up to fifty years and were allowed to pass their houses on to their heirs. As a result, farmers made long-term improvements, agricultural output soared, and rural income almost tripled. Surplus farm laborers were absorbed into small rural cooperative industries that sprang up. Although prosperity was uneven, new farmhouses mushroomed throughout China, testifying to the overall success of the program.

Deng's strategy of initiating economic reform with the farmers was a sound one, for he thereby enlisted 800 million supporters and had achieved results and obtained converts before he set about tackling the more complex problem of restructuring other sectors of the economy. *Gaige* in industry was more complicated than privatizing agriculture. In 1980 an estimated 60 percent of China's industry and technology was completely obsolete. Although Deng encouraged some private enterprise and foreign investment in joint enterprises (by 1984, 128 U.S. firms had offices in Beijing), many industries continued to be state-run. The government still allocated key resources and determined who received foreign capital and technologies. It was also difficult to adjust prices to reflect production costs and consumer demand in a society accustomed to government price setting and subsidies for basic commodities. Many found the inflation and unemployment that resulted from the reforms to be unsettling and potentially dangerous.

Some opponents of reform were senior party leaders genuinely committed to a Soviet-style centrally planned economy. Others were generals faced with a reduced share of the pie for the military, middle-ranking party bureaucrats at risk of losing their perks, and ordinary workers accustomed to the "iron rice bowl," or lifetime tenure in jobs that were low-paying but that expected little of them in return and gave them subsidized housing and food.

Deng slowly convinced many senior colleagues who opposed him to retire and placed his supporters in key positions. He persuaded military leaders to demobilize 20 percent of their forces (a million troops) and cut their share of the GNP from 11.7 percent in 1978 to 6.7 percent by 1985 with the argument that a revitalized industrial sector would make possible more sophisticated military technology later. Some factory managers were won over by the promise of more decision-making power and less state interference; this meant that the state at times allowed factories to select their own managers and to hire and fire workers based on performance.

A decade and half after Mao's death, most Chinese were undoubtedly better fed, clothed, and housed than they had been during his life. Improvements had also brought about inequality, because coastal areas adjacent to Hong Kong and across the strait from Taiwan forged ahead as a result of investments from their capitalist neighbors, leaving the interior and northern China behind. Deng hoped that in the long run the wealth of the prosperous southeast coast would trickle down to the other regions. In the short run he hoped that continued material improvements and a rising standard of living would be a sufficient sop to offset the political repression he had instituted after the Tiananmen Square massacre of 1989. He also hoped that in time the lure of trade with China would overcome international anger toward his regime's human rights violations.

North Korea remained a monocracy under Communist leader Kim Il Sung (1912–), who continued his Stalinist-style rule and cult of personality. Kim's son was groomed to succeed him. The 24 million North Koreans lived under one of the most repressive and regimented regimes, and their economy was mired in Marxist controls. Conditions deteriorated after 1991 when the Soviet Union/Russia stopped all aid, and without the Soviet Union to worry about, China also stopped its aid.

The contrasts between the prosperous capitalist economies of Japan, Taiwan, South Korea, and Hong Kong and the drab poverty of the Communist nations were very stark. While significant improvements occurred in China under Deng, even faster progress was made in Taiwan. For example, while the per capita GNP ratio between Taiwan and China was 10:1 in 1976, it had widened to about 25:1 by 1990 (over $8000 for Taiwan and $330 for China). Similar contrasts divided North from South Korea.

SOCIAL CHANGES AND CONTRASTS

Social changes in Japan, Taiwan, and South Korea resulted from rising living standards and educational levels and assimilation of Western trends. A large, confident middle class in all three nations needed little government prodding to limit family size, seek advanced education, or advocate environmental protection. Conversely, the significantly lower standard of living and educational levels in China and North Korea have made social engineering in those countries difficult. Since Mao Zedong's death the Chinese have ditched Marxist drabness and shown the same longing for material well-being and social progress as citizens in non-Communist countries. However great contrasts persist.

Japan, Taiwan, and South Korea

Sweeping changes have affected every aspect of Japanese life. Significantly, it was the first Asian nation to bring population growth under control, although (at an estimated 124 million in 1991) Japan remained one of the most densely populated lands on earth. Education reforms and legal equality gave new opportunities to Japanese women. The booming economy provided jobs and economic independence to women, although real equality between men and women in employment still lagged behind that in the United States by about ten years. Because of educational and career demands and opportunities, both Japanese men and women married late; a man's average age at marriage was twenty-seven years, and woman's was twenty-five. Many women resisted marriage in order to protest male dominance in family life, and they disregarded government propaganda and subsidies that encouraged having larger families. Farmers had the most difficult time finding wives because of the rigors and isolation of farm life; some advertised as far as Sri Lanka for wives. These tendencies worried many Japanese planners, for not only did Japan have one of the lowest birthrates (at 11 per 1000 persons per year) and population growth rates (at 0.5 percent per year, attributable to increasing longevity), but it also had the world's highest life expectancy, eighty-two years for women and seventy-six years for men. The cost of supporting this aging population loomed large. In a culture that traditionally revered the elderly, older Japanese now complained about the decline in respect.

The new Japanese were literate (99 percent) and predominantly urban. By 1972 one out of four lived in the Tokyo-Osaka industrial belt. Although among the most affluent people in the world, many Japanese lived in cramped apartments, worked long hours, and commuted great distances in crowded public transportation. Stressful lives, heavy smoking, and the newly acquired preference for red meat, fast foods, and fatty foods took their toll in a high incidence of strokes and heart attacks. Pollution was also a major problem. Still, although the Japanese had social problems caused by rapid change, up to the early 1990s their society lacked many of the ills that afflicted the West. There was virtually no drug problem, and the crime rate was low.

Since the mid-1960s Japan's humiliation stemming from its military defeat had been replaced by a growing national self-confidence sustained by its economic success; by and large, this new nationalism was diffuse, like that of other modern states, and not accompanied by a reemergence of militarism or emperor ideology. The death of Emperor Hirohito in 1990 ended a chapter in Japan's modern history. Although most people believed he was a figurehead during World War II, the issue of his actual role had never been satisfactorily settled. His son and successor, Akihito, however, had had no part in those events.

Unlike Germany, however, Japan's government did not make full reckoning with the crimes committed by the nation's leaders before and during World War II and continually attempted to cover them up. For example, it repeatedly introduced school history textbooks that soft-pedaled its past brutal imperialist policies. Japan only reluctantly admitted the kidnapping of over 200,000 young women from Korea, Taiwan, China, and other conquered lands to be the sex slaves of Japanese soldiers during World War II, countless numbers of whom died of abuse. Japan also refused to pay compensation to the survivors or families of the men it drafted from Korea and Taiwan to serve in its military. Such behavior kept alive resentment by Japan's former victims, most notably China, Taiwan, and Korea. The failure to make a clean breast of past wrongs also prevented Japan from gaining full international acceptance and playing the significant world role that its enormous economic success would otherwise have warranted.

In Taiwan, Hong Kong, and South Korea rapid economic progress had also resulted in major social changes. Each had over 90 percent literacy and among the world's best educational systems. Taiwan's women enjoyed an average life span of seventy-seven years, and men, seventy-two years. All had within a generation changed from high to low birthrates. The birthrate had dropped to under 16 per 1000 people per year, and the natural increase to just over 1 percent per year, similar to that for advanced Western nations. As a result, Taiwan developed a labor shortage in the late 1980s and had to deal with the problem of illegal immigrant workers (the minimum wage in Taiwan was $2.10 per hour as opposed to $4.25 per hour in the United States) from China and Southeast Asia. Fearful of the consequences of an aging population and labor shortages, Taiwan's government changed its planned parenthood slogan from "Two (children) are good, but one is enough" to "Two are good; three are not too many."

Both nations were confronted with problems associated with rapid progress, for example, environmental degradation, pollution, urban congestion, and snarled traffic. Social patterns had also changed rapidly. Two-salary nuclear families were becoming the norm, and retirement centers and nursing homes for the old were replacing the traditional multigenerational household. Labor shortages encouraged women to enter the workplace in growing numbers. The increasingly prosperous, sophisticated, and well-educated peoples of Taiwan and South Korea had within a generation transformed their traditional societies into modern civil societies. It was this social transformation that propelled both toward political democracy. Fear that the Communist rulers of China did not understand these social and political forces clouded Hong Kong's future.

China and North Korea

Convinced that China would not advance unless it could slow the population explosion, Deng Xiaoping enacted severe measures to ensure birth control. Couples were ordered to have only one child, and drastic sanctions were placed on those who disobeyed, from forced abortions to loss of housing to reduced educational opportunities for children with siblings.

While the government was relatively successful in cities, where controls were easy to enforce and where people tended to be more modern in attitude, enforcing the single-child policy proved very difficult in the countryside. This was partly due to conservative attitudes of country people who valued children, especially sons, but ironically was also due to Deng's successful policy of privatizing farming. The hand-tool-using Chinese farmer needed children to help with chores, and boys were valued because of their strength and because rural young couples lived with the husband's parents. Thus, unless a farming couple had a son, they might have no one to pass their farm to and no one to look after them in their old age. With little education and few opportunities, rural young people married early and wanted sons. Chinese literacy was at 70 percent (however, most Chinese had only an elementary education) and the birthrate in 1989 was 23 per 1000 people. In 1990 the estimated population stood at 1.13 billion. China's large population remained its major handicap in moving toward modernization and higher living standards.

There was, moreover, a great dichotomy among China's people. Most of the 80 percent who lived in the countryside were poorly educated compared to urban dwellers. Thus, while the students, intellectuals, and factory workers who demonstrated for political and other reforms in major cities in 1989 were bloodily put down, the countryside remained quiet and generally apathetic. Deng Xiaoping continued to make economic reforms in the wake of the Tiananmen Square massacre in the hope that a people with full stomachs would not rise up against the regime.

INTERNATIONAL AND INTRAREGIONAL RELATIONS

International relations in East Asia were very complex. They were dictated by superpower struggles, regional antagonisms, and unresolved internal conflicts. Sino-Soviet and U.S.-Soviet relations were pivotal in dictating major shifts in Sino-American and Sino-Japanese relations.

The 1960s witnessed the steady deterioration of Sino-Soviet relations, which Mao had earlier characterized as "lasting, unbreakable, and invincible." Ideology was one reason. Mao Zedong claimed that his ideas contributed to the ideological development of Marxism-Leninism and were especially applicable to revolutionary movements in the non-Western world. The Soviet Union firmly rejected such Maoist claims. Mao, moreover, asserted that he was the senior worldwide Communist leader after Stalin's death in 1953, another claim that the Soviet Union absolutely denied. In addition, there were territorial disputes between the two nations that went back to the nineteenth century. Khrushchev's de-Stalinization campaign, which he had launched without prior consultation with Mao, and his dismantling of Stalin's personality cult especially upset Mao because he was busily creating his own.

The two Communist giants were clearly on a collision course. In 1960 the Soviet Union abruptly ended all technical aid to China and recalled its technicians together with their blueprints, leaving Chinese planners in the lurch. The split widened in 1962 when Khrushchev bowed to U.S. pressure and withdrew nuclear missiles from Cuba without consulting the Chinese, who called him a coward for doing so. When China and India went to war over a disputed boundary in 1962, the Soviet Union sided with India. Relations had deteriorated to such a low point by 1964 that when China detonated a nuclear device, the Soviet Union considered launching a preemptive strike to destroy its nuclear industry. Although this did not happen, border skirmishes erupted in 1969 over territorial disputes. Chinese fear of the Soviet Union, especially the possibility that the Soviets might apply the Brezhnev Doctrine to China (i.e., as the senior Communist state, the U.S.S.R. had the right to use military force to enforce the correct practice of communism in other Communist states), led Mao to repair relations with the United States and to rejoin the international community.

Also fearful of the Soviet Union and anxious to disengage itself from the Vietnam war, the United States moved toward rapprochement with China. In

1971, when the United States dropped its opposition, China was seated in the United Nations in the place of Taiwan. President Richard Nixon visited China in 1972. In 1979 the United States established diplomatic relations with China, thereby severing formal ties with Taiwan, although the Taiwan Relations Act passed later by the Senate retained "informal" ties with that nation; trade with Taiwan increased despite the severing of formal ties.

Chinese foreign policy under Deng Xiaoping was characterized by pragmatism and flexibility. China steadily increased its trade with the West and its participation in international organizations. Politically it abandoned providing even moral support for revolutionary movements in the Third World. It softened its denunciations of both the Soviet Union and the United States, but it did condemn either the Soviet Union for its role in Afghanistan and Indochina or the United States for developing the Strategic Defense Initiative.

China never stopped professing its goal of reunification. In 1986 the Central Committee of the CCP declared that one of the objectives it intended to pursue was the unification of Taiwan with China, by force if necessary.

Even before Deng cracked down on the 1989 prodemocracy demonstrations, the Chinese leadership had taken steps to lessen outside influences on its citizens. It required all Chinese to obtain special passes before they could enter the four special economic zones along the southern coast, which were separated from the rest of the country by barbed-wire fences. Chinese officials increased ideological indoctrination in the schools and stringently screened applicants who wished to study abroad. The disintegration of the Soviet Union and the end of the Soviet empire in Eastern Europe and (Outer) Mongolia heightened the siege mentality of China's Communist leaders as they clung to power. China's relations with the West were strained by the Tiananmen Square killings, but the United States, the European Community, and Japan, all major trading partners, were unwilling to place economic sanctions on China to punish it for its human rights violations.

Japan's foreign policy remained anchored to its alliance with the United States. Although trade issues, mainly Japan's surplus trade balance with the United States, strained relations, and racial overtones sometimes threatened to poison them, the quarrels were nevertheless those between allies. Japan was the largest contributor of international aid to other Asian nations and the largest investor in the region.

Although Japan played an important part in ending the civil war in Cambodia and sent a peacekeeping force to that nation (after the Japanese Diet reluctantly passed the necessary enabling bill), it generally pursued a low-profile foreign policy in Asia. This was due in part to the legacy of World War II and a lingering hatred of Japan's ignoble conduct toward conquered people, and in part to Japan's unwillingness to own up to the past and thereby lay it to rest. Thus Japan continued to have few friends in Asia despite attempts to pursue a "no enemies" foreign policy. Similarly, while Japan desired the raw materials of the Soviet Union (now the Commonwealth of Independent States) and the latter sorely needed Japanese technology and know-how, unresolved territorial claims to the Kurile Islands (taken by the Soviet Union at the end of the World War II and now part of Russia) prevented the development of a mutually beneficial relationship between it and Russia.

The divisions between the two Koreas and the two Chinas are the region's most intractible problems. Neither Korea gave up its goal of unification on its own terms. North Korea pursued a policy of attempting to destabilize South Korea by infiltration, assassinations, and threats to disrupt the 1988 Olympic Games held in Seoul, which it boycotted after failing to obtain cosponsorship. The DMZ between the two Koreas remained one of the most tightly guarded in the world, and the United States continued to maintain a 40,000-strong military force in South Korea. The North Korean government, considered an unpredictable rogue regime by the international community, was suspected of developing nuclear weapons. North Korea lost a former mentor after the disintegration of the Soviet Union; only China remained as an ally of sorts. Several developments in 1991–1992 portended greater stability on the Korean peninsula. They were the establishment of formal relations between South Korea and China with the intention of isolating North Korea, the admission of both Koreas to the United Nations, and the opening of contacts between the two Koreas through the International Red Cross.

Since the 1970s Taiwan had been forced out of most international organizations at the insistence of China. Its economic success, however, gave it considerable clout internationally. After Japan, Taiwan was the largest investor nation in Southeast Asia; it also became a giver of loans and aid. In 1989 it reopened commercial and cultural relations with Russia, Ukraine, Belorus, the Baltic republics, and the Eastern European nations and began giving economic aid to former Communist nations. In the late 1980s Taiwan relaxed restrictions against contacts and trade with China; millions of travelers from Taiwan visited China, and Taiwanese enterprises invested billions in China, where labor costs were low. No political solutions were found acceptable to both sides, and the prosperous citizens of Taiwan feared and disliked the Communist system.

As several world regions moved to greater economic integration in the 1990s (the European Community, the North American Free Trade Agreement, and talk of ASEAN forming a tariff union), all the nations of East Asia feared future closing of economic doors to them. Japan, Taiwan, and South Korea saw the upgrading of their products to maintain competitiveness as one way to combat future barriers. Up to 1992 political and historical problems precluded them from making serious plans for an economic union.

SUMMARY

Resource-poor Japan continued its economic miracle, becoming the nation with the second largest GNP globally. Independent Japan remained a democratic, pluralistic society; it benefited from U.S. military protection and remained a firm member of the Western community of nations. In the final decades of the twentieth century, Japan played a constructive role as trading partner, loan supplier, and aid provider to other nations in Asia.

U.S. military protection and economic aid helped war-torn South Korea and Taiwan build up strong economies that continued to prosper after aid ended. In recent decades Taiwan, South Korea, and British Hong Kong emerged as "Little Japans" as they entered the ranks of developed nations. The highly educated and economically secure citizens of Taiwan and South Korea demanded and realized political participation in their governments. Hong Kong's political future remained uncertain because of its projected return to China in 1997.

Chinese politics were mired in Communist political and ideological struggles. Mao Zedong all but destroyed China's political and social infrastructure in the tumult of the Cultural Revolution that returned him to power for the last ten years of his life. Deng Xiaoping's rise and tenure of power after 1978 brought economic prosperity to Chinese farmers through the dismantling of Marxist communal farming. Industries were more difficult to privatize and modernize. Because it had lost so much ground during the Maoist years, China faced a Herculean task in catching up. Although much progress was made, it fell further behind its capitalist neighbors. In politics Deng and his supporters were orthodox Marxists refusing to give up their totalitarian power, as the Tiananmen Square massacre of reform-minded students in 1989 conclusively demonstrated. As communism crumbled in Eastern Europe and the former Soviet Union, China, North Korea, and Vietnam were the only Communist states remaining on the Eurasian continent.

The crimes of the past imperialist Japanese government prevented Japan from playing the major role in Asia that its economic power warranted. The unresolved unification questions of China and Korea continued to make East Asia politically unstable along the fracture lines.

SUGGESTED SOURCES

BUTTERFIELD, FOX, *Alive in the Bitter Sea* (1983). A moving account of life in Mao's China.*

CHENG, NIEN, *Life and Death in Shanghai* (1987). An autobiography by a survivor of the Cultural Revolution detailing the excesses of the Maoist movement.*

CRUMP, THOMAS, *The Death of an Emperor, Japan at the Crossroads* (1991). On the legacy of Hirohito and a changing Japan.*

EMMOTT, BILL, *The Sun Also Sets, the Limits to Japan's Economic Power* (1989). Important to understanding present-day Japan and its likely future.*

FELDMAN, HARVEY, and ILPYONG J. KIM, *Taiwan in a Time of Transition* (1988). Written by many experts.*

FRANZ, ULI, *Deng Xiaoping*, Tom Astin trans. (1988). Good book on Deng's life and times from the 1920s, and his colleagues.

Hirohito: The Chrysanthemum Throne (1980). Leaders of the 20th Century Series (Coronet). A video depicting the Japanese economic miracle.

KELLEY, BRIAN, and MARK LONDON, *The Four Little Dragons, A Journey to the Source of the Business Boom along the Pacific Rim* (1989). Analysis of what made these societies successful.*

LINCOLN, EDWARD J., *Japan Facing Economic Maturity* (1988). A summary of Japanese economic development since the 1970s, with prediction of possible future developments.*

LIU, BINYAN, *A Higher Kind of Loyalty,* Zhu Hong trans. (1990). An autobiography by China's foremost journalist on how the Communist dream became a nightmare.

LORD, BETTE BAO, *Legacies, A Chinese Mosaic* (1990). A moving book on China's past and present.*

MacDONALD, DONALD STONE, *The Koreans, Contemporary Politics and Society,* 2d ed. (1992). The best introductory book on Korea.*

SALISBURY, HARRISON E., *The New Emperors, China in the Era of Mao and Deng* (1992). Details how power has corrupted China's leaders.

*Paperback available.

CHAPTER 32

African Problems and Promise

In the 1970s and 1980s, Africa, like the rest of the developing world, endured a multitude of problems but also showed signs of promise for economic, social, and political improvement. East Africa was one area of major upheaval, but the chief spot that attracted international concern was southern Africa, dominated in the early 1970s by European imperial powers and white minority governments. As superpowers and their surrogates began to play a significant role, the Cold War, already a major factor over much of the world, affected eastern and southern Africa. The independent nations of Africa also faced common problems of political factionalism and of conflict between the industrial and rural sectors. Some of these problems were typical of those faced by Third World nations around the globe, but others were unique to Africa. With the collapse of the Soviet Union and the end of the Cold War, African nations, like much of Asia and Europe, experienced a resurgence of democratic movements and popular demands for more direct participation in solving political and economic problems.

TURMOIL IN NORTH AND EAST AFRICA

North African Rivalries and Negotiations

North African nations have struggled with a variety of regional rivalries while playing a substantial role in Arab, African, and international politics. Libya under Muammar al-Qadhdhafi used petroleum revenues not only to launch massive development and agricultural programs but also to champion Islamic revolutions throughout the Middle East and much of Africa. Al-Qadhdhafi's particular brand of Islamic-based social revolution, which was explained in his Green Books (similar to Mao's more famous Red Book), was often opposed by both the United States and the Soviet Union. Both nations viewed al-Qadhdhafi as a threat to their own aims in the region. In contrast, Algeria steered a neutral path between the two superpowers and became a successful negotiator between the West and the Third World. Because of its reputation as "an honest broker," Algeria was able to mediate the release of the U.S. hostages from Iran in 1980–1981.

In addition, rivalries among North African nations for the dominant role in the region contributed to increasing military expenditures, which channeled scarce monies away from much-needed social welfare programs such as education, housing, and public services. For example, as early as the 1960s Algeria and Morocco clashed over control of parts of the Sahara which is rich in natural resources. The dispute over control of the western Sahara turned into a protracted war throughout the 1970s and 1980s between the Polisario, armed revolutionaries seeking an independent Sahara Arab Democratic Republic, and Morocco. Determined to exercise sovereignty over the area, Morocco constructed a wall of earth over 1,000 miles long, created to enclose the most valuable part of the western Sahara and to impede guerrilla activity. In 1988 all the involved parties reluctantly agreed to hold a referendum for the Sahrawis (inhabitants of the Sahara) to decide their political future. Depending on its military presence and increased economic expenditures, Morocco was confident that most Sahrawis would vote for affiliation with Morocco, but by 1993 the long-awaited elections had yet to be held and the international community was still attempting to mediate a settlement. Such regional conflicts in North Africa, as elsewhere in the world, undermined programs for economic development.

In North African nations such as Algeria, Tunisia, and the Sudan, where the populations were largely Muslim, large and exceedingly popular militant Islamist movements demanded the creation of Islamic governments. By the 1990s these Islamist groups enjoyed the support of many disaffected students

The Islamic faithful, an important cultural and political force, at prayer in West Africa. *(Marc & Evelyne Bernheim/Woodfin Camp & Associates)*

and working-class people who had concluded that neither Western capitalism nor Soviet-style communism had succeeded in solving their political and economic problems. As in the Middle East, these Islamist movements were often opposed by both the military and largely urban elite who warned that Islamic governments would not sustain democratic institutions; however, public support for the creation of Islamic states remained widespread. In many nations, for example Algeria, it appeared likely that if free elections were held, the Islamist parties would win. Whether the existing military and civilian regimes could respond to the economic and social needs of their populations and withstand demands for Islamic governments remained uncertain.

Uganda's Nightmare

Uganda, one of Great Britain's most prosperous colonies, went down a calamitous road of death and devastation after it received its independence in 1962. Lacking a broad base of support, the government fell to the military leadership of Milton Obote. Subsequently, while he was attending the 1971 Commonwealth conference outside Uganda, Obote was ousted by Idi Amin. Obote finally took up residence in neighboring Tanzania.

Idi Amin, a Muslim, was an officer from the tiny Kakwa tribe in a nation where 80 percent of the population was Christian. His rule was characterized by a bizarre combination of flamboyance, cruelty, and personal eccentricity. He delighted in sending long, rambling telegrams to Queen Elizabeth and Richard Nixon and offered public advice on how they should govern. At the same time, he himself was instituting a reign of terror, massacring his political and tribal opponents by the thousands. In 1972 Amin gave the Asian population, which was mostly engaged in business, ninety days to leave Uganda. Using his Islamic allegiance, he established close ties with many Arab nations and was vociferous in his antipathy to Israel, South Africa, and Western imperialism.

The mounting violence in Uganda made its neighbors increasingly hostile. After Amin's ill-considered attempt to invade Tanzania in 1978, Tanzanian president Julius Nyerere moved Tanzanian forces into Uganda in January 1979. Libya, under al-Qadhdhafi, openly supported Amin. In the ensuing chaos, Amin escaped, eventually moving to Saudi Arabia. The new Ugandan compromise government was plagued with internal divisions, violence, economic ruin, refugees, and uncertainty. Only large amounts of foreign aid, mostly from Arab nations, saved the nation from total economic collapse. Rebuilding and developing this formerly prosperous area remained an enormous task.

War and Revolution in the Horn of Africa

Owing to its strategic geographic location, the Horn of Africa (a collective name for the eastern sector of the continent projecting into the Indian Ocean) became one of the major areas of the U.S.-Soviet competition. Ethiopia, a centuries-old Coptic Christian kingdom, regained its independence in 1941 when

British forces defeated the Italians and returned Emperor Haile Selassie to Addis Ababa. In 1952 Eritrea, with its predominantly Muslim population, was federated within Ethiopia in spite of Eritrean preference for independence and a closer association with Arab states. Eritreans and other ethnic groups within Ethiopia, particularly the Somali minority in eastern Ethiopia, viewed themselves as victims of both Ethiopian and European imperial ambitions and continued armed opposition to all Ethiopian regimes.

Haile Selassie was extremely pro-Western, and Ethiopia soon became a major pivot in U.S. policies for Africa. The United States built a radar tracking station and a major military base in Ethiopia and provided large sums of foreign aid. In addition, Israelis were brought in to train army officers and to provide technical skills. Israeli involvement in Ethiopia typified a pattern whereby each superpower encouraged its allies to further the superpower's interests in a region.

In spite of substantial foreign aid, Ethiopia remained a desperately impoverished nation. The peasants, who composed over 90 percent of the population, were among the poorest in the world. The Coptic church and the emperor's family kept tight control over a largely feudal system. With minimal natural resources and a terrain of high plateaus separated by deep valleys that made travel difficult, Ethiopia faced major obstacles to economic development. The emperor's regime was further weakened by its disregard of the widespread starvation brought on by several years of drought and famine.

In 1974, as a consequence of these problems, a group of army officers led by Mengistu Haile Mariam rebelled, ousted the emperor, and created a military government. The new Ethiopian government adopted a pro-Soviet stance and became a major center for Soviet influence and naval presence in Africa.

Neighboring Somalia, formerly an Italian colony, became independent in 1960. In 1969 the conservative Somali government was replaced by a military-led socialist regime that was originally friendly to the Soviet Union. Somalia claimed the Somali-populated Ogaden region in Ethiopia and in 1977 began aiding guerrillas in that area. Thousands fled from the war zone to gather in huge refugee camps. By the 1980s, war, drought, and famine had made living conditions in Somalia among the worst on earth. Political rivalries, corruption, and red tape prevented massive foreign aid programs and food shipments from stopping the human suffering and starvation.

As Ethiopia moved closer to the Soviet Union, Somalia moved closer to the United States. Both superpowers were anxious to control the vital shipping routes through the Red Sea and the Suez Canal. Furthermore, the Horn was a strategic area from which both the United States and the Soviet Union serviced naval units watching the petroleum-rich Arabian peninsula. With its enormous economic problems and regional rivalries, the Horn of Africa was a focal point of Cold War tensions in Africa. With the collapse of the Soviet Union and the end of the Cold War, both superpowers decreased their foreign aid to the desperately poor nations in the Horn of Africa. Although the populations in Ethiopia and Somalia called for democracy, years of civil strife, starvation, warfare, and massive human migrations had so undermined or destroyed centralized government that the political systems were unable to respond to even the basic needs of the people. In Somalia, centralized government essentially ceased to exist, and rival warlords competed for control. Only international intervention seemed to hold any promise for a return to peace and economic recovery and many opposed intervention on the grounds that foreign involvement might worsen the situation.

FREEDOM STRUGGLES IN SOUTHERN AFRICA: THE ENTRANCE OF THE COLD WAR

Independence in Mozambique, Angola, and Zimbabwe

As the Portuguese in Angola and Mozambique and the white minorities in Rhodesia and South Africa fought to keep control of those areas in the 1970s and 1980s, the black majority populations intensified their struggles for independence, increasingly resorting to guerrilla warfare. Both sides sought and received outside support. From the first, independent black African nations assisted the liberation movements of southern Africa; later, the Soviet Union and Cuba also gave support. Nations along the borders of South Africa, such as Mozambique, became known as "front-line states." These nations provided training bases, often run by Marxist and Chinese advisors, for guerrillas operating in the target areas.

On the other side, Great Britain and the United States, both of which had substantial economic investments in mining and raw materials in South Africa, continued to maintain economic ties with the white minority regime. The South African and Western governments also argued that the sale of arms was necessary because of South Africa's strategic location on the southern Cape and because of its steadfast opposition to the Soviet Union.

The Portuguese colonies of Angola and Mozambique were the chief scenes of nationalist guerrilla warfare in the early 1970s. The MPLA liberation movement in Angola and the FRELIMO rebels in Mozambique both escalated guerrilla attacks against the Portuguese army and the *prazeros* in a classic example of wars of national liberation. Both MPLA and FRELIMO received aid from the Soviet bloc and sympathetic African nations. Although Portugal received some military assistance from European NATO nations, the colonial wars severely drained its already weak economy. Finally, following a coup in 1974, the new Portuguese leaders moved to settle the conflicts. In a relatively peaceful transition, Mozambique declared its independence. The new regime, dominated by Marxist leaders from FRELIMO, launched programs for improving health care facilities and other social welfare institutions and subsequently inaugurated a massive campaign to increase literacy. In addition, the regime was openly friendly to other African liberation movements, particularly in Rhodesia.

As in Mozambique, nationalist guerrillas forced the Portuguese to leave Angola, but in this case a second Angolan war broke out before a stable government could be created. In 1975 competing nationalist groups, each supported by different ethnic and linguistic groups and by different superpowers, vied for power. South Africa, which opposed the Soviet-backed MPLA, occupied parts of southern Angola, while the United States and private mercenaries assisted rival nationalist groups. Finally, Cuban troops moved in to bolster the MPLA, which took control of the government and declared independence in 1975.

By 1978 the situation had temporarily stabilized, and the Marxist Angolan government turned its attention to rebuilding the nation's economic base, which had been largely destroyed by over a decade of warfare. On the other hand, continual internal rivalries impeded development. The revenues from Angola's petroleum resources helped in the reconstruction, but in part because of its petroleum, Angola remained a nation of interest to the superpowers and to its neighbors.

With black independence marching south toward its very border, the South African government feared for the future of apartheid. It employed a broad range of economic, political, and military efforts to cripple the support that neighboring black nations were giving to independence movements in Rhodesia and Southwest Africa and to black people in South Africa. From 1981 on, Angola was subjected to continuing retaliatory raids by South African armed forces which, coupled with a civil war fought with U.S.-supported guerrillas, impeded and ultimately largely destroyed Angola's economic and social progress. However, by the time of the 1988 negotiations among the rival parties, Angolan and Cuban forces had largely defeated the South African Defence Forces and the Western-backed liberation movements of UNITA and FLNA; and the leftist government remained in power.

During the 1980s, South Africa also conducted raids into Mozambique and gave support to a rebel insurgency group which was so cruel that the whole world, including the United States, condemned it. South Africa also used its economic power, particularly its control over much of the railroad system of southern Africa, to intimidate Zimbabwe and Botswana. In a very real way both the "enclave states" of Botswana, Lesotho, and Swaziland and the "front-line states" of Zambia and Angola were victims of the continuation of apartheid in South Africa.

Besides Mozambique and Angola, the liberation movement focused on Rhodesia. South Africa supported the Ian Smith regime, but the rest of Africa and the international community refused to recognize the white minority government. In the face of increasing violence on the domestic front and mounting international opposition, Smith finally granted token black representation in 1978, but it was a far cry from true participation. The move failed to satisfy the demands of black nationalists, who tended to become more radical as their legitimate aspirations for self-determination were continually rejected by the small white minority. Escalating tensions induced many white Rhodesian farmers to leave, however, those who remained continued to cling to power. Fearing the growing Cuban and Soviet presence in the region, Great Britain and the United States launched another series of negotiations in 1979. These protracted discussions, complicated by domestic rivalries, led to relatively free elections in the spring of 1979 and independence in 1980.

The new nation, named Zimbabwe (for an ancient African culture in that area) and led by Robert Mugabe, moved to deal with the continuing problems of superpower involvement, political opponents, and internal development. Although the infant nation faced massive domestic problems involving economic development and political divisions, coupled with continued hostility from South Africa, Zimbabwe became a relative success story. Negotiations ultimately succeeded in avoiding the worst excesses of total civil war, the parliamentary system remained intact, and the white minority continued to participate in the political system. Ian Smith even became a member of parliament. Unfortunately, protracted droughts in the late 1980s and early 1990s threatened to cripple Zimbabwe's economic progress and seemed likely to turn the formerly fertile southeastern part of the African continent into a vast dust bowl. Mugabe responded to these crises by increasing the authoritarian power of his party, and by 1991 it was uncertain whether Zimbabwe would follow along the lines of so many other African nations now governed by one-man or one-party rule, or whether it would be able to maintain its multiparty parliamentary system.

Meanwhile, South Africa took the offensive in Southwest Africa. It denied independence to the projected new black state of Namibia and retained the area as a buffer against black African and Marxist governments from the north. In the sense of being a region of Africa ruled by an outside white government, Namibia was the last African colony. South Africa had held Namibia as a League of Nations mandate since 1919 and in spite of U.N. opposition annexed the territory in 1949. In retaliation, the United Nations censured South Africa for its racist policies. In 1966 the black independence organization SWAPO launched an armed struggle against South African domination. Although South Africa responded quickly with armed force, the struggle continued. As the Namibian forces escalated their attacks, the South African regime moved swiftly to arrest and imprison SWAPO leaders, but by 1972 armed confrontations were commonplace. The United Nations declared 1975 the deadline for South African withdrawal; however, the deadline came and went with no appreciable changes in policy.

Meanwhile, SWAPO continued its attacks and boycotted South African attempts to further the establishment of Bantustans in Namibia. SWAPO had the public support of its African neighbors and the Communist bloc, but political divisions among various nationalist groups in Namibia also became apparent as the situation polarized leftist and more conservative forces. Finally U.N.-backed negotiations led to the independence of Namibia in 1989. The first national elections resulted in a huge voter turnout and a resounding victory for SWAPO, but rival political forces, particularly those formerly supported by the United States and South Africa, continued to oppose and launch armed attacks against the elected government.

Apartheid versus Equality in South Africa

Despite objections from around the world, successive Afrikaner leaders continued the segregation policies of apartheid. Black African nationalist leaders were imprisoned or forced underground or escaped into exile. After the African National Congress (ANC) was outlawed in 1960, the leaders, including Nelson Mandela and Oliver Tambo, reluctantly concluded that only the force of arms would end apartheid. Following the Rivonia Trials from 1963 to 1964, Mandela was sentenced to life imprisonment; Tambo escaped into exile. Many of the armed ANC members continued to operate from the front-line states of Zambia, Tanzania, and Angola. Sabotage bombings and attacks increased within South Africa, and in 1973 there were massive strikes.

The most serious violence occurred in Soweto in 1976, when schoolchildren demonstrated against the use of Afrikaans as the major language of instruction. The students were also protesting the Bantu Education Act, which institutionalized inferior education programs for the majority black population. The violence soon spread from Soweto to the rest of the country and indicated that many black Africans had become radicalized. The South African government responded with a new series of repressive tactics, typified by the death of Steven Biko, a well-known student nationalist spokesperson. Biko died of brain injuries inflicted by police beatings in 1977.

International organizations widely condemned South Africa for its racial policies, and in 1984 a major critic of apartheid, Bishop Desmond Tutu, was awarded the Nobel Prize for Peace. Both Tutu and the Reverend Allan Boesak called for economic boycotts of white businesses and divestment by Western interests as a means of undercutting the apartheid regime and forcing changes. While the boycott helped to call international attention to the situation, outsiders continued to purchase South African goods, to operate industries, and to sell armaments to the regime.

The South African system of apartheid and its continued domination of Namibia were annually condemned by the United Nations. In addition, many church leaders, including the Pope, and activist organizations around the world voiced their opposition to apartheid. In attempts to lessen its growing isolation in international forums, South Africa modified racial barriers to allow multiracial memberships on sports teams. By means of largely cosmetic changes, South Africans, who were keen sports enthusiasts, hoped to be readmitted to international competitions. Strict censorship regulations had prohibited many publications and mass media productions from depicting black Africans in roles of equality, but by the mid-1970s the government was pressured into allowing television broadcasts. Some job restrictions among the races and other racially based laws were modified, but the limitations on citizenship were augmented.

Although a new constitution, implemented by Prime Minister P. W. Botha in 1984, permitted Asians and colored minorities technically to became junior partners in the political system, its main result was to reinforce the complete exclusion of the black majority. During the 1987 "White Only" elections, a political button stating, "If voting could change the system, it would be illegal," encapsulated the problem. Black activists and sympathetic white citizens joined in large-scale demonstrations against apartheid, both in South Africa and in other nations, but the South African regime showed few signs of chang-

Life and Death under Apartheid

The last thing I ever dreamed of when I was daily battling for survival and for an identity other than that of inferiority and fourth-class citizen, which apartheid foisted on me, was that someday I would attend an American college, edit its newspaper, graduate with honors, practise journalism and write a book.

How could I have dreamed of all this when I was born of illiterate parents who could not afford to pay my way through school, let alone pay the rent for our shack and put enough food on the table; when black people in Alexandra lived under constant police terror and the threat of deportation to impoverished tribal reserves; when at ten I contemplated suicide because I found the burden of living in a ghetto, poverty-stricken and without hope, too heavy to shoulder; when in 1976 I got deeply involved in the Soweto protests, in which hundreds of black students were killed by the police and thousands fled the country to escape imprisonment and torture? . . .

Much has been written and spoken about the politics of apartheid: the forced removals of black communities from their ancestral lands, the Influx Control and Pass laws that mandate where blacks can live, work, raise families, be buried; the migrant labour system that forces black men to live away from their families eleven months out of a year. . . .

When I was growing up in Alexandra it meant hate, bitterness, hunger, pain, terror, violence, fear, dashed hopes and dreams. Today it still means the same for millions of black children who are trapped in the ghettos of South Africa, in a lingering nightmare of a racial system. . . .

At thirteen I stumbled across tennis, a sport so "white" most blacks thought I was mad for thinking I could excel in it; others mistook me for an Uncle Tom. Through tennis I learned the important lesson that South Africa's 4.5 million whites are not all racists. As I grew older, and got to understand them more—their fears, longings, hopes, ignorance and mistaken beliefs, and they mine—this lesson became the conviction that whites are in some ways victims of apartheid, too, and that it is the system, not they, that has to be destroyed.

＊◀◆▶ ▶

In his moving autobiography Mark Mathabane describes growing up in Alexandra, a black ghetto outside Johannesburg, South Africa. Through intelligence, extraordinary hard work, love from his family, and some luck, Mathabane managed to secure an education and obtain a tennis scholarship to an American college. Mathabane now lives in the United States where he frequently lectures on apartheid and the struggle against it.

*From Kaffir Boy: The True Story of a Black Youth's Coming of Age in Apartheid South Africa by Mark Mathabane, pp. ix–xi. Copyright © 1986 by New American Library, New York.

ing its racial policies and in 1986 adopted Emergency Powers to crush black opposition. It forced more and more black Africans into the Bantustans, now renamed "homelands" to appease world opinion. Identity cards were gradually replaced with "travel documents" (passports). South Africa thereby became the first African nation with no black African citizens.

In Althone, South African police use rhinoceros hide whips to beat anti-government demonstrators in 1985.
(*Detroit Free Press photo by David C. Turnley*)

The black liberation movement was impeded by the poverty of its people and by the overwhelming military power of the government. Old ethnic divisions which the white South African government continually sought to intensify broke out increasingly in widespread violence as rival black African groups clashed with supporters of the ANC. In particular, the ANC faced opposition from the Inkatha Freedom Party led by the "Chief" of the KwaZulu, Gatsha Buthelezi, who had received support from the Afrikaner government in the past. Mandela accused factions within the Afrikaner community and South African military of inspiring violence and financing opposition to the ANC. Although the movement had the sympathy of the rest of Africa, most African nations were too weak and poor to offer much direct assistance.

Hoping to avoid a bloody confrontation, F. W. de Klerk further modified some apartheid regulations, released Mandela from prison in 1989, removed the ban on political groups, and opened negotiations with the ANC. Mandela and de Klerk struggled to find some acceptable compromise but were limited by political considerations. De Klerk was particularly vulnerable to opposition from segments of the Afrikaner population that rejected all changes to the apartheid system. Mandela too faced criticism from more radical elements within the ANC for negotiating directly with the white regime.

As white Africans appeared to fear too much change, and black Africans too little change, the negotiations faltered with no resolution in sight. The situation in South Africa remained particularly volatile as the majority black population remained without political rights or equality. The longer the apartheid system continued without change or compromise, the greater the likelihood of massive civil war. Many black and some white South Africans, who had long hoped and worked toward a peaceful solution of full national rights for all, became increasingly pessimistic.

PROBLEMS AMONG NEW AFRICAN NATIONS

Several major problems confronted African nations after their independence. First, all African leaders had to deal with widespread poverty and often with starvation. Economic problems contributed to preexisting religious, ethnic, and regional divisions that made it difficult and often impossible to forge national unity. As previously noted, the national boundaries drawn by European colonial powers frequently did not reflect the cultural, ethnic, or linguistic patterns of the peoples living within them. Consequently, newly independent African nations often had to deal with a multitude of different and sometimes hostile ethnic groups within one nation. Border disputes among neighboring nations also deflected energy and money away from internal development to armaments and the military.

These problems, and the failures of the civilian governments to solve them, frequently led to open interference by the military. Togo experienced the first military coup d'etat in independent black Africa in 1963. The leader of that coup, Lt. General Gnassingbe Eyadema, remained in power into the 1990s. In the following two decades there were about eighty military coups in African nations. Thus, as in many other parts of the world, in particular Latin and South America, military coups and countercoups became the rule rather than the exception. The preeminence of the military in government also meant that large portions of national revenues were expended on the military sector. Military leaders often lacked the expertise to formulate and implement much-needed development projects. This was particularly true in the agricultural sector, in which the overwhelming majority of Africans worked. Hence, the tasks of nation building and economic development often proved more difficult than the struggles for independence had been.

AGRICULTURE: CRISIS AND POTENTIAL

Africa has particular environmental problems. The highest rainfalls occur around the equator, but the majority of the continent is either semiarid or desert. Rains tend to be unpredictable and often fall in such torrents that soil erosion becomes a major problem. The tsetse fly, which carries the deadly trypanosomiasis parasitic infection, infests the humid and subhumid regions where agriculture and cattle farming are climatically possible and has proved to be a major impediment to development.

In addition to these environmental issues, newly independent African nations also faced a number of political, social, and economic troubles. One African child in every seven died before his or her fifth birthday. Many African nations remained desperately poor. For example, in 1991, the average life expectancy in Malawi was only forty-seven years and the per capita income was still less than $200 per year.

Uncertainty about children surviving, as well as religious traditions, made most parents want large families, thus contributing to the high population growth in many nations. As a consequence of these environmental conditions, many African nations were not able to increase agricultural output fast enough to keep pace with the growing population. During the 1980s food output in Africa as a whole actually declined. Ironically, advanced Western technological "solutions" such as gigantic dams often exacerbated the problems and contributed to increased soil depletion and declining production. The problem of ever-larger populations, droughts, and the resultant famines was particularly acute along the Sahel, a hot, dry stretch of land running from West Africa south of the Sahara (which itself was rapidly advancing) into Ethiopia and Somalia in the east. From 1977 onward this region had one of the worst refugee problems in the world. Many people moved from their homes to escape the devastation caused by prolonged droughts (in some areas 90 percent of the livestock perished) and to avoid continuing regional conflicts.

By the late 1980s droughts had also created huge dust bowls in Botswana and southern Africa, areas that had previously been highly productive agricultural centers. In Chad, the Sudan, Ethiopia, and Mozambique (nations also plagued by civil war), over 600,000 persons had died of starvation, and the lives of 19 million starving people were threatened throughout the Sahel and East Africa. An estimated 150 million others were rapidly running out of food. Even with increased rains by mid-decade, famines continued because there was no seed to plant; massive numbers of people had left their traditional farm holdings; livestock had long since been killed or had died; and deforestation was widespread. There were numerous charges that the affluent nations were too slow to recognize the problem and that the relief agencies and the governments of the afflicted nations were inefficient in distributing food.

On the positive side, individual projects, such as Burkina Faso's public health blitz that inoculated three-quarters of its children against measles, meningitis, and yellow fever and Ethiopia's well-digging project in Bale province were remarkably successful. Other grass-roots and self-help projects that required minimal outside money or support systems often worked out well.

Despite their plethora of troubles, many Africans saw promise of improvement. Several African nations attacked their agricultural problems by introducing agroforestry (tree farms), making more efficient use of animal and human resources, pursuing land reclamation through water-harvesting in microbasins, and practicing water conservation. The best procedure for these projects appeared to be a combination of market and government projects, mainly for urban areas, and locally run projects in rural areas. In 1980 African nations elaborated such a program under the Lagos Plan of Action, but its im-

The city of Lusaka typifies the modern and rapidly expanding African city where a wide variety of imported manufactured goods are available for the few who can afford them.
(Jason Lauré)

plementation was impeded by political and military divisions. On the other hand, only decades before, India had faced similar agricultural shortages, yet had become self-sufficient in food. There was a similar potential for Africa.

AFRICA IN THE POST-COLD WAR ERA

As in Eastern Europe, the end of the Cold War provided an enormous impetus for democracy throughout much of Africa. By the early 1990s over forty African nations had moved toward more public participation in the political systems. Long-term one-party rulers, such as Zambia's Kenneth Kaunda, were defeated in open elections, and thousands joined public demonstrations demanding political reforms and an end to corruption in the Congo, Malawi, Kenya, and other nations. Military dictators were reluctant to give up their power and, as in Zaire under Mobutu, were often willing to use armed force to crush democratic opposition movements. As in Eastern Europe, the creation of democratic governments was difficult and plagued with uncertainties. One African leader underscored the difficulties by citing the African proverb, "Slowly, slowly, an egg grows feet and walks."

With the end of the Cold War, danger of direct confrontations between the United States and the Soviet Union in Africa faded away, but many remnants of the superpower rivalry continued to plague the continent. In the Horn of Africa the Soviet-backed regimes collapsed, but no clear-cut political force emerged to take their places. As a result, Ethiopia and Somalia both became battlegrounds for rival gangs and politicians. While families faced starvation, armed gangs frequently confiscated food donations provided by richer Western nations and terrorized the civilian populations. By the early 1990s up to 2,000 people were dying every week in Somalia.

The international community, led by the United Nations and the United States, opposed violence and supported democracy in both the Horn of Africa and South Africa, but as the century drew to a close, negotiations, diplomacy, and even armed intervention had thus far failed to resolve these crises.

SUMMARY

North African nations were plagued by border disputes and internal problems of development. However, Libya, with vast oil revenues, launched massive and largely successful development projects. Algeria, which also had petroleum, devoted considerable resources to domestic development; but with a much larger and generally young population to feed and provide services for, economic growth was not as rapid or extensive.

By the 1970s and 1980s military dictators had become the rule in much of sub-Saharan Africa. Some, such as Idi Amin in Uganda, were particularly repressive and were eventually overthrown. African nations, particularly in the Horn of Africa and the southern sector, had also been the scenes of outside intervention from neighboring nations and the superpowers. In the process, a number of African nations had become battlegrounds for Cold War rivalries. In southern Africa, levels of violence had continued to rise as the South African government clung to the apartheid system, which excluded the majority black population from all political activity and equal rights in the work place. Political equality for all people, particularly the black majority in South Africa, had yet to be achieved.

Mounting economic troubles also exacerbated religious, ethnic, and regional divisions that made it difficult and often impossible to forge national unity. Regional disputes also directed much-needed resources toward armed conflicts and away from economic development programs. There were some success stories in agriculture, but drought, underproduction, and famines continued to ravage much of Africa.

With the end of the Cold War, many new political forces emerged in Africa and a number of nations moved toward democracy. In nations with large Muslim populations, many supported the creation of Islamic governments. The Horn of Africa and South Africa remained two crisis points. As the South African government refused to dismantle the apartheid system and continued to deny equal rights to the black majority, violence in that nation escalated. In spite of these daunting problems, the vast natural resources, agricultural potential, and labor force in Africa made the continent important to the industrialized world and provided the potential for future improvements in the quality of life for all African peoples.

SUGGESTED SOURCES

BAYART, JEAN-FRANCOIS, *The State in Africa: The Politics of the Belly* (1992). Interdisciplinary analysis of contemporary society and politics in Africa.*

CHAZAN, NAOMI, R. MORTIMER, J. RAVENHILL, and D. ROTHCHILD, *Politics and Society in Contemporary Africa* (1988). An insightful narrative on the complexities of African politics.*

HARRISON, PAUL, *The Greening of Africa: Breaking Through in the Battle for Land and Food* (1987). Rare optimistic look at success stories in African development projects.*

LAMB, DAVID, *The Africans* (1983). A fascinating survey.*

LEGUM, COLIN, *The Battlefronts of Southern Africa* (1988). A history of the current crisis in southern Africa and the forecast for greater violence.*

MEER, FATIMA, *Higher Than Hope* (1988). Authorized biography of Nelson Mandela, a leader of the antiapartheid movement in South Africa.

A World Apart (1988). A film about the personal story of a white girl growing up in an apartheid society which her family opposes.

ZARTMAN, I. WILLIAM, *Ripe for Resolution: Conflict and Intervention in Africa* (1989). Scholarly analysis of the key crises, with useful maps.*

*Paperback available.

CHAPTER 33

Gorbachev and the Transformation of Europe, 1985–1991

The years 1985–1991 marked profound changes in Europe and in the Soviet Union. By the end of 1991 the Soviet empire had collapsed: Communist governments had fallen in Eastern Europe, the U.S.S.R. itself had disintegrated, and Boris Yeltsin, the leader of Russia, its largest and most powerful state, was no longer a Communist. Nor was Europe any longer divided into Western and Eastern Cold War blocs—even the term "Eastern Europe" seemed outdated. The Berlin Wall, which for three decades had symbolized this partition, had been smashed down and the Democratic and Federal republics (East and West Germany) reunited into a new Germany of about 78 million people. Although there were many complex reasons for this transformation, including the heroic efforts of dissidents, the most dominant cause was the activity of Soviet leader (until the end of 1991) Mikhail Gorbachev.

In Western Europe there were other important developments—aside from changes (like arms reductions) motivated by Gorbachev's policies and communism's collapse. One was the growing tendency, following the example of Great Britain's Margaret Thatcher, to cut back on state subsidies and turn government holdings over to private interests. (After the collapse of communism in Eastern Europe, where such holdings had long predominated, a larger-scale "privatization" began in that region.) There were also new steps taken to move toward a more unified twelve-nation European Community (EC).

GORBACHEV, REFORM, THE DISSOLUTION OF THE SOVIET UNION, AND THE END OF THE COLD WAR

After coming to power as general secretary of the Soviet Union's Communist party in March 1985, Mikhail Gorbachev began a process of reforming the Communist system at home and modifying its dealings with foreign powers. Once begun, the reforms assumed a momentum of their own, sometimes exceeding Gorbachev's intentions. By Christmas Day, 1991, the fifteen republics

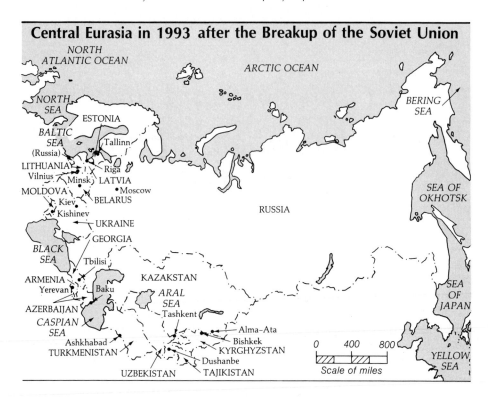

Central Eurasia in 1993 after the Breakup of the Soviet Union

of the Soviet Union had all declared their independence, and Gorbachev, without a nation to rule, resigned as president.

Domestic Reforms, 1985–1989

Soon after he came to power Gorbachev began pressing for a whole series of changes in Soviet society, despite the difficulties such changes might bring with them. His domestic program was soon characterized by three words: *glasnost* (openness), *perestroika* (restructuring), and *demokratizatsiia* (democratization).

Glasnost encompassed the ideas of more freedom of expression and less censorship and government secrecy. Writers became free to criticize without fearing punishment, and many dissidents were released from detention. Permission to emigrate and travel abroad increased significantly, and many Soviet intellectuals supported Gorbachev's policies. Films, plays, and books that had long been forbidden suddenly appeared, including Boris Pasternak's long-suppressed *Doctor Zhivago*. New historical interpretations, especially ones critical of the Stalin and Brezhnev eras, were published. According to the Soviet newspaper *Izvestia*, the old history books were full of "lies," and the government canceled all final history examinations for primary and secondary school students at the end of the 1987–1988 school year. The government tolerated some demonstrations and strikes, and Gorbachev initiated a more liberal attitude toward religious believers and broadened the legal rights of Soviet citizens. In December 1988 the government suspended the jamming of foreign radio broadcasts, including the Russian-language programs of U.S.-financed Radio Liberty.

Perestroika, although a term eventually used to symbolize all of Gorbachev's reforms, originally referred primarily to economic restructuring, for the reorganization of the Soviet economy was a top priority. During the decade before 1985 the growth of the Soviet economy had slowed considerably compared to earlier periods. It grew at less than half the rate of the 1960s; some economic supporters of Gorbachev asserted that there had been no real growth in national income during the early 1980s. Moreover, the economy was plagued with various structural defects, including poor worker productivity and shortages of both housing and consumer goods.

One persistent problem that Gorbachev and his supporters faced was deficient agricultural production. Despite having more farmers than all of the industrialized West and Japan put together, the Soviet Union was forced year after year to spend precious hard currency to import Western grain. Not only did Soviet peasants produce much less than Western farmers—roughly one-seventh per capita—but as much as one-third of the vegetable crop spoiled each year before it could reach consumers.

High defense expenditures presented another major problem. Although roughly equivalent to that of the United States, Soviet military spending represented a much greater burden since the per capita GNP of the U.S.S.R. was less than half of that of its superpower rival.

Another important factor stimulating change was the challenge of the Information Age. At a time when computers and telecommunications were becoming increasingly important in business and economic affairs, the Soviet Union was falling further behind the United States and many other nations in Europe and Asia. As late as 1988 personal computers in the Soviet Union numbered in the tens of thousands, while there were about 20 million in the United States. The director of Moscow's Institute for Space Research even admitted that to find adequate computers for his institute he had to buy U.S.-made ones on Moscow's "black market."

Earlier Soviet leaders, especially Khrushchev, had experimented with piecemeal economic reforms, but Gorbachev and his backers realized that more radical measures were needed. In an effort to stem alcoholism and its retardant effects on worker productivity, he instituted a "vodka reform" that increased alcohol prices and made it more difficult to obtain. In 1986 and 1987 the government began permitting individuals and cooperatives to offer some lawful private alternatives to state enterprises, especially in the long-neglected area of services, such as restaurants and repairs. It also established joint ventures with foreign businesses that signed agreements to provide for a variety of enterprises from fast foods to dental fillings and hotel construction. As of January 1988, state enterprises were to begin switching to a system of self-financing.

Gorbachev's long-range economic plans called for reducing centralized control of the economy and allowing more local initiatives to factories, farms,

Under Gorbachev, joint ventures with foreign businesses increased, exemplified by Moscow's Pizza Hut getting ready to open in the summer of 1990. (*Walter Moss*)

and peasants, and limited private enterprise. Further, Gorbachev and his supporters wanted to increase both worker productivity and quality control and restructure prices and salaries to more adequately reflect real market values. He increasingly called for *perestroika* to be applied to various other areas of Soviet life, such as the government, society, and culture.

Gorbachev's third watchword, *demokratizatsiia*, meant increased participation of Soviet citizens in the political process. In 1988 he brought forth a series of changes designed to reduce the role of the Communist party in the everyday political and economic life of the nation. These changes mandated secret-ballot, multiple-candidate (although not multiparty) elections to Soviet bodies at all levels and limited the term of elected government officials to a maximum of ten years in any position.

In the spring of 1989, after elections that were for the most part contested, a new Soviet congress of 2,250 deputies met in a spirited two-week televised session that presented to Soviet citizens the most open political debates they had witnessed in seven decades of Soviet rule. Before adjourning, the congress elected by secret ballot a new and more powerful 542-member Supreme Soviet, with Gorbachev as its president. Pronouncements and resolutions of this period made clear the interconnection of Gorbachev's three political slogans. He believed that all three reforms, reinforcing each other, were necessary to revitalize the Soviet Union.

By 1989 it was clear that Gorbachev desired to transform the Soviet Union more than any other Soviet leader since 1928. He wished to create a far more humane system than any of his Soviet predecessors had done and one that was neither totalitarian nor terroristic. Yet up to this point he also showed no intention of working for a Western-style multiparty government with a capitalist economy.

Gorbachev's Three Crises, 1988–1991

Partly as a result of the persistence of long-standing Soviet problems—some of which Gorbachev's reforms were attempting to correct—and partly as a result of hopes, fears, and confusion sown by the reforms themselves, Gorbachev faced three crises by the early 1990s.

One was a federal crisis that by the end of 1991 led to the dismantling of the Soviet Union. Soviet harmony among the more than 100 Soviet ethnic nationalities was always somewhat of a myth, but state repression had maintained order and kept the Russians, by far the single most populous nationality, in control. As Communist controls eased under Gorbachev, old grievances against other ethnic groups and against the Russian-dominated Soviet state quickly resurfaced among the subordinated nationalities.

Conflict between Armenians and Azerbaijanis in the Caucasus Mountains occurred sporadically in 1988, leading to deaths, massive demonstrations, strikes, and the flight of about 180,000 people from their homes before a devastating earthquake hit the region and temporarily diverted attention from nationalistic rivalries.

In the three Soviet Baltic republics of Estonia, Latvia, and Lithuania, nationalism took another form. "Popular front" organizations, created in all three republics in 1988, increasingly pushed for more national autonomy. By 1991 all three Baltic republics were insisting on complete independence. In January 1991 Soviet army troops stormed a government press building in Vilnius, Lithuania, killing fourteen people. Gorbachev denied that he had ordered the attack, but it occurred amidst other signs that he was not willing to allow his reforms to develop to the point of permitting Baltic independence.

Not only did the Baltic republics declare their sovereignty, but so too did the other republics, especially after the huge Russian republic (RSFSR) itself declared its sovereignty from the federal government in June 1990. By early 1991, the federal crisis had become inextricably intertwined with the other two crises, the political and the economic.

From 1985 to early 1990 Gorbachev battled mainly against conservative Communist party personnel who feared change. These individuals, many

Estonian demonstrators in Tallinn demanding independence, summer 1990.
(*Walter Moss*)

among the long-privileged elite, often stalled, delayed and, at times, weak-ened reforms.

Yet by the end of the 1980s, Gorbachev also faced criticism from those who thought that he was not enough of a reformer, that he was too timid. Although most deputies to the new Supreme Soviet that met in mid-1989 were opposed to sweeping reforms, a more liberal minority within the Soviet formed the "Inter-Regional Group." For a while its chief spokesman was long-time dissi-dent Andrei Sakharov, freed by Gorbachev from his Gorky exile in December 1986. But ill health led to his death at the end of 1989. Boris Yeltsin, who had served as head of the party in Moscow for two years until denounced by Gor-bachev and replaced in late 1987, then emerged as the group's leading voice.

By the end of 1989 other voices were also speaking out for an acceleration of reform. Gorbachev's policies had made possible the emergence of tens of thousands of informal, voluntary groups. Some of them, like the popular fronts in the Baltic republics, were large and primarily political. They existed on every level from city to all-union. In the years 1987–1989 about twenty substantial independent political organizations sprang up composed of either Moscow or St. Petersburg residents, and many times that number appeared in other cities or on higher levels. Although not all of them pressed for faster reform, they represented a broadening of democracy.

In early February 1990, on the eve of an important meeting of the Communist party's Central Committee, the voices of the people were heard in a massive prodemocracy demonstration in Moscow. The next day Gorbachev proposed to his fellow Communists that they agree to allow a multiparty system, and a few days later, following a bitter debate, they voted to accept his proposal.

Subsequent elections to local and republican parliaments further strengthened the hand of those desiring faster reforms, and in May 1990 Yeltsin was elected chairman of the Russian Republic's Supreme Soviet. He quickly became Gorbachev's first serious reformist competitor and continued to criticize him for being too timid in pushing reforms. The rivalry between the two men helped push Gorbachev temporarily toward the secret police and the military forces.

By early 1991 Yeltsin had become increasingly successful in portraying Gorbachev as someone more in tune with the old Communist authoritarian system than with the new, more democratic politics that by then had gone beyond Gorbachev's initial intentions. With Yeltsin and reformist mayors in cities like Moscow and Leningrad frequently challenging Gorbachev's authority within the Russian Republic itself, people on the local Russian level were often confused about whose orders they should follow. Undoubtedly one of the causes of the blossoming political crisis was the inexperience of the leaders in the give-and-take of a liberalized democratic process.

Gorbachev's third crisis, the economic one, grew yearly more acute from 1988 to 1991. By the late 1980s declining world petroleum prices were already contributing to large budget deficits for the U.S.S.R.—the world's largest oil producer. The wrenching difficulties of transforming the old command (planned) economy also brought to the fore new problems, as did the ethnic and political crises. To make matters worse, Gorbachev seemed to lack a clear vision of exactly what type of economy he wanted. If he had one, he certainly was not able to effectively explain it to Soviet citizens.

In any case, many of Gorbachev's economic "reforms" had produced more opposition than support. By late 1988, when he eased back on his unpopular antialcohol measures, there was increased grumbling about the high prices that some of the new cooperatives and private entrepreneurs were charging for other goods and services. Declining food supplies and consumer goods and increasing inflation and unemployment brought about further unpopular measures in early 1991: currency reform and price increases. Gorbachev's popularity fell to an all-time low.

The Coup That Failed and Its Aftermath

Demonstrations on behalf of reform and strikes, especially a widespread miners' strike in March 1991, helped move Gorbachev back toward reformers like Yeltsin. In June, in a popular election for the office of president of the Russian

Republic, Yeltsin further strengthened his position by trouncing his rivals. In late July, Gorbachev advocated a free market economy and called for the Communist party to abandon many of its Marxist-Leninist ideas. On August 20 he was scheduled to sign a new union treaty with the leaders of several republics, including Yeltsin. This treaty, which would have transferred considerable powers to the republics, was also later to be signed by the leaders of as many other republics as were persuaded to agree.

On August 18 some old-line Communists leaders made their move. Fearing loss of their powers and the disintegration of the Soviet Union, they put Gorbachev under house arrest while he was vacationing in the Crimea. The next morning an eight-member Emergency Committee of old-line Communists, including the defense minister and the KGB (secret police) chief, announced in Moscow that Gorbachev was sick and that it had assumed emergency powers. However, neither it nor the tanks and troops it mobilized were resolute enough to fire on resisters led by Boris Yeltsin in Moscow. By August 22, the coup had failed, and Gorbachev returned to Moscow that same morning. Coup leaders were arrested, and Yeltsin became the hero of the day.

The events that followed quickly after were almost as dramatic as the failed coup. The coup created a backlash against the Communist party, and the government suspended the party's political activities. Gorbachev followed the example that Yeltsin and others had set before the failed coup and resigned from the party. Within a few weeks the three Baltic republics announced their independence, and a reluctant Gorbachev agreed to recognize their wishes. On December 1 the Ukraine voted for independence. A week later the three founding members of the U.S.S.R. in 1922—Russia, Ukraine, and Belorussia (now Belarus)—agreed to disband the union and instead to form a "commonwealth of independent states." On December 21, eight other former Soviet republics agreed to join them. Out of the fifteen former Soviet republics only the three Baltic republics and Georgia remained outside the new commonwealth.

Gorbachev, now a president without a country, resigned his office on December 25, 1991. The exact shape of the new commonwealth was unclear, but the eleven members insisted that they were independent states. Although Russia, under president Boris Yeltsin, was clearly the most powerful of the states, the others appeared determined not to let him dominate the commonwealth.

Gorbachev's "New-Thinking" Foreign Policy and the End of the Cold War

While Gorbachev and other Soviet leaders used the term *perestroika* to symbolize his domestic reforms, they often chose the phrase "new thinking" to characterize his foreign policy. It was indeed new in many ways. Soviet détente policies of the 1970s had aimed at decreasing superpower tensions but without abandoning "ideological struggle." Gorbachev was also now willing to jettison such "struggle." While there were numerous reasons for this change in policy, Soviet economic difficulties were perhaps the greatest factor. The Cold

War and the arms race were just too expensive for the stagnant Soviet economy to continue. Gorbachev admitted that the Soviet Union bore some responsibility for the past arms race, and a 1988 party conference declared that "foreign policy activity should contribute ever more to releasing the nation's resources for peaceful construction, for *perestroika*." At about the same time, the Soviet government admitted it had been wrong not to give its full support to the United Nations because the world needed a stable structure for international affairs. In the sphere of regional conflicts, it renounced exporting revolution or counterrevolution and expressed its desire to help find solutions to conflicts in such places as Angola, Cambodia, and the Middle East.

Soviet foreign policy demonstrated its new orientation in deeds as well as in words. By the end of 1988 Gorbachev had met with U.S. President Reagan on five occasions in three years, producing agreements that reversed the deteriorating relations of the early 1980s. The most important was the Intermediate Nuclear Forces (INF) treaty, ratified in 1988, which mandated the destruction of all (about 2,800) Soviet and U.S. land-based nuclear missiles in the 300 to

Gorbachev and Reagan at their first summit (Geneva, November 1985).
(Reuters/Bettmann Newsphotos)

3,400 mile range. Other agreements provided for increased exchanges of students, cultural programs, scientific research, and nuclear testing information. Despite Gorbachev's strong objections to President Reagan's SDI—"What we need is Star Peace and not Star Wars," he quipped on one occasion—Soviet negotiators continued discussing with U.S. representatives a strategic arms reduction treaty (START) which would cut the number of long-range nuclear weapons on each side.

After the election of George Bush, Gorbachev continued his summit diplomacy and disarmament talks. In November 1990 Gorbachev, Bush, and twenty other NATO and Warsaw Pact leaders met in Paris to sign the most sweeping arms control treaty in history. It committed the signatories to destroy tens of thousands of howitzers, tanks, and other conventional weapons. In July 1991 the two leaders signed the START treaty, which promised approximately a 30 percent cut in long-range nuclear weapons over the next seven years. In late September Bush announced several additional unilateral disarmament steps, and a week later Gorbachev went even further, promising among other steps to observe a one-year moratorium on nuclear testing. By the end of 1991 it almost appeared as if the two leaders were involved in a "disarmament race." Only fears about who would become responsible for the 27,000 Soviet nuclear warheads in the disintegrating Soviet Union restrained the euphoric feeling that the arms race between the two former Cold War rivals was over.

An equally significant Soviet foreign policy turnaround came in 1989 and 1990 when one Communist government after another was toppled in Eastern Europe—and the Soviet Union did not intervene. This was due to a whole host of reasons, including the devastating impact such intervention would have had on both reforms at home and relations abroad, especially with the West.

Gorbachev stressed Soviet links with Western Europe, advocating "the end of the schism of Europe" and referring to it as our "common home." In the fall of 1988 he met with the heads of the governments of Italy, West Germany, and France and had numerous subsequent meetings with European leaders. Both the Western European nations and the United States granted some economic assistance to the disintegrating U.S.S.R. or directly to the increasingly independent republics.

Improving U.S.-Soviet relations also helped solve regional conflicts such as Afghanistan, from which the U.S.S.R. removed all its troops by early 1989. The Soviet invasion of Afghanistan in 1979 had been a major source of Sino-Soviet friction, and by withdrawing, the Soviet Union improved its relations with China. The Soviet government also eased tensions with China by reducing Soviet forces stationed along the Chinese border and encouraging Vietnam to withdraw its troops from Cambodia. In June 1989 Gorbachev visited China, and relations between the two Communist giants were normalized after almost thirty years of strain.

Gorbachev's efforts to improve Soviet-Chinese relations were symptomatic of his efforts to better Soviet relations in Asia as well as in Europe. He sought increased trade on both continents and help from Asian capitalist nations for Siberian development. Despite Japan's unhappiness over Soviet un-willingness to return the Kurile Islands taken after World War II, it did become a major source of loans.

The Gorbachev Image at Home and Abroad

Gorbachev was more admired abroad than at home. His role in ending the Cold War and Soviet control over Eastern Europe earned him the gratitude of people in numerous countries. In the Western democracies he was perceived as a Westernizer, attempting to make the U.S.S.R. more like the West. While many Soviet citizens also appreciated these accomplishments and efforts, oth-ers were embittered by the collapse of the Soviet empire and too much West-ernization. While Soviet society generally welcomed his policies of *glasnost* and democratization, it was less enthusiastic about his economic policies, which many thought only worsened conditions.

Although Gorbachev sometimes displayed great political skills amidst the many landmines along the road to reform, his defects as a politician were often overlooked in the West. Compared to someone like Yeltsin, he was never as comfortable among the common people, and he failed to realize how deeply feelings like nationalism and resentment toward Communist privileges ran among Soviet citizens. Nor was he ever able to communicate a clear vision that would have inspired the peoples of the U.S.S.R. to remain together and willingly sacrifice for a better future. Given the difficulties he faced, his own background and personality, decades of Communist rule and misrule, and the natural aspirations of many non-Russians for national independence, it is hardly surprising that he failed in this quest.

COMMUNISM IN EASTERN EUROPE, 1985–1988: ECONOMIC AND POLITICAL CHALLENGES

By early 1985 Eastern Europe, like the Soviet Union, faced growing economic and political difficulties. Although living standards varied considerably from East Germany to Rumania, on the whole, Eastern European consumers were noticeably worse off than Western Europeans in regard to the availability of both goods and services. The economic growth rate from 1980 to 1984 was ap-proximately only one-fourth that of the early 1970s. There was a growing tech-nological gap between the two parts of Europe, especially in regard to com-puters and telecommunications. This gap was broadened in the late 1970s and early 1980s as Western Europe invested much more heavily in a whole range of modernized and energy-efficient machinery. Foreign debt also promised continuing hardships, as in another way did the region's severe industrial pol-lution.

The governments of Eastern Europe found their economic problems com-pounded by lack of popular support. This was seen most clearly in Poland, where the Communist government seemed unable to reverse a significant de-

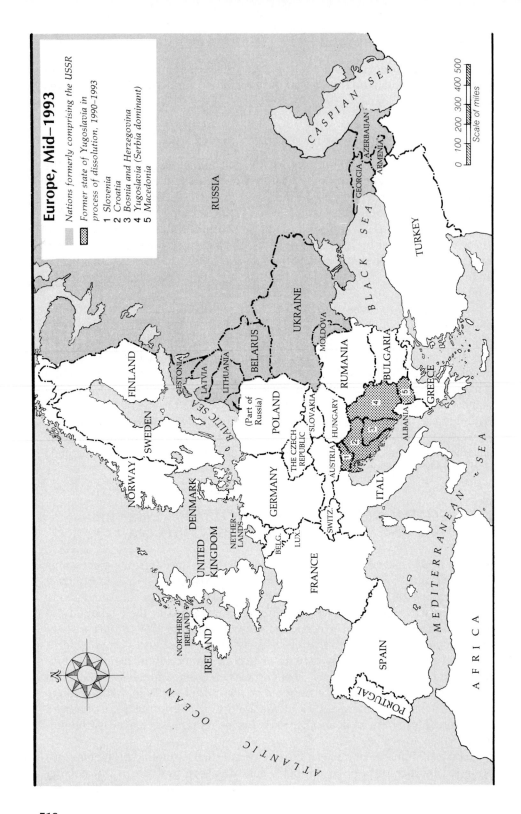

Europe, Mid–1993

Nations formerly comprising the USSR

Former state of Yugoslavia in
process of dissolution, 1990–1993

1 Slovenia
2 Croatia
3 Bosnia and Herzegovina
4 Yugoslavia (Serbia dominant)
5 Macedonia

0 100 200 300 400 500

Scale of miles

RUSSIA

FINLAND

NORWAY

SWEDEN

BALTIC SEA

ESTONIA

LATVIA

LITHUANIA

BELARUS

UKRAINE

(Part of
Russia)

POLAND

DENMARK

UNITED
KINGDOM

NETHER-
LANDS

GERMANY

THE CZECH
REPUBLIC

SLOVAKIA

HUNGARY

AUSTRIA

SWITZ.

BELG.

LUX.

FRANCE

ITALY

SPAIN

PORTUGAL

MEDITERRANEAN SEA

AFRICA

ATLANTIC OCEAN

IRELAND

NORTHERN
IRELAND

MOLDOVA

RUMANIA

BULGARIA

GREECE

ALBANIA

TURKEY

BLACK SEA

CASPIAN SEA

GEORGIA

AZERBAIJAN

ARMENIA

cline in the standard of living compared to the 1970s. The government refused to deal with the outlawed Solidarity union, and most Polish workers refused to cooperate with a government in which they had little faith. Similar conditions of popular unrest made many of the other governments of Eastern Europe reluctant to risk introducing measures of economic austerity, even though some of the funds subsidizing living standards were badly needed to pay off debts and to invest in industrial research and modernization.

Soviet insistence that they would not allow change in Communist Eastern Europe to undermine Soviet security had always been a major limitation on political and economic reform movements, as Hungary, Czechoslovakia, and Poland had learned. The appearance of Gorbachev on the Soviet scene opened up a whole new range of possibilities, however, because he actively encouraged reform. His thinking appeared to be more akin to Alexander Dubček's than to that of Brezhnev, who had intervened to overturn the Czechoslovakian leader in 1968.

Gorbachev did not ignore Soviet security interests, but he defined them differently than his predecessors. Economic stagnation in the Soviet bloc and a costly arms race appeared to him more threatening to Soviet security than Eastern European political reforms. He encouraged economic restructuring throughout the bloc and signed the INF agreement, which removed a whole class of Soviet missiles from Europe. He promised unilateral reductions of Soviet European forces and pushed for more European cooperative efforts and reductions in both nuclear and conventional forces throughout Europe. The new Soviet foreign policy was popular with most Eastern European political leaders, who for various reasons desired better relations, especially increased trade, with the West.

The attitude of political leaders to Soviet economic reforms, however, was more varied. Polish and Hungarian leaders were generally supportive. The East Germans, however, with a centralized economy that was the most prosperous in the Soviet bloc, displayed little desire to move in the direction Gorbachev advocated for the Soviet Union. In Rumania, independent-minded party chief Ceausescu was more concerned with personal power and with reducing his foreign debt than with restructuring Rumania's economy, the most miserable in the Soviet bloc. For his part, Gorbachev emphasized a willingness to tolerate different economic approaches among the nations of Eastern Europe, especially if, as in the case of the East Germans, they had achieved some success.

The Communist parties of Eastern Europe also reacted in varying ways to Gorbachev's political reforms. Again there was less enthusiasm among East German and Rumanian leaders and more support among party bosses in Poland and Hungary, who had already allowed more freedom in their nations than existed in the U.S.S.R. In Poland General Jaruzelski praised Gorbachev's policies and declared that the Soviet Union and Poland were now moving in the same direction: "Poland has not experienced such a happy convergence for the whole of the past millennium."

THE COLLAPSE OF COMMUNISM IN EASTERN EUROPE AND THE REUNIFICATION OF GERMANY, 1988–1991

Between 1988 and 1991 two momentous developments—the virtually blood-less collapse of the Communist governments in Eastern Europe and the swift reunification of Germany—brought an end to an era that had dominated east-ern and central Europe for over forty years. It began in Poland in the spring-summer of 1988, when a number of strikes and continuing economic misery (for example, high inflation that reduced real wages by about 20 percent com-pared to 1980) nudged Polish leaders further along the road to reform. The government opened round-table talks with Solidarity leader Lech Walesa and other supporters of change in Poland. In early 1989 it agreed to once again le-galize Solidarity, to revamp Poland's parliament, and to allow Solidarity to run candidates for all 100 seats of a new upper house and for 35 percent of those of the lower house.

In elections in June 1989, Solidarity candidates won over 99 percent of the seats they were allowed to contest. A few months later, for the first time in a Soviet bloc nation, a coalition government was formed with a non-Communist head—Prime Minister Tadeusz Mazowiecki. After it became clear that the So-viet Union had no intention of intervening to maintain Communist domi-nance, other Communist governments, lacking popular support, began col-lapsing like dominos in Eastern Europe.

By the end of 1989 old-line Communist leaders had been replaced throughout the former Eastern European bloc nations. In some countries re-formist Communists or coalition governments took over, as in Rumania and Bulgaria; but in others, like Czechoslovakia, power fell to people the Commu-nists had once persecuted. When Vaclav Havel, a playwright and often-im-prisoned human rights advocate, became president of Czechoslovakia in De-cember 1989, it became clear that the voice of the people in Eastern Europe could no longer be stifled. As was generally the case in the region, the changeover in Czechoslovakia (the "Velvet Revolution") was surprisingly bloodless.

In 1990 and 1991 democratic forces continued to develop in the region. In December 1990 Lech Walesa was elected Poland's president, and in October 1991 elections, the Bulgarian Socialist party (the former Communist party) was narrowly defeated and ousted from political dominance.

The internal political changes sweeping Eastern Europe affected foreign policy developments. The region's nations improved Western ties, and in 1991 the Warsaw Pact military alliance came to an end and Soviet troops began leaving Eastern European nations.

Although Albania and Yugoslavia were not part of the Soviet bloc, they were Eastern European Communist nations which experienced some of the same problems and challenges faced by bloc nations. Albania, the poorest na-tion in Europe, was slow to change but by the end of 1991 had a coalition gov-ernment with a reforming former head of the Communist party as its presi-dent. By late 1989 Yugoslavia's foreign debt, inflation, and unemployment

A Czech Student in the Velvet Revolution

Jana Markvartova is the daughter of a doctor and a lawyer, a privileged child of Czechoslovakia's elite. Before this week, she had never really talked to any of the hundreds of thousands of people who are this country's manual laborers.

Today, Miss Markvartova stood before nearly 200 workers at the Domaci Potreby household appliance factory in the polluted industrial outskirts of the city and told them how the police here had violently broken up a peaceful demonstration by students last Friday night. Then tearfully, she asked the workers to support a two-hour general strike that the students have called for Monday to demand wholesale changes in the country's leadership.

"We need your help," Miss Markvartova told the workers. "It is your work that allows us to study and to develop our minds and our ideas. But alone our ideas are nothing. We need you. We need you to join our strike."

Her efforts paid off. The workers voted overwhelmingly to support the strike.

In the last week, Miss Markvartova and students like her at Prague's universities have realized that they must reach out to workers at factories, farms and industries if their demonstrations and strikes are to succeed in forcing change on their resistant Communist Government.*

———◆◄◆►◆———

Although Gorbachev played the chief individual role in the changes that swept Eastern Europe and the Soviet Union from 1989 to 1991, there were a countless number of other individuals like the twenty-one-year-old philosophy student described above who helped bring about the collapse of Communist governments.

*From "Students Ask Workers' Aid in Czech Rally" by Esther B. Fein in *The New York Times*, November 24, 1989.

combined to make it one of the most economically troubled nations of Europe. But as in the Soviet Union, its economic problems were intertwined with federal-ethnic and political problems that soon reached crisis proportions. As central Communist control weakened, this state of Serbs, Croats, Bosnian Muslims, Slovenes, Macedonians, Albanians, and other ethnic groups began to disintegrate. Besides ethnic rivalries, often sharpened by past grievances, differing levels of economic well-being and clashing attitudes toward political and economic reforms also contributed to divisiveness. In mid-1991 Slovenia and Croatia declared their independence from a Yugoslavia they believed too dominated by Serbs, and full-scale civil war broke out as federal troops invaded Croatia. Assisted by Serb guerrilla forces in Croatia, the federal forces captured some Croatian territory, and, despite outside diplomatic pressures and frequent cease-fires, the war continued. By the end of 1991 it had produced more than 10,000 casualties.

One result of the collapsing communism in Eastern Europe was the reunification of Germany. For almost three decades the Berlin Wall had stood as a symbol of the Cold War. But in early November 1989 it was opened by a re-

As East German border guards look on, a man pounds away at the Berlin Wall, November 1989.
(Reuters/Bettmann Newsphotos)

formist East German Communist government that, because of demonstrations, had recently replaced the hard-line government of Erich Honecker. Over a million East Germans visited West Berlin and West Germany in the first few days after the opening of the wall. After elections in March 1990 brought a non-Communist coalition to power, it agreed to reunification with West Germany, which came about in October under West Germany's Helmut Kohl, head of the Christian Democratic party.

WESTERN EUROPE, 1985–1991: ECONOMICS, POLITICS, AND THE COMMON MARKET

The general prosperity that characterized Europe before 1985 continued after that date, especially in Germany, Scandinavia, and Switzerland. Economic growth increased from 1984 through 1988, with 1988 registering the most growth in over a decade. Unemployment remained high, however, hovering around 11 percent in the Common Market nations during the same five-year period. From 1989 to 1991 economic growth slowed, with Great Britain's economy actually in recession in 1990 and 1991.

Many Western European nations faced economic problems similar to those in the United States. One concern was how to maintain high wages and extensive social services while remaining globally competitive and not increasing taxes. Throughout the postwar era, the trend was for governments to grow and to provide more and more services. By the late 1980s about one out of every five Western European workers was a government employee. "Big government" was especially the trend in the Scandinavian nations, where the welfare state was the most developed. As Western European populations aged and birthrates declined, however, the proportion of the population working, and thus taxable, diminished. Many governments found it increasingly difficult to raise sufficient revenues to fund services without raising taxes, and this in turn led to voter discontent.

Faced with increased public hostility, Western European governments, like the United States in the 1980s, began to reverse, or at least to slow down, the growth of the welfare state. This approach was most strongly pursued by Great Britain's prime minister, Margaret Thatcher, who in the early 1980s had said that what irritated her most about politics in the postwar era was its drift toward collectivism. In the years 1985 to 1990, this daughter of a prosperous grocer continued her "privatization" policies, selling government-owned enterprises such as utilities to private stockholders and deregulating areas like private housing. She weakened Great Britain's once powerful unions and tightened controls over health services and unemployment and welfare benefits. And she made many enemies in Great Britain's universities by refusing to allocate more funding and by enacting legislation restricting faculty tenure. But economic growth and relatively low inflation and unemployment (5.3 percent in 1989) helped keep the "iron lady," as she was called, in power.

In November 1990, after being in office longer than any other twentieth-century British prime minister, Thatcher resigned under pressure. A declining economy and her resistance to faster European Common Market integration weakened her, along with the perception that she was too arrogant and inflexible. She also appeared to be out of touch with the common people, especially after the Conservatives in 1990 replaced local property taxes with a violently unpopular poll (head) tax, in which each individual paid the same amount regardless of income. As one objector put it: "A millionaire will pay half as much as a pensioner couple." Thatcher was replaced as Conservative party leader and prime minister by Chancellor of the Exchequer John Major. At age forty-seven, this son of a circus performer was just the sort of self-made man that Thatcher liked to champion. After dropping out of school at sixteen, he made his way in the world of banking and politics.

If Thatcher represented the most noted case of chipping away at big government, she was not alone. In the late 1980s, Spain, Portugal, and France, despite having socialist heads of state, also sold some public enterprises to private owners. Spain's prime minister, Felipe Gonzalez, was accused by many of his former political allies of betraying the poor in his quest to stimulate economic growth. Presidents Mario Soares in Portugal and François Mitterrand in France were forced by political necessity to cooperate with prime ministers from other political parties who strongly pushed privatization. Even Sweden signaled its readiness to cut back on big government. In late 1991 it rejected the Social Democratic party that had governed for fifty-three of the previous fifty-nine years and had championed the welfare state. Sweden's new conservative government promised to privatize much state-owned industry and reduce tax burdens, which in the 1980s had been the highest in Western Europe.

Despite this movement to slow and even reverse the growth of some aspects of government, a broad consensus continued to exist in Western Europe that prevented any wholesale dismantling of the welfare state. Most European governments continued to provide more "cradle-to-grave" services than did the U.S. government.

Even before the collapse of communism in Eastern Europe, Western European Communist political parties were on the decline. Some Europeans thought communism less relevant in a Europe of high technology, consumerism, and a smaller percentage of blue-collar workers. After the fall of Eastern European communism, the Italian Communist party, Western Europe's strongest, tried harder than ever to distance itself from the failed communism of Eastern Europe and changed its name to the Democratic party of the Left.

While moderate socialist and conservative parties dominated Western European politics, there were some notable groups on the edges. Two issues especially seemed to mobilize votes for fringe parties—the environment and foreign workers and immigrants.

Environmental concerns attracted voters to Green parties. In 1987–1988 the Greens won 42 seats in the 520-member West German Federal Assembly (Bundestag) and 20 in the 349-member Swedish Parliament. Smaller Green parties also existed in many other Western European nations. Although environmental concerns were most prominent, Green parties also spoke out on other topics such as women's rights and fairer treatment for foreign workers.

At the same time, right-wing nationalist parties in West Germany, France, and other nations played upon increasing hostility to foreign workers and immigrants. Low population growth, expanding economies, and a willingness to turn undesirable jobs over to foreign workers had all brought many such la-borers to Western Europe. Nations had also allowed other types of immigra-tion. Although many "illegals" made it difficult to guess how many foreign workers lived in Western Europe, there were probably over 15 million in the 1980s. By 1988 almost a million black people and Asians lived in London, and incidents of racial conflict became more common. In German cities there were many Turkish and other foreign workers. In Frankfurt, Munich, and Stuttgart combined, about one in five residents was foreign. In France, there were many Africans and Asians. By the end of 1991 over 10 percent of the population had been born outside France. All these immigrants put additional pressure on government social services and the taxes that paid for them.

In the 1988 presidential contest in France, right-wing candidate Jean-Marie Le Pen blamed many of his nation's problems, such as crime and unemploy-ment, on foreign minorities. In West Germany, the Republican party, a new right-wing organization, played a similar tune and in local elections some-times did better than the Greens.

Concerns about immigrants were heightened from 1989 to 1991 by two pressing fears. The first was that Eastern European governments would ease restrictions on emigration, unleashing a new wave of immigrants into Western Europe. The second was that the end of frontier barriers among the nations of the European Community (EC), anticipated to take place by the beginning of 1993, would also make it easier for non-EC citizens to move about, legally or illegally, within the twelve-nation community. (Portugal and Spain joined the previous ten members in 1986.)

The breakdown of frontier barriers was just one of the plans and actions that EC members had made by 1991 to bring about the integration of Europe. In 1987 member nations ratified a treaty, the Single European Act, pledging to go beyond eliminating tariffs between them and to try by 1992 to remove a va-riety of other financial, commercial, and customs barriers that hampered the free flow of goods within the EC. The act also pointed to highly integrative goals such as a common currency and more unified social, foreign, and de-fense policies. In December 1991, at Maastricht in the Netherlands, EC nations reiterated these commitments and agreed upon new specifics, including a timetable for monetary union—not later than 1999, although some community nations might not immediately join. German Chancellor Helmut Kohl stated: "Maastricht stands as a decisive breakthrough for Europe." Mitterand of France declared: "We have created a European union."

Yet many roadblocks still stood in the way of true European political and economic unity. The Maastricht-amended EC constitution still had to be rati-fied by EC nations, and some leaders still maintained reservations about turn-ing over too much authority to EC officials.

Before leaving office in late 1990, Britain's Thatcher had been the main roadblock to further unity. In 1988 she warned of efforts to "suppress nation-hood and consolidate power at the center of a European conglomerate." She spoke out against a common currency and expressed fears that EC economic and social policies would once again encourage the type of governmental paternalism that her anti-welfare state policies had aimed at curbing. Although a less vocal critic of the EC, John Major obtained an agreement at Maastricht that Great Britain could decide later if it wished to adopt a common EC currency and would be exempted from the agreement signed by the other eleven nations to expand EC authority over economic and social issues like minimum wages.

Although the Maastricht meeting occurred after communism's collapse in eastern Europe, the question of EC policy toward newly non-Communist European nations received little attention at the meeting. After the fall of communism several nations in eastern Europe expressed an interest in joining the organization. Broadening European unity by opening up the EC to former Communist countries—which were "alarmingly dilapidated" in Mitterand's words—promised to be much more difficult than embracing more prosperous nations like Austria and Sweden, who also wanted to join. EC nations disagreed on how strongly to encourage eastern European aspirations.

A NEW EUROPE

By the end of 1991 it was clear that a new Europe had emerged, no longer divided by the Berlin Wall and an ideological Cold War. Despite the economic and other difficulties of grafting East Germany onto the more prosperous West Germany, a new and powerful Germany was rising in the middle of Europe. Its position in the EC and in Europe as a whole was stronger than West Germany's had been.

Although East Germans (and West Germans) were forced to make some sacrifices during their integration process, citizens in other former Communist countries faced an even more difficult transition. Moving from a Communist system to a democratic one with a market economy proved more painful than many had imagined. Long-neglected environmental problems also needed to be faced and competed with other needs for governmental spending. National differences, long suppressed under the Communists, came to the forefront in some countries like Yugoslavia and the former Soviet Union.

In some ways post-Cold War Europe resembled post-World War I Europe. New independent nations again emerged, hoping to become more democratic and prosperous. As after World War I, however, so after the post-Cold War, it was not immediately clear how nationalist and democratic aspirations would interact and fare in eastern Europe. Of the two, nationalism certainly had deeper roots in the region. In the 1991 elections to Poland's Sejm, only about 40 percent of the electorate voted, and they selected delegates from twenty-nine different parties, an unstable parliamentary situation.

Yet despite some similarities to the post-World War I era, Europe at the end of 1991 was far different in many ways. World War II and decades of technological, environmental, economic, social, and cultural changes had seen to that. Thus, the momentous political developments of 1985–1991 could lead to a restoration of some earlier nations, but not earlier times. Europe entered 1992 aware that it was facing a new era.

SUMMARY

From 1985 until the end of 1991, Europe changed in a way that few would have dared to believe possible in the mid-1980s. When Mikhail Gorbachev came to power as the Soviet leader in 1985, the Soviet economy was stagnating and pressures for reform were building. Gorbachev recognized the need for reforms and began pushing a whole series of domestic and foreign policies that soon gathered a momentum of their own. In less than seven years these policies and numerous other forces, especially popular political movements, led to the collapse of Communist governments in Soviet bloc states in Eastern Europe, the end of the Cold War, the reunification of Germany, and the collapse of the Soviet Union itself. Along the way, numerous important arms control treaties were signed with Western powers.

While the collapse of the forced unity of the Soviet empire was widely hailed by proponents of democracy, a difficult transition, often complicated by strong ethnic rivalries and occasionally armed conflict, was still underway by the end of 1991. Although not a part of the former Soviet bloc, Yugoslavia, split by civil war in late 1991, was an extreme example of where such rivalries could lead.

Although much more prosperous and stable than their fellow Europeans to the east, Western Europeans grappled with their own problems. Following the example of Britain's Margaret Thatcher, many of their government leaders attempted to curtail the growth of "big government." Leaders also sought methods to deal with rising hostility toward foreign workers and immigrants, and most Western European heads of state, especially within the twelve-member European Community, worked toward creating greater European economic and political unity.

SUGGESTED SOURCES

ARDAGH, JOHN, *Germany and the Germans,* rev. ed. (1991). A description of German life, including the reunification of East and West Germany.*

BLACK, CYRIL E. et al., *Rebirth: A History of Europe Since World War II* (1992). A good overview of Europe, western and eastern (including the Soviet Union), up through the end of 1991.

CARRÈRE ENCAUSSE, HÉLÈNE, *The End of the Soviet Empire* (1993). An explanation by a leading French expert of the forces leading to the collapse of the Soviet Empire.

DAWISHA, KAREN, *Eastern Europe, Gorbachev and Reform: The Great Challenge,* 2d ed. (1990). An excellent overview of the background leading up to the 1989–1990 overthrow of communism in Eastern Europe; deals with events up to the spring of 1990.*

GOLDMAN, MARSHALL I., *Gorbachev's Challenge: Economic Reform in the Age of High Technology* (1987). A good account of the economic problems facing Gorbachev in his first years in power.*

GOLDMAN, MINTON F., *Commonwealth of Independent States and Central/Eastern Europe,* 4th ed. (1992). A useful overview that surveys the effects of the changes of 1989–1991, plus twenty-six 1991–1992 articles from the world press; part of the annual Global Studies Series.*

GORBACHEV, M. G., *Perestroika: New Thinking for Our Nation and the World* (1987). An elaboration of some of the major ideas of the Soviet leader during his early years in power.*

HOSKING, GEOFFREY A., PETER DUNCAN, and JONATHAN AVES, Eds., *The Road to Post-Communism: Independent Political Movements in the Former Soviet Union, 1985–1991* (1992). A valuable guide to the groups, personalities, and aims that comprised the independent political movement.*

GWERTZMAN, BERNARD, and MICHAEL T. KAUFMAN, Eds., *The Collapse of Communism*, rev. ed. (1991). A collection of articles from the correspondents of the *New York Times*, covering Eastern Europe and the Soviet Union from the winter of 1988–1989 through August 1991.*

KAISER, ROBERT, *Why Gorbachev Happened: His Triumphs, His Failure and His Fall* (1992). An examination of Gorbachev and Soviet life under him by a former correspondent stationed in Moscow; contains a convenient and detailed chronology of events from 1985 to 1991.*

SMITH, HEDRICK, *The New Russians* (1991). A perceptive look at Russian life under Gorbachev by another former correspondent; deals with events up to the early fall of 1991.*

SWANN, DENNIS, *The Economics of the Common Market*, 6th ed. (1988). A good overview; the most recent printing contains some post-1988 information.*

YELTSIN, BORIS, *Against the Grain: An Autobiography* (1990). A book that offers some revealing insights into one of Gorbachev's chief political rivals, the hero of the anti-coup forces of August 1991 and independent Russia's first president.

YOUNG, HUGO, *The Iron Lady: A Biography of Margaret Thatcher* (1990). A long and insightful work that relates the life and policies of one of Europe's most important postwar politicians.

*Paperback available.

CHAPTER 34

Postscript to a Changing Century

SCIENCE AND TECHNOLOGY

As the world approaches the end of the twentieth century, the five interrelated issues important in 1900 are still major factors around the globe. By 1992 scientists were probing deep into space in search of intelligent life on planets in other galaxies. Although these odysseys are far cries from the thirty-minute flights of the Wright brothers' experiments, they indicate humanity's continuing quest to conquer space and time. The communications revolution has swept the world, and car phones are as popular in Riyadh, Saudi Arabia, as in Detroit, Michigan.

Despite these achievements, contemporary societies face the paradox that while technology offers the possibility of incredible advances, there is a growing threat to the continued existence of life on earth. At the same time that scientists like Professor Stephen Hawking at Cambridge University in the United Kingdom might be close to explaining the creation of the universe, major human-induced ecological crises such a global warming (the greenhouse effect) and the depletion of the ozone layer (thought to be largely caused by carbon dioxide pollutants) seem to defy easy solutions. One U.S. senator summed up the feeling of many when he remarked, "We only have one planet. If we screw it up we have no place to go."

Developments in public health demonstrate another facet of this ambiguity. Although scientific and technological achievements in medicine have benefited millions, they still have not conquered a host of old and new problems. For example, diphtheria, the scourge of the early twentieth century, has been virtually eradicated, but a new virulent plague, AIDS, has spread around the world. Diseases such as tuberculosis, which had seemed almost extinct, have returned in new, more virulent strains.

In 1992 hundreds of representatives from around the world attended the much publicized "Earth Summit" at Rio de Janeiro in Brazil, called in hopes of mobilizing a world consensus on how to deal with the mounting degradation

An African child receives immunization against disease. Although health care has improved in much of the world, many children in the Third World and even in the United States still do not receive even such basic medical care.
(*Joe Loya, Save the Children*)

of the global environment. The meeting revealed sharp disagreements concerning the nature of and the solutions to this problem. Although many European and small, poor nations sought to enact stringent and far-reaching environmental protection regulations, the United States (which has about 5 percent of the world population but accounts for 25 percent of the world's GNP, consumes 25 percent of the world's energy units, and produces 32 percent of carbon dioxide emissions) joined with a number of other nations in opposing any regulations that might threaten their lifestyles or place further drains on their shaky economies. In a different split, the Northern Hemisphere, with a preponderance of technologically advanced and wealthy nations, backed such ecological issues as preserving virgin forests, protecting endangered species, and limiting population growth. These measures were often opposed for economic and cultural reasons by many poor and rural nations in the Southern Hemisphere. On a more positive note, attending nations agreed, for the first time in history, to take global environmental concerns into account when formulating domestic economic policies. Whether these decisions will result in a cleaner and safer global environment remains to be seen.

Increased technological sophistication has also contributed to the development of more deadly weapons that now have the capability of destroying life on the earth. Although the end of the Cold War diminished the likelihood of a nuclear confrontation between the United States and the Soviet Union/Russia, regional conflicts continue to pose a danger of escalating into nuclear warfare. Nuclear proliferation is yet another danger as nation after nation, from France to China to India, has developed nuclear capabilities. By the early 1990s about thirty nations had the capability to produce atomic weapons. As manifested throughout the century, the destructive potential of modern weapons often seems to exceed human abilities to control or to limit their use and proliferation. On the other hand, the 1993 START II missile reduction treaty banning landbased long-range missiles with multiple warheads provided for a two-thirds reduction in U.S. and Russian stockpiles of these fearsome weapons. However, three former Soviet republics where some of these weapons were still deployed did not sign the international accord.

In addition, humans have developed skills and knowledge in the scientific and technological fields so rapidly that societies have been unable to absorb or to understand their impact. As a result, political and social institutions have frequently failed to deal effectively with the impact of twentieth-century technology.

For many nations, the highly sophisticated technology of the industrial world is inappropriate to their social and economic needs. Early in the century, Mohandas Gandhi advocated the use of labor-intensive pragmatic approaches in rural areas. Faced with hard economic and ecological choices, many poor and even industrialized nations are recognizing the validity of Gandhi's approach. Traditional irrigation schemes are being revitalized, and labor, a surplus commodity in much of the Third World, is being used instead of machinery. Architects such as the late Hasan Fathi from Egypt have advocated the revival of age-old earthern and mud architecture to provide inexpensive yet artistically pleasing housing for the poor around much of the world. The use of mud architecture has also been adopted by some wealthy homeowners in parts of the southwestern United States and in Europe.

While modern science and technology may well possess the ability to control and to solve the most pressing problems, many societies may lack the resources, will, and determination to finance or to implement the solutions. How to cope with and, perhaps, how to resolve these paradoxes remain the greatest challenges of science and technology.

ECONOMIC TRENDS

The famine in India at the beginning of the century was caused by problems in food production and distribution, politics, and economics. So, too, in the 1990s, are famines devastating Somalia and threatening Sudan, Mozambique, and other African nations, the result of a complex web of interrelated issues. As the twentieth century draws to a close, struggles for economic power remain one of the most divisive factors in world affairs.

Economic differences between the affluent "North," (Europe, North America, and Japan) and the poor "South," (Africa, Latin America, most of the Middle East, and Asia) continue. Because of rapid economic and technical growth in the developed world, the gap continues to widen between the rich North with access to and control of modern technology and the poor South with outdated and poorly developed agricultural and industrial systems. On the positive side, by the early 1990s, India, in spite of its burgeoning population growth, successfully continued to apply the technology of the green revolution to increase its agricultural productivity, thereby eradicating the famines of the past. Unfortunately, the technological promise of the green revolution seems to work best in temperate climates and has yet to be applied in most of Africa or South America. Thus about 1.2 billion people in the South or in poor nations live in poverty with average per capita incomes of less than $800 as compared to a $2,500 per capita income in eastern Europe and the former Soviet Union or to over $6,000 in the rich nations.

Importantly, ever-increasing populations literally eat up the economic gains made by many poor nations. The world population is expected to reach 6 billion by 1998 and to double by the middle of the twenty-first century. Although by 1992, fertility in China, India, and a dozen other developing nations had declined by nearly two-thirds, the fact that their large populations were mostly young indicates considerable population growth in the future even with stringent birth control. In 1992, the Indian government announced a new birth control vaccine that it hoped would limit population growth.

In 1992 the rich, technologically advanced nations also face a host of economic problems. The socialist economies in Eastern Europe and the former Soviet Union have collapsed, ending the competition between the Marxist world and the so-called free-enterprise economies that had characterized the Cold War. Nevertheless, Western Europe, the United States, and the Asian Rim nations dominated by Japan continue to compete with one another for larger shares of the global markets in a manner similar to that of imperial colonial systems in 1900. By 1993 the European Common Market, a trading bloc of 338 million people, had lowered many barriers to the free movement of goods and services and formed a major competitive force against Japan and the western hemisphere.

In former Soviet-dominated eastern Europe, the transition from a Communist to a market economy has not been an easy one. In Poland, for example, a scarcity of banks, computers, adequate communication systems, training personnel and an inherited foreign debt, all made the changeover difficult. High inflation, rising unemployment and crime, declining production, and a huge government budget deficit resulted. Privatization, often supported by the International Monetary Fund, moved more slowly than anticipated, and many former Communist officials found ways to enrich themselves. Yet despite these problems, Poland was better positioned to make the transition to a modern market economy than were most other Eastern European nations.

Meanwhile, around the rest of the world, the gap between rich and poor nations has persisted and widened. The basic problem of the unequal distribution of wealth remains unsolved, and many nations remain trapped in a cycle of poverty while a few industrialized nations continue to prosper. The world continues to face interlocking economic and environmental problems that only international cooperation can begin to solve. The problems of hunger, poverty, population growth, military expenditures, and unequal distribution of wealth are all related. How and whether national governments and multinational organizations will move to resolve these problems remains uncertain.

SOCIAL AND POLITICAL TRENDS

Just as Emma Goldman and her allies in the early twentieth century had a vision about what sort of societies they wished to create, so too do women, racial and ethnic minorities and indigenous peoples, homosexuals, and other activist groups and individuals continue to seek sweeping political and social changes that will bring a full measure of citizens' rights. A prime example is Rigoberta Menchú, the 1992 recipient of the Nobel Prize for Peace. In the words of the Nobel Committee, Menchú "stands out as a vivid symbol of peace and reconciliation across ethnic, cultural, and social dividing lines." Given out on the 500th anniversary of the landing of Christopher Columbus, the award indicated growing awareness of the historical plight of the indigenous people of the Western Hemisphere. Menchú's courageous struggle for the rights of indigenous people, for women, and for better economic and political conditions for the downtrodden echo those of Emma Goldman at the beginning of the century.

Whereas almost no women could vote in 1900, by the early 1990s they had been enfranchised in almost all countries where elections take place. However, women continue to struggle for equality around the world. Estimates in the 1990s indicate that women do about two-thirds of the work of the world and produce about 45 percent of the world's food, but receive only 10 percent of the world's income. Women's work is often undervalued, unpaid, or underpaid. Likewise, children are often considered a source of free or cheap labor and lack basic legal or social protections. In many Western nations, working mothers have become the norm; many families rely on two incomes in order to survive. Many other women are the sole providers for one-parent households. The constantly changing structure of family life has become a major political and social issue of the late twentieth century.

The struggle between liberal and conservative forces also continues to characterize political life in Western nations. Throughout the twentieth century, the political pendulum in the United States has swung back and forth between the Left and the Right. For example, during the 1980s the Right predominated, but the 1992 election of Democrat Bill Clinton seemed to indicate a swing back toward the center. The reunification of Germany also contributed to a revival in

1992 of right-wing German nationalism and attacks against minorities and recent immigrants. However, many Germans publicly protested racist movements in huge, silent candlelight vigils held throughout the country.

The end of the Cold War and the collapse of the Soviet Union seemed to unleash a drive for democracy around the world. Open elections were held in many eastern European nations for the first time since the 1930s. Many African nations liberalized their political systems, but steps toward democracy were often impeded by military or government interference. For example, the election campaign in Kenya was relatively free of government repression, but the reelection of Daniel Arap Moi was hotly contested amid charges of corruption and election fraud. Similarly, elections in Algeria were postponed when it became clear that free elections would result in a victory for Islamist forces. In 1992, Brazil, for the first time in its history, used constitutional means to remove a president from office as opposed to the frequent military *golpes* of the past. Freely held elections in Argentina, Brazil, Chile, and other Latin American nations reinforced the move against military dictatorship and toward the creation of workable, albeit fragile, democracies. Although authoritarian and dictatorial regimes remained in power in China, in most of the Middle East and elsewhere, democratic forces were organizing everywhere and working to gain support and strength.

Just as unsatisfied national aspirations of ethnic groups destabilized the world in the early part of the twentieth century, so too in the early 1990s they threaten the cohesion of existing nation-states and cause armed conflicts around the world. The end of Soviet domination led to the revival of old ethnic hatreds and rivalries which often exploded into open warfare in former Soviet republics, especially in the Caucasus. With the collapse of Soviet hegemony over eastern Europe, new or resurrected nations like Estonia, Latvia, and the Ukraine appeared, just as they had earlier emerged from the ashes of the Russian, Austro-Hungarian, and German empires. Democratic ideals were once again endorsed, but it was not immediately clear how nationalist and democratic aspirations would interact in the former Soviet republics or in eastern Europe.

At the same time that the Soviet Union split into many parts, so too did Czechoslovakia and Yugoslavia move toward dissolution. At the beginning of 1993, Czechoslovakia ceased to exist as a unified nation and split into two separate entities. In Yugoslavia earlier Macedonian, Slovenian, and Croatian independence movements (the latter itself somewhat bloody) were followed by carnage among Serbs, Croats, and Muslims in Bosnia. The limited intervention of European and U.N. forces failed to stop the fighting. Similarly, ethnic national aspirations of the Kurds in Iran, Iraq, and Turkey, ethnic groups in the southern Sudan, and the Tamils in Sri Lanka threatened the continued unity of those nations. By the 1990s dozens of ethnic conflicts threatened the continued existence of many nations, and it seemed likely that by the end of the century many new nations would emerge out of violent confrontations. Palestinians and black South Africans continue to fight for national self-determination; by late 1993 the Israelis and Palestinians had negotiated a partial settlement of their long-standing conflict.

INTERNATIONAL RELATIONS

At the beginning of the twentieth century, the Boxer Rebellion demonstrated both the complexities of international relations and the desire of powerful nations to dominate or dictate to small or weak states. Toward the end of this century, the complex forces of nationalism and economics sometimes seem to foster international cooperation; at other times these same forces contribute to political strife and armed intervention to protect economic and national self-interests. The 1991 Gulf War demonstrated not only national rivalries for control of territory and resources among Middle Eastern governments but the willingness of most of the international community, led by the United States, to protect economic (in this case petroleum) interests by armed intervention.

The creation of an international military coalition of many nations during the 1991 Gulf War was in stark contrast to the armed intervention by single nations that was so common in former eras. The collapse of the Soviet Union, the emergence of new nations, the mounting power of multinational corporations and the petroleum-producing nations, the economic might of Japan, and the growing strength of China have all diminished any one nation's ability to control global affairs. Although the United States retains a clear-cut military supremacy and sometimes interferes directly in small nations in the Caribbean such as Grenada and Panama, it lacks the economic power and political influence to implement long-term interventions elsewhere in the world without international support.

Increasingly, national leaders have come to realize that the scope of many of the major problems facing their societies necessitates international cooperation. No one nation can solve the environmental crises caused by industrialization and overpopulation. No one nation can institute effective legislation to regulate multinational corporations, and no one nation can resolve the complex problems of inflation, indebtedness, and scarcity. In the twentieth century, nations must work together on global problems that threaten the quality of life everywhere. Ironically, many of these problems—abuses of multinational corporations, pollution, the arms race—are so huge and so complex that individuals despair of understanding or solving them and find solace in alliances with nationalistic loyalties. Thus, at the very time that fruitful international relationships are more vital than ever before, there is also an opposing tendency in much of the world toward commitment to nationalistic loyalties based on ethnic and regional identities.

The results of the referendums for approval of the Maastricht treaty, which provides for the further integration of European national economic and political systems, demonstrate the conflict between those who favor further supranational integration and those who are fearful of losing too much national sovereignty. In 1992 Danish voters rejected the treaty but accepted a revised version in May 1993. The German population favored the treaty while French voters only approved by a slim margin. The British government and public postponed final consideration of it until after the second Danish vote. Moves toward economic integration of a common market in the Western

Hemisphere have raised similar national concerns in the United States, Mexico, and Canada.

With the end of the Cold War, the United Nations has been called upon to shoulder increasing burdens in stopping, controlling, and policing disputes among ethnic and political enemies in places as far apart as Somalia, Bosnia, Cambodia, and Cyprus. In 1992 U.N. Secretary-General Boutros Boutros-Ghali called on the nations of the world to form regional peacekeeping forces, to create an "early warning" system for threats to peace, to support a joint military staff committee, and to increase their financial support for the United Nations. As the U.N. is called upon to send troops and observers to more and more "trouble spots" around the globe, its already slender financial resources have been severely strained. If the United Nations is to be a major force in ending regional conflicts and overseeing peacekeeping efforts, individual nations will have to increase their financial and military contributions to the international organization. Many nations, particularly the United States, remain reluctant to cede national interests to the United Nations or any another international organization. However, as Dag Hammarskjold, a former U.N. secretary-general, once observed, "The United Nations was created not to bring mankind to heaven, but to save it from hell."

CULTURAL TRENDS

In 1988, the grand old man of Egyptian literature, Naguib Mahfouz, received the Nobel Prize for Literature. Unaware that he had even been nominated, Mahfouz stressed that he was only one of many meritorious Arab writers. Like Nietzsche nearly a century before, Mahfouz had often been criticized by conservatives for his harsh depictions of modern life and his secular approaches to sex and family life. Mahfouz received death threats from Islamist groups and leaders from al-Azhar, the famous Islamic university, publicly complained about his work. Similarly, Christian fundamentalists in the West have urged the banning of some rock and rap videos and the censorship of films, records, and art exhibitions.

During the later decades of the twentieth century, disillusionment and fear over the uncertainties created by the modern technological age caused many to turn toward spiritual goals. Muslim, Christian, Hindu, and Jewish communities have all experienced a resurgence of religious fervor and sometimes of religious fanaticism. To some extent, the growth of militant and fundamentalist religion has been precipitated by the failure of secular societies to solve human problems.

In the twentieth century, scientific and political changes have occurred at a dizzying pace. As a result, all societies have experienced some form of "culture shock." These changes, first apparent in the industrialized nations, have spread throughout the world. Initially, Western societies eagerly embraced the changes that seemed to offer an opportunity for unlimited progress. Western artists explored revolutionary dramatic, literary, and artistic styles, and many people experimented with totally new and unconventional lifestyles. By the 1990s some conservative forces in the Western world had reacted against new, experimental artistic and cultural expressions by advocating stricter legal and governmental regulations of the arts and nonconventional lifestyles.

The effects of technology and Western modes of life have been particularly traumatic in traditional societies. Although most societies have embraced the use of manufactured goods which offer immediate improvements in daily life—refrigerators, radios, trucks—modernization has often meant Westernization, which has entailed the loss of long-held values and beliefs. Some traditional societies have refused to give up their own institutions and beliefs for new Western ways that seem to them not only foreign but also highly undesirable.

Thus, in many traditional societies, and ultimately in the West as well, attempts have been made to balance the uncertainties of modern existence by returning to traditional values. By the closing decade of the twentieth century, two contradictory cultural trends are apparent. On one hand, there is a movement toward continued change and experimentation; on the other, there is a growing trend toward the return to conservative, traditional ways. The resurgence of militant Islam throughout the Middle East—most notably in the Iranian revolution—is just one evidence of this trend. Many organized religious movements have recently experienced an increase in adherents throughout the world, and many groups have begun openly to question the value of the cultural and societal changes that occurred in previous decades.

In the social, cultural, and economic arenas, many traditional methods are also being revitalized. Artists around the globe are infusing their work with old cultural designs, music, and themes to produce new artistic expressions. The 1992 Nobel Prize winner in literature, Derek Walcott, has been referred to as "the laureate of multiculturalism." A citizen of the newly independent West Indian nation of St. Lucia, Walcott, multiracial in ancestry, loves English, the language of St. Lucia's colonial government. Walcott writes plays and poems that depict the black-dominated culture of the West Indies; his book-length epic poem, *Omerose* (1990) depicts the sweep of Western history from the days of Homer to the present, casting Homeric figures, for example, as fishermen and waitresses.

All societies, Western and traditional, have been irrevocably altered by the political, military, and scientific changes of the twentieth century. Societies that wish to maintain their traditional values must still deal with the problems of incorporating technical advances and changes within older, established institutions. Many societies continue to debate the social, cultural, and political roles of women and the family. What direction world societies will take remains one of the most perplexing and difficult problems of the century. By the early 1990s the observation of historian Eric Hobsbawm serves as a guidepost for the future: "The only certain thing about the future is that it will surprise even those who have seen furthest into it."

SUGGESTED SOURCES

A Brief History of Time (1992). Film version of Stephen Hawking's best-selling book on the origin of the universe; a moving film about Hawking's remarkable scientific investigations and long struggle with amyotrophic lateral sclerosis (Lou Gehrig's disease).

CHOMSKY, NOAM, *Deterring Democracy* (1992). Discussion by a leading dissident intellectual of shifting power alliances in the aftermath of the Cold War.*

FRENCH, MARILYN, *The War Against Women.* (1992). Sober analysis regarding economic and cultural status of women around the contemporary world.

Great Decisions. (1993). PBS eight-part television series focusing on central issues including the post-Cold War role of the United States, the United Nations, Russia and the Central Asian Republics, India and Pakistan, and problems facing children around the world.

HARRISS, JOHN, *The Family: A Social History of the Twentieth Century* (1991). Part of the Oxford series on social, cultural, and scientific developments, with lavish illustrations.

KENNEDY, PAUL, *Preparing for the Twenty-First Century* (1993). Careful analysis of challenges facing nations and societies in the contemporary world.

LUNDESTAG, GEIR, and ODD ARNE WESTAD, Eds., *Beyond the Cold War: Future Dimensions in International Relations* (1993). Scholarly discussion of future problems, including human rights, international debt, environmental crises.

REICH, ROBERT B., *The Work of Nations: Preparing Ourselves for 21st-Century Capitalism* (1992). A readable explanation of how the global economy has developed and its implications for the future.*

SEGAL, GERALD, *The World Affairs Companion: The Essential One-Volume Guide to Global Issues* (1991). A clear and comprehensive overview.*

*Paperback available.

World Geography

INTRODUCTION

The history of every nation has been and is, to a great extent, determined by its geography. Physical geography considers the patterns of landforms, climate, soils, and other natural factors that form the setting for human activities and often impose limitations on them. Cultural geography studies population, urbanization, and the significance of languages, religions, and settlement, among other phenomena, in creating the human mosaic. Finally, economic geography concerns itself with the ways in which people pursue their livelihoods. Patterns of agricultural and industrial development, resource utilization, differences in wealth and poverty, trade and transportation, and environmental impacts are analyzed with a view to understanding the complex human struggle for economic advancement, or perhaps only survival. In the following section, the world's major geographical regions are briefly summarized, with particular attention to their economic development, population growth, and changes in resource utilization.

THE WORLD POPULATION

There were approximately 1.6 billion people on the earth in the year 1900, and about two-thirds lived in Asia, which, including European Russia, accounted for about one-third of the earth's land surface. Europe contained the next largest population with nearly 400 million people. By comparison, the other land areas were sparsely populated, with 81 million in the United States and Canada, 63 million in Central and South America, 118 million in Africa, and only 6 million in Australasia and Oceania. Antarctica was (and remains) an unpopulated land. Every continent contained large areas unsuitable to human habitation because of extreme heat or cold, too much or too little rain, infertile soils, and high altitudes. As a result, approximately 90 percent of the people lived (and still live) on less than 10 percent of the land. Thanks to medical and technological advances, world population in 1990 stood at 5.3 billion, and at the current rate of increase, there will be 6.1 billion by the year 2000.

ASIA

This is the largest continent and is by far the larger part of the Eurasian land mass.

Japan

Japan lies on the eastern extremity of Asia. It is an island nation the size of California, and in 1900 had approximately 40 million people. Only 16 percent of the land was arable, and agriculture was labor-intensive. Rice was the main crop, with other cereals, tea, and mulberry for silkworms as secondary crops. As a result of government intervention and encouragement, Japan developed a core of basic and light industries. These industries were fueled by a very limited coal supply and later by abundant hydroelectricity from harnessed mountain streams. Japan lacked industrial resources and had to depend on importing raw materials and exporting manufactured products for survival. In 1900, it was the only Asian nation to have industrialized successfully and its people enjoyed the highest standard of living in Asia. Today Japan is an industrial giant that enjoys the second highest gross national product (GNP) among all nations and continues to maintain the highest standard of living in Asia and one of the highest in the world. Tokyo, the capital of Japan, vies with Shanghai in China as one of the most populous cities in the world, with about 12 million people.

China

China lies to the west of Japan. It is a giant nation in size, and in 1900 was the most populous in the world, with over 400 million people. However, most of China was unsuitable for habitation. Great mountains rim its northwest. Mount Everest, highest peak of the towering Himalayan Mountains, bestrides its southwestern border. Its northern frontier is rimmed by the Gobi and Karakorum deserts, an area inhabited by Mongol and Turkic nomadic tribes. However, following the construction of railroads, sedentary farmers from farther south steadily encroached on the old pastures of the nomads, causing friction.

Only 10 percent of the land in China was arable; most of this lay along the Yellow and Yangtze River valleys and near the coast. Over 80 percent of the population lived on this farmland and, as elsewhere in Asia, were mostly subsistence farmers. In the cool, dry north, farmers grew wheat and other cereals. In the warmer and wetter south, rice was the main crop, and double- and triple-cropping allowed more food to be harvested from tiny farms. The diet of most Chinese was protein-poor, the result of poverty and lack of grazing land. The main source of meat was the pig, a scavenging animal. Extreme changes in weather brought floods and famine, the endemic scourge of Chinese agriculture. Farmers sometimes owned their own land but often rented. Because of the custom of equal division of land among all male heirs, there were few large estates in China. The nation had significant deposits of coal and iron ore, but in 1900 China had few modern industries and railroads, and those were mostly owned and developed by foreign nations.

Today, the People's Republic of China remains an economically underdeveloped nation. Extensive petroleum deposits have been discovered. Now, as then, about 80 percent of the population remains rural (the total population has risen to over 1.1 billion). Agriculture was collectivized around 1950 but has returned to individual cultivation; it is still essentially unmechanized. Despite water conservancy works, floods and droughts still wrack the land periodically. Industrialization lags because of a lack of capital and constraints placed by the Communist system.

India

India constitutes another great geographical entity in Asia. It is a self-contained subcontinent, rimmed on the north by the Himalayan and the Hindu Kush ranges, south of which stretch the great Ganges-Brahmaputra and Indus valleys. Low-lying mountains and plateaus, flanked by coastal plains, cover central and southern India. Monsoon winds demarcate the seasons and provide rainfall critical to agriculture.

In 1900 about 30 percent of the land was arable, and it was sown with rice, wheat, other cereals, cotton, tea, and sugarcane. Most Indian farmers, whether tenant or landholder, were poor, illiterate, and debt-ridden. Most were vegetarian, because of poverty or religious prohibitions. Oxen were the chief draft animals, but many of the cattle roaming the Indian countryside and cities were "holy cows" and made little economic contribution. India had a few modern industries, mostly textile mills in Bombay and Calcutta. A system of British-built trunk roads and railroads linked the various sections of the subcontinent.

Today, there are three major nations on the subcontinent, namely, India, Pakistan, and Bangladesh. Despite ambitious economic plans, foreign aid, and local efforts, each nation remains poor and underdeveloped. All suffer from rapidly increasing populations that have defied sporadic efforts at control. Thus, increased production from irrigation projects and the Green Revolution (which introduced disease-resistant hybrid strains of grain and other crops that depend on chemical fertilizers and pesticides for their high yield) have not raised the standard of living. To date, no large petroleum deposits have been found. As a result, all three nations are heavily dependent on petroleum imports and have suffered acutely from the high cost of energy.

Southeast Asia

Southeast Asia contains two regions, the Indochinese peninsula, consisting of Vietnam, Laos, Cambodia, Malaysia, Thailand, and Burma; and the two island groups of Indonesia and the Philippines. Accessibility from the sea makes water rather than land the primary means of transportation within the area and has made the area open to outside influence in times ancient and modern. There is also great similarity in the topography and climate of Southeast Asia. The climate is either equatorial or tropical monsoon, with abundant rainfall. As a result, living patterns tend to be similar. In 1900 most people were farmers. Rice was generally the main crop and was tended by human hands, not machines. After the late nineteenth century, with Western capital and management, large areas were opened to plantation farming, most notably rubber in Malaya and Vietnam, tea and coffee in Java (an island of Indonesia), and sugarcane in Java and the Philippines. Many of the plantations depended on Chinese or Indian labor, as did newly opened mines, such as the tin mines in Malaya.

Today, Southeast Asia suffers from rapid population increases which have resulted in intense pressure on the land. Virgin forests are being destroyed at a rapid rate for timber and to provide cropland without regard to ecological results. Although the Green Revolution has helped to increase yields, it has also squeezed out small farmers who cannot afford the improvements. The dispossessed have flocked to cities and created huge slums of unemployed. Industrialization has come too slowly to absorb the large reservoir of workers. Malaysia, with a small population and abundant resources, is relatively well off. Indonesia, with major petroleum deposits, is also reasonably prosperous. Political and economic mismanagement mire the economies of the Philippines, Burma, and Vietnam.

The Middle East

The Middle East, or Southwest Asia, forms a unit because of similarities in geography and the religion of the majority of the people. Except for coastal plains, river valleys, and oases, the area tends to be arid, with much desert. Mountainous terrain dominates large parts of Persia (Iran) and Turkey and all of Afghanistan.

While in 1900 the majority of the people were farmers and village dwellers, a minority were, and remain, nomadic. In Persia and Afghanistan, the tribes followed their herds up and down the mountain slopes in a vertical migration pattern. They and their sedentary village neighbors wove colorful rugs, each tribe or village with its own distinctive pattern. Nomads called Bedouins lived in the dry plains and desert lands. They herded sheep, horses, and especially camels. Each group followed strictly defined migration routes; violations resulted in tribal wars. Nomads traded their animals to villagers for agricultural products.

Today, as a result of the discovery of large petroleum deposits, the Middle East has become an important region economically and strategically. Petroleum has made Iraq, Saudi Arabia, Iran, Kuwait, and other Persian Gulf states very prosperous. Their per capita income in some cases exceeds that of advanced Western nations. Lack of petroleum keeps the remaining nations poor. Large sums of petroleum revenue have been spent by Iran and Saudi Arabia for modernization.

AFRICA

Africa is physically dominated by plateaus and low tablelands. Such large river systems as the Nile, Congo, Niger, and Zambezi drain parts of the continent, but only parts of each of these rivers are navigable. Rainfall is sparse in the north and south and very abundant in the equatorial zones. The continent has played a subordinate role in the modern commercial world and, with few exceptions, remains underdeveloped.

North Africa

North Africa is arid, except for a relatively narrow strip along the coast and the Nile Valley, where there is adequate moisture from rainfall or irrigation for agriculture. In 1900 North Africa, where both native Arabs and Europeans lived, was the most urbanized part of the continent. There were many good harbors: Alexandria, Tripoli, and Algiers, for example. The economy was a mixture of the old and the new, represented by native subsistence farms and European-organized plantations for such crops as cotton and grapes. A few nomads roamed the marginal dry lands.

Today, the European-controlled plantations are gone, although the land continues to be used for food products. Modern industries are still of minor importance because the region lacks most of the resources necessary for developing manufacturing complexes. The Aswan High Dam has brought more acreage into cultivation along the Nile. Egypt has a huge population and little petroleum, while Libya and Algeria have huge petroleum and natural gas reserves and small populations.

West Africa

West Africa's interior is linked by rivers, but the long coastline lacks good ports. With abundant rainfall, much of the area is suitable for tropical crops, and a reliable local labor supply made possible the development of cacao, palm oil, rubber, coconut, and cotton plantations, under European domination, in the late nineteenth and early twentieth centuries. Europeans also opened up tin, gold, bauxite, and other mines in the interior. Despite commercialization, many local peoples, especially in the interior, remained primitive subsistence farmers. Sleeping sickness and river blindness carried by the tsetse fly and mosquito made herding and farming difficult. No Europeans settled in the area.

Today, continued demand for tropical products by the outside world has maintained the economy of the area. Mining has become important in Zaire, and the petroleum discovered in Nigeria has made it a rich nation. However, the general dependence of West Africa on exports makes it a victim of world economic vicissitudes.

East Africa

East Africa from Ethiopia in the north to Tanganyika (Tanzania) in the south has no uniform topography but forms a distinctive unit because it possesses the most favorable conditions in tropical Africa for human habitation and successful agriculture. Much is highland between 3,000 and 6,000 feet in elevation with a temperate climate. Coastal East Africa has long been known to Arabs, Indians, Chinese, and Europeans and was important through most of the nineteenth century for the export of gold, ivory, spices, and slaves.

In the late nineteenth century, British and German colonists found the area inhabited by indigenous black subsistence farmers who were dominated by Bantu herders and farmers. European settlers introduced commercial agriculture that produced sugar, coffee, tea, and tobacco. Indian laborers developed roads and railroads, and many stayed to become retailers and professional people. While some black East Africans became plantation workers, most remained herders and farmers.

Today, Kenya and Tanzania are relatively prosperous because of continued development brought about by local efforts and foreign aid. Wars, civil disturbances, and drought have all but ruined the economies of Ethiopia, Somalia, and Uganda.

Southern Africa

Southern Africa was modified by Europeans more than any other part of the continent. It attracted European settlers because of its equable climate and land suitable to European-style farming and grazing. It was also populated sparsely by peoples of a simple culture who were easy to subdue. By 1900 Europeans had spread from South Africa to the Rhodesias (Zambia and Zimbabwe). The discovery of gold and diamonds made the area rich and glamorous.

Today, South Africa, together with Russia, mines most of the world's gold and diamonds. Together with Namibia (formerly Southwest Africa), it is also rich in silver, uranium, copper, and a host of other minerals. South Africa also has huge coal reserves. Thus, it is the wealthiest and most advanced African nation, with extensive modern mining and manufacturing centers and large cities.

EUROPE

Europe is situated on the western tip of the Eurasian land mass. Its coastal location and the belt of prevailing westerly winds give much of Europe a temperate climate and sufficient rain. However, Eastern Europe suffers from the extremes of heat and cold typical of continental climates, while the Mediterranean basin has a dry summer climate.

There are no deserts. Even the highest mountain ranges, such as the Alps, the Pyrenees, and the Carpathians, are relatively minor barriers compared with the Himalayas in Asia and the Rockies and Andes in North and South America. The Danube and Rhine rivers, flowing into the Black Sea and Atlantic Ocean respectively, dominate the central and western portions of the continent. In 1900 Europe, along with the United States, had undisputed leadership in the world economy, including an almost monopolistic position in manufacturing: It supplied most of the world with machine-made goods and commanded most of its trade. Western Europe was the most advanced part of the continent.

Great Britain

In 1900 Great Britain was the leading economic power. The Industrial Revolution began in England in the eighteenth century; it was made possible by water power in Lancashire and Yorkshire, and coal mines in the Midlands and south Wales. Dominance of the seas permitted Great Britain to colonize and trade around the world and to bring food and raw materials from many lands. Great Britain became a global investor nation, and London became the financial center of the world.

Today, Great Britain has lost its preeminent position. The growing industrial might of the United States, Germany, Japan, and others have deprived Great Britain of old markets. It has lost its empire and investments, its industrial plants are outmoded, and its labor and management practices are antiquated. One bright spot is that with its North Sea petroleum wells flowing, Great Britain is again energy self-sufficient.

France

France is the largest nation in Europe after Russia and Ukraine, about four-fifths the size of Texas. With frontage on both the Atlantic Ocean and the Mediterranean Sea, it has long been a link between nations of the Mediterranean and northern Europe.

Since the early nineteenth century, France has had a fairly stable and slow-growing population and so has avoided the problems of overpopulation. This stability has been a disadvantage in France's effort to maintain its position in Europe because the populations of Great Britain, Germany, and Italy increased at a faster rate.

French agriculture enjoyed a strong tradition. France was one of the first nations to adopt modern farming practices in the nineteenth century, and these methods proved so successful that French farmers were reluctant to leave their farms for factories or to adopt twentieth-century practices. Unlike Great Britain, France was self-sufficient in its basic food needs.

In 1900 France lacked major iron ore deposits (the Lorraine ore fields were then under German control) and abundant coal. To compensate for these deficiencies, French industry was characterized by high-quality products. For example, although it produced all types of textiles, it was especially noted for fashion fabrics. The same situation prevailed in most other types of manufacturing, and handicrafts continued strong.

Today, France has recovered from the damage of two world wars. With the loss of empire, it is now even more dependent on imports of fuel and industrial raw materials. It is a leader in nuclear power generation. France exports textiles, automobiles, chemical and electrical equipment, weapons, and wines; the last is not high on the list by value but is one of the oldest and steadiest earners of foreign exchange.

Germany

Germany is located east of France in the center of Europe. It occupies an exceedingly favorable position for international trade, with good land, river, and sea routes radiating in all directions. Its climate is reasonably suitable for agriculture. Above all, it is abundantly supplied with coal and minerals such as iron ore, copper, lead, and zinc. In 1900 it was the second largest European country after Russia and vied with Great Britain for economic leadership in Europe.

Germany had many industrial centers, of which the most important was and is the greater Ruhr industrial district, a focal point of world industry. The Ruhr area contained the largest deposits of high-grade coal in Europe, as well as other minerals. It is situated on the Rhine River complex of water and land routes. As a result, the Ruhr attracted huge primary iron and steel plants, as well as heavy-metal fabricating mills that produced locomotives, automobiles, machinery, chemicals, cement, paper, synthetics, textiles, and electrical equipment.

Today, after forty-five years of division that began with its defeat in World War II, Germany is once again reunified, but it has been shorn of former eastern territories, including East Prussia. Partition produced dislocations in the German economy. East Germany's economy was largely integrated with that of the Soviet Union and its satellites, while that of larger and more populous West Germany was integrated with those of other members of the European Economic Community, which it dominated. Since reunification in 1989 Germany has been engaged in a massive effort to upgrade the infrastructure and productivity of the former eastern Communist sector.

Italy

In 1900 Italy was not as strong economically as Great Britain, France, and Germany but was the leader among Mediterranean states. Italy lacks natural resources, is mountainous, and has little productive farmland. Its agricultural-industrial core was and is the north Italian plain and the bordering Alpine and Apennine foothills. Here, textile, metal, and chemical industries relied on hydroelectric power or "white coal." The rest of Italy was rural and poor. Southern Italy geographically and economically was closer to other Mediterranean lands than to northern Italy. Generally speaking, the level of poverty increased as one moved south.

Today, Italy continues to have problems supporting a large population on poor agricultural land. In manufacturing Italians find competition difficult with nations more plentifully endowed with resources. Emigration, which had acted as the safety valve for an increasing population, has for the most part ended. Thus, Italy must resort to more efficient farming and manufacturing to improve its living standard.

The Iberian Peninsula and Greece

Iberia included Spain and Portugal and is a peninsula cut off from Europe by the difficult Pyrenees Mountains and more accessible to Africa across the Straits of Gibraltar. Much of the land in both nations is too rugged and dry for farming and more suitable to grazing. Most of the agriculture of this area and North Africa in 1900 was based on the cultivation of grapes, olives, and citrus fruits. Roads and railways were expensive to build and maintain. Nor was there abundant coal or iron ore. Thus, industrial development was slow.

Today, Spain, Portugal, and Greece are more prosperous than before because of the integration of their economies with those of other nations of the European Community. Tourism is booming because of the mild, sunny climate and abundant historical ruins.

Eastern Europe

Broad lowlands and rivers characterize the northern section of Eastern Europe, whereas much of the landscape in the Balkans to the south is cut up by rugged mountains. Poland, Hungary, Bulgaria, and Rumania were traditionally grain-growing areas, but only small pockets of land were cultivable in the regions of former Yugoslavia, Greece, and Albania.

Agriculture was the main mode of livelihood in 1900. Industries were developed only in Silesia (then Germany, now Poland) and Bohemia (then the Austro-Hungarian Empire, now the Czech Republic). Before World War II, all nations in the area exported food to Western Europe in exchange for industrial products.

After World War II, the Soviet Union dominated the entire area and all governments, except that of Austria. The result was state planning of the economy to coordinate with developments in the Soviet Union (except for Yugoslavia). Up to the 1960s the economies of Poland and Czechoslovakia in general emphasized industry, while the other nations concentrated on food crops and industrial raw materials. With the collapse of the Soviet Union, all Eastern European nations regained their independence and renounced communism in 1989. They are all struggling with restructuring their economies from discredited Soviet Marxist models to capitalist free market ones. All seek integration with Western Europe and hope to join the European Community.

Northern Europe

Northern Europe consists of Scandinavia (Norway, Sweden, Denmark) and Finland. Except for Denmark, which is situated on a low peninsula suitable for farming and grazing, the area is mountainous and heavily glaciated. The nature of the terrain and the northerly latitude render most of the land unsuitable for agriculture and normal grazing. There are extensive forests and, as a result of coastal indentations, much of the land is close to the sea. Therefore, forest industries and fishing have played, and still play, important roles in the economy.

Today, Scandinavia is highly industrialized. Since coal is lacking, most industries are fueled by hydroelectricity (except in Norway, which has recently developed abundant petroleum deposits beneath the North Sea). The area is notable for its effective use of natural resources such as iron ore and uranium; such use has produced a high level of prosperity. It ranks high in the world in per capita production and in economic and cultural standards. Illiteracy is virtually unknown, and health and sanitary conditions are unsurpassed anywhere.

Russia (Soviet Union)

This nation comprises large portions of both Europe and Asia. It is about as large as all of North America. Most of Russia is situated north of 50 degrees latitude, with the result that most of the land ranges from cool temperate to arctic in climate, although small areas near the Black Sea are subtropical. Some major rivers flow northward into the Arctic Ocean, while others such as the Volga and Dnieper flow into the Caspian and Black seas.

In 1900 Russia was primarily an agricultural nation. It was an exporter of grain and forest products. In Asiatic Russia, the population was very sparse. There, Great Russians and other people of European descent lived in farming, mining, or penal communities, amid nomadic or seminomadic natives of Turkic and Mongolian racial background. In Central Asia, people were Muslim in religion.

The Industrial Revolution did not come to Russia until the late nineteenth century. In 1900 it was far behind Great Britain, Germany, and France in key aspects of industrial development. Moreover, Russian industries were limited to small areas close to the western extremity of the empire. They were in the St. Petersburg (Leningrad)-Baltic coastal region where communications with the rest of the world were best; in the Moscow region because it was a focal point of water routes; and in the Ukraine-Crimea area to the south where there were coal and iron ore deposits.

During the Soviet era European Russians were moved to populate the rest of the Soviet Union, and in some areas they outnumbered the indigenous population. This was offset, however, by larger population increases among some of the hundred-plus nationalities that populated the Soviet Union, especially those of Muslim background in Central Asia, who grew to constitute almost 50 percent of the Soviet population because of higher birthrates than those among European Soviet citizens. European parts of the Soviet Union remained more developed and enjoyed a higher standard of living.

With its GNP second only to that of the United States, the Soviet Union became an economic giant. A succession of Five-Year Plans substantially built up Soviet industry. New industrial centers dotted the Soviet Union from the Baltic to the Pacific, and even above the Arctic Circle. The most important of these were in the Caucasus and Volga districts in Europe, in the Urals, in the Kuzbass mineralized area of Siberia, in Central Asia, and in the Baikal and Far Eastern districts in Asia. Much environmental degradation resulted from rapid and careless industrialization. Soviet agriculture was collectivized and poorly mechanized; because farm workers lacked incentive, it was inefficient and wasteful. Further, a difficult climate and bad soil conditions meant that yields per acre for most crops in the Soviet Union were much lower than in the United States. For example, the Soviet Union was not self-sufficient in grain, a basic staple crop. The standard of living of Soviet citizens was much lower than that of Europeans and North Americans.

In 1991 the Soviet Union broke up. Estonia, Latvia, and Lithuania along the Baltic Sea and Georgia in the south seceded outright. All other component republics of the former U.S.S.R. continued tenuous and unstable ties with one another in a Commonwealth of Independent States. Russia, still the largest and strongest of the republics, is back to its approximate boundaries of the eighteenth century. Industries and agriculture are in a state of flux and disorganization in all states of the former Soviet Union as they seek to privatize and restructure.

NORTH AMERICA

The Western Hemisphere had three distinctive divisions: North America, Middle America, and South America. North America was the first area in the New World to experience the Industrial Revolution. As a result, it possessed the most advanced economies.

Canada

In 1900 most of Canada's 11 million people were congregated in the southeastern corner. The southern prairie lands were mostly given over to grain farming, and in the north were cold forests and frozen wastes. Canada today has about 24 million people. Discovery of petroleum and minerals has made it wealthy, but lack of population and capital and a formidable climate make development difficult.

The United States

The United States is well endowed in assets. About two-thirds of its territory is lowland, and much of this possesses some of the best soils for agriculture as well as favorable climates. In 1900 U.S. farming was the most efficient in the world. Out of a population of 74 million, about 13.5 million were farmers, who grew enough to export large quantities. The economic heartland region of the United States was situated in the northeast quadrant from the east bank of the Missouri to the Atlantic, and north of the Ohio and Potomac rivers. This area was noted for agriculture, mining, manufacture, and commerce. The coastal stretch between Boston and Baltimore contained a number of large urban centers. New York City was a major world center of finance and culture.

The southeastern United States was primarily agricultural, with some industries. Land west of the Missouri River up to the Rocky Mountains was sparsely populated and devoted to agriculture and ranching. Further west lay the Rocky Mountain region of rugged terrain and forests. The economy then centered on gold, silver, tin, copper, and other minerals. Along the Pacific coast, an agricultural economy was developing.

Today, the United States is the industrial giant of the world. U.S. agriculture is the most efficient in the world, and agricultural products are still major items of export, as are machinery, manufactured goods, and technology. However, in recent years, some of its manufacturers have faced stiff competition from more efficient German and Japanese industries. Dependence on foreign sources for about half its petroleum needs has restricted industrial growth. Within the United States there has been a shift of industries and population from the old centers in northeastern "frost belt" to the "sun belt" in the South and Southwest.

MIDDLE AMERICA

Middle America consists of Mexico, Central America, and the Caribbean islands. The former two regions are situated within a major belt of high mountains, with narrow coastal plains and some interior basins, and are populated by Indians and people of Spanish-descent.

Mexico

In 1900 half of the people in Mexico were concentrated in the areas around Mexico City, where high plateaus and valleys supported agriculture. Northern Mexico is too arid for large populations, and the southern part is debilitatingly hot and humid. In 1900 corn was the staple grain, cultivated by subsistence farmers or laborers on large estates.

Sugar was a major crop. There was some mining and a little manufacturing. Today, Mexico has more factories and mines. Recent discoveries of large petroleum and natural gas fields have promoted prosperity, but population increases have been too rapid for the absorption of new workers into the labor force.

Central America

Central America is broken up into numerous small nations. Rugged terrain and areas of dense rain forest prevented good land communications in 1900. Unstable governments frightened away investors. Except for enclaves of modern plantation agriculture, most people were, and remain, subsistence farmers, not much touched by modern influences. The Panama Canal, situated at the base of Central America, provides a route of communication between the Atlantic and Pacific oceans.

The Caribbean Islands

The Caribbean islands were colonized by many European powers and were mainly populated by descendants of African slaves. The economies were export-oriented and were dominated by sugar and other tropical crops. Today, the newly independent republics depend heavily on tourism for income.

SOUTH AMERICA

Northern South America

Northern South America is dominated by Brazil. The rain forests of the Amazon River basin spread through much of the interior of Brazil and northern South America, much of which was underdeveloped in 1900. The population was concentrated along the coastal regions and engaged in sugar and coffee production and ranching. Brazil encouraged immigration from both Europe and Asia. Today, Brazil's economy is booming, with rapid development of industry and mining. Efforts are being made to open up the Amazon valley, which will, however, also have severe ecological repercussions.

Other nations in northern South America are Colombia and Venezuela, plus the Guiana colonies. In 1900 most inhabitants were farmers and herders whose use of the land was dictated by the mountains. Coffee was grown, and gold, other metals, and emeralds were mined. Today, coal and petroleum have provided the basis for the development of some manufacturing. Venezuela in particular is petroleum-rich; its exports revenues have provided boom economic conditions. Guyana, French Guiana, and Suriname remain poor.

Western or Andean South America

Consisting of Chile, Bolivia, Peru, and Ecuador, this narrow strip of land extends from the equator to 50 degrees south latitude. The rugged Andes isolated this area from the rest of South America, as few roads penetrated the mountains to connect with the rest of the continent.

Ecuador in the north was predominantly a land of Indians who persisted in a meager traditional life of farming and herding. The urban and commercial sector was dominated by mestizos (people of Indian-Spanish descent) and people of Spanish descent. Peru fell to Spanish conquistadors in the sixteenth century because of its gold and silver.

Today, foreign-owned companies have expanded the area of exploitation (little gold and silver remain) to copper, lead, and zinc and some petroleum and coal. Although guano (fertilizer made from bird droppings) was once the main export of coastal Peru, today this has been superseded by cotton and sugar and by the products of an important fishing industry. Peru's difficult terrain and tradition-minded Indians have slowed modern development.

Bolivia is a land-locked, high-altitude Andean nation. Very few Spaniards settled in this area, with the result that over half the people remain full-blooded Indians. Other than subsistence agriculture, which involved most of the population, it was tin mining that formed and continues to form the basis of Bolivia's commercial life.

Chile's favorable climate attracted many Spanish and other European settlers. In 1900 it was one of the most advanced nations in South America. Today, it has modern urban centers and diversified manufacturing. It has commercial rather than subsistence farming in the temperate coastal valleys.

Argentina, Uruguay, and Paraguay

These countries are located in southern South America. The former two nations enjoy a favorable location for trade on the Atlantic coast, temperate climate, and good soils. These two nations attracted European immigrants who came bringing new skills and technology. Except for the Chaco waste region in the north and parts of Patagonia in the extreme south, most of the land is suitable for farming and grazing. The main products in 1900 were commercially raised maize, wheat, cattle, and sheep, which were exported to Europe. Today, Argentina is an important commercial, manufacturing, and agricultural nation. In contrast, land-locked Paraguay remains underdeveloped and poor.

AUSTRALASIA

Australasia is the smallest, most recently developed, and most sparsely populated geographical area. The dominating feature of this region, the island-continent of Australia, is too arid for intensive settlement in the interior, and in 1900 the population was concentrated along the south and east coasts. Most Australians were of British descent. Agriculture prevailed mostly along the east and south coasts and on some inland plains with adequate rainfall. Ranching of both sheep and cattle took place in the more arid parts of the interior, while the vast core of the continent remained relatively empty. Until recently, Australia exported products of the land in exchange for industrial products. Today, manufacturing has become important in such coastal cities as Sydney and Melbourne, and discovery of important mineral deposits such as coal, natural gas, petroleum, and aluminum has led to the development of the Outback as well as increased Australia's importance as a resource producer. New Zealand, which was settled even more recently than Australia by the British, remains rural and pastoral. The total present population of Australasia including the people on scattered islands of Oceania is about 20 million.

Wealthy Nations, Poor Nations, 1989

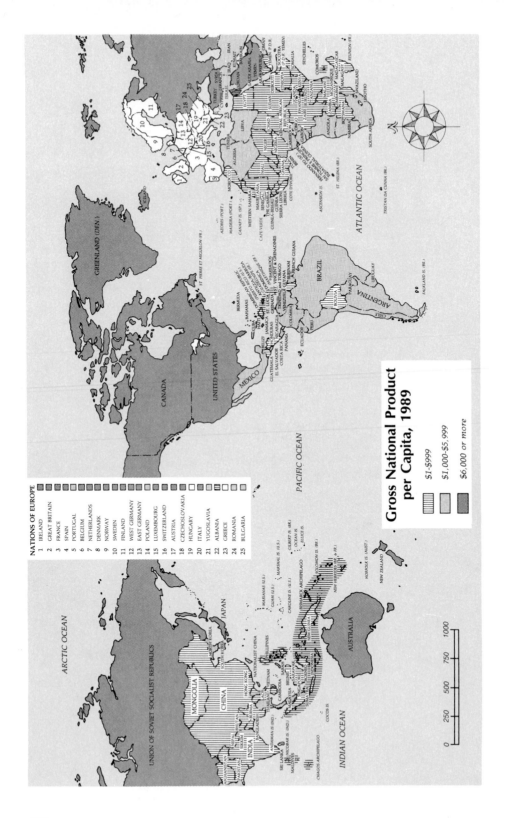

Gross National Product per Capita, 1989

	$1–$999
	$1,000–$5,999
	$6,000 or more

NATIONS OF EUROPE

1. IRELAND
2. GREAT BRITAIN
3. FRANCE
4. SPAIN
5. PORTUGAL
6. BELGIUM
7. NETHERLANDS
8. DENMARK
9. NORWAY
10. SWEDEN
11. FINLAND
12. WEST GERMANY
13. EAST GERMANY
14. POLAND
15. LUXEMBOURG
16. SWITZERLAND
17. AUSTRIA
18. CZECHOSLOVAKIA
19. HUNGARY
20. ITALY
21. YUGOSLAVIA
22. ALBANIA
23. GREECE
24. ROMANIA
25. BULGARIA

Per Capita Military Expenditures and Gross National Product by Region for 1979, 1984, and 1989 (constant 1989 dollars)

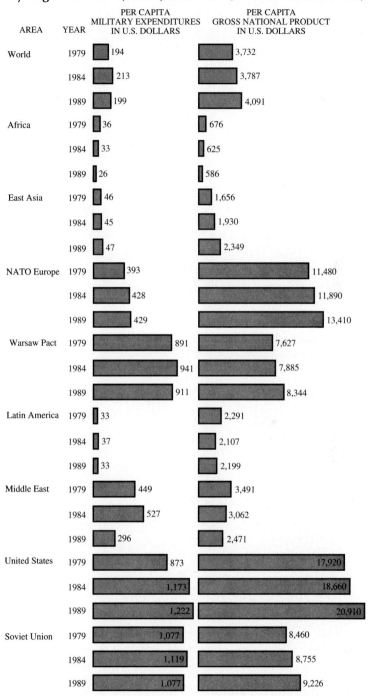

AREA	YEAR	PER CAPITA MILITARY EXPENDITURES IN U.S. DOLLARS	PER CAPITA GROSS NATIONAL PRODUCT IN U.S. DOLLARS
World	1979	194	3,732
	1984	213	3,787
	1989	199	4,091
Africa	1979	36	676
	1984	33	625
	1989	26	586
East Asia	1979	46	1,656
	1984	45	1,930
	1989	47	2,349
NATO Europe	1979	393	11,480
	1984	428	11,890
	1989	429	13,410
Warsaw Pact	1979	891	7,627
	1984	941	7,885
	1989	911	8,344
Latin America	1979	33	2,291
	1984	37	2,107
	1989	33	2,199
Middle East	1979	449	3,491
	1984	527	3,062
	1989	296	2,471
United States	1979	873	17,920
	1984	1,173	18,660
	1989	1,222	20,910
Soviet Union	1979	1,077	8,460
	1984	1,119	8,755
	1989	1,077	9,226

Figures above for 1979, 1984, and 1989 are taken from U.S. Arms Control and Disarmament Agency figures. Figures for the Warsaw Pact nations, especially the Soviet Union, are less reliable than others, but no solid consensus on what these figures actually were yet exists.

Index

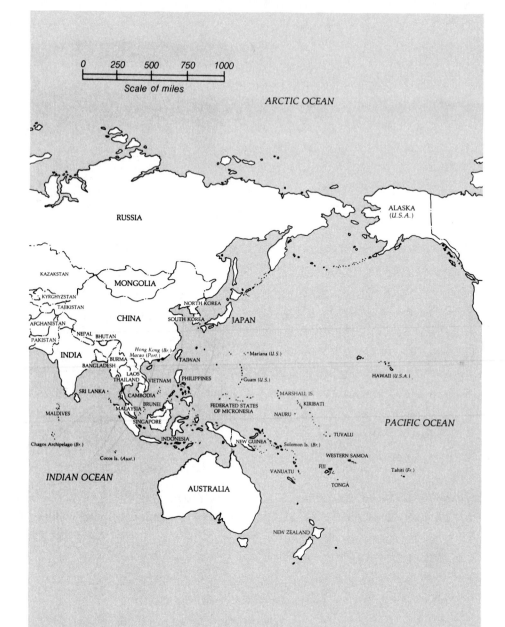

0   250   500   750   1000

ARCTIC OCEAN

RUSSIA

ALASKA
(U.S.A.)

KAZAKSTAN

KYRGHYZSTAN

TAJIKISTAN

AFGHANISTAN

PAKISTAN

NEPAL BHUTAN

MONGOLIA

CHINA

NORTH KOREA

SOUTH KOREA   JAPAN

INDIA

BURMA

BANGLADESH

Hong Kong (Br.)
Macao (Port.)

TAIWAN

Mariana (U.S.)

LAOS
THAILAND   VIETNAM

PHILIPPINES

Guam (U.S.)

HAWAII (U.S.A.)

SRI LANKA

CAMBODIA

MARSHALL IS.

KIRIBATI

MALDIVES

MALAYSIA

BRUNEI

FEDERATED STATES
OF MICRONESIA

NAURU

SINGAPORE

PACIFIC OCEAN

Chagos Archipelago (Br.)

INDONESIA

NEW GUINEA   Solomon Is. (Br.)

TUVALU

Cocos Is. (Aust.)

WESTERN SAMOA

INDIAN OCEAN

VANUATU

FIJI

Tahiti (Fr.)

AUSTRALIA

TONGA

NEW ZEALAND

The World in 1993

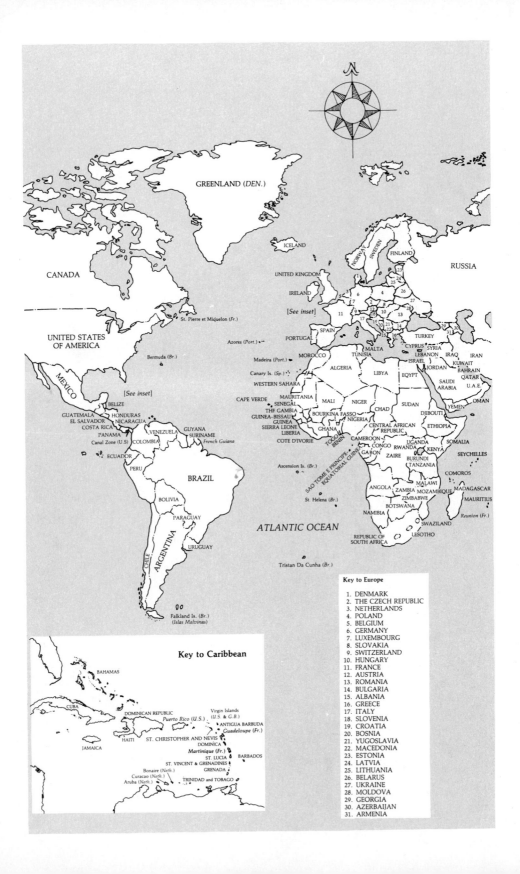

N

GREENLAND (DEN.)

ICELAND

CANADA

NORWAY
SWEDEN
FINLAND

RUSSIA

UNITED KINGDOM

IRELAND

UNITED STATES
OF AMERICA

St. Pierre et Miquelon (Fr.)

[See inset]

SPAIN

PORTUGAL

Azores (Port.)

Bermuda (Br.)

Madeira (Port.)

MOROCCO

MALTA
TUNISIA

TURKEY

CYPRUS SYRIA
LEBANON
ISRAEL JORDAN

IRAQ IRAN

KUWAIT
BAHRAIN
QATAR

MEXICO

Canary Is. (Sp.)

ALGERIA

LIBYA

EGYPT

SAUDI
ARABIA

U.A.E.

OMAN

[See inset]

BELIZE
GUATEMALA HONDURAS
EL SALVADOR NICARAGUA
COSTA RICA
PANAMA
Canal Zone (U.S) COLOMBIA

VENEZUELA
GUYANA
SURINAME
French Guiana

ECUADOR

PERU

BRAZIL

BOLIVIA

PARAGUAY

ARGENTINA
CHILE

URUGUAY

WESTERN SAHARA

CAPE VERDE

MAURITANIA
SENEGAL
THE GAMBIA
GUINEA-BISSAU
GUINEA
SIERRA LEONE
LIBERIA

MALI

NIGER

CHAD

SUDAN

YEMEN

DJIBOUTI

BOURKINA FASSO
NIGERIA

GHANA

COTE D'IVOIRE

TOGO
BENIN

CAMEROON

CENTRAL AFRICAN
REPUBLIC

ETHIOPIA

SOMALIA

Ascension Is. (Br.)

SAO TOME E PRINCIPE
EQUATORIAL GUINEA

CONGO
GABON

ZAIRE

RWANDA
BURUNDI

UGANDA
KENYA

TANZANIA

SEYCHELLES

COMOROS

St. Helena (Br.)

ANGOLA

ZAMBIA
ZIMBABWE
BOTSWANA

MALAWI
MOZAMBIQUE

MADAGASCAR

MAURITIUS

Reunion (Fr.)

NAMIBIA

SWAZILAND

ATLANTIC OCEAN

REPUBLIC OF
SOUTH AFRICA

LESOTHO

Tristan Da Cunha (Br.)

Falkland Is. (Br.)
(Islas Malvinas)

Key to Caribbean

BAHAMAS

CUBA

DOMINICAN REPUBLIC
Puerto Rico (U.S.)

Virgin Islands
(U.S. & G.B.)
ANTIGUA BARBUDA
Guadeloupe (Fr.)

JAMAICA

HAITI

ST. CHRISTOPHER AND NEVIS
DOMINICA
Martinique (Fr.)
ST. LUCIA
ST. VINCENT & GRENADINES
GRENADA

BARBADOS

Bonaire (Neth.)
Curacao (Neth.)
Aruba (Neth.)

TRINIDAD and TOBAGO

Key to Europe

1. DENMARK
2. THE CZECH REPUBLIC
3. NETHERLANDS
4. POLAND
5. BELGIUM
6. GERMANY
7. LUXEMBOURG
8. SLOVAKIA
9. SWITZERLAND
10. HUNGARY
11. FRANCE
12. AUSTRIA
13. ROMANIA
14. BULGARIA
15. ALBANIA
16. GREECE
17. ITALY
18. SLOVENIA
19. CROATIA
20. BOSNIA
21. YUGOSLAVIA
22. MACEDONIA
23. ESTONIA
24. LATVIA
25. LITHUANIA
26. BELARUS
27. UKRAINE
28. MOLDOVA
29. GEORGIA
30. AZERBAIJAN
31. ARMENIA